ELEMENTS OF PUBLIC SPEAKING, 7TH EDITION, OFFERS A **COMPLETE** LEARNING AND TEACHING PACKAGE...

W9-AEZ-952

For Students:

Website at http://awlonline.com/devito

Speech Writer's Workshop CD-ROM   0-321-07535-8
(FREE with every new copy of the text)

Discount subscription to Newsweek magazine
(ask your local sales representative for more information)

Student Guide to PowerPoint   0-321-04926-8

Studying Communication   0-673-97005-1

Public Speaking Guide for Students   0-06-501292-5

Brainstorms Booklet: A Guide to Creative Thinking
0-673-98136-3

Speech Writer's Workshop   (Mac) 0-321-02801-5

Speech Writer's Workshop   (Win) 0-321-02453-2

For Instructors:

Instructor's Manual and Testbank   0-321-06296-5

PowerPoint Presentation on CD-ROM   0-321-06306-6

Transparencies   0-321-07522-6

TestGen CD-ROM (computerized test bank)   0-321-06298-1

ESL Guide for Public Speaking   0-321-02079-0

Teaching Public Speaking   0-321-00386-1

Assessment Guide for Public Speaking   0-321-02078-2

Great Ideas for Teaching Speech (GIFTS)   0-321-02081-2

Student Speeches Video-2000 Edition   0-321-07536-6

Selection of Student Speeches Video   0-321-02253-X

Addressing Your Audience Video   0-321-40598-6

Speaker Apprehension Video   0-321-02256-4

Critiquing Student Speeches Video   0-321-02255-6

Video Guide to Public Speaking   0-321-02080-4

Take a look through the book that will prepare your students for public speaking in the 21st Century...

GIVE YOUR STUDENTS THE BACKGROUND IN **TECHNOLOGY** THEY NEED!

FREE Speech Writer's Workshop CD-ROM in every copy of the text! This effective and exciting software includes a speech handbook with tips for researching and preparing speeches, a speech workshop which guides students through the speech writing process, a topics dictionary which gives students hundreds of ideas for speeches, and a citation database.

NEW! Website at **http://awlonline.com/devito** includes web activities, annotated research links, online research information, and sylllabus builder.

Unit 7 "Researching Your Speech" (pp. 124-159) now includes thoroughly integrated coverage of technological resources – databases **(p. 136)**, e-mail and listservs **(p. 128-129)**, newsgroups **(p.130)**, chat groups **(pp.132-133)**, and the Web **(p. 120, 133-136 and integrated throughout)**. The unit discusses ways to access, evaluate **(p.151)**, and cite these new sources **(pp. 154-155)**.

NEW! Comprehensive Coverage of Presentation Software Programs now appears in **Unit 9 (p.194-205)**. Explaining how students can use programs such as PowerPoint and Corel Presentations to create handouts and slide shows, the unit includes a complete PowerPoint slide show accompanying a speech to guide students through the entire process of creating and presenting.

ALSO AVAILABLE! Student Guide to PowerPoint booklet FREE when bundled with the text.

NEW! Increased Emphasis on ETHICS. Coverage of ethics appears early in Unit 1 and is presented throughout the text with 18 "The Ethics of..." boxes, ensuring that students see this topic as an essential issue in all aspects of public speaking.
p. 46 The Ethical Responsibilities of the Speaker
p.153 Plagiarism and How to Avoid It
p. 305 When Speech is Unethical

NEW! Expanded Coverage of LISTENING. In addition to the full unit on listening (Unit 4, pp. 60-77), 14 "Listen to This" boxes are presented throughout the text to emphasize the crucial role listening has in public speaking.
p. 51 How to Listen to Help Reduce Apprehension
p.326 How to Listen without Racist, Sexist, and Heterosexist Attitudes
p.364 How to Listen to New Ideas

Extensive Coverage of the CULTURAL DIMENSIONS of Public Speaking. The new edition of the text features even more intercultural material, helping students become more effective public speakers in today's global society.
p. 13 Culture and Public Speaking
p. 80 Cultural Differences
p. 193 Table 9.2 Color and Culture
p. 474 The Special Occasion Speech in Cultural Perspective

Abundant Sample Speeches. By both students and professional speakers, sample speeches are by annotated and contain critical evaluations to help students see more clearly how the principles of public speaking are applied in real life speeches.
p. 38 Adventure Drug Events
pp. 95-7 XXX Has Got to Go

"Test Yourself" questions, interspersed through the text, promote active learning and personalize material by asking the students to answer questions about their own attitudes and beliefs.
pp. 55-6 How Shy Are You?
p. 81 Individual and Collective Cultures
pp. 238-9 How Flexible Are You as a Public Speaker?

"Practically Speaking Exercises" in the end-of-chapter material focus on applying principles to specific public speaking issues and include "Short Speech Technique" exercises that get students up and speaking right away.
p. 122 Brainstorming for Topics
p. 243 Predicting Listener's Attitudes
p. 346 Developing the Impromptu Speech

An Entire Unit on Criticism in the Classroom. A crucial yet often neglected topic, this unit helps make critiques constructive and comfortable.
Please see **Unit 5, pp. 78-97.**

THE ELEMENTS OF PUBLIC SPEAKING

SEVENTH EDITION

THE ELEMENTS OF PUBLIC SPEAKING

Joseph A. DeVito

Hunter College of the
City University of New York

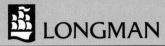 LONGMAN

An imprint of Addison Wesley Longman, Inc.

New York • Reading, Massachusetts • Menlo Park, California • Harlow, England
Don Mills, Ontario • Sydney • Mexico City • Madrid • Amsterdam

Editor-in-Chief: Priscilla McGeehon
Acquisitions Editor: Michael Greer
Development Director: Lisa Pinto
Marketing Manager: Megan Galvin
Supplements Editor: Mark Toews
Full Service Production Manager: Valerie Zaborski
Project Coordination, Text Design, Art, and Composition: Elm Street Publishing Services, Inc.
Cover Design Manager: Nancy Danahy
Cover Designer: Kay Petronio
Cover Illustration: John Clementson/Illustration Works
Photo Researcher: Julie Tesser
Senior Print Buyer: Hugh Crawford
Printer and Binder: World Color Book Services
Cover Printer: The Lehigh Press, Inc.

For permission to use copyrighted material, grateful acknowledgment is made to the copyright holders on pp. 563–565, which are hereby made part of this copyright page.

Library of Congress Cataloging-in-Publication Data

DeVito, Joseph A.
    The elements of public speaking / Joseph A. DeVito.
    —7th ed.
            p.   cm.
    Includes bibliographical references and index.
    ISBN 0-321-04422-3
    1. Public speaking.   I. Title
PN4121.D389   2000
808.5'1—dc21   99-14865
                                                                        CIP

Please visit our Web site at http://www.awlonline.com

ISBN 0-321-04422-3

12345678910 — WCV — 02010099

BRIEF CONTENTS

PART 1 ELEMENTS OF PUBLIC SPEAKING

PART 2 ELEMENTS OF SUBJECTS AND PURPOSES

PART 3 ELEMENTS OF ORGANIZATION

PART 4 ELEMENTS OF STYLE AND DELIVERY

PART 5 ELEMENTS OF PUBLIC SPEECHES

DETAILED CONTENTS

SPECIALIZED CONTENTS

SPEECHES AND OUTLINES

Speeches

THE ETHICS OF PUBLIC SPEAKING

LISTEN TO THIS

TEST YOURSELF

PRACTICALLY SPEAKING EXERCISES

PREFACE

It's a pleasure to introduce the seventh edition of a text that has proven so popular with so many instructors and students. While similar in purpose to previous editions, this new edition is dramatically different in several important ways. The general goal of the text remains the same: to provide a **comprehensive treatment of public speaking skills**. *Elements* continues to offer a serious, in-depth study of public speaking designed for the beginning college student. *Elements* is now, however, more easily accessible to the beginning public speaker and continues to be adapted easily to a variety of classroom structures.

MAJOR THEMES AND FEATURES

Among the major themes and features of this new edition are its integrated coverage of new technology, inclusion of ethics, emphasis on listening, expanded coverage of culture and gender, and continued focus on critical thinking. In addition, full units are devoted to two of the course's major difficulties—giving students enough guidance for speaking early in the semester and making the criticism of classroom speeches both comfortable and constructive for the speaker and critic alike. Unit 2, "Preparing a Public Speech: an Overview," presents an abbreviated version of the 10 steps in public speaking to get students speaking as early in the semester as possible. Unit 5, "Speech Criticism in the Classroom," presents the essentials of criticism in the classroom so that students can profit from the constructive criticism of others.

Technology

One major change in this edition is the expanded integration of **technology** into the entire text but especially in Unit 7, "Researching Your Speech" and Unit 9, "Presentation Aids."

The research unit now includes thorough coverage of the technological resources that students now have available for researching their speeches—computerized databases, e-mail and listservs, newsgroups, chat groups, and especially the World Wide Web. The unit discusses ways to access, evaluate, and cite these new sources.

Unit 9 now covers the popular presentation software programs (for example, PowerPoint and Corel Presentations) that enable students to create handouts, slides, and even a total slide show for their speeches. A complete PowerPoint slide show speech is included to illustrate these new capabilities and to guide the student through the entire process of creating and presenting such slide shows.

Further, references to many of the resources available at the Podium—Longman's public speaking Web site—are provided throughout the text. Students and instructors alike will find a wide variety of useful materials at this Web site as well as links to other relevant sites.

Ethics

A second major change is the emphasis given to ethics. Ethics is introduced in Unit 1 as an essential element of public speaking and is followed up throughout the text with 18 "The Ethics of Public Speaking" boxes that discuss such topics as the ethical responsibilities of the speaker (Unit 3), listener (Unit 4), and critic (Unit 5); plagiarism and how to avoid it (Unit 7); when speech is unethical (Unit 15), and a wide variety of other issues. A complete list of these ethics boxes is presented in the Specialized Contents, page xii.

Listening

A third major change is the attention given to listening. In addition to the full unit on listening (Unit 4), 15 "Listen to This" boxes are presented throughout the text to emphasize the crucial role that listening plays in public speaking. These boxes cover such topics as listening to reduce apprehension (Unit 3), listening to criticism (Unit 5), listening to other perspectives (Unit 6), listening to communicate power (Unit 11), listening to gender differences (Unit 15), and listening to empower others (Unit 23). A complete list of these listening boxes is presented in the Specialized Contents, pages xii–xiii.

Culture

The coverage of the cultural dimensions of public speaking has been updated and increased. The audiences students address, the speakers they hear, and the topics of public discourse are becoming increasingly intercultural. Heightened mobility, changing immigration patterns, global economic interdependency, and advances in communication technology have made intercultural communication an inevitable part of public speaking. This edition, quite simply, focuses on making public speaking in this intercultural context more effective. Here are a few examples of these cultural dimensions appearing throughout the text:

- Culture and public speaking, the importance of culture, the aim of a cultural perspective (Unit 1)
- Culture and speaker apprehension (Unit 3)
- Listening and culture (Unit 4)
- Cultural differences in criticism; individual and collectivist cultures (Unit 5)
- Cultural differences in topics and thesis expression (Unit 6)
- Cultural influences on meanings for icons and colors (Unit 9)
- Culture in audience analysis; culture and age; secular and sacred cultures; gender differences in nonverbal messages (Unit 10)

- High and low context cultures (Unit 12)
- Culture and meaning; cultural differences in directness and formality; gender differences in verbal messages (Unit 15)
- Cultural identifiers; racist, sexist, and heterosexist listening (Unit 16)
- Cultural differences in persuasion (Unit 20)
- Argument and evidence in cultural perspective (Unit 21)
- Cultural differences in motivational appeals (Unit 22)
- Culture and credibility (Unit 23)
- The special occasion speech in cultural perspective (Unit 24)
- The small group as a culture (Unit 25)

Critical Thinking

Critical thinking is interwoven throughout the text. Most of the principles of public speaking are also principles of critical thinking: for example, analyzing and adapting to audiences, evaluating and limiting speech topics and purposes, organizing the speech for ease of understanding, remembering, and persuasiveness, and so on. There are also, however, numerous specific sections on critical thinking, for example:

- Critically evaluating speeches (Unit 5)
- Critically evaluating research (Unit 7)
- Critically evaluating examples, narration, testimony, and statistics (Unit 8)
- Critically evaluating presentation aids (Unit 9)
- Critically evaluating unethical persuasive appeals (Units 20 and 21)
- Critically evaluating motivational appeals (Unit 22)
- Critically evaluating credibility appeals (Unit 23)
- Thinking critically with the six hats technique (Unit 25)
- Groupthink (Unit 25)

In addition, numerous speeches are annotated with critical thinking questions to guide the student through the process of preparing and delivering a public speech. Questions focus on such critical thinking skills as discovery, evaluation, problem solving, and application.

Further, at the end of each unit is a four-part series of questions that ask students to:

- **Review** the terms and concepts of the unit (all key terms and major topics of each unit are identified)
- **Develop strategies** that focus on choice points that speakers may meet in the preparation and presentation of public speeches
- **Evaluate speeches** focusing on identifying and assessing what other speakers did well and what they could improve; these suggestions also invite students to assess their own speeches in light of the unit topics
- **Use technology** to use a variety of databases, Web sites, and other tools to further their understanding and mastery of public speaking

Criticism

An entire unit on criticism in the classroom is included (Unit 5) to help deal with this crucial yet often neglected topic. This unit identifies the values and difficulties of criticism, discusses the standards of criticism, and offers suggestions for both giving and receiving criticism. With this as a background, students will be in a better position to critically evaluate the speeches of others as well as their own and in the process more completely learn the principles of effective public speaking. In addition, numerous sections throughout the text and the "evaluating speeches" questions at the end of each unit ask for critical evaluations.

Overview Unit

Elements continues to provide an **overview of the public speaking process** early in the text so that students can begin to give their speeches early in the semester. This unit (Unit 2) presents 10 steps for preparing and presenting a speech. The 10 steps are covered in greater detail throughout the rest of the text, enabling students to gradually perfect their public speaking abilities.

PEDAGOGY

The pedagogy in this edition continues to invite student interaction and participation in the content of the text. A variety of devices are used to achieve this goal.

Speeches for Analysis

This edition uses model speeches as an important tool for learning the principles of public speaking. Sample speeches, most by college students, but some by professional and well-established speakers, appear throughout the text and in the appendix. The speeches are accompanied by guides to critical evaluation to help the reader see more clearly how the principles of public speaking discussed in the text are applied in real life speeches. The speeches were chosen to serve a variety of goals:

- All of the speeches (except those in Unit 5 which are purposely poorly constructed) provide students with models of excellence and specific examples of the application of public speaking principles.
- With the exception of those speeches in The Special Occasion Speech unit (Unit 24), all of the speeches are accompanied by a guide to criticism, usually marginal annotations and questions that highlight and guide the students' focus. Most of these annotations focus on the general principles of public speaking and may prove useful as reviews of important principles or as an introduction to a round of speeches.
- Four of the student speeches in the Appendix are annotated with focused analysis questions. These speeches may prove useful in summarizing these subtopics of public speaking. These focused analyses cover four of the most important areas of public speaking:
  - Research and Supporting Materials
  - Audience Analysis and Adaptation
  - Organization
  - Style and Language
- Several speeches are presented not only because they're useful models but because they say something important about communication. Examples include the speech on communication apprehension (included in Unit 3, "From Apprehension to Confidence"), improving commu-

nication between patient and physician (included in Unit 4, "Listening"), and the speeches on executive eloquence and the biological influence on communication (included in the Appendix). These speeches may be discussed as supplements to the text discussion of the topic and as alternative perspectives.

■ Two speeches, presented in Unit 5, "Criticism in the Classroom," were written to illustrate what poorly constructed speeches might look like. These speeches will prove useful for applying the principles of criticism and also for highlighting some of the more common errors that speakers make.

A complete list of speeches and outlines is provided in the Specialized Contents on pages xi–xii.

Test Yourself

Seventeen self-tests, called "Test Yourself," interspersed throughout the text, not only promote active learning but also personalize the material for the reader. New to this edition are self-tests on cultural awareness (Unit 1), ethical issues in public speaking (Unit 2), collectivist and individualist orientation (Unit 5), research competencies (Unit 7), flexibility in public speaking (Unit 11), and gender differences in verbal messages (Unit 15). A complete listing of the 17 self-tests is provided in the Specialized Contents, page xiii.

End-of-Unit Questions

At the end of each unit are a four-part series of questions and suggestions for further exploration of the topics of the unit. These questions/suggestions, as already noted, focus on reviewing key terms and concepts, developing public speaking strategies, evaluating speeches, and using technology.

Practically Speaking Exercises and Short Speech Techniques

At the end of each unit are exercises to enable the student to work actively with the concepts discussed in the text. The first exercise in each unit is the short speech technique (SST), introduced for the first time in the previous edition and continued here. Each of these SST exercises provides the student with a variety of choices for preparing and delivering a two-minute speech using some aspect of unit content as the basis for the speech. Because of their short length, an entire class or good part of it could deliver their speeches with time left for discussion in one class period. This short speech exercise provides a kind of bridge connecting the content of the unit and the development of public speaking skills. The SST exercises are designed with several purposes in mind.

■ They give students the opportunity to analyze and verbalize some important aspect of the unit's content and will therefore reinforce learning. At the same time, these short speeches give students many opportunities to practice the skills of public speaking.

■ The frequent opportunities for speaking may help reduce the fear of public speaking for many beginning speakers.

- These frequent speeches also provide ample practice opportunities in organizing thoughts, adapting to an audience, and phrasing issues so that they're clearly understood.

Of course, these short speeches are no substitute for the longer, more sustained efforts that are already built into the course. The SST exercises are useful—with appropriate feedback—for mastering skills, gaining confidence, and reducing apprehension. The longer speeches work best to emphasize research, organizational patterns, detail to style, and in-depth audience analysis and adaptation. Suggestions for these longer or "regular" speeches appear throughout the text and in the instructor's manual.

The remaining exercises focus on understanding and applying principles to specific public speaking issues, rather than to the preparation of a public speech. These exercises cover such topics as predicting listeners' attitudes, unscrambling outlines, evaluating poorly constructed speeches, and analyzing cultural issues in persuasion. Those new to this edition include: Cultural Beliefs as Assumptions in Public Speaking (Unit 1), Using Performance Visualization to Reduce Apprehension (Unit 3), Limiting Topics (Unit 6), Cultural Identities (Unit 16), and Gender and Credibility (Unit 23).

Tips from Professional Speakers

"Tips from Professional Speakers" appear throughout the text. Their purpose is to emphasize the very practical aspects of public speaking by offering very practical advice. These Tips are placed in the margin where they can be appreciated as comments and expansions on the text rather than as interruptions.

Unit-by-Unit Improvements

In addition to the changes noted above (for example, the ethics and listening boxes, the inclusion of technology throughout the text), there have been numerous additional changes and improvements. Among the most important are the following:

- A new cultural awareness self-test has been added to Unit 1. Also in this unit, the nature of public speaking and how it differs from conversation has been integrated into one cohesive section. The discussion of noise has been expanded; gender as a cultural variable has been expanded, and the aim of a cultural perspective has been clarified.
- The discussion of communication apprehension in Unit 3 has been recast and expanded to focus more directly on ways to manage the fear of public speaking.
- A new self-test on individual and collectivist cultures and how these differences influence criticism in the classroom has been included in Unit 5.
- Ways to use search directories as a way of limiting topics have been included in Unit 6.
- Unit 7 has been completely updated to include additional research resources such as listservs, newsgroups, IRC groups, search engines and directories. The section on evaluating sources (especially Internet sources) has been expanded, and a new section on citing research sources has been added.

- The section on statistics in Unit 8 has been rewritten to make the use of statistics in public speaking easier and more effective.
- Unit 9 has been rewritten to include the use of PowerPoint and similar presentation software packages. A complete PowerPoint Slide Show speech is included to illustrate these most advanced public speaking techniques. In addition, discussions of the more traditional presentation aids and suggestions for using presentation aids more effectively have been expanded.
- Values are now discussed along with attitudes and beliefs in Unit 10.
- A new self-test on flexibility in public speaking has been added to Unit 11.
- A new section on the values of organization and an expanded discussion of arranging propositions and supporting materials have been added to Unit 12.
- Unit 14 has been reorganized to make the essentials of outlining clearer.
- Culture and directness and gender differences in verbal messages have been added to Unit 15.
- New sections on ethnic expressions and cultural identifiers have been added to Unit 16.
- Values have been added to beliefs and attitudes. Questions of fact, value, and policy are now discussed. Identification and consistency have now been added as principles of persuasion in Unit 20.
- Nominal groups, Delphi groups, quality circles, and focus groups are now discussed in Unit 25.

ANCILLARIES

The ancillary package for the seventh edition of *Elements of Public Speaking* includes the following instructional resources:

Resources for Instructors

Instructor's Manual/Test Bank with Transparency Masters. The Instructor's Manual includes chapter overviews, chapter objectives, a wealth of valuable classroom activities, a set of transparency masters, and suggestions for further reading. The Test Bank contains hundreds of challenging and thoroughly revised multiple choice, true-false, short answer, and essay questions along with an answer key. The questions closely follow the text chapters and are cross-referenced with corresponding page numbers.

TestGen-EQ 2.0 CD-ROM. The printed Test Bank is also available electronically through our computerized testing system, TestGen-EQ 2.0. This fully networkable test generating software is now on a cross-platform CD-ROM. TestGen-EQ's friendly graphical interface enables instructors to view, edit, and add questions, transfer questions to tests, and print tests in a variety of fonts and forms. Search and sort features allow instructors to locate questions quickly and arrange them in a preferred order. Six question formats are available, including short-answer, true-false, multiple-choice, essay, matching, and bimodal.

PowerPoint CD-ROM. New to this edition, the transparency masters will now be available as PowerPoint presentation slides on CD-ROM.

Overhead Transparency Package. A set of 75, four-color acetate transparencies is available to adopters. The set includes graphs, charts, and tables from the text.

Teaching Public Speaking. This introduction to teaching the public speaking course offers suggestions for everything from lecturing to designing classroom assignments to incorporating cultural diversity into lesson plans. Essential for graduate teaching assistants and first-time instructors, it may also provide new insight to the more experienced professor. An extensive bibliography and a listing of media resources is also included.

Great Ideas for Teaching Speech (GIFTS). This unique supplement offers instructors a myriad of creative ideas for enlivening their public speaking course. All of the assignments found in GIFTS have been successfully employed by experienced public speaking instructors in their classrooms.

ESL Guide for Public Speaking. The ESL Guide for Public Speaking provides strategies and resources for instructors teaching in a bilingual or multi-lingual classroom. It also includes suggestions for further reading and a listing of related Web sites.

Longman's Public Speaking Video Library. Longman's video collection includes a wide variety of films on topics such as preparation for public speaking, critiquing student speeches, speaker apprehension, and audience assessment. We also offer a variety of accompanying, printed video guides. Please contact your local sales representative for more information on titles and availability.

Resources for Students

The Speech Writer's Workshop Brainstorms CD-ROM. A virtual handbook for public speaking, this exciting public speaking software is now available on CD-ROM. The software includes five separate features: 1) a *speech handbook* with tips for researching and preparing speeches plus information about grammar, usage, and syntax; 2) a *speech workshop* which guides students through the speech writing process while displaying a series of questions at each stage; 3) a *topics dictionary* which gives students hundreds of ideas for speeches—all divided into sub-categories to help students with outlining and organization; 4) a *citation database* that formats bibliographic entries in MLA or APA style; and 5) *Brainstorms: How to Think More Creatively About Communication ... or About Anything Else,* by Joseph A. DeVito.

Student Guide to PowerPoint. Designed to introduce students to PowerPoint, this student guide explains how to use the program as a tool for planning, organizing, and delivering oral presentations. The supplement covers all of the requisite skills for mastering PowerPoint including outlining, designing and modifying slides; using graphics and animations; and presenting a slide show.

Studying Communication. This booklet introduces students to the field of communication and to the way in which research in the discipline is conducted. The booklet also offers students a variety of practical suggestions for how to get the most out of their study of communication including how to read a textbook, how to take a test, and how to write a paper for a communication course.

Brainstorms. This unique booklet integrates creative thinking into the communication course. *Brainstorms* explores the creative thinking process (its nature, values, characteristics, and stages) and its relationship to communication. It also provides 19 specific tools for thinking more creatively about communication (or anything else). The discussion of each tool includes its purposes, techniques, and an exercise to get started. Creative thinking sidebars and relevant quotations add to the interactive pedagogy.

Online Course Companion Web site (http://www.awlonline.com/devito). This Online Course Companion provides valuable resources for both students and instructors using *The Elements of Public Speaking,* Seventh Edition. Students will find interactive practice tests, links to related sites, and Web activities. Instructors will have access to complete text and supplement information, suggestions for classroom activities and our Syllabus Builder tool which allows them to put their course on the Web.

ACKNOWLEDGMENTS

I want to thank all the people who contributed so much to the development of this edition. I especially want to thank Laura Barthule, developmental editor, and Donna Erickson, editor, who gave excellent advice and direction throughout the project. I also wish to thank Ingrid Mount, project editor, who guided with great efficiency the process of turning a manuscript into a finished book. I'm especially grateful to Larry Schnoor, executive secretary of the Interstate Oratorical Association, who provided copies of so many speeches and speech excerpts appearing throughout this edition. I also want to thank my colleagues who reviewed the text of the previous edition and the manuscript for this edition and shared their many insights and suggestions for improvement with me. Thank you:

Ernest W. Bartow, *Bucks County Community College*

Melissa L. Beall, *University of Northern Iowa*

James Benjamin, *University of Toledo*

David M. Cheshier, *Georgia State University*

Thom Goodwin, *James Madison University*

Robert Gwynne, *University of Tennessee*

Douglas B. Hoehn, *Community College of Pennsylvania*

David D. Hudson, *Golden West College*

Lawrence Hosman, *University of Southern Mississippi*

Thomas May, *Indiana University SE*

Audrey P. Olmsted, *Rhode Island College*
Patti A. Redmond, *Sacramento City College*
Elizabeth Threnhauser, *Northeastern University*
Susan Scheiberg, *University of Southern California*
Roy Schwartzman, *University of South Carolina*
Debra S. Van Tassel, *University of Colorado at Boulder*
David E. Walker, *Middle Tennessee State*
Kent L. Zimmerman, *Sinclair Community College*

Joseph A. DeVito

Studying Public Speaking

UNIT CONTENTS	UNIT OBJECTIVES
	After completing this unit, you should be able to:
Studying Public Speaking	Describe the benefits to be derived from studying public speaking.
Elements of Public Speaking	Define public speaking, distinguish it from conversation, and explain the major elements in public speaking: speaker, messages, channels, audience, context, delivery, and ethics.
Culture and Public Speaking	Explain the role of culture in public speaking.

All the great speakers were bad speakers at first.
—Ralph Waldo Emerson

Of all your college courses, public speaking will surely be the most demanding, satisfying, frustrating, stimulating, ego-involving, and useful, both now and throughout your professional life. In this first unit we introduce the study of public speaking, explaining what it is and what its essential elements are. Public speaking is then placed in a cultural context that is introduced here and followed up throughout the remaining units.

STUDYING PUBLIC SPEAKING

Examine your own beliefs about public speaking by taking the accompanying Test Yourself: "What do you believe about public speaking?"

TEST YOURSELF
What Do You Believe About Public Speaking?

Throughout this text are 17 self-tests asking you to pause and reflect on your thoughts and behaviors. In working with these tests, focus on the statements in the test, on the issues they raise, and on the thoughts they help generate. The number you get "right" or "wrong" or the score you get (some tests yield scores for comparison purposes) are far less important.

For each of the following statements, respond with T if the statement is a generally accurate reflection of your thinking about public speaking or with F if the statement is a generally inaccurate reflection.

_____ 1. Public speaking is a useful art for formal occasions but has little place in my own professional or social life.
_____ 2. Good public speakers are born, not made.
_____ 3. The more speeches you give, the better you'll become at it.
_____ 4. You'll never be a good public speaker if you're afraid to give a speech.
_____ 5. It's best to memorize your speech, especially if you're fearful.
_____ 6. Public speaking is a one-way process, going from speaker to audience and rarely from audience to speaker.

_____ 7. If you're a good writer, you'll be a good public speaker; a poor writer, a poor speaker.

_____ 8. Like a good novel, play, or essay, a good speech is relevant to all people at all times.

_____ 9. The First Amendment allows the public speaker total freedom of expression.

_____10. The skills of public speaking are similar throughout the world.

All 10 of these statements are (generally) false. As you'll see throughout this book, these assumptions can get in the way of learning the skills of public speaking. Briefly, here are the reasons why each of the statements is generally false, reasons that will be explained in more detail throughout the rest of the text. (1) Public speaking is actually more often found in relatively informal situations than in formal ones, though clearly it's also used extensively in formal business and politics. Further, as you go up the organizational ladder, your need to speak in public will increase. (2) Effective public speaking is a learned skill; although some people are born brighter or more extroverted, all can improve their abilities and become more effective public speakers. (3) If you practice bad habits, you're more likely to grow less effective than more effective; consequently, it's important to learn and follow the principles of effectiveness. (4) Most speakers are nervous; managing, not eliminating, fear will enable you to become effective regardless of your current level of fear. (5) Memorizing your speech is probably the worst thing you can do; there are easier ways to deal with fear. (6) Audiences also send messages that effective speakers attend and adapt to. (7) Speaking and writing are really two different processes; poor writers can be great speakers and great writers can be poor speakers. However, speaking and writing do share many skills, for example, breadth of knowledge, diligence, and a desire to communicate will be assets to both speaker and writer. (8) Speeches are generally given for a specific audience and a specific occasion rather than for all time. Some speeches do, however, express universal values and themes that make them more widely relevant. (9) Actually, freedom of expression does not legalize slander, libel, defamation, or plagiarism. (10) The techniques of public speaking are actually culture specific; speakers in Asian cultures, for example, would be advised to appear modest while speakers in the United States would be advised to appear confident, competent, and authoritative.

The Benefits of Public Speaking

Fair questions to ask of any course or book are "What will I get out of this?" "How will the effort and time I put into this class and this textbook benefit me?" Here are just a few of the benefits you'll derive from these experiences.

Enhance Personal and Social Abilities. Public speaking provides training in a variety of personal and social competencies. For example, we will cover such skills as self-awareness, self-confidence, and dealing with the fear of communicating. These skills certainly apply in public speaking, but you will find them valuable in all of your social interactions. It's relevant to note that students from varied cultures studying in the United States see public speaking as a method for climbing up the socioeconomic ladder (Collier and Powell 1990).

Improve Your Academic and Career Skills. As you learn public speaking, you'll also learn a wide variety of academic and career skills. These skills

If all my possessions were taken from me with one exception, I would choose to keep the power of speech, for by it I would soon regain all the rest.
—Daniel Webster

TIPS
from professional speakers

When we consider candidates for promotion in management, much of our impression comes from the time those candidates have spoken in office meetings. Or from the memos or letters they've prepared. When we consider candidates for a state vice presidency, we think about their primary role:

• communicating with employees, customers, and regulators.

When we promote people to our holding company, U.S. West in Denver, we think about their primary role:

• communicating with shareowners, stock analysts, and subsidiaries.

Without a doubt, communication skills continue to grow more important.

Richard D. McCormick, president, Northwestern Bell. "Business Loves English," *Vital Speeches of the Day* 51 (November 1, 1984):53.

are central, but not limited, to public speaking. Among these are your abilities to:

- do research efficiency and effectively.
- explain complex concepts clearly.
- support an argument with all available means of persuasion.
- understand human motivation and be able to use your insights in persuasive encounters.
- organize a variety of messages for clarity and persuasiveness.
- present yourself to others with confidence and self-assurance.
- analyze and evaluate the validity of persuasive appeals.

Refine Your General Communication Abilities. Public speaking also develops and refines your general communication abilities by helping you improve competencies such as:

- developing a more effective communication style.
- adjusting messages to specific listeners.
- giving and responding appropriately to criticism.
- developing logical and emotional appeals.
- communicating your credibility.
- improving listening skills.
- organizing extended messages.
- refining your delivery skills.

Improve Your Public Speaking Abilities. Speakers aren't born—they're made. Through instruction, exposure to different speeches, feedback, and individual learning experiences, you can become an effective speaker. Regardless of your present level of competence, you can improve through proper training—hence this course and this book.

At the end of this course you'll be a more competent, confident, and effective public speaker. You'll also be a more effective listener—more open yet more critical, more empathic yet more discriminating. You'll emerge a more competent and discerning critic of public communication.

As a leader (and in many ways you can look at this course as one in leadership training skills), you'll need the skills of effective communication to help preserve a free and open society. These skills apply to you as a speaker who wants your message understood and accepted, as a listener who needs to evaluate and critically analyze ideas and arguments before making decisions, and as a critic who needs to evaluate and judge the thousands of public communications heard every day.

Historical Roots of Public Speaking

Public speaking is both a very old and a very new art. It's likely that public speaking principles were developed soon after our species began to talk. Much of contemporary public speaking—at least the Western tradition of public speaking—is based on the works of the ancient Greeks and Romans who articulated an especially insightful system of rhetoric or public speaking. This tradition has been enriched by the experiments, surveys, field studies, and historical studies that have been done since then.

Aristotle's *Rhetoric*, written some 2,300 years ago, was one of the earliest systematic studies of public speaking. It was in this work that the three kinds of proof—*logos* (or logical proof), *pathos* (emotional appeals), and *ethos* (appeals based on the character of the speaker)—were introduced. This three-part division is still followed today; Units 21, 22, and 23 discuss these specifically.

Roman rhetoricians added to the work of the Greeks. Quintilian, who taught in Rome during the first century, built an entire educational system—from childhood through adulthood—based on the development of the effective and responsible orator. Throughout these 2,300 years, the study of public speaking has grown and developed.

Contemporary public speaking builds on this classical heritage and also incorporates insights from the humanities, the social and behavioral sciences, and now, computer science and technology. Likewise, perspectives from different cultures are being integrated into our present study of public speaking. Table 1.1 shows some of the contributors to contemporary

TABLE 1.1 The Growth and Development of Public Speaking

How might the courses you're studying this semester contribute to your understanding of public speaking and to increasing your public speaking abilities?

Academic Roots	Contributions to Contemporary Public Speaking
Classical rhetoric	Emphasis on substance; ethical responsibilities of the speaker; using a combination of logical, ethical, and emotional appeals; the strategies of organization.
Literary and rhetorical criticism	Approaches to and standards for evaluation; insights into style and language.
Philosophy	Emphasis on the logical validity of arguments; continuing contribution to ethics.
Public address	Insights into how famous speakers dealt with varied purposes and audiences to achieve desired effects.
Psychology	How language is encoded and decoded and made easier to understand and remember; theories and findings on attitude change; emphasis on speech effects.
General Semantics	Emphasis on using language to describe reality accurately; techniques for avoiding common thinking errors that faulty language usage creates.
Communication theory	Insights on information transmission; the importance of viewing the whole of the communication act; the understanding of such concepts as feedback, noise, channel, and message.
Computer science	The virtual audience; design and presentation software; outlining software; search tools for research; easily accessed databases.
Interpersonal communication	Transactionalism; emphasis on mutual influence of speaker and audience.
Sociology	Data on audiences' attitudes, values, opinions, and beliefs and how these influence exposure to and responses to messages.
Anthropology	Insights into the attitudes, beliefs, and values of different cultures and how these influence communications.

The whole of science is nothing more than a refinement of everyday thinking.
—Albert Einstein

public speaking and illustrates the wide research and theory base from which its principles are drawn.

ELEMENTS OF PUBLIC SPEAKING

We can explain public speaking by identifying its essential elements and processes and by comparing and contrasting it to everyday conversation. In public speaking *a speaker presents a relatively continuous message to a relatively large audience in a unique context* (see Figure 1.1).

Public speaking, like all forms of communication, is a transactional process, a process whose elements or parts are interdependent, never independent (Watzlawick, Beavin, and Jackson 1967; Watzlawick 1978). Each element in the public speaking process depends on and interacts with all other elements. For example, the way in which you organize a speech will depend on such factors as the speech topic, the specific audience, the purpose you hope to achieve, and a host of other variables, all of which are explained in the remainder of this unit and in the units that follow.

Especially important is the mutual interaction and influence between speaker and listener. True, when you give a public speech, you do most of the speaking and the listeners do most of the listening. The listeners, however, also send messages in the form of feedback, for example, applause,

FIGURE 1.1

The Public Speaking Transaction.

How would you diagram the process of public speaking?

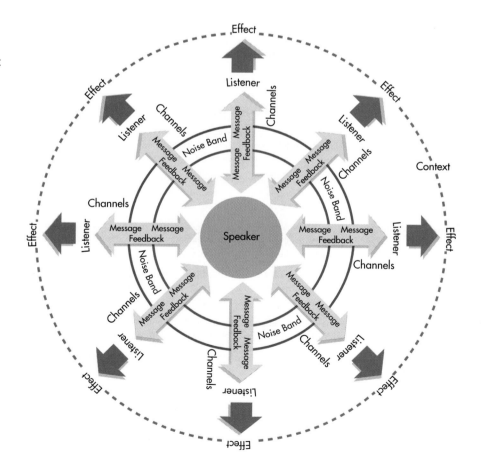

bored looks, nods of agreement or disagreement, and attentive glances. The audience also influences how you'll prepare and present your speech. It influences your arguments, language, method of organization—almost every choice you make. You would not, for example, present the same speech on saving money to high school students as you would to senior citizens.

Speaker

In conversation the speaker's role exists in short spurts; Alice says something to which Rick replies to which Alice responds, and so on. In public speaking you deliver a relatively long speech and are usually not interrupted. As a result, the public speaker occupies a more central position— you're the center of the transaction; you and your speech are the reason for the gathering.

As a speaker you bring to the public speaking situation all that you are and all that you know. Further, you bring with you all that the audience thinks you are and thinks you know. Everything about you becomes significant and contributes to the total effect of your speech. Your knowledge, speech purpose, speaking ability, and attitudes toward the audience tell the audience who you are.

Message

In both conversation and public speaking you communicate with some purpose in mind. For example, in conversation you might want to tell a friend about what happened at a recent basketball game. In this case your purpose is informative. Or you might want to convince your boss to give you a raise. Here your purpose is persuasive. In public speaking, you also communicate with a clear purpose in mind, and public speeches serve these same functions.

If you wanted to convince your friend to go to the movies, you would not simply say, "Come to the movies with me." More likely, you would offer some reasons or inducements: "It's a really exciting movie," or "Today is the last day it's playing." The number of arguments or reasons you offer will depend on how resistant you think your friend might be. The same is true in public speaking. You don't simply say, "Vote for Johnson." Rather, you would give your listeners reasons why they should vote for Johnson and perhaps reasons why they shouldn't vote for Johnson's opponent. This is where the often-dreaded research comes in; you have to discover through research the reasons why your listeners should vote for Johnson. What are Johnson's voting records, achievements, and competencies?

Technology has made an enormous body of information available to everyone. The World Wide Web alone contains more information than would ever have been in any single library, and all of it is available on your desktop. At the same time, technology has made searching for just the right information extremely easy and a great deal of fun.

Generally, in conversation you don't give any real thought to how you're going to organize your message. In public speaking, however, organization is crucial because it's an extremely useful tool for both informing and persuading an audience. Organization adds clarity to your message and therefore makes it easier for listeners to understand what you're saying. At the same time, it will help listeners remember what you said.

TIPS from professional speakers

You can become a speaker if you have these assets:

1. A voice.
2. Ordinary knowledge of language; that is, a working vocabulary and a reasonable acquaintance with grammar.
3. Something to say.
4. A desire to convey your thoughts to others.

You have been using these assets for years. You have been saying something to others, informally, dozens of times daily. Under these circumstances, you call it "conversation." Conversation is speech to the few. Public speaking is, basically, conversation adapted to a larger group.

Maurice Forley, former executive director, Toastmasters International, Inc. *A Practical Guide to Public Speaking* (North Hollywood, CA: Wilshire Book Company, 1965):2.

For it is feeling and force of imagination that makes us eloquent.
—Quintilian

Organization—for example, where you put your strongest argument or how you develop an argument to present to a hostile audience—is one of your most powerful persuasive tools.

In conversation you vary your language on the basis of the person with whom you're speaking, the topic you're talking about, and where you're located. When talking with children, for example, you might use easier words and shorter sentences than you would with friends. If you were trying to impress someone, say, at a job interview, you might use a more sophisticated style. In public speaking you also adjust your language to your audience, the topic, and the situation in the same way as in conversation. In public speaking, however, your listeners can't interrupt you to ask what a particular word means or to repeat that last sentence. Your language must be instantly intelligible.

Channels

In public speaking a speaker addresses a relatively large audience with a relatively continuous discourse. Usually, it takes place in a face-to-face situation: you deliver an oral report in your economics class, you ask your co-workers to elect you as shop steward, you try to convince your neighbors to clean up the streets or other students to donate blood. These are all public speaking situations. But, increasingly often, public speaking is mediated; often it's delivered in a television studio and heard by millions in their own livingrooms. And as it has changed so much else, the Internet has given new life to public speaking, making it much easier for the average person to reach large audiences. As video and sound capabilities become more universal, public speaking on the Net is likely to increase dramatically in frequency and in cultural significance.

Messages are the signals sent by the speaker and received by the listener or from listener to speaker. These signals pass through one or more channels on their way from speaker to listener and from listener to speaker. The channel is the medium that carries the message signals from sender to receiver. Both the auditory and the visual channels are significant in public speaking. Through the auditory channel, you send your spoken messages—your words and your sentences. At the same time, you also send messages through a visual channel—through eye contact (or the lack of it), body movement, hand and facial gestures, and clothing.

Noise

Noise interferes with your receiving a message someone is sending or with their receiving your message. Noise may be physical (others talking loudly, cars honking, illegible handwriting, "garbage" on your computer screen), physiological (hearing or visual impairment, articulation disorders), psychological (preconceived ideas, wandering thoughts), or semantic (misunderstood meanings). Technically, noise is anything that distorts the message, anything that prevents the listeners from receiving your message. All channels contain noise or interference. Each medium has a built-in source of noise.

A useful concept in understanding noise and its importance in public speaking is "signal-to-noise ratio." *Signal* refers to information that you'd find useful and *noise* refers to information that is useless (to you). So, for example, a mailing list or newsgroup that contains lots of useful information would be high on signal and low on noise; those that contained lots of useless information would be high on noise and low on signal. When you search for a topic on the Web and the search engine identifies 6,342 sources, much of them will be noise interfering with your securing the messages you want. Junk mail and the corresponding phone calls urging you to switch phone companies or get a new credit card would also be examples of noise (at least to those who don't want to switch phone companies or get a new credit card).

Public speaking involves visual as well as spoken messages, so it's important to see that noise may also be visual. The sunglasses that prevent someone from seeing the nonverbal messages from your eyes would be considered noise as would dark print on a dark background in your slides. Table 1.2 identifies these four major types of noise in more detail.

All public speaking situations will involve noise. You will not be able to totally eliminate it, but you can try to reduce its effects. Making your language more precise, organizing your thoughts more logically, and presenting your speech with reinforcement from visual aids are some ways to combat the influence of noise.

Audience

In conversation the "audience" is often one listener or perhaps a few. The audience in public speaking is relatively large, from groups of perhaps 10 or 12 to audiences of hundreds of thousands, even millions.

The audience is not the least important actor in the play and if it will not do its allotted share the play falls to pieces. The dramatist then is in the position of a tennis player who is left on the court with nobody to play with.
—Somerset Maugham

TABLE 1.2 Four Types of Noise

One of the most important skills in public speaking is to recognize the types of noise and to develop ways to combat them. Consider, for example, what kinds of noise occur in the classroom? What kinds of noise occur in Internet communication? What kinds occur at public speaking presentations at work? What can you do to combat these kinds of noise?

Types of Noise	Definition	Example
Physical	Interference that's external to both speaker and listener; it interferes with the physical transmission of the signal or message.	Screeching of passing cars, hum of computer, sunglasses.
Physiological	Physical barriers within the speaker or listener.	Visual impairments, hearing loss, articulation problems, memory loss.
Psychological	Cognitive or mental interference.	Biases and prejudices in speakers and listeners, closed-mindedness, inaccurate expectations, extreme emotionalism (anger, hate, love, grief).
Semantic	Speaker and listener assigning different meanings.	People speaking different languages, use of jargon or overly complex terms not understood by listener, dialectical differences in meaning.

If you were the speaker in this photo, what kinds of noise would you anticipate? What might you do to combat these noise sources?

In both conversation and public speaking, your listeners will influence what you say and how you say it. You would not try to convince your friend to go to the movie with the same arguments you would use to convince an instructor to accept a late paper. Usually, in conversations, you know your listeners so well that you don't even think about adjusting your messages to them. But you do make adjustments. Think, for example, of how differently you would relay the events of the day to your parents, friends, employer, and children.

In some public speaking situations—say, you're addressing work colleagues—you may know your audience quite well. In other public speaking situations, however, you may not know your audience quite so well and will have to analyze them to discover what they already know (so you don't repeat old news) and what their attitudes are (so you don't waste time persuading them of something they already believe).

In the popular mind, communication is often taken as synonymous with speaking. Listening is either neglected or regarded as something apart from "real communication." But, as emphasized in the model of public speaking presented earlier and as stressed throughout this book, listening is integral to all communication, and public speaking is certainly no exception. Public speaking isn't just the art of adjusting messages to listeners, it also involves active involvement by the listeners. The listener plays a role in encouraging or discouraging the speaker, in offering constructive criticism, in evaluating public messages, and in performing a wide variety of other functions.

If you measured importance by the time you spend on an activity, then listening would be your most important communication activity (Figure 1.2). In one study, conducted in 1926 (Rankin), listening occupied 45% of a person's communication time; speaking was second with 30%; reading (16%) and writing (9%) followed. In another study of college students, conducted in 1980 (Barker, Edwards, Gaines, Gladney, and Holley), listening also occupied the most time: 53% compared to reading (17%), speaking (16%), and writing (14%).

Because listening is so important (and so often neglected) in public speaking, it is covered in two ways. First, Unit 4: Listening discusses the nature of listening, the forms of listening, and suggestions for improving your listening effectiveness. Second, a series of "Listen to This" boxes are distributed throughout the text. These boxes relate listening to the topic of the unit and

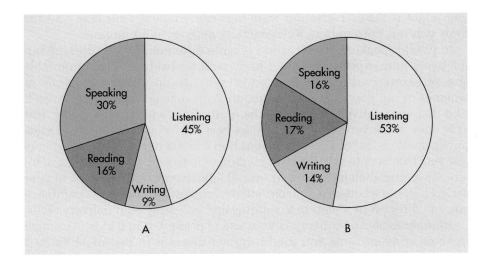

FIGURE 1.2
The Time Spent in Communication.
This figure diagrams the results of two studies (A = Rankin 1929, B = Barker, Edwards, Gaines, Gladney, and Holley 1980) and confirms the point that listening occupies an enormous part of our communication life. What percentages would you assign for your own listening, speaking, reading, and writing time?

remind us that listening is an essential part of the public speaking act. Among the topics discussed in these boxes are listening to criticism (Unit 5), listening to gender differences (Units 10 and 15), listening to new ideas (Unit 19), listening to emotional appeals (Unit 22), and listening to empower (Unit 23).

Context

Speaker and listeners operate in a physical, socio-psychological, temporal, and cultural context. The context influences you as the speaker, the audience, the speech, and the effects of the speech.

- The **physical context** is the actual place in which you give your speech (the room, hallway, park, or auditorium). A presentation in a small intimate room needs to be very different from one in a sports arena.
- The **socio-psychological context** includes, for example, the relationship between speaker and audience: Is it a supervisor speaking to workers or a worker speaking to supervisors? A principal addressing teachers or a parent addressing principals? It also includes the audience's attitudes toward and knowledge of the speaker and subject. You can't, for example, treat a supportive and a hostile audience similarly.
- The **temporal context** includes, for example, the time of day and, more importantly, where your speech fits into the sequence of events. For example, does your speech follow one that has taken an opposing position? Is your speech the sixth in a series exploring the same topic?
- The **cultural context** refers to the beliefs, lifestyles, values, and ways of behaving that the speaker and the audience bring with them and that bear on the topic and purpose of the speech. Appealing to the "competitive spirit" and "financial gain" may prove effective with Wall Street executives but ineffective with those who are more comfortable with socialist or communist economic systems and beliefs.

Delivery

In conversation you normally don't even think of how you'd deliver or present your message; you wouldn't concern yourself with how to stand or gesture or how you would raise or lower your vocal volume. Of course,

Speech is power; speech is to persuade, to convert, to compel.
—Ralph Waldo Emerson

you might if the conversation were between you and your boss and the topic was your promotion. But, generally delivery is a nonissue.

In public speaking, the situation is quite different. Public speaking is a relatively new experience and at first you'll probably feel uncomfortable and self-conscious. You may wonder what to do with your hands or whether or not you should move about. With time and experience, you'll find that your delivery will follow naturally from what you're saying, just as it does in conversation. Perhaps the best advice at this time is to view public speaking as "enlarged" conversation and not to worry about delivery just yet. This isn't to say that your method of delivery is unimportant; actually, it's a crucial element to your overall effectiveness. It's just that in your early efforts, it's better to concentrate on content. As you gain confidence you can direct your attention to refining and polishing your delivery skills.

Another aspect of delivery is your use of presentational aids. Although in some conversations you might draw a diagram in the air or show a photograph, generally, the issue of presentation aids is irrelevant in conversation. In public speaking, however, presentation aids take on great importance. Just think of what your classes would be like if the instructor limited the lecture to spoken words. Presentation aids are crucial to most public speeches and will greatly influence your effectiveness. And, just as technology has changed the complexion of research, it has also changed the nature of presentation aids—from the simple word chart to complete slide shows with audio and video components. Technology has raised the benchmark as to what constitutes effective public speaking.

Ethics

As a public speaker, you design and deliver your speeches to influence listeners: politicians give campaign speeches to secure your vote; advertisers give sales pitches to get you to buy their products; teachers give lectures to influence your thinking about history, psychology, or communication. Because your speeches will have effects, you have an obligation to consider the moral implications of your messages throughout the public-speaking process. When you develop your topic, present your research, create the persuasive appeals, and do any of the other tasks related to public speaking, there are ethical issues to be considered (Jaksa and Pritchard 1994; Bok 1978; Johannesen 1996). The listener and the critic also have ethical obligations; for example, listeners have an obligation to give a speaker a fair hearing and critics have an obligation to render a fair and unbiased evaluation.

Ethics—the morality of an act—is an integral part of all public speaking for speaker, listener, and critic. Here are just a few issues we consider throughout the text. As you read down the list, consider what you *would* do if confronted with this issue. What do you feel you *should* do (if this is different from what you *would* do)? What general principle of ethics are you using in making these *would* and *should* judgments?

- Would it be ethical to use questionable means to achieve a worthwhile end? For example, would it be wrong for a speaker to exaggerate if by doing so he or she might achieve some respectable goal, for example, getting teens to stop smoking?

- Would it be ethical to persuade an audience by scaring or threatening them if your goal was to get them to do something beneficial, such as exercise? To get them to follow a particular religious belief? To get them to do something that would benefit, say, the poor and homeless?
- Would it be ethical to assume leadership of a group to get the group to do as you wish?

Because ethics is so important in public speaking, we follow up this introductory discussion with a series of 18 ethics boxes distributed throughout the text. These boxes will serve as frequent reminders that ethics is an integral part of all aspects of public speaking. These boxed discussions will also raise ethical issues that are especially relevant to the topic of the unit in which they appear. Among the topics discussed are ethical responsibilities of the speaker, listener, and critic (Units 3, 4, and 5); plagiarism (Unit 7); accountability (Unit 12); and the ethics of propaganda techniques (Units 20 and 21), emotional appeals (Unit 22), and credibility appeals (Unit 23).

CULTURE AND PUBLIC SPEAKING

Walk through any large city, many small towns, and just about any college campus, and you will see that the United States is largely a collection of many different cultures. They may co-exist somewhat separately, but they also influence each other (Figure 1.3). We need to see public speaking within this cultural context. As demonstrated throughout this text,

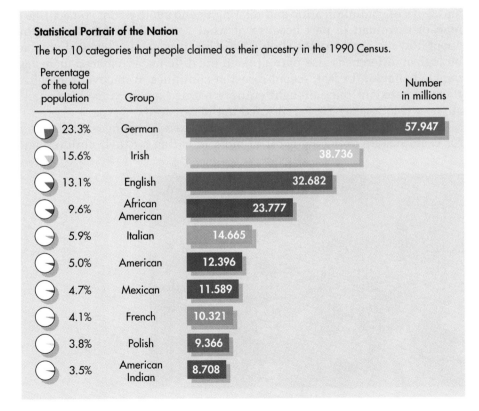

Statistical Portrait of the Nation

The top 10 categories that people claimed as their ancestry in the 1990 Census.

Percentage of the total population	Group	Number in millions
23.3%	German	57.947
15.6%	Irish	38.736
13.1%	English	32.682
9.6%	African American	23.777
5.9%	Italian	14.665
5.0%	American	12.396
4.7%	Mexican	11.589
4.1%	French	10.321
3.8%	Polish	9.366
3.5%	American Indian	8.708

FIGURE 1.3

Ancestry of United States Residents.

With immigration patterns changing so rapidly, the portrait illustrated here is likely to look very different in the coming years. For example, by the year 2030, it's predicted that the U.S. population will be 73.6 percent white, 12 percent African American, 10.2 percent Hispanic, and 3.3 percent Asian American. By the year 2050 it's predicted that the percentages will be 52.8 percent white, 24.5 percent Hispanic, 13.6 percent African American, and 8.2 percent Asian American (figures projected by the Census Bureau and reported in *The New York Times,* March 14, 1996, p. A16). To what factors might you attribute these projections? What will your own state, city, or town look like in 2030? In 2050?

cultural differences span the entire public speaking spectrum, from the way you use eye contact to the way you develop an argument or present criticism (Chang and Holt 1996).

Race, Nationality, Gender, and Culture

Culture is the collection of beliefs, attitudes, values, and ways of behaving shared by a group of people and passed down from one generation to the next through communication rather than through genes. Thus, culture does not refer to genetic traits such as color of skin or shape of eyes; culture does refer to beliefs in a supreme being, to attitudes toward family, and to the values placed on friendship or money.

Culture is not synonymous with race or nationality, although members of a particular race are often enculturated into a similar set of beliefs, attitudes, and values. Similarly, members living in the same country are often taught similar beliefs, attitudes, and values. And this similarity makes it possible for us to speak of a "Hispanic culture" or an "African American culture." Lest we be guilty of stereotyping, though, we need to recognize that within any large culture—especially a culture based on race or nationality—there will be enormous differences. The Kansas farmer may in some ways be closer to the Chinese farmer than to the Wall Street executive. Further, as an individual born into a particular race and nationality, you don't necessarily have to adopt the attitudes, beliefs, and values that may be dominant among the people of that race and nationality.

In a similar way, gender can be considered a cultural variable largely because cultures teach boys and girls different attitudes, beliefs, values, and ways of communicating and relating to one another. So, you act like a man or a woman in part because of what your culture has taught you about how men and women should act. This does not, of course, deny that biological differences also play a role in the differences between male and female behavior. In fact, recent research continues to uncover biological roots of behavior once thought entirely learned, such as happiness and shyness (McCroskey 1997, reprinted in the Appendix.

In addition, we're living in a time of great gender changes. Many men, for example, are doing a great deal more in caring for their children and

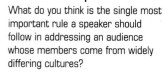

What do you think is the single most important rule a speaker should follow in addressing an audience whose members come from widely differing cultures?

the concept, if not the term, "house husband" is becoming increasingly common and perhaps a little less negative. More obvious perhaps is that many women are becoming much more visible in fields once occupied exclusively by men—politics, law enforcement, the military, and the clergy are just some examples. And, of course, women are increasingly entering corporate executive ranks; the glass ceiling may not have disappeared, but it is cracked.

The Relevance of Culture

There are many reasons for the cultural emphasis you'll find in this book, and probably in all your textbooks. Most obviously, perhaps, are the vast demographic changes taking place throughout the United States. Whereas at one time the United States was largely a country populated by Europeans, it is now a country greatly influenced by the enormous number of new citizens from South America, Africa, and Asia. The same is true on college and university campuses throughout the United States. Here are a few random facts to further support the importance of culture generally and of intercultural communication in particular (*Time* December 2, 1993, p. 14):

- Over 30 million people in the United States speak languages other than English in their homes.
- In the school systems of cities such as New York; Fairfax County, Virginia; Chicago; and Los Angeles over 100 languages are spoken.
- Over 50 percent of the residents of such cities as Miami and Hialeah in Florida, Union City in New Jersey, and Huntington Park and Monterey Park in California are foreign born.
- The foreign born population of the United States in 1990 totaled almost 20 million, approximately 8 percent of the total U.S. population; a 1997 update reports it as 25.8 million or 9.7 percent of the population (Schmidley and Alvarado 1997).
- Thirty percent of U.S. Nobel prizewinners (since 1901) were foreign born.

With these changes come different communication customs and the need to understand and adapt to these new ways of looking at communication generally and public speaking specifically.

We're also living in a time when people have become increasingly sensitive to the importance of cultural differences. From an originally assimilationist perspective (people should leave their native culture behind and adapt to their new culture), we've moved to one that values cultural diversity (people should retain their native cultural ways). And, with some notable exceptions—hate speech, racism, sexism, classism, and homophobia come quickly to mind—we seem to be more concerned with saying the right thing and with ultimately developing a society where all cultures can coexist and enrich each other.

At the same time, the ability to interact effectively in public speaking situations (as well as interpersonally and in small groups) with members of other cultures translates into financial gain. The increased economic interdependence of the United States and widely differing cultures makes it essential to gain the needed intercultural communication understanding and skills.

TIPS
from professional speakers

Life is a constant process of experimentation and learning. And because so much of life's successes depend on presenting ideas, doesn't it make sense to build your presentation skills? If you are willing to push out of your comfort zone a bit, you are ready to try on new behaviors.

Paul R. Timm, author and communication trainer and popular speaker, *How to Make Winning Presentations.* (Franklin Lakes, NJ: Career Press, 1997):8.

You may wish to continue this "cultural awareness" experience by taking the accompanying self-test "What's Your Cultural Awareness?"

TEST YOURSELF
What's Your Cultural Awareness?

The following questions are designed to stimulate you to reflect on what you know about the world and its cultures.

1. The major language of education in India is
   (a) English   (b) Hindi   (c) Urdu

2. The major ancestral group in the United States (as of the 1990 census) was:
   (a) German   (b) Irish   (c) Mexican

3. The largest number of Africans are
   (a) Christians   (b) Muslims   (c) Tribal religionists

4. The nation with the highest literacy rate (100 percent) is:
   (a) Cuba   (b) Kyrgyzstan   (c) United States

5. The nation holding the most U.S. patents granted to residents of areas outside the United States and its territories is:
   (a) France   (b) Germany   (c) Japan

6. The country with the longest expectation of life at birth is:
   (a) Canada   (b) Japan   (c) Sweden

7. Based on projected census figures for the year 2020, the country with the largest population (we're purposely omitting China—that would be too easy) will be:
   (a) India   (b) Indonesia   (c) United States

8. The nation whose per capita annual income is less than $1,000 is:
   (a) Nigeria   (b) Pakistan   (c) Philippines

9. The state with the largest number of native Americans (defined by the U.S. Department of commerce, Bureau of the Census as American Indian, Eskimo, and Aleut) is:
   (a) Arizona   (b) California   (c) Oklahoma

10. The divorce rate is highest in:
    (a) Japan   (b) Sweden   (c) United States

The answers (all, except item 6, are from current Almanacs and are as follows: (1) English. (2) Germans constitute the largest group, Irish the second, and English the third; more complete answers are given in Figure 1.3. (By the time you read this, more up-to-date data may be available. Visit http://www.census.gov/ for the latest census data or http://www.fedstats.gov/ for a wide variety of statistics.) (3) The largest number of Africans are Christian (327,204,000 Africans are Christian) with Muslims (278,250,800), and tribal religionists (70,588,000) the next largest groups. (4) Of the nations listed in this question, only Kyrgyzstan has a literacy rate of 100 percent along with such other countries as Armenia, Australia, and Andorra. Cuba has a literacy rate of 99 percent (along with North Korea, Denmark, the Czech Republic, Ireland, and Barbados). The literacy rate for the United States is 97 percent. These figures contrast sharply with those nations that have literacy rates below 50 percent, for example, Iran, Bangladesh, Senegal, Uganda, and Afghanistan. (5) Japan holds the largest number of patents, Germany is second, and France is third. (6) Japan has the longest life span, Canada is second, and Sweden is third [*Newsweek* Dec 28 1998–Jan 4 1999, p. 71]. (7) China is projected to have the greatest population with 1,424,725,000. India will rank a close second with a projected population of 1,320,746,000. The United States will be a distant third with 323,113,000, Indonesia will be fourth with 276,474,000, and Pakistan will be fifth with 275,100,000. By the year 2100, it's predicted, India will have the world's largest population. (8) All three nations listed have per capita annual incomes of less than $1,000. (9) The three states listed have the greatest Native American population; Oklahoma ranks first with 252,420, California is second with 242,164, and Arizona is third with 203,527. The three states with the fewest are Vermont (1,696), Delaware (2,019), and New Hampshire (2,134). (10) The divorce rate is highest in the United States (4.7 per 1000 population); Sweden has a divorce rate of 2.22, and Japan has a divorce rate of 1.27.

Did these questions and their answers surprise you in any way? For example, are you surprised that the United States is not in the top three in terms of life span? Are you surprised at the religions of Africa? Are you surprised that the divorce rate in the United States is twice as high as it is in Sweden? Can you trace any of these surprises to stereotypes you might have of certain countries?

The Aim of a Cultural Perspective

The principles for communicating information and for persuasion differ from one culture to another. If you're to understand public speaking, then you need to know how its principles vary on the basis of culture. Success in public speaking—as on your job and in your social life—will depend in great part on your understanding of and your ability to communicate effectively with persons who may have differing cultural perspectives.

Still another aim is to show that the principles of public speaking are specific to a given culture. What proves effective in one culture may prove ineffective in another; what is considered ethical in one culture may be considered unethical in another. For example, in some Asian cultures, it's important to avoid criticizing or embarrassing the speaker by, say, asking a question that he or she might not be able to answer. In the United States, especially in some competitive corporate and political settings, listeners may actively look for things that might be viewed negatively and might try to use this to embarrass the speaker.

This emphasis on culture does not imply that you should accept all cultural practices or that all cultural practices have to be viewed as equal (Hatfield and Rapson 1996). For example, cock fighting, fox hunting, and bull fighting are parts of the culture of some Latin American countries, England, and Spain, respectively, but you need not find these activities acceptable or equal to cultural practices in which animals are treated kindly. Further, a cultural emphasis does not imply that you have to accept or follow even the practices of your own culture. For example, even if the majority in your culture find cock fighting acceptable, you need not agree with or support the practice. Similarly, you can reject your culture's religious or political beliefs or its attitudes toward the homeless, the handicapped, or the culturally different. Of course, going against your culture's beliefs and values is often very difficult. But, it's important to realize that culture influences; it does not determine your values or

I am not an Athenian or a Greek, but a citizen of the world.
—Socrates

behavior. Often, for example, personality factors (your degree of assertiveness, independence, or optimism, for example) will prove more influential than culture (Hatfield and Rapson 1996).

The cultural differences discussed throughout this text shouldn't blind you to the great number of similarities existing among even the most widely separated cultures. Further, when reading about these differences, remember that these are usually matters of degree. Thus, for example, most cultures value honesty but not all value it to the same degree.

Advances in media and technology and the widespread use of the Internet are influencing cultures and cultural change and are perhaps homogenizing the different cultures, lessening the differences and increasing the similarities. They're also Americanizing the world's cultures because the dominant values and customs evidenced in the media and on the Internet are in large part American, a product of the current U.S. dominance in both media and technology.

UNIT IN BRIEF

Studying Public Speaking	1. increase your personal and social abilities, 2. enhance related academic and professional skills in organization, research, style, and the like, 3. refine general communication competencies, and 4. improve public speaking abilities —as speaker, as listener, and as critic—which result in personal benefits as well as benefits to society.
The Elements of Public Speaking	Public speaking is a transactional process in which (a) a speaker (b) addresses (c) a relatively large audience with (d) a relatively continuous message. Public speaking is similar and yet different from conversation in its major elements: speaker, messages, channels, audience, context, delivery, and ethics.
Culture and Public Speaking	Because of the demographic changes and the economic interdependence, cultural differences have become more significant. The aim of this perspective is to increase understanding of the role of culture in public speaking and to improve your skills in a context that is becoming increasing intercultural.

THINKING CRITICALLY ABOUT STUDYING PUBLIC SPEAKING

Throughout this book you'll cover a wide variety of skills that educators now group under the topic of "critical thinking." The objective of critical thinking training is to foster more reasoned and more reasonable decision making. It's the process of securing relevant information, analyzing and evaluating it logically, and applying what you know to a variety of situations. To help you achieve this, a series of four types of suggested questions and activities are presented at the end of each unit. As you can see, these deal with:

- reviewing and understanding the content of the unit
- evaluating alternative courses of action by developing public speaking strategies for a variety of situations
- evaluating speeches, your own as well as those of others, as a way of learning the principles of public speaking and sharpening your skills as listeners and critics
- using technology to further your study of both public speaking and technology itself

REVIEWING KEY TERMS AND CONCEPTS IN PUBLIC SPEAKING

These questions are designed to help you review the key terms and concepts covered in the unit. Each of the terms and concepts is preceded by a clear bullet that you might use to check your understanding.

1. Define the key terms covered in this unit:

   ❑ feedback (p. 6)
   ❑ public speaking (p.6)
   ❑ transactional nature of public speaking (p. 6)
   ❑ conversation (p. 7)
   ❑ speaker (p. 7)
   ❑ message (p. 7)
   ❑ channel (p. 8)
   ❑ noise (p. 8)
   ❑ audience (p. 9)
   ❑ context (p. 11)
   ❑ delivery (p. 11)
   ❑ ethics (p. 12)
   ❑ culture (p. 14)

2. Explain the key concepts discussed in this unit:

   - What benefits might you derive from the study of public speaking? What are some of the major contributors to the development of public speaking?
   - What are the essential elements of public speaking? How does public speaking differ from conversation?
   - What impact does culture have on public speaking?

DEVELOPING PUBLIC SPEAKING STRATEGIES

These questions pose choice points and ask that you consider the strategies you would use to accomplish a specific goal.

1. John has put off the required course in public speaking for as long as he could; he's now a senior and needs the course for graduation. John is simply too scared to ever get in front of a class and give a speech—or at least that's how he thinks now. What might you say to John to ease his fear (in addition to recommending that he skip to Unit 3 and read that as soon as possible)?

2. Joyce is planning to work as an editor in publishing and sees no value in taking public speaking; she argues that she'll never need this in her professional life. She's determined to put as little into the course as possible and just get by with a respectable "C." What suggestions might you make to Joyce?

EVALUATING PUBLIC SPEECHES

These suggested activities will serve two purposes: first, they'll help you evaluate your own speech preparation (that is, as a speaker) and second, they'll guide you in evaluating the speeches of others (that is, as a critic).

1. Think about a recent classroom lecture you heard. In what way did the instructor take the audience into consideration? What specifically did the instructor do or say that helped to relate the message of the lecture to the listeners?

2. Recall a recent speech or read one in the appendix. In what ways does the speech differ from conversation? Can you point to specific parts of the speech that define and characterize it as a public presentation rather than as conversation?

USING TECHNOLOGY IN PUBLIC SPEAKING

These suggestions will encourage you to use the most technologically sophisticated resources in learning about public speaking and in preparing and presenting your speeches. Bookmark those you find especially helpful or those you think you'd like to revisit.

1. Visit the Podium at http://www.awl.longman.podium, a Web site designed for use with this particular textbook. What information might prove valuable to you as you select topics for your speech, research them, organize them, put your ideas into words, and deliver them?

2. Current ethical issues are identified with links to a variety of related resources at http://www.acusd.edu/ethics/.

3. Visit a Web site devoted to a particular group of people such as http://www.lainet.com/~joejones/ (on African Americans), http://www.mit.edu:8001/afs/athena.mit.edu/user/i/r/irie/www/aar.html (Asian Americans), or http://www.latinolink.com/ (Hispanic Americans). In what way can visiting such Web sites contribute to your cultural understanding?

4. Using one of the search engines—Yahoo at http://www.yahoo.com, Excite at http://www.excite.com, Alta Vista at http://altavista.digital.com, or Infoseek at http://www.infoseek.com (see Table 7.1 for more suggestions and addresses)—search for "public speeches." What kinds of speeches are available on the Web?

PRACTICALLY SPEAKING

*These practical experiences, presented at the end of each unit, are designed to stimulate you to think more actively about the concepts and skills covered in the unit and to practice your developing public speaking skills. The first exercise in each unit is the SST, the **Short Speech Technique**. This exercise provides a vehicle for integrating lots of short speeches into the course in addition to the traditional longer and more carefully crafted speeches. These short speeches all deal with the contents of the unit and so serve the dual function of covering the text material while also affording opportunities to practice your new public speaking skills. As the course progresses, these short speeches should incorporate increasingly sophisticated application of the public speaking principles. The next unit will provide specific guidelines to follow for these and all speeches. For the short speeches in this unit, use whatever principles of public speaking you think are appropriate.*

1.1 Short Speech Technique

Prepare and deliver a two-minute speech in which you:

a. explain the role of public speaking in a particular profession.

b. tell the audience something about your attitudes and beliefs that may be of value in their understanding you as an audience member.

c. identify what you like and what you dislike in listening to a public speaker.

d. define one of the elements of public speaking.

e. explain one important cultural artifact.

f. explain one concept and how one culture defines it.

g. compare two cultures in their views of a particular concept.

h. explain how one cultural belief influences your behavior.

i. explain one similarity or one difference between any two cultural groups.

1.2. Creating Metaphors and Similes

Try your hand at creating metaphors or similes to help explain public speaking. Select an element from the Public Speaking Elements column and one from the Metaphorical Fields and explain the element with a specific metaphor drawn from the field, e.g., pairing speaker and transportation might yield a metaphor such as "The effective speaker is like a locomotive; it takes time to get up the steam for effective movement."

Public Speaking Elements	Metaphorical Fields
speaker	transportation
speech	animals
channel	environment
audience	nature
feedback	sports

Public Speaking Elements	Metaphorical Fields
context	military
noise	music
effect	economic
ethics	artistic
delivery	communication

1.3 Examining Cultural Beliefs as Assumptions

As discussed in this unit, different cultures hold widely different beliefs on religion, politics, education, family, sex, justice, and just about any topic you can think of. Further, because these beliefs will influence how an audience responds to you and to your speech, you need to take them into consideration as you prepare your speech. Assume that you're giving a speech to your public speaking class. Evaluate each of the cultural beliefs listed here in terms of how effective each would be if you used it as a basic assumption in your speech. Use the following scale:

A = the audience would favorably accept this assumption and would welcome a speaker with this point of view

B = the audience would listen fairly openly to the speaker

C = some members would listen openly and others wouldn't

D = the audience would not listen very openly to the speaker

E = the audience would definitely reject this assumption and would not welcome a speaker with this point of view

1. God is good and just.

2. A return to "traditional" values is the best hope for the world.

3. The welfare of the family must come first, even before your own.

4. The welfare of your country must come first, even before your own.

5. Sex outside of marriage is morally wrong and sinful.

6. Winning is all important; it's not how you play the game, it's whether or not you win that matters.

7. Intercultural relationships are OK in business but should be discouraged when it comes to intimate or romantic relationships; generally, the races should be kept "pure."

8. Doing good for others is the goal of life; personal happiness is secondary.

9. Money is good; the quest for financial success is a perfectly respectable one.

10. U.S. immigration should be curtailed, at least until the current immigrants are assimilated.

11. In a heterosexual relationship, "a wife is to submit graciously to the servant leadership of her husband" [a directive of the Southern Baptist Convention, Woodward, Kenneth L. "Religion: Using the Bully Pulpit? *Time* (June 22, 1998), p. 69.]

12. Keeping the United States militarily superior is the best way to preserve world peace.

What evidence do you have for your judgments? Is your evidence from observation and experience? From listening to or reading what others say? What consequences await the speaker who uses assumptions rated A? What are the consequences of using assumptions rated E?

UNIT
2

Preparing a Public Speech: An Overview

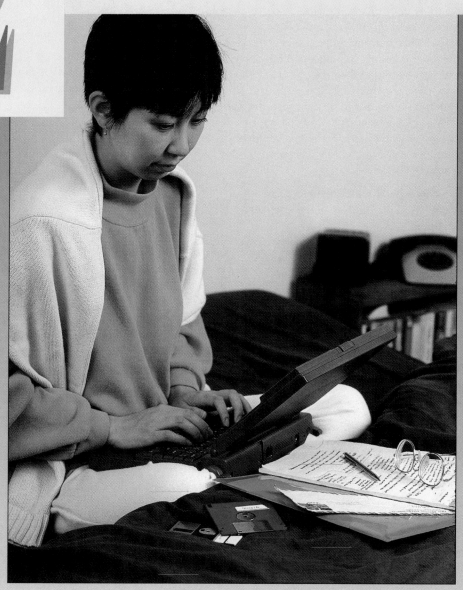

UNIT CONTENTS

UNIT CONTENTS	UNIT OBJECTIVES
	After completing this unit, you should be able to:
Select Your Topic and Purpose	Select topics and purposes that are worthwhile, interesting, and appropriate.
Analyze Your Audience	Analyze and adapt your message to your specific audience.
Research Your Topic	Locate and integrate research in your speech.
Formulate Your Thesis and Major Propositions	Construct your thesis statement and from this derive your major propositions.
Support Your Major Propositions	Support your major propositions with a wide variety of materials.
Organize Your Speech Materials	Organize your materials into a logical and coherent structure.
Word Your Speech	Style your speech so that it's instantly intelligible.
Construct Your Introduction, Conclusion, and Transitions	Develop the introduction, conclusion, and varied transitions for your speech.
Rehearse Your Speech	Rehearse your speech for greatest effectiveness and efficiency.
Deliver Your Speech	Confidently and effectively deliver your speech to your audience.

You're going to give a speech and you're anxious and unsure of what to say. What do you do? What do you speak about? How do you decide what to include in the speech? How should you organize a speech? At this point you probably have a lot more questions than answers, but that's the way it should be. This unit answers these questions with a brief overview of the public speaking process. By following the 10 steps outlined in this unit, you'll be able to prepare and present effective first speeches almost immediately.

The 10 steps for preparing a public speech will also give you a framework for structuring the remaining information in the text. In fact, you can look at the rest of the text as an elaboration on these 10 steps. As you continue reading, these principles will be enhanced and further clarified. In this way, you'll be able to gradually improve and perfect your public speaking skills.

If you're going to play the game properly, you'd better know every rule.
—Barbara Jordan

FIGURE 2.1

The Steps in Preparing and Presenting a Public Speech.

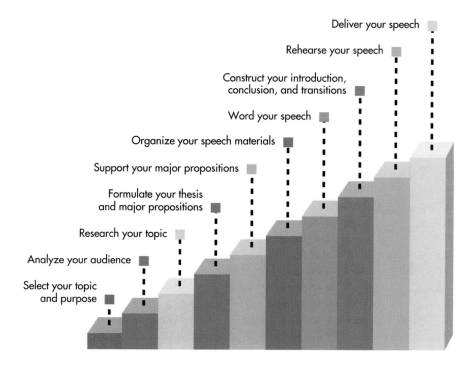

Deliver your speech

Rehearse your speech

Construct your introduction, conclusion, and transitions

Word your speech

Organize your speech materials

Support your major propositions

Formulate your thesis and major propositions

Research your topic

Analyze your audience

Select your topic and purpose

It's not wise to violate the rules until you know how to observe them.
—T. S. Eliot

Figure 2.1 presents these 10 steps in a linear fashion. The process of constructing a public speech, however, doesn't always follow such a logical sequence. You probably won't progress simply from Step 1 to 2 to 3, on through to 10. Instead, after selecting your subject and purpose (Step 1), you may progress to Step 2 and analyze your audience. On the basis of this analysis, however, you may wish to go back and modify your subject, your purpose, or both. Similarly, after you research the topic (Step 3), you may want more information on your audience. You may, therefore, return to Step 2.

Going from one step to another and then back again should not throw you off track. This is the way most people prepare speeches. So, although the steps are presented in the order a speaker normally follows, remember that you're in charge of the process. Use the order of these steps as guidelines, but break the sequence as you need to. As long as you cover all 10 steps thoroughly, you'll accomplish your goal.

SELECT YOUR TOPIC AND PURPOSE

The first step in preparing a speech is to select the topic (or subject) and the purposes you hope to achieve. Let's look first at the topic.

The Topic

Perhaps the question students in a public speaking class ask most often is, "What do I speak about?" For your classroom speeches—where the objective is to learn the skills of public speaking—there are thousands of suitable topics. Suggestions may be found everywhere and anywhere. Take a look at Table 6.2; it lists hundreds of suitable topics from abortion, academic freedom, and acupuncture to women, words, youth, and zodiac. Additional suggestions also appear in the Practically Speaking exercises at the end of this unit.

Worthwhile. The topics of public speeches should be worthwhile in that they should address issues with significant implications for the audience. Topics should also be appropriate to both you as the speaker and to your audience. Try not to select a topic just because it will fulfill the requirements of an assignment. Instead, select a topic about which you know something and would like to learn more. In the process of speech preparation, you'll not only acquire new knowledge about the topic but will also discover how to learn more about it, for example, the relevant databases, the noted authorities, and so on. If you select a topic you're interested in, you'll be more interested in talking with your audience about it, and your enthusiasm will surely show throughout your presentation.

Look also to your audience for insight into possible topics. Each person sees the world from a unique point of view, so think about what he or she may be interested in. What would he like to learn more about? On what topics would she find the time listening to your speech well spent?

Also, recognize the important role that culture plays in the topics people consider appropriate or worthwhile. For example, it would be considered inappropriate for an American businessperson to speak of politics in Pakistan, religion in Nigeria, or illegal aliens in Mexico (Axtell 1993). Because you're a college student, you can assume—to some extent—that the topics you're interested in will also prove interesting to your classmates. But beyond this exceptionally homogeneous and accepting atmosphere—an atmosphere you're not likely to see again anytime after college—culture will always play a role in the selection of the topic.

Limited in Scope. A suitable topic for a public speech is one that is limited in scope. Probably the major problem for beginning speakers is that they attempt to cover a huge topic in five minutes: the history of Egypt, why our tax structure should be changed, or the sociology of film. Such topics are too broad and try to cover too much. In these cases, all the speaker succeeds in doing is telling the audience what it already knows. Invariably, your listeners will go away with the feeling that they've gained nothing as a result of listening to your speech.

The Purpose

Generally, public speeches are designed to inform, to persuade, and to serve some ceremonial or special occasion function:

- the informative speech seeks to create understanding; the speaker clarifies, enlightens, corrects misunderstandings, or demonstrates how something works.
- the persuasive speech seeks to influence attitudes or behaviors; the speaker strengthens or changes audience attitudes or gets the audience to take action.
- the special occasion speech, containing elements of information and persuasion, introduces another speaker or a group of speakers, presents a tribute, secures the goodwill of the listeners, or entertains the audience.

TIPS from professional speakers

Most of us are mean to ourselves. We constantly tell ourselves that we are not good enough. We tell ourselves how dumb we are, how stupid we are, that we forgot to do this or forgot to do that. We do it so often that we begin to believe it! In fact, it's like what the prophets have said in the Bible, "What things you say and believe in your heart all come to pass."

The negative public relations we put out reaps negative public relations from others. You don't have to say "I'm so great" to everyone you meet, but you need to put across some self-confidence.

Lillian Glass, a vocal image consultant and frequent lecturer. *How to Win: Six Steps to a Successful Vocal Image* (New York: Putnam [Perigee Books], 1987): 161–163.

Your speech will also have a specific purpose. For example, specific informative purposes might include informing the audience of the proposed education budget or the way a television pilot is audience tested. Specific persuasive purposes might include persuading the audience to support the proposed budget or to vote for Smith. Specific purposes for special occasion speeches might include introducing the Nobel prize winner who will speak on advances in nuclear physics or defending a company policy of an all-male board of directors to the shareholders.

ANALYZE YOUR AUDIENCE

In public speaking your audience is central to your topic and purpose (see accompanying TIP). In most cases, and especially in a public speaking class, you'll be thinking of both your audience and your topic at the same time; in fact, it's difficult to focus on one without also focusing on the other. Your success in informing or persuading an audience rests largely on the extent to which you know them and the extent to which you've adapted your speech to them. Ask yourself, Who are they? What do they already know? What would they want to know more about? What special interests do they have? What opinions, attitudes, and beliefs do they have? Where do they stand on the issues you wish to address? What needs do they have?

To illustrate this process of audience analysis (a topic discussed in depth in Units 8 and 9), consider age and gender as just two factors that need to be analyzed.

Age

If you're going to speak on social security and health care for the elderly or the importance of the job interview, it's obvious that the age of your listeners should influence how you develop your speech. But age is always an important, if not so obvious, a factor. Ask yourself about the age of your listeners. What's their general age? How wide is the range? Are there different age groups that you should address? Does the age of the audience impose any limitations on the topic? On the language you'll use? On the examples and illustrations you'll select?

Gender

Men and women often view topics differently. Because each gender has special knowledge and special interests as a result of their socialization, ask yourself how the gender makeup of your audience might influence how you develop your speech. What's the predominant gender of your listeners? Do men and women view this particular topic differently? If so, how? Do men and women have different backgrounds, experiences, and knowledge concerning the topic? How will this influence the way you'll develop the topic?

For example, if you plan to speak on caring for a newborn baby, you'd approach an audience of men very differently from an audience of women. With an audience of women, you could probably assume a much greater knowledge of the subject and a greater degree of comfort in dealing with it.

With an audience of men, you might have to cover such elementary topics as the type of powder to use, how to test the temperature of a bottle, and the way to prepare a formula.

RESEARCH YOUR TOPIC

If the speech is to be worthwhile and if both you and the audience are to profit from it, you need to research the topic. First, read some general source—an encyclopedia article or a general article in a magazine or on the Web. You might pursue some of the references in the article or seek out a book or two in the library. For some topics, you might want to consult individuals; professors, politicians, physicians, or people with specialized information are useful sources and are now easy to reach through e-mail. (See Unit 7, "Research the Public Speech," for suggestions on how to use e-mail to consult with specific people.) Or, you might begin with accessing a database, assembling a bibliography, and reading the most general source first and then continuing with increasingly specific articles.

FORMULATE YOUR THESIS AND MAJOR PROPOSITIONS

What do you want your audience to get out of your speech? What single idea do you want them to retain? This single idea is the thesis of your speech. It's the essence of what you want your audience to get out of your speech. If your speech is an informative one, then your thesis is the main idea that you want your audience to understand, for example, "Human blood consists of four major elements" or "The new computerized billing

I do not object to people looking at their watches when I am speaking—but I strongly object when they start shaking them to make certain they are still going.
—Lord Birkett

Why is research necessary for a public speech? Would it ever be legitimate to give a public speech totally devoid of research?

system is easy to understand." If your speech is a persuasive one, then your thesis is the central idea that you wish your audience to accept or act on, for example, "We should support Grace Moore for Union Representative" or "Our state must institute a free needle exchange program to prevent the spread of AIDS."

Once you word your thesis, you can identify its major components by asking certain questions. For an informative speech, the most helpful questions are What? or How? For the thesis "Human blood consists of four major elements," the logical question seems to be, What are they? For the thesis "The new computerized billing system is easy to understand," the logical question seems to be, "Why is it easy?" or "How is it easy?" The answers to these questions identify the major propositions you would cover in your speech. The answer to the question, "What are the major elements of human blood?" in the form of a brief speech outline, would look like this:

> THESIS: "There are four major elements in human blood." (What are they?)
> I. Plasma
> II. Red blood cells (erythrocytes)
> III. White blood cells (leukocytes)
> IV. Platelets (thrombocytes)

In a persuasive speech, the question you'd ask of your thesis is often "Why?" For example, if your thesis is "We should support Grace Moore for Union Representative," then the inevitable question is "Why should we support Grace Moore?" Your answers to this question will identify the major parts of the speech, which might look like this:

> THESIS: "We should support Grace Moore." (Why should we support Grace Moore?)
> I. Grace Moore is an effective negotiator.
> II. Grace Moore is honest.
> III. Grace Moore is knowledgeable.

SUPPORT YOUR MAJOR PROPOSITIONS

Once you've identified your thesis and major propositions, turn your attention to supporting each of them. You must tell the audience what it needs to know about the elements in human blood. You need to convince the audience that Grace Moore is, in fact, honest, knowledgeable, and an effective negotiator.

In the informative speech, your support primarily amplifies—describes, illustrates, defines, exemplifies—the various concepts you discuss. You want the "causes of inflation" to come alive for the audience. You want them to see and feel the drug problem, the crime, or the economic hardships of the people you're talking about. Supporting materials accomplish this. Presenting definitions, for example, helps the audience understand specialized terms; definitions breathe life into concepts that may otherwise be too abstract or vague. Statistics (summary figures that explain various trends) are essential for certain topics. Presentation aids—charts,

TIPS
from professional speakers

Visual aids should be graphics, pictures of things, not, repeat, NOT—word outlines of a speaker's notes. Visuals are to help the audience. . . . I recall one time General Partridge, a four-star Air Force General, was listening to a presentation. The man briefing him put up a slide that had 17 complete sentences on it. He said, "Now I think these sentences very well summarize my main argument in support of the proposition. You can read them."

General Partridge interrupted, "Yes, I can read them, but I don't want to. Please go ahead."

Paul R. Beall, management consultant, communication teacher, lecturer, and college president, *Pass the Word: The Art of Oral Communication* (Manhattan, Kansas: Sunflower University Press, 1993): 47.

THE ETHICS OF Public Speaking

What's ethical in public speaking? What's unethical? Here are several situations that raise ethical issues. Respond to each situation with the following scale: A = ethical, B = not sure, and C = unethical.

_____ 1. In an economics course you took at another school, you received a handout that clearly explains the relationship of interest rates to stock prices, the very topic about which you're going to give your speech. Would it be ethical to use this handout to support one of your propositions without saying where you got it or who prepared it and allow your audience to draw the conclusion that you prepared it yourself?

_____ 2. You read an op-ed article in a newspaper recently and thought the writer put the issue of homelessness into clear perspective. Since you're going to give a speech on homelessness and you honestly agree with everything this person said (but just said it a lot better than you feel you could), would it be ethical for you to paraphrase this op-ed piece? You wouldn't be using the writer's exact words, you'd just use the ideas without mentioning where you got them.

_____ 3. You recently read an excellent summary of research on aging and memory in a magazine article. Would it be ethical to use this research and cite the original research studies but not mention that you got it from a summary in a popular magazine?

_____ 4. You're giving a speech to elementary school children on the dangers of smoking pot. From your research, however, you don't find the dramatic examples and startling statistics that you feel will convince these young children to stay away from pot. Since your aim is to achieve a good end, an end in which you firmly believe, would it be ethical to make up a few dramatic examples and allow the children to believe these are real cases of the problems that result from pot smoking? How

about making up a few statistics to hammer the point home?

_____ 5. In a speech on false arrests, you develop this hypothetical story about a college student getting arrested and being held in custody unlawfully for several days. As you rehearse this story, you realize it would be a lot more convincing if the audience was allowed to think that this person was you. Would it be ethical to allow your audience to believe this incident happened to you? Actually, you wouldn't be saying that it was you or that it wasn't you; you'd just be allowing the audience to form their own conclusions.

_____ 6. You're running against Pat Sanchez for student president. You're pretty evenly matched and you need something to pull ahead. A friend tells you gossip that, if more widely known, would cost Pat the election, even though it has nothing to do with the qualifications for student body president. Would it be ethical for you to bring up this information in one of your speeches?

Most public speaking textbooks would argue that all of these situations would be considered unethical, though some perhaps more unethical than others. The first three deal with plagiarism—using the words or ideas of another person as your own—a topic that is discussed in more detail in the ethics box in Unit 7. The last three deal with fabricating evidence, allowing the audience to believe what isn't true, and dealing in personal attacks.

What unifying thread runs through those situations you labeled "C"? Can you identify a general principle that would cover all the examples you labeled "C"? Do the "mitigating circumstances" contained in some of the situations influence your judgment as to what is or isn't ethical. Might any of the situations you labeled "C" ever be considered ethical? Did you label any situations "B"? If so, what is there about the situation that makes it difficult to label it as ethical or unethical?

(The next Ethics of Public Speaking box appears on page 46.)

maps, actual objects, slides, films, and so on—enliven normally vague concepts. Because presentation aids have become so important in public speaking, you may want to include these in each of your speeches. If you start using these with your first speeches, you'll develop considerable facility by the end of the semester. The best way to do this is to read Unit 9, Presentation Aids, immediately after you complete this unit and begin to incorporate such aids into all your speeches.

In a persuasive speech, your support is proof—material that offers evidence, argument, and motivational appeal and that establishes your credibility. Proof helps you convince the audience to agree with you. Let's say, for example, that you want to persuade the audience that Grace Moore is an effective negotiator (your first major proposition as noted earlier). To do this you need to give your audience good reasons for believing in Moore's effectiveness as a negotiator. Your major proposition might be supported as illustrated here:

I. Grace Moore is an effective negotiator.
  A. Moore effectively negotiated the largest raise we ever received.
  B. Moore prevented management from reducing our number of sick days.
  C. Moore has been named "Negotiator of the Year" for the past three years by our own union local.

Support your propositions with reasoning from specific instances, from general principles, and from causes and effects. These are logical supports. You can also support your position with motivational appeals. For example, you might appeal to the audience's desire for status, for financial gain, or for increased self-esteem. You also add persuasive force through your own personal reputation or credibility. If the audience sees you as competent, of high moral character, and charismatic, they're more likely to believe what you say.

ORGANIZE YOUR SPEECH MATERIALS

Organize your materials to help your audience understand and retain what you say. You might, for example, select a simple topical pattern. This involves dividing your topic into its logical subdivisions or subtopics. Each subtopic becomes a main point of your speech, and each is treated about equally. Next organize the supporting materials under each of the appropriate points. The body of the speech, then, might look like this:

I. Main point I
  A. Supporting material for I
  B. Supporting material for I
II. Main point II
  A. Supporting material for II
  B. Supporting material for II
  C. Supporting material for II
III. Main point III
  A. Supporting material for III
  B. Supporting material for III

For a persuasive speech you may wish to consider other organizational patterns. For example, a problem-solution pattern might be effective for a number of topics. Let's say you want to persuade your listeners that medical schools should require communication courses. You might use a problem-solution pattern. Your speech in outline form might look like this:

I. Doctors can't communicate. (problem)
   A. They're inarticulate in expressing ideas. (problem 1)
   B. They're ineffective listeners. (problem 2)
   C. They don't see beyond the literal meaning. (problem 3)
II. Medical schools should require communication courses. (solution)
   A. Communication courses will train doctors to express themselves. (solution 1)
   B. Communication courses will train doctors in listening skills. (solution 2)
   C. Communication courses will train doctors to listen for meaning beyond the literal. (solution 3)

WORD YOUR SPEECH

Speak properly, and in as few words as you can, but always plainly; for the end of speech is not ostentation, but to be understood.
—William Penn

Because your audience will hear your speech only once, make what you say instantly intelligible. Don't speak down to your audience, but do make your ideas, even complex ones, easy to understand at one hearing.

Use words that are simple rather than complex, concrete rather than abstract. Use personal and informal rather than impersonal and formal language. For example, use lots of pronouns (*I, me, you, our*) and contractions (*can't* rather than *cannot, I'll* rather than *I will*). Use simple and direct rather than complex and indirect sentences. Say, "Vote in the next election" instead of "It is important that everyone vote in the next election."

In wording the speech, be careful not to offend members of your audience. Remember that not all doctors are men. Not all secretaries are women. Not all persons are or want to be married. Not all persons love parents, dogs, and children. The hypothetical person doesn't have to be male.

Perhaps the most important advice to give at this point is to not write your speech out word-for-word. This will only make you sound as though you're reading to your audience, and you'll lose the conversational quality that is so important in public speaking. Instead, outline your speech and speak with your audience, using this outline to remind yourself of your main ideas and the order in which you want to present them. Units 15 and 16 offer more extensive style suggestions.

Title Your Speech

In some ways the title of a speech is a kind of frill. On the other hand, the title may be effective in gaining the interest of the audience and, perhaps, stimulating them to listen. In more formal public speech presentations, the title helps gain audience attention and interest in announcements advertising the speech.

Devise a title that's relatively short (so it's easy to remember). Two, three, or four words are often best. The title should attract the attention

The title comes last.
—Tennessee Williams

and arouse the interest of the listeners and have a clear relationship to the major purpose of your speech.

CONSTRUCT YOUR INTRODUCTION, CONCLUSION, AND TRANSITIONS

The last items to consider are the introduction, conclusion, and transitions. For now, we'll cover just enough to get you started in your early speeches; the discussion in Unit 13, "Introductions, Conclusions, and Transitions," will expand and elaborate on the ways to introduce, conclude, and tie your speech together.

Introduction

Because you must know in detail all you're going to say before you prepare the introduction, construct your introduction last. Your introduction should immediately gain the attention of the audience. Most often, your coming to the front of the room will attract their attention. However, as you start to speak, make a special effort to hold their attention or you may lose them. A provocative statistic, a little-known fact, an interesting story, or a statement explaining the topic's significance will help secure this initial attention.

Second, establish a connection among yourself, the topic, and the audience. Tell audience members why you're speaking on this topic. Tell them why you're concerned with the topic and why you're competent to address them. These are questions that most audiences will automatically ask themselves. Here's one example of how this might be done.

> You may be wondering why a twenty-five-year-old woman with no background in medicine or education is talking to you about AIDS education. I'm addressing you today as a mother of a child with AIDS, and I want to talk with you about my child's experience in class—and about every child's experience in class—your own children as well as mine.

Third, give some kind of orientation. Tell the audience what you're going to say in the order you're going to say it.

> I'm going to explain the ways in which war movies have changed through the years. To do this I'm going to discuss examples of movies depicting World War II, the Korean War, and Vietnam.

Conclusion

In concluding your speech, do at least two things: summarize your ideas and bring your speech to a close. In your summary, identify the main points again and sum up what you've told the audience.

> Let's all support Grace Moore. She's our most effective negotiator, she's honest, and she knows what negotiation and our union are all about.

In your closing, wrap up your speech. Develop a crisp ending that makes it clear to your audience that your speech is coming to an end.

I hope then that when you vote on Tuesday, you'll vote for Moore. She's our only choice.

Transitions

After you've completed the introduction and conclusion, review the entire speech to make sure that the parts flow into one another and that the movement from one part to another (say, from the introduction to the first major proposition) will be clear to the audience. Transitional words, phrases, and sentences will help you achieve this smoothness of movement. These linguistic devices are often called "connectives" because they connect pieces of the speech to each other. Here are a few suggestions:

- Connect your introduction's orientation to your first major proposition: "*Let's now look at the first of these three elements,* the central processing unit, in detail. The CPU is the heart of the computer. It consists of . . . ."
- Connect your major propositions to each other: *But, not only is* cigarette smoking dangerous to the smoker, *it's also* dangerous to the nonsmoker. Passive smoking is harmful to everyone . . . .
- Connect your last major proposition to your conclusion: *As we saw,* there were three sources of evidence against the butler. He had a motive; he had no alibi; he had the opportunity.

REHEARSE YOUR SPEECH

You've prepared your speech to deliver it to an audience, so your next step is to practice it. Rehearse your speech, from start to finish, out loud, at least four times before presenting it in class. During these rehearsals, time your speech so that you stay within the specified time limits. If you're using presentation software such as PowerPoint or Corel Presentation, you'll be able to time not only your entire speech but also the time you spend on each slide.

Practice any terms that you may have difficulty with; consult a dictionary to clarify any doubts about pronunciation.

Include in your outline any notes that you want to remember during the actual speech—notes to remind you to use your visual aid or to read a quotation.

DELIVER YOUR SPEECH

In your actual presentation, use your voice and bodily action to reinforce your message. Make it easy for your listeners to understand your speech. Any vocal or body movements that draw attention to themselves (and away from what you're saying) obviously should be avoided. Here are a few guidelines that will prove helpful. (Units 17 and 18 offer more suggestions.)

Be sincere, be brief; be seated.
—Franklin D. Roosevelt

Listen especially to two types of statements: self-destructive statements and self-affirming statements. These statements influence your self-concept, the way you feel about yourself, the degree to which you like yourself, and the extent to which you consider yourself a valuable person.

Self-destructive statements are those that damage the way you feel about yourself. They may be about yourself ("I'm a poor speaker," "I'm boring") or your world ("The audience won't like me," "People are out to get me"). Recognizing that you may have internalized such beliefs is a first step to eliminating them. A second step involves recognizing that these beliefs are, in fact, unrealistic and self-defeating. Cognitive therapists (for example, Ellis 1988, Blau & Ellis 1988, Beck 1988, Glasser 1999, Murphy 1997, Howatt 1997) argue that you can accomplish this by understanding why these beliefs are unrealistic and substituting more realistic ones. Try, for example, substituting the unrealistic belief that audiences won't like you, with the more realistic belief that most listeners are much like yourself and are supportive of other speakers.

Self-affirming statements, on the other hand, are positive and self-supportive. Remind yourself of your successes, good deeds, positive qualities, strengths, and virtues. Concentrate on your potential, not your limitations (Brody 1991). Throughout this process, be careful not to delude yourself into thinking you have no faults. Rather, be realistic; approach any real inadequacies with the belief that you can change them into strengths. Here's just a small sampling of self-affirmations that you may wish to try to say to yourself and listen to:

1. I'm a competent person.
2. I have the potential to be an effective speaker.
3. I'm growing and improving.
4. I'm empathic and supportive.
5. I can accept constructive criticism without defensiveness.
6. I don't have to repeat my past failures.
7. I can forgive myself and those who have hurt me.
8. I'm open-minded and listen fairly to others.
9. I can apologize.
10. I'm flexible and can adjust to different situations.

(The next Listen to This box appears on page 51.)

When called on to speak, approach the front of the room with enthusiasm. Even if you feel nervous (as most speakers do), show your desire to speak with your listeners. When at the front of the room, don't begin immediately; instead, pause, engage your audience eye to eye for a few brief moments, and then begin to talk directly to the audience. Talk in a volume that can be easily heard without straining. Throughout your speech maintain eye contact with your entire audience; avoid concentrating on only a few members or looking out of the window or at the floor.

Answering Questions

In many public speaking situations a question and answer period will follow. So, be prepared to answer questions after your speech. Here are a few suggestions for making this Q&A session more effective.

- If you wish to encourage questions, you might preface the question period with some kind of encouraging statement, for example, "I know you've lots of questions—especially on how the new health program will work and how we'll finance it and probably lots of others. I'll be happy to try to respond to any of your questions. Anyone?"

- Maintain eye contact with the audience. Let the audience know that you're still speaking with them.
- After you hear the question, pause, think about the question and about your answer. If you suspect the entire audience didn't hear the question, repeat it and then begin your answer.
- Control any tendency to get defensive. Don't assume that the question is a personal attack. Assume, instead, that the question is an attempt to secure more information or perhaps to challenge a position you've taken.
- If appropriate, thank the person for asking the question or note that the question is a particularly good one. This will encourage others to also ask questions.
- Don't bluff. If you're asked a question and you don't know the answer, say so.
- Consider the usefulness of a persuasive answer. Question and answer sessions often provide opportunities to further advance your purpose by connecting the question with one or more of your major assertions or points of view: "I'm glad you asked about child care because that's exactly the difference between the two proposals we're here to vote on. The plan I'm proposing . . . . "

All of these suggestions are based on the assumption that you want to encourage questions and dialogue. Generally speakers want audience questions because it gives them an opportunity to talk more about something they're interested in. And in some cases, there is an ethical obligation for the speaker to entertain questions; after all, if the audience sat through what the speaker wanted to say, the speaker should listen to what they want to say.

There are situations, however, when you might want to discourage questions—perhaps you want your audience to think about the material for a while or you don't want to go into a matter in detail before sufficient data are available or you know there are people in the audience who just want to use the question and answer period as an opportunity to voice their own ideas. If you want to discourage questions, then, obviously reverse many of these suggestions. For example, don't preface the period with an encouraging remark, don't praise the questions or the questioner, and avoid eye contact with audience members.

TIPS
from professional speakers

Practice the Q → A + 1 Formula. When you get a question which could be answered with a "yes" or "no," use my Q → A + 1 formula. Instead of responding with a one-word answer, add a "positive plus point" to keep the conversation moving. If you are asked, "Are you expanding in China?" answer, "Yes. We plan to expand our sales outlets in seven major Chinese cities in the coming year."

Elizabeth Urech, international communication specialist and founder of "Speak for Yourself," *Speaking Globally: Effective Presentations Across International and Cultural Boundaries.* (Dover, NH: Kogan Page, 1998): 135.

UNIT IN BRIEF

Select your topic and purpose.	Is the topic worthwhile and limited in scope? Is the purpose clearly defined?
Analyze your audience.	Is the speech appropriate and adapted to this specific audience?
Research your topic.	Is the speech adequately researched?
Formulate your thesis and major propositions.	Does the speech have one clearly identifiable thesis? Do all the major propositions support this thesis?

Support your major propositions.	Are the major propositions adequately supported so that they're clear and, if appropriate, persuasively presented?
Organize your speech materials.	Is the speech presented in a logical, clearly identifiable pattern that will aid comprehension?
Word the speech.	Is the speech instantly intelligible to listeners who will hear it only once?
Construct your introduction, conclusion, and transitions.	Does the introduction gain attention and orient the audience? Does the conclusion summarize and close the speech? Are the parts of the speech adequately connected with transitions?
Rehearse your speech.	Did you rehearse the speech to the point where you're comfortable giving it to an audience?
Deliver your speech.	Do your voice and bodily action reinforce your message? Do you focus your eyes and body on the listeners?

THINKING CRITICALLY ABOUT PREPARING A SPEECH

REVIEWING KEY TERMS AND CONCEPTS IN PUBLIC SPEAKING

1. Define the key terms covered in this unit:
   - ❏ speech topic (p. 24)
   - ❏ speech purpose (p. 25)
   - ❏ thesis (p. 27)
   - ❏ propositions (p. 28)
   - ❏ supporting materials (p. 30)
   - ❏ introduction (p. 32)
   - ❏ conclusion (p. 32)
   - ❏ transitions (p. 33)

2. Explain the guidelines for each of the following steps in creating a public speech:
   - selecting a topic and purpose
   - analyzing your audience
   - researching your topic
   - formulating your thesis and major propositions
   - supporting your major propositions
   - organizing your speech materials
   - wording your speech
   - constructing your introduction, conclusion, and transitions
   - rehearsing your speech
   - delivering your speech and responding to audience questions

DEVELOPING PUBLIC SPEAKING STRATEGIES

1. Stephen is a student in his 20s who wants to give a speech on his hobby, flower arranging. He wonders if this topic is going to look inappropriate—not many young men have flower arranging as their hobby and passion. Stephen especially wonders if he should say anything, perhaps in his introduction, about the topic appearing inappropriate. What would you advise Stephen to do?

2. Shasta is planning to give a speech on the need for a needle exchange program in her state. But she knows nothing of the audience other than that it's a high school PTA meeting. She knows nothing about the audience's cultural background, gender, social attitudes, or religious beliefs, for example. What can Shasta do to prepare for this very difficult situation?

3. Jake wants to describe your college campus to a group of high school students who have never seen a college campus. What organizational plan would you advise Jake to use?

EVALUATING PUBLIC SPEECHES

1. Read the introduction and the conclusion to one of the speeches in the appendix. What methods did the speaker use in introducing and concluding the speech? Were these effective? What would you have done?

2. Listen carefully to the introduction and conclusion of news show such as "60 Minutes" or "20/20." What functions does the introduction serve? What functions does the conclusion serve?

USING TECHNOLOGY IN PUBLIC SPEAKING

1. Visit Northwestern University's School of Speech Douglass website at http://douglass.speech.nwu.edu/.

Review the speeches by topic category and read one that interests you. What did the speaker do exceptionally well?

2. Visit the library and select one online research resource that you think would be useful to students preparing speeches for this class. What types of information does this source contain? Why do you think this would prove useful?

3. Visit Columbia University's website containing the Inaugural Addresses of the Presidents (http://www. columbia.edu/acis/bartleby/inaugural). Select one address and identify its thesis and its major propositions. What do you think might be a likely thesis for the next presidential inaugural address?

PRACTICALLY SPEAKING

2.1   Short Speech Technique

Prepare and present a two-minute speech in which you:

a. describe a public speech you heard recently.

b. explain a print advertisement in terms of the steps for preparing a public speech.

c. explain any one of the steps of public speaking as it might apply to intercultural conversation.

d. describe how you see your class as an audience for your next speech.

2.2 Constructing an Informative Speech

Consult the "Dictionary of Topics" in Unit 6, pages 103–109, for suggestions on informative speech topics. Select a topic and:

a. formulate a specific thesis.

b. formulate a specific purpose suitable for an informative speech of approximately five minutes.

c. analyze this class as your potential audience and identify ways that you can relate this topic to their interests and needs.

d. generate at least two major propositions from your thesis.

e. support these propositions with examples, illustrations, and definitions.

f. construct a conclusion that summarizes your main

ideas and brings the speech to a definite close.

g. construct an introduction that gains attention and orients your audience.

Discuss these outlines in small groups or with the class as a whole. Try to secure feedback from other members on how you can improve these outlines.

2.3 Constructing a Persuasive Speech

Here are 20 topics for persuasive speeches. Select any one topic and then:

- formulate a specific thesis
- formulate a specific purpose suitable for a persuasive speech of approximately five minutes
- analyze this class as your potential audience; try to predict their relevant attitudes and beliefs; and identify ways that you can relate this topic to their interests and needs
- generate at least two major propositions from your thesis
- support these propositions with examples, illustrations, definitions, facts, and opinions
- construct a conclusion that summarizes your main ideas and brings the speech to a definite close
- construct an introduction that gains attention; connects you, the audience, and the speech topic; and orients your audience

Share your outline in small groups or with the class as a whole. Try to secure feedback from other members on how you can improve these outlines.

1. Vote in the next election (college, city, state, national).
2. Capital punishment should be abolished (extended).
3. Support (Don't support) college athletics.
4. Gay men and lesbians should (not) be permitted to adopt children.
5. Military recruitment should (not) be allowed on college campuses.
6. Join the Peace Corps.
7. Sex education in elementary schools should be expanded (eliminated).
8. Volunteer to read for the blind.
9. Teachers, police, and firefighters should (not) be permitted to strike.
10. Personal firearms should be prohibited (permitted).
11. Alcohol should be prohibited (permitted) on college campuses.
12. Marijuana should (not) be legalized.
13. Marriage licenses should be denied to any couple who has not known each other for at least one year.
14. Nuclear plants should be abolished (expanded).
15. The government should (not) support the expansion of solar energy.
16. Required college courses should be eliminated.
17. The military's policy of "don't ask, don't tell" on gay men and lesbians should (not) be changed.
18. Cheating on an examination should (not) result in automatic dismissal from college.
19. This country should (not) establish a system of free legal services for all of its citizens.
20. Church property should (not) be taxed.

2.4 Analyzing a Speech

Throughout this text a number of speeches are presented. These speeches, together with their annotations and questions, illustrate the principles and skills of public speaking. With the exception of those in Unit 5, which were written to illustrate what poorly constructed speeches look like, the rest of the sample speeches are particularly good ones. Read these speeches as carefully as you would read the text; they're concrete illustrations of the principles discussed in the text and will prove extremely useful as models of excellence.

The following speech is presented as a summary of the major parts of a public speech. The annotations will guide you through the speech and will illustrate the principles considered in this unit. The questions will give you an opportunity to apply your newly acquired public speaking skills.

ADVERSE DRUG EVENTS
Ramona L. Fink
Eastern Michigan University
Coached by Michael Tew and Terry Bonnette

On March 23, 1995, the *Boston Globe* reported on the circumstances surrounding the death of one of their columnists, 39-year-old Betsy Lehman, a victim of a mathematical error. While undergoing cancer treatment at Harvard Medical Schools' Dana Faber Institute, Betsy was given four times the proper amount of the anti-cancer drug Cytoxan. While we may like to think that such gross errors could only happen on Chicago Hope, media attention to this occurrence is alerting the nation to the disturbing reality of Adverse Drug Events-or ADEs, within our nation's hospitals. While hospital errors such as cutting off the wrong limb have recently been horrifying the nation, ADEs are specific errors related to medications in hospitals and their common place occurrence is just as, if not more, horrific. As the January 11, 1996 *Business Wire* explains, "Our nation's healthcare systems have built-in

This topic is probably not one that you'd turn on the television to listen to, and yet it's a topic that everyone would probably agree is very important. How would this topic be received by members of your public speaking class? Would class members be interested in the topic? Would they want to learn more about it?

defect rates, (up to 14%), that other industries do not tolerate." Bruce Chabner, director of the Division of Cancer Treatment at the National Cancer Institute, told the *New York Times* on March 24, 1995 quite simply, "(ADEs) could happen at any place in this country, and have happened at every place in this country." Everytime we are given a drug by a hospital employee, we assume it to be a safe drug and a safe dose. Such an assumption could be deadly. In order to protect ourselves, we need to first, understand the seriousness of Adverse Drug Events' second, see how and why so many ADEs are occurring; and finally, examine practical solutions which need to be taken to reduce the risk of Adverse Drug Events.

When Betsy Lehman entered Dana Farber for cancer treatment, she knew that there were risks associated with chemotherapy; however, many fail to realize the risk associated with even the most routine drug administrations. The November 6, 1995 *American Medical News* illustrates with the horrifying story of a pharmacist who mistook morphine for the blood thinner Heparin, and did not catch that mistake until it had already been injected into three ailing infants. In a personal telephone interview with Rebecca Wilfinger, representative of the American Society of Health-System Pharmacists, on February 27, 1996, she explained that estimates of error rates range from 1% up to 20%, because different hospitals use different criteria for what constitutes an ADE. Conservatively, she explains, the American Society of Health Systems Pharmacists utilizes the 1% error rate. However, Rebecca and the December 21, 1994 *Journal o the American Medical Association* agree that even a 0.1 rate is unacceptable. The *Journal of the American Medical Association* study, which has initiated recent concern over ADEs, explains that this tiny error rate in other industries would still result in 2 unsafe plane landings each day at Chicago O'Hara International Airport; 16,000 pieces of lost mail and 32,000 bank checks deducted from the wrong bank account every hour. Every source you have or will hear me cite today concludes, that ADEs are the leading type of medical error, thus leading cause of 80-100,000 deaths each year, and according to the July 5, 1995 issue of the *Journal of the American Medical Association*, the source of additional costs, amounting to over 2,000 dollars per hospitalized patient making the annual cost to a 700 bed hospital 3.8 million.

The costs, both physical and monetary, should prompt us to ask how and why so many medication errors occur. The reasons are twofold; first, drug naming and packaging; and second, internal system errors. *Nursing*, of September 1995, explains that many pharmaceutical companies use similar packaging and drug naming as a trademark. Unfortunately, these similarities make grabbing the wrong drug an easy, and possibly deadly mistake. Examples and warnings of such errors now appear in every issue of *Nursing*. The February 1996 issue, for instance, gives the example of mix ups between Potassium Chloride and Sodium Chlorides similar packages which recently killed three and injured at least four.

Usually, speakers are advised to combine the specific with the general, the concrete with the abstract. In this way the audience can see not only the general principle but also a specific example of it. Notice that the speaker follows this general advice by combining the specific example of Betsy and the more general and abstract statements on adverse drug events. How effective do you think this was?

It's essential that the speaker successfully involve the listener in the first minute of the speech. If the listener spends an entire minute listening and doesn't see any value in continuing, then the rest of the speech, no matter how excellent, will fall on deaf ears. After this first paragraph—let's say the equivalent of one minute—how interested are you in the topic? Has the speaker successfully drawn you into her topic and her speech?

What does the speaker do to convince you that this problem can directly affect you? Would you have wanted additional evidence?

In one sentence, what is the speaker's thesis? What is the main or central idea the speaker wants to get across?

In a field where errors are unacceptable and potentially deadly, there is a tendency to lay the blame on individuals. However, the January 11, 1996 *Business Wire* explains that "Internal system and process failure are most often at fault." Humans inevitably make mistakes, but the real errors come when the system does not catch and correct those mistakes. The *Journal of the American Medical Association* study identified failures, lack of easily accessible patient information, inaccurate order transcription, inefficient medication order tracking, and poor communication between personnel.

The study also found that three quarters of these errors occur in the ordering and administration stages. The September 1995 *American Journal of Nursing* confirms that lack of knowledge about drug, dose/identity checking, and patient information availability, are the most common reasons for the errors. For instance, given thousands of different medications, a doctor may prescribe a drug he is unfamiliar with; an uninformed nurse may prepare and administer an equally unfamiliar drug; and since hundreds of patients are seen in a day, the lack of on hand, comprehensive patient information opens the door for more error. Finally, poor communication between personnel provides information gaps in what should be an integrated process. The March 16, 1995 *New England Journal* of Medicine explains, from the classic complaint of a doctor's poor handwriting, to simply being rushed and distracted, misprinting, misreading, or the simple misplacement of a decimal or zero in prescriptions in common. These gaps, inhibit inter-personnel understanding and the organization's ability to catch mistakes before administration.

Understanding the various causes of ADEs, we can now discuss the steps that need to be taken by the medical profession and by ourselves, in order to reduce the opportunity for error. On October 22, 1995 national experts in medicine, nursing, and pharmacy met in a "Panel to Identify Adverse Drug Events." Its goal, according to the October 25, 1995 *Health Line*, "was to recommend top priority changes that hospitals should make (to have a) maximum impact on preventing medication errors." *Nursing,* of January 1996, outlines the recommendations. Topping the list was the use of bar-code aided computer systems. The November 20, 1995 *Hospitals and Health Networks* explains that the system reduces errors caused by misreading doctor's quickly-scrawled orders, by having doctors directly input prescription into computers connected to a hospital wide network. The system cross-checks for proper drug and dose against the patients medical profile. As a final precaution, bar-codes on medications and patients IDs, which hold drug, dose, and patient information are scanned and automatically cross-checked immediately before administration.

Further recommendations include making sure that pharmacists are fully involved in drug treatment plans, as well as packaging, labeling and distributing drugs in unit doses, to avoid calculation and preparation difficulties. Pharmaceutical companies can have a great impact by following the example of Smith-Kline Beecham

Does the speaker provide an effective orientation to the speech? Do you feel you have a clear roadmap for the rest of the speech?

Thorough research is essential for an effective speech. But, because a speech is meant to be addressed to an audience and to influence that audience, the audience should be shown that a speech is well researched. Has this speaker effectively researched the topic? Do you feel that the speaker really knows what she's talking about? On what basis did you form these impressions?

Generally speakers are advised to use examples, illustrations, narration, statistics, and testimony to support the major propositions of the speech. What types of supporting materials did the speaker use? Were these effectively chosen and presented?

Logical reasoning, emotional appeal, and proof of the speaker's own credibility are three types of proof a speaker can use to advance her or his purpose. Was the speaker's reasoning logical? Did she appeal to your emotions? Did she establish her own credibilityóher competence, good character, and charisma?

Was the speech easy to follow? What aids did the speaker provide to help the listener follow the speech? For example, did the speaker provide transitions to enable listeners to visualize that she was moving from one point to another?

The language and style of a speech should be clear, vivid, appropriate to the topic and to the audience (let's say, members of your public speaking class), personal (rather than formal), and forceful (rather than weak). How would you describe the language of this speech in terms of these five characteristics?

Pharmaceuticals which *Nursing* of December 1995 reports has begun redesigning their easily confused medications.

These recommendations serve as guidelines for preventative action against ADEs. Acknowledging that these changes require time and funding, the July 5, 1995 *Journal of the American Medical Association* stresses that efforts to reduce ADE rates are "cost neutral or may even reduce costs."

Until such changes are made we can protect ourselves. *The People's Medical Society Newsletter* of October 1995 outlines things which we can do. First, ask questions about any prescribed treatments. Know the names and administration times and procedures of all medications given to you. Also, be aware of the color size and shape of your medications. Second, inform all of your health care providers of known allergies, and current medications and keep a written journal of this information. Finally, be assertive if something seems different from the norm. While it may not be easy to question medical professionals, it is your health and your life.

Unfortunately, we can never completely eliminate medication errors such as the one which killed Betsy Lehman. However, knowing the seriousness of ADEs, as well as how and why they occur, we have been able to identify practical solutions to reduce the opportunity for their occurrence. In taking action to protect ourselves from Adverse Drug Events, we can keep the dramas and traumas of these errors out of our real world and leave them to the worlds of televised fiction.

SOURCE: Ramona L. Fink (1996). Adverse Drug Events. Winning Orations of the Interstate Oratorical Association, pp. 47–48, ed. Larry Schnoor. Mankato, MN: Interstate Oratorical Association. Ramona L. Fink, a student from Eastern Michigan University, was coached by Michael Tew and Terry Bonnette. This speech was a semifinalist at the 1996 Interstate Oratorical Association meeting.

A conclusion should generally summarize the major topics and crisply close the speech. In addition, some conclusions provide a motivation or direction for the audience. What functions did this conclusion serve? Was it appropriate given the topic and the purpose of the speech?

Now that you have read the entire speech, was the topic limited sufficiently for the speaker to go into reasonable depth?

What other titles might have been appropriate for this speech?

UNIT
3
From Apprehension to Confidence

UNIT CONTENTS	UNIT OBJECTIVES
	After completing this unit, you should be able to:
What Is Communication Apprehension?	Define communication apprehension.
Dealing with Communication Apprehension	Identify the suggestions for dealing with communication apprehension.
Developing Confidence	Identify at least four suggestions for increasing self-confidence as a public speaker.

If you're like most students, your first concern isn't with organization or audience analysis; rather, it's with stage fright or what's called "communication apprehension." Apprehension is experienced not only by the beginning public speaker; it's even felt by the most experienced speakers. Most public speakers don't eliminate apprehension—they learn to control it.

> *Nothing is so much to be feared as fear.*
> —Henry David Thoreau

"Communication apprehension," note researchers, "is probably the most common handicap that is suffered by people in contemporary American society" (McCroskey and Wheeless 1976). According to a nationwide survey conducted by Bruskin Associates, speaking in public ranked as the number one fear of adult men and women. It ranks above fear of heights and even fear of snakes. Between 10 and 20 percent of college students suffer "severe, debilitating communication apprehension." Another 20 percent "suffer from communication apprehension to a degree substantial enough to interfere to some extent with their normal functioning" (McCroskey and Wheeless 1976).

You may wish to pause here and take the accompanying Apprehension Test.

TEST YOURSELF
How Apprehensive Are You in Public Speaking?

This questionnaire is composed of six statements concerning your feelings about public speaking. In the space provided, indicate the degree to which each statement applies to you by marking whether you:

1 = strongly agree
2 = agree
3 = are undecided
4 = disagree
5 = strongly disagree

There are no right or wrong answers. Many of the statements are similar to other statements; don't be concerned about this. Work quickly; record your first impression.

_____ 1. I have no fear of giving a speech.
_____ 2. Certain parts of my body feel very tense and rigid while giving a speech.

_____ 3. I feel relaxed while giving a speech.
_____ 4. My thoughts become confused and jumbled when I am giving a speech.
_____ 5. I face the prospect of giving a speech with confidence.
_____ 6. While giving a speech, I get so nervous that I forget facts I really know.

Compute your score as follows:

1. Begin with the number 18; this is just used as a base so that you won't wind up with negative numbers.
2. To 18, add your scores for items 1, 3, and 5.
3. Subtract your scores for items 2, 4, and 6 from your Step 2 total.
4. The result (which should be somewhere between 6 and 30) is your apprehension score for interpersonal conversations.

Any score above 18 indicates some degree of apprehension. Most people score above 18 on this test, so if you scored relatively high, you're among the vast majority of people. An apprehension test for conversations is presented on page 45 and one for group discussions and meetings appears in Unit 25, "Speaking in Small Groups." You may want to take these tests now and compare your scores. If you're like most people, your apprehension score will be highest for public speaking, lowest for conversation, and somewhere between these for group discussions or meetings. What is there about public speaking that makes it an experience most people fear?

SOURCE: from *An Introduction to Rhetorical Communication*, 7th ed., by James C. McCroskey. Copyright © 1997 by James C. McCroskey. Reprinted by permission of the author.

WHAT IS COMMUNICATION APPREHENSION?

Many people develop negative feelings about their ability to communicate orally, anticipating that their communication efforts will fail. They feel that whatever gain they might make as a result of engaging in communication isn't worth the fear they experience. As a result, apprehensive speakers avoid communication situations and, when forced to participate, speak as little as possible.

General and Specific Apprehension

Some people have a general communication apprehension that shows itself in all communication situations. These people suffer from trait apprehension—a fear of communication generally, regardless of the specific situation. Their fear appears in conversations, small group settings, and public speaking situations.

Other people experience communication apprehension in only certain communication situations. These people suffer from state apprehension— a fear that is specific to a given communication situation. For example, a speaker may fear public speaking but have no difficulty in talking with two or three other people. Or, a speaker may fear job interviews but have no fear of public speaking. State apprehension is extremely common. Most people experience it for some situations. If you haven't done so already, you may want to take the accompanying test, "How Apprehensive Are You in Conversations?" and compare your apprehension score in public speaking with that for conversation.

TIPS
from professional speakers

When the subject of nerves comes up, there is both good news and bad news. The bad news is that, more than likely, you'll be nervous. You aren't alone. Almost all speakers, including professionals, experience uneasiness before speeches. So do athletes, rock stars, actors, and other performers just before their game or performance. The good news is that, not only is this normal, but it's good!!! More news— Nervous energy IS energy. You can use it to your advantage.

Thomas J. Murphy, a teacher and author, and Kenneth Snyder, a professional speaker and trainer, *What! I Have to Give a Speech?* (Bloomington, IN: Grayson Bernard Publications, 1995): 160.

TEST YOURSELF
How Apprehensive Are You in Conversations?

This questionnaire is composed of six statements concerning your feelings about communication with other people. In the space provided, indicate the degree to which each statement applies to you by marking whether you:

1 = strongly agree
2 = agree
3 = are undecided
4 = disagree
5 = strongly disagree

There are no right or wrong answers. Some of the statements are similar to other statements; don't be concerned about this. Work quickly; record your first impression.

_____ 1. While participating in a conversation with a new acquaintance, I feel very nervous.

_____ 2. I have no fear of speaking up in conversations.

_____ 3. Ordinarily I am very tense and nervous in conversations.

_____ 4. Ordinarily I am very calm and relaxed in conversations.

_____ 5. While conversing with a new acquaintance, I feel very relaxed.

_____ 6. I'm afraid to speak up in conversations.

Compute your score as follows:

1. Begin with the number 18.
2. To 18, add your scores for items 2, 4, and 5.
3. Subtract your scores for items 1, 3, and 6 from your Step 2 total.
4. The result (which should be somewhere between 6 and 30) is your apprehension score for interpersonal conversations.

The higher the score, the greater your apprehension. A score above 18 indicates some degree of apprehension. Can you distinguish the conversations in which you're highly apprehensive from those in which you experience little to no apprehension?

Source: from *An Introduction to Rhetorical Communication*, 7th ed., by James C. McCroskey. Copyright © 1997 by James C. McCroskey. Reprinted by permission of the author.

Degrees of Apprehension

Communication apprehension exists on a continuum. Some people are so apprehensive that they're unable to function effectively in any communication situation; not surprisingly, these people will try to avoid communication as much as possible. Other people are so mildly apprehensive that they appear to experience no fear at all; they're the ones who actively seek out communication opportunities. Most of us are between these extremes. As you'll see in the next section, however, apprehension does not have to be debilitating. In fact, in many cases, apprehension may energize and motivate you to greater effectiveness.

Positive and Normal Apprehension

Apprehension in public speaking is normal. Everyone experiences some degree of fear in the relatively formal public speaking situation. In public

No passion so effectively robs the mind of all its powers of acting and reasoning as fear.
—Edmund Burke

TIPS
from professional speakers

Whether you face real or imaginary fear, physical danger, or emotional stress, the reaction is the same. And speakers benefit: The adrenaline becomes energy; their minds seem more alert; new thoughts, facts, and ideas arise. In fact, some of my best ad libs come to me in front of my toughest audiences; it's yet another gift from the adrenaline.

Nervousness can give your speech the edge—and the passion—all good speeches need. It has always been so; two thousand years ago Cicero said all public speaking of real merit was characterized by nervousness.

Dorothy Leeds, president, Organizational Technologies, Inc., a management and sales consulting firm. *Powerspeak: The Complete Guide to Persuasive Public Speaking and Presenting* (New York: Prentice Hall, 1988): 9–10.

speaking you're the sole focus of attention and are usually being evaluated for your performance. Therefore, experiencing fear or anxiety isn't strange or unique.

Although you may at first view apprehension as harmful, it's not necessarily so—as the "TIP" from Dorothy Leeds makes clear. In fact, apprehension can work for you. Fear can energize you. It may motivate you to work a little harder to produce a speech that will be better than it might have been. Further, the audience cannot see the apprehension you might be experiencing. Even though you may think that the audience can hear your heart beat faster and faster, they can't. They can't see your knees tremble. They can't sense your dry throat—at least not most of the time.

Culture and Communication Apprehension

The cultural composition of your audience can contribute to uncertainty, fear, and anxiety, all of which are intimately related to communication apprehension (Stephen and Stephen 1992).

When you're in an intercultural situation—say your audience is composed largely of people of cultures very different from your own—you're more uncertain about the situation and about their possible responses. Not surprisingly, most people react negatively to high uncertainty and develop a decreased attraction for these other people (Gudykunst and Nishida 1984; Gudykunst, Yang, and Nishida 1985). When you're sure of the situation and can predict what will happen, you're more likely to feel comfortable and at ease. But when the situation is uncertain and you cannot predict what will happen, you become more apprehensive (Gudykunst and Kim 1992).

THE ETHICS OF The Speaker

Three guidelines are often used in defining the ethics of the public speaker; as you review these guidelines, think about your own ethical standards and behaviors.

Truth. Present the truth as you understand it. Your audience has a right to expect that you speak the truth as you know it. Obviously, you shouldn't lie, but you should also avoid misrepresenting the truth because it might better fit your purpose. Avoid distorting information (no matter how small). Be truthful about the sources of your materials. Failure to properly credit sources can lead you to commit plagiarism (see Ethical Issue box in Unit 7), even though you have no intention of deceiving anyone.

Knowledge and Preparation. If you speak on a specific subject—as a teacher lecturing or as a political candidate debating—prepare yourself thoroughly. Be so informed, so knowledgeable, that the audience will be able to get the information they need to make reasoned and reasonable choices. This preparation will also ensure that you don't

present your listeners with misinformation, with information that is out-of-date and no longer valid, or with information that is inaccurate and incorrect.

Understandable. As a speaker you have an obligation to make your speech understandable to your audience (Jensen, 1985b). In talking above the level of the audience, for example, you prevent the audience from clearly understanding what you're arguing or explaining. In talking in oversimplified terms, you can fool your audience into thinking they understand what they really do not. Both approaches are unethical because they prevent the audience from learning what it needs to learn to make its choices.

Do you agree with these guidelines? Are there additional guidelines that you'd suggest the ethical speaker follow?

(The next Ethics of Public Speaking box appears on page 67.)

Why do intercultural communication situations seem to create more uncertainty, fear, and anxiety than communication between members of the same culture?

Intercultural situations can also engender fear. You might, for example, have a greater fear of saying something that will prove offensive or of revealing your own prejudices. The fear easily translates into apprehension.

Intercultural situations can also create anxiety, a feeling very similar to apprehension. Anxiety may be felt for a number of reasons (Stephan and Stephan 1985). For example, if your prior relationships with members of your audience's culture were few or unpleasant, then you're likely to experience greater apprehension than if these prior experiences were numerous and positive.

Your thoughts and feelings about the group will also influence your apprehension. For example, if you hold stereotypes and prejudices, or if you feel that you're very different from these others, you're likely to experience more apprehension than if you saw these people as similar to you.

DEALING WITH COMMUNICATION APPREHENSION

If you experience some apprehension and would like to acquire more control over it, the following guidelines should help you feel more comfortable giving speeches (Richmond and McCroskey 1997; Cheek 1989). If you continue to experience extremely high levels of communication apprehension or if you're so fearful of the speaking situation that you simply cannot function, talk with your instructor after completing this unit. There are several ways you can deal with your own public speaking anxiety: (1) reversing the factors that cause anxiety, (2) cognitive restructuring and performance visualization, (3) systematically desensitizing yourself, and (4) using some basic skills.

Reversing the Factors That Cause Apprehension

There are five factors that contribute to speaker apprehension; if you can reserve these factors or lessen their impact, you'll be able to reduce your anxiety. These five factors are the new and the different, subordinate status, conspicuousness, lack of similarity, and prior history (Beatty 1988).

New and different situations, for example, your first day at work or your first job interview, will make you anxious. Since public speaking is likely to be relatively new and different to many of you, it's a situation

The human brain starts working the moment you're born and never stops until you stand up to speak in public.
—George Jessel

that's likely to generate anxiety. As the novelty of the situation is reduced, your anxiety is also reduced. This is one reason why you're likely to experience your greatest fear during the first few minutes of the speech; as you continue, the novelty of the situation will wear off and you'll become less nervous. Gaining experience in a wide variety of public speaking situations will help you reduce their newness and thereby reduce your fear.

If you see yourself as having subordinate status, as, for example, when you feel that others are better speakers or that they know more than you do, your anxiety increases. Thinking positively about yourself and being thorough in your preparation reduces this particular cause of anxiety. In a similar way, if you feel that members of another group are competing with you or evaluating you, then you're likely to experience more apprehension than if the situation were more cooperative and equal. Thinking more positively about yourself and being thorough in your preparation are helpful techniques for reducing this particular cause of anxiety.

When you feel conspicuous or when you feel you're the center of attention, as you normally would in, say, addressing a large audience, your anxiety may increase. Realizing that you're only one of a number of speakers the audience will hear today may help reduce this feeling of conspicuousness. Similarly, thinking of public speaking as a type of conversation (some theorists call public speaking "enlarged conversation") may help reduce this feeling. Or, if you're comfortable talking in small groups, visualizing your audience as an enlarged small group will likely dispel some of the anxiety you feel.

When you feel you lack similarity with your audience, that you have little in common with your listeners—as you might when addressing an audience from cultures different from your own or when addressing people from another department within a large corporation—you may feel that your audience doesn't empathize with you and so you may become anxious. Try emphasizing the commonalties you share with your listeners as you plan your speeches as well as during the actual presentation. This will help you see yourself as a part of the audience and may also suggest areas of similarity you might integrate into your speech.

A prior history of apprehension is likely to increase anxiety and a kind of spiral may be established: you experience apprehension in one situation that leads you to feel greater apprehension in the second that creates greater apprehension in the third, and on and on. Your objective is to prevent this spiral or break it if it already exists by engaging in public speaking experiences that have positive consequences and prove rewarding. As you build up your positive public speaking experiences you'll feel more comfortable, and the comfort and control that you feel in one speech will help you feel even more comfortable and more in control in the next, and on and on.

Cognitive Restructuring and Performance Visualization

The assumption of this approach is that your own unrealistic beliefs cause apprehension. For example, set yourself unachievable goals (*Everyone must love me, I have to be thoroughly competent, I have to be the best in everything*), and you logically fear failure. This fear of failure (and the irrational beliefs behind it) are at the foundation of your apprehension

(Markway, Carmin, Pollard, and Flynn 1992). **Cognitive restructuring**, then, advises you to substitute your irrational beliefs with more rational ones (*It would be nice if everyone loved me but I don't need that to survive, I can fail. Although it would be nice, I don't have to be the best in everything*). Your last step is to practice your new, more rational beliefs.

The process may go something like this: unrealistic beliefs give rise to anxiety because you know you can never achieve these unrealistically high goals and that you will fail at some point. There's not a speaker in the world who wouldn't fail given these unrealistic beliefs. You then focus on the inevitable failure; you can almost see yourself failing. This image leads to a loss of confidence and further visions of failure.

Maintain realistic expectations for yourself and your audience. You don't have to be perfect. Be the best you can be—whatever that is. Compete with yourself. Your second speech does not have to be better than the speech of the previous speaker. It should, however, be better than your own first speech. Focus on your success, on your successfully meeting your new and realistic goals.

Recognize, too, that even if you give six 10-minute speeches in this class, you will only have spoken for 60 minutes . . . one hour . . . 1/24th of a day . . . 1/35,064th of your four-year college life. Let your apprehension motivate you to produce a more thoroughly prepared and rehearsed speech. Let it not, however, upset you to the point where it harms your other activities.

A special type of cognitive restructuring is performance visualization, designed specifically to reduce both the outward manifestations of communication apprehension and negative thinking (Ayres and Hopf 1993). In performance visualization you work toward developing a positive attitude and a positive self-perception by visualizing yourself in the role of an effective public speaker. Once you can visualize yourself as this effective speaker, you devote attention to modeling your performance on that of this effective speaker, in a way imitating this effective speaker. If you wish to try performance visualization, take a look at Practically Speaking 3.3 on page 56; it provides specific instructions for working with performance visualization.

Systematic Desensitization

Systematic desensitization is a technique for dealing with a variety of fears, including those involved in public speaking (Wolpe 1957; Goss, Thompson, and Olds 1978; Richmond and McCroskey 1997). The general idea is to create a hierarchy of behaviors leading up to the desired but feared behavior (say, speaking before an audience). One specific hierarchy might look like this:

- Giving a speech in class
- Introducing another speaker to the class
- Speaking in a group in front of the class
- Answering a question in class
- Asking a question in class

You'd begin at the bottom of this hierarchy and rehearse this behavior mentally over a period of days until you could clearly visualize asking a question in class without any uncomfortable anxiety. Once you can accomplish this, you can move to the second level. Here you'd visualize

---

TIPS
from professional speakers

Shortly before you get up to make your remarks is the time to visualize yourself delivering a confident, well-received speech. It works—if you've done your homework well and have earned the right to psych yourself up.

Think of times you've succeeded at your endeavors in any field rather than the times you've failed. Think in terms of how good it'll be to succeed rather than how bad it'll be to fail. Think about your purpose in delivering the speech.

Concentrate on what you want to do. Concentrate on the emotions you want to spread outward, not on the emotions you want to keep inside. Concentrate on what you're saying, not how you're saying it or how you look.

Ed McMahon, television emcee and frequent public speaker, *The Art of Public Speaking* (New York: Ballantine, 1986): 101–102

Fears must be faced.
—James Baldwin

and mentally practice the somewhat more threatening "answering a question." Once you can do this, you can move to the third level, and so on, until you get to the desired behavior.

In creating your hierarchy, try to use small steps. This enables you to get from one step to the next more easily. Each success makes the next step easier. You might then go on to engage in the actual behaviors after you've comfortably visualized them: ask a question, answer a question, and so on.

Skill Acquisition

The fourth general approach to dealing with communication apprehension is to acquire specific skills and techniques for greater control over apprehension and for increased speaking effectiveness. Here are some useful techniques.

Prepare and Practice Thoroughly. Much of the fear you experience is a fear of impending failure. Adequate and even extra preparation will lessen thoughts of failure and the accompanying apprehension. Jack Valenti (1982), president of the Motion Picture Association of America and speechwriter for Lyndon Johnson, put it this way: "The most effective antidote to stage fright and other calamities of speechmaking is total, slavish, monkish preparation."

Because apprehension is greatest during the beginning of the speech, try memorizing the first few sentences of your speech to eliminate any possibility of not saying them correctly or forgetting them. If there are complicated facts or figures, be sure to write these out and plan to read them. Again, this procedure will help lessen your fear of making a mistake.

Gain Experience. Learning to speak in public is similar to learning to drive a car or ski down a mountain. With experience, the initial fears and anxieties give way to feelings of control, comfort, and, eventually, pleasure. Experience will prove that you can speak effectively in public despite your fears and anxieties; it will show you that the feelings of accomplishment will outweigh any initial anxiety.

Move About and Breathe Deeply. Physical activity—gross bodily movements as well as the small movements of the hands, face, and head—eases or lessens apprehension. Using a presentation aid, for example, will temporarily divert attention from you and will allow you to get rid of your excess energy.

Deep breathing relaxes the body. By breathing deeply a few times before getting up to speak, you'll sense your body relax. This will help you overcome your initial fear of getting out of your seat and walking to the front of the room. If, during the speech, you find yourself getting a bit more nervous than you anticipated, take a deep breath during a pause.

Avoid Chemicals as Tension Relievers. Unless prescribed by a physician, avoid any chemical means for reducing apprehension. Tranquilizers, marijuana, alcohol, or artificial stimulants, for example, are likely to create problems rather than reduce them. They're likely to impair other functions which will only increase your apprehension. For example, chemicals are likely to impair your ability to remember the parts of your speech, to accurately read audience feedback, and to regulate the timing of your speech. All of these will, in turn, heighten the very apprehension you're trying to reduce.

The skill to do comes from doing.
—Cicero

LISTEN TO THIS How to Listen to Reduce Apprehension

As a listener you can do a great deal to assist speakers with their apprehension. Here are a few suggestions:

Positively Reinforce the Speaker. A nod, a smile, an attentive appearance throughout the speech will help put the speaker at ease. Resist the temptation to pick up a newspaper or talk with a friend. Try to make the speaking experience as easy as possible for the speaker.

Ask Questions in a Supportive Manner. If there's a question period, ask information-seeking questions rather than fire critical challenges. Instead of saying "Your criticism of heavy metal music is absurd," say "Why do you find the lyrics of heavy metal harmful?" Ask questions in a way that won't encourage defensiveness.

Don't Focus on Errors. If the speaker fumbles, don't focus on it. Don't put your head down, cover your eyes, or otherwise communicate your awareness of the fumble. Instead, continue listening to the content of the speech; let the speaker know that you're focused on what is being said.

(The next Listen to This box appears on page 64.)

DEVELOPING CONFIDENCE

Confidence separates the effective from the ineffective public speaker. Confidence also seems to separate the speaker who experiences enjoyment from the speaker who feels only discomfort and anxiety. Fortunately, confidence is a quality that everyone can develop and increase. Here are a few suggestions for developing your self-confidence as a public speaker.

Prepare Thoroughly

Preparation is probably the major factor in instilling confidence in a speaker, as it is in reducing apprehension. Preparation includes everything you do from the time you begin thinking about your speech to the time you deliver it. The more you know about your topic and your audience, the more confident you'll feel and the more confidence you'll project. Thorough preparation will also lessen any fears you might have of not being able to answer audience questions.

Familiarize Yourself with the Public Speaking Situation

Familiarize yourself with the arrangement of the room in which you'll speak, the type of audience you'll address, and so on. Familiarity with any situation increases your ability to control it. The public speaking situation is no exception. Perhaps a day or two before you're to speak, stand in front of the room and look it over. Try to imagine the entire speaking situation as it will be when you deliver your speech. Then, when you do go to the front of the room to give your first speech, you'll face the familiar instead of the unexpected. If possible, rehearse in the room in which you'll give your speech.

Develop the Desire to Communicate

Avoid rehearsing fear responses (*I'm going to forget my speech. No one will like my speech. I'm going to look foolish*). Replace any thoughts of fear with thoughts of control. Replace self-critical statements with thoughts of

Look . . . ours is a business of appearances, and it's terribly important to appear to be self-confident. The minute you give evidence of doubt, people are going to eat you alive.
—Ted Koppel

In what way is the display of confidence important to the success of a talk show host such as Rosie O'Donnell, pictured here with Hillary Clinton?

You've got to take the initiative and play your game . . . confidence makes the difference.
—Chris Evert

confidence. Tell yourself that the experience can be an enjoyable one—it really can be! With time, you'll find that you're operating with a more positive and confident view of the entire public speaking experience.

Rehearse

Rehearsing your speech and its presentation—and thus sensing your control over it—will increase self-confidence. Rehearse your speech often and aloud. If possible, rehearse in front of a few supportive listeners. Rehearsals that approximate the actual speaking situation will especially help reduce the novelty of the situation and will help build your confidence as a public speaker.

Rehearse your speech as a confident, fully-in-control public speaker. Rehearse with a positive attitude and perspective. When you then present the actual speech, you'll find that you can present the speech as you rehearsed it, with confidence.

Each public speaking experience—like each rehearsal—should add to your self confidence. After five or six speeches, you should be looking forward to future speaking engagements.

Engage in Self-Affirmation

Because the way you talk to and about yourself will influence what you think of yourself, it's often helpful to engage in self-affirmation. Try telling yourself that you're competent and that you'll be successful. Read through the list of self-affirming phrases presented here and try to feel what they're attempting to convey.

- I'm a generally competent person and speaker.
- I have some good personality characteristics that will come across effectively in public speaking.
- Neither I nor my speech have to be loved by everyone.
- I am worthwhile listening to because I'm me.
- My past failures and inadequacies don't have to influence everything I do.
- I am creative and that will come across in my speaking.

What, me worry?
—Alfred E. Neuman

- I think critically and will be able to analyze and present complex ideas to others.
- I'm a self-starter.
- I can be effective in most things I do, including public speaking.
- I'm flexible and can adjust to different situations and different audience responses.

With confidence, you have won even before you have started.
—Marcus Garvey

Project Your Confidence

Throughout your speech, try to project your confidence; make the audience see you as a confident, fully-in-control speaker. Here are a few suggestions:

- Remain emotionally controlled. If the audience sees you allowing emotions to get the best of you, you'll appear lacking in confidence.
- Avoid weak verbal expressions. For example, asking for agreement with tag questions—"It seems like a good idea, don't you think?"—or using lots of indefinite modifiers such as "pretty good" or "fairly inexpensive" will make your audience see your message and yourself as less sure and less confident than you'd want. At the same time, avoid weak nonverbals. Self-touching movements—playing with your hair, touching your face, or aimlessly shifting from one foot to the other—will also make you seem to lack confidence.
- Demonstrate your own consistency; show your audience that you have the confidence in your own convictions to stick with them over time.

Develop a Communicator Self-Image

A "communicator self-image" implies a view of yourself as a capable, proficient, and confident communicator. See yourself as an advocate who is effective in getting your message across to others. Think of yourself as a confident public speaker. In addition, act as a confident speaker would. For example, maintain eye contact with your listeners and stand tall. Acting confident will go a long way toward actually increasing your confidence. This process occurs in three steps: (1) You act as if you're confident. (2) You come to think of yourself as confident. (3) You become confident.

Build your positive qualities by acting as if you already have them. This "acting as if" will help you make these positive qualities a more integral part of your thoughts and behaviors.

TIPS
from professional speakers

The best and simplest way to improve is to pay attention to other presenters and analyze what they do. Observe the greater ones and also the beginners. Determine what it is that makes the good ones good and the bad ones bad. Do this every time you hear a speech or see a presentation. Then examine your own style and make adjustments.

Peter Urs Bender, frequent speaker and seminar leader, *Secrets of Power Presentations* (Willowdale, Ontario, Canada: Firefly Books, 1995): 29.

UNIT IN BRIEF

Communication Apprehension	Communication apprehension is a fear of speaking and may involve trait apprehension (fear of communication generally) or state apprehension (fear of a specific communication situation).
	In addition to culture, the following influence apprehension: novelty, subordinate status, conspicuousness, dissimilarity, and prior history.

Dealing with Communication Apprehension	Reverse the factors that contribute to apprehension.
	Use cognitive restructuring and performance visualization: substitute rational beliefs for irrational beliefs and effective for ineffective models.
	Use systematic desensitization; mastering a behavior by mastering its less threatening parts.
	Acquire skills; learn the specific techniques for managing apprehension.
Developing Confidence	Prepare thoroughly.
	Familiarize yourself with the public speaking situation.
	Develop the desire to communicate.
	Rehearse often and with a positive attitude.
	Engage in self-affirmation.
	Project your confidence.
	Develop an image of yourself as a successful speaker.

THINKING CRITICALLY ABOUT APPREHENSION AND CONFIDENCE

REVIEWING KEY TERMS AND CONCEPTS IN APPREHENSION AND CONFIDENCE

1. Define the key terms used in this unit:

   ❑ apprehension (p. 43)
   ❑ cognitive restructuring (p. 48)
   ❑ performance visualization (p. 49)
   ❑ systematic desensitization (p. 49)
   ❑ skill acquisition (p. 50)
   ❑ confidence (p. 51)
   ❑ self-affirmation (p. 52)
   ❑ communicator self-image (p. 53)

2. Explain the key concepts discussed in this unit:

   ■ What is the nature of and the dimensions of communication apprehension?
   ■ What suggestions may be offered for dealing with communication apprehension?
   ■ What guidelines can you follow to increase your self-confidence as a public speaker?

DEVELOPING PUBLIC SPEAKING STRATEGIES

1. Margaret has been asked to coach a small group of highly apprehensive students for their first public speech. Interestingly enough, Margaret is highly apprehensive herself and, in fact, that's why she was chosen for this coaching task. She wonders if she should tell the students that she, too, is a high apprehensive?

2. Nash has to give a sales presentation to persuade supermarket managers to carry his new line of soft drinks. Nash is apprehensive largely because so much

depends on this one presentation. If the managers refuse to carry his drinks, his business will go bankrupt. He has to appear confident—in his drinks and in himself. What advice would you give Nash?

3. Luanda is frightened of talking on the telephone. She wants to create a systematic desensitization hierarchy to help her reduce her fear. What advice would you give Luanda? How would you create such a hierarchy?

EVALUATING PUBLIC SPEECHES

1. Reflect on one of the speeches you've heard recently in class, on television, or in your community or school. Was the speaker noticeably apprehensive? What signs could you see that revealed this apprehension?

2. If you're apprehensive about giving a speech, what kinds of things can you do to prepare for this and to more effectively manage your own apprehension?

USING TECHNOLOGY IN PUBLIC SPEAKING

1. Access the ERIC database (ERIC stands for Educational Resources Information Center and contains abstracts to articles in over 750 journals) and search for articles on communication apprehension. What are some of the topics that research on communication apprehension has addressed?

2. Visit the Gallup Organization's Web site at http://www.gallup.com/ and look for information on common fears that people have. Where does public speaking rank?

3. Visit http://www.as.wvu.edu/~jmccrosk/66.htm and read the paper by James McCroskey on communication apprehension. What concepts does McCroskey discuss that might be helpful in reducing your own communication apprehension?

PRACTICALLY SPEAKING

3.1   Short Speech Technique

Prepare and deliver a two-minute speech in which you:

a. explain how apprehension might influence job performance in your field of work.

b. explain how apprehension might impact on a student's dating and general social life.

c. explain how uncertainty, fear, and anxiety operate in communication generally and in intercultural communication especially.

d. describe a fictional character in literature, film, or television who displays a great deal of confidence.

3.2 How Shy Are You?

Earlier you assessed your own communication apprehension in public speaking. A common misconception is that people who experience high degrees of communication apprehension are also shy. Actually, research has not been able to find a relationship between shyness and communication apprehension, even though many of the symptoms are similar. Here's a shyness scale that will enable you to measure your own degree of shyness.* Respond to these statements, as noted in the directions, and then consider the questions presented after the test.

The following 14 statements refer to talking with other people. If the statement describes you very well, circle "YES." If it describes you, somewhat, circle "yes." If you're not sure whether it describes you or not, or if you don't understand the statement, circle "?" If the statement is a poor description of you, circle "no." If the statement is a very poor description of you, circle "NO." There are no right or wrong answers. Work quickly; record your first impression.

1. I am a shy person.	YES yes ? no NO
2. Other people think I talk a lot.	YES yes ? no NO
3. I am a very talkative person.	YES yes ? no NO
4. Other people think I am shy.	YES yes ? no NO
5. I talk a lot.	YES yes ? no NO
6. I tend to be very quiet in class.	YES yes ? no NO
7. I don't talk much.	YES yes ? no NO
8. I talk more than most people.	YES yes ? no NO
9. I am a quiet person.	YES yes ? no NO
10. I talk more in a small group (3-6) than others do.	YES yes ? no NO
11. Most people talk more than I do.	YES yes ? no NO
12. Other people think I am very quiet.	YES yes ? no NO

13. I talk more in class than   YES yes ? no NO
    most people do.
14. Most people are more shy   YES yes ? no NO
    than I am.

Give your responses the following numbers:

YES = 1
yes = 2
? = 3
no = 4
NO = 5

Score your responses as follows:

1. Add the scores for items 1, 4, 6, 7, 9, 11, and 12.

2. Add the scores for items 2, 3, 5, 8, 10, 13, and 14.

3. Complete the following formula: Shyness = 42 plus the total from Step 1 minus the total from Step 2. (As with the apprehension tests, the starting number—here 42—is used to facilitate scoring and making all numbers positive.)

You may interpret your score as follows:

Above 52 = a high level of shyness
Below 32 = a low level of shyness
Between 32 and 52 = a moderate level of shyness

Consider, for example: (1) In what situations are you most shy? Least shy? Why? (2) Can you think of early experiences that contributed to your level of shyness? (3) How does your level of shyness impact on your meeting other people? Your work relationships? Your classroom behavior? Your interactions with other students? Your interactions with your instructors? (4) How do you respond to shy people as potential relationship partners? As other students? As colleagues at work? As your public speaking instructor? (5) Would you like to change your degree of shyness? How might you use the suggestions for managing communication apprehension to alter your shyness behavior?

SOURCE*From "Communication Apprehension of Elementary and Secondary Students and Teachers" by James C. McCroskey, J. F. Andersen, Virginia Richmond, and L. R. Wheeless in *Communication Education* 30:122–132. Reprinted by permission of James C. McCroskey.

3.3. Using Performance Visualization to Reduce Apprehension

Performance visualization is a technique designed specifically to reduce the outward manifestations of speaker apprehension and also to reduce negative thinking (Ayres and Hopf 1993, 1995). Try reducing your own communication apprehension by following these two simple suggestions.

1. The first part of performance visualization is to develop a positive attitude and a positive self-perception. So, visualize yourself in the role of being an effective speaker. Visualize yourself communicating as a fully and totally confident individual. Look at your listeners and speak. Throughout your conversation see yourself as fully in control of the situation. See your listeners in rapt attention from the time you begin to the time you stop. Throughout this visualization, avoid all negative thoughts. As you visualize yourself as an effective speaker, take special note of how you walk, look at your listeners, respond to questions, and especially how you feel about the whole experience.

2. The second part of performance visualization is designed to help you model your performance on that of an especially effective speaker. View a particularly competent speaker and make a mental movie of it. Try selecting one on video so you can replay it several times. As you review the actual and mental movie, begin to shift yourself into the role of speaker. Become this effective speaker.

3.4. Analyzing a Speech

Read the following brief speech on stage fright and respond to the questions posed in the annotations.

STAGE FRIGHT AND NERVOUSNESS IN PUBLIC SPEAKING
Eva-Maria Jokinen

The following speech was delivered by Eva-Maria Jokinen to a class in Finland. The class, as the speaker mentions, is made up of people studying to be interpreters and translators. They are taking the course in public speaking as part of this training. This speech is particularly useful because it presents a unique perspective on the topic of this unit and also enables us to look at a public speech by someone from a different culture from most readers.

Good morning everybody! It is nice to see you all here!

In our future professions as translators and especially as interpreters we are all going to speak in front of people in many different kinds of situations. And that's what we have been practicing here during this public speaking course. Also the theme on which I will talk today in closely tied to public speaking, or at least I have always thought so. We have probably all suffered from some kind of stage fright and nervousness during this course. And that's what I am going to talk about.

The Collins Dictionary defines stage fright as "nervousness or panic that may beset a person about to appear in front of an audience." We have all seen what can happen if the speaker is very nervous. He looks confused and doesn't look at the audience. Perhaps he keeps drumming his fingers on the table or he shifts body weight from one foot to the other, back and forth. Women often fiddle with their hair. The audience can find these kind of things very annoying. Things like that can also cause disaster. I know a true story about an interpreter who was very nervous and twisted the wire in the interpreting booth around her finger. She kept doing that until, all of a sudden, the connection between the speaker's mike and all interpreters was lost. It took the organizers half an hour to find out what was wrong; and yes, it was she who had caused everything by twisting the wire around her finger.

We are usually afraid of the unknown and the things we think are physically or mentally threatening. When we speak in front of people we feel mentally threatened. Maybe we don't trust ourselves enough. We are afraid that we will do badly, or that we can't remember what we were going to say. We are afraid that our hands will start trembling and the audience will notice it. Naturally all these things can make us very embarrassed. And that is the thing that is so frightening and threatening.

Stage fright is actually a very normal reaction. It is our body preparing itself for a big event; therefore it produces some extra adrenaline. It is just the adrenaline that causes the symptoms of stage fright. But since we are individuals, the symptoms too are individual. Some people have just a little queasy feeling in their stomachs; others may feel a slight weakness at the back of the knees. Cold or sweaty palms are also fairly common. Or perhaps your heart just beats a shade faster than normal.

Some people feel the symptoms before they get to the podium, and when they finally are there, the symptoms disappear. Usually the symptoms are worse at the beginning of the speech, then they gradually vanish. But there are people who say that the feeling doesn't go away until they've finished their speech and are off the podium.

In a public speaking class where there are several speeches per class period, introductory greetings are probably best when they are kept relatively short. Do you agree with this generalization? If not, what else might the speaker have said?

How does this introduction serve the three purposes mentioned in Unit 2: to gain attention, to establish a connection among yourself, your audience, and your topic, and to provide an orientation?

Notice that the speaker uses the masculine pronoun generically, something that would be considered inappropriate in classroom speeches in most of the United States.

Does the explanation of stage fright and its symptoms ring true to your own experience? If not, what would you have changed?

Stage fright is also very common. Even professional performers often suffer from it. Some great performers say that stage fright actually makes you do well and gives you an extra kick. But for some people stage fright is not a positive thing. I, for example, have many times not been able to sleep well the night before my speech because of it. But even if one really can't eliminate stage fright, it is possible to lessen it, learn to live with it, and change it into a positive feeling.

First you must of course know what you are afraid of. The point is: in order to lessen or eliminate the feeling or fear and nervousness you must know what it is that you really are afraid of.

Secondly, you must figure out why you are afraid of that thing. Perhaps the reason for your nervousness is that you're not sure if you can remember everything you are going to say. Or maybe there are some important persons in the audience on whom you want to make a good impression.

Thirdly, learn to discuss your fears with other people. You will find it relieving to share your feelings with somebody. That way you can discuss and analyze your fears and the reasons for them. You will probably also find out that you're not alone: other people suffer from nervousness and stage fright, too.

The next step is learn to get rid of the reasons for your fears. If you are afraid that you will not be able to remember your speech, the only way to get rid of that feeling is to practice. Make sure that you can remember the main points of your speech even when you're asleep. That way you will feel more confident in your speech delivery; you will know where you are going all the time. Get to know the room where you are going to speak and check any possible equipment you are going to use in advance; that will also make you feel more confident. Or perhaps it is the audience that makes you nervous. You feel that it is you against them. You're alone, they have each other. Positive thinking will help; you are there to co-operate with the audience, and to give them information on something. And the audience is there to hear what you want to say; they're interested in your topic. They're not there to judge or criticize you.

Since this is a particularly brief speech, these four steps to managing stage fright are covered rather briefly. If this speech were two or three or four times longer, how would you have expanded on these four steps? Can you provide examples, illustrations, or testimony, for example, that might expand on these suggestions?

The most important thing, however, is that no matter how afraid you are, how nervous and unsure you might feel, don't make excuses not to speak in many interesting situations just because of stage fright. Force yourself to go to situations where you must appear in front of an audience. It won't be easy, but if you just keep doing it often enough, the day will come when you'll get used to it. Notice that I said "get used to it," not "get rid of it," because that day may never come. However, you can reduce your fears, which will make you more confident and turn stage fright and nervousness into a positive feeling.

How does this conclusion serve the functions identified in Unit 2: to summarize; to connect speaker, audience, and topic; and to provide closure?

Listening

UNIT CONTENTS	UNIT OBJECTIVES
	After completing this unit, you should be able to:
The Listening Process	Describe the five-stage process of listening and the relevance of both culture and gender to listening.
Obstacles to Effective Listening	Explain the major obstacles to effective listening.
Principles of Effective Listening	Explain the principles for effective listening.

One of the best ways to persuade others is with our ears—by listening.
—Dean Rusk

Preparing and presenting a public speech is the task you're most concerned with and most anxious about. But that's really only half the process—the other half is critical listening. Before reading about this area of human communication, examine your own listening habits by taking the accompanying listening self-test, "How Good a Listener Are You?"

TEST YOURSELF
How Good a Listener Are You?

Respond to each question using the following scale:
1 = always
2 = frequently
3 = sometimes
4 = seldom
5 = never

_____ 1. I consider listening and hearing to be essentially the same, so I listen by simply keeping my ears open.

_____ 2. I allow my mind to wander away from what the speaker is talking about.

_____ 3. I simplify messages I hear by omitting details.

_____ 4. I focus on a particular detail of what the speaker is saying instead of the general meanings the speaker wishes to communicate.

_____ 5. I allow my attitudes toward the topic or speaker to influence my evaluation of the message.

_____ 6. I assume that what I expect to hear is what is actually said.

_____ 7. I stop listening when the speaker attacks my personal beliefs.

_____ 8. I listen to what others say but I don't feel what they are feeling.

_____ 9. I judge and evaluate what the speaker is saying before I fully understand the meanings intended.

_____ 10. I rehearse my questions and responses while the speaker is speaking.

Add up the scores for all 10 statements. Your score should be somewhere between 10 and 50. Since all statements describe ineffective listening tendencies, high scores reflect effective listening and low scores reflect ineffective listening. If you scored significantly higher than 30, then you probably have better-than-average listening skills. Scores significantly below 30 represent lower-than-average listening skills. Regardless of your score, however, most people can significantly improve their listening skills. As you read this unit try to think of specific instances where your ineffective listening got you into trouble.

THE LISTENING PROCESS

In the popular mind, listening is often thought to be the same as hearing; it's just something that takes place when you're in hearing range of speech. Actually, listening and hearing are not the same. Listening is a lot more complex than hearing, as illustrated in our five-stage model.

The Five Stages of Listening

The process of listening can be described as a series of five stages or steps: receiving, understanding, remembering, evaluating, and responding. This process is represented in Figure 4.1.

Receiving. Unlike listening, hearing begins and ends with this first stage of receiving. Hearing is something that just happens when you get within earshot of some auditory stimuli. Listening is quite different; it begins (but does not end) with receiving the messages the speaker sends. The messages are both verbal and nonverbal; they consist of words as well as gestures, facial expressions, variations in volume and rate, and much more.

At this stage you recognize not only what is said (verbally and nonverbally) but also what is omitted. The politician's summary of accomplishments in education as well as the omission of the failures in improved health care programs are both received at this stage.

Receiving messages is a highly selective process. You don't listen to all the available auditory stimuli. Rather, you selectively tune in to certain messages and tune others out. Generally, you listen carefully to messages that you feel will prove of value to you or that you feel are particularly interesting. At the same time you give less attention to messages that have less value or interest. Thus, you may, for example, listen carefully when

The wisest mind has something yet to learn.
—George Santayana

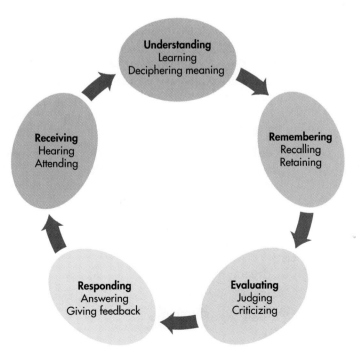

FIGURE 4.1

A Five-Stage Model of the Listening Process.

This five-stage model draws on a variety of previous models that listening researchers have developed (for example, Barker and Gaut 1996; Steil, Barker, and Watson 1983; Brownell 1987; and Alessandra 1986).

your instructor tells you what will appear on the examination but will listen less carefully to an extended story or to routine announcements. When receiving, you should:

- focus your attention on the speaker's verbal and nonverbal messages, on what is said and on what isn't said.
- avoid focusing your attention on distractions in the environment.
- focus your attention on what the speaker is saying rather than on any questions you may wish to ask later.

Understanding. Understanding is the stage at which you learn what the speaker means. This understanding includes both the thoughts that are expressed as well as the emotional tone that accompanies these thoughts, for example, the urgency or the joy or sorrow expressed in the message. To enhance understanding:

- relate the new information the speaker is giving to what you already know (In what way will this new proposal change our present health care?).
- see the speaker's messages from the speaker's point of view; avoid judging the message until you fully understand it as the speaker intended it.
- rephrase (paraphrase) the speaker's ideas into your own words as you continue to listen.

Remembering. Messages that you receive and understand need to be retained for at least some period of time. In public speaking situations you can augment your memory by taking notes or by taping the messages.

What you remember is actually not what was said, but what you think (or remember) was said. Memory for speech isn't reproductive; you don't simply reproduce in your memory what the speaker said. Rather, memory is reconstructive; you actually reconstruct the messages you hear into a system that seems to make sense to you. This is well illustrated in the accompanying box, "Do You Really Remember What You Hear?"

In remembering:

- identify the thesis or central idea and the major propositions.
- summarize the message in a more easily retained form, being careful not to ignore crucial details or qualifications.
- repeat names and key concepts to yourself.
- identify the organizational pattern and use it (visualize it) to organize what the speaker is saying.

Do You Really Remember What You Hear? To illustrate the reproductive nature of memory, try to memorize the following list of 12 words (Glucksberg and Danks, 1975). Don't worry about the order of the words. Only the number remembered counts. Take about 20 seconds to memorize as many words as possible. Don't read any further until you've tried to memorize the list of words.

Word List

bed	dream	comfort
rest	wake	sound
awake	night	slumber
tired	eat	snore

Now close the book and write down as many of the words from this list as you can remember.

How did you do? If you're like many students, you not only remembered a good number of the words on the list but you also "remembered" at least one word that was not on the list: sleep. You did not simply reproduce the list; you reconstructed it. In this case you gave the list a meaning and part of that meaning included the word "sleep." This happens with all types of messages; the messages are reconstructed into a meaningful whole and in the process a distorted version of what was said is often "remembered."

Evaluating. Evaluating consists of judging the messages' and the speaker's credibility (Unit 23), truthfulness, or usefulness in some way. At this stage your own biases and prejudices become especially influential; they influence what you single out for evaluation and what you'll just let pass, what you judge good and what you judge bad. In some situations, the evaluation is more in the nature of critical analysis, a topic explored in detail in Unit 5. When evaluating:

- resist evaluation until you fully understand the speaker's point of view.
- distinguish facts from inferences (see Unit 15), opinions, and personal interpretations that you're making as well as those made by the speaker.
- identify any biases, self-interests, or prejudices that may lead the speaker to slant unfairly what he or she is presenting.
- identify any biases that may lead you to remember what supports your attitudes and beliefs and to forget what contradicts them.

Responding. Responding occurs in two phases: (1) nonverbal (and occasionally verbal) responses you make while the speaker is talking and (2) responses you make after the speaker has stopped talking. Responses made while the speaker is talking should support the speaker and show that you're listening. These include what nonverbal researchers call backchanneling cues (Burgoon, Buller, and Woodall 1995) such as nodding your head, smiling, leaning forward, and similar signals that let the speaker know that you're attending to the message.

Responses made after the speaker has stopped talking are generally more elaborate and might include questions of clarification ("I wasn't sure what you meant by reclassification"); expressions of agreement ("You're absolutely right on this and I'll support your proposal when it comes up for a vote"); and expressions of disagreement ("I disagree that Japanese products are superior to those produced in the United States"). When responding:

- support the speaker throughout the talk by using a variety of backchanneling cues; using only one backchanneling cue—for example, nodding constantly—will make it appear that you're not listening but are on automatic pilot.
- support the speaker in your final responses by saying something positive.
- own your own responses; state your thoughts and feelings as your own; use I-messages (for example, say "I think the new proposal will entail greater expense than you outlined" rather than "Everyone will object that the plan costs too much").

TIPS from professional speakers

Be a responsive listener. Be responsive in your demeanor, posture, and facial expression. Let your whole being show you're interested in other people and their ideas.

As you listen, look at the other person and show some signs of hearing and understanding. Nod your head occasionally—gently, not vigorously. Nod slightly with a yes for agreement or a no when it's something sad or unhappy. Show through your posture, whether seated or standing, that you are concentrating on listening totally . . . .

To understand this important principle of being responsive, it helps to ask, "How do we turn people off?" The answers come quickly: by not looking at them, not asking questions, not showing any positive response, by looking at our watch or out the window, shuffling papers, interrupting, and giving other negative types of feedback.

Robert L. Montgomery, professional speaker, trainer, author, and president of his own consulting firm. *Listening Made Easy.* New York: American Management Associations, 1981, pp. 75–76.

LISTEN TO THIS How to Listen with Questions

As explained in the 5-stage model, responding is an essential part of listening. In public speaking, part of responding is in asking questions. Here are a few guidelines for responding to the speaker with questions.

1. **Keep questions short and easily understood.** Generally, ask single questions rather than multiple ones. If it's necessary to ask a two-part question, make it clear at the start that this is a two-parter.
2. **Ask questions supportively**, as requests for information rather than as attacks.
3. **Speak so that all can hear you.** Persons in the front row often speak just so that the speaker can hear, forgetting that people in the back also need to hear the question.
4. **Consider asking the persuasive question.** Although this isn't always appropriate, there are situations when it's appropriate to voice your own position in your question and say, for example, "It seems to me that the Rockland proposal will reduce cost. What do you think about it?"

(The next Listen to This box appears on page 83.)

Listening and Culture

Listening is difficult, in part, because of the inevitable differences in the communication systems between speaker and listener. Each person has had a unique set of experiences, so each person's communication and meaning system is going to be different from each other person's. When speaker and listener come from different cultures, the differences and their effects are even greater. Here are just a few areas where misunderstandings can occur.

Language and Speech. Even when speaker and listener speak the same language, they speak it with different meanings and different accents. No two speakers speak exactly the same language. Every speaker speaks an idiolect—a unique variation of the language. Speakers of the same language will, at the very least, have different meanings for the same terms because they have had different experiences.

Speakers and listeners who have different native languages and who may have learned English as a second language will have even great differences in meaning. Translations are never precise and never fully capture the meaning in the other language. If your meaning for "house" was learned in a culture in which everyone lived in their own house with lots of land around it, then communicating with someone whose meaning was learned in a neighborhood of high-rise tenements is going to be difficult. Although you'll each hear the same word, the meanings you'll each develop will be drastically different. In adjusting your listening—especially when in an intercultural setting—understand that the speaker's meanings may be very different from yours even though you each speak the same language.

Still another part of speech is that of accents. In many classrooms throughout the country, there will be a wide range of accents. Those whose native language is a tonal one (such as one of the Chinese languages), where differences in pitch signal important meaning differences, may speak English with variations in pitch that may seem unnatural to others. Those whose native language is Japanese may have trouble distinguishing the sound of "l" from "r" since Japanese does not make this distinction.

As a general rule, do you think that people are more easily informed (or persuaded) by persons who are culturally similar to them or by those who are culturally different from them? Can you identify exceptions? What implications do your responses have for intercultural understanding?

The directness or indirectness with which a speaker presents his or her ideas varies greatly from one culture to another. Some cultures—Western Europe and the United States, for example—favor a direct style in communication; they advise us to "say what you mean and mean what you say." Many Asian cultures, on the other hand, favor an indirect style; they emphasize politeness and maintaining a positive public image rather than absolute truth. Listen carefully to persons with different styles of directness. Consider the possibility that the meanings the speaker wishes to communicate with, say, indirectness, may be very different from the meanings you'd communicate with indirectness.

The case of feedback provides a good example of the difference between direct and indirect styles. Members of some cultures give very direct and very honest feedback. Speakers from these cultures—the United States is a good example—expect the feedback to be an honest reflection of what their listeners are feeling. In other cultures—Japan and Korea are good examples—it's more important that speakers be positive than truthful and so they may respond with positive feedback even though they don't feel it. Listen to feedback, as you would all messages, with a full recognition that different cultures view feedback very differently.

Nonverbal Behavioral Differences. Speakers from different cultures have different display rules—cultural rules that govern which nonverbal behaviors are appropriate and which are inappropriate in a public setting. As you listen to another person, you also "listen" to their nonverbals. If these are drastically different from what you expect on the basis of the verbal message, they may be seen as a kind of noise or interference, or they may be seen as contradictory messages. Also, different cultures may give very different meanings to the same nonverbal gesture.

For example, Americans consider direct eye contact an expression of honesty and forthrightness, but the Japanese often view this as a lack of respect. The Japanese will glance at the other person's face rarely and then only for very short periods (Axtell 1990a). Among some Latin Americans and Native Americans, direct eye contact between, say, a teacher and a student is considered inappropriate, perhaps aggressive; appropriate student behavior is to avoid eye contact with the teacher.

Ethnocentrism. One problem that hinders effective listening is the tendency to see others and their behaviors through your own cultural filters. Ethnocentrism is the tendency to evaluate the values, beliefs, and behaviors of your own culture as being more positive, logical, and natural than

Listening is a magnetic and strange thing, a creative force. The friends who listen to us are the ones we move toward. When we are listened to, it creates us, makes us unfold and expand.
—Karl Menninger

those of others. The nonethnocentric, on the other hand, would see both himself or herself and others as different but equal, with neither being inferior nor superior.

Ethnocentrism exists on a continuum. People are not either ethnocentric or not ethnocentric; rather, most are somewhere between these polar opposites. And, of course, your degree of ethnocentrism varies depending on the group on which you focus. For example, if you're Greek American, you may have a low degree of ethnocentrism when dealing with Italian Americans (because of the similarities in the cultures of Greeks and Italians) but a high degree when dealing with Japanese Americans (because of the greater differences between the Greek and the Japanese cultures). Most important for our purposes is that your degree of ethnocentrism (and we are all ethnocentric to at least some degree) will influence your listening effectiveness.

Table 4.1, drawing from a number of researchers (Lukens 1978; Gudykunst and Kim 1984; Gudykunst 1991), summarizes some of the interconnections. This table identifies five degrees of ethnocentrism; in reality, of course, there are as many degrees as there are people. The "communication distances" are general terms that highlight the attitude that dominates that level of ethnocentrism. Under "listening" are some of the major ways people might listen given their particular degree of ethnocentrism.

Recognizing the tendency toward ethnocentrism is the first step in combating any excesses. In addition, try following the suggestions for effective listening offered in this unit, especially when you're in an intercultural public speaking situation. Also, expose yourself to culturally different experiences. At the same time, resist the temptation to evaluate these through your own cultural filters. For many this will not be an easy experience. But, in light of the tremendous advantages to be gained through increased intercultural experiences, the effort seems well worth it.

TABLE 4.1 The Ethnocentrism Continuum

How would you describe your own level of ethnocentrism?

Degree of Ethno-centrism	Communication Distance	Listening
Low	Equality	Treats others as equals; it comes naturally to listen fairly to culturally different speakers and openly to different cultural ways.
	Sensitivity	Makes an effort to decrease the distance between self and culturally different others and to lessen any conscious ethnocentrism.
	Indifference	Lacks concern for others; prefers to listen to culturally similar speakers and to not seriously consider other cultural customs or perspectives.
	Avoidance	Actively avoids and limits listening to culturally different speakers or to culturally different perspectives.
High	Disparagement	Engages in hostile behavior; belittles others; views different cultures and ways of behaving as inferior to one's own.

Listening and Gender

According to Deborah Tannen (1990) in her best-selling *You Just Don't Understand: Women and Men in Conversation,* women seek to build rapport and establish a closer relationship, and they use listening to achieve these ends. Men, on the other hand, will play up their expertise, emphasize it, and use it to dominate the interaction. Women play down their expertise and are more interested in communicating supportiveness. Tannen argues that the goal of a man in conversation is to be accorded respect and so he seeks to show his knowledge and expertise. A woman, on the other hand, seeks to be liked and so she expresses agreement.

Men and women also show that they're listening in different ways. In conversation, a woman is more apt to give many listening cues such as interjecting *yeah, uh-uh,* nodding in agreement, and smiling. A man is more likely to listen quietly, without giving many listening cues as feedback. Tannen argues, however, that men do listen less to women than women listen to men. The reason, says Tannen, is that listening places the person in an inferior position whereas speaking places the person in a superior one.

We can try to apply these gender differences to listening in public speaking. Men may seem to assume a more argumentative posture while listening, as if getting ready to argue. They may also appear to ask questions that are more argumentative or that are designed to puncture holes in your position as a way to play up their expertise. Women are more likely to ask supportive questions and perhaps offer criticism that is more positive than men. Women also use more cues in listening in a public speaking context. They let the speaker see that they're listening. Men, on the other hand, use less listening cues in conversation and probably also in public speaking. Men and women act this way to both men and women; their customary ways of listening don't seem to change depending on whether the speaker is male or female.

There's no evidence to show that these differences represent any negative motives on the part of men to prove themselves superior or of women

---

THE ETHICS OF The Listener

Like speakers, listeners also have ethical obligations. Here are two that should get you thinking about this often overlooked ethical issue.

Honest Hearing. Give the speaker an honest hearing, without prejudices or preconceptions. Avoid prejudging the speaker before listening to the entire speech. At the same time, empathize with the speaker; try to understand emotionally as well as intellectually what the speaker means. Then, accept or reject the speaker's ideas on the basis of the information offered rather than on the basis of some bias or incomplete understanding.

Honest Responding. Just as the speaker should be honest with the listener, the listener should be honest with the speaker. This means giving open and honest feedback. In a learning environment, such as your public speaking class, it means giving honest and constructive criticism to help the speaker improve. It also means reflecting honestly on the questions that the speaker raises. Much as you've a right to expect an active speaker, the speaker has a right to expect a listener who will actively deal with, rather than just passively hear, the message.

Do you agree with these two ethical guidelines? Can you identify instances where you do not follow these guidelines?

(The next Ethics of Public Speaking box appears on page 85.)

to ingratiate themselves. Rather, these differences in listening are largely the result of the way in which men and women have been socialized.

OBSTACLES TO EFFECTIVE LISTENING

The first step in improving listening abilities is to recognize and combat the various obstacles to effective listening (Nichols and Stevens 1957; Nichols 1961; Murphy 1987; Roach and Wyatt 1988; Nichols, 1995).

Preoccupation with Other Issues

Probably the most serious and most damaging obstacle to effective listening is the tendency to become preoccupied with yourself. Sometimes the preoccupation with yourself centers on assuming the role of speaker. You begin to rehearse your responses, and think of what you'll say to answer the speaker. Perhaps you think of a question you want to ask the public speaker. While focusing on yourself, you inevitably miss what the speaker is saying. Similarly, you may become preoccupied with external issues. You think about what you did last Saturday or your plans for the evening. Of course, the more you entertain thoughts of external matters, the less effectively you listen.

Assimilation

Another obstacle to listening is assimilation: the tendency to reconstruct messages so they reflect your own attitudes, prejudices, needs, and values. It's the tendency to hear relatively neutral messages ("Management plans to institute drastic changes in scheduling") as supporting your own attitudes and beliefs ("Management is going to screw up our schedules again").

Friend-or-Foe Factor

You may also distort messages because of the friend-or-foe factor, the tendency to listen for positive qualities about friends and negative qualities about enemies. For example, if you dislike Fred, then it will take added effort to listen objectively to Fred's speeches or to criticism that might reflect positively on Fred.

Hearing What You Expect to Hear

Another obstacle is the failure to hear what the speaker is saying and instead hear what you expect. You know that your history instructor frequently intersperses lectures with long personal stories and so when she says, "I can remember . . . ," you automatically hear a personal story and perhaps tune out.

Prejudging the Speech or Speaker

Whether in a lecture auditorium or in a small group, avoid the tendency to prejudge some speeches as uninteresting or irrelevant. All speeches are, at least potentially, interesting and useful. If you prejudge them and tune them out, you'll never be proven wrong; at the same time, however, you close yourself off from potentially useful information. Most important, perhaps, is

[Listening is] a very dangerous thing. If one listens one may be convinced.
—Oscar Wilde

that you're not giving the other person a fair hearing. Avoid jumping to conclusions before you've heard the speaker; the conclusions that you reach may in reality be quite different from the conclusions the speaker draws.

Rehearsing Your Responses

Often a speaker may say something with which you disagree. Then, during the remainder of the speech, you rehearse your response or question, you imagine the speaker's reply to your response, and then you think of your response to the speaker's response. The dialogue goes back and forth in your mind. Meanwhile, you miss whatever else the speaker said. You may even miss the very part that would answer your question. If appropriate, jot down the point or question and go back to listening.

Filtering Out Unpleasant Messages

Resist the temptation to filter out difficult or unpleasant messages: you don't want to hear that something you believe is untrue or that people you care for are unpleasant, and yet these are the very messages you need to listen to with great care. These are the messages that will lead you to examine and re-examine your implicit and unconscious assumptions. If you filter out this kind of information, you risk failing to correct misinformation. You risk losing new and important insights.

PRINCIPLES OF EFFECTIVE LISTENING

Effective listening is extremely important because you spend so much time listening. In fact, if you measured importance by the time you spend on an activity, listening would be your most important communication activity. Most of your communication time is spent in listening. You'll improve your listening if you listen actively, for total meaning, with empathy, and with an open mind.

Listen Actively

Perhaps the most basic suggestion for listening improvement is to recognize that listening isn't a passive activity. You cannot listen without effort; listening is a difficult process. In many ways it's more demanding than speaking. In speaking you control the situation; you can talk about what you like in the way you like. In listening, however, you have to follow the pace, the content, and the language of the speaker.

The best preparation for active listening is to act like an active listener. Recall, for example, how your body almost automatically reacts to important news. Immediately, you sit up straighter, cock your head toward the speaker, and remain relatively still and quiet. You do this almost reflexively because this is how you listen most effectively. This isn't to say that you should be tense and uncomfortable but only that your body should reflect your active mind. To listen actively:

- Think of what the speaker is saying. Because your mind can process information faster than the average rate of speech, there's often a time lag. Use this time to summarize the speaker's thoughts, formulate

TIPS
from professional speakers

Select a position in the room that provides for a better listening environment. Stay away from entrances or exits; do not select a place too far away from the speaker. Do not sit next to a group that may be talking during the speech. When people enter a room, they tend to sit at the back. Change that habit. Take a front row seat, and see how your listening skills improve.

Marjorie Brody and **Shawn Kent**, both communication consultants and trainers, *Power Presentations: How to Connect with Your Audience and Sell Your Ideas.* New York: Wiley, 1993, p. 31.

questions, and draw connections between what the speaker says and what you already know.

- Work at listening. Listening is hard work so be prepared to participate actively. Avoid what James Floyd (1985) calls "the entertainment syndrome," the expectation to be amused and entertained by a speaker. Remove distractions or other interferences (newspapers, magazines, stereos) so that your listening task will have less competition.

- Assume there's value in what the speaker is saying. Resist assuming that what you have to say is more valuable than the speaker's remarks.

- Take notes if appropriate. In some instances, you'll want to take notes while the speaker is speaking. Taking notes may be helpful if you want to ask a question about a specific item of information or if you want to include a specific statement in your critical evaluation (see Unit 5). Try not to distract the speaker. Have your pen and paper on your desk rather than shuffle through your book bag. Write only what you need to. Resist the temptation to turn the exercise into a writing one rather than a listening one.

Listen for Total Meaning

The meaning of a message isn't only in the words used, it's also in the speaker's nonverbal behavior. Sweating hands and shaking knees communicate as surely as words do.

The meanings communicated in a speech will also depend on what the speaker does not say. For example, the speaker who omits references to the homeless or to drugs in a speech on contemporary social problems communicates meaning by these very omissions. Exactly what inferences listeners draw from such omissions depends on a variety of factors. Some possible inferences might be that the speaker is poorly prepared, the speaker's research was inadequate, the speaker forgot part of the speech, the speaker is trying to fool the audience by not mentioning this, the speaker is trying to cover up certain issues and thinks we won't notice, or the speaker thinks we are uninformed, stupid, or both.

As a listener, therefore, be particularly sensitive to the meanings that significant omissions may communicate. As a speaker, recognize that most inferences audiences draw from omissions are negative. Most such inferences will reflect negatively on your credibility and on the total impact of the speech. Be careful, therefore, to mention significant issues that the audience expects to be discussed. In listening for total meaning:

- Focus on both verbal and nonverbal messages. Recognize both consistent and inconsistent "packages" of messages and take these cues as guides for drawing inferences about the meaning the speaker is trying to communicate. Ask questions when in doubt.

- See the forest, then the trees. Connect the specifics to the speaker's general theme rather than merely remembering isolated facts and figures.

- Balance your attention between the surface and the underlying meanings. Don't disregard the literal (surface) meaning of the speech in your attempt to uncover the more hidden (deeper) meanings.

Listen with Empathy

It takes two to speak the truth—one to speak, and another to listen.
—Henry David Thoreau

Try to feel what the speaker feels—empathize with the speaker. To empathize with others is to feel what they feel, to see the world they see, to walk in their shoes. Only when you achieve this will you be able to fully understand another's meaning (Eisenberg and Strayer 1987). Listen to feelings as well as to thoughts and ideas; listen to what the speaker is feeling and thinking:

- See the speaker's point of view. Before you can understand what the speaker is saying, you have to see the message from the speaker's point of view. Try putting yourself in the role of the speaker and feel the topic from the speaker's perspective.
- Understand the speaker's thoughts and feelings. Don't consider your listening task complete until you've understood what the speaker is feeling as well as thinking.
- Avoid "offensive listening." Offensive listening is the tendency to listen to bits and pieces of information that will enable you to attack the speaker or find fault with something the speaker has said.

Listen with an Open Mind

Listening with an open mind is difficult. It isn't easy to listen to arguments attacking your cherished beliefs. It isn't easy to listen to statements condemning what you fervently believe. Listening often stops when such remarks are made. Yet it's in these situations that it's particularly important to continue listening openly and fairly. To listen with an open mind, try these suggestions.

- Avoid prejudging. Delay both positive and negative evaluation until you've fully understood the intention and the content of the message being communicated.
- Avoid filtering out difficult, unpleasant, or undesirable messages. Avoid distorting messages through oversimplification or leveling, the tendency to eliminate details and to simplify complex messages to make them easier to remember.
- Recognize your own biases. They may interfere with accurate listening and cause you to distort message reception through assimilation, the tendency to interpret what you hear (or think you hear) in terms of your own biases, prejudices, and expectations. Biases may also lead to sharpening—when an item of information takes on increased importance because it seems to confirm your stereotypes or prejudices.

It is the province of knowledge to speak. And it is the privilege of wisdom to listen.
—Oliver Wendell Holmes

UNIT IN BRIEF

The Listening Process

Listening is a five stage process:
Receiving the verbal and nonverbal messages.
Understanding the speaker's thoughts and the emotions.
Remembering and retaining the messages.
Evaluating or judging the messages.
Responding or reacting to the messages.

Cultural differences in verbal and nonverbal messages and ethnocentrism can create listening difficulties. Gender differences can also lead to listening difficulties.

Obstacles to Listening	Don't become preoccupied with yourself or external issues.
	Beware of assimilation.
	Watch for the friend-or-foe factor.
	Be aware of the tendency to hear what you expect to hear and not to hear what you don't expect to hear.
	Avoid prejudging the speech or speaker.
	Avoid rehearsing your own responses.
	Avoid filtering out unpleasant messages.
Principles of Effective Listening	**Listen actively** (use listening time, work hard, assume value, and, if appropriate, take notes).
	Listen for total meaning (focus on both verbal and nonverbal messages, connect specifics to the general thesis, attend to both surface and deep meanings).
	Listen with empathy (see speaker's point of view, understand speaker's feelings and thoughts, avoid offensive listening).
	Listen with an open mind (avoid prejudging and filtering out difficult messages, recognize your own biases).

THINKING CRITICALLY ABOUT LISTENING

REVIEWING KEY TERMS AND CONCEPTS IN LISTENING

1. Define the key terms used in this unit:

❏ listening (p. 61)　❏ responding (p. 63)
❏ receiving (p. 61)　❏ ethnocentrism (p. 65)
❏ understanding (p. 62)　❏ assimilation (p. 68)
❏ remembering (p. 62)　❏ empathy (p. 70)
❏ evaluating (p. 63)

2. Explain the key concepts discussed in this unit:

- What is listening? How can you describe the stages of the listening process? What is the relationship of culture to listening? What is the relationship of gender to listening?
- What are the major obstacles to effective listening?
- What are the four principles or dimensions of effective listening and how might they be used to achieve different listening goals?

DEVELOPING PUBLIC SPEAKING STRATEGIES

1. Cathy is planning to give a speech in favor of gay marriage. Cathy herself is heterosexual and she wonders if her affectional orientation should be identified in the speech. On the one hand, she thinks it may help her cause; she thinks that if the audience sees her as a lesbian, they won't listen with an open mind to what she has to say. At the same time, Cathy also believes that logically her own affectional orientation

is really irrelevant to the validity of her argument. Also, by mentioning this, she may offend and alienate the gay men and lesbians in the audience who may feel she doesn't want to be identified as a lesbian. What advice would you give Cathy?

2. Mark is listening to Sidney giving a speech laced with unbelievable cultural insensitivity. Mark wonders if he should continue to listen attentively and thus encourage Sidney to further destroy cultural understanding or if he should show that he's not listening and perhaps wake Sidney up. What do you think Mark should do?

EVALUATING PUBLIC SPEECHES

1. Read one of the speeches in the appendix and look for specific parts in the speech where you might have perked up your listening or where you might have wandered off, losing concentration. What distinguishes messages you want to listen to from messages you don't want to listen to?

2. Interview two or three people in your class and ask them how they found listening to your speeches. Ask them what you might specifically do to encourage even more active and empathic listening.

USING TECHNOLOGY IN PUBLIC SPEAKING

1. Visit one of the many humor sites on the Net (for example, http://www.vote-smart.org/other/humor.html or http://www.mit.edu:8001/activities/voodoo/chm.html —a collection of college humor magazines). Read a few of the jokes, anecdotes, or stories. What techniques do humor writers use that you can use in your speeches to make your audience want to listen?

2. Log on to a chat or IRC group and lurk for 10 or 15 minutes. How would you describe "listening" in a chat group?

3. Visit the International Listening Association's Web site at http://www.listen.org. What resources are available to someone learning about listening?

PRACTICALLY SPEAKING

4.1 Short Speech Technique

Prepare and deliver a two-minute speech in which you:

a. explain how a current television or print advertisement relies on or makes use of one of the distortions discussed under critical listening.

b. explain the role of listening in effective interpersonal relationships.

c. describe a communication breakdown (problem) occasioned by ineffective listening.

d. describe what a speaker can do to make listening easier.

4.2 Your Own Listening Barriers

Most people put on blinders when they come upon particular topics or particular spokespersons. Sometimes these blinders prevent information from getting through fairly and objectively. For example, you may avoid listening to certain people or reading certain newspapers because they frequently contradict your beliefs. Sometimes these blinders color the information you take

in, influencing you to take a positive view of some information (because it may support one of your deeply held beliefs) and a negative view of other information (because it may contradict such beliefs).

Read over the following situations and identify any barriers that may get in the way of your listening to these people and these messages fairly and objectively. Some situations may seem likely and others extremely unlikely. For this exercise, however, assume that all speakers are speaking on the topic indicated and that you're in the audience. Ask yourself the following questions about each of the 20 situations presented.

- What are your initial expectations?
- How credible do you find the speaker—even before he or she begins to speak?
- Will you begin listening with a positive, a negative, or a neutral attitude? How will these attitudes influence your listening?
- What will you be saying to yourself as you begin listening to the speaker? Will this influence what you receive, understand, and remember of the

speech? Will this influence how you evaluate and respond to the speech?

■ What do you think your final assessment of the speech will be? On a 10-point scale (10=extremely sure; 1=extremely unsure), how sure are you that this will be your assessment?

■ Can you identify at least one barrier that you (or someone else) might set up for each of these speech situations?

1. Elizabeth Taylor on the need to contribute to AIDS research.

2. Gloria Steinem criticizing (or praising) the contemporary women's movement.

3. President Bill Clinton speaking on the role of the military in defending American democracy.

4. A noted and successful business leader on the futility of a college education in today's economy.

5. Edward Kennedy on the importance of moderation.

6. Spike Lee on race relations.

7. Ross Perot or Bill Gates on financial mistakes the government must avoid.

8. A Mexican business leader urging American businesses to consider relocating to Mexico.

9. Oprah Winfrey on the mistakes of modern psychology.

10. A representative from General Motors, Toyota, or Mercedes Benz urging greater restrictions on foreign imports.

11. A Catholic priest on why you should remain a virgin until marriage.

12. A homeless person petitioning to be allowed to sleep in the local public library.

13. A representative of the leading tobacco companies voicing opposition to (or support for) the legalization of marijuana.

14. An Iranian couple talking about the need to return to fundamentalist values.

15. A person with AIDS speaking in favor of lower drug prices.

16. A successful Japanese business leader talking about the mistakes of contemporary American businesses.

17. A lesbian mother speaking against lesbians being granted custody of their children.

18. A person without sight or hearing speaking in favor of including persons with disabilities in the definition of multiculturalism used on campus.

19. A man (or woman) speaking on the failings of the opposite sex and how to tolerate them without going crazy.

20. An 85-year-old multimillionaire speaking on why social security must be given to everyone regardless of income or need.

4.3 Analyzing a Speech

Here is a speech that will serve two purposes. First, it's on listening and provides an interesting perspective on the importance of listening, in this case to the medical profession. Second, it is a useful model for analyzing effectiveness.

Read the speech and respond to the accompanying questions.

MENDING THE BODY BY LENDING AN EAR
THE HEALING POWER OF LISTENING

Address by CAROL KOEHLER, Ph.D., Assistant Professor of Communication and Medicine. Delivered to the International Listening Association Business Conference, at the Ritz-Carlton Hotel, Kansas City, Missouri, March 19, 1998

How did this introduction gain your attention? How did it establish a speaker-audience-topic connection? How did it orient the audience?

I would like to start this morning by telling you two different stories. Each story has the same two characters and happens in the same location. Both stories occur within a twenty-four hour period.

Over the Christmas holidays my husband and I were invited to a formal black tie wedding. this was to be an elegant event so we put on our best evening clothes. Adding to that, I wore my mother's diamond jewelry and this fabulous mink coat that I inherited. Just before we left the house I telephoned my 86-year-old mother-in-law for her daily check up. When she answered, her voiced sounded a little strange so my husband and I decided to stop at her apartment to make sure she was all right before we went to the wedding.

When we arrived she seemed slightly disoriented (she was 86 years old but wonderfully healthy, sharp-witted and self-sufficient). We called her physician to ask his advice and he said to bring her to the local Emergency Room and have her checked out. We did that. This was a Saturday night so the Emergency Room was pretty active. When we arrived, I in my mink and my husband in his tux, we looked noticeably different from the general population in the waiting room. While my husband filled out forms, the doctors took my mother-in-law into a makeshift curtained room. When I noticed that the staff had removed both her glasses and her hearing aid, I realized she would experience some anxiety, so at that point I decided to stay with her to keep her from being frightened. As I went into the room, a young doctor said, "Mam, you can't go in there." Without missing a beat I said "Don't be ridiculous." With that I went and found a chair in the waiting room, brought it into the examination room and sat down. I remember thinking the staff looked a little bewildered but no one challenged me at any time. When my mother-in-law's hands felt a little cool, I asked for a heated blanket and one was brought immediately. So it went for the entire evening, we missed the wedding but finally got my mother-in-law in a permanent room about 2 a.m.

The next morning I went to the hospital about 10 o'clock in the morning, dressed in tennis shoes, a sweat suit and no makeup. As I arrived at my mother-in-law's room, an unfamiliar doctor was just entering. I introduced myself and asked him to speak up so my mother-in-law would be aware of why he was there and what he was doing. I told him that she tends to be frightened by the unexpected and without her glasses or hearing aid, she was already frightened enough. This thirty something male doctor proceeded to examine my mother-in-law without raising his voice so that she could hear, and without acknowledging me or my request in any way. Actually he never really looked at either one of us.

In both those scenarios, I was listened to, not by ears alone, but by eyes, by gender, and age judgments, and by social status assessments. That started me thinking . . .

Why did a recent article in the Journal of the *American Medical Association* indicate high dissatisfaction in traditional doctor-patient appointments? Why is it *The Wall Street Journal* claims that perception of physician concern and not physician expertise is the deciding factor in the rising number of malpractice suits? Why did *The New England Journal of Medicine* report that the care and attention quotient is causing "alternative" medical practices to grow by leaps and bounds? Given this litany of events, what does it really mean to listen? And why, in the name of science, don't we produce better listeners in the medical profession?

Were the two stories effective in making the speaker's point that listening is broader than hearing and that people often listen not only with their ears but with their eyes?

In this paragraph the speaker cites the Journal of the American Medical Association, The Wall Street Journal, and The New England Journal of Medicine. Was this sufficient to convince you that listening is an important skill for the health care professional? Would these citations have been more effective if the speaker had given the dates? The authors of the articles?

The reasons are so obvious that they are sometimes overlooked. First, listening is mistakenly equated with hearing and since most of us can hear, no academic priority is given to this subject in either college or med school (this by the way flies in the face of those who measure daily time usage). Time experts say we spend 9% of our day writing. 16% reading, 30% speaking and 45% listening—just the opposite of our academic pursuits. Second, we perceive power in speech. We put a value on those who have the gift of gab. How often have you heard the compliment, "He/she can talk to anyone"? Additionally, we equate speaking with controlling both the conversation and the situation. The third and last reason we don't listen is that we are in an era of information overload. We are bombarded with the relevant and the irrelevant and it is easy to confuse them. Often it's all just so much noise.

How can we address this depressing situation? Dan Callahan, a physician and teacher, argues that primacy in health care needs to be given to the notion of care over cure. Caring as well as curing humanizes our doctor patient relationships.

Let's talk about what that might mean for health care. What comes to mind when someone is caring? (The audience responded with the words "warm," "giving," "interested," "genuine" and "sincere.") Now, what comes to mind when you think of the opposite of care? (the audience volunteered "cold," "uninterested," "egotistical," "busy," "distracted" and "selfish.")

What might a caring doctor be like? If we take the word CARE and break it down, we find the qualities that are reflective of a therapeutic communicator, in other words, someone who listens not with ears alone.

C stands for concentrate. Physicians should hear with their eyes and ears. They should avoid the verbal and visual barriers that prevent real listening. It may be as simple as eye contact (some young doctors have told me they have a difficult time with looking people in the eye, and my advice is, when you are uncomfortable, focus on the patient's mouth and as the comfort level increases, move to the eyes. In the placement of office furniture, try and keep the desk from being a barrier between you and the patient. Offer an alternative chair for consultations—one to the side of your desk and one in front of the desk. Let the patient have some control and power to decide their own comfort level.

A stands for acknowledge. Show them that you are listening by using facial expressions, giving vocal prompts and listening between the lines for intent as well as content. Listen for their vocal intonation when responding to things like prescribed medication. If you hear some hesitation in their voice, say to them, I hear you agreeing but I'm getting the sound of some reservation in your voice. Can you tell my why? And then acknowledge their response. Trust them and they will trust you.

R stands for response. Clarify issues by asking "I'm not sure what you mean." Encourage continuing statements by saying "and then what? or tell me more." The recurrent headache may mask other problems. Provide periodic recaps to focus information. Learn to take

Did the speaker effectively make the point that listening is unwisely neglected in education? If not, what additional evidence and argument would you have liked to hear?

Notice that the speaker involves the audience with very specific questions, calling for single word answers. In a short speech, you really don't want to invite the audience to discourse at length on the issues you're discussing. If you were a member of the audience, would you have appreciated this opportunity to contribute to the speech? Were there other opportunities to directly involve the audience that also might have been effective?

The speaker organized her speech around the acronym CARE. How effective do you think this organizational strategy was?

How would you evaluate the supporting materials used in the discussion of CARE? Did the examples help you understand the points the speaker was making? Were the recommendations for more effective listening clear and meaningful?

If the speaker wanted to use a presentation aid, what type would you have suggested for this speech?

cryptic notes and then return your attention to the patient. (Note taking is sometimes used as an avoidance tactic and patients sense this). Use body language by leaning toward the patient. Effective listening requires attention, patience, and the ability to resist the urge to control the conversation.

E stands for exercise emotional control. This means if your "hot buttons" are pushed by people who whine, and in walks someone who does that very thing, you are likely to fake interest in the patient. With our mind elsewhere, you will never really "hear" that person. Emotional blocks are based on previous experiences. They are sometimes activated by words, by tone of voice, by style of clothes or hair, or by ethnicity. It is not possible for us to be free of those emotional reactions, but the first step in controlling them is to recognize when you are losing control. One of the most useful techniques to combat emotional responses is to take a long deep breath when confronted with the urge to interrupt. Deep breathing redirects your response and as a bonus, it is impossible to talk when you are deep breathing. Who of us would not choose the attentive caring physician?

As it nears time for me to take that deep breath, I would just like to reiterate that listening is a learned skill and learning to listen with CARE has valuable benefits for health care professionals and patients. As a wise man named J. Isham once said, "Listening is an attitude of the heart, a genuine desire to be with another which both attracts and heals."

Thank you very much.

How did the conclusion summarize the speech? Did it contain a motivation? How did the speaker obtain closure?

Did the speaker convince you that health care professionals should devote more attention to listening?

UNIT 5
Criticism in the Classroom

UNIT OBJECTIVES

After completing this unit, you should be able to:
Define *criticism* and explain its values.

Explain the influence of culture on criticism.

Explain the standards and principles for expressing criticism.

In learning the art of public speaking, much insight will come from the criticism of others as well as from your criticism of others. This unit considers the nature of criticism in a learning environment, the influence of culture on criticism, and the standards and principles for evaluating a speech and for making criticism easier and more effective.

THE NATURE AND VALUES OF CRITICISM

Critics and criticism are essential parts of any art. *Criticism* comes from the Latin *criticus*, which means "able to discern," "to judge." Speech criticism, therefore, is the process of evaluating a speech, of rendering a judgment of its value. Note that there is nothing inherently negative about criticism; criticism may be negative, but it may also be positive.

Criticism, especially in a public speaking courses where the objective is to learn skills, can be of tremendous value. Perhaps its major value in the classroom is that it helps to improve your public speaking skills. Through the constructive criticism of others, you'll learn the principles of public speaking more effectively. You'll be shown what you do well and what you could improve and, ideally, how you can improve. As a listener-critic you'll also learn the principles of public speaking through assessing the speeches of others. Just as you learn when you teach, you also learn when you criticize.

Criticism also helps identify standards for evaluating the wide variety of speeches you'll hear throughout your life. This critical frame of mind and the guidelines for critical evaluation will prove useful in assessing all communications: the salesperson's pitch to buy a new car, the advertiser's plea to buy Tylenol rather than Excedrin, and the network's editorial.

When you give criticism—as you do in a public speaking class—you're telling the speaker that you've listened carefully and that you care enough about the speech and the speaker to offer suggestions for improvement.

Of course, criticism can be difficult—for the critic (whether student or instructor) as well as for the person criticized. As a critic, you may feel embarrassed or uncomfortable to offer criticism. After all, you might think, "Who am I to criticize another person's speech; my own speech won't be any better." Or you may be reluctant to offend, fearing that your criticism may make the speaker feel uncomfortable. Or you may view criticism as a confrontation that will do more harm than good.

> *To escape criticism—do nothing, say nothing, be nothing.*
> —Elbert Hubbard

from professional speakers

For most people, giving criticism (even in a constructive way) is risky. When people first offer such feedback, they watch closely to gauge others' responses. The reaction they receive will usually determine whether they will offer feedback again. This means that you have an opportunity to avoid turning off further feedback that could be valuable to you.

Paul R. Timm, author and communication trainer and popular speaker, *How to Make Winning Presentations* (Franklin Lakes, NJ: Career Press, 1997): 32.

Assume that you just heard a speech you consider poor and are called upon to comment on it. What difficulties would you experience in expressing your honest opinion? What would be your first three sentences?

TIPS
from professional speakers

Travel. Read about other countries and other cultures. Learn another language. Entertain people who are visiting from other countries. Host an international student. Attend lectures on other countries that are given by people from other countries. Eat at an ethnic restaurant. Join a chamber of commerce from another country. Join an ethnic social group to participate in traditions from other countries. Correspond with people from other countries.

All of these experiences expose you to different ideas, different ways of thinking, different values. This sort of exposure develops your international attitude and makes you a better international communicator.

Nancy L. Hoft, technical communication consultant and president of International Technical Communication Services, *International Technical Communication: How to Export Information about High Technology* (New York: Wiley, 1995): 133.

Still another obstacle is that in offering criticism, you put yourself on the line; you state a position with which others may disagree and which you may be called upon to defend. Considering these difficulties, you may conclude that the process isn't worth the effort and may decide to leave the criticism to others.

But, reconsider this opinion. By offering criticism you help the speaker by giving her or him another perspective on the speech that should prove useful in future speeches. When you offer criticism, you're not claiming to be a better speaker; you're simply offering another perspective. It's true that by offering criticism, you're stating a position with which others may disagree. But, that's one of the things that will make this class and the learning of the principles exciting and challenging.

Criticism is also difficult to receive. After working on a speech for a week or two and dealing with the normal anxiety that comes with giving a speech, the last thing you want is to stand in front of the class and hear others say what you did wrong. Public speaking is ego-involving, and it's normal to personalize criticism. If you learn how to give and how to receive criticism, however, it will become an effective teaching and learning tool. And it will help you sharpen your skills and improve every aspect of the public speaking process. It will also serve as an important support mechanism for the developing public speaker—as a way of patting the speaker on the back for all the positive effort.

CULTURAL DIFFERENCES

There are vast cultural differences in what is considered proper when it comes to criticism. For example, criticism will be viewed very differently depending on whether members come from an individualist culture (which emphasizes the individual and places primary value on the individual's goals) or a collectivist culture (which emphasizes the group and places primary value on the group's goals). The accompanying self-test will help you gauge your own cultural tendency toward individualism or collectivism, concepts based on extensive analyses of 91 cultures (Hofstede 1980, 1997).

TEST YOURSELF
Individual and Collectivist Cultures

Indicate how accurately the following statements describe you. Use the following scale:

1 = almost always true
2 = more often true than false
3 = true about half the time and false about half the time
4 = more often false than true
5 = almost always false.

_____ 1. My own goals rather than the goals of my group (for example, my extended family, my organization) are the more important.

_____ 2. I feel responsible for myself and to my own conscience rather than for the entire group and to the group's values and rules.

_____ 3. Success to me depends on my contribution to the group effort and the group's success rather than to my own individual success or to surpassing others.

_____ 4. Being kind and polite is usually more important than telling the truth and so I might say things that are not true in a logical sense if they allow the other person to appear in a positive light.

_____ 5. In my communications I prefer a direct and explicit communication style; I believe in "telling it like it is," even if it hurts.

Statements 1, 2, and 5 are phrased so that a person with an individualist orientation would agree with them; statements 3 and 4 are phrased so that a person with a collectivist orientation would agree with them. Therefore, in computing your total score, it will be necessary to reverse some of the individual scores:

1. Reverse the scores for items 3 and 4 such that
   if your response was 1 reverse it to a 5
   if your response was 2 reverse it to a 4
   if your response was 3 keep it as 3
   if your response was 4 reverse it to a 2
   if your response was 5 reverse it to a 1
2. Add your scores for all five items, being sure to use the reverse scores for items 3 and 4 in your calculations. Your score should be between 5 (indicating a highly individualist orientation) to 25 (indicating a highly collectivist orientation).
3. Position your score on the following scale:

5	12/13	25
highly individualist	about equally individualist and collectivist	highly collectivist

As you read the descriptions of these two orientations, consider how your own culture's teaching about individualism and collectivism may influence the ways in which you express and receive criticism.

Individual and collective tendencies are not mutually exclusive; this isn't an all-or-none orientation but rather one of emphasis. For example, in a basketball game, you may follow an individualist orientation and compete with other members of your basketball team for most baskets or most valuable player award. At the same time, however, you will—in a game—act with a collective orientation to benefit the entire group, in this case, enabling your team to win the game. In actual practice both individual and collective tendencies will help you and your team each achieve your goals. At times, however, these tendencies may conflict. For example, do you shoot for the basket and try to raise your own individual score or do you pass the ball to another player who is better positioned to score the basket and thus benefit your team?

In an individualist culture you're responsible for yourself and perhaps your immediate family; in a collectivist culture you're responsible for the entire group. Success, in an individualist culture, is measured by the extent to which you surpass other members of your group; you would take pride in standing out from the crowd. And your heroes—in the media, for example—are likely to be those who are unique and who stand apart. In a collectivist culture success is measured by your contribution to the achievements of the group as a whole; you would take pride in your similarity to other members of your group. Your heroes, in contrast, are more likely to be team-players who don't stand out from the rest of the group's members. In an individualist culture you're responsible to your own conscience and responsibility is largely an individual matter. In a collectivist culture you're responsible to the rules of the social group and responsibility for an accomplishment or a failure is shared by all members. Competition is promoted in individualist cultures while cooperation is promoted in collectivist cultures.

Those who come from cultures that are highly individual and competitive (the United States—take a look at the marginal quotations—Germany, and Sweden are examples) may find public criticism a normal part of the learning process. Those who come from cultures that are more collective and that emphasize the group rather than the individual (Japan, Mexico, and Korea are examples) are likely to find giving and receiving public criticism uncomfortable. Thus, people from individual cultures may readily criticize others and are likely to expect the same "courtesy" from other listeners. After all, this person might reason, if I'm going to criticize your skills to help you improve, I expect you to help me in the same way. Persons from collective cultures, on the other hand, may feel that it's more important to be polite and courteous than to help someone learn a skill. Cultural rules to maintain peaceful relations among the Japanese (Midooka 1990) and politeness among many Asian cultures (Fraser 1990) may conflict with the classroom cultural norm to express honest criticism. In some cultures, being kind to the person is more important than telling the truth, and so members may say things that are complimentary but untrue in a logical sense.

Collectivist cultures place a heavy emphasis on face-saving, on allowing people to always appear in a positive light. In such cultures contributing to another person's loss of face by, say, public criticism, violates an important cultural norm and may result in the critic also losing face. The closest equivalent to loss of face in the United States is embarrassment, though loss of face is much more intense and long lasting. Also, whereas embarrassment can often be humorous (especially if you're not the one being embarrassed), loss of face is never humorous to anyone (James 1995).

In cultures where face-saving is important, members may prefer not to say anything negative in public and may even be reluctant to say anything

Behind the concept of equality is a belief in individualism born of historic forces that are peculiarly American—the conditions of colonization and frontier life on this continent.
—Allan Nevins

The individual is the central, rarest, most precious capital resource of our society.
—Peter F. Drucker

positive for fear that the omissions may be construed as negatives. Japanese executives, for instance, are reluctant to say "no" in a business meeting for fear of offending the other person. But, their "yes," properly interpreted in light of the context and the general discussion, may mean "no." In cultures in which face-saving is especially important, such communication rules as the following would prevail:

- don't express negative evaluation in public; instead compliment the person.
- don't prove someone wrong, especially in public; express agreement even if you know the person is wrong.
- don't correct someone's errors; don't even acknowledge them.
- don't ask difficult questions lest the person not know the answer and lose face or be embarrassed; generally, avoid asking questions.

These differences can create special problems if you interpret unexpected behavior through your own cultural filters and fail to see that another meaning may have been intended. For example, if a speaker who expects comments and criticism gets none, he or she may interpret the silence to mean that the audience didn't care or wasn't listening. But, they may have been listening very intently. They may simply be operating with a different cultural rule, a rule that says it's impolite to criticize or evaluate another person's work, especially in public.

LISTEN TO THIS   How to Listen to Criticism

Although criticism is a valuable part of public speaking and of life in general, listening to it is difficult. Here are some suggestions for making listening to criticism easier and more effective.

Accept the Critic's Viewpoint. When a listener offers criticism, it's the listener's perception. Because of this, the critic is always right. If the critic says that he or she wasn't convinced by the evidence, it doesn't help to identify the 10 or 12 references that you used in your speech; this critic was simply not convinced. Instead, consider why these references were not convincing to your critic. Perhaps you didn't emphasize the credibility of the source or didn't stress their recency or didn't emphasize their connection to your proposition.

Listen Openly. Because public speaking is so ego-involving, it's tempting to block out criticism. If you do, however, you'll lose out on potentially useful suggestions for improvement. So, express support for the critic, and show an openness in hearing the criticism. Make the critic know that you're really listening to what he or she has to say.

Respond Without Defensiveness. Defensiveness seals off effective communication and prevents you from receiving the very information that may prove helpful to your future efforts. The more you defend yourself, the less attention you can give to the critic's comments.

Separate Speech Criticism from Self Criticism. If you're to improve your skills and yet not be psychologically crushed by negative evaluations, separate criticism of your speech from criticism of yourself. Recognize that when some aspect of your speech is criticized, your personality or your worth as an individual isn't being criticized. Externalize critical evaluations; view them dispassionately.

Seek Clarification. Ask for clarification if you don't understand the criticism or if you don't understand how you'd improve your future efforts. For example, if you're told that your specific purpose was too broad, and it's unclear how you might improve it, ask the critic how you might narrow the specific purpose. Your critics should welcome such attempts at clarification.

(The next Listen to This box appears on page 117.)

The difficulties that these differences may cause may be lessened if they're discussed openly. Some people may become comfortable with public criticism once it's explained that the cultural norms of most public speaking classrooms include public criticism (cf. Verderber 2000) just as they may incorporate informative and persuasive speaking or written outlines. Others may feel more comfortable offering written criticism as a substitute for oral and public criticism. Or, perhaps private consultations can be arranged.

STANDARDS AND PRINCIPLES OF CRITICISM

What standards do you use when you criticize a speech? How do you measure the excellence of a speech? On what basis do you say that one speech is weak, another is good, and still another is great? And once you make these judgments, how do you express criticism?

Standards of Criticism

Three major standards quickly suggest themselves: effectiveness, universality, and conformity to the principles of the art.

Effectiveness. The effectiveness standard judges the speech in terms of whether or not it achieves its purpose. If the purpose is to sell soap, then the speech is effective if it sells soap and is ineffective if it fails to sell soap. And, not surprisingly, this is the standard that advertisers apply in evaluating advertising campaigns. Similarly, politicians often evaluate their speeches with this standard; the speech would be considered effective if it helps secure votes and ineffective if it doesn't. Increased sophistication in measuring communication effects—with telephone, e-mail, and Web site surveys, for example—makes this standard tempting to apply.

There are, however, problems with this approach. In many instances—in the classroom, for example—the effects of a speech can't always be measured. Sometimes the effect of a speech is long term and you may not be present to see it take hold. Also, some effects are simply not measurable; you can't always measure changes in attitude and belief.

Sometimes audiences may be so opposed to a speaker's position that even the greatest speech will have no observable effect. It may take an entire campaign to get such an audience to change its position even slightly. At other times audiences may agree with the speaker and even the weakest speech will secure their compliance. In situations like these, the effectiveness standard will lead to inaccurate and inappropriate judgments.

Universality. The universality standard (Murphy 1958) asks to what extent does the speech address values and issues that have significance for all people in all times. By this standard Martin Luther King Jr.'s "I Have a Dream" would be judged positively because it argues for beliefs, values, and actions that most of the civilized world view positively.

A similar standard is that of **historical justification.** This standard asks to what extent was the speech's thesis and purpose justified by subsequent historical events. By this standard William Jennings Bryan's famous "Cross of Gold" speech (delivered in 1896)—although it won Bryan the Democratic nomination for president—would be judged negatively because it argued for a monetary standard that the world has since rejected.

Another similar standard is that of **ethical merit**. This standard asks to what extent does the speech argue for what is true, moral, humane, or good. By this standard the speeches of Adolf Hitler would be judged negatively because they supported ideas most people find repugnant. Other situations would not be so easy to judge with the ethical merit standard. For example, consider how different cultures would respond to such seemingly simple theses as the following:

- Try eating beef.
- Try eating pork.
- Try eating dog meat.
- Get divorced when things don't work out.
- Never get divorced.
- Support gay or lesbian marriage proposals.
- Defeat gay or lesbian marriage proposals.

Obviously, different cultures will respond with very different attitudes; some will judge some speeches ethical and others unethical.

Conformity to the Principles of the Art. A more useful standard is to evaluate the speech on the basis of its conformity to the principles of the art. With this standard a speech is positively evaluated when it follows the principles of public speaking established by the critics, theorists, researchers, and practitioners of public speaking (and as described throughout this text) and negatively evaluated as it deviates from these principles. These principles include, for example, speaking on a subject that is worthwhile, relevant, and interesting to listeners; designing a speech for a specific audience; and constructing a speech that is based on sound research. A list of critical guidelines for analyzing public speeches that is based on these principles is given later in this unit (pp. 89–91).

A good writer is not, per se, a good critic. No more than a good drunk is automatically a good bartender.
—Jim Bishop

THE ETHICS OF The Critic

Just as the speaker and listener have ethical obligations, so does the critic. Here are a few guidelines. First, **the ethical critic separates personal feelings about the speaker** from the evaluation of the speech. A liking for the speaker shouldn't lead you to give positive evaluations of the speech, nor should disliking the speaker lead you to give negative evaluations of the speech.

Second, **the ethical critic separates personal feelings about the issues** from an evaluation of the validity of the arguments. The ethical critic recognizes the validity of an argument even if it contradicts a deeply held belief and at the same time recognizes the fallaciousness of an argument even if it supports a deeply held belief.

Third, **the ethical critic is culturally sensitive**, aware of his or her own ethnocentrism, and doesn't negatively evaluate customs and forms of speech simply because they deviate from her or his own. Similarly, the ethical critic does not positively evaluate a speech just because it supports her or his own cultural beliefs and values. The ethical critic does not discriminate against or favor speakers simply because they're of a particular sex, race, nationality, religion, age group, or affectional orientation.

Do you agree with these ethical responsibilities? Do you generally follow these when you give criticism? If not, why not?

(The next Ethics in Public Speaking box appears on page 101.)

How is criticism in the classroom different from the criticism that accompanies a presentation in business? In what ways are they the same?

This standard is, of course, not totally separate from the effectiveness standard since the principles of public speaking are largely principles of effectiveness. When you follow the principles of the art, your speech will in all likelihood be effective.

The great advantage of this standard (especially in a learning situation such as this) is that it will help you master the principles of public speaking. When your speech is measured by its adherence to these principles, you'll be learning the principles by applying them to your unique situation.

The principles of public speaking are presented throughout this book, and it's by these, supplemented by whatever principles your instructor adds, that your public speech efforts will be evaluated. In your early speeches, follow the principles as closely as you can, even if their application seems mechanical and unimaginative. After you've mastered their application, you can begin to play with the principles, altering them to suit your own personality, the uniqueness of the situation, and your specific goals.

Principles of Expressing Criticism

Before reading the specific suggestions for making critical evaluations a more effective part of the total learning process and for avoiding some of the potentially negative aspects of expressing criticism, take the following test. It asks you to identify what's wrong with selected critical comments.

TEST YOURSELF
What's Wrong With These Comments?

For the purposes of this exercise, assume that each of the following 10 comments represents the critic's complete criticism. What's wrong with each?

1. I loved the speech. It was great. Really great.
2. The introduction didn't gain my attention.
3. You weren't interested in your own topic. How do you expect us to be interested?
4. Nobody was able to understand you.

5. The speech was weak.
6. The speech didn't do anything for me.
7. Your position was unfair to those of us on athletic scholarships; we earned those scholarships.
8. I found four things wrong with your speech. First, . . .
9. You needed better research.
10. I liked the speech; we need more police on campus.

Before reading the following discussion, try to explain why each of these statements is ineffective. How would you restate the basic meaning of each of these comments but in a more constructive manner?

Say Something Positive. Egos are fragile and public speaking is extremely personal. Speakers are all like Noel Coward when he said, "I love criticism just as long as it's unqualified praise." Part of your function as a critic is to strengthen the already positive aspects of someone's public speaking performance. Positive criticism is particularly important in itself, but it's almost essential as a preface to negative comments. There are always positive characteristics about any speech, and it's more productive to concentrate on these first. Thus, instead of saying (as in the self-test) "The speech didn't do anything for me," tell the speaker what you liked first, then bring up some weakness and suggest how it might be corrected.

When criticizing a person's second or third speech, it's especially helpful if you can point out specific improvements ("You really held my attention in this speech," "I felt you were much more in control of the public speaking today than in your first speech").

Remember, too, the irreversibility of communication. Once you say something, you can't take it back. Remember this when offering criticism, especially criticism that may be too negative. If in doubt, err on the side of gentleness.

Be Specific. Criticism is most effective when it's specific. Statements such as "I thought your delivery was bad," "I thought your examples were good," or, as in the self-test, "I loved the speech . . . Really great" and "The speech was weak," are poorly expressed criticisms. These statements don't specify what the speaker might do to improve delivery or to capitalize on the examples used. In commenting on delivery, refer to such specifics as eye contact, vocal volume, or whatever else is of consequence. In commenting on the examples, tell the speaker why examples were good. Were they realistic? Were they especially interesting? Were they presented dramatically?

In giving negative criticism, specify and justify—to the extent that you can—positive alternatives. Here's an example.

I liked the fact that you included lots of statistics. But, I thought the way in which you introduced your statistics was somewhat vague. I wasn't sure where the statistics came from or how recent or reliable they were. It might have been better to say something like "The U.S. Census figures for 2000 show that. . . ." In this way we would know that the statistics were as recent as possible and the most reliable available.

Be Objective. In criticizing a speech, transcend your own biases as best you can, unlike our self-test example, "Your position was unfair . . . ; we earned those scholarships." See the speech as objectively as possible. Assume, for example, that you're strongly for women's rights to abortion and you encounter a speech diametrically opposed to your position. In this situation, you would need to take special care not to dismiss the speech because of your own attitudes. Examine the speech from the point of view of a detached critic, and evaluate, for example, the validity of the arguments and their suitability to the audience, the language, and the supporting materials. Remember, you're evaluating the speech in terms of the extent to which it conforms to the principles of the art of public speaking. Conversely, take special care not to evaluate a speech positively because it presents a position with which you agree, as in "I liked the speech; we need more police on campus."

Limit Criticism. Cataloging a speaker's weak points, as in "I found four things wrong with your speech," will overwhelm, not help, the speaker. If you're the sole critic, your criticism will naturally need to be more extensive. If you're one of many critics, limit your criticism to one or perhaps two points. In all cases, your guide should be the value your comments will have for the speaker.

Be Constructive. Your primary goal should be to provide the speaker with insight that you feel will prove useful in future public speaking transactions, a point made clear in the accompanying "TIP." For example, to say "The introduction didn't gain my attention" doesn't tell the speaker how he or she might have gained your attention. Instead, you might say "The example about the computer crash would have been more effective in gaining my attention in the introduction."

Focus on Behavior. Focus criticism on what the speaker said and did during the actual speech. Try to avoid the natural tendency to read the mind of the speaker, to assume that you know why the speaker did one thing rather than another. Compare the critical comments presented in Table 5.1. Note that those in the first column, "Criticism as Attack," try to identify the reasons the speaker did as he or she did; they try to read the speaker's mind. At the same time, they blame the speaker for what happened. Those in the second column, "Criticism as Support," focus on the

---

TABLE 5.1 Criticism as Attack and as Support

Can you develop additional examples to illustrate criticism as attack and as support?

Criticism as Attack	Criticism as Support
"You weren't interested in your topic."	"I would have liked to see greater variety in your delivery. It would have made me feel that you were more interested."
"You should have put more time into the speech."	"I think it would have been more effective if you looked at your notes less."
"You didn't care about your audience."	"I would have liked it if you looked more directly at me while speaking.

specific behavior. Note, too, that those in the first column are likely to encourage defensiveness; you can almost hear the speaker saying "I was so interested in the topic . . ." Those in the second column are unlikely to create defensiveness and are more likely to be appreciated as honest reflections of how the critic perceived the speech.

Anyone can be accurate and even profound, but it is damned hard work to make criticism charming.
—H. L. Mencken

Own Your Own Criticism. In giving criticism, own your comments; take responsibility for your criticism. The best way to express this ownership is to use "I-messages" rather than "you-messages." Instead of saying "You needed better research," say "I would have been more persuaded if you had used more recent research."

Avoid attributing what you found wrong to others. Instead of saying "Nobody was able to understand you," say "I had difficulty understanding you. It would have helped me if you had spoken more slowly." Remember that your criticism is important precisely because it's your perception of what the speaker did and what the speaker could have done more effectively. Speaking for the entire audience ("We couldn't hear you clearly" or "No one was convinced by your arguments") will not help the speaker, and it's likely to prove demoralizing.

I-messages will also prevent you from using "should messages," a type of expression that almost invariably creates defensiveness and resentment. When you say "you should have done this" or "you shouldn't have done that," you assume a superior position and imply that what you're saying is correct and that what the speaker did was incorrect. On the other hand, when you own your evaluations and use I-messages, you're giving your perception; it's then up to the speaker to accept or reject them.

Use Conformity to the Principles of the Art Guidelines. The following series of questions will help you look at a speech through the standards of the principles of the art of public speaking; they're in the nature of a beginner's guide to speech criticism. These questions come from the topics in Unit 2 and are discussed in greater detail in the units to follow. Throughout the text additional principles will be introduced, and those identified here will be amplified. So, view the following questions as a *preliminary* guide to *some* of the issues to come. You'll also find it helpful to use these questions as a checklist for your own speeches. They'll help you make sure that you've followed the principles of public speaking.

The Subject and Purpose. The speech subject should be worthwhile, relevant, and interesting to the audience. The speech purpose should be clear and sufficiently narrow so that it can be achieved in the allotted time. Here are some questions to guide your criticism:

1. Is the subject a worthwhile one?
2. Is the subject relevant and interesting to the audience and to the speaker?
3. Is the information presented beneficial to the audience in some way?
4. What is the general purpose of the speech (to inform, to persuade, to secure goodwill, etc.)? Is this clear to the audience?
5. Is the specific topic narrow enough to be covered in some depth in the time allotted?

The Audience, Occasion, and Context. A public speech is designed for a specific audience and occasion and takes into account the characteristics of the audience.

6. Has the speaker taken into consideration the age; sex; culture; occupation, income, and status; and religion and religiousness of the audience? How are these factors dealt with in the speech?
7. Is the speech topic appropriate to the specific occasion and the general context?

Research. A public speech needs to be based on accurate and reliable information. The topic needs to be thoroughly researched and the speaker needs to demonstrate a command of the subject matter.

8. Is the speech adequately researched? Do the sources appear to be reliable and up-to-date?
9. Does the speaker have a thorough understanding of the subject?
10. Is the speaker's research and understanding communicated effectively to the audience?

The Thesis and Major Propositions. The public speech should have one clear thesis to which the major propositions in the speech are clearly related.

11. Is the thesis of the speech clear and limited to one central idea?
12. Are the main propositions of the speech clearly related to the thesis? Is there an appropriate number of major propositions in the speech (not too many, not too few)?

Supporting Materials. The speech's propositions need to be supported by a variety of appropriate supporting materials that explain or prove their validity.

13. Is each major proposition adequately supported? Are the supporting materials varied and appropriate to the speech and to the propositions?
14. Do the supporting materials amplify what they purport to amplify? Do they prove what they purport to prove?

Organization. The speech materials need to be organized into a meaningful whole to facilitate audience understanding.

15. Is the body of the speech organized in a pattern that is appropriate to the speech topic? To the audience?
16. Is the pattern of organization clear to the audience? Does it help the audience follow the speech?

Style and Language. The language and style of the speech should help the audience understand the speaker's message. It should be consistent in tone with the speech topic and purpose.

17. Does the language help the audience understand clearly and immediately what the speaker is saying? For example, are simple rather than

complex and concrete rather than abstract words used? Is personal and informal language used? Are simple and active sentences used?

18. Is the language offensive to any person or group of persons?

Criticism is hard to take, particularly from a relative, a friend, an acquaintance or a stranger.
—Franklin P. Jones

The Conclusion, Introduction, and Transitions. The conclusion should summarize the major points raised in the speech and should provide clear and crisp closure. The introduction should gain attention and orient the audience. Transitions should connect the various parts of the speech so that they flow into one another and should provide guideposts for the audience to help them follow the speaker's train of thought.

19. Does the conclusion effectively summarize the main points identified in the speech and effectively wrap up the speech, providing recognizable closure?
20. Does the introduction gain the attention of the audience and provide a clear orientation to the subject matter of the speech?
21. Are there adequate transitions? Do the transitions help the audience better understand the development of the speech?

Delivery. Effective delivery should help maintain audience attention and help the speaker emphasize the ideas in the speech.

22. Does the speaker maintain eye contact with the audience?
23. Are there any distractions (of mannerism, dress, or vocal characteristics) that will divert attention from the speech?
24. Can the speaker be easily heard? Are the volume and rate of speech appropriate?

UNIT IN BRIEF

The Nature and Values of Criticism	Criticism is a process of judging and evaluating a work. Among the values of criticism are that it helps (1) identify strengths and weaknesses and thereby helps you improve as a public speaker, (2) identify standards for evaluating all sorts of public speeches, and (3) show that the audience is listening and is concerned about the speaker's progress.
Cultural Differences	Cultures differ in their views of criticism and in the rules they consider appropriate. Members from individualist cultures may find public criticism easier and more acceptable than people from collectivist cultures. Interpreting critical responses (or the lack of) through your own cultural filters may prevent you from understanding the meaning intended.

Standards and Principles of Criticism	Standards of criticism ■ Effectiveness (How effectively did the speaker accomplish the purpose?) ■ Universality (Does the speech apply to all people in all times?) ■ Conformity to the principles of the art (How effectively did the speaker apply the principles of public speaking?) Suggestions for Offering Criticism ■ Say something positive ■ Be specific ■ Be objective ■ Limit criticism ■ Be constructive ■ Focus on behavior ■ Own your own criticism ■ Use conformity to the principles of the art guidelines

THINKING CRITICALLY ABOUT CRITICISM IN THE CLASSROOM

REVIEWING KEY TERMS AND CONCEPTS OF SPEECH CRITICISM

1. Review and define the key terms used in this unit:

   ❑ criticism (p. 79)
   ❑ individualism (p. 81)
   ❑ collectivism (p. 81)
   ❑ effectiveness standard of criticism (p. 84)
   ❑ universality as a standard of criticism (p. 84)
   ❑ conformity to the principles of the art standard (p. 85)

2. Explain the key concepts discussed in this unit:

   ■ What is criticism and what are its values?
   ■ What are some cultural differences that impact on speech criticism in the classroom?
   ■ What are the major standards used in critically evaluating speeches and what guidelines should be followed in expressing criticism?

DEVELOPING PUBLIC SPEAKING STRATEGIES

1. Ralph and Tony are best friends and are in public speaking class together. Ralph is a very effective speaker and wants to help Tony. What principles of criticism would you advise Ralph to be especially sensitive to in helping Tony?

2. Mirta has been asked to serve as a guest judge for a debate in a sixth grade class. The plan is for the students to conduct the debate and then to have the guest judge deliver a five to 10 minute critique of the various speeches and question-answer exchanges. The audience will consist of students, a few teachers, and the parents of the debaters. What advice would you give Mirta for presenting her critiques?

EVALUATING PUBLIC SPEECHES

1. Read one of the speeches in the appendix and evaluate it using each of the three standards discussed here: effectiveness, universality, and conformity to the principles of the art.

2. Review one of your own speeches and try to criticize it, using the standards and suggestions identified here, as objectively as you can.

USING TECHNOLOGY IN PUBLIC SPEAKING

1. Visit Mississippi State University's Historical Text Archive at http://www.msstate.edu/Archives/History and read one of the presidential inaugural addresses. How would you evaluate the speech using any standard you think is appropriate?

2. Visit the Web site for the Congressional Record (http:P//thomas.loc.gov/home/abt.cong.rec.html). Read one of the speeches and evaluate it according to the standards identified in this unit.

PRACTICALLY SPEAKING

5.1 Short Speech Technique

Prepare and deliver a two-minute speech in which you:

a. explain what you think would be the ideal critical evaluation for a speaker to receive from a critic.

b. explain why criticism is so difficult to give or to receive (select one).

c. explain what you think is the most appropriate standard to use for criticizing the classroom speech, the religious sermon, the college lecture, the political campaign speech, or the advertiser's pitch (select one or compare two).

d. offer a critical evaluation of any one of the speeches contained in this text or of a speech from some other source.

5.2 Analyzing and Criticizing a Poorly Constructed Informative Speech

The sample speeches presented throughout this book are good ones and are designed to illustrate the effective application of the principles of public speaking. Here, however, is an especially poor speech, constructed to illustrate clearly and briefly some of the major faults with informative speeches. This exercise can be returned to several times throughout the course. As the course progresses, the responses will become more complete, more insightful, and more effective.

After you've reviewed the speech and the comments on the right, phrase your criticism in the form of a relatively formal critique of one to two minutes. Assume that this is a student's first speech and you're the public speaking instructor. What do you say?

THREE JOBS

Well, I mean, hello. Er . . . I'm new at public speaking so I'm a little nervous. I've always been shy. So, don't watch my knees shake.

Eum, let me see my notes here. [Mumbles to self while shuffling notes: One, two, three, four, five, -oh, they're all here.] Okay, here goes.

Three jobs. That's my title and I'm going to talk about three jobs.

The Health Care Field. This is the fastest growing job in the country, one of the fastest, I guess I mean. I know that you're not interested in this topic and that you're all studying accounting. But, there are a lot of new jobs in the health care field. The *Star* had an article on health care and said that health care will be needed more in the future than it is now. And now, you know, like they need a lot of health care people. In the hospital where I work—on the West side,

The title seems adequate though it's not terribly exciting. After reading the speech, try to give it a more appealing title. Generally don't use your title as your opening words.

This nervous reaction is understandable but is probably best not to share it with the listeners. After all, you don't want them to be uncomfortable for you.
Going through your notes makes the audience feel that you didn't prepare adequately and may just be wasting their time.

This is the speaker's orientation. Is this sufficient? What else might the speaker have done in the introduction?

Here the speaker shows such uncertainty that we question his or her competence.
And we begin to wonder, why is the speaker talking about this to us?

Reading the Star may be entertaining but it doesn't constitute evidence. What does this reference do to the credibility you ascribe to the speaker?

uptown—they never have enough health aides and they always tell me to become a health aide, like you know, to enter the health care field. To become a nurse. Or maybe a dental technician. But I hate going to the dentist. Maybe I will.

Everything in the speech must have a definite purpose. Asides such as not liking to go to the dentist are probably best omitted.

I don't know what's going to happen with the president's health plan, but whatever happens, it won't change the need for health aides. I mean, people will still get sick; so, it really doesn't matter what happens with health care.

Here was an opportunity for the speaker to connect the topic with important current political events but fails to say anything that isn't obvious.

The Robotics Field. This includes things like artificial intelligence. I don't really know what that is but its like growing real fast. They use this in making automobiles and planes and I think in computers. Japan is a leading country in this field. A lot of people in India go into this field but I'm not sure why.

Introducing these topics like this is clear but is probably not very interesting. How might each of the three main topics have been introduced more effectively?

Notice how vague the speaker is—"includes things like" "and I think in computers," "I'm not sure why." Statements like this communicate very little information to listeners and leave them with little confidence that the speaker knows what he or she is talking about.

The Computer Graphics Field. This field has a lot to do with designing and making lots of different products, like CAD and CAM. This field also includes computer aided imagery—CAI. And in movies, I think. Like *Star Wars* and *Terminator 2*. I saw *Terminator 2* four times. I didn't see *Star Wars* but I'm gonna rent the video. I don't know if you have to know a lot about computers or if you can just like be a designer and someone else will tell the computer what to do.

Again, there is little that is specific. CAD and CAM are not defined and CAI is explained as "computer aided imagery" but unless we already knew what these were, we would still not know even after hearing the speaker. Again, the speaker inserts personal notes (for example, seeing Terminator 2 four times) that have no meaningful connection to the topic.

I got my information from a book that Carol Kleiman wrote, *The 100 Best Jobs for the 1990s and Beyond.* It was summarized in last Sunday's News.

The speaker uses only one source and, to make matters worse, doesn't even go to the original source but relies on a summary in the local newspaper. Especially with a topic like this, listeners are likely to want a variety of viewpoints and additional reliable sources.

My conclusion. These are three of the fastest growing fields in the U.S. and in the world I think—not in third-world countries, I don't think. China and India and Africa. More like Europe and Germany. And the U.S.—the U.S. is the big one. I hope you enjoyed my speech. Thank you.

Note too that the speech lacked any statistics. This is a subject where statistics are essential. Listeners will want to know how many jobs will be available in these fields, what will these fields look like in five or 10 years, how much do these fields pay, and so on.

Using the word conclusion to signal that you're concluding isn't a bad idea, but work it into the text instead of using it as a heading in a book chapter.

I wasn't as nervous as I thought I'd be. Are there any questions?

Again, the speaker makes us question his or her competence and preparation by the lack of certainty.

Again, personal comments are best left out.

5.3 Analyzing and Criticizing a Poorly Constructed Persuasive Speech

Like the informative speech in Practically Speaking 5.2, this speech was written to illustrate some really broad as well as some rather subtle errors that a beginning speaker might make in constructing a persuasive speech. First, read the entire speech without reading any of the questions in the right- hand column. Then, after you've read the entire speech, re-read each paragraph and respond to the critical thinking questions. What other questions might prove productive to ask?

XXX HAS GOT TO GO

You probably didn't read the papers this weekend but there's a XXX movie, I mean video, store that moved in on Broadway and Fifth Streets. My parents, who are retired teachers, are protesting it and so am I. My parents are organizing a protest for the next weekend.

What do you think of the title of the speech?
Visualizing yourself as a listener, how would the opening comment make you feel?
Does the speaker gain your attention?
What thesis do you think the speaker will support?
Does mentioning "my parents" help or hurt the speaker's credibility?

There must be hundreds of XXX video stores in the country and they all need to be closed down. I have a lot of reasons.

What is the speaker's thesis?
What impression are you beginning to get of the speaker?

First, my parents think it should be closed down. My parents are retired teachers and have organized protests over the proposed new homeless shelter and to prevent the city from making that park on Elm Street. So, they know what they're doing.

How do the speaker's parents sound to you? Do they sound like credible leaders with a consistent cause? Professional protesters (with perhaps a negative agenda)?
What evidence is offered to support the assertion that we should believe the speaker's parents? Is this adequate? What would you need to know about people before believing them?

The XXX video place is un-Christian. No good Christian people would ever go there. Our minister is against it and is joining in the protest.

What does this statement assume about the audience? How would this statement be responded to by your public speaking class? What do you think of the speaker explaining XXX video stores as un-Christian?

These stores bring crime into the neighborhood. I have proof of that. Morristown's crime increased after the XXX video store opened. And in Martinsville, where they got rid of the video store, crime did not increase. If we allow the video store in our own town, then we're going to be like Morristown and our crime is going to increase.

What do you think of the reasoning used here? Are there other factors that could have influenced Morristown's crime increase? Is there any evidence that getting rid of the video store resulted in the stable crime rate in Martinsville? What assumption about the audience does the speaker make in using Martinsville and Morristown as analogies?

These stores make lots of garbage. The plastic wrappings from the videos will add to our already overextended and over-utilized landfill. And a lot of them are going to wind up as litter on the streets.

Do you agree with this argument about the garbage? Is this argument in any way unique to the video store? Is it likely that people will open the wrappers and drop them on the street?

The XXX Video House stays open seven days a week, 24 hours a day. People will be forced to work at all hours and on Sunday and that's not fair. And the store will increase the noise level at night with the cars pulling up and all.

What validity do you give to each of these arguments? Given the 24-hour policy, how might you construct an argument against the video store? Are there advantages of a neighborhood store's 24-hour policy that the audience may be thinking of and thus counter the speaker's argument? If there are, how should the speaker deal with them?

The XXX Video House—that's it's name, by the way—doesn't carry regular videos which most people want. So, why do we want them?

Upon hearing this, would you be likely to extend this argument and start asking yourself, "Do we now close up all stores that most people don't want?"

The XXX Video House got a lease from an owner who doesn't even live in the community, someone by the name of, well, it's an organization called XYX Management. And their address is Carlson Place in Jeffersonville. So, they don't even live here.

Is there a connection between who the owner is and whether the video store should or shouldn't be closed? Could the speaker have effectively used this information in support of the thesis to close the video store?

A neighboring store owner says he thinks the store is in violation of several fire laws. He says they have no sprinkler system and no metal doors to prevent the spread of a fire. So, he thinks they should be closed down too.

What credibility do you ascribe to the "neighboring store owner"? Do you begin to wonder if the speaker would simply agree to have the store brought up to the fire code laws?

Last week on *Oprah* three women were on and they were in the XXX movie business and they were all on drugs and had been in jail and they said it all started when they went into the porno business. One woman wanted to be a teacher, another wanted to be a nurse, and the other wanted to be a beautician. If there weren't any XXX video stores then there wouldn't be a porn business and, you know, pornography is part of organized crime and so if you stop pornography you take a bite out of crime.

What is the cause and what is the effect that the speaker is asserting? How likely is it that the proposed cause actually produced the effect? Might there have been causes other than the pornography that might have led these women into drugs?

What credibility do you give to people you see on talk shows? Does it vary with the specific talk show?

Do you accept the argument that there would be no pornography business without video stores? What would have to be proven to you before you accept this connection?

How do you respond to the expression "take a bite out of crime"?

One of the reasons I think it should be closed is that the legitimate video stores—the ones that have only a small selection of XXX movies somewhere in the back—lose business. And if they continue to lose business, they'll leave the neighborhood and we'll have no video stores.

Is the speaker implying that this is the real reason against XXX video stores?

Do you start wondering if the speaker is against XXX video—as it seemed in the last argument—or just against stores that sell these exclusively? What effect does this impression have on your evaluation of the speaker's credibility and the speaker's thesis?

That's a lot of reasons against XXX movie houses. I have a quote here: Reason is "a portion of the divine spirit set in a human body." Seneca.

How do you feel about the number of "reasons"? Would you have preferred fewer reasons more fully developed or more reasons?

What purpose does this quotation serve?

In conclusion and to wrap it up and close my speech, I want to repeat and say again that the XXX video stores should all be closed down. They corrupt minors. And they're offensive to men and women and especially women. I hope you'll all protest with the Marshalls—my mother and father—and they'll be lots of others there too. My minister, I think, is coming too.

Might the speaker have introduced it differently?
Now, what is the speaker's thesis?
What do you think of the argument that XXX video stores are offensive? What effect does it have coming here in the conclusion?
Do you think you'd go to the protest? Why?

UNIT 6

Topic, Purpose, and Thesis

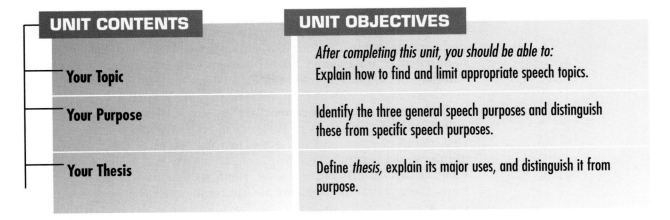

UNIT CONTENTS	UNIT OBJECTIVES
	After completing this unit, you should be able to:
Your Topic	Explain how to find and limit appropriate speech topics.
Your Purpose	Identify the three general speech purposes and distinguish these from specific speech purposes.
Your Thesis	Define *thesis*, explain its major uses, and distinguish it from purpose.

Now that the fundamentals of public speaking have been established, you can begin to focus on the principles of public speaking in greater detail. This unit covers selecting a topic and narrowing it down so that you can cover it in the allotted time, selecting a purpose, and framing the central idea or thesis of your speech.

YOUR TOPIC

A suitable speech topic should be (1) worthwhile and deal with matters of substance, (2) appropriate to you and your audience, and (3) sensitive and appropriate to the culture in which the speech takes place.

The topics should be **worthwhile**. Such topics should address issues that have significant implications for the audience. Topics that are worthwhile have consequences (social, educational, political, and so on) that are significant for your listeners. The topic must be important enough to merit the time and attention of a group of intelligent people. Speeches on trivial topics—how to best polish your shoes or pack a suitcase, the latest Sally Jesse Raphael show, or how to recognize a hairpiece, for example—are best left for the informal social group. They're simply not worth the collective time of 20 or 25 intelligent college students studying public speaking. Of course, even these topics are worthwhile to polish and suitcase designers, television producers, or toupee manufacturers and for these audiences such topics would not be considered "trivial." In fact, it would be difficult to find any topic that is trivial to all people.

A suitable topic is **appropriate** to you as the speaker, to the audience you'll address, and to the occasion. When you select a topic you're interested in, you'll enjoy thinking and reading about it, and this will come through in your speech. Look also at your topic in terms of its appropriateness to the audience. What are they interested in? What would they like to learn more about? On what topics would they think the time listening to your speech well spent? A speech on employment interview techniques might be appropriate to students in your class but inappropriate for an audience of retired persons. It's a lot easier to maintain audience attention when the topic interests them.

The topic should also be appropriate for the occasion. For example, time limitations will exclude certain topics because they're too complex. You

You will always find a few Eskimos ready to tell the Congolese how to cope with the heat.
—Stanislaw Lec

couldn't explain the problems with our educational system or solutions to the drug problem in a five minute speech. While the classroom offers few problems created by the "occasion," it imposes a number of serious restrictions outside the classroom. Some occasions call for humorous subjects that would be out of place in other contexts. Others call for speeches of personal experience that may be inappropriate in other contexts.

Topics need to be **culture-sensitive**. In many Arab, Asian, and African cultures discussing sex in an audience of both men and women would be considered obscene and offensive. In other cultures (Scandinavia, for example), sex is expected to be discussed openly and without embarrassment or discomfort. When people speak to members of their own cultures, there are rarely problems of cultural inappropriateness. A problem does arise when, for example, the Scandinavian—operating with norms from his or her own culture—talks openly about sex to a mixed Arab audience—thus violating a serious social and religious taboo.

Each culture has its own taboo topics, subjects that should be avoided, especially by visitors from other cultures. Table 6.1 lists several examples that Roger Axtell in *Do's and Taboos Around the World* (1993) recommends that visitors from the United States avoid. These examples are not intended to be exhaustive but rather to illustrate that each culture defines what is and what is not an appropriate topic for discussion.

Your college or communication classroom very likely has its own cultural norms as to what would be considered an appropriate topic. Consider, for example, if the following speeches would be considered "appropriate" by members of your public speaking class or by your general college community.

- A speech that seeks to convert listeners to a specific religion?
- A speech supporting neo-Nazi values?

TABLE 6.1 Taboos Around the World

Can you identify the taboos of your public speaking class or, at least, of a significant number of students?

Culture	Taboos
Caribbean	Race, local politics, religion
Columbia	Politics, criticism of bullfighting
Egypt	Middle-Eastern politics
Iraq	Religion, Middle-Eastern politics
Japan	World War II
Libya	Politics, religion
Mexico	Mexican-American war, illegal aliens
Nigeria	Religion
Pakistan	Politics
Philippines	Politics, religion, corruption, foreign aid
South Korea	Internal politics, criticism of the government, socialism, or communism
Spain	Family, religion, jobs, negative comments on bullfighting

THE ETHICS OF Objectivity and Subjectivity

In analyzing the ethics of a particular speech, some people take the position that ethics is objective and some that it's subjective. An **objective view** of ethics argues that the morality of an act—say a public speech—is absolute and exists apart from the values or beliefs of any individual or culture. An objective view holds that there's a set of standards that applies to all people in all situations at all times. If lying, false advertising, using false evidence, or revealing secrets you've promised to keep—to take just a few examples—are considered unethical, then, according to the objective view, they would be considered unethical regardless of the circumstances surrounding the act or of the values and beliefs of the culture in which they occur.

A **subjective view** argues that absolute statements of morality are ethnocentric and that the ethics of a message depends on the culture's values and beliefs as well as the particular circumstances. Thus, a subjective position would claim that lying may be wrong to win votes or sell cigarettes, but that it may be quite ethical if the end result is positive, such as trying to make people feel better by telling them they look great or that they'll get well soon.

Do you hold objective or subjective views on ethics? Did your culture teach you that one of these views was correct and the other incorrect? Which view do you feel is supported in your typical college class?

[The next Ethics in Public Speaking box appears on page 153.]

- A speech against interracial adoption and interracial marriage?
- A speech supporting the legitimacy of killing those who defend or perform abortions?
- A speech arguing in support of same-sex marriage or a speech that supports the Defense of Marriage act?
- A speech that teaches listeners how to cheat on their income tax or pad their expense accounts?

Finding Topics

Perhaps the first question you have is "What do I speak about? I'm not knowledgeable about international affairs, the Middle East, or environmental issues. I'm not up on issues such as mass transit, national health insurance, or gay rights." This situation is not uncommon; many, if not most, college students feel the same way.

The answer to "What do I speak about?" will change as your life situation changes, and you'll most likely speak on topics that grow out of your job or your social or political activities. In the classroom, however, where the objective is to learn the skills of public speaking, there are literally thousands of subjects to talk about. Searching for speech topics is a relatively easy process. Here are four ways to generate topics: surveys, news items, brainstorming, and the idea generator.

Surveys. Look at some of the national and regional polls concerning what people think is important—the significant issues, the urgent problems. For example, a survey conducted by the Roper organization for H&R Block in 1978, in *The American Public and the Income Tax System,* found that Americans felt the following were among the most significant issues: lowering the crime rate, making the tax system fair, improving the educational system, improving the nation's defense capabilities, setting up a

We cannot have expression till there is something to be expressed.
—Margaret Fuller

program to provide national health insurance for everyone, lowering unemployment, improving and protecting the environment, lowering Social Security taxes, and improving public transportation. The concerns look very much those of today.

A more recent survey of 10,000 executives and meeting planners identified the 10 topics they consider the most important and that will continue to be important for the next few years: dealing with change, customer service, global marketplace opportunities, future strategies, total quality, new technologies, productivity and performance in business, diversity, legal issues, and health and fitness (Weinstein 1995).

Survey data are now easier than ever to get since many of the larger poll results are available on the Internet. For example, the Gallup organization maintains a Web site at http://www.gallup.com/ that includes national and international surveys on political, social, consumer, and other issues speakers often talk about. Another way is to go to the search directories such as Hotbot or Yahoo (see Table 7.1, page 134 for other suggestions) and examine the major directory topics and any subdivisions of those you'd care to pursue—a process that's explained later in this unit. Many search engines and browsers provide lists of "hot topics," which are often useful starting points. These topics are exactly the topics that people are talking about; therefore, they often make excellent speech topics.

Or, you can conduct a survey yourself. Roam through the nonfiction section of your bookstore (online, if you prefer—for example, www.amazon.com, www.barnesandnoble.com, or www.borders.com) and you'll quickly develop a list of the topics book buyers consider important. A glance at your newspaper's best seller list will give you an even quicker overview.

Naturally, all audiences are different. Yet, such surveys are useful starting points for giving you some insight into what others think is important and, hence, what might be of interest to them.

News Items. Another useful starting point is a good newspaper or magazine. Here you'll find the important international and domestic issues, the financial issues, and the social issues all conveniently packaged in one place. The editorial page and the letters to the editor are also useful in learning what people are concerned about.

News magazines such as *Time* and *Newsweek,* and financial magazines such as *Forbes, Money,* and *Fortune* (in print or online) will provide a wealth of suggestions. Similarly, news shows like "20/20," "60 Minutes," "Meet the Press", and even the ubiquitous talk shows (and their corresponding websites) often identify the very issues that people are concerned with and on which there are conflicting points of view.

Brainstorming. Another useful method is to brainstorm, a technique designed to enable you to generate lots of topics in a relatively short time (Osborn, 1957; DeVito 1996). You begin with your "problem," which in this case is "What will I talk about?" You then record any and all ideas that occur to you. Allow your mind to free associate. Don't censor yourself; instead, allow your ideas to flow as freely as possible. Record all your thoughts, regardless of how silly or inappropriate they may seem. Write them down or record them on tape. Try to generate as many ideas as possible. The more ideas you think of, the more chance of there being a suitable topic in the

TIPS
from professional speakers

Pick a topic that you know something about. This doesn't mean you have to know more than everyone in the audience about the topic, but you should at least be familiar with your topic. No professional speaker would get up in front of an audience and speak on a topic that was totally unfamiliar. You shouldn't, either. For a beginning speaker there will be enough nervousness just facing an audience. You don't want to compound that nervousness by trying to remember information you don't really know.

Thomas J. Murphy, a teacher and author, and Kenneth Snyder, a professional speaker and trainer, *What! I Have to Give a Speech?* (Bloomington, IN: Grayson Bernard Publications, 1995): 25.

pile. After you've generated a sizable list—it should take you no longer than 5 minutes—read over the list or replay the tape. Do any of the topics on your list suggest other topics? If so, write these down as well. Can you combine or extend your ideas? Which ideas seem workable? The use of this technique in small groups is explained in Unit 25, "Small Group Communication."

The Idea Generator: Dictionary of Topics. This system is actually a method for both discovering topics and for limiting them. It consists of using a dictionary of general topics and a series of questions that you can ask of any subject. The first part of the idea generator, "Ideas: The Dictionary of Topics," will prove helpful in finding a suitable topic. It consists of a dictionary-like listing of subjects within which each topic is broken down into several subtopics. These subtopics should begin to suggest potential subjects for your informative and persuasive speeches (Table 6.2, pp. 103–109). The second part of the idea generator, "Topoi: The System of Topics," will prove useful in helping you limit your topic, to which we now turn.

> *There is no such thing as an uninteresting subject; there are only uninteresting people.*
> —Gilbert Keith Chesterton

TABLE 6.2 Ideas: The Dictionary of Topics

Presented here are ideas for speech topics. This list is not intended to provide specific topics for any of your speeches; it should, however, alleviate any anxiety over "having nothing to talk about." The list should stimulate you to think of subjects dealing with topics you're interested in but may not have thought of as appropriate to a public speech. Each topic is broken down into several subtopics that should stimulate you to see these as potential ideas for your informative and persuasive speeches.

Abortion arguments for and against; techniques of; religious dimension; legal views; differing views of

Academic freedom nature of; censorship; teachers' role in curriculum development; and government; and research; restrictions on

Acupuncture nature of; development of; current practices in; effectiveness of; dangers of

Adoption agencies for; procedures; difficulties in; illegal; concealment of biological parents; search for birth parents.

Advertising techniques; expenditures; ethical; unethical; subliminal; leading agencies; history of; slogans

Age ageism; aging processes; aid to the aged; discrimination against the aged; treatment of the aged; different cultural views of aging; sex differences

Aggression aggressive behavior in animals; in humans; as innate; as learned; and territoriality

Agriculture science of; history of; in ancient societies; technology of; theories of

Air pollution; travel; embolism; law; navigation; power; raids

Alcoholism nature of; Alcoholics Anonymous; Al Anon; abstinence; among the young; treatment of

Amnesty in draft evasion; in criminal law; and pardons; in Civil War; in Vietnam War; conditions of

Animals experimentation; intelligence of; aggression in; ethology; and communication

Arts theater; dance; film; painting; support for; apathy; social aspects of; economic aspects of; styles in the arts

Athletics professional; Little League; college; support for; corruption in; benefits of; little-known sports; records; Olympics

Automobiles development of; economics of; advances in; new developments; mass production

Awards Academy; sports; Tony; Cleo; Emmy; scholarship; athletic

Bermuda Triangle nature of; myths; structure of; losses

Bicycling as exercise; as transportation; touring; Olympic; development and types of cycles, social aspects; ecological aspects

Birth defects; control; rites; racial differences; natural

Blind number of blind persons; training of the blind; Braille; communication and the blind; prejudice against; adjustment of; famous blind persons

Books binding; burning; collecting; rare; making; publishing; writing

Boxing professional; amateur; great fights; styles of; famous fighters; economics of

Brain trust; washing; damage; genius; intelligence; aphasia

Business cycles; associations; laws; in performing arts; finance

Cable television; underground; development of; economics of

Calorie nature of; and exercise; and diets; and weight gain

Capitalism nature of; economics of; development of; depression and inflation; philosophy; alternatives to

Cards playing; tarot; fortune telling; development of games; rules for games

Censorship arguments for and against; and violence; and sex; television; literacy

Chauvinism and patriotism; and sexism; and learning; changing conceptions of

Cities problems of; population patterns; and tourism; crime; government of

Citizenship different conceptions of; acquiring loss of; naturalization; tests; in different countries

College functions of; economics of; differences among; historical development of; and job training; and education

Communication public; media; intrapersonal; interpersonal; satellite

Computer memory; music; programming; and communication; chess; personal; and education

Copyright laws; infringements; rules; practices

Credit nature of; public; agricultural; card use; unions; bureau

Crime prevention; types of; and law; and punishment

Cults types of; programming; deprogramming; influences of; power of

Culture cultural relativism; lag; drift; diffusion; change; shock; and communication

Death legal aspects of; and religion; and suicide; and life; reincarnation

Debt management; retirement; limit; and credit cards

Defense national; mechanisms; self; techniques; karate

Depression nature of; and suicide; among college students; dealing with

Diet water; Scarsdale; dangers of; alternatives to; fasting; Cambridge

Disasters natural; wartime; prevention of; famous; economics of

Discrimination sensory; and prejudice; racial; religious

Diseases major diseases of college students; prevention; detection; treatment; recovery

Divorce rate; throughout world; causes of; advantages of; disadvantages of; proceedings

Drugs addiction; treatment; allergies; poisoning; problems; effects; legalizing

Earthquakes nature of; famous; Alaskan; San Francisco; volcanoes; seismic readings

Ecology nature of; approaches of; applications of

Economics principles of; macro; micro; schools of; of education; in education

Education system of; social; religious; medical; legal; economics of; segregation; desegregation

Emigration migration; changing population patterns; uses of; problems with

Employment theory; and unemployment; service insurance

Energy conservation; nature of; types of; crisis; sources of; nuclear; solar; fusion

Entertainment industry; benefits; abuses; tax; functions of; and communication

Environment biological; influences; versus innate factors in learning; pollution of

Ethnicity meaning of; and prejudice; theories of; and culture

Ethology nature of; animal behavior patterns; pioneers; theories of

Evolution philosophical; theological; of human race; theories of; and revolution

Exercise importance of; methods of; dangers of; gymnastics

Farming techniques; government subsidies; equipment; effect of droughts

Federal Communications Commission (FCC) structure of; powers; functions; and television programming; rulings of; licenses

Feminism meaning of; implications of; changing concepts of

Folk literature; medicine; music; poetry; society; tales; wisdom

Food health; preservatives; additives; red dye; and allergies; preparation; stamps

Football rules; college; professional; abuses in; training in

Freedom of speech laws protecting; and Constitution; significance of; abuses of; and censorship; and economics

Freedom of the press and Constitution; revealing sources; importance of; investigative reporting

Gambling types of; legal aspects of; casino; houses; and chance; legalization of

Game(s) history of; theory; shows; children's psychological; destructive

Gay and lesbian rights; lifestyle; laws against; prejudice against; and religion; statistics; relationships; marriage; domestic partnerships; language

Gender roles; identification; differences

Government federal; state; city; powers of

Guilt causes of; symptoms; dealing with; effects of; and suicide; and religion

Health services; human; education; laws; audiology

Heroes nature of; and adolescence; fictional; social role of; real-life heroes

Hospital(s) structure; function; and preventive medicine; and concern for community; and cost

Housing urban; cost; inflation discrimination in; subsidized; underground

Humor theories of; nature of; situational; verbal; cultural differences

Hypnotism nature of; and memory; and age regression; potentials of; uses of; dangers of; medical uses of

Immigration migration; patterns; laws governing

Imports and exports; laws regulating; and tariffs; and protection of workers

Income personal; national; and employment theory; tax; statement

Industrialization social aspects; economics of; political aspects of; development of; psychological aspects

Infant mortality causes of; prevention of; racial differences; preventive medicine

Intelligence quotient; tests; theories of; cultural differences

Journalism as profession; investigative; photojournalism; education

Kidnapping nature of; famous; laws governing; penalties; Act; Lindberg

Labor types of; division of; hours; in pregnancy; economics of; and management; unions

Languages artificial; sign; natural; learning of; loss of; pathologies of

Laws international; criminal; of nature

Libraries functions; support; science; design; largest; collections; types of

Life definition of; extraterrestrial; cycle; insurance; support; systems

Literacy rate; world distribution; definition; problems in raising rate of

Love nature of; theories of; romantic; family; and hate; and interpersonal relationships; of self; and materialism

Magic nature of; and religion; significance of; types of; and science; history of; and magicians; and sleight of hand

Marriage and divorce; vows; traditions; open; contracts; bans; changing views of; laws against; same-sex; Defense of Marriage Act

Media forms of; contributions of; abuses; regulations; popularity of; influences of; and violence; and censorship

Medicine preventive; forensic; and health insurance; history of; holistic; and poisoning; alchemy; industrial

Men education of; problems of; and women; and chauvinism; changing roles of; and sexism; and prejudice; and homosexuality; in groups; as fathers

Military organizations; preparedness; confrontations and conflicts; governments; law

Morality nature of; cultural variations in views; teaching of; and crime

Music festivals; forms; instruments; compositions; styles; drama

Myth(s) nature of; origin of; symbolism of; and ritual; contemporary significance of

Narcissism nature of; and Narcissus; Freudian view of; and autoeroticism; and love of others

National Organization for Women (NOW) structure of; functions of; influences of; contributions of; beliefs of

Newspapers functions of; advertising; reporters; famous; structure of; economics of

Noise pollution; white; and communication; redundancy and; combating; causes of; types of

Nuclear plants; explosion; family; war; reaction; weapons; arguments for and against nuclear plants

Nutrition nature of; functions of food; essential requirements; animal; human; and starvation; and diet

Obscenity nature of; laws prohibiting; and pornography; effects of; influences on

Occupational diseases; psychology; satisfaction; therapy

Peace Corps; treaty; pipe; economics of

Personality development of; measurement of; theories of; disorders; tests

Photography nature of; types of; art of; color; development of; infrared; technology; holography

Police functions of; structure of; crime prevention; and education; community relations; civilian review; abuses by

Pollution air; atmospheric research; chemical radiation; water; and food; sources; effects; laws governing

Population(s) beliefs; theories; Malthusianism; Marxism; and education; and elderly; and family size; world; innate factors; racial typing; evolution; mutation

Pornography and censorship; types of; influences of; restrictions on

Prison reform; systems; security; routine; effect on crime; personality; behavior; and sex; and conditioning

Psychic phenomena ESP; psychokinesis; reliability of; and frauds; theories of

Psychoanalysis development of; leaders; impact of; training in; theories of

Public relations in colleges; and propaganda; public opinion; advertising

Public schools support of; changing curriculum; and parochial schools; problems with; PTAs

Publishing economics of; history of; copyright; and media exposure; trade and textbook; magazine and newspapers

Racing auto; dog; horse; corruption in; jockeys; fame

Racism nature of; self-hatred; genetic theory; human rights; education; religious; UN position; in United States

Radio development of; advertising; air traffic control; police; surveillance; radioactivity

Religion different religions; leaders in; influence of; beliefs of; and agnosticism; and atheism; and God; social dimensions of; and art; and architecture

Salaries minimum wage; professional; white-and blue-collar; racial variation; and unions; and inflation

Sales advertising; methods; forecasting; and excise taxes; effects on consumers

Satellite communication; launchings; research

Sciences history of; procedures in; empirical data; methods of; fiction

Security personal; Social; national

Segregation genetic; racial; leaders in fight against; legal aspects; and legal decisions; effects of; education

Self-concept meaning of; and communication; and depression; and conditioning

Self-defense in criminal law; international laws; and war; martial arts

Self-disclosure benefits of; cautions in; influences of; influences on; effects of; types of; conditions conducive to

Sex education; roles; therapy; surrogate; change; and love; and the concepts of deviation; variations; and learning

Social Security; facilitation; class; control; differentiation; Darwinism; equilibrium; groups; movement; realism

Solar system; wind; radiation; energy; heating

Space exploration; flight; probes; age

Sports nature of; psychology of; fans; in college; professional; records; Little League; figures; salaries; international competition; Olympics; invention of; stadiums

Strikes famous; violence; unions; essential-service occupations; teacher; causes and effects

Subconscious Freud; development of concept; defense mechanisms

Subversive activities definition of; political; legislation penalties for

Suicide causes; among college students; laws regulating; methods; aiding the suicide of another; philosophical implications; religious dimension

Superstition beliefs; mythology; influences on history

Supreme Court judicial review; decisions; make-up of; chief justices; jurisdiction

Taxation alcohol; cigarette; history of; purposes of; historical methods of; types of; without representation; evasion; tariffs

Teaching methods; teachers; machines; programmed learning; behavioral objectives; and conditioning

Technology benefits of; and undeveloped areas; as threat to workers; and economics; history of

Telepathy nature of; evidence for; tests of; and fraud

Television development of; history of; working of satellite; commercials; propaganda; and leisure time; programming; economics of; effects of; and violence; and radio; and film; producing; Nielsen ratings

Test-tube babies developments in; opposition to; methods; dangers; variations

Theater Greek; Roman; commedia dell'arte; American; British; Eastern; Italian; French; performers; styles of; and television; and film; Broadway; and critics

Theology forms; development of; different religions; education

Therapy physical; psychological; language; techniques of; schools of

Time management; travel; records

Tobacco production of; smoking; effects of; causes of; methods of stopping; nicotine dangers of; economics of

Translation computer; missionary impetus; problems in; history of; kinds of

Transplants nature of; rejection; donor selection; legal aspects; ethical aspects; future of; advances in

Transportation history; urban; water; air; land

Trust nature of; and love; and self-disclosure; types of; and communication

UFOs evidence for; types of; reported sightings; theories of; agencies in charge of

Unemployment urban; seasonal; and violence; insurance; disguised

Unions development of; problems with; advantages of; arguments for and against; unionism

United Nations (UN) development of; functions of; agencies; and League of Nations; structure; veto powers; Security Council; Declaration of Rights

Urban living; problems; benefits; stress; crime; transportation; development; decay

Vaccine nature of; types; vaccination; immunization

Values and attitudes; and communications; social; economic; changing; religious; axiology; sex differences

Vietnam country; people; war; language; rehabilitation

Virtue natural; religious; nature of; changing conceptions of; learning and

Vitamins deficiency; excess; types of

Voice qualities; voiceprints; and personality; training; and persuasion; paralanguage

Wages minimum; and inflation; and fringe benefits; average; differences among cultures

War conduct of; financing; destruction by; causes of; debts; games; casualties; effects of

Weapons hand and missile; firearms artillery; rockets; automatic; nuclear; biological; psychological

Weather forecasting; hurricanes; control of; rain; snow; heat; cold; and population patterns; and health; and psychology; diving

Weight lifting techniques in; as exercise; as sport; leading weight lifters; competition; dangers in; benefits of; societal attitudes toward; and sexual attraction

Witchcraft meaning of; white and black; and magic; structure of; functions of; theories of; in primitive societies; contemporary

Women and sexism; biology; learning and programming; in different societies; accomplishments of; prejudices against; ERA; social roles

Words history; coinage; foreign contributions; semantics; and meaning

Youth problems of; crime; education; hostels; music; communication problems; generation gap

Zodiac nature of; different conceptions of; constellations; myths surrounding; and horoscopes

Nothing is interesting if you're not interested.
—Helen MacInness

Limiting Topics

Probably the major error beginning speakers make is to try to cover a huge topic in too short a time. The inevitable result is that nothing specific is covered; everything is touched on but only superficially. No depth is achieved with a broad topic, so all you can succeed in doing is telling the audience what it already knows. To be suitable for a public speech, a topic must be limited in scope; it must be narrowed down to fit the time constraints and to permit some depth of coverage.

Another reason for narrowing your topic is that it will help you to focus your collection of research materials. If your topic is too broad, you'll be forced to review a lot more research material than you're going to need. On the other hand, if you narrow your topic, you can also narrow your search for research materials. Put in terms of signal and noise (introduced in Unit 4), narrowing your topic will help you access more signal and less noise. Here are four methods for narrowing and limiting your topic: *topoi*, tree diagrams, fishbone diagrams, and search directories.

The Idea Generator: *Topoi*, The System of Topics. The second half of the idea generator is "*Topoi*, the system of topics," a technique that comes from the classical rhetorics of ancient Greece and Rome. Using this method of *topoi*, you'd ask yourself a series of questions about your general subject. The process will enable you to see divisions or aspects of your general topic on which you might want to focus. In Table 6.3 the columns on the left contain seven general questions (Who? What? Why? When? Where? How? and So?) and a series of subquestions (which will vary depending on your topic). The right column illustrates how some of the questions on the left might suggest specific aspects of the general subject of "homelessness." By asking these general and specific questions about a subject, you'll see how you can divide and analyze a topic into its significant parts.

Tree Diagrams. Tree diagrams help you divide your topic repeatedly into its significant parts. Starting with the general topic, you divide it into its

TABLE 6.3 *Topoi,* The System of Topics

These questions should enable you to use general topics to generate more specific ideas for your speeches. Try this system on any one of the topics listed in the Dictionary of Topics in Table 6.2. You'll be amazed at how many topics you'll be able to find. Your problem will quickly change from "What can I speak on?" to "Which one of these should I speak on?"

General Questions	Subject Specific Questions
Who?	
Who is he or she?	Who are the homeless?
Who is responsible?	Who is the typical homeless person?
To whom was it done?	Who is responsible for the increase in homelessness?
	Who cares for the homeless?
What?	
What is it?	What does it mean to be homeless?
What effects does it have?	What does homelessness do to the people themselves?
What is it like?	What does homelessness do to the society in general?
What is it different from?	What does homelessness mean to you and me?
What are some examples?	
Why?	
Why does it happen?	Why are there so many homeless people?
Why does it not happen?	Why did this happen?
When?	
When did it happen?	When did homelessness become so prevalent?
When will it occur?	When does it occur in the life of a person?
When will it end?	
Where?	
Where did it come from?	Where is homelessness most prevalent?
Where is it going?	Where is there an absence of homelessness?
Where is it now?	
How?	
How does it work?	How does someone become homeless?
How is it used?	How can we help the homeless?
How do you do it?	How can we prevent others from becoming homeless?
How do you operate it?	
How is it organized?	
So?	
What does it mean?	Why is homelessness such an important social problem?
What is important about it?	Why must we be concerned with homelessness?
Why should I be concerned with this?	
Who cares?	

parts. Then you take one of these parts and divide it into its parts. You continue with this process until the topic seems manageable—one that you can reasonably cover in some depth in the allotted time.

Take the topic of television programs as the first general topic area. You might divide this topic into such subtopics as comedy, children's programs, educational programs, news, movies, soap operas, quiz shows, and sports. You might then take one of these topics, say comedy, and divide it into subtopics. Perhaps you might consider it on a time basis and divide television comedy into its significant time periods: pre–1960, 1961–1979, 1980 to the present. Or, you might focus on situation comedies. Here you might examine a topic such as women in television comedy, race relations in situation comedy, or family relationships in television comedies. The resultant topic is at least beginning to look manageable. Television programs, without some limitation, would take a lifetime to cover adequately.

The construction of tree diagrams (actually, they resemble upside down trees) might clarify the process of narrowing a topic. Let's say, for example, that you want to do a speech on mass communication. You might develop a tree diagram with branches for the division that interests you most, as shown in Figure 6.1. Thus, you can divide mass communication into film, television, radio, newspapers, and magazines. If television interests you most, then develop branches from television. Comedy, news, soaps, sports, and quiz shows would be appropriate. Now, let's say that it's the soaps that most interest you. In this case you'd create branches from soaps, perhaps prime-time and daytime. Keep dividing the topic until you get something that is significant, appropriate to you and your audience, and manageable in the allotted time.

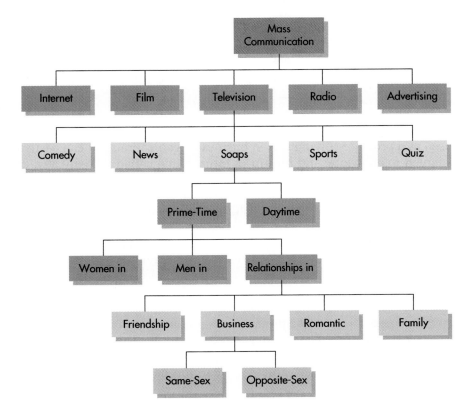

FIGURE 6.1

A Tree Diagram for Limiting Speech Topics.

How would you draw a tree diagram for limiting topics beginning with such general subjects as immigration, education, sports, transportation, or politics?

FIGURE 6.2

Fishbone Diagram for Limiting Topics.

How would you draw a fishbone diagram for limiting such topics as family, psychology, religion, crime, or economics?

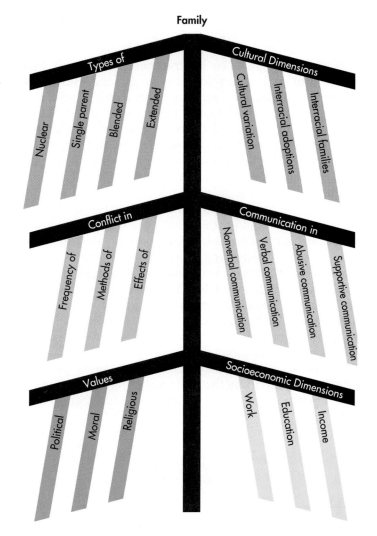

Family

Types of — Nuclear, Single parent, Blended, Extended

Cultural Dimensions — Cultural variation, Interracial adoptions, Interracial families

Conflict in — Frequency of, Methods of, Effects of

Communication in — Nonverbal communication, Verbal communication, Abusive communication, Supportive communication

Values — Political, Moral, Religious

Socioeconomic Dimensions — Work, Education, Income

Fishbones. Another useful diagram is the fishbone. The fishbone is widely used as a problem-solving tool in business organizations but can easily be adapted to analyzing and limiting a topic. Often called the Ishikawa diagram after its developer, Kaoru Ishikawa (Higgins 1994; Lumsden and Lumsden 1993), the diagram resembles the bones of a fish. The major topic appears at the head of the fish. The bones emanating from the spine are the major subtopics. The smaller bones coming out of these larger bones are the subdivisions of the subtopics. Let's say, for example, that you wanted to give a speech on "Family." Your fishbone diagram might come to look like that in Figure 6.2.

Once dissected in this way, you can easily see a variety of topics on which you might speak. Let's say you wanted to give your speech on family values. Your major propositions are already identified: political, moral, and religious. Or, you might want to limit your topic still further and focus exclusively on moral values. If so, you would then need to dissect the bones of "moral values" so that you could identify your major propositions. You might, for example, focus on types of moral values or on their decay or improvement or on their differences in different cultures.

Search Directories. A more technologically sophisticated way of both selecting and limiting your topic is to let a search directory do some of the work for you. A search directory is a nested list of topics. You go from the general to the specific by selecting a topic, and then a subdivision of that topic, and then a subdivision of that topic. The process is illustrated in Table 6.4.

YOUR PURPOSE

The purpose of your speech is your goal; it's what you hope to achieve during your speech. It identifies the effect that your want your speech to have on your audience. In constructing your speech, first identify your general purpose and then identify your specific purpose.

General Purposes

The three major purposes of public speeches are to inform, to persuade, and to serve some special occasion function. In the informative speech you seek to create understanding: to clarify, to enlighten, to correct misunderstandings, to demonstrate how something works. In this type of speech you'd rely most heavily on materials that amplify—examples, illustrations, definitions, testimony, audiovisual aids, and the like. In the persuasive

---

TABLE 6.4 Using Search Directories to Find and Limit Your Topic

This figure is based on material found on AltaVista (June 7, 1999). Your search-and-limit mission begins with selecting a topic from the first level, say, "Society & Politics." This gives you the list of topics in column 2. Selecting "Crime & Justice" produces the list in column 3. Selecting "crime prevention" produces a long list of Web sites and links to other sites, which is reproduced in Table 6.5.

First level topics	Second level topics	Third level topics
Automotive	Community & Culture	Crime by Type
Business & Finance	**Crime & Justice**	**Crime Prevention**
Computers & Internet	Environment	Criminal Law
Health & Fitness	Gender & Sexuality	Criminology
Hobbies & Interests	Government	District Attorneys
Home & Family	International Affairs	Famous Crimes
People & Chat	Issues & Policy	Law Enforcement
Reference & Education	Law	Missing Persons
Shopping & Services	News & Magazines	News & Research
Society & Politics	Politics	Prisons & Sentencing
Sports & Recreation	Religion & Belief	Services
Travel & Vacations	World Cultures	Victims & Complainants

TABLE 6.5 Results from a AltaVista Search Directory

Try using a search directory to locate and limit your next speech topic.

AltaVista ™   **Categories**   AltaVista Home

Search the LookSmart Directory:

Search [   ]   [Go!]

Search AltaVista for: [   ]   [Search]

World - **Society & Politics** - **Crime & Justice** - **Crime Prevention**

[Submit]   ◄   Click here to submit a site in this category   ⚠ **SmartTip**

National Crime Prevention Council
Non-profit organization helping to prevent crime. With prevention tips for home security to peer pressure to domestic violence.

Police Notebook, The
Great selection of articles on public safety issues including crime prevention, fire safety, personal security, first aid, and safe surfing.

CrimeStoppers International
Program in the US, UK and Australia in which the community and media join with law enforcement to solve and prevent crimes.

CAVEAT
Canadians Against Violence Everywhere Advocating its Termination is a volunteer education and advocacy group.

Children's Safety Network
Resources and technical assistance to maternal and child health agencies seeking to reduce unintentional injuries and violence to children.

Citizen Safety Center
Practical tips offered by the Office of Florida Attorney General and Florida's law enforcement community.

Crime Prevention Unit
Contains links to sites concerned with reducing opportunities for crime. Includes info on home incarceration.

Crime Prevention
Drawn from a brief to the Canadian Government by the Canadian Society for the Prevention of Cruelty to Children.

Crime-Free America
News stories, crime data and a forum to discuss the impact of crime in America and explore effective ways of preventing it.

Criminal Justice Resources
Index to US federal agencies, includes US and international stats and crime prevention pages, plus reports.

Denton County (TX) Crime Stoppers

speech you try to influence attitudes or behaviors: to strengthen or change existing attitudes or to get the audience to take some action. In this type of speech you'd rely heavily on materials that offer proof—on evidence, argument, and psychological appeals, for example.

In the persuasive speech you try to strengthen or change your listeners' attitudes and beliefs or perhaps move them to take some action. You would also communicate information, and so in the persuasive speech you'd use materials that amplify, illustrate, and define as well. In persuading an audience, however, you must go beyond simply providing information. You need to convince them to think or behave in a particular way by giving them a variety of logical, motivational, and ethical reasons.

The special occasion speech contains elements of both information and persuasion. You might, for example, introduce another speaker or a group of speakers, present a tribute, try to secure the goodwill of the listeners, or "just" entertain your listeners.

Specific Purposes

After you've established your general purpose, construct your specific purpose, which identifies more precisely what you aim to accomplish. For example, in an informative speech, your specific speech purpose would identify the information you want to convey to your audience. Here are a few examples on the topic of AIDS:

GENERAL PURPOSE: to inform

SPECIFIC PURPOSES: to inform my audience of the recent progress in AIDS research

to inform my audience of our college's plans for AIDS Awareness Day

to inform my audience of the currently used tests for HIV infection

In a persuasive speech, your specific purpose identifies what you want your audience to believe, to think, or, perhaps, to do. Here are a few examples, again on the topic of AIDS:

GENERAL PURPOSE: to persuade

SPECIFIC PURPOSES: to persuade my audience to contribute to AIDS research

to persuade my audience that they should be tested for HIV infection

to persuade my audience to become better informed about how AIDS can be transmitted

In formulating your specific purpose, keep the following three guidelines in mind.

Use an Infinitive Phrase.   Begin the statement of your specific purpose with the word "to" and elaborate on your general purpose, for example: *to inform my audience of the schedule of events for AIDS Awareness Day or*

TIPS from professional speakers

Consider the variety of ways a single topic—safety—might be handled. A speech to inform might explain the operation of a new item of safety equipment. A speech to stimulate might be given when presenting a safety award. A speech to convince might be given to community groups in an effort to persuade them to believe your organization operates with no danger to them. A speech to cause action might be delivered to a meeting of top management to get a favorable vote on the budget for your safety campaign.

Jerry Tarver, author and lecturer, "Face-to-Face Communication." In Carol Reuss and Donn Silvis, eds., *Inside Organizational Communication*, 2nd ed. (New York: Longman, 1985): 207.

My only concern was to get home after a hard day's work.
—Rosa Parks

to persuade my audience to contribute a book for the library fund raiser or to introduce the main speaker of the day.

Limit Your Specific Purpose. Limit your specific purpose in two ways. First, avoid the common pitfall of trying to accomplish too much in too short a time. For example, "to persuade my audience of the prevalence of AIDS in our community and that they should contribute money for AIDS services" contains two specific purposes. Select either "to persuade my audience of the prevalence of AIDS in our community" or "to persuade my audience to contribute money to services for persons with AIDS." Beware of specific purposes that contain the word "and;" it's often a sign that you have more than one purpose.

Second, limit your specific purpose to what you can reasonably develop in the allotted time. Specific purposes that are too broad are useless. Note how broad and overly general the following purposes are:

to inform my audience about clothing design

to persuade my audience to improve their health

Note how much more reasonable the following restatements are for a relatively short speech:

to inform my audience of the importance of color in clothing design

to persuade my audience to exercise three times a week

Use Specific Terms. Phrase your specific purpose with precise terms. The more precise your specific purpose, the more effectively it will guide you in the remaining steps of preparing your speech. Instead of saying "to persuade my audience to do something about AIDS," which is overly general, say "to persuade my audience to contribute food to homebound persons with AIDS."

YOUR THESIS

Your thesis is your main assertion; it's what you want the audience to absorb from your speech. The thesis of Lincoln's Second Inaugural Address

What three theses would you like to hear other students speak on? What three theses would you like to see other students avoid?

LISTEN TO THIS   How to Listen to Galileo and the Ghosts

"Galileo and the Ghosts" is a technique for seeing a topic or problem through the eyes of a particular group of people (DeVito 1996). It will help you see aspects of your topic that you might not see otherwise.

The technique involves setting up a mental "ghost-thinking team," much like executives and politicians hire ghostwriters to write their speeches or research institutes maintain think-tanks. In this ghost-thinking technique, you select a team of four to eight "people" you admire, for example, historical figures like Galileo or Aristotle, fictional figures like Wonder Woman or Captain Picard, or persons from other cultures or of a different sex or affectional orientation. Selecting people who are very different from you will increase the chances that widely different perspectives will be raised.

You pose a question or problem and then ask yourself how this team of ghosts would answer your question or solve your problem, allowing yourself to listen to what they have to say. Of course, you're really listening to yourself but to yourself acting in the role of another person. The technique forces you to step outside your normal role and to consider the perspective of someone totally different from you.

As you "listen" to your ghosts, your perception of the problem will probably change. Have your ghosts then view this new perception and perhaps analyze it again. Continue the process until you achieve a solution or decide that this technique has yielded all the insight it's going to yield.

(The next Listen to This box appears on page 218.)

was that Northerners and Southerners should work together for the entire nation's welfare; the thesis of the *Rocky* movies was that the underdog can win; the thesis of Martin Luther King Jr.'s "I Have a Dream" speech was that true equality must be granted to African Americans and to all people.

Let's say, for example, that you're planning to present a speech against using animals for experimentation. Your thesis statement might be something like this: "Animal experimentation should be banned." This is what you want your audience to believe as a result of your speech. Notice that in persuasive speeches, the thesis statement puts forth a point of view, an opinion. The thesis is arguable and debatable.

In an informative speech the thesis statement focuses on what you want your audience to learn. For example, a suitable thesis for an informative speech on jealousy might be: "There are two main theories of jealousy." Notice that here, as in all informative speeches, the thesis is relatively neutral and objective.

Be sure to limit the thesis statement to one central idea. Statements such as "Animal experimentation should be banned and companies engaging in it should be prosecuted" contain not one but two basic ideas.

Using Thesis Statements

The thesis statement serves three useful purposes. First, it helps you generate your main ideas or assertions. Second, it suggests suitable organizational patterns and strategies. Third, it focuses the audience's attention on your central idea. Let's look at each of these functions in more detail.

To Generate Main Ideas. Each thesis contains an essential question within it; this question allows you to explore and subdivide the thesis. Your objective is to find this question and pose it of your thesis. For example, let's take a hypothetical bill before Congress—call it the Hart bill—and let's say your thesis is: "The Hart bill provides needed services for senior citizens." Stated in this form, the obvious question suggested is "What are they?" The answer to this question suggests the main parts of your speech, for example, health, food, shelter, and recreational services. These four areas then become the four main points of your speech. An outline of the main ideas would look like this:

    I. The Hart bill provides needed health services.
    II. The Hart bill provides needed food services.
    III. The Hart bill provides needed shelter services.
    IV. The Hart bill provides needed recreational services.

The remainder of the speech would then be filled in with supporting materials. Under I, you might identify the several needed health services and explain how the Hart bill provides for these services. This first main division of your speech might, in outline, look something like this:

    I. The Hart bill provides needed health services.
      A. Neighborhood clinics will be established.
      B. Medical hotlines for seniors will be established.

In the completed speech, this first major proposition and its two subordinate statements might be spoken like this:

The Hart bill provides senior citizens with the health services they need so badly. Let me give you some examples of these badly needed health services. One of the most important services will be the establishment of neighborhood health clinics. These clinics will help senior citizens get needed health advice and services right in their own neighborhoods,

A second important health service will be the health hotlines. These phone numbers will be for the exclusive use of senior citizens. These hotlines . . .

To Suggest Organizational Patterns. The thesis provides a useful guideline in selecting your organizational pattern. For example, let's suppose your thesis is: "We can improve our own college educations." Your answer to the inherent question "What can we do?" will suggest a possible organizational pattern. If, for example, you identify the remedies in the order in which they should be taken, then a time-order pattern would be appropriate. If you itemize a number of possible solutions, all of which are of about equal importance, then a topical pattern would be appropriate. These and other patterns are explained in detail in Unit 12, "The Body of the Speech."

To Focus Audience Attention. The thesis sentence also focuses the audience's attention on your central idea. In some speeches you may wish to state your thesis early in your speech, for example, in the introduction or perhaps early in the body of the speech. There are instances, however, when you may not want to state your thesis. Or, you may want to state it late in your speech. For example, if your audience is hostile to your thesis, it may be wise to give your evidence and arguments first and gradually move the audience into a more positive frame of mind before stating your thesis.

In other cases, you may want the audience to infer your thesis without actually spelling it out. Audiences, especially uneducated ones, are not persuaded by speeches in which the speaker does not explicitly state the thesis. Listeners often fail to grasp what the thesis is and so don't change their attitudes or behaviors.

Make your decision as to when (or if) to state your thesis on the basis of what will be more effective in helping you achieve your specific purpose with your specific audience. Here are a few guidelines to help you make the right decision.

1. In an informative speech, state your thesis early, clearly, and directly.
2. In a persuasive speech where your audience is neutral or positive, state your thesis explicitly and early in your speech.
3. In a persuasive speech where your audience is hostile to your position, delay stating your thesis until you've moved them closer to your position.
4. Recognize that there are cultural differences in the way a thesis should be stated. In some Asian cultures, for example, making a point too directly or asking directly for audience compliance, may be considered rude or insulting.

Wording the Thesis

State your thesis as a simple declarative sentence. This will help you focus your thinking, your collection of materials, and your organizational pattern. You may, however, phrase your thesis in a number of different ways when you present it to your audience. At one extreme, you may state it to your audience as you phrased it for yourself, for example, "Animal experimentation must be banned" or "I want to tell you in this brief speech why animal experimentation must be stopped." Or, you may decide to state your thesis as a question, for example, "Why should we ban animal experimentation?" or "Are there valid reasons for banning animal experimentation?"

In persuasive speeches where you face a hostile or mildly opposed audience, you may wish to state your thesis in vague and ambiguous terms, for example, "I want to talk about animal experimentation" or "Is there are problem with our current policy regarding animal experimentation? Let's look at what our policy is and see if it should be changed." In these cases you focus the audience's attention on your central idea, but you delay presenting your specific point of view until a more favorable time.

Thesis and Purpose: Some Differences

The thesis and purpose are both guides to help you select and organize your speech materials. Because they both serve similar goals, they are often confused, and so it may help to identify some of the ways in which they are different.

First, the thesis and purpose differ in their form of expression. The thesis is phrased as a complete declarative sentence, for example, "The education budget must be increased." The purpose, on the other hand, is phrased as an infinitive phrase, for example, "to inform" or "to persuade."

Second, they differ in their focus. The thesis is message-focused; it identifies the central idea of your speech; it summarizes—it epitomizes—the content of your speech. In contrast, the purpose is audience-focused; it identifies the change you hope to achieve in your audience, for example, to gain information, to change attitudes, or to act in a certain way.

Third, they differ in their concern for practical limitations. The thesis epitomizes the speech without regard to practical limitations of, say, time or the attitudes of the audience. The purpose, on the other hand, takes into consideration the time you have to speak and the attitudes of the audience toward you and your topic. The purpose, therefore, needs to be phrased with the practical limitations in mind. In this sense, the purpose specifies what you hope to achieve once you've established your thesis. For example, the thesis might be, "Colleges are not educating students for today's world." The speech, however, may have several different purposes, for example: (1) to persuade my audience that colleges must change to keep pace with today's world, (2) to persuade my audience to adapt the Illinois Educational Proposal, or (3) to persuade my audience to quit college.

Here are a few more examples to clarify further the difference between thesis and purpose:

THESIS: You can reduce your phone bills.
PURPOSE: To inform my audience of three ways to save on their phone bills.

THESIS: Computer science knowledge is essential.
PURPOSE: To persuade my audience to take a computer science course.

Especially in your early stages of mastering public speaking, formulate both the thesis statement and the purpose. With both the thesis and the purpose clearly formulated, you'll be able to construct a more coherent and more understandable speech.

UNIT IN BRIEF

Your Topic

Speech topics should be:
- Worthwhile
- Appropriate to the speaker, audience, and occasion
- Culture-sensitive

Speech topics may be found through:
- Surveys
- News items
- Brainstorming
- Dictionary of topics

Speech topics may be limited by:
- *Topoi,* the system of topics
- Tree diagrams
- Fishbone diagrams
- Search directories

Your Purpose	Speech purposes are both:
	■ General (for example, to inform or persuade)
	■ Specific (for example, to inform my audience of the new health plan options)
	Specific purposes should be:
	■ Phrased as an infinitive phrase
	■ Limited to one main point and to what can reasonably be accomplished
	■ Phrased with precise terms
Your Thesis	Speech theses should be:
	■ Phrased as complete declarative sentences
	■ Clear and specific
	■ Limited to one central idea or focus
	Speech theses may be used to:
	■ Generate main ideas
	■ Suggest organizational patterns
	■ Focus audience attention

THINKING CRITICALLY ABOUT TOPICS, PURPOSES, AND THESES

REVIEWING KEY TERMS AND CONCEPTS IN PUBLIC SPEAKING TOPICS, PURPOSES, AND THESES

1. Define the key terms used in this unit:

❑ topic (p. 99)
❑ taboos (p. 100)
❑ brainstorming (p. 102)
❑ *topoi* (p. 109)
❑ tree diagrams (p. 110)
❑ fishbone diagrams (p. 112)
❑ search directories (p. 113)
❑ general purpose p. 113)
❑ specific purpose (p. 115)
❑ thesis (p. 116)

2. Review the key concepts discussed in this unit.

■ What are the characteristics of an effective speech topic? How might speech topics be found and limited?
■ What are the types of speech purposes? How should speech purposes be formulated?
■ What is the speech thesis? How might it be used? How should it be phrased?

DEVELOPING PUBLIC SPEAKING STRATEGIES

1. Jill wants to give a speech on women's rights but she can't seem to narrow it down to manageable proportions. Everything she comes across seems important and cries out for inclusion in the speech. What advice would you give Jill to help her narrow and focus her general topic?

2. George and Iris want to give their speeches on opposite sides of Megan's Law—the law requiring that residents be notified if a convicted sex offender is living in close proximity. George is against the law and Iris is for it. If George and Iris were giving their speeches to your class, what would you advise each of them to do concerning the statement of their theses?

EVALUATING PUBLIC SPEECHES

1. Read one of the speeches contained in this text or on one of the many websites identified throughout the text and identify the specific topic, purpose, and thesis. Would you consider the topic worthwhile, appropriate, and culture-sensitive if, say, given in your class?

2. Mentally review the speeches you've heard in this class. Did the speakers narrow their topics to manageable proportions? If not, what specific suggestions might you offer for helping them narrow their topics more effectively?

USING TECHNOLOGY IN PUBLIC SPEAKING

1. If you're still having trouble finding a topic, visit http://www.compassnet.com/~rdeneefe/topicgen.htm. It's a random topic generator that will suggest topics for conversation, writing, or public speaking.

2. Visit one of the news Web sites (for example, http://www.cnn.com/, http://www.sfgate.com/, or http://www.usatoday.com/). How many topics for public speaking can you derive from just this one Web site?

3. A useful list of over 250 debate topics that can be modified for both informative and persuasive speeches can be found at the International Islamic University Malaysia's Web site at http://www.iiu.edu.my/stadd/spice/topics.html.

PRACTICALLY SPEAKING

6.1 Short Speech Technique

Prepare and deliver a two-minute speech in which you:

a. explain what makes a good speech topic.

b. explain the thesis of a particular movie or television sitcom.

c. explain the thesis of one or a few recent lectures you've heard.

d. evaluate the topics of recent talk shows against the criteria for a worthwhile and appropriate topic.

e. explain the cultural factors operating in this class that need to be taken into consideration by the speaker selecting a topic and purpose.

6.2 Brainstorming for Topics

Together with a small group of students or with the class as a whole, sit in a circle and brainstorm for suitable speech topics. Be sure to appoint someone to write down all the contributions, or use a recorder.

After this brainstorming session, consider these questions:

1. Did any members give negative criticism (even nonverbally)?

2. Did any members hesitate to contribute really wild ideas? Why?

3. Was it necessary to restimulate the group members at any point? Did this help?

4. Did some useful speech topics emerge in the brainstorming session?

6.3 Limiting Topics

Here are a few overly general topics. Using one of the methods discussed in this unit (or any other method you're familiar with), limit the topic to one that would be reasonable for a five to 10 minute speech.

1. Dangerous sports.
2. Race relationships.
3. Parole.
4. Censorship on the Internet.
5. Ecological problems.
6. Problems faced by college students.
7. Morality.
8. Health and fitness.
9. Ethical issues in politics.
10. Urban violence.

Researching Your Speech Topic

UNIT CONTENTS	UNIT OBJECTIVES
	After completing this unit, you should be able to:
General Principles of Research	Explain the general principles for conducting research.
General Internet Resources	Explain the values of e-mail, newsgroups, chat groups, and the World Wide Web for researching speech topics.
Databases	Explain the major databases for general reference works, news items, articles and posts, and books.
"Experts" and the Interview	Explain the advantages of using experts and the general principles for interviewing.
Critically Evaluating Research	Explain the suggested standards for critically evaluating research.
Integrating Research in Your Speech	Explain the ways to cite your sources and avoid the suspicion of plagiarism.

Suppose that you're to speak on immigration policies. Where do you go for information? How can you learn about the different immigration policies? How do you find the evidence and arguments bearing on current policies and proposed changes? What are the legal issues involved? What were the prominent legal battles? What are the moral implications of the varied immigration policies and proposals? How does granting asylum to political dissidents impact on immigration policy? Research will enable you to answer these and hundreds of other questions.

You'll probably use traditional printed books, journals, magazines, newspapers, and pamphlets alongside computerized sources such as e-mail, newsgroups, the World Wide Web, and a vast array of computerized databases on CD ROM and online. Because the information available on just about any topic is so vast, it's understandably daunting for many people. At the same time, however, the same technology that has produced this tremendous expansion of available information has also made searching it easy and efficient.

Because research is so important in public speaking (as well as in your other courses and in your professional career) and because research methods are changing so rapidly, it's important to cover this topic in some detail. In this unit, then, we first cover some general principles of research and provide guidelines for doing all kinds of research. Second, we focus on the Internet and cover the four major resources available to the researcher (e-mail, Usenet groups, chat groups, and the World Wide Web) and offer suggestions on how to use them for researching your topic. Third, we examine a variety of databases—organized collections of information—for finding general reference works, news items, articles and posts, and books, and we offer guides for accessing these effectively and efficiently. Fourth, we consider how "experts" may be used in the research process and offer suggestions for conducting the research interview. Fifth, we focus on ways to evaluate your sources, the critical standards you should apply to the information your research uncovers. Sixth, we suggest ways you might integrate your research into your speech and ways to cite it at the end of your speech outline.

Before beginning this research excursion, consider your own research competencies by taking the accompanying self-test. You may wish to return to this self-test at the end of this unit or even at the end of the course to see if there's any change.

TEST YOURSELF
What Are Your Research Competencies?

Indicate your research competencies by responding to each of the items with the following scale:

A = Finding this would be simple; I'd be able to find it with a relatively direct search.

B = Finding this would be possible, but would take some effort; I'd probably not be able to find it with a direct search but would make a few wrong turns before I eventually found it.

C = Finding this would be impossible without asking someone for help; I wouldn't really know where to begin.

_____ 1. an article on India that appeared in the *New York Times* sometime in 1999
_____ 2. 10 newsgroups dealing with the topic of computers
_____ 3. 10 listservs dealing with topics relating to your professional goal
_____ 4. the most recent stock quotation for IBM
_____ 5. 10 abstracts of articles dealing with hepatitis
_____ 6. the communication courses offered at Kansas State University
_____ 7. the population of Toronto and Tokyo
_____ 8. the speeches given during the last session of Congress
_____ 9. the biography of a state political figure
_____ 10. recent law cases dealing with sexual harassment

One way to review this test and this topic generally is to share your responses and your own research strengths and weaknesses in a small group of five or six others or with the entire class. As you discuss the various responses also consider: Which avenues of research are the most efficient? Which are the most reliable? Which will prove the most credible with your peers?

There are two types of knowledge. One is knowing a thing. The other is knowing where to find it.
—Samuel Johnson

GENERAL PRINCIPLES OF RESEARCH

After you've selected your topic, you'll need to find information on it—statistics, arguments for or against a proposition, examples, biographical data, or research findings, for example. Here are some general principles to help you do your research more efficiently and effectively.

Examine What You Know

Begin your search by examining what you already know. Before Edward Gibbon, the famed English historian and author of *The History of the Decline and Fall of the Roman Empire,* would begin to write a new book, he would take a long walk or sit alone and try to recall everything he knew about the topic. Only after doing this did he move on to other sources of information. Winston Churchill followed the same procedure when preparing his speeches.

Write down what you know, for example, about books or articles on the topic or persons who might know something about the topic. In this way you can attack the problem systematically and not waste effort and time.

Also consider what you know from your own personal experiences and observations. In assessing these experiences and observations do realize that we all have a self-serving bias and that we often remember and explain things in a way that makes us look good.

Work from the General to the Specific

After you've examined all you know about a topic, continue your search by getting an authoritative but general overview of the topic. An encyclopedia article will serve this purpose well. Although a bit more difficult—you'll have to sift through lots of noise—you could also search the Web (querying a few search engines) for some general overview. This will help you see both the topic as a whole and how its various parts fit together. Many of these articles contain references or links to direct the next stage of your search for more specific information. After securing this overview, consult increasingly specific and specialized materials, for example, newspaper articles, statistical reports, biographical information, or research reports (all are discussed in the next sections of this unit).

Take Accurate Notes

The more accurate your notes are, the less time you'll waste going back to sources to check on a date or spelling. Accurate records will also prevent you from going to sources you've already consulted but may have forgotten.

If you want to collect your material on paper, a looseleaf notebook works well to keep everything relating to a speech or article in the same place. Another advantage of this format is that you can photocopy book pages and articles and print material from the Internet and insert them in the appropriate places (don't waste time copying long quotations and statistics). If you want to file your material electronically, create a folder and title it something like **PublicSpeaking/Speech1:Immigration**. This will work especially well if you have a scanner and can scan into your folder material you find in print. In this notebook or folder, you can retain the sources consulted, quotations, ideas, arguments, suggested references, preliminary outlines, and material you've printed or downloaded in this one place.

Key your notes to the topics in your preliminary speech outline. For example, let's say that your speech is to be on immigration. Your preliminary outline looks like this:

Immigration
    I. Political aspects
   II. Legal aspects
  III. Moral aspects

You might then classify your notes under these three major topics. Simply head the page with "political, "legal," or "moral." Taking notes with your preliminary outline will help focus your research and will remind you of those topics for which you need more information.

Because this is a preliminary outline, you'll need a large category for miscellaneous information. Here you'd put all the interesting information that you're not sure you'll use and yet don't want to lose.

Make sure your notes are complete (and legible). If you have to err, then err on the side of having notes that are too detailed. You can always cut the quotation or select one example out of the three at a later time. As you take notes, be sure to identify the source so that you can find that reference again should you need it. You might also want to include its location so you can find the source again.

Use Research Time Effectively

Manage the time you have effectively and efficiently. If you're going to give two speeches on the same topic, do the research for both at the same time. Don't wait until you've finished the first speech to begin researching the second. You might, for example, divide your notebook into two sections or create another folder and insert the material with appropriate cross-references.

When searching the Net, it's easy to get lured into taking long detours. These are often excellent learning experiences and so shouldn't be discouraged. It will help, however, if you keep your purpose clearly in mind—even to the point of writing it down—as you surf the Net or lurk among the newsgroups.

Access your college library from home, if you can; it will save you time if you can go to the library with your searches already completed.

Learn the Available Sources of Information and Research Tools

You can make research a lot easier if you learn the available sources of information and the relevant research tools. Learn what is available, where, and in what form. For example, spend a few hours in the library learning where some of the most useful materials are located or how they can be accessed. Learn the computer search facilities that are available at your college library and at neighboring public or college libraries for

I find that a great part of the information I have was acquired by looking up something and finding something else on the way.
—Franklin P. Adams

accessing newspapers, research articles, corporate reports, magazines, or any type of media you may wish to use. Learn, too, the search engines and search directories and how to use them efficiently. Just as you'd keep a list of the books you use in your research, keep a list of the Web sites that are most appropriate for topics you're interested in. For example, if you were especially interested in health issues, then you'd want to become familiar with the National Institute of Health's Web site (http://www.nih.gov). Bookmark the general Web address for the site or your actual query. In this latter case, when you want to return to this search, the search engine will perform the varied operations it went through in the first place but it will pull up the up-dated sources.

One recommended short-cut to learning the available sources of information is to consult your librarian. Librarians are experts in the very issues that may be giving you trouble. They'll be able to help you access biographical material, indexes of current articles, materials in specialized collections at other libraries, and a wide variety of computerized databases.

GENERAL INTERNET RESOURCES

Although you'll no doubt use a variety of research sources—both print and electronic—it's important to realize at the start that it's a lot easier to do your research by computer. For all its convenience and efficiency, however, the Internet isn't the only useful place to go for information; a great deal of useful information is available on microfiche, microfilm, and, of course, in print.

Perhaps the greatest advantage is that in computer research you browse through a larger number of sources in less time and with greater accuracy and thoroughness than you could do manually. And, in many cases, you can do this research at your own convenience since electronic sources are available 24 hours a day and from your own home.

Researching by computer enables you to do combined searches, something you can't do manually. If, for example, you're researching drugs and violence, you don't have to review all the references to drugs to see if any also deal with violence (as you would with print indexes). You can request a computer search for all and only the references dealing with "drugs and violence." Similarly, you can more easily locate related information. For example, many computerized information sources are hypertext-based and thus allow you to select highlighted terms to go to related documents. An added convenience is that you can download the information to your computer or print it out instead of copying it longhand as had to be done just a few years ago. There are four major Internet avenues you'll want to consider in researching your speeches: e-mail, newsgroups, chat groups, and the World Wide Web (see Figure 7.1). An older and less often used part of the Internet is gopherspace, which contains a wide variety of documents that may prove interesting. Figure 7.1 provides a sample gopher menu and the means for accessing gopher.

E-mail and Listservs

Through e-mail you can write to specific people, to a group, or to what is called a listserv—an e-mail list of several to perhaps hundreds of people who exchange messages on a relatively specific topic at a rate of perhaps

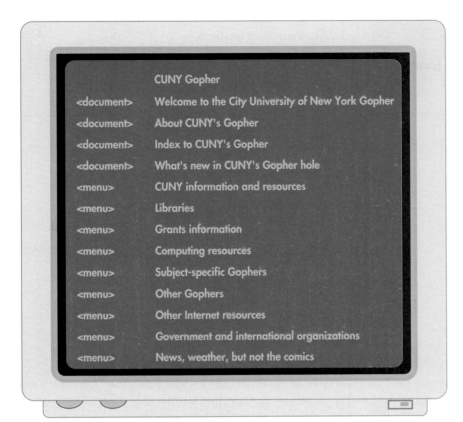

FIGURE 7.1

A Sample Gopher Menu.

Because of the popularity and enormity of the Web, it has almost become synonymous with the Internet. But the Web is really only a part of the Internet. Some researchers find gopher useful. As shown here, gopher provides you with a system of menus through which you get around the Internet, exploring gopher-space. Try accessing gopher://gopher.utah.edu:3000/7. In what ways might the public speaker find gopher useful in doing research?

several to hundreds a week. Some listserv messages will be from other members and some will be postings from, for example, the press, which some member copies and distributes.

E-mail may prove useful in public speaking in several ways. For example, you can write to specific people who may be experts in the topic you're researching. Internet services are now making it quite easy to locate a person's e-mail address. Try, for example, the Netscape people page— which you can access from Netscape's home page or by going to http://guide.netscape.com/guide/people.html—or Yahoo's directory (http://www.yahoo.com/search/people/) and their links to numerous other directories such as Yahoo's white pages (http://www.yahoo.com/Reference/White-Pages/). Another useful people search tool is http://www.procd.com/hl/direct.htm. Also, try the sites that specialize in e-mail addresses such as Four11 (http://www.four11.com), WhoWhere? (http://www.whowhere.com), and Switchboard (www.switchboard.com). Four11 also provides a directory of regular telephone numbers as well as special directories for government personnel and for celebrities.

You can use e-mail to join a mailing list or listserv that focuses on the topic you're researching and learn from the collective insights of all members. You can explore potentially useful listservs by visiting the Liszt Web site (www.liszt.com), a directory of information about a wide variety of listservs and whether new members are welcomed (see Figure 7.2). In joining a listserv remember to lurk before contributing; get a feel for the

group and for the types of messages they send. Read the frequently asked questions (FAQs) to avoid asking questions that have already been answered. The types of questions listserv members seem to favor are those that ask for ideas and insights rather than those that ask for information readily available elsewhere.

If your class is set up as a listserv, you'd be able to communicate with everyone else through e-mail. You'd be able, for example, to distribute an audience analysis questionnaire to see what your audience knows about your topic or what their attitudes are about a variety of issues. The sample questionnaires presented in the next unit would be excellent to distribute via e-mail and would enable you to find out what you need to know about your audience to adjust your speech to them. You'd also be able to set up a critique group with a few others from your class to get feedback on your speech or outline, or even moral support. Such a group would also be helpful for people who want to ask questions or try out an idea before presenting it in the actual speech.

When working in small groups, e-mail can also be of great value. For example, meetings can be planned and coordinated, announcements can be distributed, questions can be raised and answered, and ideas can be debated within a listserv.

Newsgroups

Newsgroups are discussion forums for the exchange of ideas on a wide variety of topics. There are thousands of newsgroups on the Internet (the overall system of newsgroups is referred to as Usenet) where you can post your messages (also called "articles" or "posts"), read the messages of others, and respond to the messages you read. Messages, replies to them, replies to the replies, and so on constitute a thread, a collection of messages unified by a focus on a specific topic. Newsgroups are much like list-servs in that they bring together a group of people interested in communicating about a common topic. Some newsgroups also include messages from news services such as the Associated Press or Reuters.

Newsgroups are hierarchically organized with a general topic at the top, and more specific topics as you go down the hierarchy. Currently there are eight major newsgroup hierarchies: computers and computing, Usenet and newsgroups, recreation, science, social issues, and three miscellaneous categories, designated as Alt., Misc., and Talk. Much like a listserv, you'd join a newsgroup and then have access to all the postings of the group's members. Unlike the listserv, which sends messages directly to your e-mail account (and can quickly result in information overload), the newsgroup's postings remain on the server so you can access them when you want.

Some newsgroups (and listservs) are moderated—someone evaluates submitted posts and decides whether or not to publish them. Other newsgroups (and listservs) are unmoderated; in these, your article is posted automatically. Usually, but not always, the moderated groups are focused more on content and are more serious; the unmoderated groups are more social and less serious.

Newsgroups are useful to the public speaker for a variety of reasons. The most obvious reason is that newsgroups are useful sources of information; they contain news items, letters, and papers on just about any topic you can think of. Because there are so many newsgroups, you should have no problem finding several that deal with topics on which you'll be speaking. You can also save the news items you're particularly interested in to your own file. Internet search engines such as Deja News (http://www.dejanews.com/) or any of a variety of others (see Figure 7.3) will search the available newsgroups for the topics you request. You simply submit key

FIGURE 7.3

Deja.com, formerly known as Deja News.

This site has one of the best search engines for locating newsgroups. Try searching with Deja.com. Can you locate any newsgroups that focus on one of your speech topics?

words that best describe your research topic, and the program will search its database of newsgroups and provide you with a list of article titles and authors along with the date on which they were written and the relevance score for each article. You then click on any of the titles that seem most closely related to what you're looking for. Reading through the Usenet FAQ file—http://sunsite.unc.edu/usenet-i/info-center-faq.html—will help you get the maximum benefit from your Usenet connections.

Newgroups offer lots of advantages to the researching public speaker. For example, those newsgroups that get news feeds are especially useful because the information is so current and very likely in greater detail than you'd find in newspapers, which have to cut copy to fit space limitations. You're also more likely to find a greater diversity of viewpoints than you'd find in most newspapers or news magazines.

Another advantage is that through newsgroups you can ask questions and get the opinions of others for your next speech. Newsgroups also provide an easily available and generally receptive audience to whom you can communicate your thoughts and feelings.

Chat Groups

Chat groups such as you'll find on the commercial Internet Service Providers and the increasingly popular Internet Relay Chat groups enable you to communicate with others in real time (called *synchronous conversation* as opposed to *asynchronous conversation* in which there's a delay between the message-sending and the message-receiving). These types of groups use the same general principles and so will be discussed under the general label of "chat groups." Real time communication obviously has its advantages; you can ask questions, respond to feedback, and otherwise adjust your message to the specific receivers. One great disadvantage, however, is that you may not find anyone you want to talk with when you log on. Unlike e-mail, you can't leave a message. Chat groups, like listservs and newsgroups, are subject specific and, because there are so many of

One cyberlibrarian draws a distinction between "technophiles" who think everything on the Web is accurate and trustworthy and "technophobes" who think just the reverse; they try to discredit all Internet information and prefer printed sources (James-Catalano 1996). How do you feel about information on the Internet? Do these attitudes influence the way you use and evaluate Internet information?

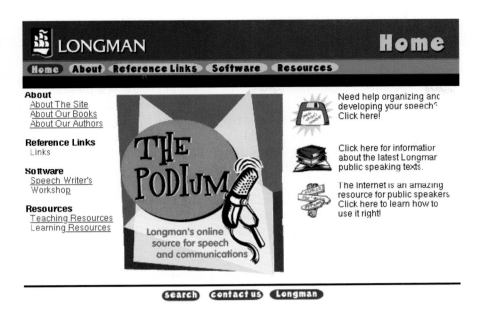

FIGURE 7.4
The Podium Web site.

Log on to the Podium (http://longman.awl.com/podium). What can you learn about public speaking from this Web site?

them (they number in the thousands), you're likely to find some dealing with the topics you're researching.

Another advantage of chat rooms and IRC channels is that you can establish one yourself. With other members of your class, you can then discuss the topics you're interested in. Like listservs, chat groups are ideally suited for offering feedback and support. The problem with chat groups is that everyone has to be online at the same time; with listservs you can send and receive mail at your convenience.

The World Wide Web

The World Wide Web is the most interesting and most valuable part of the Internet for research; it's a collection of documents—some containing graphic, audio, and video components. Some documents appear in abstract form and increasingly in full text form. Newpapers, news-magazines, and numerous books are available in full text through some publisher or library. Some Web sites are available to the general public and others are available only by subscription. Figure 7.4 presents a page of a Web site, "The Podium," that is devoted to public speaking.

In some instances you may know the Web address of the source you want to consult. In this case you'd access the Web site by simply entering the address in your Web browser. Fortunately, Web addresses are becoming more standardized, making it easier for you to predict many relevant addresses. For example, the Web address of most corporations follow the same general format: www.NameOfCorporation.com, for example, www.Microsoft.com. You can access these Web sites for copies of speeches, annual reports, or other information you might need for your speech.

Generally, this information will be sent to your e-mail address so you'd be able to print out whatever they send.

In most cases, however, searching the Web efficiently for speech topics requires the use of search engines and subject directories and some knowledge of how they operate (see Table 7.1). A search engine is a program that searches a database or index of Internet sites for the specific words you submit. These search engines are easily accessed through your Internet browser. And, in fact, the popular browsers—Netscape and Internet Explorer, for example—have search functions as a part of their own home pages; they also provide convenient links to the most popular search engines and directories.

You use all the search engines in essentially the same way; you type in a word or phrase and the program searches its databases and presents you with a list of sites (sometimes with an indication of how relevant the

---

TABLE 7.1 Popular Search Engines and Directories for Surfing the Internet

Netscape and Internet Explorer assume that the address begins with http:// so you can really leave this out; Netscape also assumes the www and the .com so you can leave these out as well. Most of these engines support some degree of Boolean operators enabling you to narrow your searches more effectively (see Table 7.2).

Search Engines and Directories	Features
Yahoo (see Figure 7.5) http://www.yahoo.com	A search engine and a directory; enables you to search the Web, Usenet groups, and e-mail directories; contains news articles and Internet events (see Figure 7.5).
Excite http://www.excite.com	A search engine and a directory; also provides news summaries and evaluations of Web sites; enables you to search for Web sites and newsgroups by keywords and concepts—for example, if you ask it to search for "military personnel," it will also search for soldier, sailor, marine, and so on.
Alta Vista http://altavista.digital.com	Enables search of both the Web and Usenet groups; extremely comprehensive.
Infoseek http://www.infoseek.com	A combination search engine and directory; it also contains directories of e-mail addresses as well as several useful reference books—dictionary, thesaurus, and book of quotations; searches the Web, Usenet groups, and wire services.
Lycos http://www.lycos.com	A search engine and a directory for Web, gopher, and FTP sites; performs searches of the Web partly based on the popularity of the Web sites; its database is built not from all the words in a document but rather on key words such as titles and headings.
HotBot http://www.hotbot.com	Searches the Web and usenet groups; uses a unique series of pull down menus to help you narrow your search.
Webcrawler http://www.webcrawler.com	Both a search engine and a directory; searches a database of especially popular Web sites.
MetaCrawler http://www.metacrawler.com/	One of a variety of meta-search engines; submits your search request to several search engines at the same time, performs parallel searches, and then provides a collated list of sites based on the key words you submitted.

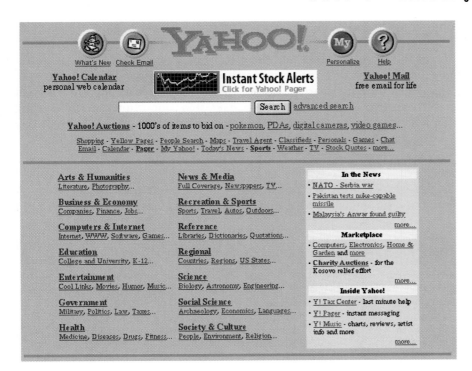

FIGURE 7.5

Yahoo!

Log on to Yahoo! and search for your next speech topic. Compare the results you get when you submit exactly the same words to one of the other search engines listed in Table 7.1. How are they the same? How are they different?

source will be to you—based in part on the number of times the words you typed in appear in the document—and sometimes with a brief description of the site) you can click on to visit.

A **directory** serves a similar function but does it differently. A directory is a list of subjects or categories of Web links. As mentioned in our discussion of limiting topics in Unit 6 (see Tables 6.4 and 6.5), you begin the process by selecting the category you're most interested in, and then a subcategory of that, and then a subcategory of that until you reach the specific topic you're interested in. A directory doesn't cover everything; rather, the documents that it groups under its various categories are selected by the directory's staff from those they feel especially worthwhile, and they group them as seems reasonable.

Many search engines also provide directories. Yahoo, Excite, Infoseek, and others, for example, are both search engines and directories. Other popular directories include Magellan (http://www.mckinley.com/) and Point (http://www.pointcom.com/).

Because the databases these engines search are so vast and because they may search for all occurrences of the words you submit, they invariably pull up lots of noise—documents that are totally unrelated to what you're looking for. Because of this it's important to narrow your search and ask the search engine to look for specific rather than general topics. Further, most of the search engines and directories—despite their frequent updates—will include a variety of expired links. Expect this; it's one of the inevitable problems created by a system that is so vast in size and that's constantly changing.

Because each search engine or directory uses a somewhat different database and a different method for searching, no two will yield the same results, even when the exact same request is submitted to each. So, when conducting research, be sure to use several of these search engines and directories. A good practice is to bookmark or list among your "favorites" each of the search engines and directories in Table 7.1; in this way you'll have a wide arsenal of resources to choose from, depending on your specific needs. In using search engines you'll find Boolean operators a great help in narrowing your searches to manageable proportions and to focusing it on what you want and away from what you don't want (see Table 7.2).

DATABASES

A database is simply organized information contained in one place. A dictionary, an encyclopedia, an index to magazines, and a collection of

---

TABLE 7.2   Boolean Operators and Truncation Symbols to Narrow Internet Searches

Let's say you're interested in researching the topic of drugs and violence in high schools for your next speech. Using Boolean operators and truncation symbols can help you get the material you need more efficiently, even though different search engines don't all use these shortcuts in the same way. Some search engines have pull down menus that enable you to limit your search by selecting one of the menu items. So, learn the most popular Boolean operators and truncation symbols but be sure to check with the specific search engine for its own unique search methods. These shortcuts will also help you search many CD ROM databases. If you want to learn more about Boolean logic and how it can be used to surf the Web, visit http://arlo.wilsonhs.pps.k12.or.us/boolean.html.

Search Operators	Search
AND, + drugs AND violence + drugs + violence	Limits the search to only those documents that contain both words—in any order.
OR drugs OR violence drugs violence	Searches for documents containing either word; usually, if you type the two words with a space between them, an OR search will be performed as the default.
NOT violence and schools NOT elementary violence and schools -elementary	Limits the search to documents containing both violence and schools but excludes those that also contain the word "elementary," thus enabling you to exclude all those articles that focus on elementary schools. Do note, however, that by excluding articles containing the word "elementary" you might also exclude articles that focus on high schools but also and perhaps casually mention elementary schools as well. Similarly, an article titled "Elementary Issues about Drugs and Violence in High Schools" would be lost.
NEAR drugs NEAR violence	Limits your search to documents containing the two items in close proximity to each other, though each search engine defines "near" differently.
Nesting drugs AND (violence OR assault)	Limits your search to documents with the word drugs and either violence or assault.
wild card communicat*	(Generally) will search for all forms of the word: communicating, communicate, communication, communicated, and communicates.
quotation marks "drugs and violence in high schools"	Searches for that complete phrase and retrieves only those articles that have that exact phrase.

abstracts from hundreds of journals are all examples of databases. Databases may be in print, for example, *Psychological Abstracts,* or computerized, for example, *Psychlit.*

Once you've selected your topic, consult a directory of the available databases to locate the appropriate database(s). Your library will have directories of the available databases for which access may be secured. In these directories, you'd discover the particular database that would contain the subject area you want to research. Librarians will be familiar with the various databases; make use of their expertise. Some databases may be reserved for faculty or graduate students; some may have to be done by the librarian. Some databases are extremely expensive and are beyond the budgets of many libraries, so even though you may find the right database, you may not have access to it.

Here we look at databases under four headings: general reference sources, news items, articles and posts, and books.

General Reference Sources

General reference sources are often your first stop in conducting research. These resources provide you with some basic information that can help you think more clearly about your topic and provide you with leads to more specialized sources. Here we discuss just a few general sources: encyclopedias, biographical dictionaries, almanacs, and a somewhat dissimilar source, museum collections and exhibits.

Encyclopedias. One of the best places to start researching your topic is a standard encyclopedia. It will give you a general overview of the subject and suggestions for additional reading. The most comprehensive and the most prestigious is the *Encyclopaedia Britannica,* available in print (32 volumes), on CD ROM, and online. A variety of other encyclopedias are also available on CD ROM, for example, *Compton's Multimedia Encyclopedia, Grolier's, Collier's,* and *Encarta.* CD ROM and online encyclopedias have great advantages; they allow you to locate articles, maps, diagrams, and even definitions of difficult terms (through the built-in dictionary) more easily and efficiently than hard copy volumes. For example, you'd locate articles simply by typing in terms that describe the topic you want to explore. Video illustrations and audio capabilities enable you to see the exploding volcano and the heart pumping blood and to hear the pronunciation of foreign terms and the music of particular instruments. Hypertext capabilities enable you to get additional information on any term or phrase that is highlighted in the video display. Simply select the highlighted phrase and you'll get this other article on screen. You can then, of course, shift back and forth among these articles. Most of the CD ROM encyclopedias have accompanying Web sites that provide periodic updates of the articles and additional materials, thus ensuring both recency and completeness.

The Encyclopedia Americana, and *The Academic American Encyclopedia* are excellent and comprehensive print encyclopedias. These works provide much insight into just about any subject you might look up. The *Americana* consists of 30 volumes and, as its title implies, focuses on American issues. The articles are generally shorter and easier to read than those in the *Britannica.* The *Academic American Encyclopedia* is

It's [success in the media] in the preparation—in those dreary pedestrian virtues they taught you in seventh grade and you didn't believe.
—Diane Sawyer

addressed specifically to high school and college students. It contains many essays on topics frequently discussed in the classroom.

There are also many specialized encyclopedias. Those devoted to religion include the *New Catholic Encyclopedia* (15 volumes) which contains articles on such topics as philosophy, science, and art, showing how these have been influenced by and have influenced the Catholic Church; *Encyclopaedia Judaica* (16 volumes plus yearbooks) which emphasizes Jewish life and includes biographies and detailed coverage of the Jewish contribution to world culture; and *Encyclopedia of Islam* and *Encyclopaedia of Buddhism* which cover the development, beliefs, institutions, and personalities of Islam and Buddhism, respectively. Supplement these with appropriate Web sites devoted to specific religions, for example, http://www.utm.edu/martinarea/fbc/bfm.html (Southern Baptist), http://www.catholic.org/index.html (Catholic), http://www.geocities.com/RodeaDrive/1415/indexd.html (Hinduism), http://www.utexas.edu/students/amso (Islam), and http://jewishnet.net (Jewish-related sites).

For the physical, applied, and natural sciences, review the 20-volume *McGraw-Hill Encyclopedia of Science and Technology.* This is complemented by annual supplements. *Our Living World of Nature* is a 14-volume popular encyclopedia dealing with natural history from an ecological point of view. *The International Encyclopedia of the Social Sciences* concentrates on the theory and methods of the social sciences in 17 well-researched volumes. Other widely used encyclopedias include the *Encyclopedia of Bioethics* (4 volumes), the *Encyclopedia of Philosophy* (8 volumes), and the *Encyclopedia of Religion* (16 volumes).

Biographical Material. A speaker often needs information about particular individuals. For example, you might want to look up authors of books or articles to find out something about their education, training, or other writings. Or you may wish to discover if there have been any critical evaluations of their work in, say, book reviews or articles about them or their writings. Knowing something about your sources enables you to more effectively evaluate their competence, present their credibility to the audience, and answer audience questions about your sources.

First, consult the *Biography and Genealogy Master Index*—in print, on CD ROM, or online; it indexes over 350 biographical indexes. This index will lead you to the best index for the information you want. There are numerous specialized works to which this index will send you. Following are just a few to give you an idea of the breadth and depth of biographical research. *The Dictionary of American Biography* (DAB) contains articles on famous deceased Americans from all areas of accomplishment, for example, politics, sports, education, art, and industry. For living individuals, the best single source is *Current Biography.* This is issued monthly and in cumulative annual volumes. Beginning in 1940, *Current Biography* contains articles of one to two pages in length, most with photographs and brief bibliographies. The essays in *Current Biography* are written by an editorial staff and, therefore, include both favorable and unfavorable comments. *Who's Who in America* also covers living individuals.

In addition, there are a host of other more specialized works whose titles indicate their scope: *The Dictionary of Canadian Biography, The*

The United States Government is the largest publisher in the world. Its publications originate in the various divisions of its 13 departments, each of which is a prolific publisher. The Departments of Agriculture, Commerce, Defense, Education, Energy, Health and Human Services, Housing and Urban Development, Interior, Justice, Labor, State, Treasury, and Transportation each issue reports, pamphlets, books, and assorted documents dealing with their various concerns. Because of the wealth of published material, it would be best to first consult one of the guides to government publications. A few of the more useful ones that should be in your college library include Government Reference Books (1968 to date), A Bibliography of United States Government Bibliographies, and U. S. Government Books: Recent Releases (published quarterly). The Congressional Record (http://thomas.loc.gov/home/abt. cong.rec.html) (1873 to date) is issued daily when Congress is in session. The Record contains all that was said in both houses of Congress. It also contains materials that members of Congress wish inserted. How might you use the Congressional Record in your next speech?

Dictionary of National Biography (British), *Directory of American Scholars, International Who's Who, Who Was Who in America, Who's Who* (primarily British), *Dictionary of Scientific Biography, American Men and Women of Science, Great Lives from History* (25 volumes), *Notable American Women, National Cyclopedia of American Biography* (1888-1984), *Who's Who in the Arab World, Who's Who in the World, Who's Who in Finance and Industry, Who's Who in American Politics, Who's Who Among Black Americans, Who's Who of American Women,* and *Who's Who Among Hispanic Americans.*

The *Official Congressional Directory* (1809 to date) and the *Biographical Directory of the American Congress* provide biographical information on government personnel, maps of congressional districts, and various other helpful information to those concerned with the workings of Congress.

Not surprisingly, there are many Internet sources for biographical information. For example, http://mgm.mit.edu:8080/pevzner/Nobel.html provides links to biographical information on all Nobel Prize winners. If you want information on members of the House of Representatives, try http://www.house.gov. And http://www.biography.com/ will provide you with brief biographies of some 15,000 famous people, living and dead.

Still another way to search for information on a person is to simply type in the name of the person into one of the search engines or use one of the directories identified in Table 7.1.

Almanacs. Should you want information on the world's languages, household income, presidential elections, the countries of the world, national defense, sports, noted personalities, economics and employment, the environment, awards and prizes, science and technology, health and medicine, maps, world travel information, or postal rates, an almanac will prove extremely useful. Numerous inexpensive versions published annually are among the most up-to-date sources of information on many topics. The most popular are *The World Almanac and Book of Facts* (also available on CD ROM), the *Information Please Almanac, The Universal Almanac,* and *The Canadian Almanac and Directory.*

The annual *Statistical Abstract of the United States* contains the most complete statistical data on population, vital statistics, health, education, law, geography and environment, elections, finances and employment, defense, insurance, labor, income, prices, banking, and a wide variety of other topics. Other valuable statistical sources include *Vital Statistics of the United States* (especially useful for demographic statistics) and *Morbidity and Mortality Weekly Report* (useful for health-related issues). For international statistics see *United Nations Statistical Yearbook, World Statistics in Brief,* and *UNESCO Statistical Yearbook.* Useful Web sites include http://cedr.1b1.gov/cdrom/doc/lookup_doc.html for United States census data and http://www.cs.cmu.edu/Web/references.html, which provides links to a wide variety of relevant reference materials.

Museum Collections and Exhibits. Not too long ago, museums weren't even listed in reference lists and research discussions, largely because really good museums were so far away from most people that the possibility of visiting the particular museum needed was remote. Now, however, you have the world of museums literally at your fingertips. Museums contain collections of all sorts of information pertaining to the museum's major focus, for example, art, natural history, or science. Visiting a few of the museum Web sites will be time well spent. Here are a few especially good ones: Franklin Institute Science Museum at http://sln.fi.edu/, London's Museum of Natural History at http://www.mhm.ac.uk, and the Smithsonian Institution at http://www.si.edu/. The Smithsonian Wed site will provide guidance for visiting its 16 museums, the *Smithsonian Encyclopedia,* and lots more. An especially helpful site if you don't know what museum you'd like to visit is http://www.comlab.ox.ac.uk/archive/other/museums/usa.html, which contains links to museums, archives, and galleries throughout the United States.

News Sources

Often you'll want to read reports on accidents, political speeches, congressional actions, obituaries, financial news, international developments, United Nations actions, or any of a host of other topics. Or you may wish to locate the time of a particular event and learn something about what else was going on in the world at that particular time. For this type of information you may want to consult a reliable newspaper. Many speeches rely to some extent on news, whether local, national, or international. Especially relevant are newspaper indexes, newspaper databases, newspaper and magazine Web sites, news wire services, and news networks online.

Newspaper Indexes. One way to start a newspaper search is to consult one of the newspaper indexes, for example, the *National Newspaper Index,* which covers 27 newspapers, including the *Christian Science Monitor, The New York Times, The Wall Street Journal, The Los Angeles Times,* and *The Washington Post.* Each of these newspapers also has its own index.

Electronic Newspaper Databases. Many newspapers can be accessed online or through CD ROM databases to which your college library probably subscribes. The *New York Times* database, for example, contains complete editorial content of the paper, one of the world's most comprehensive newspapers. All aspects of news, sports, editorials, columns, obituaries, New York and regional news, and the *New York Times Book Review* and *Magazine* are included. You can search this database by subject terms, personal names, or company names. Many features also contain brief 25-word abstracts. A sample entry from the *New York Times* database is included in Figure 7.6.

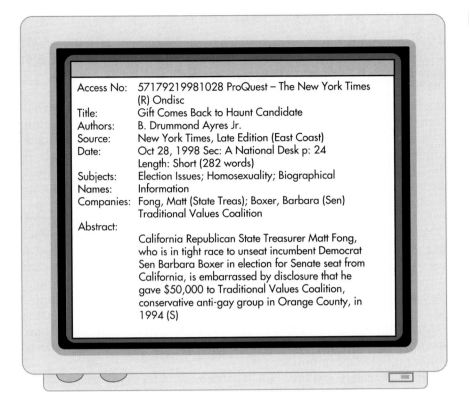

FIGURE 7.6

A Sample Citation from the *New York Times Index*.

For what types of speech topics would the *New York Times Index* be especially useful?

Access No:	57179219981028 ProQuest – The New York Times (R) Ondisc
Title:	Gift Comes Back to Haunt Candidate
Authors:	B. Drummond Ayres Jr.
Source:	New York Times, Late Edition (East Coast)
Date:	Oct 28, 1998 Sec: A National Desk p: 24 Length: Short (282 words)
Subjects:	Election Issues; Homosexuality; Biographical
Names:	Information
Companies:	Fong, Matt (State Treas); Boxer, Barbara (Sen) Traditional Values Coalition
Abstract:	California Republican State Treasurer Matt Fong, who is in tight race to unseat incumbent Democrat Sen Barbara Boxer in election for Senate seat from California, is embarrassed by disclosure that he gave $50,000 to Traditional Values Coalition, conservative anti-gay group in Orange County, in 1994 (S)

Newspaper and News Magazine Web sites. Most newspapers now maintain their own Web sites from which you can access current and past issues. Here are a few to get you started: http://www.latimes.com/ (*Los Angeles Times*), http://www.usatoday.com/ (*USA Today*), http://journal.link.wsj.com/ (*The Wall Street Journal*), http://www.washingtonpost.com/ (*Washington Post*). A particularly useful Web site is http://www.newslink.org/menu.html, which provides access to a variety of online newspapers and magazines. http://nt.excite.com/?uid= offers a variety of news items and allows you to search the news index.

News Wire Services. Three wire services should prove helpful. The Associated Press can be accessed at http://www1.trib.com/NEWS/Apwire.html, Reuters at http://www.reuters.com/, and PR Newswire at http://www.prnewswire.com/. The advantage of getting your information from a news wire service is that it's more complete than a newspaper. Newspapers often must cut copy to fit space requirements and, in some cases, may put a politically or socially motivated spin on the news.

News Networks Online. All of the television news stations maintain extremely useful Web sites. Here are some of the most useful: Access CNN at http://www.cnn.com/, ESPN at http://espn.sportszone.com/, ABC News at http://www.abcnews.com/newsflash, CBS News at http://www.cbs.com/news/, MSNBC News at http://www.msnbc.com/news.

Articles and Posts Sources

Very often you'll want to read articles in professional research journals, in magazines, or in postings online. Here we consider first, academic research articles and second, general research articles and posts.

Academic Research Articles. Academic research forms the core of what we know about people and the world. These are reports of studies conducted by academicians around the world. For the most part, these articles are conducted by unbiased researchers using the best research methods available. Further, this research is subject to careful critical review by experts in the specific field of the research. This research is the most valid and the most reliable you're likely to find.

Each college library subscribes to a somewhat different package of CD ROM and online databases. Unlike the personal CD ROM encyclopedias and almanacs, these CD ROMs (and their corresponding online databases) are vastly larger. All of these databases contain information on the nature and scope of the database and user-friendly directions for searching, displaying, printing, and saving the retrieved information to disk. Many contain examples that you can work through to get to know the system and an explanation of the technical terminology used in the database. Here are just a few examples of databases that your college library is likely to have, either on CD ROM or online.

America: History and Life. This database contains citations and abstracts of the major scholarly literature in history. In scope and contents, this online source is identical to the print version, *America: History and Life.* This database contains abstracts (approximately 75-100 words in length) from over 2,100 journals in 40 different languages. Approximately 900 of these journals are printed in the United States and Canada. Foreign journals are surveyed for all articles dealing with American history and life. One of the useful features of this database (and various others) is that articles and the commentaries written in response to them are combined so that you can access all the relevant articles at the same time. This database also contains reviews from about 140 mainly U.S. and Canadian journals, as well as reviews of works on microfilm, film, and video.

Psychlit and Sociofile. These two databases are similar in format and so can be considered together. Psychlit is a database of citations from approximately 1,300 journals in psychology and related fields in 27 languages published in some 50 different countries. Sociofile is the sociological counterpart and contains citations from about 1,600 journals in sociology and related fields in 30 different languages published in approximately 55 countries. Both databases also contain citations for books, book chapters, and dissertations of psychological and sociological relevance. Abstracts of around 250 words are provided for each article or book.

Medline. The Medline database is the computerized version of *Index Medicus;* it's the National Library of Medicine's bibliographic database, the definitive source in the United States for biomedical literature. This database is enormous and contains citations from over 3700 journals "selected for inclusion because of their importance to health professions." The index is international in scope; 75% of the citations are published in English. Medline covers such categories as anatomy, diseases, chemicals, drugs,

FIGURE 7.7

A Sample Citation from Medline.

The research reported in this database is not limited in application to speeches specifically on medicine. Browse through this database. Can you identify types of information indexed here that would be appropriate for speeches on politics or economics or education?

equipment, psychiatry, biological sciences, information science and communications, and health care. Articles since 1975 contain abstracts of about 250 words.

You can also limit your search to, for example, an abridged index that covers 118 journals in English, dental information, or nursing information. An example from Medline appears in Figure 7.7.

ERIC. Should you be preparing a speech on some topic related to education—bilingualism, school violence, leadership training, teacher preparation, test anxiety, communication apprehension, and multiculturalism are a few examples—the Educational Resources Information Center (ERIC) database will prove useful. ERIC is a network of 16 contributing clearinghouses, each of which specializes in a separate subject area. Together they survey over 750 journals and provide complete citations and abstracts of 200 to 300 words. In addition, 850 ERIC Digest records that contain the full text of the original work are also available. In addition to journal articles, ERIC also includes dissertations, convention papers, books, computer programs, nonprint media, and speeches. A sample citation from ERIC appears in Figure 7.8.

Other frequently available databases include the Linguistics and Language Behavior Abstracts database, which contains references to studies on language, the Social Science database, which covers the social and behavioral

FIGURE 7.8

A Sample Citation from ERIC.

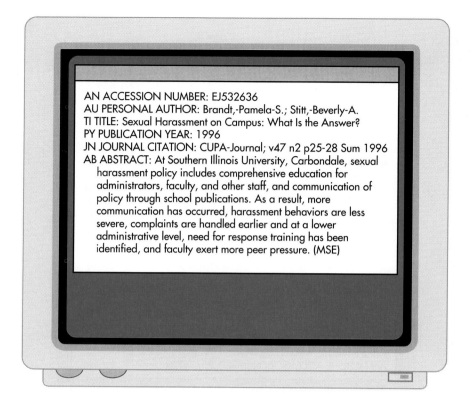

AN ACCESSION NUMBER: EJ532636
AU PERSONAL AUTHOR: Brandt,-Pamela-S.; Stitt,-Beverly-A.
TI TITLE: Sexual Harassment on Campus: What Is the Answer?
PY PUBLICATION YEAR: 1996
JN JOURNAL CITATION: CUPA-Journal; v47 n2 p25-28 Sum 1996
AB ABSTRACT: At Southern Illinois University, Carbondale, sexual harassment policy includes comprehensive education for administrators, faculty, and other staff, and communication of policy through school publications. As a result, more communication has occurred, harassment behaviors are less severe, complaints are handled earlier and at a lower administrative level, need for response training has been identified, and faculty exert more peer pressure. (MSE)

sciences, and the Legal Resource Index, which covers periodicals devoted to law. The LEXIS/NEXIS System allows you to retrieve the complete text of articles from hundreds of newspapers, magazines, journals, and even newsletters in addition to a wide variety of legal and statutory records.

Other research sources combine the academic and the more popular articles. The *Education Index,* for example, published since 1929, indexes articles from about 330 journals and magazines relevant to education at all levels. It also indexes most of the speech communication journals and government periodicals. ERIC, discussed previously, is a more comprehensive and efficient database to search.

The *Social Sciences Index* covers periodicals in such areas as psychology, economics, sociology, and political science. Although more specialized indexes cover these subjects in greater depth, this one is useful for its cross-disciplinary coverage. Among the more specialized indexes that will prove useful to many speakers are the *Business Periodicals Index, Art Index, Applied Science and Technology Index, Biological and Agricultural Index, General Science Index, Index to Legal Periodicals, Humanities Index, Music Index,* and *PAIS* (Public Affairs Information Service).

General Research and Opinion Posts

In preparing a speech you may wish to research dinosaurs, animal language, conservative politics, the growth of cities, immigration patterns, changes in the media, business innovations, management practices, abstract art, Brazilian trade practices, U.S.–China relationships, AIDS, or just about any popular topic. A useful source is the magazine. Articles in magazines differ greatly from those in professional journals. For example, they're most often written by professional writers rather than researchers. Magazine articles may be summaries of the research by others or they may be largely opinion. Often, they're simplified accounts of rather complex issues written for the general public rather than an audience of professional researchers. Further, they seldom undergo the rigorous review process that accompanies publication in a professional academic journal. As a result, articles appearing in popular magazines are much less reliable than those appearing in such professional research journals as, say, *Communication Monographs, Journal of Experimental Psychology,* or *The New England Journal of Medicine.* Nevertheless, magazine articles and general posts are often very helpful for speakers. Here are a few suggestions for finding the information you want.

Indexes. The *Readers' Guide to Periodical Literature,* available in print and electronic formats, covers magazine articles for the period from 1900 to the present. This guide indexes by subject and by author (in one convenient alphabetical index) articles published in about 180 different magazines. *Readers' Guide* is valuable for its broad coverage, but it's limited in that it covers mostly general publications and only a few of the more specialized ones. The "First Search Help for Readers' Guide to Periodical Literature" at http://www.uni_stuttgart.de/ub/oclc/help/ReadersGuide_scope_help.htm will help you get the most from this valuable research tool. The *Alternative Press Index* (also available on CD ROM to which your library might subscribe) indexes approximately 250 "alternative, radical, and left publications." This index is valuable for speakers dealing with such issues as the Third World, minority rights, socialism, and the like.

Listservs, Usenet Groups, and the World Wide Web. Listservs, newsgroups, and the World Wide Web, as explained earlier in this unit, contain a wide variety of articles, many more than you could possibly use in any one speech. Explore relevant listservs through Liszt (www.liszt.com), newsgroups through DejaNews (www.DejaNews.com), and the vast array of World Wide Web documents with the help of the numerous search engines.

Book Sources

There are two major ways to find books—through a library and through a bookstore.

Libraries. Each library catalogs its books, journals, and government documents in a slightly different way, depending on its size and the needs of its users. All, however, make use of some form of computerized catalog. These are uniformly easy and efficient to use. The catalog is the best place to find out what books are in your college library or a library whose books you can secure on interlibrary loan, for example.

Generally, you'd access your material by looking up your major subject heading(s). A good way to do this is to make a list of the five or six major

Some books are to be tasted, others to be swallowed, and some few to be chewed and digested.
—Francis Bacon

concepts that appear in your speech and look each of these up in the library catalog. Create a complete bibliography of available sources and examine each one. Sometimes, you may want to locate the works by or about a particular person. In this case, you'd simply look up the author's name, much as you would a concept.

Both general and specialized online libraries are available. The Library of Congress (http://www.loc.gov/) provides an online catalog of all its holdings as well as links to Internet search engines and a variety of useful indexes for researching a wide variety of topics (see Figure 7.9). Useful directories to libraries, most in North America and Europe, can be found at http://www.llv.com/~msauers/libs/libs/html. And an especially rich source of links to reference cites can be found at http://www.state.wi.us/agencies/dpi/www/lib_res.html.

Bookstores. Not surprisingly, bookstores are good places to look for books. Browsing through any large bookstore is almost sure to give you insights into your topic. If you're talking about something that people are interested in today, there's likely to be a book dealing with it on the bookshelf of most bookstores. Visit too some of the online bookstores, for example, Amazon.com, BarnesandNoble.com, or Borders.com. Visit the Library of Congress (http://lcweb.loc.gov) to discover any book at all—the Library of Congress maintains records on all books published in the United States. In addition, other useful sites include: http://aaup.pupress.princeton.edu/ (Association of American University Presses), http://www.cs.cmu.edu/Web/People/spok/banned-books.html (contains links to texts of books that have been banned in the United States and elsewhere), and http://www.booksite.com/ (contains search tools for locating over 2 million books).

The LIBRARY of CONGRESS

SEARCH THE CATALOG | SEARCH OUR WEB SITE | WEB SITE MAP

USING the LIBRARY
Catalogs, Collections & Research Services

THOMAS
Congress At Work

COPYRIGHT OFFICE
Forms & Information

BICENTENNIAL
1800-2000
Libraries • Creativity • Liberty

HELP & FAQs
General Information

AMERICAN MEMORY
America's Story in Words, Sounds & Pictures

EXHIBITIONS
An On-Line Gallery

THE LIBRARY TODAY
News, Events & More

Above, the interior of the dome of the Main Reading Room of the Library of Congress.

101 INDEPENDENCE AVE. S.E.
WASHINGTON, D.C. 20540
(202) 707-5000

Comments: lcweb@loc.gov
NOTICE

USING the LIBRARY | THOMAS | COPYRIGHT OFFICE | AMERICAN MEMORY | EXHIBITIONS | The LIBRARY TODAY | BICENTENNIAL | HELP & FAQs | TOP of PAGE

"EXPERTS" AND THE INTERVIEW

Another useful source of information is the "expert." As used here, "expert" refers to anyone with specialized knowledge, anyone who has information about something that others don't have. Usually this means people who are extremely knowledgeable about a particular topic; images of world-renown scientists come quickly to mind. But, it can also refer to a teenager who witnessed an accident, experienced homelessness, or won the national spelling bee.

The faculty is one of the best, if rarely used, sources of information for almost any speech topic. Regardless of what your topic is, a faculty member of some department knows a great deal about the topic. At the very least, faculty members will be able to direct you to appropriate sources. Experts in the community can serve similar functions. Local politicians, religious leaders, doctors, lawyers, museum directors, and the like are often suitable sources of information.

Beyond your college lies a world of experts—religious and business leaders, politicians, educators at other colleges and research institutes, medical personnel, and researchers in almost any field imaginable. Ask yourself if your speech and your audience could profit from the insights of experts. If your answer is yes—and few topics could not so profit—then consider the steps suggested here for interviewing such experts in person, by telephone, or, as is becoming increasingly popular, over the Internet, especially in e-mail or chat groups.

Select the Person You Wish to Interview

There are several ways to locate an expert. Let's say that you want to speak on family therapy. You might, for example, look through your college cata-log. There you find that a course in family communication is offered by Professor Bernard Brommel. You think it might be worthwhile to interview him. Or, you visit a variety of newsgroups and discover that one particular person has posted extremely well-reasoned articles, and you'd like to inter-view her to get her opinion on family communication and the role it plays in family therapy. If you want to contact a book author, you can always write to the author in care of the publisher or editor (listed on the copyright page), though many authors are now including their e-mail addresses. You can often find the address and phone number of most professional people by calling the professional association for a directory listing (the *Encyclopedia of Associations* lists just about every professional association in the country). You can also write to the person via the association's Web site. Newsgroup and listserv writers are, of course, the easiest to contact since their e-mail address is included with their posts. Lastly, you can often find experts through *The Yearbook of Experts, Authorities,* and *Spokespersons* and a variety of Web sites, for example, http://www.experts.com and http://www.usc.edu/dept/news_service/experts_directory.html.

You're now on your first step; you've selected one of the people you hope to interview. Your next step is to learn something about the person. Consult an online library or bookstore to see if this person wrote a book, or go through a CD ROM database to see if this person wrote any research articles. Search through the databases covering family communication; ERIC, Psychlit, and Sociofile (discussed earlier) would probably cover just about any research in the field of family communication. Search the Web and Usenet groups to see if the person has a Web page or posts to newsgroups (see Table 7.1 for shortcuts for doing this). You may find that the person encourages people to correspond via e-mail.

Secure an Appointment

Phone the person or send an e-mail requesting an interview. In your call or letter, identify the purpose of your request and that you'd like a brief interview by phone or that you'd like to send this person a series of questions by e-mail. For example, if you call, you might say: "I'm preparing a speech on family therapy and I would appreciate it if I could interview you to learn more about the subject. The interview would take about 15 minutes." (This time limitation helps since Brommel now knows it will not take very long and is more likely to agree to being interviewed.) Generally, it's best to be available at the interviewee's convenience, so be flexible (for example, "I can interview you any day after 12 p.m."). If you're doing this by e-mail, write the person and ask if she or he would be willing to answer a few questions (it might help to specify the number and type of questions) by e-mail. If you want to interview someone you met in a chat group, you might ask to arrange a phone interview or to talk privately ("whisper") online at some mutually convenient time.

Phrase Your Questions

If this is an in-person or telephone interview, prepare the questions you wish to ask in advance. This will ensure that you use the time available to your best advantage. Of course, as the interview progresses other questions will come to mind and should be asked. Having a prepared list of questions, though, will help you feel more relaxed and will help you obtain the information you need more easily.

In face-to-face interviews be especially alert to nonverbal cues that tell you the interviewee wishes to say more (so avoid interrupting) or that he or she has finished (so go on to another question). Try to avoid cutting short the interviewee's discussion, but at the same time try to avoid awkward and prolonged silences.

Be on Time

Be on time whether the interview is in-person, a phone call, or an agreement to chat ("whisper") in a chat room. Attitudes toward time, promptness, and lateness vary greatly from culture to culture. These attitudes are extremely important and to one who values promptness, lateness in others is rarely tolerated or excused. Being on time will thus enable you to make the right impression, to use the time set aside to your advantage, and will demonstrate your seriousness of purpose.

Establish Rapport with the Interviewee

Open the in-person, telephone, e-mail, or chat group interview with an expression of thanks for making the time available to you and again state your purpose. Many people receive lots of requests and it helps if you

TIPS
from professional speakers

Requesting a fact limits a person's thinking. He or she generally answers with the fact and grows silent again. If you want to have the person expand so that you can gather a wide range of information and impressions, suggest a topic rather than ask a question: "Tell me what you think about the way the President is handling the economy." "What do you know about nuclear energy—have you given it any thought for heating your home?" "How about employee morale around here?"

Dianna Booher, business communications consultant and author and president of Booher Consultants, *Communicate with Confidence: How to Say It Right the First Time* (New York: McGraw-Hill, 1994): 168-69.

remind the person of your purpose. You might say something like this: "I really appreciate your making time for this interview. As I mentioned, I'm preparing a speech on family therapy and your expertise and experience in this area will help a great deal."

Ask for Permission to Tape or Print the Interview

It's a good idea to keep an accurate account of the interview so ask permission to tape the interview if it's in person or by telephone. Taping will enable you to focus your total attention on the interview and will eliminate your worry about taking notes and having to ask the interviewee to slow down or repeat. It will also provide you with a much more accurate record of the interview than will handwritten notes. But, always ask permission first. Some people prefer not to have informal interviews taped. If the interview is by e-mail and you want to quote the interviewee's responses, ask permission first. An agreement to be interviewed does not include permission to print or distribute the interview or even parts of it.

Ask Open-ended and Neutral Questions

Use questions that provide the interviewee with room to discuss the issues you want to raise. Thus, asking "Do you have formal training in the area of family therapy?" which requires a simple "yes" or "no," will not be very informative. On the other hand, asking, an open-ended question such as "Can you tell me something of your background in this field?" allows Brommel to tell you about his background in as much detail as he thinks appropriate.

Ask questions phrased in a neutral manner. Try not to lead the interviewee to give the answers you want. Asking, "What do you think of the administration's recent policy?" gives the interviewee free range and does not bias the answer as would, for example, "What problems do you think the administration's recent policy is likely to create?"

Close the Interview with a Note of Appreciation

Thank the person for making the time available for the interview and for being informative, cooperative, helpful, or whatever. In short, let the person know that you do, in fact, appreciate the effort made to help you with your speech. On the more practical side, this will also make it a great deal easier if you want to return for a second interview.

Follow Up on the Interview

Follow up on the interview with a brief note of thanks. Or, perhaps you might send (e-mail works very well here) the person you interviewed a copy of your speech, again with a note of thanks for the help.

CRITICALLY EVALUATING RESEARCH

Collecting research materials—whether from traditional print sources, from listservs or the Web, or from interviews with experts—is only part of

TIPS from professional speakers

It's amazing how many people pose question after question in their conversations, as if they were rhetorical, and never pause for an answer. When you ask a question and then rush ahead with an answer yourself or move on to the next topic, the other person notices the pattern and decides you don't intend to take any answer seriously. Nervousness also plays a big part in someone's talking right through where the pauses should go. Be aware of that habit; ask, pause, wait.

Dianna Booher, business communications consultant and author and president of Booher Consultants, *Communicate with Confidence: How to Say It Right the First Time* (New York: McGraw-Hill, 1994): 169.

the process; the other part is critically evaluating them. Although evaluating specific amplifying materials and arguments is discussed in later units (see Units 8 and 21, for example), some general questions to ask of all researched information are suggested here.

Is the Information Current?

Generally, the more recent the material, the more useful it will be. With some topics, for example, unemployment statistics, developments in AIDS research, and tuition costs, the currency of the information is crucial to its usefulness. Check important figures in a recent *Almanac,* newspaper, or frequently updated Internet source.

The date of the newspaper, the copyright date of a book, or the date of a cited article or e-mail will help you identify when the information was written or last updated. Unfortunately, not all Internet documents are dated and so at times you won't be able to tell when the document was written. You may, however, be able to write to the author and ask, since many Internet writers include their e-mail address.

Is the Information Fair and Unbiased?

Bias isn't easy to determine, but do try to examine any sources of potential bias. Obvious examples come quickly to mind: cigarette manufacturers' statements on the health risks from smoking; newspaper and network editorials on the fairness of news reporting; and the National Rifle Association's arguments against gun control. Other examples, however, are not so easy to see as potentially biased. Try checking the credibility of your sources in a biographical dictionary or in relevant newspaper articles. Reviewing the research in the area will enable you to see how other experts in this area view this author. It will also enable you to see if this author's view of the situation takes into consideration all sides of the issue and if these sides are represented fairly and accurately. In some cases, the author presents her or his credentials, and these can easily be checked should you wish to.

Distinguish between primary and secondary source material. Primary sources include, for example, the original research study as reported in an academic journal or a corporation's annual report. Secondary sources would include, for example, summaries of the research appearing in popular magazines and television news reports on a corporation's earnings. When using secondary sources, examine the information for any particular spin the writer may be giving the material. If possible, you may wish to check with the primary source to see what might have been left out or if the conclusions are really warranted on the basis of the primary evidence.

Look at the writer's sources to see if they represent all sides of an issue. If, for example, all the information comes from either liberal or conservative publications, then the arguments are likely to be biased. Some authors may even indicate their bias and their point of view.

Like public speeches, articles, books, and news posts aim at times to inform and at times to persuade; frequently, they aim to achieve both purposes. Often the purpose is quite clear. A news report on the Federal Reserve Board's meeting is largely informational. An newspaper editorial on needed changes in the educational system is largely persuasive. With these types of examples, there's usually little trouble; you know which is which and you approach each with a different attitude and a different readiness to accept the information. In most cases, however, articles—like speeches—mix informational and persuasive purposes, and it's often difficult to tell where information stops and persuasion begins. This difficulty notwithstanding, it's crucial to distinguish the two. Try to identify specific persuasive words and sentences. Look for weasel words—words whose meanings are difficult to pin down. For example, the medicine that claims to work better than Brand X doesn't specify how much better or in what respect it performs better. Is it possible that it performs better in one respect and less effective on nine other measures? "Better" is a weasel word. "Like" is another word often used for weaseling as when a claim is made that "Brand X will make you feel like a new man" Exactly what such a claim means is impossible to pin down. Other weasel words are "helped," "virtually," "as much as," and "more economical." Try looking for weasel words; you'll often find them lurking in the promises of advertisers and politicians.

Recognize that anyone can "publish" on the Internet. An article on the Internet can be written by world-renown scientists or by elementary school students, by fair and objective reporters or by those who would spin the issues to serve political, religious, or social purposes. It's not always easy to tell which is which. Find out what the author's qualifications are. Look carefully at any statistics or figures. Are these cited from reliable and recent sources? One useful technique used by many Web writers is to include in their document Internet links to the sources from which they derived, say, their statistics, predictions, or arguments. If you find these links, it's often worth checking them to see if the author did, in fact, fairly and accurately present the information. Very likely, however, the links are there because the information in them is accurately represented.

Many Web sites are constructed by people who admire others—Web sites devoted to film and television stars, for example—and these are likely to be highly biased just as are Web sites of religious and political organizations. This, of course, isn't any different from biographical books being written by admiring writers or pamphlets written by supporters of a particular cause. All of these sources will, however, contain lots of useful and reliable information. They may just not be totally revealing of the negatives of the star or of alternative points of view. They may also exaggerate their own positive qualities and de-emphasize their negative qualities or may engage in boldfaced lying. So, be on the lookout for materials that are self-promotional in focus.

Recognize also, however, that much information on the Internet is identical to the information you regularly read in print. Encyclopedias, newspapers and newsmagazines, and professional journals that appear on the Internet are identical to the print copies; there is no need to draw distinctions between print and Internet information when dealing with sites such as these.

Is the Information Sufficient?

Ask yourself if the collected information is sufficient to illustrate your point, to prove that one proposal is better than another, or to show why

How dangerous it always is to reason from insufficient data.
—Sherlock Holmes

your system will work better than the existing system. The opinion of one dietician is insufficient to support the usefulness of a particular diet; the statistics from five private colleges on tuition increases are insufficient to illustrate national trends in rising tuition costs.

Try to read articles on all sides of the issue. Balance any one-sided article with articles dealing with each of the other sides, and remember there are usually more than two sides to any complex issue.

Consider, also, if the author provides you with the information you'd need to check up on the accuracy and reliability yourself. For example, does the author cite the sources for the statistics given? Does the author tell you how she or he conducted the research that lead to the conclusions?

Is the Evidence Reliable and the Reasoning Logical?

The most important question in evaluating research must focus on the evidence and reasoning used in arriving at a conclusion. Ask yourself if the conclusions have been arrived at logically rather than, say, emotionally. Does the author offer clear evidence and sound arguments to support conclusions rather than, say, anecdotes or testimonials from like-minded people?

Another way to estimate reliability is look at the publisher. Note especially if the publisher is a special interest group with a specific corporate, religious, political, or social agenda. If so, try to balance this perspective with information that represents the other sides of the issue.

On the other hand, if an article appears in a journal sponsored by the American Psychological Association or the National Communication Association, for example, you can be pretty sure that the article has been carefully reviewed by experts before publication. If an article appears in *The New York Times, The Washington Post, The Wall Street Journal,* or any of the major newsmagazines or news networks, again, you can be pretty sure that the information is reliable. Both textbook and trade book publishers go to enormous effort to ensure the accuracy of what appears in print. A textbook, for example, is normally reviewed by perhaps 10 to 20 professionals in the specific field before it ever sees the light of day.

Do realize that this claim of accuracy is a generalization that has on occasion been proven false. Recently, for example, two writers for *The Boston Globe* were found to have fabricated stories they presented in their columns as true. *The Cincinnati Enquirer* paid Chiquita Corporation over $10 million for stories the newspaper later said were "untrue." And, in perhaps the most widely publicized example, both CNN and *Time* magazine apologized for claiming that the United States military had used lethal gas in Laos that was intended to kill American defectors (*The New York Times,* Section 4, July 5, 1998, p. 2). So, inaccuracies do creep into even the most respected sources.

With the Internet, it's especially difficult to distinguish reliable from unreliable sources. Some sources are highly reliable and others are collections of personal anecdotes and unsupported ramblings. Many Web sites are clearly commercial, designed to promote and sell a product or service, but you should have no trouble identifying these. In some cases Web sites have a commercial banner running across the top; again, however,

THE ETHICS OF Plagiarism [and How to Avoid it]

Plagiarism occurs when you use material from another source without properly crediting it. It can take a number of different forms.

Using the exact words of another person. If you're going to use another person's exact words, then cite it exactly as it was written or spoken and credit the source. For example, in a speech on nonverbal communication in different cultures, you might say something like this: "According to Roger Axtell, in his *Gestures: The Do's and Taboos of Body Language Around the World,* touching varies from one culture to another. Axtell says, for example, "In the Middle East, two Arab male friends may even be seen walking down the street hand-in-hand and all its signifies is friendship.""

In your outline, give the full bibliographic reference just as you would in a history paper. Be sure you use quotation marks for any citation in which you use the person's exact words, just as you would in a written essay. And, when delivering your speech, make it clear to your listeners that you're using the person's exact words as was done in the previous example. You can do this by changing your inflection, stepping forward, or reading the specific words from your notes. In this way, the audience will know that the exact words belong to someone else.

Using the ideas of another person. Even if you're not quoting directly, you still need to acknowledge your source if you're using the ideas, arguments, insights, or examples taken from another source. If you're using the ideas of another, simply acknowledge this in your speech and in any written materials, such as your outline. Weave into your speech the sources of your materials, with subtlety and without disturbing the natural flow and rhythm of your speech. For example, you might say, "A recent article in *Time* magazine noted that . . . ." Or, "Professor Fox, in her lecture last week on Western Civilization, argued that . . . ." Or, "This week Nielsen reported that the number of homes watching cable . . ."

Using the organizational structure of another. Even if you're "only" following the organizational structure of another source, you need to acknowledge your indebtedness. In these cases, you can say something like "I'm here following the arguments given by Professor Marishu in her lecture on culture and racism" or "This pattern for explaining how a car is designed comes from the work of Edward Frid in his new book, *Designing a Car.*"

What would you say in an actual speech to acknowledge the information described in each of the situations presented in the Ethics box in Unit 2?

(The next Ethics in Public Speaking box appears on page 171.)

---

this obvious commercial purpose is easily identified, just as it is in a newspaper when an advertisement is positioned next to a news report or in television when a commercial interrupts the news. Generally, the same relationship exists between advertiser and medium; the advertisements don't determine the content, but they do at times influence content and, generally, advertisers buy space or time in newspapers, television programs, and Web sites that are related to and consistent with their product or service.

Some Internet sources contain "about" files that will help you learn more about the author and perhaps the author's sources. Sometimes you'll be able to contact the author via e-mail.

INTEGRATING RESEARCH IN YOUR SPEECH

After you've collected your research and integrated it into your speech, you need to make sure that you cite it correctly in your list of references and in your actual speech.

The ultimate goal of all research is not objectivity, but truth.
—Helene Deutsch

Citing Research

In citing references, first find out what style manual is used in your class or at your school. Different schools and different departments within the college often rely on different formats for citing research, which, quite frankly, makes a tedious process even worse. Table 7.3 presents a wide

---

TABLE 7.3 Source Citation

The suggested citation formats for Internet information are taken from Harnack and Kleppinger (1997) who adapted their system from that of the American Psychological Association. The suggested citation formats for print sources are taken from the American Psychological Association Manual. For a useful citation guide for both APA and MLA style manuals for citing Internet sources, see Janice Walker's "Citing Your Sources" at http://longman.awl.com/podium/citation_walker_citing.htm.

Source	Sample Citation
Newspaper article Author name. Year of publication, Title of article, Title of newspaper, Month and day of publication: page number(s).	Goleman, Daniel. (1995). For man and beast, language of love shares many traits. *The New York Times* (February 14): C1, C9.
Journal or magazine article Author name (date of publication). Title of article. Title of journal or magazine, volume number, pages.	Neuliep, James W., & McCroskey, James C. (1997). The development of a U.S. and generalized ethnocentrism scale. *Communication Research Reports*, 14, 385-398.
Book *Author name (if edited)* (date of publication). Title of book. City and state of publication: Publisher.	Jandt, Fred E. (1998). *Intercultural communication: An introduction*, 2nd ed. Thousand Oaks, CA: Sage Publications.
WWW article Author's name (date of publication). Title of article. Title of complete work where applicable <URL address> (date of visit).	Doe, John (1996). How to surf the net. *NetSuggest*. <http:www.netsuggest.com> (July 4, 1998).
E-mail or listserv Author (e-mail writer) <author's e-mail address> "Subject Line from the E-mail." Date of the e-mail. Type of e-mail (for example, personal e-mail, office communication). (Date you accessed the e-mail).	DeVito, Joseph. <jdevito@shiva.hunter.cuny.edu> "Research in Public Speaking." July 22, 1998. Personal mail. (July 23, 1998).
Newsgroup post Author name <author e-mail address> (publication date) Subject line. <name of newsgroup> (date of visit).	DeVito, Joseph. <jdevito@shiva.hunter.cuny.edu> "Research?" (August 1, 1999). <alt.communication.research> (September 15, 1999).
Personal communication Author name (date of communication). Identification of discussion. Personal communication.	Doe, Jane (1998). Phone conversation on multiculturalism. Personal communication.

variety of sources and the ways in which they're cited in one widely used system, the APA (American Psychological Association) format.

Integrating Research

By integrating and acknowledging your sources of information in the speech, you'll give fair credit to those whose ideas and statements you're using. At the same time you'll help establish your own reputation as a responsible researcher. Here are a few suggestions for integrating your research into your speech.

Mention the sources in your speech by citing at least the author and, if helpful, the publication and the date. Here's how C. Kenneth Orski (1986) did it:

> *In assessing what the future may hold for transportation, I will lean heavily on a technique pioneered by John Naisbitt, author of* Megatrends. *Naisbitt believes that the most reliable way to anticipate the future is to try to understand the present. To this end he methodologically scans 6000 daily local newspapers from around the country.*

Avoid useless expressions such as "I have a quote here" or "I want to quote an example." Let the audience know that you're quoting by pausing before the quote, taking a step forward, or referring to your notes to read the extended quotation. Marilyn Loden (1986) again does this effectively:

> *Mary Kay Ash believes in feminine leadership. Recently she said: "A woman can no more duplicate the male style of leadership than an American businessman can exactly reproduce the Japanese style."*

If you feel it's crucial that the audience know you're quoting and you want to state that this is a quotation, you might do it this way:

> *Recently, Mary Kay Ash put this in perspective, and I quote: "A woman can no more duplicate the male style of leadership. . ."*

Use "signal verbs" in your speech to let the audience know your own evaluation of the material (Harnack and Kleppinger, 1997). Let's say, for example, that in an Internet article by Pat Doe you read the statement "Low self-esteem influences speaker apprehension." You can preface that information with a variety of signal verbs such as *has proven that, says, argues that, speculates that, has found that, thinks,* and *wonders if,* for example, and say "Pat Doe *speculates that* low self-esteem influences speaker apprehension." This, of course, is quite different from saying "Pat Doe *has proven that* low self-esteem influences speaker apprehension." (You might then go on to explain briefly how this was proven.) Select the verb that best represents what Pat Doe said and meant and at the same time the support or lack of support that you're attributing to Pat's statement. You may find it helpful to modify your verb in some way, for example, "convincingly argues," or "wildly speculates" to further indicate your support or lack of it.

UNIT IN BRIEF

General Principles of Research	Examine what you know. Work from the general to the specific. Take accurate notes. Use research time efficiently. Learn the available sources of information.
General Internet Resources	E-mail and listservs (mailing lists) Usenet groups (newgroups) Chat groups World Wide Web
Databases	General reference works (Encyclopedias, biographical data, almanacs, museum collections and exhibits) News sources (Newspaper indexes, newspaper CD ROM databases, newspapers and news magazine Web sites, news wire services, online news networks) Articles and posts (academic research articles, general research and opinion posts) Books (libraries, bookstores)
"Experts" and the Interview	Select the person. Secure an appointment. Prepare questions. Arrive on time. Establish rapport. Ask permission to tape. Ask open-ended and neutral questions. Close with appreciation. Follow up the interview.
Critically Evaluating Research	Is the information recent? Is the information fair and unbiased? Is the information directly relevant to your topic? Is the information sufficient? Is the evidence reliable and the reasoning logical?
Integrating Research in Your Speech	Mention your sources. Credit your sources for exact words as well as for ideas (to avoid even the suspicion of plagiarism). Provide smooth transitions between your words and the words of others.

THINKING CRITICALLY ABOUT PUBLIC SPEAKING RESEARCH

REVIEWING KEY TERMS AND CONCEPTS IN PUBLIC SPEAKING RESEARCH

1. Review and define the key terms used in this unit:
   - ❏ e-mail (p. 128)
   - ❏ newsgroups (p. 130)
   - ❏ chat groups (p. 132)
   - ❏ IRC channels (p. 132)
   - ❏ synchronous conversation (p. 132)
   - ❏ asynchronous conversation (p. 132)
   - ❏ World Wide Web (p. 133)
   - ❏ search engine (p. 134)
   - ❏ directory (p. 135)
   - ❏ Boolean operator (p. 136)
   - ❏ database (p. 136)

2. Review the key concepts discussed in this unit.
   - ▪ What are the general principles of research?
   - ▪ What are the values of e-mail, newsgroups, chat groups, and the World Wide Web for research in public speaking?
   - ▪ What are the major databases for general reference works, news items, articles and posts, and books?
   - ▪ What guidelines should be followed in conducting the research interview?
   - ▪ What principles should you follow in evaluating research?
   - ▪ How should research be cited and integrated into your speech?

DEVELOPING PUBLIC SPEAKING RESEARCH STRATEGIES

1. You have to give a speech in your sociology class on the cultural makeup of one of America's cities. Your speech is due next week and you have many other projects due, so your time is severely limited. How would you go about researching this topic in the shortest amount of time? You'll need at least six really recent sources.

2. You want to give a speech on television talk shows and want to include biographical information on some of the talk show hosts. What sources might you go to in order to get authoritative and current information on these hosts? What sources might you go to in order to get "fan" type information? How do you distinguish the two types of sources and information?

EVALUATING PUBLIC SPEECH RESEARCH

1. Evaluate the research in one of your own speeches or in one that you've read for recency, fairness, relevance, sufficiency, and reliability and logic.

2. Evaluate the way in which research is used in one of the speeches in the appendix. How effectively is the research integrated? How might its integration have been improved?

USING TECHNOLOGY IN PUBLIC SPEAKING RESEARCH

1. Visit http://www.refdesk.com/ (a collection of links to a wide variety of references sources). To what types of reference materials do these links connect you? Log on to one of the links that might prove useful in your research.

2. Visit a Web site that focuses on evaluating research on the Internet and compare that to what is suggested in this unit. What would you add to what is discussed in this unit? Here are three excellent Web sites dealing with evaluating research: "Evaluation of Information Sources by Alastair Smith at http://www.vuw.ac.nz, "Evaluating Information Found on the Internet" by Elizabeth Kirk at http://milton.mse.jhu.edu:8001/research/education/net.html (both suggested by Harnack and Kleppinger 1997) and "Evaluating Your Sources" by Janice Walker at http:longman.awl.com/podium/citation_walker_eval.htm.

3. Visit Argus Clearinghouse at www.clearinghouse.com and explore the kinds of information that might be relevant to your next speech. Do note that Argus, both a directory and a key word search engine, searches for lists of Web sites by title and key words—not the Web sites themselves—so be sure to use words that would be key words or that would appear in the title.

4. If you're new to IRC groups—or even if you're not—you might find it interesting to visit http://www2.ari.net/saunderf/mystery/mystery.html. It will give you an interesting introduction to the world of IRC.

PRACTICALLY SPEAKING

7.1   Short Speech Technique

Prepare and deliver a one-to-two minute speech in which you:

a. explain the value of one reference book for research.

b. explain one computer program that will prove helpful in research.

c. explain an advertisement that is reportedly based on research and evaluate the research.

d. explain how you used a computerized database either one discussed in this unit or some other database.

7.2 Accessing Information

In order to gain some familiarity with the various ways of locating information, each student should select or be assigned one of the following items of information and should report back to the class (in a brief two-minute speech) the answer and the reference work(s) he or she used to find the answer. In discussing how the answer was found, try to trace the process followed, identifying both productive and unproductive sources that were consulted and the reasons for consulting each source. If any of these prove too easy, then try identifying two or three totally different research paths that would all allow you to find the information you need.

1. The flag of Indonesia.
2. The ethnic population of Nebraska.
3. The current stock price of CocaCola.
4. The ingredients of a Harvey Wallbanger.
5. The first capital of the United States.
6. The current president of the National Communication Association, The American Psychological Association, or the International Communication Association.
7. The world's largest library and the number of volumes it contains.
8. The Academy Award winner in 1952 for best actor.
9. The literacy rate for China.
10. The main languages of Cambodia.
11. The prime interest rate for today.
12. The faculty-student ratio for Harvard University.
13. The largest amount of money grossed by a film.
14. The profits or losses for IBM last year.
15. The author of the quotation: "Though it be honest, it is never good to bring bad news."
16. The birthplace and real name of John Wayne.
17. The full name of the journals usually abbreviated QJS, JC, CM, CE.
18. The use and origin of the word *cyberspace*.
19. The early years of John Travolta.
20. The percentage of popular votes from Arkansas that Bill Clinton received in the election of 1996.
21. The text of John Kennedy's Inaugural Address.
22. The political configuration of Europe today.
23. The graduate program in communication at Indiana University.
24. The tuition at Brown University.
25. The amount of money charged for a full-page, four-color advertisement in *TV Guide*.
26. The major Hudson River artists.
27. The rules for playing chess.
28. Contemporary speeches on U.S. energy problems.
29. The speeches of the President of the United States.
30. The birthplace and political biography of one of your state senators.
31. The principles and beliefs of Islam.
32. The history of the Boy Scouts in Canada.
33. The author and source of the quotation, "My only love sprung from my only hate!"
34. The title of the Ph.D. dissertation of someone teaching at your school.
35. A recent psychological study on "learned helplessness."

7.3 Conducting Electronic Research

This exercise illustrates the wide variety of information you can easily secure from computer searches and provides the opportunity for exploring your online resources. Look up and bring to class a copy of an abstract for one of the following:

■ an article on public speaking that appears in the ERIC database in the last 5 years.

■ an article on a psychological study on fear—from

the Psychlit database.

- an article on persuasion from the Sociofile database.
- an article from a business journal dealing with communication skills.
- an article from any online newspaper dealing with college education.
- two articles on diabetes, one from *Medline* and one from the Web.
- a list of Listservs or Usenet groups concerned with ecological issues.
- a copy of a speech given in acceptance of an award.
- a list of 10 Web sites on divorce identified by any one of the major search engines.
- an article on immigration patterns during the last 20 years from *America: History and Life*.
- a review of a novel published in the last two years.

UNIT
8

Supporting Materials

UNIT CONTENTS	UNIT OBJECTIVES
	After completing this unit, you should be able to:
Examples	Explain the nature of examples and give suggestions for critically evaluating and using them in a public speech.
Narration	Explain the nature of narration and give suggestions for critically evaluating and using it in a public speech.
Testimony	Explain the nature of testimony and give suggestions for critically evaluating and using it in a public speech.
Statistics	Explain the nature of statistics and give suggestions for critically evaluating and using them in a public speech.
Some Additional Forms of Amplification	Explain the usefulness of quotations, definitions, comparisons and contrasts, facts and series of facts, and repetition and restatement.

Once you've identified your specific purpose and your main assertions and know where and how to search for information, you should then devote your attention to supporting your assertions, largely with the material you've uncovered in your research. This unit focuses on how to use examples, narration, testimony, and statistics, as well as such materials as quotations, definitions, comparisons, statements of facts, and repetition and restatement to support your ideas.

EXAMPLES

Examples are specific instances that are explained in varying degrees of detail. A relatively brief specific instance is referred to as an **example**. A longer and more detailed example is referred to as an **illustration**, and one told in story-like form is referred to as a **narration**, which is covered in the next section.

Examples are useful when you want to make concrete an abstract concept or idea. Specific examples can make the audience see what you mean by such abstract concepts as "persecution," "denial of freedom," "love," and "friendship." Your examples also encourage listeners to see *your* mental pictures of these concepts rather than seeing their own.

In a speech on free speech and song lyrics, Sam Brownback (1998, p. 454), United States Senator from Kansas, uses some powerful specific examples to make his point:

Women are objectified, often in the most obscene and degrading ways. Songs such as Prodigy's single "Smack My Bitch Up" or "Don't Trust a Bitch" by the group "Mo Thugs" encourage animosity and

Few things are harder to put up with than the annoyance of a good example.
—Mark Twain

even violence towards women. The alternative group Nine Inch Nails enjoyed both critical and commercial success with their song "Big Man with a Gun" which describes forcing a woman into oral sex and shooting her in the head at pointblank range.

Shock-rock bands such as "Marilyn Manson" or "Cannibal Corpse" go ever further, with lyrics describing violence, rape, and torture. Consider just a few song titles by the group "Cannibal Corpse"; "Orgasm by Torture", or "Stripped, Raped and Strangled." As their titles indicate, the lyrics to these songs celebrate hideous crimes against women.

Here D. Stanley Eitzen (1998, p. 123) uses a series of examples to support his point that college sport is big business:

Big-time college sport is organized so that separating the business aspects from the play on the field is impossible. The intrusion of money into collegiate sport is evident in the following representative examples:

—Some university athletic budgets are now as much as $33 million.

—Each school in the 1997 Rose bowl received $8.25 million, which it divided with other schools in its conference.

—Coors Brewing Company paid $5 million to the University of Colorado when the university agreed to name the new field house "Coors Events Center."

—Notre Dame has a $38 million contract to televise its football games. The sale of Notre Dame merchandise brings the school another $1 million in royalties and an appearance in a bowl game raises another $3 to $6 million.

Here, Carol W. Kinsley (1994, p. 41) uses an example to explain what community service learning is:

One of Michelle Herbert's recent projects at Liberty School involved her fifth-grade writing class in visits to a retirement home. They acted as pen-pals, writing letters, drawing pictures, and relating their own experiences to the residents. They also corresponded with the residents via computer e-mail. As part of their experience, they recorded their impressions and reflections in a journal after every session.

Finally, Holger Kluge (1997, p. 172) uses a personal example to illustrate how men and women often fail to understand each other.

I remember the time my wife told me she had a splitting headache. I suggested she take some Tylenol. And she got upset with me! She wasn't looking for a solution to her problem. She knew how to get rid of a headache. She was looking for sympathy, empathy and understanding. But being a man, I had only seen a problem that needed fixing.

Critically Evaluating Examples

"For example" is not proof.
—Yiddish proverb

Ask yourself (as speaker, listener, and critic) the following questions about examples.

1. Is the example typical or representative? Generally, use an example that is representative of the class of objects about which you're speaking. Training schools that advertise on television frequently show a particularly successful graduate. The advertiser assumes, of course, that the audience will see this example as representative. Perhaps this person is representative; more often than not, however, representativeness isn't achieved or perhaps even desired by the advertiser.

At times you may want to draw an example that is purposefully far-fetched. Perhaps you wish to poke fun at a particular proposal or show the inadequacies of an alternative point of view. The important point is that both you and the audience see the example in the same way.

2. Is the example relevant? Use examples that relate directly to the proposition you wish to explain. Leave out irrelevant examples, however interesting or entertaining. Be certain too that the audience sees the relevance. Notice how Marvin Alisky (1985) uses his example to make his point:

In his play Pygmalion, *George Bernard Shaw observes, "If you treat a girl like a flower girl, that's all she will ever be. If you treat her like a princess she may become one."*

If we treat those around us like extensions of our modern technology, that is all they will be. If we treat them like important assets with individual and changing needs, then they will become assets to our organizations and communities.

Using Examples

In using examples, keep in mind that their function is to make your ideas vivid and easily understood. Examples are useful for explaining concepts; they're not ends in themselves. Make them only as long as necessary to ensure that your purpose is achieved.

Use enough examples to make your point. Make sure that the examples are sufficient to recreate your meaning in the minds of your listeners, but be careful not to use too many. If you use too many examples the audience may become bored and may lose the very point you wish to make.

Make the relationship between your assertion and your example explicit. Remember that this relationship is clear to you because you've constructed the speech. The audience is going to hear your speech only once. Show the audience exactly how your example relates to the assertion or concept you're explaining. Consider the following excerpt in which Stella Guerra (1986) uses a series of examples to illustrate the progress made by women in government and the military. Notice how much more effective these examples are than if she had simply said, "Women have made great progress in government and in the military."

In short, we are continuing to help America forge an environment that says "opportunities are abundant." In this environment of prosperity we've seen many firsts:

- The first female brigadier general
- The first female astronaut
- The first female sky marshall
- The first female ambassador to the United Nations
- The first female justice of the Supreme Court
- The first female director of Civil Service
- The first female U.S. Customs rep in a foreign country
- The first female to graduate at the very top of the class in a service academy—Navy '84; Air Force '86

The list goes on and on—and this same progress can be seen in all sectors of our society.

Make clear the distinction between real and hypothetical examples. Don't try to foist a hypothetical example on the audience as a real one. If they recognize it, they'll resent your attempt to fool them. Use statements such as the following to let the audience know when you're using a hypothetical example.

- We could imagine a situation such as . . .
- I think an ideal friend would be someone who . . .
- A hypothetical example of this type of friendship would be like this . . .

If the example is real, let the audience know this as well. Help the audience see what you want them to see with such statements as "A situation such as this occurred recently; it involved . . . ," or "I have a friend who . . . ," or simply "An actual example of this was reported . . ."

NARRATION

Narratives are stories, and they are often useful as supporting materials in a speech. Narratives give the audience what it wants: a good story. Listeners seem to perk up automatically when a story is told. If the narrative is a personal one, it will likely increase your credibility and show you as a real person. Listeners like to know about speakers, and the personal narrative meets this desire. Notice how you remember the little stories noted personalities tell in television interviews.

The main value of narration is that it allows you to bring an abstract concept down to specifics. For example, to illustrate friendship and love, you might recount the mythical story of Damon and Pythias. After being sentenced to death for speaking out against the government by the tyrant Dionysius, Pythias asked to be allowed to return home to put his affairs in order. His friend, Damon volunteered to remain in his place. If Pythias did not return, Damon would be executed. At the appointed time, Pythias did not return. Without animosity toward his friend, Damon prepared for his own execution. But, before the sentence could be carried out, Pythias returned, apologized for his unavoidable delay, and asked that his friend be set free. So impressed was Dionysius by this friendship that he pardoned Pythias and asked if he could join the two of them in this extraordinary friendship. This brief story illustrates friendship and love in a way that a definition could never do.

Narratives may be of different types, and each serves a somewhat different purpose. Following Clella Jaffe (1998), we distinguish three types of narrative: explanatory, exemplary, and persuasive.

Explanatory narratives explain the way things are. The biblical book of Genesis, for example, explains the development of the world. Here, Jamie Lee Wagner (Schnoor, 1994, p. 7), a student from Arizona State University, uses an explanatory narrative to introduce her topic of sleep deprivation.

> On September 9, 1993, a Greyhound bus bound for my hometown of Phoenix, Arizona, swerved off the road and flipped over. The accident injured 42 of the passengers, including David Mata who was forced to have both of his hands amputated. The driver, the man responsible for the passengers' safety, had fallen asleep behind the wheel. And he was just one of the 100 million Americans who suffers from sleep deprivation, ranging in severity from occasional jet lag to chronic insomnia.

Exemplary narratives provide examples of excellence, examples to follow or admire. The stories of the lives of saints and martyrs are exemplary narratives, as are the Horatio Alger success stories. Similarly, many motivational speakers such as Susan Powter and Tony Little often include exemplary narratives in their speeches and will tell the story of how they were when they were out of shape. Here, for example, is just a part of a narrative used by Kathleen B. Cooper (1994, p. 85), chief economist for Exxon Corporation:

> My story began like many others: I married early—after only one year of college. And I headed off to work to "put hubby through" doing clerical work, as was also so common then. What happened to get me back on the road to finish college? One extraordinarily boring job experience. It made me realize that I would probably work for most or all of my life, and I did not want to go through life without enjoying my work.

Persuasive narratives try to strengthen or change beliefs and attitudes. When Sally Struthers tells us of the plight of the starving children, she's using a persuasive narrative. The parables in religious writings are persuasive in their urging listeners to lead life in a particular way. Here, Richard A. Gephardt (1995, p. 199), a Missouri Congressman, uses a persuasive narrative to emphasize the importance of economic recovery:

> A few weeks ago, I met a man in Jefferson Country, Missouri, who had lost his job, and couldn't find a way of earn a living. His economic crisis shattered his marriage, as well as his self-confidence. He had loaded all of his worldly possessions into his car, and was headed down the road to nowhere.
>
> He looked at me with tears in his eyes, and said: "They took away more than my paycheck. They took away my pride. And that was all

I had left to give." Your job is more than what you do—*it's who you* are. *It's your identity.*

Often, the same narrative can serve a variety of functions. For example, consider the story from Greek mythology of Narcissus, the beautiful boy who so admired himself that he ignored the advances of the nymph Echo and only wanted to stare at and admire his own reflection in a lake. As a result of his total self-absorption, he pined away and died, being "reborn" as the narcissus flower. The story is explanatory because it explains the myth of how the narcissus flower developed; it's exemplary because it portrays the evil that befalls a narcissistic personality; and it's persuasive because of its obvious injunction: Don't be self-absorbed.

Narratives can be first person or third person accounts. In first person narratives the speaker tells a story that happened to her or him. Kathleen Cooper's narrative given earlier is a good example. In third person narratives, the speaker tells a story about someone else—a parent's decision to give up a child to adoption, a person's first day in the military, a family conflict. Wagner's and Gephardt's narratives, given earlier, are good examples of third person narratives.

Critically Evaluating Narratives

Like examples, narratives need to be assessed critically.

1. Is the narrative relevant? If the narrative isn't relevant to the speech purpose, then it shouldn't be used. Regardless of how humorous, heart wrenching, or instructive the story is, use it only if it supports your purpose.

2. Is the narrative fairly presented? Although narratives are commonly thought of as true, narratives can be hypothetical, or they can be composites of a variety of stories. Novelists, for example, often combine the lives of numerous people into one character. Regardless of the type of narrative you use, it should be clear to your audience when your story is real, when it's hypothetical, and when it's a composite drawn for purposes of illustration.

Using Narratives

When using narratives as support, keep them relatively short and few in number. In most cases, one or possibly two narratives are sufficient in a short 5-7 minute speech. Especially if the narrative is a personal one, be sure you don't get carried away and elaborate more than necessary.

Maintain a reasonable chronological order. Events happen in time and are best recounted in a time sequence. Avoid shifting back and forth through time. Start at the beginning and end at the end.

Make explicit the connection between your story and the point you're making. Be sure that the audience will see the connection between the story and the purpose of your speech. If they don't, you not only lose the effectiveness of the story but you also lose their attention as they try to figure out why you told that story.

Consider using a climax order in which you build to a highpoint. If possible, create suspense. If you do, your audience is likely to pay you greater attention than normal.

Use dialogue only if you can carry it off. Be especially careful of speaking in the dialogue of a person who is very different form you—say another sex or race. You can easily revert to stereotypes or what can easily be perceived as stereotyping. The man who recites the dialogue of a frail woman and who raises his pitch too high or uses too many facial expressions, may easily create a humorous effect. Generally, dialogues are easier to incorporate into your speech if the person is like you. And, with perhaps only the rarest of exceptions, avoid using foreign accents.

Literature is strewn with the wreckage of men who have minded beyond reason the opinion of others.
—Virginia Woolf

TESTIMONY

Testimony refers to the opinions of experts or to the accounts of witnesses. Testimony helps amplify your speech by adding a note of authority to your arguments. Testimony may, therefore, be used in either of two ways. First, you might be concerned with the opinions, beliefs, predictions, or values of some authority or expert. You might, for example, want to state an economist's predictions concerning inflation and depression, or you might want to support your analysis by citing an art critic's evaluation of a painting or art movement.

As you might think, testimony is also valuable when you wish to persuade an audience. Thus, you may use the testimony of a noted economist to support your predictions about inflation, or you may wish to cite an education professor's opinion about the problems confronting education in an effort to persuade your listeners that certain changes must be made in our schools.

In the following excerpt, for instance, Rebecca Winter (Schnoor, 1996, p. 30), a student from Kansas State University, uses the testimony of two industry leaders to support her argument that daycare is good business.

Providing daycare or daycare assistance is good business. The February 8, 1995, The Wall Street Journal *points to several progressive firms like Marriot International. Marriot's program stopped a 300 percent yearly turnover rate.* 48 Hours *reports that Toyota's program is responsible for the 60 percent of employees who have a perfect attendance record. As Toyota's vice president of human resources said, "It's not a fringe benefit anymore. It's a necessity." As Marriot's director of work-life pro-*

With your next speech topic in mind, if you could interview anyone, whom would you choose? What questions would you ask?

grams said, "You don't manage people as a second class work force. They're integral to the job, a part of the fabric of the company."

Second, you might want to use the testimony of an eyewitness to some event or situation. You might, for example, cite the testimony of someone who saw an accident, the person who spent two years in a maximum-security prison, or the person who had a particular operation.

Critically Evaluating Testimony

Test the adequacy of your testimony by asking yourself the following questions.

1. Is the testimony presented fairly? In using the testimony of others, present it fairly. Include, for example, any qualifications made by the expert. When presenting the ideas of an authority, present them as that authority would want.

2. Is the person an authority on this subject? Authorities, especially today, reign over very small territories. Doctors, professors, and lawyers—to name just a few—are experts on very small areas of knowledge. A doctor may be an expert on the thyroid gland but may know little about skin, muscles, or blood. A professor of history might know a great deal about the Renaissance but little about American history. When an authority is used, be certain that the person is in fact an authority on your specific subject.

3. Is the person unbiased? This question should be asked of both expert and witness accounts. Try to discover if there are any biases in the sources being cited. The real estate salesperson who tells you to "Buy! Buy! Buy!" and the diamond seller who tells you "Diamonds are your best investment" obviously have something to gain and are biased. Be suspicious of the conclusions of any biased source. This does not mean that normally biased sources can't provide unbiased testimony. Surely they can. This does mean that once a bias has been detected, you should be on the lookout for how this bias might figure into the testimony.

Using Testimony

When you cite testimony, stress first the competence of the person and whether that person is an expert or a witness. To cite the predictions of a world-famous economist of whom your audience has never heard will mean little unless you first explain the person's competence. You might say, for example:

This prediction comes from the world's leading economist, who has successfully predicted all major financial trends over the past 20 years.

Now the audience will be prepared to lend credence to what this person says.

Similarly, establish the competence of a witness. Consider the following two excerpts.

My friend told me that in prison drugs are so easy to get that all you have to do is pay the guard and you'll get whatever you want.

My friend, who was a guard in three different prisons over the past 15 years, told me that in prisons drugs are so easy to get that all you have to do is pay the guard and you'll get whatever you want.

Notice that in the second statement, you establish the credibility of your source. Your audience is much more likely to believe this second testimony.

Second, stress the unbiased nature of the testimony. If the audience perceives the testimony to be biased—whether or not it really is—it will have little effect. You want to check out the biases of a witness so that you may present accurate information. But, you also want to make the audience see that the testimony is, in fact, unbiased. You might say something like this:

Researchers and testers at Consumer Reports, *none of whom have any vested interest in the products examined, found wide differences in car safety. Let's look at some of these findings. In the October 1998 issue, for example, ...*

Third, stress the recency of the statement to the audience. Notice that in the first excerpt that follows, we have no way of knowing when the statement was made and therefore no way of knowing how true this statement would be today. In the second excerpt, however, the recency of the statement is stressed. As demonstrated by these examples, recency is often a crucial factor in determining whether or not we will believe a statement.

General Bailey has noted that the United States has over twice the military power of any other world power.

General Bailey, who was interviewed last week in The Washington Post, *noted that the United States has twice the military power of any other world power.*

STATISTICS

Let's say you want to show that significant numbers of people are now getting their news from the Internet, that the cost of filmmaking has skyrocketed over the last 20 years, or that women buy significantly more books and magazines than men. To communicate these types of information, you might use statistics—summary figures that help you communicate the important characteristics of an otherwise complex set of numbers. Statistics help the audience see, for example, the percentage of people getting their news from Internet, the average cost of films in 1999 versus previous years, and the difference between male and female book and magazine purchases.

Types of Statistics

For most speeches and most audiences, simple statistics work best. Examples of some simple statistics include measures of central tendency, correlation, difference, and percentages.

Measures of Central Tendency. Measures of central tendency tell you the general pattern in a group of numbers. The *mean* is the arithmetic average of a set of numbers. For example, if the mean grade on an examination was

There are three kinds of lies: lies, damned lies, and statistics.
—Mark Twain

89, it means that if you added up all the scores and divided by the number of students taking the exam, the result would be 89.

The *median* is the middle score; 50 percent of the cases fall above and 50 percent fall below it. For example, if the median score on an examination was 78, it means that half the class scored higher than 78 and half scored lower.

The *mode* is the most frequently occurring score. It's the single score that most people received. If the mode of the mid-term was 85, it means that more students received 85 than any other single score.

Measures of Correlation. Measures of correlation tell you how closely two or more things are related. For example, there's a high positive correlation between smoking and lung cancer; smokers have a greater incidence of lung cancer than nonsmokers and heavy smokers have a greater incidence than light smokers. As your smoking increases, so does the likelihood of lung cancer. Correlations can also be negative. For example, there's a high negative correlation between the amount of money you have and the likelihood that you'll be convicted of a crime. As the amount of money increases, the likelihood of criminal conviction decreases; as the amount of money decreases, the likelihood of conviction increases.

Recognize that high correlations (whether positive or negative) do not mean causation. The fact that two things vary together (that is, are highly correlated) does not mean that one causes the other. They may each be caused by some third factor. So, although you know that smoking does cause lung cancer, it's not the correlation itself that tells you this. The correlation merely tells you that as smoking increases so does the incidence of lung cancer, and as smoking decreases so does the incidence of lung cancer. The same is true with negative correlations. The high negative correlation between money and the likelihood of criminal conviction does not tell you that a lack of money is the cause of a high conviction rate; it merely tells you that as one goes up (say, money), the other goes down (say, conviction rate). So, beware of research that argues that a high correlation proves causation; it doesn't.

Measures of Difference. Measures of difference tell you the extent to which scores differ from the average or from each other. For example, the *range* tells you how far the lowest score is from the highest score. The range is computed by subtracting the lowest from the highest score. If the lowest score on the mid-term was 76 and the highest was 99, the range was 23 points. Generally, a high range indicates great diversity, whereas a low range indicates great similarity. The range may be used to show, for example, the discrepancy in income between management and labor or between college and high school graduates.

Percentages. Percentages allow you to express a score as a portion of 100. So, if 78 percent of the people favored coffee over tea, that would mean that 78 people out of every 100 favored coffee over tea. Percentages would prove useful if you wanted to show, say, the growth of cable television over the past 10 years, the amount of the proposed tuition increase, or the divorce rate in different parts of the world. In some cases, you might want to compare percentages. For example, you might compare percentages among the various ways in which people get their news. You might note, for instance, that 60 percent get their news from television while only 47

What type of statistical graph would you use to illustrate each of the following propositions: (1) school violence is increasing; (2) inflation is under control; (3) the military budget is much too large; (4) the divorce rate is increasing?

percent get it from newspapers to illustrate the importance of television news. To illustrate the growth of the Internet as a news medium, you might note that in 1995 only 4 percent of the people got their news from the Internet but in 1998 that percentage grew to 20 percent (*The New York Times,* July 27, 1998, p. D8). Here, for example, Howard R. Veit (1998, p. 563) uses percentages to show the growth in managed health care:

> *Given the growth in managed care enrollment, it is not surprising that the AMA reports that in 1997, 92% of physicians were in practices that held contracts with one or more managed care companies. In 1990, that figure was 65%, and in 1986, it was about 43%.*

THE ETHICS OF Means and Ends

Would it be ethical for you, as a public speaker, to say things that would normally be considered unethical? What about making up statistics if the end you hoped to achieve was a worthy one, such as keeping children from using drugs? Those taking an objective position (see Ethics of Public Speaking box, Unit 6) would argue that the ends don't justify the means, that the lie, for example, is always wrong regardless of the specific situation. Those taking a subjective position would argue that at times the end would justify the means and at times it wouldn't; it would depend on the specific means and ends in question.

You'll probably make at least some of your public speaking decisions on the basis of a means-ends analysis. Consider your own feelings about means and ends by asking yourself if it would it be ethical to:

1. Pretend to be culturally similar to an audience (without actually saying so, but just allowing them to

believe it) to better achieve your purpose, which will ultimately benefit the audience members?

2. Exaggerate your skills and experience to make yourself more credible to obtain a job in which you know you'll be a great asset to the company?

3. Misrepresent yourself in an Internet newsgroup to spice things up?

4. Make up statistics to support your point of view in a public speech because you know that what you're advocating will benefit the audience?

5. Work on an advertising team writing an ad using only emotional and credibility appeals (nothing logical about it) to get children to buy expensive sneakers? To get teens to avoid potentially dangerous sexual practices?

(The next Ethics of Public Speaking box appears on page 214.)

Critically Evaluating Statistics

In critically evaluating statistics, whether those you find in research or those that other speakers use, ask the following questions.

Are the statistics based on a large enough sample? The size of the sample is always important. This is one reason why few advertisers ever report the size of their sample. Advertisers may tell you, for example:

Buy Blotto milk for the health of your baby. Four out of five nutritionists surveyed chose Blotto.

In this and similar claims, however, you're not told how large the entire sample was. If they merely tested groups of five until they found one group where four would endorse Blotto, you wouldn't put much confidence in those statistics. (Note, too, that the statement does not say *what* they chose Blotto milk over. We assume it was other brands of milk but nowhere is this made explicit.) The sample must be large enough to expect that if another group were selected, the results would be the same as those reported in the statistics. Enough nutritionists should have been surveyed so that if you went out and selected 100 at random, 80 would endorse Blotto.

Is the sample a fair representation of the entire population? If you wish to make inferences about an entire class of people, sample the group fairly and include representatives of all subgroups. Thus, it would be unfair to make inferences about the attitudes of college professors if you surveyed only those who taught communication.

Is the statistic based on recent sampling? Recency is particularly important since things change so rapidly. To report mean income, church attendance, or smoking statistics without ensuring recency is meaningless. Here, for example, Amir Brown (Schnoor, 1997, p. 131), a student from Rice University, uses recent statistics to argue that children's playgrounds are unsafe:

The June 7, 1996, issue of the San Francisco Examiner *reports that the Consumer Federation of America conducted a survey of 562 playgroups in 25 states and the District of Columbia. The survey found that 85% of the playgroups had improper protective surfacing. . . . In addition, the survey found that 92% of the playgrounds had monkey bars or slides that were higher than the recommended six feet. . . . The Consumer Federation of America also discovered that 46% of the playgrounds had equipment with small gaps which can trap children's heads, protrusions and open S hooks, which are used to hold swings and ropes and chains.*

Are the statistics collected and analyzed by an unbiased source? Remember our advertisers! They're intent on selling a product; they make their living that way. When they say "four out of five," ask who collected the data and who analyzed it?

Are contrary statistics omitted? Unfortunately, many advertisements for colleges omit statistics that are often relevant to their argument. For example, in many college ads you'll read of the success of some of its graduates. Often, however, the statistics on less successful students are omitted. Thus, for example, you may read that 7 students were accepted into prestigious medical schools and 9 into high ranking law schools. But, these ads rarely tell you how many pre-med and pre-law students failed to gain placement in any professional school. The percentage of students who did and who did not get into such schools would give you a much fairer picture of the college's success rate. In evaluating statistics, always ask if what isn't said might be relevant.

I could prove God statistically.
—George Gallup

Using Statistics

Keep in mind that the audience will ask essentially the same questions that a good researcher would ask in analyzing statistics found, say, on the web or that a critical listener would ask when hearing statistics in a speech. Answer these questions for your audience. For example, answer their questions about whether the source is biased by stressing the unbiased nature of the source who collected and analyzed the statistics. Answer their questions about how representative the sample is by telling them that the statistic is based on a fair representation of the entire population about which you're speaking. Answer their questions about recency by giving them the date when the statistics were collected or when the survey was completed. In addition, express your statistics so that they're clear, meaningful, connected to your proposition, reinforced, and used with moderation.

Make the Statistics Clear. Be sure to make the statistics clear to an audience that will hear the figures only once. Round off figures so they're easy to comprehend and retain. Don't say that the median income of workers in this city is $31,347. This may be accurate, but it will be difficult to remember. Instead, say that it's "around $31,300" or even "a bit more than $31,000."

Make the Statistics Meaningful. Numbers need to be made meaningful to the audience. First, when using statistics it's often helpful to remind the audience of what the statistic itself means. So, for example, if you say that "the median co-op apartment in San Francisco is $243,000" remind the audience that median means the middle price—that half of the homes are above $243,000 and half are below.

Second, try to present the numbers so that the audience can appreciate the meaning you want to convey. To say, for example, that the Sears Tower in Chicago is 1,559 feet tall does not visualize its height. So, consider saying something like:

> *The Sears Tower is 1,559 feet tall. Just how tall is 1,559 feet? Well, it's as tall as the length of more than four football fields. That's how tall. It's as tall as 260 6-foot people standing on each other's heads.*

Connect the Statistics with the Proposition. Make explicit the connection between the statistics and what they show. To say, for example, that college professors make an average of $62,000 per year needs to be related specifically to the proposition that teachers' salaries should be raised or lowered, depending on your point of view.

Visually (and Verbally) Reinforce the Statistics. Because numbers are difficult to grasp and remember when they're presented without some kind of visual reinforcement, it's often helpful to complement your oral presentation of statistics with some type of presentation aid—perhaps a graph or a chart. In this way, your audience will both see and hear the numbers and will be better able to see their relevance and remember them. At the same time, consider the value of using repetition and restatement when you have the least suspicion that your statistics may be difficult to grasp on one hearing. For example, in using the percentage increases for people getting their news from the Internet, it might be helpful to say: "Between 1995 and 1998, the percentage of people getting their news from the Internet grew from 4 percent to 20 percent; 20 people out of every hundred now get their news from the Internet compared with only 4 out of a hundred just a few years ago—that's an increase of 500 percent!"

Use Statistics in Moderation. If you were giving a speech on, for example, the results of scientific studies on reducing diseases, birth, and mortality rates throughout the world, or the growth of consumer spending, you'd have to rely quite heavily on statistics. In most cases, however, statistics should be used sparingly. Most listeners' capacity for numerical data presented in a speech is limited, so use statistics in moderation.

SOME ADDITIONAL FORMS OF AMPLIFICATION

There are a variety of other forms of amplification that can be used. Here's just a brief mention of some of these.

Quotations

Quotations are useful for adding spice and wit as well as authority to your speeches. Quotations can, however, become cumbersome. Too often they're not related directly to the point you're trying to make and their relevance gets lost. If the quotation is in technical language that listeners will not understand, it then becomes necessary to interject definitions as you go along. Therefore, unless the quotation is short, comprehensible to the audience, and related directly to the point you're trying to make, use your own words; paraphrase in your own words the essence of the idea. And credit the person you're quoting.

Here, for example, James H. Carr (1995, p. 219) uses a quotation from Martin Luther King Jr.:

> *This is as true today as it was just over thirty years ago when Dr. Martin Luther King Jr. stood on the steps of the Lincoln Memorial at the great civil rights march of 1963 and stated, "We have . . . come to this spot to remind America of the fierce urgency of now . . . now is the time to open the doors of opportunity to all."*

> *Now is the time for us to think rationally and act compassionately. Now is the time for us to consider the future of our great nation if we continue to place a priority on punishing people after their lives have been destroyed, rather than providing meaningful educational training and employment opportunities.*

Here Clifton Wharton (1995, p. 207) uses his own words and also credits the source:

> *A Michigan Senator, Arthur Vandenberg, once said that politics stop at the water's edge—meaning that the nation unites once action is taken. Unfortunately, we have forgotten that bit of wisdom.*

Definitions

Definitions clarify and explain the meaning of specific terms and are especially helpful when complex terms are introduced or when you wish to provide a particular perspective on a subject. As will be explained in Unit 19 definitions can be of varied types. For example, you might define a term by providing a simple dictionary definition or you might define it by tracing its etymology or historical development. Or, you might define a term by using the authority of an expert.

Comparisons and Contrast

Another form of amplification is comparison and contrast. You might want to compare or contrast one thing with another—living conditions in Germany and Japan, extroverted and introverted personalities, or computers and typewriters. This form of amplification is discussed in Unit 21 under "Reasoning from Analogy."

Simple Statement of Fact or a Series of Facts

It's often useful to cite facts or a series of facts to explain a statement or position. In a speech on the growing problem of drug trafficking, Lee Brown (1995, p. 177) uses a series of facts:

> *There are other critical developments:*
>
> *—Worldwide opium production has quadrupled in the last decade.*
>
> *—Poppy growing areas are expanding in Afghanistan and the new republics of the former Soviet Union.*
>
> *—Heroin addict populations, particularly in Asia, are increasing.*
>
> *—South American heroin from Colombia is now being shipped by the cocaine cartels to the United States.*

Repetition and Restatement

Still another way to amplify your thoughts is to use repetition or restatement. Repetition involves repeating your idea in the same words at strategic places throughout your speech. Restatement involves repeating your idea in different words.

Repetition and restatement are especially helpful in public speeches because of the inevitable lapses in audience attention. When you repeat or

---

TIPS

from professional speakers

Restatement is the art of being redundant without being repetitious. To restate is not to merely repeat the same thing in the same way; to restate is to find different ways of communicating a message. Using a variety of types of support—an example, a quotation, a comparison with a statistic—to develop an idea affords a likelihood that more of our listeners will understand or embrace our ideas.

Caryl Rae Krannich, communication and career expert, frequent speaker and trainer, *101 Secrets of Highly Effective Speakers: Controlling Fear, Commanding Attention* (Manassas Park, VA: Impact Publications, 1998): 47.

restate your ideas, you provide listeners with one more opportunity to grasp what you're saying.

Restatement is especially important when addressing a culturally mixed audience who may not have learned your language as their first language. Consequently, they may not easily understand certain idioms and figures of speech. Restating these ideas in different words increases the chances of audience comprehension.

UNIT IN BRIEF

Examples: specific instances explained in varying degrees of detail.	Examples should be: ■ representative ■ relevant Examples are most effective when: ■ used to explain a concept rather than as ends in themselves ■ the relationship between the concept and the example is explicit ■ the distinction between a real and a hypothetical example is clear
Narration: a story that illustrates an assertion and can be explanatory, exemplary, or persuasive and presented in first or third person.	Narratives should be: ■ relevant to the subject and purpose ■ presented fairly Narratives are most effective when they're: ■ relatively short ■ presented in chronological order ■ clearly connected to the speech purpose ■ presented in climax order ■ presented in dialogue only when most effective (otherwise, use your own words)
Testimony: the opinions of experts or the accounts of witnesses often used to lend authority or otherwise amplify assertions.	Testimony should be: ■ presented fairly ■ authoritative on the specific subject ■ unbiased Testimony is most effective when: ■ the competence of the authority is stressed ■ the unbiased nature of the testimony is stressed ■ the recency of the observation or opinion is stressed

Statistics: a figure that summarizes the important characteristics of an otherwise complex set of numbers.

Statistics should be:
- based on a large enough sample
- based on a representative sample
- based on recent sampling
- collected and analyzed by unbiased sources
- complete; don't omit contrary but relevant statistics

Statistics are most effective when they're:
- clear
- meaningful to the audience
- connected to the proposition they support
- visually and verbally reinforced
- used in moderation

THINKING CRITICALLY ABOUT SUPPORTING MATERIALS

REVIEWING KEY TERMS AND CONCEPTS IN SUPPORTING MATERIALS

1. Review and define the key terms used in this unit:
   - ❑ examples (p. 161)
   - ❑ narration (p. 164)
   - ❑ testimony (p. 167)
   - ❑ statistics (p. 169)
   - ❑ quotations (p. 174)
   - ❑ definitions (p. 175)
   - ❑ comparison and contrast (p. 175)
   - ❑ series of facts (p. 175)
   - ❑ repetition (p. 175)
   - ❑ restatement (p. 175)

2. Review the key concepts discussed in this unit:
   - What are examples and how might they be used to support an idea?
   - What is narration and how might it be used in a speech?
   - What is testimony? What are the guidelines for using testimony?
   - What are statistics? What are the main kinds of statistics that are useful to a public speaker? What guidelines should be followed in evaluating statistics?
   - How might quotations, definitions, comparison and contrast, statements of facts, and repetition and restatement be used in speeches?

DEVELOPING PUBLIC SPEAKING STRATEGIES FOR SUPPORTING IDEAS

1. Karla is planning to give a speech on road rage and wants to show that it's a real problem needing a real solution. What kinds of statistical information would help her establish the severity of the problem?

2. You want to present the testimony of a retired judge to bolster your position that probation should be abolished. For your purpose, what would be the ideal qualifications of this judge? How might you weave these qualifications into your speech?

EVALUATING PUBLIC SPEECHES

1. Review one of the speeches in this text or on the Web, focusing on the types of supporting materials the speaker used. What kinds can you identify? Were they effective in achieving the speaker's purpose?

2. Revisit one of the speeches presented in Unit 5 (pp. 93-98), the two poorly constructed speeches. Review these for supporting materials. What are some of the problems with the support used in these speeches? What distinguishes the support in one of the effective speeches from the support in one of these two poorly constructed speeches?

USING TECHNOLOGY IN PUBLIC SPEAKING

1. Visit one of the Web sites devoted to quotations (for example, http://www.cc.columbia.edu/acis/bartleby/bartlett/ or http://www.yahoo.com/Reference/Quotations/) and select a quotation that can be used with your next speech.

2. Search for information on the author of the quotation you found in No. 1, using one of the search engines discussed in Unit 7 (see Table 7.1) or a specific Web site such as http://www.biography.com/. Might knowing something about the author help you in introducing your quotation?

3. Excellent aids for using and interpreting statistics may be found at http://nilesonline.com/stats/. This will prove useful in understanding and evaluating research results and in using statistics in your own speeches.

PRACTICALLY SPEAKING

8.1 Short Speech Technique

Prepare and deliver a two-minute speech in which you

a. develop two examples (real or hypothetical) to illustrate one of these propositions: rewards come to those who work hard; having faith will solve all problems; being optimistic leads to happiness; use time, don't waste it; practice makes perfect; good neighbors are nosy neighbors.

b. tell a personal story to illustrate a specific point, being sure to follow the suggestions offered in this unit.

c. retell a fairy tale or folktale to illustrate a moral or general principle.

d. explain the kind of testimonials that would convince you to buy a particular brand of toothpaste, cereal, car, dog food, or hearing aid.

e. explain a print ad that relies on statistics and show how the advertiser uses statistics to make a point.

8.2 Amplifying Statements

Here are some rather bland, uninteresting statements. Select one of them and amplify it using at least three different methods of amplification. Identify each method used. Since the purpose of this exercise is to provide greater insight into forms and methods of amplification, you may, for this exercise, manufacture, fabricate, or otherwise invent facts, figures, illustrations, examples, and the like. In fact, it may prove even more beneficial if you go to extremes in constructing these forms of support.

1. Abortion is wrong/Abortion is moral.
2. The Sears Tower in Chicago is the world's tallest building.
3. Dr. Kirk was a great instructor.
4. My grandparents left me a fortune in their will.
5. The college I just visited seems ideal.
6. The writer of this article is a real authority.
7. I knew I was marrying into money as soon as I walked into the house.
8. Considering what they did, punishment to the fullest extent of the law would be mild.
9. The fortune teller told us good news.
10. The athlete lived an interesting life.

Presentation Aids

UNIT CONTENTS	UNIT OBJECTIVES
	After completing this unit, you should be able to: Identify the functions of presentation aids.
Functions of Presentation Aids	
Types and Media of Presentation Aids	Identify the types and media of presentation aids.
Preparing and Using Presentation Aids	Explain the suggestions for preparing and using presentation aids.
Computer Assisted Presentations	Explain the advantages of and guidelines for preparing and delivering computer assisted presentations.

When you're planning to give a speech, consider using some kind of presentation aid—a visual or auditory means for clarifying ideas. Presentation aids are not necessary or even desirable in all speeches and should only be used when they contribute to making your speech more effective. Using presentation aids when they aren't relevant will only detract from the message you want to communicate.

In many instances, however, presentation aids will significantly improve your speech. Ask yourself how you can visualize with your aid what you want your audience to remember. How can you reinforce your ideas with additional media? For example, if you want your audience to see the increases in sales tax, consider showing them a chart of rising sales tax over the last 10 years. If you want them to see that Brand A is superior to Brand X, consider showing them a comparison chart identifying the superiority of Brand A.

This unit will provide you with the tools for developing and using presentation aids ranging from the simple word chart to a professional-looking slide show. More specifically, this unit explains the functions of presentation aids and the types (graphs, words, maps, models) and media (video, transparencies, slides) you can choose from. A wide variety of suggestions for preparing and using presentation aids are offered to help you effectively develop and present them. The last major section of this unit focuses on computer-assisted presentations and covers the advantages of computer presentations, the ways you can use them, guidelines for using presentation software, rehearsal suggestions, and working through the presentation.

FUNCTIONS OF PRESENTATION AIDS

In oratory the greatest art is to hide art.
—Jonathan Swift

Presentation aids are not added frills. They're integral parts of your speech and will prove useful for gaining attention and maintaining interest, adding clarity, reinforcing your message, and contributing to your credibility and confidence.

Presentation Aids Gain Attention and Maintain Interest

We are a generation that grew up on multimedia entertainment. We are used to it and we enjoy it. It's not surprising, then, that we as members of the audience appreciate it when a speaker makes use of such aids. We perk up when the speaker says, "I want you to look at this chart showing the employment picture for the next five years" or "Listen to the vocal range in this voice."

Presentation aids also help maintain attention and interest because they break up the speech and provide some variety in what we see and hear. Audiences will appreciate this and will respond more favorably when you provide them with this variety, with this differently packaged message.

Presentations Add Clarity

Let's say you want to illustrate the growth of the cable television industry in the United States over the last 20 years. You could say, for example, "In 1977 there were 12 million subscribers, in 1982 there were 29 million subscribers, in 1987 there were . . ." This gets pretty boring fast. Further, the numbers you want the audience to appreciate are difficult to retain in memory so that by the time you get to mentioning the 1997 figures, they've already forgotten the 1977 figures. And so, the very growth that you want your audience to see is lost when you just present the figures orally. Note how much easier this same information is communicated in the bar graph in Figure 9.1. At a glance your audience can see the rapid growth for each five-year period over the last 20 years.

Presentation Aids Reinforce Your Message

Presentation aids add a reinforcement to your message that helps ensuring that your listeners understand and remember what you've said. With an aid you present the same information in two different ways—verbally as audience members hear you explain the aid and visually as they see the chart, map, or model. The same is true with audio aids. The audience hears you speak of vocal variety but they also hear examples of it from the recording. This one-two punch helps the audience understand more clearly. At the same time it aids audience memory and makes your speech and your ideas more memorable.

Presentation Aids Contribute to Credibility and Confidence

If you use appropriate and professional-looking presentation aids—and we explain how you can do this later—the audience is likely to perceive you as especially credible, as someone who cares enough about the topic and them (the audience) to do this "extra" work. With this impression they're much more likely to listen more carefully to and believe what you say.

Presentation aids also help to reduce apprehension and make you appear more confident. Because you have to concentrate on the speech and on the presentation aids, you're less likely to focus on yourself. Just the movement involved in using presentation aids seems to relax many

TIPS from professional speakers

Visual aids should be used to reinforce the speech, not replace it. The aid should not deflect attention from the actor, nor should it detract from the message. One corporate head of a utilities conglomerate effectively used a chart comparing tonnage on trucking, rail, and shipping lines, but he did it this way. He had the chart posted at the rear of the audience room. Then, toward the end of his speech, he strode off the podium to the back of the room. People turned expectantly around, fixing their eyes on the clearly marked chart even before the speaker reached it. Though the red, green, blue, and black colors marking the comparative traffic totals were self-explanatory, the speaker exploited the audience's focusing on the chart as a good way to encapsulize and end his talk.

James C. Humes, professional speech writer and consultant. *Standing Ovation: How to Be an Effective Speaker and Communicator* (New York: Harper & Row, 1988): 147–148.

FIGURE 9.1

Growth of the Cable Television Industry in the United States Over Twenty Years.

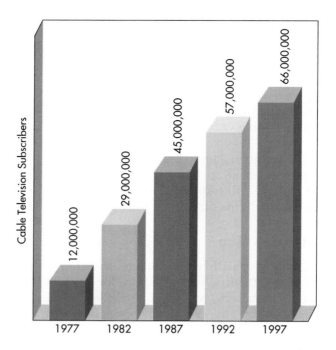

speakers. With greater relaxation comes greater confidence, and the audience recognizes this.

TYPES AND MEDIA OF PRESENTATION AIDS

Once you have in mind the ideas you want to reinforce with presentation aids, you can search for the most appropriate types and media of aids. Let's first look at some of the more popular types and media of presentation used by speakers.

Types of Presentation Aids

Among the presentation aids you have available are the actual object, models of the object, graphs, word charts, maps, people, photographs and illustrations, and tapes and CDs.

The Actual Object. As a general rule (to which there are many exceptions), the best presentation aid is the object itself. Bring it to your speech if you can. Notice that infomercials sell their product not only by talking about it but by showing it to potential buyers. You see what George Forman's Lean Mean Grilling Machine looks like and how it works. You see the jewelry, the clothing, and the new mop from a wide variety of angles and in varied settings. If you want to explain some tangible thing and you can show it to your audience, do so.

If you're talking about the workings of a computer or a lie detector, kinds of rocks, or computer games, it might be possible to use these as presentation aids. In a speech on the uses of different types of glues, for example, one student brought in the glues and the pieces of plastic, wood, and metal with which he explained how each glue worked differently on different materials.

In some cases, however, the actual object isn't available—the new car hasn't been produced yet, for example. In other cases, the object is too large to bring to class or too small for an audience to see. In these cases, you may wish to consider using a model.

Models. Models—replicas of the actual object—are useful for a variety of purposes. For example, if you wanted to explain complex structures such as the hearing or vocal mechanism, the brain, or the structure of DNA, you would almost have to use a model. You may remember from science classes that these models (and the pictures of them in the textbooks) made a lot more sense than just the verbal explanations. These models helped clarify relative size, position, and how each part interacts with each other part. These were good examples of large models used to help listeners visualize objects that are too small (and unavailable) to appreciate otherwise.

In other cases, small models of large objects—objects that are too large to bring to your speech—are helpful. For example, in a speech on native styles of dress, one student brought in a collection of dolls, each dressed in the style of a different culture. In a speech on stretching exercises, one student used a 14-inch wooden artist's model. In a speech on driving safety, a student used a toy garage and miniature toy cars. And in a speech on how to buy a diamond ring, one enterprising student brought in a crystal-looking water faucet knob that enabled her to illustrate the qualities to look for in buying a diamond ring—size, quality, and clarity.

Graphs. Graphs are useful for showing differences over time, for showing how a whole is divided into parts, and for showing different amounts or sizes. The bar graph illustrating the growth of the cable television industry presented in Figure 9.1 is a good example of a graph designed to show differences over time.

Figure 9.2 contains a variety of graphs that can be drawn free-hand or can be generated with the graphics capabilities of any word processing or presentation software.

When using graphs keep in mind that your primary task is to communicate your data clearly and in a way that focuses audience attention on the meaning of the data. Therefore, keep the graphs as simple as possible. In a pie chart, for example, don't have more than four or five segments. Similarly, in a bar graph limit the number of items to four or five. As in the graphs shown in Figure 9.2, be sure you add the legend, the labels, and the numerical values you wish to emphasize.

Notice that each of the graphs serves a somewhat different purpose. The pie chart (Figure 9.2a) is especially useful if you want to show how some whole is divided into its parts and the relative sizes of the parts. From the pie chart you can easily see the relative percentage of students of different cultural groups at a particular time. Only use a pie chart to show a division that's numerically significant; that is, the sizes of the pie's slices should bear some relationship to numerical values. So, illustrating the three branches of government with a pie chart would only be appropriate if you wanted to show that each branch is equal in power. Pie graphs are especially helpful when you have three to five values to illustrate; any more than five creates a pie that's difficult to read at a glance.

TIPS
from professional speakers

It can be difficult to figure out how to communicate a concept using a picture or graph. If you write the message title for each visual aid first, you'll have a sense of whether you need a word slide or a picture/graph slide. Then, if you need a picture or graph, use the verb of the message to guide you.

- Does the verb talk about a trend? Use a trend line.
- Does the verb talk about growth or shrinking? Use an up or down arrow.
- Does the verb focus on comparison? Use a bar chart.
- Does the verb focus on segmenting? Use a pie chart.
- Does the verb refer to a human relationship or people activity? Use a cartoon.

Lin Kroeger, communication consult to managers and executives, *The Complete Idiot's Guide to Successful Business Presentations*. (New York: Simon & Schuster, Alpha Books, 1997): p. 124.

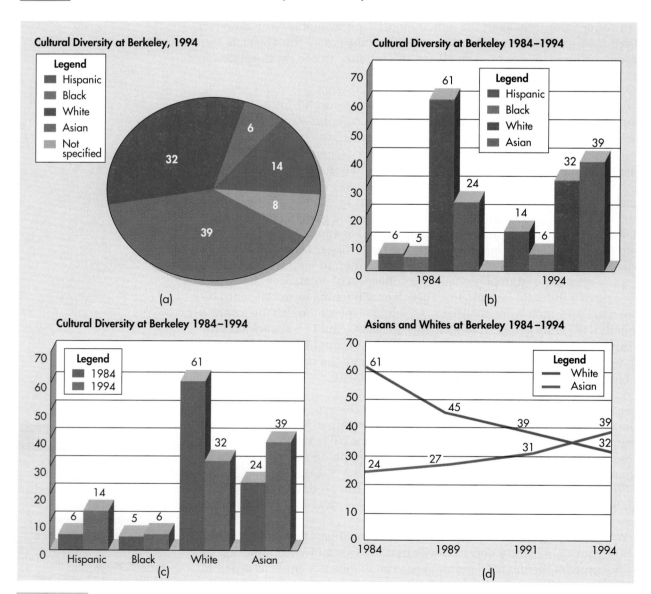

Cultural Diversity at Berkeley, 1994

Legend
- Hispanic
- Black
- White
- Asian
- Not specified

(a)

Cultural Diversity at Berkeley 1984–1994

Legend
- Hispanic
- Black
- White
- Asian

(b)

Cultural Diversity at Berkeley 1984–1994

Legend
- 1984
- 1994

(c)

Asians and Whites at Berkeley 1984–1994

Legend
- White
- Asian

(d)

FIGURE 9.2

Assorted Graphs.

These graphs are discussed in the text. As you read that brief discussion, think about how you might use similar graphs in your own speeches.

Data for these four graphs come from the University of California at Berkeley as reported in *The New York Times* (June 4, 1995): 22.

The two bar graphs (Figures 9.2b and c) both illustrate the same data but in different ways. Both graphs enable you to see at a glance the changing cultural composition of the Berkeley student body. Notice that Figure 9.2b is divided into the two years studied, making it especially easy to see the differences between 1984 and 1994. The colors symbolize the different cultural groups and so the viewer has to match up the colors to see increases or declines for a particular cultural group. Figure 9.2c is divided into the four cultural groups, making it especially easy to see the differences within each cultural group for 1984 and 1994. As with the pie chart, try not to create bar graphs that will require more than five color distinctions.

The line graph is illustrated in Figure 9.2d and shows how comparisons can be illustrated with this most simple graph. Notice that the graph is especially clear because it focuses on only two groups. Had it focused on eight or 10 groups, it would have been difficult for an audience to understand.

Word Charts. Word charts (which can also contain numbers and even graphics) are useful for many different types of information. For example, you might use a word chart to identify the key points that you cover in one of your propositions or in your entire speech—in the order in which you cover them, of course. Slide 5 in Figure 9.5 (page 196) is a good example of a simple word chart that identifies the major topics discussed in the speech. Or, you could use word charts to identify the steps in a process, for example, the steps in programming a VCR, in dealing with sexual harassment, or in installing a new computer program.

In a speech on weights and measures, one student used charts to identify the several types of weights and measures discussed in the speech. One chart on linear measures is shown in Figure 9.3.

Another use of charts is for information you want your audience to write down. Emergency phone numbers, addresses to write to, or titles of recommended books and websites are examples of the type of information that listeners will welcome in written form.

Maps. Maps are useful for illustrating a wide variety of issues. If you want to illustrate the location of cites, lakes, rivers, or mountain ranges, for example, maps will obviously prove useful as presentation aids. One speaker, for example, used a map to show the size and location of the rain forests.

But maps can be used for a lot more. Maps are helpful for illustrating population densities, immigration patterns, varied economic conditions, the spread of diseases, and hundreds of other issues you may wish to develop in your speeches. For example, in a speech on natural resources, one speaker used a variety of maps to illustrate the location of large reserves of oil, gas, and precious metals. Another speaker used maps to illustrate the concentration of wealth while another used maps to show differences in the mortality rate throughout the world.

You can also use maps to illustrate numerical differences. Let's say you wanted to show the wide variation in literacy rates throughout the world. You might color the countries on a map that have 90–100 percent literacy red, the countries that have 80–89 percent literacy green, and so on. When you use maps in this way, it's often useful to complement them with charts or graphs that, for example, give the specific literacy rates for the specific countries on which you want to concentrate.

Although theses maps may seem overly complex to construct, computer programs now make the creation of such maps relatively simple. Further, a wide variety of maps may be downloaded from the Internet, which you can then show as slides or transparencies. Chances are you'll find a map on the Internet for exactly the purpose you need.

People. Oddly enough, people can function effectively as "presentation aids." For example, if you wanted to demonstrate the muscles of the body, you might use a bodybuilder. If you wanted to demonstrate different voice patterns, skin complexions, or hairstyles, you might use people as your

Linear Measures

12 inches	1 foot
3 feet	1 yard
$5\frac{1}{2}$ yards	1 rod
40 rods	1 furlong (220 yards or 660 feet)
8 furlongs	1 mile (1,760 yards or 5,280 feet)
3 miles	1 league

aids. Aside from the obvious assistance they provide in demonstrating their muscles or voice qualities, people help secure and maintain the attention and interest of the audience.

And don't overlook yourself as a (kind of) presentation aid. For example, if you're giving a speech on boxing strategies, exercise techniques, or sitting and standing postures that can lead to backaches, you might demonstrate them yourself. As an added plus, going through these demonstrations is likely to reduce your apprehension and make you more relaxed.

Photographs and Illustrations. Photographs and illustrations prove useful for lots of speeches—to show, for example, types of trees, styles of art or architecture, or types of exercise machines. You might want to show the horrors of war with photos from wars throughout history. Or you could talk about the art of decoration with photographs of homes decorated by world-famous decorators. The best way to use photographs is to have them converted to slides. If you're using a computer presentation program (explained later) and you have a scanner, you can import your photos into your presentation with relative ease. Or you can avail yourself of the services of a print or photo shop and have the photographs converted to slides. Once they're converted into slides, you'll be able to project them in a large enough format for everyone to see clearly. You'll also be able to point to specific parts of the photo as you explain the devastation of war or the fine art of combining colors and textures. You can also have photographs converted to transparencies for use with a transparency projector, although you'll lose some of the detail that may be crucial in, say, a speech on styles of decorating.

If you want to use photographs but can't convert them into slides, then you might try to have the photos enlarged to a size large enough for the entire audience to see. It will also help if you mount these on cardboard so that they won't roll up as you're speaking and will prove generally easier to handle. Most copy shops provide this service, though the cost may be considerable, especially if you have several photos to convert and you need them in color. Nevertheless, this is an option that may prove useful in some situations.

If you can't convert the photos to slides or transparencies or have them enlarged, you might reassess their possible value; in small format the pho-

Maps are undervalued by most public speakers. Most speakers are unaware of the wide variety of maps available and the functions they might serve. How might maps have been used in any of the speeches you've heard this semester?

tographs may actually detract from what you're saying. If you hold up photos that are too small for the audience to see, members may crowd around you to get a better view and then gradually return to their seats—diverting attention from your speech. Or they may not bother to try to see them and therefore miss the point you want to make.

The other option, to pass pictures around the room, is generally a bad idea. This method also draws attention away from what you're saying. Listeners will wait for the pictures to circulate to them, will wonder what the pictures contain, and will miss a great deal of your speech in the interim.

Illustrations may at times be more useful than photographs. For example, Figure 9.4 presents an illustration of the human ear to show the structures of the ears, their shape, and how they're related to each other, something a photograph simply could not do. The same principles apply to illustrations as apply to photographs—try to convert them to slides or have them enlarged so that everyone can see them without straining.

Tapes and CDs. To deliver a speech about music and not provide the audience with samples would seem strange. Very likely the audience's attention will be drawn away from your speech while they wondered why you've not provided the actual music. Tapes and CDs, of course, can be useful for many other types of speeches as well. A speech on advertising would be greatly helped by having actual samples of advertisements as played on radio or television; the audience could see exactly what you're talking about. It would also provide variety by breaking up the oral presentation.

The Media of Presentation Aids

Once you've decided on the type of presentation aid you'll use, you need to decide on the medium you'll use to present it. Some of these media are low tech, for example, the chalkboard, transparencies, and flip charts. These media are generally more effective in smaller, informal types of situations, especially those that arise without prior notice when you simply don't have the time to prepare high-tech resources. Low-tech devices are also useful for highly interactive sessions—for example, the flip chart is still one of the best ways to record group members' contributions. Other

The camera makes everyone a tourist in other people's reality, and eventually in one's own.
—Susan Sontag

FIGURE 9.4

The Human Ear.

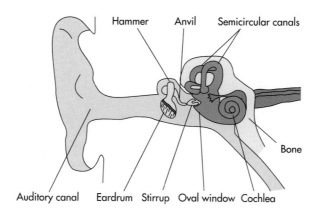

Hammer   Anvil   Semicircular canals

Bone

Auditory canal   Eardrum   Stirrup   Oval window   Cochlea

media are high tech, for example, slides and slide shows. High-tech materials are generally more effective with larger, more formal groups, where you will do most of the talking and the audience will do most of the listening. High-tech materials may also be your only choice if the material you have to communicate is extremely complex or if the norms of your organization simply require that you use high-tech presentation formats.

The best advice anyone could offer is to encourage you to learn both low- and high tech resources. The decisions you make concerning which types of media to use should be based on the message you want to communicate and on the audience to whom you'll be speaking.

The Chalkboard. The easiest to use, but not necessarily the most effective, device is the chalkboard. All classrooms have such boards, and you have seen them used by teachers with greater or lesser effect; in some way, you have had some "experience" with them. The chalkboard may be used effectively to record key terms or important definitions or even to outline the general structure of your speech. Don't use it when you can present the same information with a preplanned chart or model. It takes too long to write out anything substantial. Be careful if you do write on the board not to turn your back to the audience. In this brief time, you can easily lose the attention of your audience.

Chartboards. Chartboards are useful when you have just one or two relatively simple charts that you want to display during your speech. If you want to display them for several minutes, be sure you have a way of holding them up. Bring masking tape if you intend to secure them to the chalkboard or enlist the aid of an audience member to hold them up. Use a light colored board; white generally works best. Write in black; it provides the best contrast and is the easiest for people to read. Be sure to remove any masking tape from the chalkboard after your speech.

Flip Charts. Flip charts, large pads of paper (usually about 24 by 24 inches) mounted on a stand, can be used to record a variety of types of information that you reveal by flipping the pages as you deliver your speech. For example, if you were to discuss the various departments in an organization, you might have the key points relating to each department on a separate page of your flip chart. As you discuss the advertising department, you'd show the chart relevant to the advertising department. When you move on to discuss the human resources department, you'd flip to the chart dealing with personnel. You may find this device useful if you have a large number of word charts that you want to have easy control over. Do be sure that the chart is positioned so that everyone in the audience can see it clearly and that the folding legs are positioned securely so it doesn't collapse when you flip the first page. Sometimes it's useful to tear off the pages and hang them up, so be sure to bring masking tape with you. Make sure you write large enough so that the people in the back can read it without straining

Flip charts are especially useful to record ideas at small group meetings (see Unit 25, Speaking in Small Groups). Unlike the chalkboard, the flip chart lets you retain a written record of the meeting; should you need to, you can easily review the groups' contributions.

Slide and Transparency Projections. Slides are helpful in showing a series of visuals that may be of very different types, for example, photographs, illustrations, charts, or tables. The slides can easily be created with many of the popular computer programs (see the final section of this unit, Computer Assisted Presentations). To produce actual 35mm slides, you'll need considerable lead time, so be sure to build this into your preparation time.

If you don't have access to slide projectors, or if you don't have the lead time needed to construct the slides, consider less sophisticated transparencies. You can create your visual in any of the word processing or spreadsheet programs you normally use and probably find a printer that will enable you to print transparencies. Another alternative is to use a copier that will provide transparencies.

When using any presentational aid, but especially with slides and transparencies, do check to make sure that you have the proper equipment, for example, projector, table, a working outlet nearby, control over the lighting in the room, and whatever else you'll need to have the audience see your projections clearly.

An advantage of transparencies is that you can write on the transparencies (and on slides in computer presentations as we note later) while you're speaking. You can circle important items, underline key terms, and draw lines connecting different terms.

Videotapes. Videotapes serve a variety of purposes in public speaking. Basically, you have two options with videotapes. First, you can tape a scene from a film or television show with your VCR and show it at the appropriate time in your speech. Thus, for example, you might videotape examples of sexism in television sitcoms, violence on television talk shows, or types of families depicted in feature films and show these excerpts during your speech. As you can see, however, this type of video takes a great deal of time and preplanning so if you're going to use this, do plan well in advance. As a teacher, I use a variety of films and film excerpts to illustrate some of the breakdowns in interpersonal communication, the studies in teaching animals to communicate, the nature of nonverbal communication, and various other topics.

Second, you can create your own video with a simple camcorder. One student created a video of ethnic store signs to illustrate the "interculturalization" of the city. With the help and agreement to be videotaped of a few friends, another student created a three-minute video of religious holidays as celebrated by members of different religions and carefully coordinated each excerpt with her discussion of each holiday.

Videos are best used in small doses; in many instances 20- or 30-second excerpts will sufficiently illustrate your point. Using long excerpts will have your listeners focusing on the film rather than on your message. Use just enough video so that your listeners understand the point you're making, not the plot of the entire movie. Further, since your purpose in giving classroom speeches is to learn the art of public speaking, using overly long videos reduces the time you have available for practicing the very skills you're here to learn.

Handouts. Handouts are printed materials that you distribute to members of the audience. They are especially helpful in explaining complex material and also in providing listeners with a permanent record of some aspect of your speech. Handouts are also useful for presenting complex information that you want your audience to refer to throughout the speech. Handouts encourage listeners to take notes—especially if you leave enough white space or even provide a specific place for notes—which keeps them actively involved in your presentation. Handouts reward the audience by giving them something for their attendance and attention. A variety of handouts can be easily prepared with many of the computer presentation packages that we consider in the last section of this unit.

You can distribute handouts at the beginning, during, or after your speech, but do realize that which ever system you use comes with potential difficulties. If you distribute them before or during your speech, you run the risk of your listeners reading the handout and not concentrating on your speech. On the other hand, if they're getting the information you want to communicate—even if primarily from the handout—that isn't too bad. And, in a way, handouts allow listeners to process the information at their own pace, which is also probably a good thing.

You can encourage listeners to listen to you when you want them to and to look at the handout when you want them to by simply telling them: "Look at the graph on the top of page 2 of the handout; it summarizes recent census figures on immigration" or "We'll get back to the handout in a minute; now, however, I want to direct your attention to this next slide [or the second argument]."

If you distribute your handouts at the end of the speech, they'll obviously not interfere with your presentation, but they may not get read at all. After all, listeners might reason, they heard the speech, why bother going through the handout as well. To counteract this very natural tendency, you might include additional material on the handout and mention this to your audience. When you distribute your handout you might say something like: "This handout contains all the slides shown here and also additional slides that provide economic data for Thailand, Cambodia, and VietNam, which I didn't have time to cover. When you look at the data, you'll see that it mirrors exactly the data provided in my talk of the other countries." When you provide additional information on your handout, it's more likely that it will get looked at and thus provide the reinforcement you want.

PREPARING AND USING PRESENTATION AIDS

Once you have the idea you want to present in an aid and you know the medium you want to use, direct your attention to preparing and using the aid so it serves your purpose.

Preparing Presentation Aids

In preparing presentation aids make sure that they add clarity to your speech, that they're appealing to the listeners, and that they're culturally sensitive.

Clarity. This is the most important test of all. Make sure that the aid is clearly relevant to your speech purpose—in the minds of your listeners. It may be attractive, well designed, easy to read, and possess all the features one could hope for in a presentation aid, but if the listeners don't understand how it relates to your speech, leave it at home.

Make sure your aid is large enough to be seen by everyone from all parts of the room. Use typefaces that are easy to see and easy to read (see Table 9.1 for some typeface suggestions and problems to avoid).

Use colors that will make your message instantly clear; light colors on dark backgrounds or dark colors on light backgrounds provide the best contrast and seem to work best for most purposes. Be careful of using yellow which is often difficult to see, especially if there's glare from the sun.

Use direct phrases (not complete sentences); use bullets to highlight your points or your support (see Figure 9.5). Just as you phrase your propositions in parallel style, phrase your bullets in parallel style; in many cases this comes down to using the same part of speech (for example, all nouns or all infinitive phrases). And make sure that any connection between a graphic and its meaning is immediately clear. If it isn't, explain it.

Use the aid to highlight a few essential points; don't clutter it with too much information; four bullets on a slide or chart, for example, is about as much information as you should include. Make sure the aid is simple rather than complicated; like your verbal message, the aid should be instantly intelligible.

Give the aid a title—a general heading for the slide or chart or transparency—to further guide your listener's attention and focus.

Appealing. Presentation aids work best when they're appealing. Sloppy, poorly designed, and worn-out aids will detract from the purpose they're intended to serve. Presentation aids should be attractive enough to engage the attention of the audience, but not so attractive that they're distracting. The almost nude body draped across a car may be effective in selling underwear but would probably detract if your object is to explain the profit-and-loss statement of Microsoft Corporation.

Culturally Sensitive. Make sure your presentation aids are easily interpreted by people from other cultures and that the aid is culturally sensitive. Just as what you say will be interpreted within a cultural framework, so too will the symbols and colors you use in your aid (see Table 9.2). For example, the symbols you use that you may assume are universal may not be known by persons new to a culture (see accompanying self-test). And,

Simplicity is the essence of the great, the true and the beautiful in art.
—George Sand

TABLE 9.1 Some Typefaces

You have available an enormous number of typefaces to choose from. Generally, select typefaces that are easy to read and that are consistent in tone to the message of your speech.

Typeface	Comments
Melior Garamond Goudy Old Style **Rockwell**	Serif typefaces—a style that resembles writing by pen and illustrated especially in the "m" and "n" which begin with a slight upsweep—are easy to read and useful for blocks of text. Melior is the type face used for the text body in this book.
Arial Black **Futura** **Bauhaus** **Arial Rounded**	Sans-serif typefaces (a style that is more bold and does not include the serif or upsweep) are useful for titles and headings but would make reading long text difficult. Futura is used in Slides 1 and 12 in Figure 9.5.
Braggadocio **Britannic** **Broadway**	These extremely bold typefaces are tempting to use but, as you can see, they're not easy typefaces to read. They're most appropriate for very short titles.
Impact Abadi MT **Bernard MT** Onyx	These are compressed typefaces and are useful when you have to fit a lot of text into a small space. These typefaces, however, are difficult to read and so should probably be avoided when creating your slides. It would be better to use an easier-to-read typeface and spread out the text over additional slides.
Westminster Ransom MATISSE ITC Jokerman	Decorative styles like these, although difficult to read for extended text, make great headings or titles.
Mistral Monotype Corsiva Lucida Calligraphy Harrington French Script	These typefaces are interesting and will give your aid a personal look, as if you wrote it longhand. But, they'll be difficult to read. If you're going to read the slides word-for-word along with the audience, then typefaces that are a bit more difficult to read may still be used with considerable effect. But, for general purposes avoid these type faces in your presentation aids.

of course, when speaking to international audiences, you need to use universal symbols or explain those that are not universal. Also, be careful that your icons don't reveal an ethnocentric bias. For example, using the American dollar sign to symbolize "wealth" may be quite logical in your public speaking class but might be interpreted as ethnocentric if used with an audience of international visitors.

TEST YOURSELF

Can You Distinguish Universal from Culture-Specific Icons?

Here are 10 icons and the meaning intended to be conveyed. Write U if you think the symbol is universal throughout all cultures and CS if you think the symbol is culture specific. What reasons do you have for each of your choices?

_____ 1. ♀ ♂ male/female

_____ 2. 🎓 college/college graduation

_____ 3. 🌍 the world

_____ 4.   💡   good idea/creativity

_____ 5.   ♿   wheel chair access

_____ 6.   🍀   good luck

_____ 7.   ⚠   fire

_____ 8.   ⚛   atom/atomic/radioactive

_____ 9.   🚭   no smoking

_____ 10.   ♪   music

Icons 1, 5, 7, 8, 9, 10 would be considered universal; the others are specific to different cultures. Icon 3 is universal in depicting the world, although the positioning of the globe (with North America at the center, for example) would be considered culture-specific.

Also, the meanings that different colors communicate will vary greatly from one culture to another. Table 9.2 illustrates some of these different meanings. Before you look at the table, consider the meanings your own culture(s) gives to such colors as red, green, black, white, blue, yellow, and purple.

Using Presentation Aids

Keep the following guidelines clearly in mind when using presentation aids.

TABLE 9.2 Color and Culture

This table, constructed from the research reported by Henry Dreyfuss (1971), Nancy Hoft (1995), and Norine Dresser (1996), illustrates only some of the different meanings that colors may communicate and especially how they're viewed in different cultures. As you read this table, consider the meanings you give to each of these colors and where your meanings came from.

Color	Cultural Meanings and Comments
Red	In China, red signifies prosperity and rebirth and is used for festive and joyous occasions, in France and the United Kingdom masculinity; in many African countries blasphemy or death; and in Japan it signifies anger and danger. Red ink, especially among Korean Buddhists, is used only to write a person's name at the time of death or on the anniversary of the person's death and creates many problems when American teachers use red ink to mark homework.
Green	In the United States green signifies capitalism, go ahead, and envy; in Ireland, patriotism; among some Native Americans, femininity; to the Egyptians, fertility and strength; and to the Japanese, youth and energy.
Black	In Thailand black signifies old age, in parts of Malaysia, courage, and in much of Europe and North America, death.
White	In Thailand white signifies purity, in many Muslim and Hindu cultures, purity and peace; and in Japan and other Asian countries, death and mourning.
Blue	In Iran blue signifies something negative; in Egypt, virtue and truth; and in Ghana, joy; and among the Cherokee it signifies defeat.
Yellow	In China yellow signifies wealth and authority; in the United States, caution and cowardice, in Egypt, happiness and prosperity; and in many countries throughout the world, femininity.
Purple	In Latin America purple signifies death; in Europe royalty, in Egypt, virtue and faith; in Japan, grace and nobility; and in China, barbarism.

Know Your Aids Intimately. When planning to use a presentation aid, learn it intimately. This is especially true when you're planning to use several aids. Be sure you know in what order they're to be presented and how you plan to introduce them. Know exactly what goes where and when. Do all your rehearsing with your presentation aids; this will help you introduce them and use them more smoothly and effectively.

Test the Aids Before Using Them. Test the presentation aids prior to your speech. Be certain that they can be easily seen from all parts of the room. Using an aid that the audience can't see is probably the greatest error speakers make; they underestimate, for example, how large the print must be to be seen by those in the back of the room.

Rehearse your speech with the presentation aids incorporated into the presentation. Practice your actual movements with the aids you'll use. If you're going to use a chart, how will you use it? Will it stand by itself? Will you tape it to the board (and do you have tape with you)? Will you ask another student to hold it for you? Will you hold it yourself? The need to rehearse with your presentation aids is a good reason for building adequate lead time into your preparation. In this way, your aids will be available when you begin rehearsals. This is especially important if you're using slides that have to be produced or enlargements that have to be made.

Integrate your aids into your speech seamlessly. Just as a verbal example should flow naturally into the text and seem an integral part of the speech, so should the presentation aid. It should not appear as an afterthought but as an essential part of the speech.

Don't Talk to Your Aid. Avoid the common mistake that many speakers make when using presentation aids—they talk to the aid instead of the audience. Both you and the aid should be focused on the audience. Talk to your audience at all times. Know your aids so well that you can point to what you want without breaking eye contact with your audience. Or, at the least, break audience eye contact only for very short periods of time.

Use the Aid When It's Relevant. Use your aid only when it's relevant. Show it when you want the audience to concentrate on it and then remove it. If you don't remove it, the audience's attention may remain focused on the visual when you want them to focus on what you'll be saying next. As you'll see, one of the great advantages of the computer-generated slide show is that parts of a word chart can be hidden when they're no longer immediately relevant.

COMPUTER ASSISTED PRESENTATIONS

There are a variety of presentation software packages available; PowerPoint, Corel Presentations, and Lotus Freelance are among the most popular and are very similar in what they do and how they do it. Figure 9.5 illustrates what a set of slides might look like; the slides are built around the speech outline that will be discussed in Unit 14 and were constructed in PowerPoint. As you review this figure, try to visualize how you'd use a slide show to present your next speech.

Slide 1

Speech title

Have You Ever Been
Culture Shocked?

FIGURE 9.5
A Slide Show Speech.

Slide 1
This first slide introduces the topic with the title of the speech. Follow the general rules for titling your speech: Keep it short, provocative, and focused on your audience. If you put a graphic on this page, make sure that it doesn't detract from your title. What graphics might work well here?

Slide 2

The thesis
of the speech

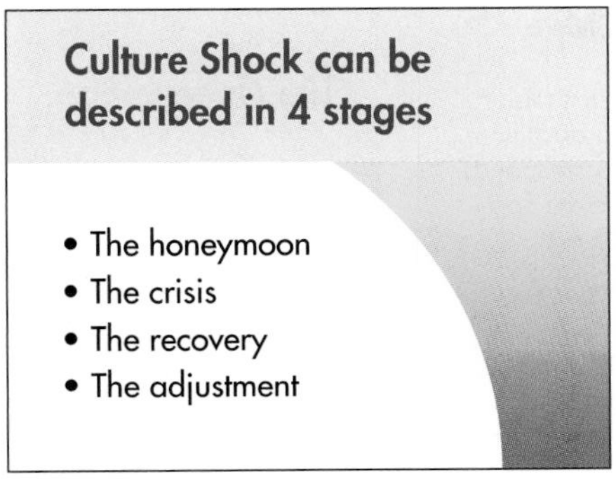

Culture Shock can be
described in 4 stages

- The honeymoon
- The crisis
- The recovery
- The adjustment

Slide 2
You may or may not want to identify your thesis directly right at the beginning of your speech. Consider the arguments for and against identifying your thesis—both cultural and strategic—and the suggestions for when and how to state the thesis on pages 117–120. As a listener, do you prefer when speakers state their thesis right at the beginning or do you prefer it when the theses is only implied and left for you to figure out?

Slide 3

Attention-getting
device;
corresponds
to the
Introduction's
"I A-B"

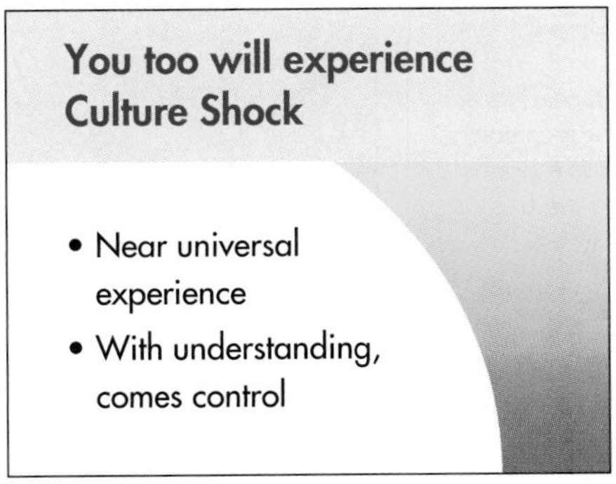

You too will experience
Culture Shock

- Near universal
  experience
- With understanding,
  comes control

Slide 3
This slide gains attention by relating the topic directly to the audience; it answers the listener's obvious question, "Why should I listen to this speech?".

Slide 4

S-A-T
connection;
corresponds
to the
Introduction's
"II A-B"

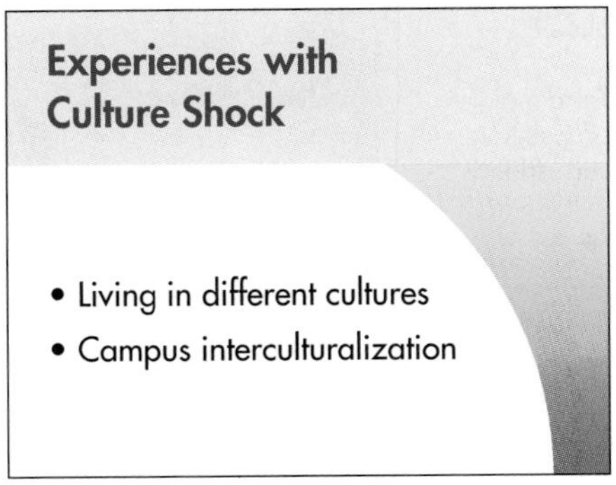

Experiences with
Culture Shock

- Living in different cultures
- Campus interculturalization

Slide 4
This slide connects the speaker, the audience, and the topic. Because you talk about yourself in this part of your speech, some speakers may prefer to eliminate a verbal slide and use a graphic or photo. Another alternative is to include your S-A-T connection with the previous attention-getting slide.

FIGURE 9.5
(continued)

Slide 5
In this slide you give your orientation by identifying your major propositions. These four bullets will become your four major propositions.

Slide 5

Orientation; corresponds to the Introduction's "III A-D"

Culture Shock

- The honeymoon
- The crisis
- The recovery
- The adjustment

Slide 6
This is your first major proposition and you'd introduce it, perhaps, by saying, "The honeymoon occurs first." If you want your audience to keep track of the stage number, you could use numbers in your slide, e.g., "1. The Honeymoon" or "Stage 1: the Honeymoon." The graphic of the heart is meant to associate culture shock with good times and a romantic-like experience. As a listener, would you prefer the speaker to explain this graphic or say nothing about it?

Slide 6

First major proposition; corresponds to the Body's "I A-B"

The Honeymoon

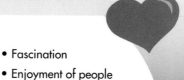

- Fascination
- Enjoyment of people and culture

Slide 7
This is your second proposition and follows the previous slide in format. Again, a graphic is used. Can you find a better graphic?

Slide 7

Second major proposition; corresponds to the Body's "II A-B"

The Crisis

- Problems arise
- Life becomes difficult

Slide 8
This is your third major proposition that again follows the format of the previous two slides.

Slide 8

Third major proposition; corresponds to the Body's "III A-B"

The Recovery

- Learning to cope
- Intercultural competence

Slide 9

Fourth major proposition; corresponds to the Body's "IV A-B"

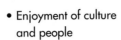

The Adjustment

- Enjoyment of culture and people
- Appreciation of the culture and people

FIGURE 9.5
(continued)
Slide 9
This is your fourth major proposition and, as noted later in the text, the sound of applause is programmed to come on with this slide, reinforcing the idea that we do adjust to culture shock. Examine the sound effects you have available; what other sound effects would you use in this speech?

Slide 10

Summary; corresponds to the Conclusion's "I A-D"

Culture Shock

- The honeymoon
- The crisis
- The recovery
- The adjustment

Slide 10
This is the summary of your four major propositions; notice that it's the same as your orientation (Slide 5). This slide violates the general rule of using graphics in moderation. What do you think of the repetition of graphics? Do you think they add reinforcement? Do they detract from the verbal message?

Slide 11

Motivation; corresponds to the Conclusion's "II A-C"

**Culture Shock
Want to know more?**

- Comm325, Intercultural Communication
- Sunday's "60 Minutes"
- Two great books:
  - Lustig and Koester, *Intercultural Communication*
  - Samovar and Porter, *Communication between Cultures*

Slide 11
This part of the summary ideally motivates your listeners to pursue the topic in more detail. Notice that this is just about too much information for one slide, and you might want to consider breaking it into three slides—giving each bullet it's own slide. What are the advantages and disadvantages of using just one slide? Of using three slides?

Slide 12

Closure; corresponds to the Conclusion's "III"

Culture Shock

Slide 12
This slide is intended to wrap up the speech—it contains the title and two graphics that will support the speaker's concluding statement: "By knowing about culture shock you'll be in a better position to deal with it at school and on the job." Notice that the conclusion is tied to the Introduction by a similarity in font and text color; it helps signal that this is the last slide and the end of the speech.

The Advantages of Computerized Presentations

Computer assisted presentations possess all the advantages of aids already noted (for example, maintaining interest and attention, adding clarity, and reinforcing your message). In addition, however, they have advantages all their own, so many in fact that you'll want to seriously consider using this technology in your speeches. Because they're state-of-the-art, they give your speech a professional, up-to-date look and, in the process, add to your credibility. They show you're prepared and care about your topic and audience.

Computer assisted presentations also allow for great choice and flexibility. For example, slides may be easily added, deleted, or reordered; changes in fonts and colors can be made with a few keystrokes; and a wide variety of graphics and special effects can be added, changed, or deleted with little effort. Computer assisted presentations also enable you to rehearse and precisely time your presentation. Still another advantage, explained more fully later, is that they allow you to create a variety of printed materials that you may wish to use as speaker's notes or as handouts for your listeners.

Ways of Using Presentation Package Software

Computer presentation software enables you to produce a variety of aids; the software will produce what you want. For example, you can construct your slides on your computer and then have 35 mm slides developed from disk. To do this you'd have to have a slide printer or send them out (you can do this via modem) to a lab specializing in converting electronic files into 35mm slides. You may have access to a slide printer at your school, so do check first. Similarly, your local office supply store or photocopy shop such as Staples, Office Max, or Kinko's may have exactly the services you need.

Or, you can create your slides and then show them on your computer screen. If you're speaking to a very small group, it may be possible to have your listeners gather around your computer as you speak. With larger audiences, however, you'll need a computer projector or LCD Projection Panel. Assuming you have a properly equipped computer in the classroom, you can copy your entire presentation to a floppy or ZIP disk and bring it with you the day of the speech.

Computer presentation software also enables you to print out a variety of materials: slides, slides with speaker's notes, slides with room for listener notes, and outlines of your speech. In using any of these options, you may wish to consider the advantages of using a header or a footer to identify the title of your speech, the date, your name, the page number, or any other information you feel would be valuable to your listeners.

You can print out your complete set of slides to distribute to your listeners, or you can print out a select portion of the slides. You can even print out slides that you didn't have time to cover in your speech but which you'd like your audience to look at later. The most popular options are to print out two, three, or up to six slides per page. The two-slide option provides for easy readability and is especially useful for slides of tables or graphs that you want to present to your listeners in an easy-to-

TIPS from professional speakers

The graphics software programs today provide templates for visual aids. The templates predetermine the fonts, the sizes of the images, and the spacing of information if you're using words. Let those templates be your guide! If you find yourself having to shrink the letters to fit more onto the visual aid, you're probably overloading the visual aid. Simplify it. Make it into two or three visuals.

Lin Kroeger, communication consultant to managers and executives, *The Complete Idiot's Guide to Successful Business Presentations.* (New York: Simon & Schuster, Alpha Books, 1997): p.131.

read size. The three-slide option is probably the most widely used; it prints the three slides down the left side of the page with space for listeners to write notes on the right. This option is useful if you want to interact with your audience and you want them to take notes as you're speaking. Naturally, you'd distribute this handout before you begin your speech, during your introduction, or ideally at that point when you want your listeners to begin taking notes. A sample printout is provided in Figure 9.6. If you want to provide listeners with a complete set of slides, then the six-slide option may be the most appropriate. You can, of course, also print out any selection of slides you wish—perhaps just those slides that contain graphs or perhaps just those slides that summarize your talk.

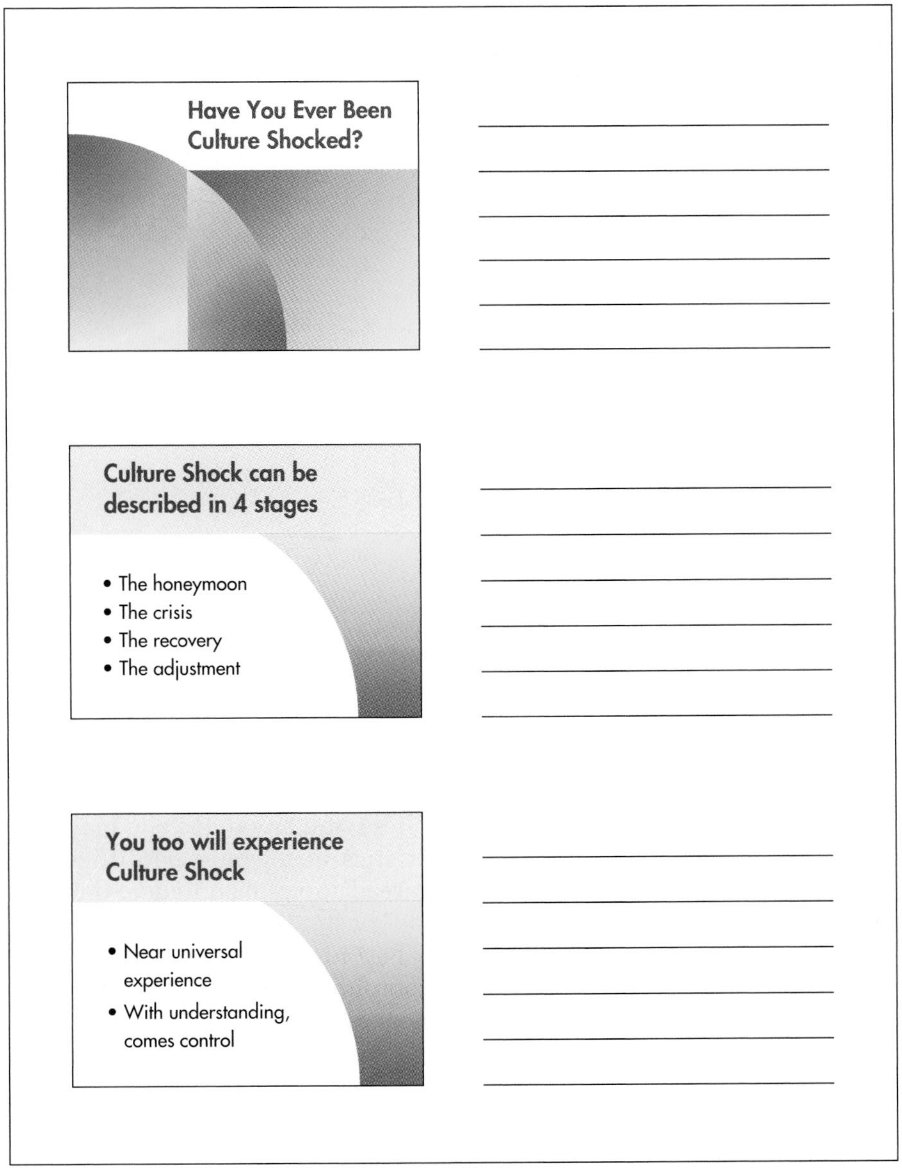

FIGURE 9.6
A Handout of Slides with Space for Listener's Notes.

Have You Ever Been Culture Shocked?

Culture Shock can be described in 4 stages

- The honeymoon
- The crisis
- The recovery
- The adjustment

You too will experience Culture Shock

- Near universal experience
- With understanding, comes control

FIGURE 9.7
Slide and Speaker's Notes.

PAUSE!

Scan the audience

Slide #1

Have you ever been Culture Shocked?

PAUSE!

I have.

And many of you have too.

If you haven't, you will.

The world (and especially bright college graduates like ourselves) are becoming increasingly mobile.

We'll all spend time in different cultures.

Understanding culture shock $\rightarrow$ better to deal with it

Preventive medicine.

Forewarned is forearmed.

Slide #2

Another useful option is to print out your slides with your speaker's notes. With this option, you have your slides and any notes you may find useful—examples you want to use, statistics that would be difficult to memorize, quotations that you want to read to your audience, delivery notes, or anything that you care to record. The audience will see the slides but not the speaker's notes. It's generally best to record these notes in outline form, with key words rather than complete sentences. This will prevent you from falling into the trap of reading your speech. A sample printout is provided in Figure 9.7.

Another useful printout is the speech outline. Two outline options are available: the collapsed outline and the full outline. The collapsed outline contains only the slide titles and would be useful if you want to give your audience a general outline of your talk. If you want your listeners to fill in the outline with the information you'll talk about, then you can distribute this collapsed outline at the beginning of your speech. The complete outline (slide titles plus bullets) option provides listeners with a relatively complete record of your speech and might be useful if you cover lots of technical information that listeners will have to refer to later. Perhaps you are giving a speech on company health care or pension plans and you want to provide your listeners with detailed information on each option. The outline is also useful if you want to provide listeners with addresses and phone numbers that they may need. This complete outline would normally be distributed after you've completed your speech since outlines that are so complete may lead your audience to read and not to listen.

Overhead transparencies can also be created from your computer slides. They can be made on many printers and most copiers by just substituting transparency paper for computer paper. Transparencies are low tech and are certainly not state-of-the-art. Nevertheless, they're often very useful when all you have available is a transparency projector. If you construct your slides with a computer presentation package, you'll produce professional-looking transparencies.

Suggestions for Using Presentation Software

Perhaps the best suggestion for designing slides is to use the templates provided by the presentation software or allow the design wizards to help you choose colors and type faces. These are created by professional designers who are experts at blending colors, fonts, and designs into a clear and appealing rendering.

Another general guideline to follow in designing your slides is to give each item in your outline that has the same level head (for example, all the Roman numeral heads) the same typeface, size, and color throughout your presentation. Similarly, use the same font for all the A level, B level, etc. This will help your listeners follow the organization of your speech. If you're using one of the predesigned templates, this will be done for you. Notice that this principle is followed for the most part in the slides in Figure 9.5. It's broken in one case to connect the introduction with the conclusion by doing these in a color and typeface different from the rest of the slides. Another way this rule might be broken is to design your internal summaries a bit differently from the regular slides to signal their unique function. This would prove especially effective in a long speech in which there are frequently internal summaries.

Clarity should be your number one concern. Design your slides so that they help you communicate the information you want to convey rather than to simply amaze the audience with intricate and complex design. For example, choose typeface styles, sizes, and colors to help you clearly distinguish the major propositions from the supporting materials.

Be brief. Your objective in designing these slides is to provide the audience with key words and ideas that will reinforce what you're saying in your speech; you don't want your audience to spend their time reading rather than listening. Generally, put one complete thought on a slide. Don't try to put too many words on one slide; use few words for the slides and expand on these during your speech. Try not to use more than two levels of thought in a slide—a major statement and two or three or four subordinate phrases (bulleted)—is about all you can put on one slide. Avoid using subheads of subheads of subheads. Consider using tables or graphs instead of large blocks of text to explain an idea.

Generally, use a sans serif type for headings. Sans serif type is bolder and more attention getting, but is often difficult to read for extended text. Similarly, use all capital letters sparingly; these are difficult to read as well, but they may be used for emphasis or titles. Use a serif type for your bulleted text; it isn't as dramatic but is easier to read (revisit Table 9.1).

In designing your slides consider the advantages of word art—printing a word or phrase in an arc or on a slant, for example. Again, this technique should be used sparingly. Like all caps or sans serif type, word art is generally more difficult to read, but it does help to gain attention and it often makes for a great opening slide.

Use colors—for type and for background—that provide the kinds of contrasts you want. Remember that many people have difficulty distinguishing red from green, so if you want to distinguish ideas, it is probably best to avoid this contrast. Similarly, if you're going to print out your slides in shades of gray, make sure the colors you choose provide clear contrasts. Also, be careful that you don't choose colors that recall holidays that have nothing to do with your speech—red and green recalling Christmas, orange and black recalling Halloween, or purple and yellow recalling Easter. Remember, too, the cultural attitudes toward different colors; for example, among some Asian cultures, writing a person's name in red means that the person has died.

Use visuals as appropriate. Presentation software packages make inserting visuals so easy that it often leads to the inclusion of too many visuals. Most presentation packages provide a variety of graphic pictures, animated graphics, photos, and videos which are useful for a wide variety of speeches. With the help of a scanner, you can add your own visuals. Use visuals when you have room on the slide and when the visual is directly related to your speech's thesis and purpose. Also, try to use graphics that are consistent with one another; generally it's better to use all shadow figures or all stick figures or all Victorian images than to mix them. In deciding whether or not to include a visual, ask yourself if the inclusion of this graph or photo will advance the purpose of your speech. If it does, use it; if it doesn't, don't. In using video, remember that these take up enormous amounts of space. If you're using flopping disks, a three or four second video can take up a full third or even half of your disk space; if you're using Zip disks, you'll have enough room for just about any speech you'd make. You can also draw a variety of shapes that may be useful if you want to, say, draw flowcharts or communication models.

As verbal transitions help you move from one part of your speech to another, presentational transitions help you move from one slide to the next with the desired effect—blinds folding from left or right or top or bottom or a quick fade. Don't try to use too many different transitions in the same talk; it will detract attention from what you're saying. Listeners will wonder what type of transition will accompany the next slide. Generally, it's best to use the same transitions for all your slides in a single presentation. You might vary this a bit by, say, having the last slide introduced by a somewhat different transition, but any more variation is likely to work against the listeners focusing on your message. In choosing transitions select one that is consistent with your speech purpose; don't use a frivolous black and yellow checkerboard transition in a speech on child abuse, for example.

A wide variety of sound effects come with most presentation packages. Here you can have individual sounds—foghorn, drum roll, or doorbell, for example, and excerpts from musical compositions. Consider using sound effects in your speech, perhaps especially with your transitions. As with graphics, though, go easy; overdoing it is sure to make your speech seem carelessly put together. In the slides in Figure 9.5, I programmed "applause" (one of the readily available sound effects) to come on as Slide No. 9—the adjustment—comes on. As you read through the slides you might find additional places where sound could be used effectively.

Use build effects to help you focus your listeners' attention. Build effects refer to the way in which your bulleted items come to the screen. For example, you can have each bulleted phrase fly from the top of the screen into its position; with the next mouse click, the second bullet flies into position. Or you can have your bullets slide in from right to left or from left to right. And so on.

In listing four or five bulleted items, consider the value of hiding or dimming the previous bullet as you introduce the next one. Making the previous bullet disappear or fade into a lighter color when the next bullet appears further focuses your listeners' attention on exactly the point you're discussing. Do be careful that you allow the audience time to read each bullet, otherwise they'll be disappointed when it disappears.

Charts and tables are especially useful, as noted earlier, when you want to communicate complex information that would take too much text for one slide to explain. You have a tremendous variety of chart types (for example, pie, bar, and cumulative charts) and tables to choose from. If you're using presentation software that's part of a suite, then you'll find it especially easy to import files from your word processor or spread sheet. Also, consider the advantages of chart animation. You can display bullets as you discuss each one, and you can also display the chart in parts so that you can focus the audience's attention on exactly the part of the chart you want. You can achieve somewhat the same effect with transparencies by covering up the chart and gradually revealing the parts you want the audience to focus on.

Sometimes layering will prove useful. Layering is the technique of positioning material on top of other material and is often useful for showing

In addition to those suggestions offered here, what other suggestions would you offer the speaker in this photo?

connections among concepts. You can then reverse the layers to bring objects in the back to the front or vice versa.

Try tying the conclusion back to the introduction in some visually interesting way. It's a convenient way to signal to your audience that you're coming to a close. It's especially easy to do this when using computer presentation packages. In Figure 9.5 this was done simply by using the same color for the conclusion as was used when introducing the topic. Repeating a graphic or using one background for the first and the last slides and a different background for those in the middle serves a similar purpose.

If there's a question-and-answer period following your speech, consider preparing a few extra slides for responses to questions you anticipate being asked. Then when someone asks you a predicted question, you can say: "I anticipated that someone might ask that question; it raises an important issue. The data I've been able to find are presented in this chart." You'd then show the slide and explain it more fully. This is surely going the extra mile, but it can easily make your speech a real standout.

Lastly, make use of the spell check. You don't want professionally prepared slides with misspellings; it can ruin your credibility and seriously damage the impact of your speech.

Rehearsal

Presentation packages are especially helpful for rehearsing your speech and timing it precisely. As you rehearse, the computer program records the time you spend on each slide and will record that time under each slide; it will also record the presentation's total time. You can see these times at the bottom of each slide in a variety of views, but they won't appear in the printed handout, such as used in Figure 9.5. You can use these times to program each slide so you can set it to run automatically. Or, you can use these times to see if you're devoting the amount of time to each of your ideas that you want to. If you find in your rehearsal that your speech is too long, these times can help you see the topics that are perhaps taking up too much time and that might be shortened.

Presentation software allows you to rehearse individually selected slides as many times as you want. But do make sure that you go through the speech from beginning to end toward the end of your rehearsal period. Rehearse with this system as long as improvements result; when you find that rehearsal no longer serves any useful purpose, then stop.

Another type of rehearsal is to check out the equipment available in the room you'll speak in and its compatibility with the presentation software you're using. If possible, rehearse with the very equipment you'll have available on the day you're speaking. In this way, any incompatibilities or idiosyncrasies can be identified are remedied. Further, you'll discover how long it takes to warm up the slide projector or load PowerPoint and not have to use up your speaking time for these warm ups.

The Actual Presentation

During your actual presentation, you can control your slides with your mouse, advancing to the next one or going back to a previously shown slide. If you set it to run automatically, where each slide is programmed to be shown for different amounts of time, you won't be tied to the mouse—if you don't have a remote mouse. You can, of course, override the automatic programming by simply clicking your mouse to either advance or go back to a slide that perhaps went by too quickly.

As with any presentation aid, do make sure that you focus on the audience; don't allow the computer or the slides to get in the way of your immediate contact with the audience.

Consider using the pen—actually your mouse—to write on and highlight certain words or figures in the slides. It's not very easy to write with

UNIT IN BRIEF

Functions of Presentation Aids	Maintain interest and attention. Add clarity. Reinforce your message. Contribute to credibility and confidence.
Types and Media of Presentation Aids	**Types of Presentation Aids:** The actual object, models, graphs, word charts, maps, people, pictures and illustrations, tapes and CDs. **Media of Presentation Aids:** chalkboard, chartboards, flip charts, slide and transparency projections, videotapes, handouts.
Preparing and Using Presentation Aids	**Preparing Presentation Aids:** Create presentation aids that are clear, appealing, and culturally sensitive. **Using Presentation Aids**: Know your aids intimately, test your aids before using them, don't talk to your presentation aid, use the aid when it's relevant.
Computer Assisted Presentations	CAPs possess all the advantages of "regular" presentation aids, allow for great choice and flexibility, facilitate rehearsal and precise timing, and facilitate the printing of handouts. Presentation software enables you to construct computer slide presentations, 35mm slides, handouts, and transparencies. In using CAPs strive for consistency and clarity, consider using charts and tables, use transitions, build effects, and sound effects in moderation. Use the rehearsal functions built into the presentation software. During the actual presentation make sure you leave enough time for listeners to read each slide; focus on your audience; use the pen when appropriate.

THINKING CRITICALLY ABOUT PRESENTATION AIDS

REVIEWING KEY TERMS AND CONCEPTS IN PUBLIC SPEAKING

1. Review and define each of the key terms used in this unit:

   ❏ presentation aid (p. 180)
   ❏ pie chart (p. 183)
   ❏ models (p. 183)
   ❏ line graph (p. 184)
   ❏ bar graph (p. 184)
   ❏ flip chart (p. 188)
   ❏ transparency and opaque projections (p. 189)
   ❏ handouts (p. 190)
   ❏ slide show (p. 194)
   ❏ transitions (p. 202)
   ❏ text build (p. 203)

2. Review and explain the key concepts covered in this unit:

   - What are the functions of presentation aids?
   - What are the main types and media of presentation aids?
   - What suggestions can you offer for preparing and using presentation aids?
   - How can you most effectively prepare and run a computerized slide show?

DEVELOPING STRATEGIES FOR PRESENTATION AIDS IN PUBLIC SPEAKING

1. Jamie, a student at a Community College in Texas, wants to give a speech on the cruelty of cock fighting. The audience is predominantly Hispanic, most coming from Mexico where cock fighting is a legal and popular sport. Among the visuals Jamie's considering are extremely vivid photographs of cocks literally torn to shreds by their opponents who have razor blades strapped to their feet. Would you advise Jamie to use these photographs if the audience was, say, moderately in favor of cock fighting? What if they were moderately against cock fighting? What general principle underlies your recommendations?

2. Shana wants to illustrate the rise and fall in the prices of 12 stocks over the last 10 years. She wants to show that the investment club (an audience of 16 members who are active participants in the club's investments) should sell three of the stocks and keep the other nine. This is the first time Shana will be using visual aids and she needs advice on what types of aids might best serve her purpose. What suggestions do you have for Shana?

3. Kim plans on giving her speech as a slide show but worries that using slides for each topic she discusses might be too much repetition. Yet she wants to gain some experience in using this technique since it is widely used in advertising and marketing, fields in which Kim hopes to get a job. How can Kim use a slide show where the slides complement rather than repeat what she'll be saying?

EVALUATING PUBLIC SPEECHES

1. Read one of the speeches in this text, on the Web, or in some other source, or listen to one and focus specifically on the use and misuse of presentation aids. If the speaker used presentation aids, could you offer suggestions for making them more effective? If the speaker did not use such aids, could you suggest ways in which presentation aids might have been used to further the speaker's purpose?

2. Read one of the speeches in this text, on the Web, or in some other source, or listen to one and develop at least two presentation aids that you think would have added to the speech's effectiveness.

3. Using as an example your own last speech, the speech you're working on now, or any of the speeches you've heard or read, respond to the following checklist for presentation aids:

   - Did the aid serve the functions it was supposed to serve? Did it maintain interest and attention? Did it add clarity? Did it help reinforce the message? Did it contribute to the speaker's credibility?
   - Was the type of aid appropriate and effective? Was the media used appropriate and effective? How might the use of presentation aids been improved?
   - Was the aid well prepared? Were there any problems with the aid?
   - Was the aid used effectively? Did it accomplish the purposes the speaker wanted to accomplish?

USING TECHNOLOGY IN PRESENTATION AIDS IN PUBLIC SPEAKING

1. Create a slide show for one of the units in this text. In what ways would a slide show be a more effective way of communicating the information? In what ways might it be less effective? What kinds of handouts would you distribute? When would you distribute them?

2. Explore the fonts you have available. Classify these into (a) those that would make good headings, (b) those that are easy to read and so appropriate for text, and (c) those that are best for the display of, say, one or two letters. Test out your classification by asking others for their opinions.

3. Visit the Web sites for Microsoft PowerPoint, Corel Presentations, and Lotus Freelance. What helpful hints can you glean from these Web sites that would be useful to the public speaker?

4. Visit one of the Web sites for quotations (for example: http://www.columbia.edu/acis/bartleby/bartlett [Barlett's Quotations], http://us.imdb.com/ [a database of quotations from films], and http://isleuth.com/quote.html [a combined reference of different collections of quotations]), select a quotation suitable for use with the slide show of the speech on culture shock, and explain how you'd use this on a new slide or on one of the 12 presented in Figure 9.5.

5. Access one of the databases for professional journals or magazines discussed in Unit 7 ("Research") and search for information on presentation aids, using the key terms "visual," "visuals in public speaking," "visual aids," or "presentation aids," or more specific headings such as "organizational chart" or "graphics." Select one abstract or article and in a brief two-minute speech report to the class what the article says about presentation aids and the procedures you followed in locating this article.

PRACTICALLY SPEAKING

9.1 Short Speech Technique

Prepare and deliver a two-minute speech in which you:

a. explain a print ad that contains a visual and explain how the visual complements the text (or how the text complements the visual).

b. explain a product's packaging as a presentation aid for the product itself.

c. select some object in the room and use it as a presentation aid to illustrate any thesis you'd like.

d. explain what an ideal ad would look like for any popular product.

9.2 Analyzing Presentation Aids

Select a print advertisement and analyze the visuals. For purposes of this exercise, consider the text of the ad as the spoken speech and the visual in the ad as the presentation aid for the speech.

1. What types of aids were used?
2. What functions did the presentation aids serve?
3. Were the aids clear?
4. Were they relevant?
5. Were the aids appealing?
6. Where the aids culturally sensitive?

The Audience: Sociological Analysis and Adaptation

UNIT CONTENTS	UNIT OBJECTIVES
	After completing this unit, you should be able to:
Approaching Audience Analysis and Adaptation	Define audience, attitude, belief, and value and explain the importance of audience analysis to effective public speaking.
Analyzing Audience Characteristics	Identify at least five characteristics that need to be considered in audience analysis and adaptation.
Analyzing Context Characteristics	Explain the context characteristics and how they relate to audience analysis and adaptation.

Public speaking audiences can vary from thousands of people at Yankee Stadium listening to a politician or religious leader to 20 students in a classroom listening to a lecture, to five people listening to a street orator. The characteristic that seems best to define an audience is common purpose; a public speaking audience is a group of individuals gathered together to hear a speech.

You may deliver a speech to inform or persuade your audience. Or, you may give a speech to introduce a speaker, to present or accept an award, to secure the goodwill of your audience, or to pay tribute to someone. A teacher lectures on Gestalt psychology to increase understanding; a minister talks against adultery to influence behaviors and attitudes; a football coach gives a pep talk to motivate the team to improve—all of these persons are trying to produce change. If speakers are to be successful, then they must know their audience. If you're to be successful, you must know your audience. This knowledge will help you in:

- selecting your topic
- phrasing your purpose
- establishing a relationship between yourself and your audience
- choosing examples and illustrations
- stating your thesis, whether directly or indirectly
- selecting arguments and motives to which you'll appeal

APPROACHING AUDIENCE ANALYSIS AND ADAPTATION

Your first step in audience analysis is to construct an audience profile in which you analyze the sociological or demographic characteristics of your listeners (for example, their culture, age, gender). Through an analysis and understanding of these characteristics, you'll gain insight into their attitudes, beliefs, and values. This in turn, will enable you to better tailor your speech to these specific listeners. In approaching this analysis, then, we first need to explain the nature of attitudes, beliefs, and values and, second, some of the ways you can seek audience information.

Attitudes, Beliefs, and Values

Attitude refers to your tendency to act for or against a person, object, or position. If you have a positive attitude toward the death penalty, you're likely to argue or act in favor of instituting the death penalty (for example, vote for a candidate who supports the death penalty). If you have a negative attitude toward the death penalty, then you're likely to argue or act against it. Attitudes influence how favorably or unfavorably listeners will respond to speakers who support or denounce the death penalty.

Belief refers to the confidence or conviction you have in the existence or truth of some proposition. For example, you may believe that there's an after-life, that education is the best way to rise from poverty, that democracy is the best form of government, or that all people are born equal. If your listeners believe that the death penalty is a deterrent to crime, for example, then they'll be more likely to favor arguments for (and speakers who support) the death penalty than would listeners who don't believe in the connection between the death penalty and deterrence.

Value refers to your perception of the worth or goodness (or worthlessness or evil) of some concept or idea. For example, you probably have positive values for financial success, education, and contributing to the common welfare. At the same time, you probably have negative values for chemical weapons, corrupt politicians, and selling drugs to children. Because the values an audience holds influence how it responds to ideas that are related to those values, it's essential that you learn the values of your specific audience. For example, if your audience places a high positive value on child welfare, then it's likely to vote for legislation that protects children or that allocates money for breakfasts and lunches in school. They might consider signing a petition, volunteering their time, or donating their money to advance the welfare of children. If you find that your audience places a negative value on big business, you might want to reconsider using the testimony of corporate leaders or the statistics compiled by corporations.

In short, the attitudes, beliefs, and values that your listeners have will influence how receptive they'll be to your topic, your point of view, and your evidence and arguments. It's essential, therefore, that you learn about your listeners' attitudes, beliefs, and values and use this information as you prepare your speech.

What is the single most important characteristic about your public speaking audience to keep in mind? How will this one characteristic influence your speech preparation and presentation?

Seeking Audience Information

In learning about your audience, you'll need to analyze first their demographic or sociological characteristics and then their psychographic or psychological makeup. In this unit we examine the sociological characteristics and in the next, the psychological.

You can seek out audience information using a variety of methods: observation, data collection, interviewing, and inference (Sprague and Stuart 1996).

Observe. Think about your audience. What can you infer about, say, their economic status from their clothing and jewelry? Might their clothing reveal any conservative or liberal leanings? Might clothing provide clues to attitudes on economics or politics? What do they do in their free time? Where do they live? What do they talk about? Are different cultures represented? Does this give you any clue as to what their interests or concerns might be?

Collect Data Systematically. A useful means for securing information about your audience is to use a questionnaire. Let's say you took a course in Web design and were thinking about giving an informative speech on ways to design effective Web pages. One thing you'd need to know is how much your audience already knows. This will help you judge the level at which to approach the topic, information that you can assume, terms you need to define, and so on. You might also want to know how much experience the audience members have had with Web pages, either as users or as designers. To help you answer these and other relevant questions you might compose a questionnaire such as that appearing in Figure 10.1.

As already noted in our discussion of e-mail, if your class is set up as a listserv, these questionnaires would be extremely easy to distribute since you could do it with one e-mail questionnaire sent to the listserv. Other members of the class could then respond to you, and you could tabulate the results and incorporate this into your speech. Do caution other members of the listserv that in returning questionnaires they should go directly and only to you. If they're sent to the listserv then everyone in the class would get everyone else's responses; in a class of 25 students, each person would receive 625 responses. If your class is not established as a listserv, you can still distribute questionnaires before class begins or as students are leaving.

Audience questionnaires are even more useful as background for your persuasive speeches. Let's say you plan to give a speech in favor of allowing single people to adopt children. To develop an effective speech, you need to know your audience's attitudes toward single-parent adoption. Are they in favor? Opposed? Do they have reservations? If so, what are they? To help you answer such questions, you might use a questionnaire such as that presented in Figure 10.2.

Interview Members of Your Audience. In a classroom situation, this is easily accomplished. But, if you're to speak to an audience you'll not meet prior to your speech, you might interview those who know the audience

TIPS from professional speakers

As to how you find out what they [audience members] know, there's no great mystery and no arcane methodology.

- Ask questions
- Read
- Go online
- Find an ally/channel and ask more questions
- Network
- Get on the phone
- Read
- ASK MORE QUESTIONS

Don Pfarrer, public speaking coach and author, *Guerrilla Persuasion: Mastering the Art of Effective and Winning Business Presentation* (Boston, Mass.: Houghton Mifflin, 1998): 45-46.

FIGURE 10.1

Audience Questionnaire for an Informative Speech.

How would you construct a questionnaire for your next speech?

Audience Questionnaire

I'm planning to give my informative speech on ways to effectively design Web sites and I'd like to know what you know and what you'd like to know. I'd appreciate it if you'd complete this questionnaire and return it to jdevito@shiva.hunter.cuny.edu.

1. How much do you know about the World Wide Web?

_____ a great deal

_____ something but not very much

_____ very little

_____ virtually nothing

2. Have you ever tried to design your own Web site?

_____ yes, and was quite successful

_____ yes, but I really need help

_____ no, but have thought about it

_____ no, and hope to never have to

3. How interested are you in learning more about Web design?

_____ very interested

_____ neither interested nor uninterested

_____ uninterested

4. Is there anything special about Web design that you'd like to learn?

Thanks,

Joe

members better than you. For example, you might talk with the person who invited you to speak.

If you do survey your audience—with a questionnaire or by interview—be sure to mention this in your speech. It will alert your listeners to your thoroughness and your concern for them. It will also satisfy their curiosity since most people will be interested in how others responded. You might say something like this:

I want to thank you all for completing my questionnaire on single-parent adoption. Half of you were neutral; 40 percent were in favor, and 10 percent were opposed. The major reason in favor of single-parent adoption was that it would provide homes for an enormous number of

Audience Questionnaire

I'm planning to give my persuasive speech on adoption, and I'd like to know your attitudes on a few issues relating to this topic. I'd appreciate it if you'd complete this questionnaire and return it to jdevito@shiva.hunter.cuny.edu.

1. How do you feel about single people adopting children?

_____ strongly in favor of it

_____ in favor of it

_____ neutral

_____ opposed to it

_____ strongly opposed to it

2. How do you feel about interracial adoption? About gay men and lesbians adopting? Please explain.

3. What are your main reasons for your current attitudes?

4. What underlying values and beliefs do you think contribute to your current attitude?

Thanks,

Joe

FIGURE 10.2

Audience Questionnaire for a Persuasive Speech.

What are the disadvantages to stating your position on the issue in your questionnaire? Can you identify any possible advantages?

children who would otherwise not be adopted. The major reason against such adoption was the belief that a child needs two parents to grow up emotionally healthy. Let's look more carefully at each of these concerns.

Use "Intelligent Inference and Empathy". Use your knowledge of human behavior and human motivation and try to adopt the perspective of the audience (Sprague and Stuart 1996). For example, let's say you're addressing the entire teaching staff of your college on the need to eliminate (or expand) affirmative action. What might you infer about your audience? Are they likely to be in favor of affirmative action or opposed to it? Can they be easily classified in terms of their liberal-conservative leanings? How informed are they likely to be about the topics and about its

THE ETHICS OF Public Speaking in a Democracy

One interesting approach to ethics that has particular relevance to public speaking is Karl Wallace's (1955, Johannesen 1996) "Ethical Basis of Communication," which, although written over 40 years ago, is amazingly current in its viewpoint. This ethic is based on the essential values of a free and democratic society, for example, the opportunity for any person to grow and develop to the limits of his or her ability, equality of opportunity, and the essential dignity and worth of an individual. Consequently, this approach will not prove culturally universal. Four principles define this approach.

1. The speaker must have a thorough knowledge of the topic, an ability to answer relevant questions, and an awareness of the significant facts and opinions bearing on the issues discussed.

2. The speaker must present both facts and opinions fairly, without bending or spinning them to personal advantage. The speaker must allow the listener to make the final judgment.
3. The speaker must reveal the sources of these facts and opinions and must assist the listeners to evaluate biases and prejudices in the sources.
4. The speaker must acknowledge and respect opposing arguments and evidence. The speaker must advocate a tolerance for diversity. Any attempt to hide valid opposing arguments from the audience is unethical.

What do you think of these principles? Do you think these principles would apply to other political systems, such as a totalitarian state?

(The next Ethics of Public Speaking box appears on page 237.)

advantages and disadvantages? How would you feel about affirmative action if you were teaching at your college?

ANALYZING AUDIENCE CHARACTERISTICS

Caution: All generalizations are false. The generalizations in the following discussion seem true in most cases but may not be valid for any specific audience. Beware of using these generalizations as stereotypes. A stereotype is a fixed impression of a group of people. It's an image of a group that you have in your mind and that you use in thinking about or talking with members of this group. Although we often think of stereotypes as negative ("They're lazy and only interested in getting high"), they may be positive ("They're all smart and extremely loyal").

Stereotypes are especially difficult and can easily create problems in audience analysis. One problem with stereotypes is that there's often some element of truth in them and this gives the impression that the stereotype as a whole is true. Stereotypes are also convenient thinking shortcuts to use when meeting people for the first time or when making a quick assessment of your audience. But stereotypes can distort your perceptions by preventing you from seeing characteristics that are present (because the stereotype leads you to think it isn't there). Thus, the stereotype of "ignorant" or "uneducated" may lead you to fail to appreciate the validity of an argument or the value of a proposal if proposed by "one of them." Similarly, stereotypes can distort your perceptions by leading you to see characteristics that aren't there (because the stereotype leads you to believe it's absent). Thus, the stereotype of "religious" may lead you to see "fidelity" or "humanitarianism" when it simply isn't there.

So, be careful. As soon as you begin to use a sociological characteristic with the expressed or implied "all," consider the possibility that you may be stereotyping. Don't assume that all women or all older people or all highly educated people think or believe the same things. They don't. Nevertheless, there are characteristics that seem to be more common among one group than another, and it's these characteristics that are explored in these generalizations. Use them to stimulate your thinking about your specific and unique audience. Most important, test what is offered here against your own experience.

Let's look at six major sociological or demographic variables: (1) cultural factors, (2) age; (3) gender; (4) educational and intellectual levels; (5) occupation and income and (6) religion and religiousness.

It is always easier to believe than to deny. Our minds are naturally affirmative.
—John Burroughs

Cultural Factors

Nationality, race, and cultural identity are crucial in audience analysis. Largely because of different training and experiences, the interests, values, and goals of various cultural groups will also differ. Further, cultural factors will also influence each of the remaining factors; for example, attitudes toward age and gender will differ greatly from one culture to another. Consider the following questions as you think about culture and your audience.

1. Are the attitudes and beliefs held by different cultures relevant to your topic and purpose? Find out what these are. For example, the degree to which listeners are loyal to family members, feel responsibility for the aged, and believe in the value of education will vary from one culture to another. In many Asian cultures the aged are revered, are held in the highest esteem, and are frequently asked for advice and guidance by the young. Among some in the United States—though certainly not all or even necessarily a majority, the aged are often ignored and devalued. Build your appeals around your audience's attitudes and beliefs.

2. Will the varied cultures differ in their goals or suggestions to change their lives? For example, groups that have experienced recent oppression may be more concerned with immediate goals and immediate means of effecting change in their lives. Many want revolutionary rather than evolutionary change. They may have little patience with the more conservative posture of the majority that tells them to be content with small gains. You see this division even within groups where there are those who want to take it slowly and those who want more dramatic change; you see it in disputes within the African American community, the Hispanic community, and the gay and lesbian community. And, of course, you see this in other countries throughout the world; in China, there are those who want democracy now and those who are content with changes coming more slowly. Among the Israelis as among the Palestinians, there are those who want revolutionary and those who want evolutionary changes.

3. Will the cultures have different views toward education, employment, and life in general? Some cultures value formal education and take great pride in their members graduating from college and earning advanced degrees. Other cultures may place greater value on practical experience, on hard work, or on living for the pleasure of the moment. How might these different cultural views impact on how they see your topic and your specific purpose?

Generally, do you think you're at an advantage speaking to a same-sex or an opposite-sex audience? As a listener, are you more responsive to a same-sex speaker or an opposite-sex speaker?

4. Are the differences within cultures relevant to your topic and purpose? Speakers who fail to demonstrate an understanding of these differences will be distrusted. Speakers, especially those who are seen to be outsiders, who imply that all African Americans are athletic and all lesbians are masculine will quickly lose credibility. Many African Americans are poor athletes and many lesbians are extremely feminine. Avoid any implication that you're stereotyping audience members (or the groups to which they belong). It's sure to work against achieving your purpose.

Age

Different age groups have different attitudes and beliefs largely because they have had different experiences in different contexts. Take these differences into consideration in preparing your speeches.

For example, let's say that you're an investment counselor and you want to persuade your listeners to invest their money to increase their earnings. Your speech would have to be very different if you were addressing an audience of retired people (say in their 60s) and an audience of young executives (say in their 30s). You might, for example, begin your speech to the retired audience as follows:

> I want to talk with you about investing for your future. Now, I know what you're thinking. You're thinking to yourself, our future is now. You're thinking that you need more income now, not in the future. Well, that is what investing is all about. It's about increasing your income now, tomorrow, and next week and next month. Let me show you what I mean.

In your speech to the young executives, you might begin with something like this:

> I want to talk with you about investing for your future. In 30 years—years that will pass very quickly—many of you will be retiring. You'll quickly learn that your company pension plan will prove woefully

The dead might as well try to speak to the living as the old to the young.
—Willa Cather

inadequate. Social security will be equally inadequate. With only these sources of income, you'll have to lower your standard of living drastically. But that need not happen. In fact, with extremely small investments made now and throughout your high-income earning years, you'll actually be able to live at a much higher standard than you ever thought possible.

Note that in both of these examples the speaker made inferences about the audience attitudes toward investments based on age. The speaker demonstrated a knowledge of the audience and their immediate concerns. As a listener hearing even these brief excerpts, you'd probably feel that the speaker is addressing you directly and specifically. As a result, you'd probably give this speaker more attention than you'd give to one who spoke in generalities and without any clear idea of who was listening.

Here are some questions about age that you might find helpful in analyzing and adapting to your audience. In examining these questions, recognize that culture will greatly influence attitudes toward age. Among Native Americans and Chinese, for example, there is great respect for the aged. In the United States youth is valued and the aged are, perhaps, tolerated. Programs for the aged, scholarships for students, or parental and child responsibilities are likely to be met very differently by members of these different cultures.

1. Do the age groups differ in the goals, interests, and day-to-day concerns that may be related to your topic and purpose? Graduating from college, achieving corporate success, raising a family, and saving for retirement are concerns that differ greatly from one age group to another. Learn your audience's goals. Know what they think about and worry about. Connect your propositions and supporting materials to these goals and concerns. Show the audience how they can more effectively achieve their goals and you'll win a favorable hearing.

2. Do the groups differ in their ability to absorb and process information? With a young audience, it may be best to keep up a steady, even swift pace. If possible use visuals. Make sure their attention doesn't wander. With older persons, you may wish to maintain a more moderate pace.

3. Do the groups differ in their respect for tradition and the past? Is one age group (traditionally the young) more likely to view innovation and change positively? Might appeals to tradition be more appropriate for an older audience? Might appeals to discovery, exploration, newness, and change find a more receptive hearing among the young?

4. Do the groups differ in the degree to which they're motivated by their peer group? Although all people have the need to be evaluated positively by their peer group, young people often have especially strong needs for positive evaluation by peers; group identification is particularly important to the young. Use this motive in your speeches. Show them why agreement with you will result in peer approval.

Gender

Gender is one of the most difficult audience variables to analyze. The rapid social changes taking place today make it difficult to pin down the effects of gender. At one time, researchers focused primarily on biological

When I was a boy of fourteen, my father was so ignorant I could hardly stand to have the old man around. But when I got to be twenty-one, I was astonished at how much the old man had learned in seven years.
—Mark Twain

How to Listen to Gender Differences in Silent Messages

Consider these few findings from research on non-verbal sex differences (Burgoon, Buller, and Woodall 1995; Eakins and Eakins 1978; Pearson, West, and Turner 1995; Arliss 1991).

1. Women smile more than men.
2. Women stand closer to each other than do men and are generally approached more closely than men.
3. Both men and women, when speaking, look at men more than at women.
4. Women both touch and are touched more than men.
5. Men extend their bodies, taking up greater areas of space, than women.

What problems might these differences create when men listen to female speakers and women listen to male speakers?

(The next Listen to This box appears on page 234.)

sex differences. Now, however, many researchers are focusing on psychological sex roles. When we focus on a psychological sex role, we consider a person feminine if that person has internalized those traits (attitudes and behaviors) that society considers feminine and rejected those traits society considers masculine. We consider a person masculine if that person has internalized those traits society considers masculine and rejected those traits society considers feminine. Thus, a biological woman may display masculine sex-role traits and behaviors and a biological man may display feminine sex-role traits and behaviors.

Because of society's training, biological males generally internalize masculine traits and biological females generally internalize feminine traits. So, while there's probably great overlap between biological sex and psychological sex roles, they're not equivalent. At times, in fact, they may be quite different. Although we use the shorthand "men" and "women," remember that psychological sex roles may be more significant than biological sex roles in accounting for these differences.

Attitudes toward men and women and even the traits that are considered masculine and feminine will vary from one culture to another. In the United States, Australia, and Western Europe, women and men are considered equal in most areas. In much of the rest of the world—Asia and the Arab world, for example—men make the business decisions and the important family decisions. In Islamic cultures, women are seen in "traditional" roles of mother and housewife, not as business partner. And men and women don't compete with each other whether at school or at work. With even these few examples, it's easy to see the difficulties a female speaker would have addressing men from these cultures on topics heard every day in the United States—abortion, no-fault divorce, lesbians in the military, and sexual equality, for example.

Let's say that you're a marriage counselor and are delivering a speech on how to communicate more effectively. Your speech should be very different if delivered to a group of women versus a group of men. Women, it has been argued, will probably be more receptive to the topic and more willing to talk about their relationships than men (Tannen 1990). In your speech to an audience of women, you might say:

Many of you are probably in relationships with those who have difficulty expressing themselves, especially when it comes to romance. Oh, they're good men, of course, but they don't know how to talk romance. They don't know the language of romance. You do; women have been taught this language and feel comfortable with it. And so, you have to assume the role of teacher and teach your partner this new and different language. But you must do it with subtlety; that is what I want to talk about.

To an audience of men, however, you might introduce your topic very differently. You might, for example, say something like this:

Most of you are probably in relationships with women who do all or most of the talking about the relationship. They're the ones who talk romance. Somehow you're not comfortable talking like this; you have difficulty using the language of romance. You're men of action. But maybe there are ways of talking this language that will make it less painful. In fact, I'm going to show you how to talk the language of romance so that you'll love each and every syllable.

Note that in these two examples, the speaker begins with and builds on the feelings the audience is assumed to have. The audience is made to see that the speaker knows who they are and does not intend to contradict or criticize their feelings but rather takes these feelings into consideration in the speech.

Although it's not possible to make generalizations about all men or all women, you may be able to make some assumptions about the men and women in your *specific audience*. Here are some questions to guide your analysis of this very difficult audience characteristic.

1. Do men and women differ in the values they consider important and that are related to your topic and purpose? Traditionally, men have been found to place greater importance on theoretical, economic, and political values. Traditionally, women have been found to place greater importance on aesthetic, social, and religious values. Of course, you are unlikely to ever find yourself speaking to an audience of all "traditional" men and "traditional" women. Rather, your audience is likely to be composed of men and women whose values overlap. Be careful of assuming that the women in your audience, because they're women, are therefore religious and that the men, because they're men, are not or that the men are interested in sports and the stock market but that the women are not.

2. Will your topic be seen differently by men and by women? Although both men and women may find the topic important, they may nevertheless view it from different perspectives. For example, men and women don't view such topics as abortion, date rape, performance anxiety, anorexia, equal pay for equal work, or exercise in the same way. So, if you're giving on speech on date rape on campus, you need to make a special effort to relate the topic and your purpose to the attitudes, knowledge, and feelings that the men and women in your audience bring with them. For example, you may find it relevant to recall that in at least one study over 50 percent of the women on this one college campus said that they were verbally threatened, physically coerced, or physically abused and over 12 percent

Love enters a man through his eyes; a woman through her ears.
—Polish proverb

said they were raped (Barrett 1982, Kersten and Kersten 1988). Further, it might also be relevant to recall that in another study over 40 percent of the men indicated that they had engaged in coercive sexual relationships (Craig, Kalichman, and Follingstad 1989). From these differences you may wish to infer that the men and women in your audience will look at this problem and respond to possible solutions very differently.

3. Will men or women respond differently to the language and style of your speech? Research shows that men and women differ in language usage a lot less than the stereotypes might have us believe. And yet, research does support at least two differences: women are more polite in their speech and are more indirect, especially when stating something that is unpleasant or negative. Depending on your specific audience, you may want to make the inference—based on this research—that women will be less favorable to slang or to expressions you might label "vulgar." Your best bet, of course, is to avoid slang or any expression that may be interpreted as vulgar and avoid this especially when your audience is mixed. You may also want to infer that women will prefer a more indirect form of criticism or argument, a less confrontational style of speaking, than will men.

Educational and Intellectual Levels

An educated person may not be very intelligent and, conversely, an intelligent person may not be well educated. In most cases, however, the two go together. Further, they seem to influence the reception of a speech in similar ways and so are considered together. The shorthand "educated" is used here to refer to both qualities.

Let's say you're an advertising executive and are giving a speech on how spokespersons for television commercials are chosen. If your audience is highly educated and knowledgeable, you might say something like this:

The credibility of the spokesperson depends on three essential dimensions. First, it depends on the person's perceived competence. Second, it depends on the person's moral character. Third, it depends on the person's charisma. Rhetorical scholarship and experimental research have found support for these three factors.

If your audience is less educated and less knowledgeable, you might communicate essentially the same information this way:

What makes us believe one person and disbelieve another person? Research tells us that there are three main characteristics. First, we believe someone we think has knowledge or competence. Second, we believe someone who is moral, who is essentially a good person. Third, we believe someone who is dynamic and outgoing.

The first example assumes that the audience knows such technical terms as *credibility, rhetorical,* and *charisma.* The second example does not take this knowledge for granted and instead uses everyday language to explain the same concepts. When technical vocabulary is used, the terms are explained (as in ". . . we think has knowledge or competence"). In looking at the education and intelligence of your audience, consider asking questions such as the following.

1. Is the educational level related to the audience's level of social or political activism? Generally, the more educated are more responsive to the needs of others. They more actively engage in causes of a social and political nature. Appeals to humanitarianism and broad social motives should work well with an educated audience. However, when speaking to less-educated groups, concentrate on the value your speech has to their immediate needs and to the satisfaction of their immediate goals.

2. Will the interests and concerns of the audience differ on the basis of their educational level? Generally, the educated are more concerned with issues outside their immediate field of operation. They're concerned with international affairs, economic issues, and the broader philosophical and sociological issues confronting the nation and the world. The educated recognize that these issues affect them in many ways. Often the uneducated don't see the connection. Therefore, when speaking to a less-educated audience, draw the connections explicitly and relate such topics to their more immediate concerns.

Note, too, that groups from different educational levels will be familiar with different sources of information. Thus, for example, only a relatively educated audience would be familiar with such periodicals as *Architectural Digest, Byte,* and *Barron's.* The educated and the less educated will probably also read different newspapers and watch different television shows. Recognize these differences and use the relevant sources appropriately.

3. Will the educational levels influence how critical the audience will be of your evidence and argument? The more educated will probably be less swayed by appeals to emotion and to authority. They'll be more skeptical of generalizations (as you may and should be of my generalizations in this unit). They'll question the validity of statistics and frequently demand better substantiation of your propositions. The educated are more likely to apply the tests of evidence discussed in later units (see Units 21–23, for example). Therefore, pay special attention to the logic of your evidence and arguments in addressing an educated audience.

4. Will the educational level relate to what the audience knows about your topic? As a speaker you'll be able to assume more background knowledge when addressing an educated than an uneducated audience. Fill in the necessary background and detail for the less educated.

Occupation and Income

Occupation and income, although not the same, are most often positively related. Therefore, they can be dealt with together. Let's say you're a politician delivering campaign promises to a wide variety of audiences. One of your positions is to lower condo taxes. Now, if you're speaking to a group of high income Wall Street executives in their twenties, you might emphasize that lower taxes on condos will benefit them because they will have low monthly payments and, as a result, will be able to buy bigger and better apartments. On the other hand, if you're speaking to a group of low income residents who already own their own modest homes, you might

'Tis education forms the common mind, just as the twig is bent, the tree's inclined.
—Alexander Pope

No man forgets his original trade: the rights of nations, and of kings, sink into questions of grammar, if grammarians discuss them.
—Samuel Johnson

emphasize how lower condo taxes will bring more high income people into the city, more businesses, and thus lower the overall taxes for the entire city. In thinking about the occupation and income of your audience, consider asking such questions as these.

1. How will job security and occupational pride be related to your topic and purpose? Appeal to these when appropriate and attack them only with extreme caution. If you can show your audience how your topic will enhance their job, give them greater job security or mobility, or make them more effective and efficient workers, you'll have a most attentive and receptive audience.

2. Will people from different economic levels view long-range planning and goals differently? Higher income people are generally more future-oriented. They train and plan for the future. Their goals are clear and their efforts are directly addressed to achieving these goals. Even their reading matter relates directly to these goals. For example, high income individuals read *Forbes, Fortune,* and *The Wall Street Journal* to help them achieve their financial goals. When speaking to a lower-income audience, relate future-oriented issues to their more immediate and demanding situations.

3. Will the different groups have different time limitations? More financially secure people may be more likely to devote their time to social and political issues. Lower income people may be more concerned with meeting their immediate needs. Time is extremely valuable to the poor. The speaker who asks anything that would take their time is demanding a great deal—perhaps more than many can afford. Relate any request for them to see "the larger picture" to the fulfillment of their present needs.

Religion and Religiousness

Today there's great diversity among religions. Attitudes of religions vary widely on numerous issues: abortion, same-sex marriage, women's rights, and divorce. Attitudes also vary within a religion; almost invariably there are conservative, liberal, and middle-of-the-road groups within each. In some Christian communities, for example, gay men and lesbians may be ordained ministers and same-sex marriages may be performed. In other Christian communities the attitudes are vastly different. Only recently, for example, Bob Jones University, a fundamentalist Christian school in South Carolina, sent a letter to one of its gay alumni saying, "With grief we must tell you that as long as you are living as a homosexual, you, of course, would not be welcome on the campus" (*The New York Times,* October 25, 1998, p. 40).

Although religious attitudes and teachings are often slow to change, it would be a mistake to assume that these are static. In some cases, the changes are in the direction of increased conservatism; in other cases (for example, Europe), the changes are in the direction of increased liberalism.

Some cultures may be viewed as secular cultures where religion does not dominate the attitudes and views of the people or greatly influence political or educational decisions (Dodd 1995). Liberal Protestant cultures such as those in the Scandinavian countries would be clearly secular. Other cultures are sacred; in these cultures religion and religious beliefs and values dominate everything a person does and influence politics, education, and just about every issue. Islamic cultures would be traditional examples of sacred cultures. Technically, the United States would be a secular culture (the Constitution, for example, expressly separates church and state) but in some areas of the country, religion exerts powerful influence on schools (from prayers to condom distribution to sex education) and politics (from the selection of its political leaders to its concern for social welfare to its gay rights legislation).

Generalizations here, as with gender, are changing rapidly. In thinking about the religiousness of your audience, consider the following questions.

1. Will the religious see your topic or purpose from the point of view of religion? Religion permeates all topics and all issues. On a most obvious level, we know that such issues as birth control, abortion, and divorce are closely connected to religion. Similarly, premarital sex, marriage, child-rearing, money, cohabitation, responsibilities toward parents, and thousands of other issues are clearly influenced by religion. Religion is also important, however, in areas where its connection isn't so obvious. For example, religion influences one's ideas concerning such topics as obedience to authority, responsibility to government, and the usefulness of such qualities as honesty, guilt, and happiness.

2. Does your topic or purpose attack the religious beliefs of any segment of your audience? Even those who claim total alienation from the religion in which they were raised may still have strong emotional (though perhaps unconscious) ties to that religion. These ties may continue to influence their attitudes and beliefs.

When dealing with any religious beliefs (and particularly when disagreeing with them), recognize that you're going to meet stiff opposition. Proceed slowly and inductively. Present your evidence and argument before expressing your disagreement.

3. Do the religious beliefs of your audience differ in any significant ways from the official teachings of their religion? Don't assume that a religious leader's opinion or pronouncement is accepted by the rank-and-file members. Generally, opinion polls show that official statements by religious leaders take a more conservative position, while members are more liberal.

4. Can you make reliable inferences about people's behavior based on their religiousness? One of the common beliefs about religious people is that they're more honest, more charitable, and more likely to reach out to those in need than the nonreligious. A review of research, however, finds even this seemingly logical connection not true (Kohn 1989). For example, in a study of cheating among college students, religious beliefs bore little relationship to honesty; in fact, atheists were less likely to cheat than those who identified themselves as religious. Other studies have found that religious people were not any more likely to help those in need, for example, to give time to work with retarded children or to comfort someone lying in the street. So, be careful of making assumptions about people's behavior on the basis of their religiousness. You're much more likely to be accurate in judging attitudes than behaviors.

Other Factors

No list of audience characteristics can possibly be complete, and the list presented here is no exception. You'll need another category—"other

There is only one religion, though there are a hundred versions of it.
—George Bernard Shaw

TIPS
from professional speakers

Once you have gathered that [demographic] information and thought it through, the answers to these further questions will give you the detailed information you need to make your presentation more relevant to your audience's needs and interests:

- What can you say that will be of most use or interest to participants?
- What can you say about how well they perform the task you are there to discuss ?
- What other positive points can your talk include?
- How can you let the audience know you are sincere and realistic?
- How else can you help them see the benefits of your message?

Stephen C. Rafe, president of Rapport Communications and professional speech coach and advisor. *How to Be Prepared to Think on Your Feet* (New York: HarperBusiness, 1990): 58.

factors"—to identify any additional characteristics that might be significant to your particular audience. Such factors might include the following.

Expectations. How will your audience's expectations about you influence their reception of your speech? Whether you intend to fulfill these expectations or explode them, you need to take them into consideration.

Relational Status. Will the relational status of your audience members influence the way in which they view your topic or your purpose? Will singles be interested in hearing about the problems of selecting preschools? Will those already in long-term relationships be interested in the depression many people who are not in close relationships experience during the holidays?

Special Interests. Do the special interests of your audience members relate to your topic or purpose? What special interests do the audience members have? What occupies their leisure time? How can you integrate these interests into your examples and illustrations or use them to help select quotations?

Organizational Memberships. How might the organizational memberships of your audience influence your topic or purpose? Might you use these organizational memberships in selecting your supporting materials?

Political Affiliation. Will your audience's political affiliations influence how they view your topic or purpose? Are they politically liberal? Conservative? What does this mean to the development of your speech?

ANALYZING CONTEXT CHARACTERISTICS

In addition to analyzing specific listeners, devote attention to the specific context in which you'll speak. Consider the size of the audience, the physical environment, the occasion, the time of your speech, and where your speech fits into the sequence of events.

Size of Audience

Generally, the larger the audience, the more formal the speech presentation should be. With a small audience, you may be more casual and informal. In a large audience you'll have more variety of religions, a greater range of occupations and income levels, and so on. All the variables noted earlier will be more intensified in a large audience. Therefore, you'll need supporting materials that will appeal to all members.

Physical Environment

The physical environment—indoors or outdoors, room or auditorium, sitting or standing audience—will obviously influence your speech presentation. Take a few minutes to erase or lessen the problem of entering the public speaking environment totally cold. Spend some time in front of the room. See the room from the perspective of the speaker (and from the perspective of the listener) before you're ready to speak.

Also, consider the equipment that is available. Is there a chalkboard, flip chart, or transparency projector? Is there a slide projector and screen? Is there a computer with the projector for showing computer slides? Are chalk and markers available? And, as stressed in the previous unit, check the compatibility of the equipment in the room with that on which you prepared your materials. And, if at all possible, try to rehearse in the room you'll be speaking in with the same equipment that you'll have when you deliver your speech.

Another factor in speech effectiveness is audience density. Generally, listeners are easier to persuade if they're sitting close together than if they're spread widely apart. With listeners close together, it's easier to maintain eye contact and to concentrate your focus.

Occasion

The occasion greatly influences the nature and the reception of the speech. Whether the speech is a class exercise (as most of your early speeches will be) or some invited address (as most of your professional life speeches will be) will influence much of the speech. If the speech is given as a class assignment, you'll probably be operating under a number of restrictions—time limitations, the type of purpose you can employ, the types of supporting materials, and various other matters. When your speech is invited because of who you are, you have great freedom to talk about what interests you, which by virtue of the invitation will also interest the audience.

The occasion will dictate, in part, the kind of speech required. A wedding speech will differ drastically from a speech at a funeral, which will differ drastically from one at a political rally. In constructing the speech, focus on each element in relation to the occasion. Ask yourself in what way the particular public speaking variable (language, organization, supporting materials) might be made more responsive to this particular occasion.

Time of the Speech

If your speech is to be given in an early morning class, say around 8AM, then take into consideration that some of your listeners will still be half asleep. Tell them you appreciate their attendance; compliment their attention. If necessary, wake them up with your voice, gestures, attention-gaining materials, visual aids, and the like. If your speech is in the evening when most of your listeners are anxious to get home, recognize this as well.

Sequence of Events

Also consider where your speech fits into the general events of the time. A useful procedure is to scan a recent news magazine as well as the morning newspaper to see if any items relate to what you'll say in your speech. If so, you might make reference to the story as a way of gaining attention, adding support to your argument, or stressing the importance of the topic.

Think too about where your speech fits in with the other speeches that will be heard that day or during that class. If you're to speak after one or more other speakers, try especially hard to build in some reference to a previous speech. This will stress your similarity with the audience mem-

Every crowd has a silver lining.
—P. T. Barnum

bers and will also demonstrate important connections between what you're saying and what others have said.

UNIT IN BRIEF

Approaching audience analysis and adaptation	Public speaking audience: a group of people gathered together to hear a speech. Attitude: the tendency to act for or against something. Belief: the conviction in the truth or falsity of some statement. Value: the worth you perceive an idea or object to have.
Factors to consider in analyzing an audience	1. Cultural factors 2. Age 3. Gender (biological sex and psychological sex role) 4. Educational and intellectual levels 5. Occupation and income 6. Religion and religiousness 7. Expectations, relationship status, special interests, organizational memberships, political affiliation
Factors to consider in analyzing the context	1. Size of the audience 2. Physical environment 3. Occasion 4. Time 5. Sequence of events

THINKING CRITICALLY ABOUT THE SOCIOLOGY OF AUDIENCES

REVIEWING KEY TERMS AND CONCEPTS IN THE SOCIOLOGY OF AUDIENCES

1. Define the key terms used in this unit:

- ❏ audience (p. 209)
- ❏ audience analysis (p. 209)
- ❏ attitude (p. 209)
- ❏ belief (p. 210)
- ❏ value (p. 210)
- ❏ sociological analysis (p. 214)
- ❏ context factors (p. 224)

2. Review and explain the key concepts covered in this unit:

- ■ What are some of the ways you can gain information on your audience?

- ■ What are the major characteristics of audiences that you should analyze as a way of learning something about their attitudes, beliefs, values, and behaviors?
- ■ What characteristics of the context should you investigate and make plans to adapt to?

DEVELOPING PUBLIC SPEAKING STRATEGIES

1. On the basis of the following facts, what assumptions can you make about your audience's attitudes toward (1) saving for retirement, (2) supporting gay marriage,

and (3) requiring the use of only English on the job?

- The audience consists of people whose background is approximately 50 percent European American, 20 percent Asian American, 15 percent African American, 15 percent Hispanic.
- The audience is about 80 percent female.
- The average age is 21, with a range of 18-23.
- The audience is first or second generation American; they or their parents were born in foreign countries.
- The parents of these audience members are all blue-collar workers, some with a college education in their native country.
- The audience is all in college, studying a variety of subjects and working at a variety of part-time jobs.
- The audience is about 50 percent Christian, 15 percent Muslim, 15 percent Jewish, and 10 percent Buddhist, and 10 percent "none" or "other."

2. How would you tailor your speech to the audiences described above if you were speaking on each of the following issues:

- Support the National Rifle Association in its efforts to fight gun control.
- The values of cross cultural friendship and romantic relationships.
- The need for the college to make condoms available to all students.

EVALUATING PUBLIC SPEECHES

1. Read one of the speeches included in this text or on the Web and identify specific ways in which this speech would have to be adapted if it were to be presented to your class. What assumptions are you making about your audience as you identify these adaptations?

2. Review the speech you're working on now, focusing particularly on how you're tailoring your speech to the attitudes, beliefs, and values of your audience. In what ways would your speech have to differ if it were to be presented to an audience of first year high school students? To an audience of the parents of class members?

USING TECHNOLOGY IN PUBLIC SPEAKING

1. Visit the Gallup Organization's Web site at http://www.gallup.com/ for a wide variety of information on all sorts of polls—economic, business, political, lifestyle, attitudes, buying habits, and more. Can you find a poll that would have provided useful information for a speech presented in this class?

2. Visit http://www.odci.gov/cia/publications/nsolo/wfb-all.htm for the CIA World Factbook, a source that contains information on every country in the world. Can you locate any information here that would have been of value to one of your previous speeches?

PRACTICALLY SPEAKING

10.1 Short Speech Technique

Prepare and deliver a two-minute speech in which you:

a. explain how men and women see the world differently or similarly.

b. explain the importance of culture in public speaking.

c. explain a particularly strong belief that you hold.

d. explain some of the things you don't understand about the influence of culture, age, gender, or any sociological factor on audience analysis.

e. explain the differences among attitudes, beliefs, and values (with lots of examples).

10.2 Analyzing an Unknown Audience

This experience should familiarize you with some of the essential steps in analyzing an audience on the basis of relatively little evidence and in predicting their attitudes.

The class should be broken up into small groups of five or six members. Each group will be given a different magazine; their task is to analyze the audience (i.e., the readers or subscribers) of that particular magazine in terms of the characteristics discussed in this unit. The only information the groups will have about their audience is that they're avid and typical readers of the given magazine. Pay particular attention to the types of articles published in the magazine, the advertisements, the photographs or illustrations, the editorial statements, the price of the magazine, and so on. Magazines that differ widely from each other are most appropriate for this experience.

After the audience has been analyzed, try to identify at least three favorable and three unfavorable attitudes that they probably hold on contemporary issues. On what basis do you make these predictions? If you had to address this audience advocating a position with which they disagreed, what adaptations would you make? What strategies would you use in preparing and presenting this persuasive speech?

Each group should share with the rest of the class the results of their efforts, taking special care to point out not only their conclusions but also the evidence and reasoning they used to arrive at the conclusions.

The Audience: Psychological Analysis and Adaptation

UNIT CONTENTS

How Willing Is Your Audience?

How Favorable Is Your Audience?

How Active Is Your Audience?

How Knowledgeable Is Your Audience?

How Homogeneous Is Your Audience?

Analysis and Adaptation During the Speech

UNIT OBJECTIVES

After completing this unit, you should be able to:
Adapt your speech to an unwilling audience.

Adapt your speech to an unfavorable audience.

Adapt your speech to a passive audience.

Adapting your speech to the knowledgeable and the not knowledgeable audience.

Adapt your speech to the heterogeneous audience.

Explain the suggestions for analyzing and adapting to the audience during the speech.

The previous unit examined the demographic characteristics of an audience and discussed how you can discover some of their attitudes, beliefs, and values that may be relevant to your speech. This unit continues the discussion of audience analysis but focuses on psychological characteristics such as how willing the audience is to listen to you and how favorable they are to your topic and purpose.

You may view audiences along such scales as those in Figure 11.1 By indicating on each scale where you think a particular audience is, you can construct an audience profile. Since each audience is unique, each audience will have a unique profile.

HOW WILLING IS YOUR AUDIENCE?

Audiences gather with varying degrees of willingness to hear a speaker. Some are anxious to hear the speaker and might even pay a substantial admission price. The "lecture circuit," for example, is a most lucrative

FIGURE 11.1

The Dimensions of An Audience.

What kind of an audience will your class be for your next speech? Can you position them on the following scales?

The Audience

Willing	___ :	___ :	___ :	___ :	___ :	___ :	___ Unwilling
Favorable	___ :	___ :	___ :	___ :	___ :	___ :	___ Unfavorable
Passive	___ :	___ :	___ :	___ :	___ :	___ :	___ Active
Knowledgeable	___ :	___ :	___ :	___ :	___ :	___ :	___ Not Knowledgeable
Homogeneous	___ :	___ :	___ :	___ :	___ :	___ :	___ Heterogeneous

aspect of public life. While some audiences are willing to pay to hear a speaker, others don't seem to care one way or the other. Still other audiences need to be persuaded to listen (or at least to sit in the audience). A group of people who gather to hear Shirley MacLaine talk about supernatural experiences are probably there willingly; they want to be there and they want to hear what MacLaine has to say. On the other hand, some groups gather because they have to. For example, the union contract may require members to attend meetings where officers give speeches. Administrators may put pressure on instructors to attend college and department meetings. These people may not wish to be there, but they don't want to risk losing their jobs or their vote.

Your immediate concern, of course, is with the willingness of your fellow students to listen to your speeches. How willing are they? Do they come to class because they have to or do they come because they're interested in what you'll say? If they're a willing group, then you have few problems. If they're an unwilling group, all is not lost, you just have to work a little harder in adapting your speech.

Adapting to the Unwilling Audience

The unwilling audience demands special and delicate handling. Here are a few suggestions to help change your listeners from unwilling to willing.

Secure their interest and attention as early in your speech as possible. Reinforce this throughout the speech by using little-known facts, quotations, startling statistics, examples, narratives, audiovisual aids, and the like. These devices will help you secure and maintain the attention of an initially unwilling audience. Here, for example, Judith Maxwell (1987), Chair of the Economic Council of Canada, uses humor to gain the interest and attention of her audience. She then quickly connects this humor to the topic of her talk:

> Yogi Berra said something once that's relevant to a discussion of economic forecasting. "If you don't know where you're going, you could wind up somewhere else." Whether we are business economists or economists in the public sector, what society expects from us is advice on how to "know where we are going." Our mission is to help captains of industry or captains of the ship of state plot an orderly path forward. In that sense, we are navigators.

Reward the audience for their attendance and attention. Do this in advance of your main arguments. Let the audience know you're aware they're making a sacrifice in coming to hear you speak. Tell them you appreciate it. One student, giving a speech close to midterm time, said simply:

> I know how easy it is to cut classes during midterm time to finish the unread chapters and do everything else you have to do. So I especially appreciate your being here this morning. What I have to say, however, will interest you and will be of direct benefit to all of you.

Once acknowledged, it's difficult for an audience to continue to feel unwilling.

Never hold any one by the button or the hand in order to be heard out; for if people are unwilling to hear you, you had better hold your tongue than them.
—Lord Chesterfield

Relate your topic and supporting materials directly to your audience's needs and wants. Show the audience how they can save time, make money, solve their problems, or become more popular. If you fail to do this, then your audience has good reason for not listening.

HOW FAVORABLE IS YOUR AUDIENCE?

Audiences vary in the degree to which they're favorable or unfavorable toward your thesis or point of view. Within the same audience you may have some who agree with you and others who disagree and perhaps still others who are undecided. If you intend to change an audience's attitudes, beliefs, or behaviors, you must understand their present position.

Audiences also differ in their attitudes toward you and toward your topic. At times the audience may have no real feeling, positive or negative. At other times they'll have very clear feelings that must be confronted. Thus, when Richard Nixon addressed the nation after Watergate, it was impossible to avoid the audience's unfavorable attitude toward him as a person. When Bill Clinton addressed the nation after testifying to the grand jury, it was impossible to avoid the audience's sense of betrayal and that he had to do something to win back his supporters. (This speech is reprinted in Unit 24, pages 469–470.)

Sometimes the degree of favorableness will depend not only on the specific speaker but also on some of the speaker's characteristics. Thus, a group of police officers may resent listening to a convicted felon argue against unlawful search and seizure. On the other hand, they might be quite favorable toward essentially the same speech given by a respected criminologist.

Similarly, audiences may have favorable or unfavorable responses to you because of your racial or ethnic origin, religion, affectional orientation, or social status. Find out, therefore, how the audience sees not only your speech purpose but also you as a speaker. If you conclude that your audience is unfavorable, the following suggestions should help.

Adapting to the Unfavorably Disposed Audience

The unfavorably disposed audience is a difficult one to confront and so needs special handling. Here are a few suggestions for dealing with this type of audience.

Clear up any possible misapprehensions that may be causing the disagreement. Often disagreement is caused by a lack of understanding. If you feel this is the case, then your first task is to clear this up. So, for example, if the audience is hostile to your team approach because they wrongly think it will result in a reduction in their autonomy, then tell them very directly, saying something like:

> *I realize that many people oppose this new team approach because they feel it will reduce their own autonomy and control. Well, it won't; as a matter of fact, with this approach, each person is actually given greater control, greater power, greater autonomy.*

Build on commonalities; emphasize not the differences but the similarities. Stress what you and the audience share as people, as interested citizens, as fellow students. Theorist and critic Kenneth Burke (1950) argues that we achieve persuasion through identification with the audience. Identification involves emphasizing similarities between speaker and audience. When an audience sees similarity or "common ground" between itself and you, it becomes more favorable to both you and your speech.

Here, for example, Alan Nelson (1986) identifies with the city of his audience in his introduction:

> *Returning to the Golden Gate, my home area, reminds me of another harbor and a beautiful statue . . . the Statue of Liberty, which has stood for 100 years in New York Harbor, is being rededicated this year and represents the heritage of America.*

Organize your speech inductively. Try to build your speech from areas of agreement, through areas of slight disagreement, up to the major differences between the audience's attitudes and your own position. Let's say, for example, that you represent management and you wish to persuade employees to accept a particular wage offer. You might begin with such areas of agreement as the mutual desire for improved working conditions or for long-term economic growth. Once areas of agreement are established, it's easier to bring up differences such as, perhaps, the need to delay salary increases until next year. In any disagreement or argument, there are still areas of agreement; emphasize these before considering areas of disagreement.

Strive for small gains. Don't try to convince a pro-life group to contribute money for the new abortion clinic or a pro-choice group to vote for repealing abortion laws in a five-minute speech. Be content to get them to see some validity in your position and to listen fairly. About-face changes take a long time to achieve. To attempt too much persuasion, too much change, is likely to result in failure or resentment.

Acknowledge the differences explicitly. If it's clear to the audience that they and you are at opposite ends of the issue, it may be helpful to acknowledge this directly. Show the audience that you understand their position and that you respect it but that you'd like them to consider a different way of looking at things. Say something like:

> *I know you don't all agree that elementary school teachers should have to take tests every several years to maintain their licenses. Some teachers are going to lose their licenses, and that isn't pleasant. And we all feel sorry that this will happen. What isn't widely known, however, is that the vast majority of teachers will actually benefit from this proposal. And I'd like an opportunity to sketch out the benefits that many of us will enjoy as a result of this new testing procedure.*

HOW ACTIVE IS YOUR AUDIENCE?

Most individuals are active listeners. They don't merely take in the information and use it as we might want them to. Rather, they work actively with it: they analyze, evaluate, question, and challenge it.

There is, however, another kind of audience—the audience that public speakers dread. This audience simply doesn't care about you, about your

TIPS
from professional speakers

Effective speakers attempt to establish common ground with their listeners when speaking to potentially hostile audiences. They help their listeners identify with them and realize they have similar goals. By emphasizing their areas of agreement, speakers stand a better chance that their audience will listen with an open mind and may be persuaded to accept the speaker's point of view.

Caryl Rae Krannich, communication and career expert, frequent speaker and trainer, *101 Secrets of Highly Effective Speakers: Controlling Fear, Commanding Attention* (Manassas Park, VA: Impact Publications, 1998): 68-69.

speech, or about your position. Its members may be physically present at your speech, but emotionally and intellectually, they're somewhere else. These listeners need to be awakened and made to feel concern.

Adapting to the Passive Audience

Here are a few suggestions for dealing with the passive audience and to move them into a state of greater activity and involvement.

Show the audience why they should listen to your speech. Show them why they need to be concerned with what you're saying. During your first few minutes, answer your listeners' unspoken questions: Why should I listen? Why should I care about what you're saying? Why should I bother to clutter up my mind with this information, with these arguments? The techniques for gaining attention (Unit 13) and for motivating listeners (Unit 22) should prove helpful with this task.

Involve the audience directly in your speech. Ask questions and pose problems directly to the audience members, pausing so they can consider a response. Here's how Nadine Jackson-Smith (1988) involved the audience. Notice too how she emphasizes commonalities by identifying with the audience. She began her speech in this way:

> By the power vested in me as your luncheon speaker, I hereby declare each and every one of you to be persons of excellence; persons of high ability, standing conspicuously among the best of your time.
>
> As Oscar Wilde was fond of saying, . . . "I have the simplest of tastes; I am always satisfied with the best."

LISTEN TO THIS How to Listen for Power

Much as you can communicate power and authority with words and nonverbal expression, you also communicate power through listening. In a business meeting or interview, for example, you're probably being evaluated when you listen as well as when you speak. If you want to project power and confidence, consider these suggestions.

Respond visibly but in moderation. An occasional nod of agreement or a facial expression that says "that's interesting" are usually sufficient. Responding with too little or too much reaction is likely to be perceived as powerless. Too little response says you aren't listening and too much response says you aren't listening critically.

Avoid adaptors. Playing with your hair or a pencil or drawing pictures on a Styrofoam cup signal your discomfort and hence your lack of power. The lack of adaptors, on the other hand, make you appear in control of the situation and comfortable in the role of listener.

Maintain an open posture. When around a table or in an audience, resist covering your face, chest, or stomach with your hands. This type of posture is often interpreted as indicating defensiveness and may therefore signal that you're feeling vulnerable and hence powerless.

Follow the cultural norms of the group. Or have good reason for violating them. If the norm is to avoid interrupting the speaker, then don't interrupt unless you have a great reason. If the norm is to ask only supportive questions, then avoid asking questions that may be perceived as unsupportive.

Take modest notes when appropriate. Taking too many notes may communicate a lack of ability to distinguish between what is and what isn't important. Taking too few notes may communicate a lack of interest or unwillingness to deal with the material.

(The next Listen to This box appears on page 304.)

Good Afternoon.
I am pleased to be here with you today, because it brings back memories of my first real job. I worked as a secretary at the University of Washington and my office was located in the same wing as the Assistant Attorney General for Student Affairs.

Use supporting materials that gain attention and secure interest. Once you get the audience to pay attention, they'll begin to listen willingly. They'll begin to internalize some of your arguments and information. Be sure to continue to maintain their interest and attention throughout your speech.

Focus on a few (even one) very strong issues. Don't diffuse your energies and time on many issues, none of which may awaken the truly passive audience. You want your audience to stop thinking there's no reason to be concerned. If you give them four or five poorly developed reasons, they may still feel there's no reason to care. If, however, you devote most time to your one strongest argument, it will be difficult for them to continue to be passive.

HOW KNOWLEDGEABLE IS YOUR AUDIENCE?

Listeners differ greatly in the knowledge they have. Some listeners will be quite knowledgeable about the topic; others will be almost totally ignorant. Mixed audiences are the most difficult ones.

If you're unaware of the audience's knowledge level, you won't know what to assume and what to explain. You won't know how much information will overload the channels and how much will put the audience to sleep. Perhaps you want to show that their previous knowledge is now inadequate. Perhaps you want to demonstrate a new slant to old issues. Or perhaps you want to show that what you have to say will not repeat but will instead build on the already extensive knowledge of the audience. However you accomplish this, you need to make the audience see that what you have to say is new. Make them realize that you won't simply repeat what they already know.

Adapting to the Unknowledgeable Audience

Treat audiences that lack knowledge of the topic very carefully. Never confuse a lack of knowledge with a lack of ability to understand.

Don't talk down to your audience. This is perhaps the greatest communication error that teachers make. After having taught a subject for years, they face, semester after semester, students who have no knowledge of the topic. As a result, many teachers often talk down to the audience and, in the process, lose them. No one wants to listen to a speaker putting them down.

Don't confuse a lack of knowledge with a lack of intelligence. An audience may have no knowledge of your topic but be quite capable of following a clearly presented, logically developed argument. Try especially hard to use concrete examples, presentation aids, and simple language. Fill in background details as required. Avoid jargon and specialized terms that may not be clear to someone new to the subject. Never overestimate your audience's knowledge, but never underestimate their intelligence.

Everybody is ignorant, only on different subjects.
—Will Rogers

How would you analyze your class in terms of their willingness, favorableness, activity, and knowledge for a speech on "How to Get the Job you Want."

Adapting to the Knowledgeable Audience

Audiences with much knowledge also require special handling because their response may well be, "Why should I listen to this? I already know about this topic."

Let the audience know that you're aware of their knowledge and expertise. Try to do this as early in the speech as possible. Emphasize that what you have to say will not be redundant. Tell them that you'll be presenting recent developments or new approaches. In short, let them know that they won't be wasting their time listening to your speech.

Emphasize your credibility, especially your competence in this general subject area (see Unit 23). Let the audience know that you have earned the right to speak. Let them know that what you have to say is based on a firm grasp of the material.

Here, for example, Richard Colino (1986) establishes his credibility early in his speech:

> I'm pleased to be here today to discuss the impact of the Information Age on national policies—a subject which merits more analysis and debate than it gets. I'm the Director General and Chief Executive of the International Telecommunications Satellite Organization, better known as INTELSAT. However, my commentary on a series of issues and themes today represents my personal, rather than official INTELSAT, views.

HOW HOMOGENEOUS IS YOUR AUDIENCE?

If you face a delicate situation, don't go into it wearing your spurs or you'll rip it apart. Instead, dress for the occasion. Cloak yourself in diplomacy. Vest yourself with wisdom, and wear a smile.
—Ann McKay Thompson

Audiences vary in homogeneity—the degree to which they have similar characteristics, values, attitudes, knowledge, and so on. Homogeneous audiences consist of individuals who are very much alike; heterogeneous audiences consist of widely different individuals.

Obviously, it's easier to address a homogeneous group than a heterogeneous group. If your listeners are alike, your arguments will be as effective for one as for another. The language appropriate for one will be appropriate for another, and so on, through all the elements of the public speaking transaction.

With a heterogeneous group, however, this does not apply. The argument that works with one subgroup will not necessarily work with another. The language that is appropriate for the educated members will not be appropriate for the uneducated, so when you address a heterogeneous audience you'll have to make some tough decisions.

Homogeneity–heterogeneity also relates to the four dimensions just considered. Thus, audience homogeneity–heterogeneity applies to their willingness to listen, their favorableness, their passivity, and their knowledge. For example, some audiences will be extremely similar (homogeneous) in their willingness to listen; others may contain members who differ widely in their willingness to listen.

Adapting to the Heterogeneous Audience

The most difficult audience to address isn't the unwilling or the unfavorable or the unknowledgeable. It's the mixed audience: the audience consisting of some who care and some who don't, of some who know and some who don't. At times, addressing this type of audience will seem an impossibility. It isn't, so don't despair. Teachers face this type of audience every day, as do politicians and advertisers. Some general principles (rather than specific adaptation guidelines) for dealing with the heterogeneous audience follow. These should help you in this difficult but not impossible task.

The greater the heterogeneity of the audience, the more difficult will be your analysis and adaptation. A heterogeneous audience will require a much more complex audience analysis and a much more careful plan of adaptation than a homogeneous audience. Consider, for example, a PTA audience

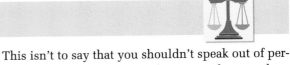

THE ETHICS OF Audience Focus

When advertisers conduct audience research, they're interested in learning about their audience so they can develop more effective persuasive strategies to help them make a greater profit by enabling them to sell more products or services. And while the profit motive isn't unethical, it does raise ethical issues when it takes precedence over audience welfare, for example, when advertising is directed at selling products that are dangerous or unhealthy or simply overpriced. Cigarettes and cigars, cereals and snacks loaded with sugar and high cholesterol fats, and certain brand name sneakers come to mind most quickly. This is quite different from the purpose of audience research as explained here. The objective of the public speaker is surely to be more persuasive, but the audience's best interests and welfare must come first.

This isn't to say that you shouldn't speak out of personal interest. It is to argue, however, that speakers should never exploit their audiences or speak out of a self-interest that may be harmful to the listeners. If a speaker asks an audience to listen to a speech and to do certain things, it should be for their ultimate benefit. It would be unethical, for example, to persuade an audience to take up arms in a self-destructive war, to buy homes in a flood zone, or to donate money to an embezzling organization.

Can you locate a specific print or television or Web advertisement that violates this "focus on the audience" principle?

(The next Ethics of Public Speaking box appears on page 249.)

composed of parents (differing widely in income, education, and cultural background) and teachers (differing widely in background, training, and age). Each of these groups will have different points of view, backgrounds, and expectations. As a speaker you'll have to recognize these differences and take special care to appeal to all groups.

When the audience is too heterogeneous, it's sometimes helpful to subdivide it and appeal to each section separately. A common example is the audience consisting of men and women. Say the topic is abortion on demand. To limit yourself to arguments that would appeal equally to men and women might seriously damage your case. Consider, therefore, concentrating first on arguments that women can relate to and then on those to which men can relate. You thus avoid using supporting materials that fall in between the groups and that are effective with neither.

Homogeneity does not equal attitudinal sameness. The audience that is similar in age, sex, educational background, and so on, will probably also share similar attitudes and beliefs. However, this isn't always true. Heterogeneity increases with the size of the group. As any group expands in size, its characteristics become more diverse—keep this in mind when you're analyzing your audiences.

ANALYSIS AND ADAPTATION DURING THE SPEECH

In your classroom speeches, you'll face a known audience, an audience you've already analyzed and for which you've made appropriate adaptations. At other times, however, you may face an audience that you've not been able to analyze beforehand or one that differs greatly from the audience you thought you'd address. In these cases you'll have to analyze and adapt to them as you speak. Before considering the suggestions for making this process easier and more effective, think about your own flexibility as a public speaker by taking the accompanying self-test.

TEST YOURSELF
How Flexible Are You as a Public Speaker?

Visualize yourself in each of the following situations. Reflect for one minute on each situation and identify as many different appropriate ways of handling the situation that you can think of in this one minute. Jot down brief abbreviations for each of the possibilities you think of. Record the number of ways you might appropriately handle each situation in the spaces provided.

_____ 1. You're preparing a speech on abortion and were planning to use some posters on both sides of the issue. Unfortunately, the person who was going to lend you the posters went on vacation and you now have no way of getting them. These were going to be great visual aids. What might you do?

_____ 2. Right in the middle of delivering a speech on violence on television, one of the listeners in the back row yells out in a perfect Austrian accent "Hasta la vista, baby!" The entire class busts out laughing. What might you do?

_____ 3. While giving your speech, one of the members of your audience not only falls asleep but starts snoring so loudly that everyone begins to concentrate on the snoring rather than on what you're saying. What might you do?

_____ 4. In your speech on e-mail programs you had planned to show the class three different programs. The first two went along without any problems. When you tried to show the third one, you got an error message that you didn't understand. What might you do?

_____ 5. One of your speeches requires that, as part of your supporting material, you interview someone with special knowledge of your speech topic. You've developed a really great speech on the dangers of taking too many vitamins and your interviewee is going to be a nurse who suffered from taking an excessive amount of vitamins and has just written a book on the topic. Unfortunately, the nurse is called out of town for several weeks and won't be available for the interview. What might you do?

The number of ways of handling each situation is a measure of your flexibility. The more ways you can think of, the more flexible you are. If possible, share your responses with others in small groups or with the class as a whole. You should find that the group is a lot more flexible than any one person; that is, the group as a whole will come up with more possibilities than would any one individual. Can you think of other situations where flexibility would come in handy?

Ask "What If" Questions

As you prepare your speech, have your audience clearly in mind. For example, let's say you have been told that you're to explain the opportunities available to the nontraditional student at your college. You have been told that your audience will consist mainly of working women in their 30s and 40s who are just beginning college. As you prepare your speech with this audience in mind, ask yourself, for example:

- what if the audience has a large number of men?
- what if the audience consists of women much older than 40?
- what if the audience members come with their spouses or their children?

Keeping such questions in mind will force you to consider alternatives as you prepare your speech. And you'll find them readily available if you face this new or different audience.

Speak Extemporaneously

As explained in more detail in Unit 17, when you speak extemporaneously, you prepare a delivery outline that includes your main assertions and your supporting materials in the order in which they'll be presented. Avoid memorizing your speech, however, or committing yourself to any exact wording. In this way you'll maintain the flexibility to delete examples that may be inappropriate or to add examples that may be more relevant to this new audience. If you memorize your speech, you'll find it impossible to make these essential last-minute adjustments.

Do Extra

The more preparation you put into your speech, the better prepared you'll be to make on-the-spot adjustments and adaptations. For example, if you

TIPS
from professional speakers

The audience thinks, reacts, modifies, and synthesizes from the moment the speaker gains its attention. A speaker who fails to sense these movements and changes will soon drift out of touch. And what you want is precisely *touch.*

Don Pfarrer, public speaking coach and author, *Guerrilla Persuasion: Mastering the Art of Effective and Winning Business Presentation* (Boston, Mass.: Houghton Mifflin, 1998): 61.

anticipate a knowledgeable audience you may decide not to include background material or definitions in your speech. You should have these ready, though, just in case you discover that your listeners are not as knowledgeable as you thought. The more alternatives you consider as you prepare your speech, the more alternatives you'll have available as you deliver your speech.

Focus on Listeners as Message Senders

As you're speaking, look at your listeners. Remember that just as you're sending messages to your audience, they're also sending messages to you. Just as they're responding to what you're communicating, you need to respond to what they're communicating. Pay attention to these messages and, on the basis of what these tell you, make the necessary adjustments.

Do remember that members of different cultures will operate with different display rules—cultural rules that state what types of expressions are appropriate to reveal and what expressions are inappropriate to reveal and should be kept hidden. Some display rules call for open and free expression of feelings and responses; these listeners will be relatively easy to read. Other display rules call for little expression, and these listeners will be extremely difficult to read.

If your listeners are talking among themselves or reading their newspapers, then it should be clear that they're not paying attention and that you have to do something to win them back. But not all audience behaviors are so obvious. Wanda Vassallo, in the accompanying tip, offers a wide variety of suggestions that you may wish to look for. These are more subtle behaviors and their meanings are harder to decode. You may wish to use Vassallo's suggestions as starting points, but remember that any bit of nonverbal behavior may mean many different things.

There are a wide variety of adjustments that could be made to each type of audience response. For example, if your audience shows signs of boredom, you might increase your volume, move closer to them, or tell them that what you're going to say will be of value to them. If your audience shows signs of disagreement or hostility, you might stress some similarity you have with them. If your audience looks puzzled or confused, you might pause a moment and rephrase your ideas, provide necessary definitions, or insert an internal summary. If your audience seems impatient, you might say, for example, "my last argument . . ." instead of your originally planned "my third argument . . . ."

Address Audience Responses Directly

Another way of dealing with audience responses is to confront them directly. To those who disagree, you might try the following:

> *I know you disagree with this position, but all I ask is that you hear me out and see if this new way of doing things will not simplify your accounting procedures.*

To those who seem puzzled, you might say:

> *I know this plan may seem confusing, but bear with me; it will become clear in a moment.*

TIPS

from professional speakers

These are some generally accepted messages listeners give a speaker by what they do.

Folding arms across chest—closed mind or hostile response

Moving chair forward, leaning forward toward speaker—open-mindedness, interest in message

Crossing legs—competitive attitude, opposition

Stroking chin—undecided, contemplating

Open hands—willingness to listen

Hands behind head—taking it all in

Fidgeting, looking around—bored

Swinging foot in circle, tapping foot—bored, impatient

Wrinkled brow—puzzled, contemplating

Wringing hands—nervous, anxious

Twiddling thumbs—bored

Shrugging shoulders—indifference

Gritting teeth—anger

Rolling eyes—disgust

Dropping mouth open—disbelief

Covering mouth with hand—surprise, shock

Biting lip—concentration, thinking

Looking off in distance—indifference, daydreaming

Touching nose with index finger quickly—doubt

Glancing sideways, drawing back—suspicion

Steepling hands—confidence

Wanda Vassallo, speaker, writer, and minister. From *Speaking With Confidence: A Guide for Public Speakers.* Copyright © 1990 by Wanda Vassallo. Reprinted by permission of Betterway Publications, Inc.

To those who seem impatient, you might respond:

I know this has been a long day but give me just a few more minutes and you'll be able to save hours reorganizing your files.

By responding to your listeners' reactions and feedback, you acknowledge your audience's needs. You let them know that you hear them, that you're with them, and that you're responding to their very real needs.

My play was a complete success. The audience was a failure.
—Ashleigh Brilliant

UNIT IN BRIEF

Audience	Suggestions
Unwilling audience	1. Secure their attention as early as possible. 2. Reward the audience for their attendance and attention. 3. Relate your topic and supporting materials to the audience's needs and interests.
Unfavorable audience	1. Build on the similarities you have with the audience. 2. Build your speech from areas of agreement up to the major differences. 3. Strive for small gains.
Passive audience	1. Give your audience reasons why they should listen to your speech. 2. Involve the audience as directly as possible in your speech. 3. Use lots of attention-gaining and interest-securing materials. 4. Focus on the few strongest issues.
Unknowledgeable audience	1. Avoid talking down to them (or to any audience). 2. Don't confuse a lack of knowledge with a lack of intelligence.
Knowledgeable audience	1. Let the knowledgeable audience know that you're aware of their expertise. 2. Emphasize your credibility.
Heterogeneous audience	1. Give special attention to analyzing the differences among heterogeneous listeners. 2. Consider appealing to each of the major groups within the audience separately. 3. Don't assume that homogeneous listeners will all have the same attitudes and values.
Adapting during the speech	1. Ask "what if" questions as you prepare your speech. 2. Speak extemporaneously. 3. Do more than you anticipate is necessary. 4. Focus on your audience as message senders, not merely message receivers. 5. Address audience responses directly.

THINKING CRITICALLY ABOUT THE PSYCHOLOGY OF AUDIENCES

REVIEWING KEY TERMS AND CONCEPTS IN PSYCHOLOGICAL ANALYSIS AND ADAPTATION

1. Review and define the key terms used in this unit:

   - ❑ psychological analysis (p. 230)
   - ❑ audience willingness (p. 230)
   - ❑ audience favor (p. 232)
   - ❑ audience activity (p. 233)
   - ❑ audience knowledge (p. 235)
   - ❑ audience homogeneity and heterogeneity (p. 236)

2. Review and explain the key concepts discussed in this unit:

   - ■ How do you adapt to an unwilling audience?
   - ■ How do you adapt to an unfavorable audience?
   - ■ How do you adapt to a passive audience?
   - ■ How do you adapt to knowledgeable and unknowledgeable audiences?
   - ■ How do you adapt to a heterogeneous audience?
   - ■ How do you adapt to the specific audience during the speech?

DEVELOPING STRATEGIES IN AUDIENCE ANALYSIS AND ADAPTATION

1. Jim is scheduled to give a speech on careers in computer technology to a group of high school students who have been forced to attend Career Day on Saturday. The students must attend at least three of the speeches. The audience is definitely an unwilling one. What advice can you give Jim to help him deal with this type of audience?

2. Cara is scheduled to give a speech arguing that the school board president should be dismissed for incompetence. She really has a convincing case; there's no doubt that the president has been incompetent and should be dismissed. Nevertheless, Cara faces two major problems: First, the school board wants to keep things the way they are since the president allows them to do what they want to do, gives them the budget they want, and most importantly, supports their annual reappointment to the board. Second, the president is extremely well liked by the entire community and if the board votes to dismiss, the community isn't going to like it. What advice would you give Cara?

EVALUATING PUBLIC SPEAKING ANALYSIS AND ADAPTATION

1. Using a scale such as that presented in Figure 11.1, how would you rate your class for any one of the speeches in the appendix? If you were giving this speech to your class, what psychological factors would you worry about most? How would you adapt your speech in light of this analysis?

2. Read a speech from the appendix, the Web, or any other source, or listen to one and look for ways in which the speaker adapted to the audience's level of willingness, favor, activity, knowledge, and homogeneity?

USING TECHNOLOGY IN AUDIENCE ANALYSIS AND ADAPTATION

1. Visit a newsgroup (use one of the search engines discussed in Unit 7, Table 7.1) that is concerned with the topic for your next speech and lurk about for a while. After you get a feel for the group, think of this group as a second audience for your next speech. How would your speech differ if you presented it in class and if you posted it to this newsgroup?

2. Access the Psychlit, Sociofile, or ERIC databases and search for the key terms and concepts discussed in this unit: for example, attitude, value, belief, and audience psychology. On the basis of this search, what might you add to this unit's discussion?

PRACTICALLY SPEAKING

11.1 Short Speech Technique

Prepare and deliver a two-minute speech in which you:

a. describe your class in terms of how willing, favorable, active, knowledgeable, or homogeneous you see them to be about any specific topic or speaker.

b. describe the ideal audience for your next speech.

c. describe the worst possible audience for your next speech.

d. describe the audience of a popular magazine or television show or recent hit movie.

e. describe the student body of your college as an audience for your next speech.

11.2 Predicting Listeners' Attitudes

Described here are five public speaking situations. Each student should analyze the audience based on the five dimensions identified in this unit, then complete a set of scales (such as that presented in Figure 11.1) for each of the situations. On the basis of this analysis, what one suggestion would you give the speaker to help her or him better adapt the speech to this audience?

a. Film students listening to Quentin Tarantino talk about how to break into films.

b. High school athletes listening to a college athletic director speaking against sports scholarships.

c. Pregnant women listening to an advertising agency executive speak on how advertisers try to protect the consumer.

d. Office managers listening to an organizational communication consultant speaking on ways to increase employee morale and productivity.

e. Chicago high school seniors listening to a college recruiter speak on the advantages of a small rural college.

The Body of the Speech

This is the first of a three-unit sequence on organizing and outlining your speech. In these units you'll see how to select and word your major propositions, how you can organize them, and how to outline your thoughts into a coherent speech outline. The introduction, conclusion, and transitions are considered in depth in Unit 13. The functions and types of outlining and guidance in preparing the outline are presented in Unit 14.

Don't agonize. Organize.
—Florence R. Kennedy

WHY ORGANIZE?

There are four very good reasons why organization is important and why an effective public speaker has to learn its principles: to aid speech preparation, to make the speech easy to understand, to make the speech easy to remember, and to contribute to your credibility.

Organization Aids Speech Preparation

If you view organization as a living thing, something that is constantly undergoing change, it will provide you with guidelines for preparing your speech. For example, as you organize your speech you'll be able to see if you've adequately and fairly supported each of your main points and if you're devoting approximately equal time to each of your main propositions. If you rehearse with presentation software, the software program will calculate the time you spend on each point, and you'll be able to see at a glance if you're spending about equal time with each or if one point is being given too much time.

Organization Makes Your Speech Easy to Understand

As a student, you know that it's easier for you to understand a lecture if you have an idea of the pattern that the instructor is following. The same is true for those listening to your speeches. An organized presentation will be easier to follow.

Organization Makes Your Speech Easy to Remember

Perhaps the most obvious reason for organizing a speech is that it will be easier for your listeners to remember. Notice that when you organize information for a speech, you're grouping that information into chunks, and chunks make it easier for you to remember varied types of information. For example, you group the nine digits of your social security number and the ten digits of a long distance phone number into chunks that help you remember the information.

So, when you organize perhaps 30 pieces of specific information (for example, statistics, statement of thesis, examples, illustrations, testimonials, transitions) into, say, three or four or five chunks, you're making it much easier for the audience to remember what you want them to remember. After all, you don't really want them to remember each of your examples—you want them to remember your thesis and your major propositions.

Another way organization helps listeners remember is by providing them with a kind of template or pattern. Into this template the audience will be able to fit the individual pieces of your speech. An added bonus here is that organization will also help you remember your speech more easily. You'll be less likely to forget a carefully organized speech than you would a disorganized one.

Organization Contributes to Your Credibility

Still another reason to organize is that a well-organized presentation contributes to the speaker's credibility. The audience sees the well-organized speaker as more competent, more knowledgeable, and more in control of the information in the speech (see Unit 23).

MAJOR PROPOSITIONS

The major propositions are your principal assertions, your main points. If your speech were a play, the propositions would be its acts. Let's look at how you can select and word your propositions.

In discussing the thesis (Unit 6), you saw how you can develop your main points or propositions by asking strategic questions. To see how this works in detail, imagine that you're giving a speech to a group of high school students on the values of a college education. Your thesis is: "A college education is valuable." You then ask, "Why is it valuable?" From this question you generate your major propositions. Your first step might be to brainstorm this question and generate as many answers as possible without evaluating them. You may come up with answers such as the following:

1. It helps you get a good job.
2. It increases your earning potential.
3. It gives you greater job mobility.
4. It helps you secure more creative work.
5. It helps you to appreciate the arts more fully.
6. It helps you to understand an extremely complex world.

7. It helps you understand different cultures.
8. It allows you to avoid taking a regular job for a few years.
9. It helps you meet lots of people and make new friends.
10. It helps you increase your personal effectiveness.

There are, of course, other possibilities, but for purposes of illustration, these 10 possible main points will suffice. Not all 10 are equally valuable or relevant to your audience, however, so you should look over the list to see how to make it shorter and more meaningful. Try these suggestions:

1. Eliminate those points that seem least important to your thesis. On this basis you might want to eliminate Number 8 since this seems least consistent with your intended emphasis on the positive values of college.

2. Combine those points that have a common focus. Notice, for example, that the first four points all center on the values of college in terms of jobs. You might, therefore, consider grouping these four items into one proposition:

A college education helps you get a good job.

This point might be one of the major propositions that could be developed by defining what you mean by a "good job." This main point or proposition and its elaboration might look like this:

I. A college education helps you get a good job.
   A. College graduates earn higher salaries.
   B. College graduates enter more creative jobs.
   C. College graduates have greater job mobility.

Note that A, B, and C are all aspects or subdivisions of a "good job."

3. Select points that are most relevant to or that interest your audience. On this basis you might eliminate Numbers 5 and 7 on the assumption that the audience will not see learning about the arts or different cultures as exciting or valuable at the present time. You might also decide that high school students would be more interested in increasing personal effectiveness, so you might select Number 10 for inclusion as a second major proposition:

A college education increases your personal effectiveness.

Earlier you developed the subordinate points in your first proposition (the A, B, and C of I) by defining more clearly what you meant by a "good job." Follow the same process here by defining what you mean by "personal effectiveness." It might look something like this:

I. A college education helps increase your personal effectiveness.
   A. A college education helps you improve your ability to communicate.
   B. A college education helps you acquire the skills for learning how to think.
   C. A college education helps you acquire coping skills.

Follow the same procedure you used to generate the subordinate points (A, B, and C) to develop the subheadings under A, B, and C. For example, point A might be divided into two major subheads:

> A. A college education helps improve your ability to communicate.
>   1. College improves your writing skills.
>   2. College improves your speech skills.

Develop points B and C in essentially the same way by defining more clearly (in B) what you mean by "learning how to think" and (in C) what you mean by "coping skills. "

4. Use two, three, or four main points. For your class speeches, which will generally range from five to 15 minutes, use two, three, or four main propositions. Too many main points will result in a speech that is confusing, contains too much information and too little amplification, and proves difficult to remember.

5. Word each of your major propositions in the same (parallel) style. Phrase points labeled with Roman numerals in a similar (parallel) style. Likewise, phrase points labeled with capital letters and subordinate to the same Roman numeral (for example, A, B, and C under point I or A, B, and C under point II) in a similar style. Parallel style is used in the example on college education.

This parallel styling helps the audience follow and remember your speech. Notice in the following that the first outline is more difficult to understand than the second, which is phrased in parallel style.

Not This:
Mass Media Functions
  I. The media entertain.
  II. The media function to inform their audiences.
  III. Creating ties of union is a major media function.
  IV. The conferral of status is a function of all media.

This:
Mass Media Functions
  I. The media entertain.
  II. The media inform.
  III. The media create ties of union.
  IV. The media confer status.

6. Develop your main points so they're separate and discrete. Don't allow your main points to overlap each other. Each section labeled with a Roman numeral should be a separate entity.

Not This:
  I. Color and style are important in clothing selection.

This:
  I. Color is important in clothing selection.
  II. Style is important in clothing selection.

For every human problem, there is a neat, plain solution—and it is always wrong.
—H. L. Mencken

THE ETHICS OF Accountability

Ethical public speaking requires accountability. As a speaker you have to take responsibility for what you say, and, of course, listeners will hold you accountable for what you say. Communication researcher Jon Hess (1993) suggests that, because you'll be held accountable, you should do the following:

- If you're not sure if certain information is correct, tell your audience. They have a right to know.
- Make clear when you're using facts and when you're using your own opinions.

- Avoid misleading the audience in any way. Fooling the audience or encouraging them to believe what isn't true is unethical.

What impressions do you get from speakers who fail to distinguish facts from opinions? Can you identify specific examples where speakers seem to deliberately cloud the distinction between facts and opinions?

[The next Ethics of Public Speaking box appears on page 276.]

ORGANIZATIONAL PATTERNS

Once you've identified the major propositions you wish to include in your speech, you need to devote attention to how you'll arrange these propositions in the body of your speech. When you follow a clearly identified organizational pattern, your listeners will be able to see your speech as a whole and will be able to see more clearly the connections and relationships among your various pieces of information. Should the audience have a momentary lapse in attention—as they surely will at some point in just about every speech—they'll be able to refocus their attention if your speech is clearly organized.

Temporal Pattern

Organizing your propositions on the basis of some temporal (time) relationship is a popular and easy-to-use organizational pattern. It's also a pattern that listeners find easy to follow. Generally, when you use this pattern, you organize your speech into two, three, or four major parts, beginning with the past and working up to the present or the future, or beginning with the present or the future and working back to the past.

The temporal (sometimes called "chronological") pattern is especially appropriate for informative speeches in which you wish to describe events or processes that occur over time. It's also useful when you wish to tell a story, demonstrate how something works, or how to do something. A speech on the development of language in the child might be organized in a temporal pattern and could be divided something like this:

The Development of Language
I. Babbling occurs around the fifth month.
II. Lallation occurs around the sixth month.
III. Echolalia occurs around the ninth month.
IV. "Communication" occurs around the twelfth month.

TIPS from professional speakers

Effective speakers recognize the importance of organization. You've got an important goal—a message you want your listeners to understand, believe, or act on. You have good main points and you've selected great supports to develop your ideas. Now organize your message clearly, and it's far more likely that your listeners will understand your message, accept your message, remember your message, and be interested in your message. Are you apt to be interested in something you don't understand? How hard will you work to make sense out of a speech that is hard to follow? If you don't see the speaker's point, you will probably soon take a mental exit. Your listeners are no different.

Caryl Rae Krannich, communication and career expert, frequent speaker and trainer, *101 Secrets of Highly Effective Speakers: Controlling Fear, Commanding Attention* (Manassas Park, VA: Impact Publications, 1998): 47–48.

Here you would cover each of the events in a time sequence beginning with the earliest stage and working up to the final stage—in this case the stage of true communication. Most historical topics lend themselves to organization by time. The events leading up to the Civil War, the steps toward a college education, or the history of writing would all be appropriate for temporal patterning. A time pattern would also be appropriate in describing the essential steps in a multistep process in which temporal order is especially important. The steps involved in making interpersonal contact with another person might look something like this:

> Making Interpersonal Contact
>   I. Spot the person with whom you want to make contact.
> II. Make eye contact.
> III. Give some positive nonverbal sign.
> IV. Make verbal contact.

Spatial Pattern

You can also organize your main points on the basis of space. This pattern is especially useful when you wish to describe objects or places. Like the temporal pattern, it's an organizational pattern that listeners will find easy to follow as you progress, from top to bottom, left to right, inside to outside, or from east to west, for example. The structure of a place, object, or even animal is easily placed into a spatial pattern. You might describe the layout of a hospital, school, skyscraper, or perhaps even the structure of a dinosaur with a spatial pattern of organization. Here's an example of an outline describing the structure of the traditional townhouse and using a spatial pattern:

> The Townhouse
>   I. The first floor is the kitchen.
> II. The second floor is the living and dining rooms.
> III. The third floor is the master bedroom suite.
> IV. The fourth floor is the children's rooms.
>   V. The fifth floor is the maid's rooms.

Topical Pattern

Perhaps the most popular pattern for organizing informative speeches is the topical pattern. When your topic conveniently divides itself into subdivisions, each of which is clear and approximately equal in importance, this pattern is most useful. A speech on important cities of the world might be organized into a topical pattern, as might speeches on problems facing the college graduate, great works of literature, or the world's major religions. Each of these topics would have several subtopics or divisions of approximately equal importance; consequently, a topical pattern seems most appropriate. For example, the topical pattern is an obvious choice for organizing a speech on the powers of the government. The topic itself divides into three parts: legislative, executive, and judicial. A sample outline might look like this:

The Powers of Government
  I. The legislative branch is controlled by Congress.
 II. The executive branch is controlled by the president.
III. The judicial branch is controlled by the courts.

Problem-Solution Pattern

The problem–solution pattern is especially useful in persuasive speeches where you want to convince the audience that a problem exists and that your solution would solve or lessen the problem.

Let's say that you believe that jury awards for damages have gotten out of hand. You might want to persuade your audience, then, that jury awards for damages should be limited. A problem–solution pattern might be appropriate here. In this first part of your speech you identify the problem(s) created by these large awards and in the second part, the solution. A sample outline for such a speech might look something like this:

  I. Jury awards for damages are out of control. [the general problem]
     A. These awards increase insurance rates. [a specific problem]
     B. These awards increase medical costs. [a second specific problem]
     C. These awards place unfair burdens on business. [a third specific problem]

 II. Jury awards need to be limited. [the general solution]
     A. Greater evidence should be required before a case can be brought to trial. [a specific solution]
     B. Part of the award should be turned over to the state. [a second specific solution]
     C. Realistic estimates of financial damage must be used. [a third specific solution]

Cause-Effect/Effect-Cause Pattern

Similar to the problem–solution pattern is the cause–effect or effect–cause pattern. This pattern is useful in persuasive speeches in which you want to convince your audience of the causal connection existing between two events or elements. In the cause–effect pattern you divide the speech into two major sections, causes and effects. For example, a speech on the reasons for highway accidents or birth defects might lend itself to a cause–effect pattern. Here you might first consider, say, the causes of highway accidents or birth defects and then some of the effects, for example, the number of deaths, the number of accidents, and so on.

Let's say you wanted to demonstrate the causes for the increase in AIDS in your state. You might use an effect–cause pattern which might look something like this:

  I. AIDS is increasing. [general effect]
     A. AIDS is increasing among teenagers. [a specific effect]
     B. AIDS is increasing among IV drug users. [a second specific effect]
     C. AIDS is increasing among women. [a third specific effect]

What organizational pattern do most of the speeches you hear follow? What patterns do most of the college lectures you hear follow? What advice would you give your instructors on organizing college lectures?

II. Three factors contribute to this increase. [general causal statement]
  A. Teenagers are ignorant about how the HIV virus is transmitted. [a specific cause]
  B. IV drug users share tainted needles. [a second specific cause]
  C. Men and women are not practicing safe sex. [a third specific cause]

As you can see from this example, this type of speech is often combined with the problem-solution type. For example, after identifying the causes, the speaker might then treat the causes as problems and offer solutions for each problem/cause (for example: education programs for teens, free needle exchange, and education programs for men and women).

The Motivated Sequence

Developed by Alan H. Monroe in the 1930s and widely used in all sorts of oral and written communications, the motivated sequence is a pattern of arranging your information so as to motivate your audience to respond positively to your purpose (Gronbeck, McKerrow, Ehninger, and Monroe 1997). In fact, it may be reasonably argued that all effective communications follow this basic pattern whether it's called the motivated sequence or given some other name.

As you'll see, the motivated sequence is especially appropriate for speeches designed to move an audience to action (to persuade your listeners to do something). However, it's also useful for a wide variety of informative speeches.

The previous organizational patterns provided ways of organizing the main ideas in the body of the speech. The motivated sequence is a pattern for organizing the entire speech. Here the speech (introduction, body, and conclusion) is divided into five parts or steps: (1) attention, (2) need, (3) satisfaction, (4) visualization, and (5) action.

Step 1. Gain Attention
The attention step makes the audience give you their undivided attention. If you execute this step effectively, your audience should be anxious and ready to hear what you have to say. You can gain audience attention through a variety of means (more fully identified in Unit 13):

1. Ask a question (rhetorical or actual).
2. Make reference to audience members.
3. Make reference to recent happenings.
4. Use humor.
5. Use an illustration or dramatic story.
6. Stress the importance of the topic to this specific audience.
7. Use presentation aids, tell the audience to pay attention, use a quotation, refer to yourself, refer directly to your thesis or purpose, make reference to a little known fact or statistic.

Step 2. Establish Need

In the second part of your speech, you demonstrate that a need exists. The audience should feel that something has to be learned or something has to be done because of this demonstrated need. You can establish need in four parts:

1. State the need or problem as it exists or will exist.
2. Illustrate the need with specific examples.
3. Further support the existence of the need with additional illustrations, statistics, testimony, and other forms of support (identified in Units 8, 9, 21–23).
4. Show how this need affects your specific listeners, for example, how it affects their financial status, their career goals, or their individual happiness.

Step 3. Satisfy the Need

Present the "answer" or the "solution" to satisfying the need that you demonstrated in Step 2. On the basis of this satisfaction step, the audience should now believe that what you're informing them about or persuading them to do will effectively satisfy the need. In this step you answer the question: How will the need be satisfied by what I am asking the audience to learn, to believe, to do? This satisfaction step usually involves:

1. A statement (with examples and illustrations if necessary) of what you want the audience to learn, believe, or do.
2. A statement of how or why what you're asking them to learn, believe, or do will lead to satisfying the need identified in Step 2.

Step 4. Visualize the Need Satisfied

Visualization intensifies the audience's feelings or beliefs. In this step you take the audience beyond the present time and place and enable them to imagine the situation as it would be if the need were satisfied as you suggested in Step 3. There are two basic ways of doing this:

1. Demonstrate the benefits that the audience will receive if your ideas are put into operation.
2. Demonstrate the negative effects that the audience will suffer if your plan isn't put into operation.

Of course, you could combine these two methods and demonstrate both the benefits of your plan and the negative consequences of the existing plan or of some alternative plan.

TIPS
from professional speakers

Explain very carefully *how* they [the audience] can apply the information you have presented. For instance, if you have been convincing them they *should* give blood, tell them *where*. And make it sound easy to get there! The enthusiasm of the audience frequently fades quickly, and your stimulus is most important.

Frank Snell, advertising executive and teacher, *How to Stand Up and Speak Well in Business.* (New York: Simon and Schuster [Cornerstone], 1974): 135.

Step 5. Ask for Action

Tell the audience what they should do to ensure that the need (as demonstrated in Step 2) is satisfied (as stated in Step 3). That is, what should the audience do to satisfy the need? Here you want to move the audience in a particular direction, for example, to speak in favor of additional research funding for AIDS or against cigarette advertising, to attend the next student government meeting, to contribute free time to read for the blind. You can accomplish this step by stating exactly what the audience members should do, using an emotional appeal, or giving the audience guidelines for future action. These and other methods of concluding and motivating an audience are covered in depth in Units 13 and 22.

Here's a much abbreviated example of how these five steps would look in a speech designed to inform an audience about the workings of home computers.

[Attention]

> *By the time we graduate, there will be more home computers than automobiles. (You might then go on to explain the phenomenal growth of computers in education until you have the complete attention of your audience revolving around the importance and growth of computers.)*

[Need]

> *Much as it's now impossible to get around without a car, it will be impossible to get around the enormous amount of information without a home computer. (You might then go on to explain how knowledge is expanding so rapidly that it will be extremely difficult to keep up with any field without computer technology.)*

[Satisfaction]

> *Learning a few basic principles of home computers will enable us to process our work more efficiently, in less time, and more enjoyably. (You might then explain the various steps that your listeners could take to satisfy the needs you already identified.)*

[Visualization]

> *With these basic principles firmly in mind (and a home computer), you'll be able to stay at home and do your library research for your next speech just by punching in the correct codes. (You might then go through in more or less detail the speech research process so that your listeners will be able to visualize exactly what the advantages of computer research will be.)*

[Action]

> *These few principles should be supplemented by further study. Probably the best way to further your study is to enroll in a computer course. Another useful way is to read the brief paperback,* The Home Computer for the College Student. *(You might then identify the*

several computer courses that are available and that would be appropriate for a beginning student. Further, you might identify a few other books or perhaps distribute a brief list of books that would be appropriate reading for the beginning student.)

Notice that in an informative speech you could have stopped after the satisfaction step because you would have accomplished your goal of informing the audience about some principles of home computers. But, in some cases, you may feel it helpful to complete the steps to emphasize your point in detail.

In a persuasive speech, on the other hand, you must go at least as far as visualization (if your purpose is limited to strengthening or changing attitudes or beliefs) or to the action step (if you're attempting to motivate behavior).

Because your organizational pattern serves primarily to help your listeners follow your speech, you might want to tell your listeners (in your introduction or as a transition between the introduction and the body of your speech) what pattern you'll be following. Here are a few examples:

- In explaining the layout of the townhouse, we'll start at the bottom and work our way to the top.
- I'll first explain the problems with jury awards and then propose three workable solutions.
- First, we'll look at the increase in AIDS and then we'll look at three of the causes.

Additional Organizational Patterns

The six patterns just considered are the most common and useful for organizing most public speeches. There are other patterns, however, that might be appropriate for different topics.

Structure–Function. The structure–function pattern is useful in informative speeches in which you want to discuss how something is constructed (its structural aspects) and what it does (its functional aspects). This pattern might be useful, for example, in a speech to explain what an organization is and what it does, the parts of a university and how they operate, or the sensory systems of the body and their various functions. This pattern might also be useful in discussing the nature of a living organism: its anatomy (that is, its structures) and its physiology (that is, its functions). Here's an example of an outline using a structure–function pattern:

I. The brain consists of two main parts [explanation of structure]
   A. The cerebrum consists of . . .
   B. The cerebellum consists of . . .

II. The brain enables us to do a variety of things [explanation of functions]
   A. The cerebrum enables us to move, think, and feel.
   B. The cerebellum enables us to coordinate actions and maintain balance.

Comparison and Contrast. Arranging your material in a comparison–and–contrast pattern is useful in informative speeches in which you want to analyze two different theories, proposals, departments, or products in terms of their similarities and differences. In this type of speech you would not only be concerned with explaining each theory or proposal, but you also would focus primarily on how they're similar and how they're different. Here's an example of a simplified outline comparing (in general) liberal and conservative political philosophies (Lineberry, Edwards, and Wattenberg, 1994):

I. Government regulation
   A. The liberal attitude toward government regulation is . . .
   B. The conservative attitude toward government regulation is. . .

II. Redistribution of income
   A. Liberals view the redistribution of income . . .
   B. Conservatives view the redistribution of income . . .

III. Disadvantaged groups
   A. Liberals feel that disadvantaged groups . . .
   B. Conservatives feel that disadvantaged groups . . .

Pro and Con, Advantages and Disadvantages. The pro–and–con pattern, sometimes called the advantages–disadvantages pattern, is useful in informative speeches in which you want to explain objectively the advantages (the pros) and the disadvantages (the cons) of each plan, method, or product.

Both the comparison–and–contrast and the pro–and–con patterns might be developed by focusing on the several qualities or aspects of each plan or product. For example, if you were comparing two health plans, your major propositions might center on such topics as costs to the worker, hospital benefits, and sick leave. Under each of these major propositions, you'd show what Health Plan A provides and then what Health Plan B provides.

Your outline might look something like this:

I. Costs to the worker
   A. Health Plan A would cost each worker . . .
   B. Health Plan B would cost each worker . . .

II. Hospital benefits
   A. Health Plan A provides . . .
   B. Health Plan B provides . . .

III. Sick leave
   A. Health Plan A provides . . .
   B. Health Plan B provides . . .

Both the comparison–and–contract and the pro–and–con patterns are also useful in persuasive speeches where you wish to highlight the weaknesses in one plan or product and the strengths of another, much like advertisers do when they compare their product with Brand X.

Claim and Proof. The claim–and–proof pattern is especially useful in a persuasive speech in which you want to prove the truth or usefulness of a particular proposition. It's the pattern that you see frequently in trials where the claim made by the prosecution is that the defendant is guilty and the proof is the varied evidence: the defendant had a motive; the defendant had the opportunity; the defendant had no alibi. In this pattern your speech would consist of two major parts. In the first part you explain your claim (tuition must not be raised, library hours must be expanded, courses in AIDS education must be instituted). In the second part you offer your evidence or proof as to why tuition must not be raised, for example. Your outline might look like this:

I. A program of free needle exchange must be instituted [this is your claim, the proposition you want your audience to accept]
   A. A free needle exchange program would consist of . . .
   B. A free needle exchange program would be established by . . .

II. Needle exchange must be established for two main reasons.
   A. It will save lives [under this heading you would offer your proof that this program does in fact save lives].
   B. It will save money [under this heading you would offer proof that this program would save money].

Multiple Definition. The multiple definition pattern is useful for informative speeches in which you want to explain the nature of a concept (What is a born-again Christian? What is a scholar? What is multiculturalism?). In this pattern each major heading would consist of a different type of definition (see Unit 19, p. 362) or way of looking at the concept. For example, if you were going to define "creative thinking," you might develop an outline that looked something like this:

I. According to Webster's . . . [a dictionary definition]
II. Edward deBono says that . . . [a creative thinking theorist's definition, definition by authority]
III. A good example of creative thinking [definition by example]
IV. Creative thinking is not . . . [definition by negation]

Who? What? Why? Where? When? This 5W pattern is the pattern of the journalist. It is useful in informative speeches when you wish to report or explain an event, for example, a robbery, political coup, war, or trial. Here the major parts of your speech would each deal with the answers to several or all of these five questions. A speech on, say, the United States Constitution might be organized something like this:

I. The Constitution is a document that sets forth . . . [answers the question What?]
II. The Constitution was necessitated by . . . [answers the question Why?]
III. The Constitution was written . . . [answers the questions When? and Where?]
IV. The Constitution was written by . . . [answers the question Who?]

TIPS

from professional speakers

One way to think about this three-step approach [introduction, body, and conclusion] is to imagine a "speech sandwich." . . . To make your speech sandwich appetizing, you need to add some spices or condiments. Otherwise it will taste bland. So in the meat of your speech, add:

- a few flavorful facts,
- some scintillating statistics,
- appetizing anecdotes,
- mouth-watering metaphors, and
- a pinch of humor.

Delicious! Anybody would want to take a bite.

Diane DiResta, international communications coach and speaker, *Knockout Presentations: How to Deliver Your Message with Power, Punch, and Pizzazz* (Worcester, MA: Chandler House Press): 143–144.

ADDING AND ARRANGING SUPPORTING MATERIALS

Once you've identified your main propositions, you need to support them with the materials you've been collecting—the examples, illustrations, statistics, testimonies, definitions, and presentation aids that were discussed in Units 8 and 9.

One-level and Two-level Patterns

Generally, you'll find it useful to arrange your support in a one- or a two-level pattern. Let's use a speech on exercise and its importance for health, and arrange hypothetical supporting materials into each pattern. Notice that in the one-level pattern, the supporting materials relate directly to the proposition. There is no order within the major proposition; each of the supports (A–D) is separate and equal.

One-level Pattern

I. Physical exercise is essential to mental health.
   A. Example.
   B. E-mail survey data.
   C. Testimony from researcher.
   D. Statistics from research study.

II. Physical exercise is essential to physical health.
   A. Research Study 1.
   B. Research Study 2.
   C. Statistics from the United States.
   D. Statistics from Africa.
   E. Statistics from South America.

In the two-level pattern, the supporting materials relate to the proposition indirectly through a secondary proposition. Notice that the supporting materials are arranged into categories that are expressed in the A and B heads.

Two-level Pattern

I. Physical exercise is essential to mental health.
   A. Scientific research supports this.
      1. Statistics from research study.
      2. Testimony from researcher.
   B. My own observations support this.
      1. Example.
      2. E-mail survey of this class.

II. Physical exercise is essential to physical health.
   A. Controlled experiments support this.
      1. Study 1
      2. Study 2
   B. Longevity statistics support this.
      1. Statistics from the United States.
      2. Statistics from Africa.
      3. Statistics from South America.

Both patterns are useful; the one you select should depend on your purpose. For example, if your purpose is to have your audience remember your major propositions, then either pattern would work. You might argue, of course, that the one-level pattern has somewhat of an advantage in that it doesn't add additional information and that each of the supporting materials relates directly to and reinforces the proposition. If, however, your purpose is to have the audience know that both controlled experiments and longevity statistics support the role of exercise in physical health, then the two-level pattern would work best. One argument in favor of the two-level pattern is that it groups your supports together into memorable chunks. For instance, the audience is unlikely to remember the specific statistics from each of the areas, but they are likely to remember that longevity statistics support the importance of exercise since you've already given them the category to aid their memory.

Cultural Considerations in Organization

Cultural considerations are important in organization as they are in all other aspects of public speaking. One factor that's especially important is whether the culture is a high context or a low context one (Hall and Hall 1987). **High-context cultures** (Japanese, Arabic, Latin American, Thai, Korean, Apache, and Mexican are examples) are those in which much of the information in communication is in the context or in the person rather than in the actual spoken message. Both speaker and listener already know the information from, say, previous interactions, assumptions each makes about the other, or through shared experiences. **Low-context cultures** (German, Swedish, Norwegian, and American are examples) are those in which most information is explicitly stated in the verbal message. In formal communications, the information would be in written form as well, as it is with contracts, prenuptial agreements, or apartment leases.

To appreciate the distinction between high and low context, consider giving directions. If someone knows the neighborhood (a high-context situation), you can assume the person knows the local landmarks. So, you can give directions such as "next to the laundromat on Main Street" or "the corner of Albany and Elm." With a newcomer (a low-context situation), you can't assume that you have a common body of shared information and so you have to use only those directions that even a stranger would understand, for example, "make a left at the next stop sign" or "go two blocks and then turn right."

Extending this distinction to speech organization, we note that high-context cultures would probably prefer an organization in which the supporting materials are offered and the audience is allowed to infer the general principle or proposition themselves. Low-context culture members, on the other hand, would prefer an organization in which the proposition is clearly and directly stated and the supporting materials are clearly linked to the proposition.

Persons from the United States speaking in Japan, to take one well-researched example, need to be careful lest they make their point too obvious or too direct and insult their audience. Speakers in Japan are expected to lead their listeners to the conclusion through example, illustration, and various other indirect means (Lustig and Koester 1999). Persons from Japan speaking in the United States need to be careful lest their indirectness be perceived as unnecessarily vague, underhanded, or an attempt to withhold information.

Balance

In supporting your propositions, use the principle of balance. Devote about equal time to each of your main points. A useful rule of thumb is to give about equal time to each item having the same symbol in your outline. Give each Roman numeral about equal time, each item denoted by a capital letter about the same amount of time, and so on. Break this rule only when you have an especially good reason.

Notice also the type of supporting materials you're using. Be careful of using only examples or only statistics. Generally, a mix of varied supporting materials works best. Variety holds the audience's attention and also provides a rhythm to your speech that all the same types of supports can't create.

Climax and Anticlimax

Climax and anticlimax orders refer to the use of inductive (beginning with specifics and working up to a generalization) or deductive approaches (beginning with a generalization and from it deriving a series of specifics). In climax order you first present your evidence (your specifics) and then climax it with your conclusion or thesis. For example, you might say to a college class:

> *The athletic program will have to be cut because of inadequate funds; the student union, which operates at a loss each year will have to be closed; and class size will have to be increased 40 percent because a number of faculty will have to be fired since there is no money to pay them.*

You'd then climax these bits of information with the main issue: tuition must be raised.

In anticlimax order you'd start out with the thesis that tuition must be raised (your general statement or conclusion) and then give your reasons (the specifics). Whether you choose the climax or the anticlimax order depends a great deal on the attitudes and points of view of your audience. Here are some suggestions:

- Lead with the information the audience will object to least.
- If you anticipate great objection to your thesis, present your arguments and somehow soften the blow that is soon to come.
- If you anticipate little or no objection to your thesis or if your audience already supports it, lead with it and present the reasons or support for it later.

Primacy and Recency

The rule of primacy states that what you hear first will be remembered best and will have the greatest effect. The rule of recency states that what

What strategies of arrangement would you use if you were giving a pro-choice speech to an anti-abortion audience? What strategies would you use if you were giving a speech in favor of domestic partnership insurance to the leadership of a variety of gay rights organizations?

you hear last or most recently will be remembered best and will have the greatest effect.

Research findings on this controversy offer a few useful conclusions.

- What is in the middle is remembered least and has the least general effect. Thus, if you have a speech with three points, put the weakest one in the middle.
- If your listeners are relatively neutral and have no real conviction either way, lead with your best argument and in this way get the listeners on your side early.
- Lead with your best argument with an audience that is favorable to your point of view.
- If you're faced with a hostile audience or with an audience that holds very different views than you, put your most powerful argument last and work up to it gradually, assuming that you can count on the listeners staying with you until the end.

Research on memory tells us that the audience will remember very little of what you say in a speech. Interesting as your speech may be, listeners will forget most of what you say Therefore, repeat your main assertions—whether you put them first or last in your speech—in your conclusion.

The Known and the Unknown

Generally, it's wise to organize information from the known to the unknown, the familiar to the unfamiliar, the accepted to the unaccepted. So, if you know that your audience is favorable toward one of your arguments but unfavorable toward another, it's probably best to begin with the argument they're favorable toward. In this way you create a positive atmosphere and get them on your side. Once you've achieved a favorable hearing, then you can raise the argument on which you hope to change their opinion.

In a similar way, you want to consider if the audience is familiar with, say, a part of your speech and if so, should this influence how you order your points. For example, let's say that you want to give a speech on the effects of exercise. You assume that your audience is familiar with the effects of exercise on physical health but not with the effects of exercise on mental health. So, you have a choice. Do you begin with the familiar on the theory that this will help you create common ground? But, do you also risk boring the audience with what they already believe? Or, do you begin with what they don't know, on the theory that you'll demonstrate that what you have to say isn't common knowledge and that your speech will provide something new and different? But, do you also risk their rejection of this one point and, consequently, of your entire thesis? The answer is that it depends on your topic, you, and your audience. Each situation is different and each situation calls for a unique analysis.

The Independent and the Interdependent

Some propositions are relatively independent of each other. For example, in an informative speech on stocks and bonds, the information that you give on bonds is really not dependent on the information you give on stocks; the two concepts are relatively independent of each other. But, consider, for example, a speech given to account executives in a United States brokerage firm on investing in Canadian stocks and bonds. Let's say that your two propositions are that "Wealth can be made by investing in Canada" and that "Canada is economically stable." In this case, it's obvious that you first have to show that Canada is economically stable and then show that wealth can be made by investing in Canada. If you did it the other way around, your audience would likely wonder if the underlying fundamentals of a stable economy can be presumed. In the speech on culture shock used as an example in Unit 14 (pp. 292-295), you can see that the four stages are interdependent—each stage is dependent upon its prior stage—and so these four stages have to be presented in the order in which they occur.

Ask yourself if the audience has to know one part of your speech to understand another part. If the answer is yes, then look for what information depends on other information and place it in an order that will make sense to a listener.

UNIT IN BRIEF

Why Organize

The advantages of an organized speech are:
- It aids speech preparation.
- It's easier for listeners to follow.
- It's easier to listeners to remember.
- It contributes to the speaker's credibility.

Major Propositions

1. Select those that are most important to your thesis.
2. Combine those that have a common focus.
3. Select those that are most relevant to your audience.
4. Few in number (two, three, or four) work best.
5. Phrased them in parallel style.
6. Have separate and discrete items.

Organizational Patterns	Temporal: main ideas are arranged in a time sequence. Spatial: main ideas are arranged in a space pattern, for example, left to right. Topical: main ideas (equal in value and importance) are itemized. Problem–solution: main ideas are divided into problems and solutions. Cause–effect: main ideas are arranged into causes and effects. Motivated sequence: attention, need, satisfaction, visualization, and action steps. Additional patterns include structure-function, comparison and contrast, pro and con (advantages and disadvantages), claim and proof, multiple definition, and who-what-why-where-when.
Adding and Arranging Supporting Materials	Consider: ■ one-level and two-level patterns ■ cultural differences ■ balance ■ climax and anticlimax ■ primacy and recency ■ the known and the unknown ■ the independent and the interdependent

THINKING CRITICALLY ABOUT ORGANIZATION

REVIEWING KEY TERMS AND CONCEPTS IN ORGANIZATION

1. Review and define the key terms used in this unit:

- ❏ temporal pattern (p. 249)
- ❏ spatial pattern (p. 250)
- ❏ topical pattern (p. 250)
- ❏ problem–solution pattern (p. 251)
- ❏ cause–effect pattern (p. 251)
- ❏ motivated sequence (p. 252)
- ❏ structure–function (p. 255)
- ❏ comparison and contrast (p. 256)
- ❏ pro– and con– pattern (p. 256)
- ❏ claim and proof pattern (p. 257)
- ❏ multiple definition (p. 257)
- ❏ 5W pattern (p. 257)
- ❏ high- and low-context cultures (p. 259)
- ❏ climax and anticlimax order (p. 260)
- ❏ primacy and recency (p. 260)

2. Review and explain the key concepts discussed in this unit:

- ■ Why should a speech be organized?
- ■ What cultural considerations need to be taken into account in organizing a speech?
- ■ How might you select and word your major propositions?
- ■ What are the major organizational patterns you might use to order your propositions?
- ■ What are the major guidelines for adding and arranging supporting materials?

DEVELOPING PUBLIC SPEAKING STRATEGIES IN ORGANIZATION

1. Nancy is a health professional who has been asked to give several speeches on "the ideal exercise plan." Among the audiences she will address are a group of high school students and a group of people in their 70s. Nancy has collected lots of material and now wants to organize it into a pattern that will be easy to understand and remember. What suggestions would

you offer Nancy for organizing the speeches for each of these two audiences?

2. You're giving a speech on "healthy living" and your three major propositions will concern diet, exercise, and positive mental attitude. How would you use your insights on primacy and recency and climax and anti-climax order if you were giving the speech to a group of college athletes? If you were giving the speech to a group of elementary school children?

EVALUATING PUBLIC SPEECH ORGANIZATION

1. Read a speech in this text, on the Web, or from some other source, or listen to one and identify the organizational structure the speaker followed. Was this an effective and logical pattern to use? What other patterns might have been appropriate?

2. Listen to a television advertisement—you may have to tape it because you'll want to review it a few times—and analyze it in terms of the motivated sequence. Can you identify each of the five steps?

USING TECHNOLOGY IN ORGANIZING PUBLIC SPEECHES

1. Explore the outlining capabilities of your word processor. You might have to go back to your manual for this since this isn't a feature that many people use, despite its usefulness. How might such features help you develop your speech outline?

2. Visit any search engine and put into outline form all the information on its home page (see Table 7.1 for suggestions). Construct the outline as if it were the body of a speech in which you were going to explain the information on a search engine's home page.

PRACTICALLY SPEAKING

12.1 Short Speech Technique

Prepare and deliver a one-to-two minute speech in which you:

a. describe the differences between high- and low-context cultures as they apply to your public speaking class.

b. describe something in or some part of this room using a spatial pattern.

c. select an ad and analyze it in terms of the motivated sequence.

d. describe the events portrayed in a recently seen television program using a temporal pattern.

e. discuss a recent newspaper editorial or op-ed letter in terms of a problem–solution or cause–effect pattern.

12.2 Generating Major Propositions

One of the skills in organizing a speech is to ask a question of your thesis and from the answer generate your major propositions. Here we present 20 thesis statements suitable for a variety of informative or persuasive speeches. For each thesis statement, ask a question and generate two, three, or four major propositions that would be suitable for an informative or persuasive speech. Here's an example to get you started:

THESIS STATEMENT: Mandatory retirement should (shouldn't) be abolished.

QUESTION: Why should mandatory retirement be abolished?

I. Mandatory retirement leads us to lose many of the most productive workers.
II. Mandatory retirement contributes to psychological problems of those forced to retire.
III. Mandatory retirement costs corporations economic hardship because they have to train new people.

1. Buy (Don't buy) American.
2. Tax (Don't tax) property assets owned by religious organizations.
3. Require (Don't require) adoption agencies to reveal the names of birth parents to all children when they reach 18 years of age.
4. Permit (Don't permit) condom advertisements in all media.
5. Require (Don't require) sex education courses in elementary school.

6. Permit (Don't permit) gays and lesbians to adopt children.

7. Ban (Don't ban) all sales of wild-animal fur.

8. Make (Don't make) the death penalty mandatory for those convicted of selling drugs to minors.

9. Reinstate (Don't reinstate) the draft.

10. Eliminate (Expand) affirmative action programs.

11. Give (Don't give) political asylum to women who have been abused.

12. Elected political officials should (not) be allowed to serve as lobbyists at any time after their term of office has expired.

13. Courses on women's issues should (not) be required for all students at this college.

14. Expand (Reduce, Eliminate) ROTC Programs.

15. Abolish (Expand, Reduce) intercollegiate athletic competition.

16. Legalize (Don't legalize) soft drugs.

17. Build (Don't build) houses for the homeless.

18. Become (Don't become) computer literate.

19. Support (Don't support) mandatory instruction in AIDS prevention in all elementary and high schools.

20. Grant (Don't grant) full equality to gay men and lesbians in the military.

UNIT 13

Introductions, Conclusions, and Transitions

UNIT CONTENTS	UNIT OBJECTIVES
Introductions	*After completing this unit, you should be able to:* Explain the methods for gaining audience attention; establishing a connection among speaker, audience, and topic; and orienting the audience.
Conclusions	Explain the methods for summarizing, motivating your audience, and closing the speech.
Transitions and Internal Summaries	Explain the types and functions of transitions and internal summaries.

Now that you have the body of your speech organized, devote your attention to the introduction, conclusion, and transitions that will tie the parts of your speech together.

INTRODUCTIONS

Together with your general appearance and your nonverbal messages, the introduction gives your audience its first impression of you and your speech. As you know, first impressions are very resistant to change, so your introduction is an especially important part of the speech. Your introduction sets the tone for the rest of the speech, telling your listeners what kind of a speech they'll hear.

Although you obviously will deliver the introduction to your speech first, you should construct it only after you've constructed the entire speech (body and conclusion). Begin collecting suitable material for your introduction as you prepare the entire speech, but wait until all the other parts are completed before you put the pieces together. In this way you'll be better able to determine which elements should be included and which should be eliminated.

Your introduction should serve three functions: gain attention, establish a speaker-audience-topic connection, and orient the audience as to what is to follow. Let's look at how you can accomplish each of these functions.

Gain Attention

Your introduction should gain the attention of your audience and focus it on your speech topic. You of course need to maintain that attention throughout your speech. Here are a few ways you can secure attention.

Ask a Question.   Questions are effective because they're a change from the more common declarative statements, and listeners automatically pay attention to change. Rhetorical questions, questions to which you don't expect an answer, are especially helpful in focusing the audience's

TIPS
from professional speakers

By carefully crafting your opening and closing statements, you will start your speech in such a way that will instantly capture your audience's attention and end it with a bang that will leave them applauding. Then the only thing left for you to do will be to smile, bow, and look forward to your next speaking engagement!

Don Gabor, communication trainer and author, *Talking with Confidence for the Painfully Shy* (New York: Crown Trade Paperbacks, 1997): 115.

attention on your subject: "Do you want to live a happy life?" "Do you want to succeed in college?" "Do you want to meet the love of your life?" Also useful are polling-type questions, questions that ask the audience for a show of hands: "How many of you have suffered through a boring lecture?" "How many of you intend to continue school after graduating from college?" "How many of you have suffered from loneliness?" As these questions illustrate, some questions are more likely to be responded to openly than others. The question about loneliness, for example, may yield no raised hands because people might be embarrassed to reveal this openly and not because they haven't experienced it.

Here, for example, the speaker uses a very simple question to introduce his topic of the Internet's future (Conrades 1998, p. 378):

> *I'd like to start by asking you . . . suppose they held an Internet conference and nobody came? At first glance, that seems improbable. After all, the number of Internet-related seminars, trade shows, road shows, and expos is growing almost as fast as the network itself. It may not be long though, before the Net is such an indispensable part of our organizations, our business processes, and our lifestyles . . . it essentially disappears.*

Refer to Audience Members. Reference to the audience makes them perk up and pay attention because you're involving them directly in your talk. Harvey C. Jacobs (1985) gains attention by referring to members of the audience (and complimenting them) in his introduction:

> *Winston Churchill once gave this advice to public speakers: "One, never walk up a wall that's leaning against you; two, never try to kiss a person who's leaning away from you; and, three, never speak to a group that knows more about the subject than you do." You work much closer to the readers than I do. You know readers very well, I'm sure. Editors are often referred to as the ivory tower crowd, while circulation people are out in the trenches trying to peddle the product we editors and reporters create.*

Refer to Recent Happenings. Referring to a previous speech, recent event, or prominent person currently making news helps gain attention because the audience is familiar with this and will pay attention to see how you're going to connect it to your speech topic. Soon after the financial problems of Orange County, California, came to light, Arthur Levitt (1995, p. 194), Chair of the U.S. Securities and Exchange Commission, in a speech on consumer protection referred to recent events in his introduction:

> *This visit was scheduled well before a problem erupted in Orange County. It is a significant problem, and it may cause grief and loss to many. But our markets have been tested before—and they will surely be tested again. Problems will be dealt with, risk will be spread, plans will be developed to recoup losses. No other market in the world could have absorbed such a shock.*

Use Humor. A clever (and appropriate) anecdote is often useful in holding attention. Humor is also risky; if it falls flat, it can make the audience (and the speaker) uncomfortable. If you feel uncomfortable telling humorous stories or jokes in a public speaking situation, avoid this method. Similarly, avoid humor if you feel your joke or story will make any members of your audience uncomfortable or ill-at-ease. Further, make sure that your humor is integral to your speech topic. Here, for example, is an especially good example of humor used to express thanks for the introduction (Hankin, 1997, p. 22):

> *Thank you, John, for that all too generous introduction. If, as Mark Twain said, a man can live a month on one compliment, you have just assured me of immortality, and you will go to heaven for your charity unless you go somewhere else for your exaggerations.*

Use an Illustration or Dramatic Story. Much as people are drawn to soap operas, so are we drawn to illustrations and stories about people. Here's an example from a speech by Todd Prins (Schnoor, 1994, p. 73):

> *An eight-year-old boy became just another victim when his mother turned unintentionally away from him for just a few seconds unaware that there was a real danger present in her home. This was enough time for her child to be burned on over half of his body. Because of the injuries he received, he was hospitalized for sixteen days before he died.*

Do be sure to make the connection between your opening illustration and the topic and purpose of your speech. Don't expect the audience to make the connections themselves. They may not do it, and your great illustration will have no effect.

Stress Importance of Topic. People pay attention to what they feel is important to them and ignore what seems unimportant and irrelevant. For example, in addition to telling them that budget cuts will hurt education in the state (again, too general to relate to), tell them what this means to them specifically. You might, for example, say:

> *Budget cuts in the abstract mean little. So, let me tell you what these cuts will mean to us. First, our class size is going to be increased from thirty to fifty. Just think what that will mean in a course like Public Speaking. Second, all our laboratory courses will be eliminated. Those of us majoring in Biology, Chemistry, Physics, Physiology, and similar sciences will receive no practical experience. All these courses will be conducted as pure lecture courses. Third, our tuition— already too high to suit me and I'm sure most of you as well—will be increased by thirty percent!*

Use Visual or Audio Presentation Aids. Presentation aids are valuable because they're new and different. They engage our senses and thus our attention. When used in the introduction they serve to quickly secure the attention of the audience and let the audience know that this speech is going to be something special. Unit 9 discussed presentation aids in depth.

TIPS from professional speakers

You have to be careful with humor. It should be appropriate to the audience and to the subject. It can serve to warm up the speaker or the audience, or it can be pointed. But be careful of how sharp the point is. Sarcasm, literally "flesh rending," can backfire, creating sympathy for the opposite point of view. Or, though appropriate for the immediate audience, it may generate bad publicity.

Henry Ehrlich, business and political speechwriter, *Writing Effective Speeches* (New York: Paragon House, 1992): 62.

The beginning is the most important part of the work.
—Plato

My way is to begin with the beginning.
—Don Juan

Tell the Audience to Pay Attention. A simple, "I want you to listen to this frightening statistic," or "I want you to pay particularly close attention to . . . ," used once or twice in a speech, will help gain audience attention.

Use a Quotation. Quotations are useful because the audience is likely to pay attention to the brief and clever remarks of someone they have heard of or read about. Do make sure that the quotation is directly relevant to your topic. If you have to explain its relevance, it probably isn't worth using.

Refer Directly to Your Topic. If your topic focuses on the interests of the audience, you might begin by referring directly to it. If it's one whose relevance you have to prove, then this approach probably would not be appropriate. In his speech to announce the new developments in Haiti, President Clinton (1994, p. 740) began his speech by referring directly to the issue:

> *My fellow Americans, I want to announce that the military leaders of Haiti have agreed to step down from power. The dictators have recognized that it is in their best interest and in the best interest of the Haitian people to relinquish power peacefully, rather than to face imminent action by the forces of the multinational coalition we are leading.*

Cite a Little-Known Fact or Statistic. Little-known facts or statistics will help perk an audience's attention. Headlines on unemployment statistics, crime in the schools, and political corruption sell newspapers because they gain attention.

Establish a Speaker-Audience-Topic Relationship

In addition to gaining attention, use your introduction to establish a connection among yourself as the speaker, the audience members, and your topic. Try to answer your listeners' inevitable question: Why should we listen to you speak on this topic? You can establish an effective speaker-audience-topic relationship in a number of ways.

Establish Your Credibility. The introduction is a particularly important time to establish your competence, character, and charisma. This recommendation to stress your competence must be viewed in cultural perspective. In some cultures, it would be considered an inappropriate show of immodesty to stress one's own competence so directly. The speaker in many Asian cultures, for example, would be expected to stress his or her lack of competence verbally but to demonstrate competence nonverbally. Unit 23, "Speaker Credibility," covers in detail the ways to make yourself more credible and believable.

Here, for example, the speaker establishes his credibility and in doing so establishes a connection among himself, the audience, and the topic (Jacobs 1997, p. 461):

> *I will discuss both the challenges and the opportunities of diversity. As an African American, as a person who has spent most of his adult*

years working to inject minorities into the mainstream of American life, and as someone who has been fortunate to join the senior management of a great global corporation, I believe that no organization can achieve its full potential unless it is capable of benefiting from diversity.

Refer to Others Present. Not only will this help you to gain attention, it will also help you to establish an effective speaker-audience-topic relationship. In this example Harvey Mackay (1991) refers not only to the audience but also to their present thoughts and feelings:

I'm flattered to be here today, but not so flattered that I'm going to let it go to my head. Yes, I was delighted to be asked to be your commencement speaker. But I also know the truth: by the time you're my age ninety-nine out of a hundred will have completely forgotten who spoke at your graduation.

And, I can accept that. Because I can't remember the name of my commencement speaker either. What I do remember from graduation day is the way I felt: excited, scared and challenged. I was wondering what the world was like out there, and how I would manage to make an impact.

Refer to the Occasion. Often your speech will be connected directly with the occasion. By referring to the reason the audience has gathered, you can establish a connection among yourself, the audience, and the topic. Here Joan David Ratteray (1987) refers to the occasion in her speech, "Escape to Freedom":

Thank you, Mr. Lustig. I am glad to be in Ohio today, for this is a State that has meant so much to Black Americans, a State that in the past has been a symbol of freedom . . . . I understand from your local newspapers that it was in this State also that a black man named John Brown, in the early 19th century, started some of the first independent schools for black children. And it was here that Harriet Tubman was buried with full military honors. Thus, the "Underground Railroad" and the State of Ohio are inextricably linked in the history of America's search for freedom.

I have come to tell you today that I have found another "underground railroad" in America. This time it's helping inner-city youth all across this country escape the slavery imposed on them by traditional mass education in our inner cities.

Express Your Pleasure or Interest in Speaking. Yukio Matsuyama (1992) effectively establishes a speaker-audience-topic relationship by humorously expressing his pleasure in addressing the audience:

I feel very happy to be invited here today. It is always a great pleasure for me to talk about Japan with those Americans who have a sincere interest in Japanese affairs and who don't find us inscrutable, but only intractable.

Here Susan Peterson (1995, p. 188) expresses her interest in the subject and makes her connection with the audience:

> *I don't always admit in public that I once was a television news correspondent. These days the reactions can be somewhat unpredictable! Actually, it's now a relief to come home to the Midwest for Christmas and not have to defend Dan Rather or Barbara Walters anymore. Though I was once proud to be a television journalist, I am prouder still to be a business owner, and particularly a woman business owner. We have one incredible network.*

Compliment the Audience. Pay the audience an honest and sincere compliment, and they'll not only give you their attention, they'll feel a part of your speech.

In some cultures—Asian cultures such as Japan and Korea are good examples—the speaker is expected to compliment the audience. It's one of the essential parts of the introduction. Visitors from the United States are often advised when speaking in a foreign country to compliment the country itself, its beauty, its culture. Obviously, if done to an extreme or if the speaker appears insincere, the compliment is probably best omitted. In this example Donna Anderson (1994, p. 138) compliments the audience directly by noting the group's accomplishments:

> *First, I want to compliment the organizers of these two days. Yours is the most comprehensive program on the important subject of retiree activity that I've encountered—and I have been deeply engaged in this area of activity for nearly 17 years.*

Express Similarities with the Audience. By stressing your own similarity with members of the audience, you create a bond with them and become an "insider" instead of an "outsider." Here Janice Payan (1990) uses this technique most effectively:

> *Thank you. I felt as if you were introducing someone else because my mind was racing back 10 years, when I was sitting out there in the audience at the Adelante Mujer conference. Anonymous. Comfortable. Trying hard to relate to our "successful" speaker, but mostly feeling like Janice Payan, working mother, glad for a chance to sit down.*

> *I'll let you in on a little secret. I still am Janice Payan, working mother. The only difference is that I have a longer job title, and that I've made a few discoveries these past 10 years that I'm eager to share with you.*

> *The first is that keynote speakers at conferences like this are not some sort of alien creatures. Nor were they born under a lucky star. They are ordinary Hispanic women who have stumbled onto an extraordinary discovery.*

Orient the Audience

The introduction should orient the audience in some way as to what is to follow in the body of the speech. Preview for the audience what you're going to say. The orientation may be covered in a variety of ways.

Give a General Idea of Your Subject

- Tonight I'm going to discuss atomic waste.
- My concern today is with pollution.
- I want to talk with you about the problems our society has created for the aged.

Here Nannerl Keohane (1991) orients her audience by giving a general idea of the topic:

My topic is leadership—a sorely needed skill in our country and our world these days; and particularly women leaders—an even scarcer phenomenon; and how we might prepare more women to be leaders in the future.

Give a Detailed Preview. S. J. Buchsbaum (1991) provides a detailed orientation that previews what he will cover in his speech:

Today, I want to review the problem of networked computer security, and establish some common perspectives on key aspects of this problem—along with some widely applicable security approaches. I will then discuss current forms of these security approaches in computer networks—ranging from very large computer networks, such as the AT&T telecommunications and information network to the more limited computer networks that are pervading our corporate and national infrastructures. And I'll conclude with a look at emerging technological capabilities for improving computer network security.

Identify Your Goal. Here, Harold Carr (1987) identifies the thesis he hopes to establish:

I'll argue today—and certainly will be happy to debate with you during the question session—that communications during a "crisis"—however you define that term—shouldn't be all that different from communications during routine times.

Some Common Faults of Introductions

The introduction is perhaps the most important single part of the speech, so be especially careful to avoid the most common faults.

Don't Apologize (Generally). As the accompanying tip warns, apologies are to be avoided. Generally, at least. In much of the United States and Western

---

TIPS
from professional speakers

Never—but never—apologize. Follow the positive road all the way. "An apology," said Oliver Wendell Holmes, "is only egotism wrong side out." It starts the audience looking for the shortcomings in you and your message. All the things you may be tempted to apologize for should have been taken care of, and would have with a little planning, long before D-Day. If you failed to take the time needed to research, develop, and rehearse your talk, or if you did not know, or learn, enough about your subject, you won't improve matters by pointing this out. Instead, you will lessen the audience's interest and put them on the lookout for anything about you or your talk that may be deficient.

Dorothy Sarnoff, speech consultant and trainer and developer of the "Speech Dynamics and Cosmetics" course, *Speech Can Change Your Life* (New York: Dell, 1970): 214.

Europe, an apology is seen as an excuse for a lack of competence or effectiveness. To apologize in your speech is therefore to encourage your audience to look for faults and to alert them that your speech could have and should have been better. So, the general advice to avoid apologizing is reasonable in these cultures. In many other cultures (Japanese, Chinese, and Korean are good examples), however, the speaker is expected to begin with an apology. It's a way of complimenting the audience and placing them in a superior position. The speaker who doesn't apologize or act humbly may be seen as arrogant and as one who feels superior to the audience.

Don't Make Hollow Promises. A related fault is to promise something that you will not in fact deliver. The speaker who promises to tell you how to solve your love life problems, how to make a fortune in the stock market, or how to be the most popular person on campus, and fails to deliver such insight, quickly loses credibility.

Don't Rely on Gimmicks. Avoid gimmicks that gain attention but are irrelevant to the nature of the speech or are inconsistent with your treatment of the topic. Thus, for example, slamming a book on the desk, yelling obscenities, or telling a joke that bears no relation to the rest of your speech may accomplish this very limited goal of gaining attention. The audience, however, quickly sees them for what they are—gimmicks and tricks that have fooled them into paying attention. Such actions are resented and will set up barriers between you and your listeners.

Don't Preface Your Introduction. Don't preface your speech with such common but ineffective statements as:

- I'm really nervous, but here goes. . .
- Before I begin my talk, I want to say . . .
- I hope I can remember everything I want to say.

Here's a sample introduction with accompanying comments that summarize our discussion of the introduction.

Speech Introduction	Comments
At 8:30 in the morning and with the weather below freezing, I sure appreciate your being here.	Here the speaker gains attention by paying the audience an honest compliment. Do realize that this can be overdone; in moderation it's an effective opener.
I fully intend to justify your being here by telling you of one of the most dangerous things going on right here at Hudson Valley College and at colleges throughout the country.	The speaker tells the audience that there's a serious problem and tries to arouse their curiosity by coaxing them to figure out what this dangerous thing is. The speaker further relates the problem to the immediate audience.
What is this that is so dangerous— it's nothing. That's right, it's nothing. Our college and the colleges throughout the country are doing virtually nothing to combat the AIDS crisis, and this has put our lives in jeopardy.	Here the speaker sets up an apparent contradiction to further involve the audience and to entice them to ask—how could something dangerous be nothing?

Asian culture has been called the "culture of courtesy" and North American and Eastern European culture the "culture of realism" (Culick 1962). Is this still true today? If so, what implications does this have for constructing introductions to speeches for these different audiences? More than likely, your audience will consist of people from both cultures. How will you tailor an introduction to such a mixed audience?

My sister's college did nothing and my sister is now HIV positive. I don't want that to happen to another person and that's why I'm talking about a topic that is very difficult for me personally to discuss. But, it's so important that I feel I really have no choice.

From this disclosure, we know that the topic is especially important to the speaker. The speaker also tries to relate this topic and problem to this specific audience. We can easily hear the speaker's involvement and the speaker's concern for the topic and the audience.

Today, I want to explain why "nothing" is so important and why it has created such a serious problem and what we can do to help solve the problem—not of AIDS, but of AIDS prevention right here at Hudson Valley College.

This brief orientation clearly explains what the speaker is going to cover and also reveals the organizational pattern to be used. We know that the speaker is first going to discuss the problem and then the solution. Note too that the speaker very specifically limits the purpose to what can reasonably be accomplished and this is most clearly seen in limiting the solution: to AIDS prevention at Hudson Valley College.

CONCLUSIONS

Your conclusion is especially important because it's often the part of the speech that the audience remembers most clearly. It's your conclusion that in many cases determines what image of you is left in the minds of the audience. Devote special attention to this brief but crucial part of your speech. Let your conclusion serve three major functions: to summarize, motivate, and provide closure.

Summarize

The summary function is particularly important in an informative speech, less so in persuasive speeches or in speeches to entertain. You may summarize your speech in a variety of ways.

Restate Your Thesis or Purpose. In this type of brief summary, you restate the essential thrust of your speech, repeating your thesis or perhaps the goals you hoped to achieve. In this excerpt Margaret Milner Richardson

THE ETHICS OF Clear and Present Danger

In the United States it's illegal to create what is termed "a clear and present danger." This principle—which actually provides for great freedom in speech—derives from a Supreme Court decision in Schenck v. U.S., 1919, with Oliver Wendell Holmes presiding. Charles Schenck had been convicted of distributing circulars urging citizens to oppose the draft. When the case reached the Supreme Court, the decision was reversed, with Holmes writing: "The question in every case is whether the words used, are used in such circumstances and are of such a nature as to create a clear and present danger that they will bring about the substantive evils that Congress has a right to prevent. It is a question of proximity and degree." In some instances—as during the anti-Communist McCarthy era of the 1950s—the clear and present danger ruling was used to convict people solely for being Communist Party members. In a later case in which five Russians were convicted of distributing political fliers (in *Abrams v. United States*), Holmes, in a dissenting opinion, argued that even ideas we "loathe" should not be suppressed "unless they so imminently threaten immediate interference with the lawful and pressing purposes of the law that an immediate check is required to save the country." In most instances, however, the "clear and present danger" law protects speech that does not present imminent danger and so gives the speaker great freedom—but not total freedom; specifically, it does not protect speech that might prove dangerous to the welfare of the people and the country.

Would you consider violating the clear and present danger principle to be unethical? Can you think of illegal acts that you'd consider ethical? Can you think of legal acts that you'd consider unethical?

(The next Ethics in Public Speaking box appears on page 305.)

(1995, p. 203), Commissioner of Internal Revenue, concludes her speech by restating her purpose:

> *Thank you for taking this journey with me into the future. By sharing with you our vision of the future, I hope you will not only understand where we have been as an agency but where we will be in the future. You are an indispensable part of that future. I look forward to working with you to bring tax administration into the twenty-first century.*

Restate the Importance of the Topic . Another method for concluding is to tell the audience again why your topic or thesis is so important. In a speech entitled "Corporate Fitness Programs Pay Off," Brenda W. Simonson (1986) restates her thesis:

> *It is estimated that within the next five years, 25 percent of all major corporations in the United States will have established some sort of fitness programming. Indeed, corporate fitness programming has come of age. There's no doubt about it—healthy employees work more and cost less, and that's why managers will embrace fitness, not as a fringe benefit, but as an integral part of their regular personnel and healthcare policies. The message is clear—fitness means profits.*

Restate Your Major Propositions. In this type of summary you restate your thesis and the major propositions you used to support it. In his conclusion, Carl Wayne Hensley (1994, p. 319) restates his major propositions as questions:

Now, do you see why I assert that mediation provides a sensible approach for settling divorce-related issues? Do you see why I believe that mediation has to become a way of life in America when the divorce rate is so overwhelming? Do you understand that mediation helps the couple manage conflict, helps the couple engage in a win-win exchange, and helps the couple stabilize individually? Do you see more clearly that mediation does provide a sensible approach for settling divorce-related issues?

Motivate

A second function of the conclusion—most appropriate in persuasive speeches—is to motivate your audience to do what you want them to do. In your conclusion you have the opportunity to give the audience one final push in the direction you wish them to take. Whether it's to buy stock, vote a particular way, or change an attitude, you can use the conclusion for a final motivation, a final appeal. Here are two excellent ways to motivate.

Ask for a Specific Response. Specify what you want the audience to do after listening to your speech. Clarence Darrow (Peterson, 1965), in his summation speech in defense of Henry Sweet, an African American man charged with murder, directed his conclusion at motivating the jury to vote not guilty in a case that drew national and worldwide attention because of the racial issues involved. A vote of not guilty was in fact quickly returned by a jury of 12 white men.

Gentlemen, what do you think of our duty in this case? I have watched day after day these black, tense faces that have crowded this court. These black faces that now are looking to you 12 whites, feeling that the hopes and fears of a race are in your keeping. This case is about to end, gentlemen. To them, it is life. Not one of their color sits on this jury. Their fate is in the hands of 12 whites. Their eyes are fixed on you, their hearts go out to you, and their hopes hang on your verdict. This is all. I ask you, an behalf of this defendant, on behalf of these helpless ones who turn to you, and more than that—on behalf of this great state, and this great city, which must face this problem and face it fairly—I ask you, in the name of progress and of the human race, to return a verdict of not guilty in this case!

Reiterate Speaker-Audience Agreement. In a speech designed to strengthen attitudes, it may prove of value to repeat what you and the audience believe. Here, for example, Boutros Boutros-Ghali (1994, p. 130), Secretary-General of the United Nations, concluded his speech on transnational crime by reminding the audience of the areas of agreement:

It is because we support these values and recognize the need to unite against transnational crime that we have come together today. I therefore see this meeting as an opportunity for us to re-state our commitment to the triumph of the rule of law over the law of the jungle. But I

also see it as an expression of our faith in international cooperation to achieve the lofty ideals of the Charter of the United Nations.

Provide Directions for Future Action. Another type of motivational conclusion is to spell out, most often in general terms, the direction you wish the audience to take. Here's an example by David Archambault (1992), president of the American Indian College Fund, in a speech to the Rotary Club:

Let us make this anniversary a time of healing and a time of renewal, a time to wipe away the tears. Let us—both Indian and non-Indian— put our minds together and see what life we can make for our children. Let us leave behind more hope than we found.

Provide Closure

The third function of your conclusion is to provide closure. Often your summary will accomplish this, but in some instances it will prove insufficient. End your speech with a conclusion that is crisp and definite. Make the audience know that you have definitely and clearly ended. Some kind of wrap-up, some sort of final statement, is helpful in providing this feeling of closure. You may achieve closure through a variety of methods.

Use a Quotation. A quotation is often an effective means of providing closure. Here, for example, Linda Reivitz (1985) uses a quotation in a humorous but pointed way to conclude her speech on women's equality:

I would like to close today with a salute to former President Grover Cleveland, who in 1905 said, "Sensible and responsible women do not want to vote." May all those who display equal enlightenment as that attain an equal place in history.

Another good example can be seen in the conclusion of Martin Luther King Jr.'s famous "I Have a Dream" speech where King uses the words of an old spiritual to close his speech:

When we allow freedom to ring, when we let it ring from every village and every hamlet, from every state and every city, we will be able to speed up that day when all of God's children, black men and white men, Jews and Gentiles, Protestants and Catholics, will be able to join hands and sing in the words of the old Negro spiritual, "Free at last! Free at last! Thank God almighty, we are free at last!

Refer to Subsequent Events. You may also achieve closure by referring to future events to take place either that day or soon afterwards. Notice how effectively United States Secretary of State Madeleine K. Albright (1998) uses this method in a speech on NATO:

Our task is to make clear what our alliance will do and what our partnership will mean in a Europe truly whole and free, and in a world that looks to us for principles and purposeful leadership for peace, for prosperity, and for freedom. In this spirit, I look forward to our discussion today and to our work together in the months and years to come.

Refer Back to the Introduction. It's sometimes useful to connect your conclusion with your introduction. Here Jill Reiss (Schnoor 1994, p. 3), a student from George Mason University, after noting the hard work that Thomas Edison put into his inventions, concludes her speech by referring to Edison again:

> *Today we've examined what ecofoam peanuts are, how they compare to other alternatives, and their problems as well as their promises as an environmentally conscious product. American Excelsior, like Thomas Edison, has been willing to invest the perspiration necessary to bring its inspirations to work.*

Pose a Challenge or Question. You may close your speech by leaving the audience with a provocative question to ponder or a challenge to consider. David T. Kearns (1987), Chief Executive Officer of Xerox, provides crisp closure with his briefly stated request:

> *Ladies and gentlemen, let me leave you with this thought. Today's kindergartners will be the first high school graduates of the 21st century. Let's give them a head start on their future. Let's start now.*

Another method is to pose a question and answer it by recapping your thesis and perhaps some of your major arguments or propositions. Here Jeff Sculley (Reynolds and Schnoor, 1991), a student from Bradley University, in an after-dinner speech on homophobia, asks a question as a way of summing up his speech and then answers it:

> *How can we avoid this horrible fate? By simply giving up on hatred and fear, and remembering that the greatest guarantor of our civil liberties is mutual toleration.*

Thank the Audience. Speakers frequently conclude their speeches by thanking the audience for their attention or their invitation to you to address them. Here, for example, John Dalton (1994, p. 298) expresses his appreciation to the audience:

> *I am very grateful to you for the opportunity to share my concerns with you, and I hope that you will give me the benefit of your own knowledge and expertise as I continue to address these matters. If at the end of my tenure as Secretary of the Navy I am remembered for having encouraged the men and women of the Navy and Marine Corps to value and adhere to personal integrity and sacrificial service to others, I will be* deeply satisfied *indeed.*
>
> *Thank you very much, and God bless you.*

Begin low, speak low;
Take fire, rise higher;
When most impressed
Be self-possessed;
At the end wax warm,
And sit down in a storm.
—John Leifchild

How is a lawyer's summation speech, say in defending a client charged with murder, similar to and different from a conclusion to a persuasive speech?

Some Common Faults of Conclusions

Because the conclusion is such an important part of your speech, be careful to avoid the common problems.

Don't Introduce New Material. You may, of course, give new expression to ideas covered in the body of the speech, but don't introduce new material in your conclusion. Instead, use your conclusion to reinforce what you've already said in your discussion and to summarize your essential points.

Don't Dilute Your Position. Here are some expressions you'll want to avoid:

■ I know this isn't that important, but . . .
■ We really don't know enough about inflation to offer any real advice, but anyway . . .
■ This information is probably dated, but it was all I could find.

Statements such as these are ineffective and only detract from the credibility you've already established.

Ethically, of course, you do have the obligation to qualify your assertions as warranted by the evidence, but do this in the body of your speech, not in the conclusion.

Don't Drag Out Your Conclusion. End your speech crisply. Avoid dragging out your conclusion. Beginning speakers often preface each statement of their conclusion with terms that lead the audience to think that this is the last statement. Expressions such as "in summary," "in conclusion," or "therefore" will often lead the audience to expect an ending. When you're ready to end, end. Don't linger at the podium.

A sample conclusion with accompanying commentary that summarizes our discussion of the conclusion appears on page 281.

TRANSITIONS AND INTERNAL SUMMARIES

Remember that your audience will hear your speech just once. They must understand it as you speak it or lose it. Transitions and internal summaries help listeners understand your speech more effectively and efficiently.

Speech Conclusion	Comments
The apathy and indecision of the administration and the opposition from various religious groups have created a situation in which nothing is being done to help prevent the spread of HIV infection.	Here the speaker summarizes the problem—the administration and the opposition from certain religious groups.
We need to change that by signing the petition being circulated today by Hudson Valley Aids Awareness in all the cafeterias on campus. We also need to become better informed by reading the pamphlet I'll distribute in a minute. It's your life; don't do nothing.	The speaker here offers two solutions—sign the petition and become more informed. Note that both of these are behaviors that the speaker can logically expect to succeed in motivating.
Let's tell the administration and those who oppose our becoming informed that we are not going to allow NOTHING to continue. We want something.	This is the speaker's closing statement; it repeats the main theme of the speech, which is to do something, and it uses the term "nothing" to effectively connect the introduction, conclusion, and the specific thesis of the speech.

Transitions

Transitions are words, phrases, or sentences that connect the various parts of your speech. They provide the audience with guideposts that help them follow the development of your thoughts and arguments. Use transitions in the following places at the very least:

- between the introduction and the body of the speech
- between the body and the conclusion
- between the main points in the body of the speech

In addition, use transitions to serve a wide variety of other functions. Here are some examples:

To announce the start of a major proposition or piece of evidence:

First, . . .
A second argument . . .
A closely related problem . . .
If you want further evidence, look at . . .
Next, consider . . .
My next point . . .
An even more compelling argument . . .

To signal that you're drawing a conclusion from previously given evidence and argument:

Thus, . . .
Therefore, . . .
So, as you can see . . .
It follows, then, that . . .

TIPS
from professional speakers

Perhaps the simplest way to transition from one topic to the next is to simply announce that you are doing so. For example: "Now that I have explained the history of widget production in the United States, let me now present some exciting new technologies on the horizon of widget-making."

Paul R. Timm, author and communication trainer and popular speaker, *How to Make Winning Presentations* (Franklin Lakes, NJ: Career Press, 1997): 68.

To alert the audience to your introducing a qualification or exception:

But, . . .
However, also consider . . .

To remind listeners of what has just been said and that it's connected with another issue that will now be considered:

In contrast to . . . , consider also . . .
Not only . . . , but also . . .
In addition to . . . , we also need to look at . . .
Not only should we . . . , but we should also . . .

To signal the part of your speech you're approaching:

By way of introduction . . .
In conclusion . . .
Now, let's discuss why we are here today . . .
So, what's the solution? What should we do?

You can enhance your transitions by pausing between your transition and the next part of your speech. This will help the audience see that a new part of your speech is coming. You might also take a step forward or to the side after saying your transition. This will also complement the movement from one part of your speech to another.

Internal Summaries

Closely related to the transition (and in some cases a special type of transition) is the internal summary. An internal summary is a statement that summarizes what you've already discussed. It's a statement that usually summarizes some major subdivision of your speech. Try to incorporate a number of internal summaries into your speech—perhaps working them into the transitions connecting, say, the major arguments or issues.

An internal summary that is also a transition might look something like this:

The three arguments advanced here were (1) . . . , (2) . . . , (3) . . . . Now, what can we do about them? I think we can do two things. First, . . .

Another example:

Inadequate recreational facilities, poor schooling, and a lack of adequate role models seem to be the major problems facing our youngsters. Each of these, however, can be remedied and even eliminated. Here's what we can do.

Note that these brief passages remind the listeners of what they have just heard and preview for them what they'll hear next. The clear connection in their minds will fill in any gaps that may have been created through inattention, noise, and the like.

Every speech ought to be put together like a living creature, with a body of its own, so as to be neither without head, nor without feet, but to have both a middle and extremities, described proportionately to each other and to the whole.
—Plato, *Phaedrus*

UNIT IN BRIEF

Introductions	Purposes: to gain attention; establish a connection among speaker, audience, and topic; and orient the audience. Avoid the major problems of apologizing (generally), pretending, making hollow promises, relying on gimmicks, and prefacing your introduction.
Conclusions	Purposes: to summarize your speech or some aspect of it, motivate your audience, and provide crisp closure. Avoid the common problems of introducing new material, diluting the strength of your position, and dragging out the conclusion.
Transitions and Internal Summaries	Purposes: to connect the parts of your speech and give your listeners guides to help them follow your speech. Use them between the introduction and the body, between the major propositions, and between the body and the conclusion.

THINKING CRITICALLY ABOUT INTRODUCTIONS, CONCLUSIONS, AND TRANSITIONS

REVIEWING KEY TERMS AND CONCEPTS IN INTRODUCING, CONCLUDING, AND CONNECTING THE PARTS OF YOUR SPEECH

1. Review and define the key terms used in this unit:

   - ❑ introduction (p. 267)
   - ❑ attention (p. 267)
   - ❑ speaker-audience-topic connection (p. 270)
   - ❑ orientation (p. 273)
   - ❑ conclusion (p. 275)
   - ❑ summary (p. 275)
   - ❑ motivation (p. 277)
   - ❑ closure (p. 278)
   - ❑ transition (p. 281)
   - ❑ internal summary (p. 282)

2. Review and explain the key concepts discussed in this unit:

   - What purposes should an introduction serve? What means can you use to achieve these purposes? What are the common faults with introductions?
   - What purposes should a conclusion serve? What means can you use to achieve these purposes? What are the common faults with conclusions?
   - What are transitions and internal summaries and how might they best be used?

DEVELOPING STRATEGIES FOR INTRODUCING, CONCLUDING, AND CONNECTING THE PARTS OF THE PUBLIC SPEECH

1. Harley is running for president of the tenants association (as are three others). Each speaker has been asked to give a brief talk stating his or her qualifications and what each would do for the building if elected president. The entire building and the other three candidates all belong to the same race; Harley is the only one who isn't of this race. Harley wonders if this issue of racial differences should be mentioned in the speech? What would you advise Harley to do?

2. Your speech has run overtime and you've been given the 30-second stop signal. You haven't even begun your conclusion, what should you do? Should you just continue your speech and go overtime? Or, should you wrap up in 30-seconds? If you do choose to abide by the time limit, what do you use the 30-seconds for?

EVALUATING INTRODUCTIONS, CONCLUSIONS, AND TRANSITIONS IN PUBLIC SPEECHES

1. Read or listen to the introduction and conclusion of a speech. What purposes did the introduction serve? What purposes did the conclusion serve? How might these two elements have been made more effective?

2. Look over the introduction and conclusion you used in an earlier speech. How would you evaluate them now that you've read about these elements in more detail?

3. Read or listen to a speech and try to identify as many transitions and internal summaries as you can. Were these sufficient to assist an audience in moving from one point to another?

USING TECHNOLOGY IN PUBLIC SPEAKING INTRODUCTIONS AND CONCLUSIONS

1. Visit http://www.lm.com/~chipp/spkrhome.htm. What advice does this Web site give for introducing and concluding your speech?

2. Visit one of the online magazine sites and read the introductions and conclusions to two or three or four of the articles—select any topic you're interested in. How do these differ from speech introductions and conclusions?

PRACTICALLY SPEAKING

13.1 Short Speech Technique

Prepare and deliver a two-minute speech in which you:

a. explain how a particular television commercial attempts to get your attention.
b. explain how a television news program tries to maintain your attention throughout.
c. describe the introductions and conclusions used on television talk shows.
d. describe the introductions and conclusions used on news programs.
e. construct a connection among the speaker, audience, and topic for one of these situations.
   1) a college recruiter addressing your class on coming to work for a large corporation.
   2) a peace corps volunteer addressing your class on the values of becoming a peace corps volunteer.
   3) a candidate for college president addressing your class on why you should vote for him or her.

13.2 Constructing Introductions

Prepare an introduction to one of the topics listed, making sure that you (1) secure the audience's attention and

interest, (2) establish a connection among speaker, audience, and topic, and (3) orient the audience as to what is to follow. Be prepared to explain the methods you used to accomplish each of these aims.

1. College isn't for everyone.
2. It's better never to love than to love and lose.
3. Maximum sentences should be imposed even for first offenders of the drug laws.
4. All alcoholic beverages should be banned from campus.
5. Abortion should be declared illegal.
6. Contribute to the Olympics.
7. Donate your organs to medicine after your death.
8. Switch to the new spreadsheet program.
9. Earn an M.B.A. Degree.
10. Laws restricting Sunday shopping should be abolished.

13.3 Constructing Conclusions

Prepare a conclusion to a hypothetical speech on one of the topics listed, making sure that you (1) summarize the speech's main points, (2) motivate the audience, and

(3) provide closure. Be prepared to explain the methods you used to accomplish each of these functions.

1. Children should be raised and educated by the state.
2. All wild-animal killing should be declared illegal.
3. Properties owned by churches and charitable institutions should be taxed in the same way that all other properties are taxed,
4. Suicide and its assistance by others should be legalized.
5. Teachers—at all levels—should be prevented from going on strike.
6. Gambling should be legalized in all states,
7. College athletics should be abolished.
8. Same-sex marriages should be legalized.
9. Divorce should be granted immediately when there's mutual agreement.
10. Privatization of elementary and high schools should be encouraged.

Outlining the Speech

The outline is a blueprint for your speech; it lays out the elements of the speech and their relationship to each other. With this blueprint in front of you, you can see at a glance all the elements of organization considered in the previous units—functions of the introduction and conclusion, transitions, major propositions and their relationship to the thesis and purpose, and adequacy of the supporting materials. Like a blueprint for a building, the outline enables you to spot weaknesses that might otherwise go undetected.

Begin outlining at the time you begin constructing your speech. Don't wait until you've collected all your material; begin outlining as you're collecting material, organizing it, and styling it. In this way you'll take the best advantage of one of the major functions of an outline—to tell you where change is needed. Do you need a more complete orientation? Do you have a sufficient number of transitions? Do your major propositions clearly support your thesis? Change and alter the outline as your prepare the speech.

FUNCTIONS AND TYPES OF OUTLINES

Outlines serve several important functions and may be of different types.

Functions of Outlines

An outline will help you organize your speech. As you outline the speech, you clarify the major points, the major supporting materials, and the transitions. Once these can be easily examined visually, you may see, for example, if your assertions are properly coordinated, if your supporting materials do, in fact, support your assertions, and so on. If you're using a temporal or a spatial organizational pattern, for example, you can quickly see from the outline if the temporal or spatial progression is clear or is in need of further refinement.

Speech outlines provide an efficient way to assess the strengths and weaknesses of the speech as it's being constructed. Let's say you're preparing a speech on censorship and your major points concern sex and violence. Your outline will tell you at a glance if your supporting materials are adequately and evenly distributed between the two points. The outline may tell you that more material has to be collected on the sex issue, or that your speech is almost totally devoted to statistical information and you

The outline is the framework of the speech. It bears the same relationship to the finished talk that steel girders and uprights bear to the finished office building.
—Charles Henry Woolbert

Your presentation structure, to be of any use whatsoever, must be simple enough to be remembered. It must be simple enough so that you'll remember what you want to say, and your audience will have no difficulty remembering what you told them.

Ron Hoff, leading speaker and advertising and marketing director, *"I Can See You Naked": A Fearless Guide to Making Great Presentations* (Kansas City, MO: Andrews and McMeel, 1988): 144.

need a human interest element, and so on. In short, the outline can guide your collection of information.

The outline, when it's constructed from the beginning of the speech preparation process, helps you check the speech as a whole (or at least as much as you've constructed so far). When you work for a long time on a speech and when each part is constructed over a long period of time, it becomes difficult to "see the forest for the trees." The outline enables you to stand back and examine the entire forest.

Types of Outlines

Outlines may be extremely detailed or extremely general. Since you're now in a learning environment where the objective is to make you a more proficient public speaker, your instructor may wish to suggest one type of outline over another. And, of course, just as the type of outline will depend on the specific speaker, the type of outline that proves best for instructional purposes will vary with the instructor.

The more detail you put into the outline, the easier it will be to examine the parts of the speech for all the qualities and characteristics that were discussed in the previous units. In the beginning, outline your speeches in detail and in complete sentences. The usefulness of an instructor's criticism will often depend on the completeness of the outline.

Here are some tips that will help you construct your first few outlines.

- Begin constructing the outline as soon as you have the topic clearly in mind.
- Revise it constantly. Every new idea, every new bit of information will result in some alteration of basic structure. At this point keep the outline brief and perhaps in key words or phrases.
- Once you feel pretty confident that you're near completion, construct an outline in detail—using complete sentences—and follow the procedures and principles discussed in the next sections of this unit.

CONSTRUCTING THE OUTLINE

After you've completed your research and have an organizational plan for your speech mapped out, put this plan (this blueprint) on paper. That is, construct what is called a "preparation outline" of your speech using the following guidelines.

Preface the Outline with Identifying Data

Before you begin the outline proper, identify the general and specific purposes as well as your thesis. You may also want to include a working title, one that you may change as you continue to polish and perfect your speech. This prefatory material should look something like this:

Title: What Do Media Do?

General purpose: to inform

Specific purpose: to inform my audience of four major functions of the mass media

Thesis: The mass media serve four major functions.

These identifying notes are not part of your speech proper. They're not, for example, mentioned in your oral presentation. Rather, they're guides to the preparation of the speech and the outline. They're like road signs to keep you going in the right direction and to signal when you've gone off course.

Outline the Introduction, Body, and Conclusion as Separate Units

Each of these three parts of the speech, although intimately connected, should be labeled separately and should be kept distinct in your outline. Like the identifying data mentioned previously, these labels are not spoken to the audience but are further guides to your preparation.

By keeping the introduction, body, and conclusion separate, you'll be able to see at a glance if they do, in fact, serve the functions you want them to serve. You'll be able to see where further amplification and support are needed. In short, you'll be able to see where there are problems and where repair is necessary.

At the same time, make sure that you examine the speech as a whole. See the speech from the attention gaining devices of the introduction, through the speaker-audience-topic connection and the orientation, to the major propositions and their supporting materials, to the summary, motivation, and closure of the conclusion.

Insert Transitions and Internal Summaries

Insert [using square brackets] transitions between the introduction and the body, the body and the conclusion, the major propositions of the body, and wherever else you think they might be useful. Insert your internal summaries (if these are not integrated with your transitions) wherever you feel they'll help your audience understand and remember your ideas.

Append a List of References

Some instructors require that you append a list of references to your speeches. If this is requested, then do so at the end of the outline or on a separate page. Some instructors require that only sources cited in the speech be included in the list of references, whereas others require that the full list of sources consulted be provided (those mentioned in the speech as well as those not mentioned).

Whatever the specific requirements, remember that these sources will prove most effective with your audience if you carefully integrate them into the speech. It will count for little if you consulted the latest works by the greatest authorities but never mention this to your audience. So, when appropriate, weave into your speech the source material you've consulted. In your outline, refer to the source material by author's name, date, and page in parentheses and then provide the complete citation in your list of references.

In your actual speech it might prove more effective to include the source with your statement. It might be phrased something like this:

According to John Naisbitt, author of the nationwide bestseller, Megatrends, the bellwether states are California, Florida, Washington, Colorado, and Connecticut.

Regardless of what specific system is required (find out before you prepare your outline), make certain to include all sources of information, not just written materials. Personal interviews, information derived from course lectures, and data learned from television should all be included in your list of references.

Use a Consistent Set of Symbols

The following is the standard, accepted sequence of symbols for outlining.

        I.
          A.
            1.
              a.
                (1)
                  (a)

Begin the introduction, the body, and the conclusion with Roman numeral I. Treat each of the three major parts as a complete unit.

Not This:	This:
Introduction	Introduction
I.	I.
II.	II.
Body	Body
III.	I.
IV.	II.
V.	III.
Conclusion	Conclusion
VI.	I.
VII.	II.

Use Visual Aspects to Reflect the Organizational Pattern

Use proper and clear indentation. This will help visually set off coordinate and subordinate relationships.

Not This:

    I. Television caters to the lowest possible intelligence.
   II. Talk shows illustrate this.
  III. "General Hospital"

This:

    I. Television caters to the lowest possible intelligence.
       A. Talk shows illustrate this.
          1. "Jerry Springer"
          2. "Ricki Lake"
          3. "Regis and Cathy Lee"
       B. Soap operas illustrate this.
          1. "As the World Turns"
          2. "General Hospital"
          3. "The Young and the Restless"

Use One Discrete Idea Per Symbol

If your outline is to reflect the organizational pattern among the various items of information, use just one discrete idea per symbol. Compound sentences are sure giveaways that you have not limited each item to a single idea. Also, be sure that each item is discrete, that is, that it does not overlap with any other item.

Not This:

    I. Education might be improved if teachers were better trained and
      if students were better motivated.

This:

    I. Education would be improved if teachers were better trained.
   II. Education would be improved if students were better motivated.

Note that in **This** items I and II are single ideas but in **Not This** they're combined.

Not This:

   I.Teachers are not adequately prepared to teach.
    A. Teacher education programs are inadequate.
    B. Course syllabi are dated.

This:

    I. Teachers are not adequately prepared to teach.
      A. Teacher education programs are inadequate.
         1. Support for A
         2. Support for A
      B. In-service programs are inadequate.
         1. Support for B
         2. Support for B

Can you identify the organizational principles used in this textbook for organizing each unit?

Note that A and B are discrete in **This** but overlap in **Not This**. In **Not This** B is actually a part of A (one of the inadequacies of teacher education programs is that course syllabi are dated).

Use Complete Declarative Sentences

Phrase your ideas in the outline in complete declarative sentences rather than as questions or as phrases. This will further assist you in examining the essential relationships. It's much easier, for example, to see if one item of information supports another if both are phrased in the declarative mode. If one is a question and one is a statement, this will be more difficult.

THREE SAMPLE OUTLINES

Now that the principles of outlining are clear, here are some specific examples to illustrate how those principles are used in specific outlines. Presented here are a full-sentence preparation outline with annotations to guide you through the essential steps in outlining a speech, a skeletal outline that provides a kind of template for a speech outline, and a delivery outline that illustrates the type of outline you might use in delivering your speech.

A Preparation Outline with Annotations

Here's a relatively detailed outline similar to the ones you might prepare in constructing your speech. The sidenotes will clarify both the content and the format of a full sentence outline.

HAVE YOU EVER BEEN CULTURE SHOCKED?

Usually the title, thesis, general, and specific purpose of the speech are prefaced to the outline. When the outline is an assignment that is to be handed in, more information may be requested.

THESIS: Culture shock can be described in four stages.
GENERAL PURPOSE: to inform.
SPECIFIC PURPOSE: to inform my audience of the four phases of culture shock.

Note the general format for the outline; the headings are clearly labeled and the indenting helps you see clearly the relationship that one item bears to the other. For example, in Introduction II, the outline format helps you to see that A and B are explanations (amplification, support) for II.

Introduction

I. Many of you have or will experience culture shock.
   A. Many people experience culture shock, that reaction to being in a culture very different from what you were used to.

B. By understanding culture shock, you'll be in a better position to deal with it if and when it comes.

Note that the introduction, body, and conclusion are clearly labeled and separated visually.

II. I have lived in four different cultures myself.
   A. I've always been interested in the way in which people adapt to different cultures.
   B. With our own campus becoming more culturally diverse every semester, the process of culture shock becomes important for us all.

Here the speaker attempts to connect the speaker, audience, and topic by stressing intercultural experiences and an abiding interest in the topic. Also, the speaker makes the topic important to the audience by referring to their everyday surroundings.

III. Culture shock occurs in four stages (Oberg 1960).
   A. The Honeymoon occurs first.
   B. The Crisis occurs second.
   C. The Recovery occurs third.
   D. The Adjustment occurs fourth.

Note that references are integrated throughout the outline just as they would be in a term paper. In the actual speech, the speaker might say: "Anthropologist Kalervo Oberg who coined the term 'culture shock' said it occurs in four stages."

The introduction serves the three functions noted: it gains attention (by involving the audience and by stressing the importance of the topic to the audience's desire to gain self-understanding), it connects the speaker, audience, and topic in a way that establishes the credibility of the speaker, and it orients the audience as to what is to follow. This particular orientation identifies both the number of stages and their names. If this speech were a longer and more complex one, the orientation might also have included brief definitions of each stage.

[Let's follow the order in which these four stages occur and begin with the first stage, the Honeymoon.]

This transition cues the audience into a four-part presentation. Also, the numbers repeated throughout the outline will aid the audience in keeping track of where you are in the speech. Most important, it tells the audience that the speech will follow a temporal thought pattern.

BODY
   I. The Honeymoon occurs first.
      A. The honeymoon is the period of fascination with the new people and culture.
      B. You enjoy the people and the culture.
         1. You love the people.
            a. For example, the people in Zaire spend their time very differently from the way people in New York do.
            b. For example, my first 18 years living on a farm were very different from life in a college dorm.
         2. You love the culture.
            a. The great number of different religions in India fascinated me.
            b. Eating was an especially great experience.

Notice the parallel structure in the outline. For example, note that I, II, III, and IV in the body are all phrased in exactly the same way. Although this may seem redundant, it will help your audience closely follow your speech and will also help you in logically structuring your thoughts.

Notice that there are many examples in this speech. These examples are identified briefly in the outline and would be elaborated on in the speech.

[But, like many relationships, life isn't all honeymoon; soon there comes a crisis.]

Notice too the internal organization of each major point. Each main assertion in the body contains a definition of the stage (IA, IIA, IIIA, and IVA) and examples (IB, IIB, IIIB, and IVB) to illustrate the stage.

II. The Crisis occurs second.
   A. The crisis is the period when you begin to experience problems.

Because this is a specific fact, some style manuals require that the page number should be included.

    1. One-third of American workers abroad fail because of culture shock (Samovar and Porter 1991, p. 232).

    2. The personal difficulties are also great.

  B. Life becomes difficult in the new culture.

    1. Communication is difficult.

    2. It's easy to offend people without realizing it.

[As you gain control over the crises, you begin to recover.]

Note that each statement in the outline is a complete sentence. You can convert this outline into a phrase or key word outline for use in delivery. The full sentences, however, will help you clearly see relationships among items.

III. The Recovery occurs third.

  A. The recovery is the period where you learn how to cope.

  B. You begin to learn intercultural competence (Lustig and Koester 1999).

    1. You learn how to communicate.

      a. Being able to go to the market and make my wants known was a great day for me.

      b. I was able to ask for a date.

    2. You learn the rules of the culture.

      a. The different religious ceremonies each have their own rules.

      b. Eating is a ritual experience in lots of places throughout Africa.

The transitions are inserted between all major parts of the speech. Although they may seem too numerous in this outline, they'll be appreciated by your audience because the transitions will help them follow your speech.

[Your recovery leads naturally into the next and final stage, the adjustment.]

IV. The Adjustment occurs fourth.

  A. The adjustment is the period where you come to enjoy the new culture.

  B. You come to appreciate the people and the culture.

[Let me summarize the stages you go through in experiencing culture shock.]

Notice that these four points correspond to I, II, III, and IV of the body and to I A, B, C, and D of the introduction. Notice how the similar wording adds clarity.

CONCLUSION

  I. Culture shock can be described in four stages.

    A. The Honeymoon is first.

    B. The Crisis is second.

    C. The Recovery is third.

    D. The Adjustment is fourth.

In this step the speaker motivates the listeners to continue learning about culture shock. It is optional in informative speeches.

  II. Culture shock is a fascinating process; you may want to explore it more fully.

A. Lots of books on culture shock are on reserve for Communication 325: Culture and Communication.

B. Sunday's "60 Minutes" is going to have a piece on culture shock.

III. By knowing the four stages, you can better understand the culture shock you may now be experiencing on the job, at school, or in your private life.

This step provides closure; it makes it clear that the speech is finished. It also encourages reflection on the part of the audience as to their own culture shock.

References

Lustig, Myron W. and Jolene Koester (1999). *Intercultural Competence: Interpersonal Communication across Cultures,* 3rd ed New York: Longman.

Oberg, Kalervo (1960). Culture Shock: Adjustment to New Cultural Environments. *Practical Anthropology* 7:177–182.

Samovar, Larry A. and Richard E. Porter (1991). *Communication Between Cultures.* Belmont, CA: Wadsworth.

This reference list includes the sources that appear in the completed speech.

A Skeletal Outline

Here's a skeletal outline—a kind of template for structuring a speech. This particular outline would be appropriate for a speech using a time, spatial, or topical organization pattern. Note that in this skeletal outline there are three major propositions (I, II, and III in the Body). These correspond to the III A, B, and C in the introduction (where you'd orient the audience) and to the I A, B, and C in the conclusion (where you'd summarize your major propositions). The transitions are signaled by square brackets. As you review this outline—the faintly printed watermarks will remind you of the functions of each outline item—you'll be able to see how it can be adapted for use with other organization patterns, for example, problem–solution, cause–effect, or the motivated sequence.

Skeletal Outline

THESIS: your main assertion; the core of your speech.
GENERAL PURPOSE: your general aim (to inform, to persuade, to entertain).
SPECIFIC PURPOSE: what you hope to achieve from this speech.

Introduction

I. _____ *gain attention* _____

II. _____ *establish s-a-t connection* _____

III. _____ *orient audience* _____

In all chaos there is a cosmos, in all disorder a secret order.
—Carl Jung

A. _____ *first major proposition; same as I in body* _____

B. _____ *second major proposition; same as II in body* _____

C. _____ *third major proposition; same as III in body* _____

[Transition: *connect the introduction to the body*]

Body

I. _____ *first major proposition* _____

  A. _____ *support for I (the first major proposition)* _____

  B. _____ *further support for I* _____

[Transition: *connect the first major proposition to the second*]

II. _____ *second major proposition* _____

  A. _____ *support for II (the second major proposition)* _____

  B. _____ *further support for II* _____

[Transition: *connect the second major proposition to the third*]

III. _____ *third major proposition* _____

  A. _____ *support for III* _____

  B. _____ *further support for III* _____

[Transition: *connect the third major proposition (or all major propositions) to the conclusion*]

Conclusion

I. _____ *summary* _____

  A. _____ *first major proposition; same as I in body* _____

  B. _____ *second major proposition; same as II in body* _____

  C. _____ *third major proposition; same as III in body* _____

II. _____ *motivation* _____

III. _____ *closure* _____

TIPS
from professional speakers

Include whatever facts and phrases you personally need in your outline, such as key thoughts and transitional sentences that will help you achieve a smooth, clean delivery. You shouldn't have to struggle to remember anything while speaking. A number of my clients write out all their transitional sentences since these tend to slip the mind; for others this might be unnecessary. Remember: These notes are for you. Let your needs and habits be your only criteria in formulating your visual guide.

Lilyan Wilder, communication consultant, *Talk Your Way to Success* (New York: Simon & Schuster [Fireside], 1986): 104.

References:

1. _____

2. _____

3. _____

The skill to do comes from doing.
—Cicero

A Delivery Outline

Now that you've constructed a preparation outline, you need to construct a delivery outline, an outline that will assist you in delivering the speech. Resist the temptation to use your preparation outline to deliver the speech. If you use your preparation outline, you'll tend to read from the outline instead of presenting an extemporaneous speech where you attend to and respond to audience feedback.

Instead, construct a brief delivery outline, one that will assist rather than hinder your delivery of the speech. Here are some guidelines in preparing this delivery outline.

Be Brief. Don't use full sentences. Instead, use key words that will trigger in your mind the ideas you wish to discuss with your audience. Follow, too, the principles for constructing the preparation outline: (1) use a consistent set of symbols (the same ones you used in your preparation outline) and (2) use the visual aspects to reflect and reinforce the organizational pattern. Try to limit yourself to one side of one sheet of paper.

Be Clear. Be sure that you can see the outline while you're speaking. Don't write so small that you'll have to squint to read it; on the other hand, don't write so big that you'll need reams of paper to deliver a five-minute speech. Use different colors, underline, and use any symbols or guidance system that will help you communicate your ideas to your audience most effectively.

Be Delivery Minded. This is your outline. You want it to help you deliver your speech most effectively. Therefore, include any guides to delivery that will help while you're speaking. For example, you might note in the outline when you'll use your presentation aid (PA) and when you'll remove it. A simple "Show PA" or "Remove PA" should suffice. You might also wish to note some speaking cues such as "slow down" when reading a poetry excerpt, or perhaps a place where an extended pause might help.

Rehearse with the Delivery Outline. In your rehearsals, use the delivery outline only. Don't rehearse with your full-sentence outline. This is simply a specific application of the general rule: Make rehearsals as close to the real thing as possible.

Here's a sample delivery outline constructed from the preparation outline on culture shock, presented on pages 292–295. Note these features in the following sample delivery outline.

- It's brief enough so that you'll be able to use it effectively without losing eye contact with the audience. It uses abbreviations (for example, CS for culture shock) and phrases rather than complete sentences.
- It's detailed enough to include all essential parts of your speech, including transitions.
- It contains delivery notes specifically tailored to your own needs, for example, pause suggestions and guides to using visual aids.
- It's clearly divided into introduction, body, and conclusion and uses the same numbering system as the preparation outline.

[Delivery Outline]
PAUSE!
LOOK OVER THE AUDIENCE!

 I. Many experience CS
  A. CS: the reaction to being in a culture very different from your own.
  B. By understanding CS, you'll be better able to deal with it.

PAUSE/SCAN AUDIENCE

 II. CS occurs in 4 stages (WRITE ON BOARD)
  A. Honeymoon
  B. Crisis
  C. Recovery
  D. Adjustment

[Let's examine these stages of CS]
PAUSE/STEP FORWARD

 I. Honeymoon
  A. Fascination w/people and culture
  B. Enjoyment of people and culture
   1. Zaire example
   2. Farm to college dorm

[But, life isn't all honeymoon—the crisis]

 II. Crisis
  A. Problems arise
   1. 1/3 Am workers fail abroad
   2. Personal difficulties
  B. Life becomes difficult.
   1. Communication
   2. Offend others

[As you gain control over the crises, you learn how to cope]
PAUSE

III. Recovery
    A. Period of learning to cope.
    B. You learn intercultural competence.
        1. Communication becomes easier.
        2. You learn the culture's rules.

[As you recover, you adjust]

IV. Adjustment
    A. Learn to enjoy (again) the new culture.
    B. Appreciate people and culture.

[These then are the 4 stages; let me summarize]
PAUSE BEFORE STARTING CONCLUSION

I. CS occurs in 4 stages: honeymoon, crisis, recovery, & adjustment.

II. By knowing the 4 stages, you can better understand the culture shock you may now be experiencing on the job, at school, or in your private life.

PAUSE

ANY QUESTIONS?

UNIT IN BRIEF

Functions and Types of Outlines	The functions of outlines are to: 1. help you organize your thoughts into a coherent pattern, 2. help you assess the strengths and weaknesses of your speech, and 3. help you check and review the speech as a whole. Outlines may vary from word and phrase outlines to those with complete sentences.
Guidelines for Outlining	Preface the outline with identifying data. Outline the introduction, body, and conclusion as separate units. Insert transitions and internal summaries. Append a list of references (if required). Use a consistent set of symbols. Use visual aspects to reflect and reinforce the organizational pattern. Use one discrete idea per symbol. Use complete declarative sentences.

THINKING CRITICALLY ABOUT OUTLINING

REVIEWING KEY TERMS AND CONCEPTS IN OUTLINING

1. Review and define the key terms used in this unit:

   ☐ outline (p. 287)
   ☐ preparation outline (p. 292)
   ☐ skeletal outline (p. 294)
   ☐ delivery outline (p. 296)

2. Review and explain the key concepts discussed in this unit:

   ■ What functions do outlines serve? What are the major types of outlines?
   ■ What guidelines can you suggest for constructing the outline?

DEVELOPING STRATEGIES FOR OUTLINING PUBLIC SPEECHES

1. Luis is giving a speech on the three major advantages and the three major disadvantages of vitamins. Can you construct a template that would help Luis outline his speech?

2. What alternative organizational strategies might have worked for the speech on Culture Shock presented in this unit? For example, could you organize the material into a problem–solution pattern? Into a temporal pattern?

EVALUATING THE OUTLINING OF PUBLIC SPEECHES

1. How would you evaluate the outline on culture shock presented in this unit?

2. Review one of the poorly constructed speeches in Unit 5. How might outlining have helped prevent some of the problems with this speech?

USING TECHNOLOGY IN OUTLINING PUBLIC SPEECHES

1. Dave wants to set up a system of folders so he can conveniently store all the information he collects for his next three speeches, all of which will be built around the general topic of suicide. The first speech will deal with cultural views of suicide, the second with the current laws governing physician-assisted suicides, and the third will be a persuasive speech on physician-assisted suicides. Dave wants to store all his outlines, research, speech critique forms, and anything else in a series of folders that he's heard about but doesn't really know how to use. What advice can you give Dave to help him organize his speech folders? (The assumption here is that these are computer folders but physical folders would also work, though not as efficiently.)

2. Create templates on your computer for organizing the types of speeches you're likely to prepare. Share this with others and discuss the advantages and disadvantages of using a template in preparing a public speech.

PRACTICALLY SPEAKING

14.1 Short Speech Technique

Prepare and deliver a two-minute speech in which you:

a. Explain how you'd outline a speech on the geography of the United States.

b. Explain how you'd outline a speech on the structure of a table lamp.

c. Explain how you'd outline a speech on the need for improved AIDS education on campus.

d. Explain how you'd outline a speech on why parents should contribute to UNICEF.

e. Explain how the author outlined a chapter in any one of your textbooks.

14.2 Organizing a Scrambled Outline

This exercise provides an opportunity to work actively with the principles of organization and outlining discussed in the previous units. Your task is to unscramble the following statements from the outline on culture shock presented earlier and fit them into a coherent and logical outline consisting of an introduction, a body, and a conclusion. Don't look back at the outline until you've completed your unscrambling.

1. Culture shock occurs in four stages.

2. The crisis occurs second.

3. Many of you have or will experience culture shock.

4. The adjustment occurs fourth.

5. The honeymoon occurs first.

6. Culture shock is a fascinating process; you may want to explore it more fully.

7. By knowing the four stages, you can better understand the culture shock you may now be experiencing on the job, at school, or in your private life.

8. I lived in four different cultures myself.

9. The recovery occurs third.

10. Culture shock can be described in four stages.

If that was too easy, try this one. Like the above, it contains the major statements from a speech outline. Try unscrambling these. One possible unscrambled outline is provided on page 317.

Friendship

1. We develop an acquaintanceship.

2. Friendship is an interpersonal relationship between two persons that is characterized by mutual positive regard.

3. We meet.

4. In order to understand friendships we need to see what a friendship is and its stages of development.

5. Friendship is one of the most important of our interpersonal relationships.

6. We develop an intimate friendship.

7. Friendships develop through various stages.

8. Friendships don't develop full-blown but rather go through various stages—from the initial meeting to intimate friendship.

9. We develop a casual friendship.

10. By understanding friendship we will be in a better position to develop and maintain productive and enjoyable friendships.

11. Friendship—an interpersonal relationship characterized by mutual positive regard—is one of our most important assets.

12. We develop a close relationship.

13. Friendship is vital to all of us.

UNIT 15

Characteristics of Style

You're a successful public speaker when your listeners create in their minds the meanings you want them to create. You're successful when your listeners adopt the attitudes and behaviors you want them to adopt. The language choices you make—for example, the words you select and the sentences you form—will greatly influence the meanings your listeners receive and, thus, how successful you are.

HOW LANGUAGE WORKS

Your use of language will greatly influence your ability to inform and persuade an audience. Five qualities of language are especially important: directness, abstraction, objectivity, formality, and accuracy.

Language Varies in Directness

Consider the following sentences:

1A. We should all vote for Halliwell in the next election.
1B. Vote for Halliwell in the next election.
2A. It should be apparent that we should abandon the present system.
2B. Abandon the present system.
3A. Many people would like to go to Xanadu.
3B. How many of you want to go to Xanadu?

The B sentences are clearly more direct than the A sentences. Note, for example, that the B sentences address the audience directly. The A sentences are more distant, more indirect. Indirect sentences address only an abstract, unidentified mass of people. The sentences might as well address just anyone. When you use direct sentences, you address your specific and clearly defined listeners.

If you want to achieve directness, use active rather than passive sentences. Say "The professor invented the serum" rather than "The serum was invented by the professor." Use personal pronouns and personal references. Refer to your audience as "you" rather than "the audience" or "my listeners."

The following test will help you listen to gender differences more accurately.

Here are 10 statements about the speech of women and men. For each of the following statements, indicate whether you think the statement describes "women's speech" (write W), "men's speech" (M), or "women's and men's speech equally" (WM).

_____1. This speech is logical rather than emotional.
_____2. This speech is vague.
_____3. This speech is endless, less concise, and jumps from one idea to another.
_____4. This speech is highly businesslike.
_____5. This speech is more polite.
_____6. This speech uses weaker forms (for example, the weak intensifiers like "so" and "such") and fewer exclamations.
_____7. This speech contains more tag questions (for example, questions appended to statements that ask for agreement, such as "Let's meet at ten o'clock, *OK*?").
_____8. This speech is more euphemistic (contains more polite words as substitutes for some taboo or potentially offensive terms) and uses fewer swear terms.
_____9. This speech is generally more effective.
_____10. This speech is less forceful and less in control.

After responding to all 10 statements, consider the following: (1) On what evidence did you base your answers? (2) How strongly do you believe that your answers are correct? (3) What effect might these language differences have on listening to women and men? *Don't read any further* until you've responded to the above statements and questions.

The 10 statements were drawn from the research of Cheris Kramarae 1981; also see Coates and Cameron 1989), who argues that these "differences"—with the exception of statements 5 and 8 (women's speech is often more "polite")—are actually stereotypes of women's and men's speech which are not in fact confirmed in analyses of actual speech. According to Kramarae, then, you should have responded "WM" for statements 1, 2, 3, 4, 6, 7, 9, and 10 and "W" for statements 5 and 8.

Reexamine your answers to the 10 statements. Were your answers based on your actual listening to the speech of women and men, or might they have been based on what you think you heard, based on your beliefs about women's and men's speech?

(The next Listen to This box appears on page 326.)

Cultural Differences in Directness. The preference for directness will vary considerably with the culture of the speaker and the audience. Many Asian and Latin American cultures, for example, stress the values of indirectness largely because it enables a person to avoid appearing criticized or contradicted and thereby lose face. In most of the United States, however, you're taught that directness is the preferred style. "Be up front" and "tell it like it is" are commonly heard communication guidelines. Many Asian Americans and Latin Americans may, in fact, experience a conflict between the recommendation of style manuals to be direct and the cultural recommendation to be indirect.

In conversation, people adapt to the language style of the other person. This "communication accommodation" makes you more effective and more well liked (Giles, Mulac, Bradac, and Johnson 1987; Buller, LePoire, Aune, and Eloy 1992; Martin and Anderson 1995). In conversation, however, the adaptation takes place almost automatically and without pre-planning. To accommodate to the style of the audience in public speaking, however, you have to work at it. If your normal tendency is to be extremely direct and your audience has a decided preference for indirectness, you might work on tempering your customary style, making it somewhat

THE ETHICS OF Speech

The purpose of this ethics box is to suggest just a few types of speech that many people are beginning to see as unethical. For example, it's considered unethical (and it's illegal as well) to defame another person, to falsely attack his or her reputation and thus damaging it. When this attack is done in print or in pictures, it's called **libel**; when done through speech, it's called **slander**.

Whereas just decades ago it would have been considered quite respectable to use **racial, sexist,** or **homophobic language** in conversation or tell jokes at the expense of various cultural groups, today it would be considered unethical to demean another person because of that person's sex, age, race, nationality, affectional orientation, or religion. It would also be considered unethical to speak in cultural stereotypes—fixed images of groups that deny differences and that promote generally negative pictures. Public speakers are generally expected to follow a more socially conscious speech than would be expected in, say, a small group of culturally similar persons.

Sexual harassment (against either sex by either sex) would be considered unethical and a form of speech that would not be protected by the first amendment. Thus, for example, making unwanted sexual overtures to others, telling unwelcomed jokes that revolve around sex, or commenting on others' sexual anatomy in ways that would be considered offensive or unreasonable would be considered unethical.

Another form of speech that would be considered unethical is **verbal abuse**. Verbally abusing people because of their position on a particular issue or because of their cultural identification would be considered unethical.

What other forms of speech would you consider unethical?

(The next Ethics in Public Speaking box appears on page 356.)

more indirect. On the other hand, if you're normally indirect but you think directness might work better for you in a particular situation, then consider phrasing your ideas in a more direct style.

Language Varies in Abstraction

Consider the following list of terms:

- entertainment
- film
- American film
- recent American film
- *Titanic*

At the top is the general or abstract entertainment. Note that entertainment includes all the other items on the list plus various other items—television, novels, drama, comics, and so on. Film is more specific and concrete. It includes all of the items below it as well as various other items such as Indian film or Russian film. It excludes, however, all entertainment that is not film. American film is again more specific than film and excludes all films that are not American. Recent American film further limits American film to a time period. *Titanic* specifies concretely the one item to which reference is made.

Choose words from a wide range of abstractions. At times a general term may suit your needs best; at other times a more specific term may serve better. Generally, the specific term is the better choice.

The more general term—in this case, entertainment—conjures up a number of different images. One person in the audience may focus on television, another on music, another on comic books, and still another on radio. To some, "film" may bring to mind the early silent films. To others, it brings to mind postwar Italian films. To still others, it recalls Disney's animated cartoons. As you get more specific—less abstract—you more effectively guide the images that come to your listeners' minds. Specific rather than abstract language will aid you in both your informative and persuasive goals.

Language Varies in Objectivity

The best way to explain how language varies in objectivity is to introduce two new terms: denotation and connotation. The **denotative meaning** of a term is its objective meaning, the meaning you find in a dictionary. This meaning points to specific references. Thus, the denotation of the word "book" is, for example, the actual book, a collection of pages bound together between two covers. The denotative meaning of "dog" is a four-legged canine; the denotative meaning of "to kiss" is, according to the *Random House Dictionary,* "to touch or press with the lips slightly pursed in token of greeting, affection, reverence, etc."

Connotative meaning, however, is different. The connotative meaning is your affective, your emotional meaning for the term. The word "book" may signify boredom or excitement. It may recall the novel you have to read or perhaps this textbook that you're reading right now. Connotatively, "dog" may mean friendliness, warmth, and affection. "To kiss" may, connotatively, mean warmth, good feeling, and happiness.

All words (other than function words such as prepositions, conjunctions, and articles) have both denotative and connotative meaning. The relevance of this to you, as a public speaker, is considerable. Seldom do listeners misunderstand the denotative meaning of a term. When you use a term with which the audience isn't familiar, you define it and thus make sure that the term is understood. Similarly, arguments seldom center on denotation. Differences in denotative meaning are fairly easy to handle.

Differences in connotative meanings, however, pose difficulties. You may, for example, use the term "neighbor" and wish to communicate security and friendliness. To some of your listeners, however, the term may connote unwanted intrusions, sneakiness, and nosiness. Notice that both you and your listeners would surely agree that denotatively, "neighbor" means one who lives near another. What you and they disagree on—and what then leads to misunderstanding—is the connotation of the term.

Consider such terms as "politician," "jock," "lady," "police," "sex," and "religion." You can easily appreciate the varied connotative meanings that an audience may have for these terms. In public speaking, remember that your connotative meaning for a term isn't necessarily the same as that of your audience. Select words with your audience's meanings in mind.

Cultural differences add to the complexity and difficulty in accurately communicating meaning. The meaning of the word "dog" will obviously differ greatly for the person from the United States where "dog" signifies a "beloved pet," and for the person from a culture where "dog" signifies "eating delicacy." "Beef" to a person from Kansas or Texas (where cattle

Political campaign speaking—although extremely important to the welfare of the community and the country—is often quite boring. What stylistic suggestions would you offer a political candidate giving a campaign speech to your public speaking class?

provide much of the state's wealth) will mean something very different than it does to a person from India where the cow is a sacred animal.

As a speaker, consider the audience's evaluation of key terms before using them in your speech. When you're part of the audience, as in a public speaking class, you probably have a good idea of the meanings members have for various terms. When you address an audience very different from yourself, however, this prior investigation becomes crucial. When there's any doubt, select another word or qualify the word to make clear exactly what you wish to communicate.

Language Varies in Formality

Language varies from formal to informal or colloquial. Linguist Mario Pei (1956), for example, identified five levels of formality. He illustrates these (from the most formal to the most informal) with the "same" sentence.

1. Those individuals do not possess any.
2. Those men haven't any.
3. Those men haven't got any.
4. Those guys haven't/ain't got any.
5. Dem guys ain't got none.

Formal style is the style of written prose and the style of strangers speaking in a formal context. As the above examples illustrate, formal style uses longer words ("individuals" rather than "men") and infrequently used words ("possess" rather than "have" or "got").

In formal style, sentences may contain written language expressions such as "the former," "the latter," and "the aforementioned." When you're reading, you can easily locate what "the former" or what "the latter" refers to by simply looking back at the previous sentence. When listening to a speech, however, you can't go back and re-listen to the previous sentence. You have to pause to discover which item was the former and which the latter. In the process you probably lose attention and miss much of what the speaker is saying.

No single guideline for selecting an appropriate level of formality-informality can be offered. As a general rule, however, speak at a level a bit more formal than the conversational level of the audience. Therefore, use

TIPS

from professional speakers

Bear the following in mind as you make your assessment:

■ Asians are more formal than Westerners.

■ Older people are more formal than younger people.

■ People in large organizations are more formal than people in smaller organizations.

■ People in older, established organizations are more formal than people in younger, entrepreneurial organizations.

■ People in older industries (for example, mining) are more formal than people in newer industries (for example, computer technology).

David L. James, international business consultant and former director of business programs at the East-West Center in Hawaii, *The Executive Guide to Asia-Pacific Communications* (New York: Kodansha International, 1995): 30.

common words but avoid slang. Use informal constructions (for example, contractions and personal pronouns), but avoid forms that your audience would consider incorrect (for example, "ain't got none").

Also note that the expected level of formality will vary greatly with the culture of the individuals. For example, it has been shown that Bahamian students expect public speakers to be more formal than most students in the United States (Masterson, Watson, and Chichon 1991). Generally, it seems fair to say that Africans, Europeans, and Asians expect a greater degree of formality than do people from, say, Canada and the United States. In the accompanying tip David James offers a number of generalizations about formality. Does your own experience support or contradict these generalizations?

Language Varies in Accuracy

Language can reflect reality faithfully or unfaithfully. It can describe reality (as science tells us it exists) with great accuracy or distortion. For example, we can use language to describe the many degrees that exist in, say, wealth, or we can describe it inaccurately in terms of two values, rich and poor. We can discuss the ways in which language may vary in terms of the five thinking errors, central to the area of language study known as "General Semantics" (Korsybski, 1933; DeVito, 1974; Hayakawa and Hayakawa, 1990), and now so much a part of critical thinking instruction (K. Johnson, 1991). These five errors are polarization, fact-inference confusion, allness, static evaluation, and indiscrimination.

Polarization. Polarization refers to the tendency to look at the world in terms of opposites and to describe it in terms of extremes—good or bad, positive or negative, healthy or sick, intelligent or stupid, rich or poor, and so on. It's often referred to as the "fallacy of either-or." So destructive is either-or thinking that the American Psychiatric Association (1980) identifies it as one of the major behaviors characteristic of "borderline personality disorder"—a psychological disorder that lies between neurosis and psychosis and that is characterized by unstable interpersonal relationships and confusion with one's own identity.

Most people, events, and objects, of course, exist somewhere between the extremes of good and bad, health and sickness, intelligence and stupidity, wealth and poverty. Yet there's a strong tendency to view only the extremes and to categorize people, objects, and events in terms of these polar opposites.

Problems arise when polar opposites are used in inappropriate situations; for example, "That politician is either for us or against us." Note that these options don't include all possibilities. The politician may be for us in some things and against us in other things, or he or she may be neutral. Beware of speakers implying and believing that two extreme classes include all possible classes—that an individual must be pro-rebel forces or anti-rebel forces, with no other alternatives.

False words are not only evil in themselves, but they infect the soul with evil.
—Plato

Fact-Inference Confusion. You can make statements about the world you observe, and you can make statements about what you have not observed. In form or structure these statements are similar and can't be distinguished by any grammatical analysis. For example, you can say, "This proposal contains 17 pages" as well as "This proposal contains the seeds of self-destruction." Both sentences look similar in form, yet they're very different types of statements. You can observe the 17 pages, but how do you observe "the seeds of self-destruction"? Obviously, this isn't a descriptive but an inferential statement, a statement you make on the basis not only of what you observe but on what you conclude.

You may wish at this point to test your ability to distinguish facts from inferences by taking the accompanying fact-inference test based on similar tests by Haney (1973).

The greatest obstacle to discovery is not ignorance—it is the illusion of knowledge.
—Daniel J. Borstein

TEST YOURSELF
Can You Distinguish Facts from Inferences?

Read the following report and the observations based on it. Indicate whether you think the observations are true, false, or doubtful on the basis of the information presented in the report. Write T if the observation is definitely true, F if the observation is definitely false, and ? if the observation may be either true or false. Judge each observation in order. Don't reread the observations after you've indicated your judgment, and don't change any of your answers.

A well-liked college instructor had just completed making up the final examinations and had turned off the lights in the office. Just then a tall, broad figure with dark glasses appeared and demanded the examination. The professor opened the drawer. Everything in the drawer was picked up and the individual ran down the corridor. The president was notified immediately.

_____ 1. The thief was tall, broad, and wore dark glasses.
_____ 2. The professor turned off the lights.
_____ 3. A tall figure demanded the examination.
_____ 4. The examination was picked up by someone.
_____ 5. The examination was picked up by the professor.
_____ 6. A tall, broad figure appeared after the professor turned off the lights in the office.
_____ 7. The man who opened the drawer was the professor.
_____ 8. The professor ran down the corridor.
_____ 9. The drawer was never actually opened.
_____ 10. Three persons are referred to in this report.

Number 3 is True, Number 9 is False and all the rest are ? Review your answers by referring back to the story. To get you started, note that the teacher and the professor need not be the same person. Also, there might not have been a thief; the dean may have demanded to see the instructor's examination. ❏

There's nothing wrong with making inferential statements. You must make them in order to talk about much that is meaningful. The problem arises in acting as if those inferential statements are factual statements. When you hear inferential statements, treat them as inferential and not as factual. Recognize that such statements may prove to be wrong, and be aware of that possibility.

Allness. Because the world is infinitely complex, we can never know all or say all about anything—at least we can't logically say all about anything. Beware of speakers who present information as if it's all that there is or as if it's all you need to know to make up your mind: *There's only one way to save social security. Never let financial considerations get in the way of romance. Always be polite.*

Disraeli's observation, "to be conscious that you are ignorant is a great step toward knowledge," is an excellent example of a nonallness attitude. If, as a critical listener, you recognize that there's more to learn, more to see, and more to hear, you'll treat what the speaker says as part of the total picture, not the whole or the final word.

Static Evaluation. Often when you form an abstraction of something or someone—when you formulate a verbal statement about an event or person—that statement remains static and unchanging. But, the object or person to whom it refers has changed. Everything is in a constant state of change.

As critical listeners, respond to the statements of speakers as if they contained a tag that identified the time frame to which they refer. Visualize each such statement as containing a date. Look at that date and ask yourself if the statement is still true today. Thus, when a speaker says that 10 percent of the population now lives at or below the poverty level, ask yourself about the date to which that statement applies. When was the statistic compiled? Does the poverty level determined at that time adequately reflect current conditions?

Indiscrimination. Nature seems to abhor sameness at least as much as vacuums. Nowhere in the universe can you find two things that are identical; everything is unique. Language, however, provides you with common nouns (such as teacher, student, friend, enemy, war, politician, and liberal) which lead you to focus on similarities. Such nouns lead you to group all teachers together, all students together, and all politicians together. These words divert attention away from the uniqueness of each individual, each object, and each event. Indiscrimination, then, occurs when you focus on classes of individuals, objects, or events rather than on the unique individual, object, or event.

Of course, there's nothing wrong with classifying. No one would argue that classifying is unhealthy or immoral. On the contrary, it's an extremely useful method of dealing with any complex matter. Classifying helps us deal with complexity. It puts order into our thinking. The problem arises from applying some evaluative label to that class, and then using that label as an "adequate" map for each individual in the group. Put differently, indiscrimination is a denial of uniqueness.

Beware, therefore, of speakers who group large numbers of unique individuals under the same label. Beware of speakers who tell you that "Democrats are . . . " that "Catholics believe . . . " that "Mexicans always . . . ." Ask yourself, which Democrats, how many Catholics, which Mexicans, and so on.

ORAL STYLE

Oral style is a quality of spoken language that differentiates it from written language. You don't speak as you write. The words and sentences you use differ. The major reason for this difference is that you compose speech instantly. You select your words and construct your sentences as you think of your ideas. There's very little time in between the thought and the utterance. When you write, however, you compose your thoughts after considerable reflection. Even then you probably often rewrite and edit as you go along. Because of this, written language has a more formal tone. Spoken language is more informal, more colloquial.

Generally, spoken language consists of shorter, simpler, and more familiar words than does written language. There's more qualification in speech than in writing. For example, when speaking you probably make greater use of such expressions as *although, however, perhaps,* and the like. When writing, you probably edit these out.

Spoken language has a greater number of self-reference terms (terms that refer to the speaker herself or himself): *I, me, our, us,* and *you.*

Spoken language also has a greater number of "allness" terms such as *all, none, every, always, never.* You're probably more careful when you write to edit out such allness terms when you realize that such terms are probably not very descriptive of reality.

Spoken language has more pseudo-quantifying terms (for example, *many, much, very, lots*), and terms that include the speaker as part of the observation (for example, *it seems to me that . . . or as I see it . . .*). Further, speech contains more verbs and adverbs; writing contains more nouns and adjectives.

Spoken and written language not only do differ, they should differ. The listener hears a speech only once; therefore, speech must be *instantly intelligible.* The reader, on the other hand, can reread an essay or look up an unfamiliar word. The reader can spend as much time as he or she wishes with the written page. The listener, however, must move at the pace set by the speaker. The reader may reread a sentence or paragraph if there's a temporary attention lapse. The listener doesn't have this option.

For the most part, it's wise to use "oral style" in your public speeches. The public speech, however, is composed much like a written essay. There is considerable thought and deliberation and much editing and restyling. Because of this, you'll need to devote special effort to retaining and polishing your oral style. The following unit presents specific suggestions for achieving this goal.

To further clarify the differences, examine the following contrasting examples of "Oral and Written Style."

Simplicity is the essence of the great, the true and the beautiful in art.
—George Sand

Written Style

There are three major ways of lying that have been identified. The omission of information that is true is referred to as concealment. An example of this type of lie would occur when an individual answers one's parents, who ask "What did you do last night?", with the phrase, "Listened to records," but without any reference to drinking.

Oral Style

We can identify three major ways of lying: concealment, falsification, and misidentification. First, in concealment you omit true information. A good example of this occurs when your parents ask, "What did you do last night?" If you answer "listened to records" but omit "drinking," then you've lied by concealment. Second, in falsifica-

To present false information as if it were the truth would be considered an instance of falsification. An example of this latter type of lie would be if someone who owed money said, "The check is in the mail" when it really was not. Misidentifying the causes of an emotion, as in saying, "I'm not crying; I just got something in my eye," would be considered an example of misdirection.

tion you present false information as if it were true. A popular example of falsification is when your friend who borrowed money tells you, "The check is in the mail" when it isn't. Third, in misdirection you misidentify the causes of an emotion. For example, let's say you don't want others to know you're crying. You might lie by misdirection and say, "I just got something in my eye."

Note some of the differences between these two styles. The oral style version uses the active voice; the written style version relies on the more indirect passive voice. In the oral style version we included a preview of the three types of lies to help the audience follow the discussion. No such preview is presented in the written style version, largely because the reader can easily glance ahead or back for orientation. In the oral version the sentences are shorter, and there are guide phrases to help the listener follow the discussion (for example, first, second, third).

The language in the oral version is more informal and more personal; it makes use of personal pronouns (we, you) and contractions (you've, isn't, you're). It also involves the listener in the examples (your parents, your friend borrows money, you don't want others to know you're crying).

The written version depersonalizes the examples and makes use of "written style" expressions such as "the individual," "one," and "latter." Note, too, that in the oral version the key terms (concealment, falsification, and misdirection) are repeated to help the audience remember and follow the examples. Further, the oral version uses parallel structure as you can see in these three sentences used in the oral version:

1. First, concealment involves omitting true information.
2. Second, falsification involves presenting false information as if it were true.
3. Third, misdirection involves misidentifying the causes of an emotion.

Notice, for example, that

- guide phrases begin each sentence—first, second, third;
- key terms are introduced next—concealment, falsification, misdirection;
- the verb "involves" is used in all three sentences;
- the gerund (the -ing form of the verb) is used to begin the defining phrase.

THE HUMOROUS STYLE

It's important to understand the role of humor in public speaking as a speaker (to use it more effectively), as a listener (to better appreciate the speaker's strategies), and as a critic (to better evaluate and judge the speech). Although humor is an important element in some public speeches, it's not a necessary element, nor is it always desirable. It's effective in some situations, with some speakers, and with some audiences. Analyze each specific speaking sit-

A difference of taste in jokes is a great strain on the affections.
—George Eliot

uation, then make a judgment as to whether or not to try humor. It's extremely difficult to use humor effectively. At the same time, it may be extremely effective in the right situation. With this disclaimer, consider humor—its role in public speaking and some guidelines for its effective use.

Some writers would suggest that humor is more appropriate in some cultures than in others, that certain cultures have a sense of humor and others don't. Humor is probably a universal in all cultures, but each culture may have different rules as to when and where humor is appropriate (Axtell 1999). At business meetings in some cultures humor *may* be inappropriate, but in some American high tech corporate cultures, it *may* be both appropriate and expected. Questions about the cultural appropriateness of humor should probably be resolved by omitting it. You can err less by not using humor than by using it inappropriately. So, when in doubt, leave it out.

Humor can serve a number of important purposes, however. In a speech that is long and somber, humor breaks up the mood and lightens the tone. At times, humor serves as a creative and useful transition. Humor is excellent support material. It can help you emphasize a point, crystallize an idea, or rebut an opposing argument.

Some of you are probably excellent humorists. You can look at a situation, find the humor in it, and convey this humor to an audience easily and clearly. Others are probably ineffective humorists. In between these extremes lie most of us. All of us, however, could probably improve the humor in our communications. Effective humor in public speaking is relevant, brief, spontaneous, tasteful, and appropriate.

Relevance

Like any other type of supporting material, the humorous anecdote or story must be germane to your topic and your purpose. If it's not, don't use it. If you must go to exceptional lengths to make the story fit, or if you have to seriously distort the proposition it should support, then reconsider

TIPS
from professional speakers

Don't tell jokes. You are (probably) not a comedian, and if you tell a series of set "funny stories," you are almost sure to fail. This does not mean you should avoid humor. In fact you should use humor whenever possible, but it should arise naturally from the context of who you are, where you are, and what you have to say. That is what "wit" is all about.

Charles Osgood, CBS news correspondent, *Osgood on Speaking: How to Think on Your Feet Without Falling on Your Face* (New York: Morrow, 1988): 51.

How would you characterize the humor of Jim Carrey?

your material. Here's an example of humor that is especially relevant for a speech on relationship communication (Hensley 1992, p. 115):

A woman went to an attorney and said, "I want to divorce my husband." Lawyer: Do you have any grounds? Woman: About 10 acres. Lawyer: Do you have a grudge? Woman: No, just a carport. Lawyer: Does your husband beat you up? Woman: No, I get up about an hour before he does every morning. Lawyer: Why do you want a divorce? Woman: We just can't seem to communicate.

Brevity

Humor works best in public speaking when it's brief. If it occupies too great a portion of your speech, the audience may question your sincerity or seriousness. Humor in special occasion speeches, however, may logically occupy a greater part of the entire speech than in informative or persuasive speeches. Here, for example, Amy Cram, a student from Casper College (Schnoor, 1997, p. 157) uses humor, very briefly, to introduce her topic of sex education:

One of my father's favorite sayings is "Remember when sex was safe and motorcycles were dangerous?" While his fondness over some of his sayings leaves something to be desired, there is a certain amount of truth in it.

And here professional comedian Bob Newhart (1997), in a speech given at the commencement of The Catholic University of America, uses humor in creating a bond with the audience.

I'm honored and moved to be asked to be the 1997 commencement speaker. These may appear to be tears but they are actually allergies. My son graduated from here in 1989 with a degree in English literature, specializing in the poetry of Yeats. As you all know, when you pick up the classified pages you just see page after page for jobs for Yeats scholars.

Spontaneity

Humor works best when it seems spontaneous. If humor appears studied or too well practiced, it may lose its effectiveness. In telling a humorous anecdote, for example, always keep your eyes on the audience, not on your notes. Never, never read your punch line. At the same time that humor should appear spontaneous, recognize the difficulty of getting a laugh. So, test your humor on your friends or family first to gauge their reactions and improve your delivery.

Don't telegraph your humorous material by long prefaces or by telling the audience that you're going to tell a funny story—you'll be lost if it fails to get the expected laugh. Let the humor of the story speak for itself.

Try also to develop a spontaneous retort just in case your humorous story turns out to be a dud. Don't look surprised, hurt, or as though you've lost control of yourself and your material. Instead develop a clever response.

TIPS
from professional speakers

- Don't embarrass other people (unless it is a formal roast).
- Don't use ethnic or racial jokes.
- Don't use dialects.
- Don't make jokes about religion.
- Avoid any scatological or profane language.

Roger E. Axtell, professional speaker and intercultural communication expert, *Do's and Taboos of Public Speaking: How to Get Those Butterflies Flying in Formation* (New York: Wiley, 1992): 86.

Standup comedians such as David Letterman and Jay Leno are masters of these rejoinders, which are often more humorous than their best jokes.

Tastefulness

Humor should be tasteful. Reject vulgar and "off-color" expressions. Coarseness is never a substitute for wit. If there's even the smallest possibility that your humor might make your listeners uncomfortable, then eliminate it. Avoid poking fun at any group, race, religion, nationality, sex, sexual minority, occupation, or age group. Especially avoid ethnic jokes; they have no place in a public speech.

At the same time, be careful of telling jokes at your own expense, of poking too much fun at yourself. Although we are often our own best foils, in a public speaking situation poking fun at yourself can damage your credibility. The audience may see you as a clown rather than as a responsible advocate.

Avoid sarcasm and ridicule. It's rarely humorous and it's often difficult to predict how an audience will respond, Your listeners may well wonder when your sarcasm or ridicule will be directed at them.

Appropriateness

Like all forms of support, humor must be appropriate to you as the speaker. Tell jokes in your own style—not in the style of Roseanne or Jay Leno. Invest time in developing a style that is your own and with which you're comfortable.

Similarly, use humor that is appropriate to your audience and to the occasion. Jokes about babies or anecdotes about the singles' scene are not likely to prove effective with a group of retired teamsters. The topic of the joke and its implications must be relevant and appropriate to all elements of the public speaking act.

TIPS
from professional speakers

If you have any doubts about a joke and how well it will go over, don't tell it. And steer clear of any jokes that are based on age, race, or sex. Otherwise, you risk offending and alienating others.

Connie Brown Glaser (communication consultant) and Barbara Steinberg Smalley (freelance writer), *More Power to You! How Women Can Communicate Their Way to Success* (New York: Warner Books, 1992): 89–90.

UNIT IN BRIEF

Language Can Vary on a Number of Dimensions:	Direct and indirect. Abstract and specific. Objective and subjective. Formal and informal. Accurate and inaccurate (polarization, fact-inference confusion, allness, static evaluation, and indiscrimination).
Compared to Written Style, Oral Style Is Characterized by:	Shorter, simpler, and more familiar words. More self-reference and "allness" terms. More pseudoquantifying terms and terms including the speaker. More verbs and adverbs and can be achieved by incorporating the above characteristics and by using short sentences, guide phrases, informal terms, sentences that involve the listener, and parallel structure.

Humor in a Public Speech Is Most Effective When It's:	Relevant to your topic and your purpose. Brief. Spontaneous or seemingly spontaneous. Tasteful rather than vulgar, off-color, or sarcastic. Appropriate to you as a speaker, to your audience, to the topic, and to the occasion.

THINKING CRITICALLY ABOUT STYLE IN PUBLIC SPEAKING

REVIEWING KEY TERMS AND CONCEPTS IN STYLE IN PUBLIC SPEAKING

1. Review and define the key terms used in this unit:

   ❑ language directness (p. 303)
   ❑ language abstraction (p. 305)
   ❑ language objectivity (p. 306)
   ❑ denotation (p. 306)
   ❑ connotation (p. 306)
   ❑ language formality (p. 307)
   ❑ language accuracy (p. 308)

   ❑ polarization (p. 308)
   ❑ fact-inference confusion (p. 308)
   ❑ allness (p. 310)
   ❑ static evaluation (p. 310)
   ❑ indiscrimination (p. 310)
   ❑ oral style (p. 310)

2. Review and explain the key concepts discussed in this unit:

   ■ How does language work in terms of directness, abstraction, objectivity, formality, and accuracy?
   ■ What are the major differences between oral and written style?
   ■ What functions does humor serve in public speaking? How might it best be used?

DEVELOPING STYLISTIC STRATEGIES

1. John has this great joke that is only tangentially related to his speech topic. But the joke is so great that it will immediately get the audience actively involved in his speech and this, he thinks, outweighs the fact that it isn't integrally related to the speech. John asks your advice; what do you suggest?

2. Mary comes from a background very different from the students in this class—Mary's family dressed for dinner, women were encouraged to be accepting rather than assertive, and politeness was emphasized above all else. If Mary communicates this image of herself, she thinks that the class will see her as an outsider as a speaker but also as a person. She wonders if there's anything she can do in her speeches to present herself in a light that others will respond to positively. What advice would you give Mary?

EVALUATING STYLE IN PUBLIC SPEECHES

1. Read a speech and focus especially on the use of language. How would you classify the language in terms of directness, abstraction, objectivity, formality, and accuracy? Can you identify specific terms and phrases that illustrate and support your classification?

2. Look over one of your previous speeches. Can you identify at least five phrases or sentences that can be restyled to be made more effective?

USING TECHNOLOGY IN STYLING PUBLIC SPEECHES

1. If you have any doubts as to the preferred gender-free term to use, visit http://www.eecis.udel.edu/~chao/gfp/ for an extensive FAQ file on gender and language.

2. Whether or not you speak English as a second language, visit a Web site devoted to this (for example, http://www.lang.uiuc.edu/r-li5/esl/). What can you learn from this Web site that could supplement what was covered in this unit?

3. Visit the language and culture listserv, a group that focuses on social interaction and has much of interest to the public speaker. To access:

   ■ mail to: listproc@cs.uchicago.edu
   ■ body: subscribe language-culture
   ■ Your first name Your last name

PRACTICALLY SPEAKING

15.1 Short Speech Technique

Prepare and deliver a two-minute speech in which you:

a. tell a humorous story.

b. describe an object in highly abstract and then highly concrete language.

c. describe the language of a noted personality (television, politics, arts, etc.).

d. describe an incident in highly objective and highly subjective language.

e. describe the humorous style of a particular comedian or style of comedy.

15.2 Making Concepts Specific

One of the major skills in public speaking is learning to make your ideas specific so that your listeners will understand exactly what you want them to understand.

Here are fifteen sentences. Rewrite each of the sentences making the italicized terms more specific.

1. The *woman* walked up the *hill* with her *children*.
2. The *teacher* was *discussing economics*.
3. The *player scored*.
4. The *teenager* was *listening* to a *record*.
5. No one in the *city* thought the *mayor* was right.
6. The *girl* and the *boy* each received *lots* of *presents*.
7. I read the *review* of the *movie*.
8. The *couple* rented a *great car*.
9. The *detective* wasn't much help in solving the *crime*.
10. The *children* were playing an old *game*.
11. The *dinosaur approached* the *baby*.
12. He *walked* up the *steep hill*.
13. *They* played *games*.
14. The *cat climbed* the *fence*.
15. The *large house* is in the *valley*.

Unscrambled Outline on Friendship (Practically Speaking 14.2, page 301.)

Here's one way—there may be others—in which these statements could have been arranged into a coherent outline:

Introduction

I. Friendship is one of the most important of our interpersonal relationships. (5)

II. Friendship is vital to all of us. (13)

III. In order to understand friendships we need to see what a friendship is and its stages of development. (4)

Body

I. Friendship is an interpersonal relationship between two persons that is characterized by mutual positive regard. (2)

II. Friendships develop through various stages. (7)

   A. We meet. (3)

   B. We develop an acquaintanceship. (1)

   C. We develop a casual friendship. (9)

   D. We develop a close relationship. (12)

   E. We develop an intimate relationship. (6)

Conclusion

I. Friendship—an interpersonal relationship characterized by mutual positive regard—is one of our most important assets. (11)

II. Friendships don't develop full-blown but rather go through various stages—from the initial meeting to intimate friendship. (8)

III. By understanding friendship we will be in a better position to develop and maintain productive and enjoyable friendships. (10)

UNIT 16

Effective Style in Public Speaking

UNIT CONTENTS	UNIT OBJECTIVES
Choosing Words	*After completing this unit, you should be able to:* Define and identify the suggestions for achieving clarity, vividness, appropriateness, a personal style, and forcefulness.
Phrasing Sentences	Identify the specific suggestions for constructing effective sentences.
Making Your Speech Easy to Remember	Explain the principles for making your speech easy to remember.

Now that the general principles of language and style are understood, specific suggestions can be identified for improving your speech style.

CHOOSING WORDS

The words you use in your public speeches should be chosen carefully. Choose words to achieve clarity, vividness, appropriateness, a personal style, and forcefulness.

Clarity

Clarity in speaking style should be your primary goal. Here are some guidelines to help you make your speech clear.

Be Economical. Don't waste words. The best way to achieve economy is to avoid redundancies and meaningless words. Notice the redundancies in the following expressions:

at 9 A.M. *in the morning*

we *first* began the discussion

the full *and complete* report

I *myself personally*

blue *in color*

*over*exaggerate

you, *members of the audience*

clearly unambiguous

approximately 10 inches *or so*

cash *money*

By withholding the italicized terms you eliminate unnecessary words. You thus move closer to a more economical and clearer style.

As to the adjective: When in doubt, strike it out.
—Mark Twain

Use Specific Terms and Numbers. Picture these items:

- a bracelet
- a gold bracelet
- a gold bracelet with a diamond clasp
- a braided gold bracelet with a diamond clasp

Notice that as we get more and more specific, we get a clearer and more detailed picture. Be specific. Don't say "dog" when you want your listeners to picture a St. Bernard. Don't say "car" when you want them to picture a limousine. Don't say "movie" when you want them to think of *Citizen Kane.*

The same is true of numbers. Don't say "earned a good salary" if you mean "earned $90,000 a year." Don't say "taxes will go up" when you mean "taxes will increase 22 percent." Don't say "the defense budget was enormous" when you mean "the defense budget was $17 billion."

Use Guide Phrases. Listening to a public speech is difficult work. Assist your listeners by using guide phrases to help them see that you're moving from one idea to another. Use phrases such as "now that we have seen how. . . , let us consider how. . . ," and "my next argument. . . ." Terms such as *first, second, and also, although,* and *however* will help your audience follow your line of thinking.

Guide phrases are especially useful when your listeners aren't native speakers of the language you're speaking. And, of course, guide phrases also prove valuable if you're speaking in a language that you have not fully mastered. The guide phrases help compensate for the lack of language and speech similarity between speaker and audience.

Use Short, Familiar Terms. Generally, favor the short word over the long one. Favor the familiar word over the unfamiliar word. Favor the more commonly used term over the rarely used term. Here are a few examples:

Poor choices	Better choices
innocuous	harmless
elucidate	clarify
utilize	use
ascertain	find out
erstwhile	former
eschew	avoid
expenditure	cost or expense

Use Repetition and Restatement. Repetition and restatement will help listeners follow what you're saying and will make your speech clearer and more easily understood. These are not the same as redundancy, which involve using unnecessary words that don't communicate any information. Repetition means repeating something in exactly the same way, usually at different points in your speech. This will help the audience better remember the idea and remind them of how it's connected with what

TIPS from professional speakers

Avoid showy language. Speak the way you talk in everyday conversation. Your everyday speech is spontaneous, new, like freshly baked bread. Speech is alive. It has music to it. In one of his speeches, F. D. Roosevelt changed "We are endeavoring to construct a more inclusive society" to the way it would be spoken: "We're going to make a country where no one is left out." Say it the easy way, "trippingly on the tongue."

Elayne Snyder, corporate consultant and speech coach, *Persuasive Business Speaking* (New York: American Management Association, 1990): 145.

you're now saying. Restatement means rephrasing an idea or statement in different words. This is especially helpful when the idea is new or even moderately complex. Hearing the same idea expressed in two different ways helps clarify the concept.

Another type of restatement is the internal summary—periodic summary statements or reviews of subsections of your speech. These summaries help the audience appreciate the speech as a progression of ideas and show them how one idea leads to another. Be careful not to overuse these techniques; you don't want to bore the audience by repeating material that doesn't need to be repeated.

Distinguish Between Commonly Confused Words. Many words, because they sound alike or are used in similar situations, are commonly confused. Try the accompanying self-test; it covers 10 of the most frequently confused words.

TEST YOURSELF
Can You Distinguish Between Commonly Confused Words?

Underline the word in parentheses that you would use in each sentence.

_____ 1. She (accepted, excepted) the award and thanked everyone (accept, except) the producer.

_____ 2. The teacher (affected, effected) his students greatly and will now (affect, effect) an entirely new curriculum.

_____ 3. Are you deciding (between, among) red and green or (between, among) red, green, and blue?

_____ 4. I (can, may) scale the mountain but I (can, may) not reveal its hidden path.

_____ 5. The table was (cheap, inexpensive) but has great style; the chairs cost a fortune but look (cheap, inexpensive).

_____ 6. We (discover, invent) uncharted lands but (discover, invent) computer programs.

_____ 7. He was (explicit, implicit) about his past experiences and discussed them at length, but because he was (explicit, implicit) concerning his present feelings, I never knew what to say.

_____ 8. She (implied, inferred) that she'd seek a divorce; we can only (imply, infer) her reasons.

_____ 9. The wedding was (tasteful, tasty) and the food most (tasteful, tasty).

_____10. The student seemed (disinterested, uninterested) in the lecture. The teacher was (disinterested, uninterested) in who received what grades.

Here are the principles that govern the correct usage for these 10 pairs of terms:

1. Use *accept* to mean to receive and *except* to mean with the exclusion of.
2. Use *to affect* to mean to have an effect or to influence, and *to effect* to mean to produce a result.
3. Use *between* when referring to two items and *among* when referring to more than two items.
4. Use *can* to refer to ability and *may* to refer to permission.
5. Use *cheap* to refer to something that is inferior and *inexpensive* to something that costs little.

6. Use *discover* to refer to the act of finding something out or to learn something previously unknown and use *invent* to refer to the act of originating something new.
7. Use *explicit* to mean specific and *implicit* to mean the act of expressing something without actually stating it.
8. Use *to imply* to mean to state indirectly and *to infer* to mean to draw a conclusion.
9. Use *tasteful* to refer to one's good taste and use *tasty* to refer to something that tastes good.
10. Use *uninterested* to mean a lack of interest and use *disinterested* to mean objective or unbiased.

What other commonly confused words can you think of?

Assess Idioms Carefully. Idioms are expressions that are unique to a specific language and whose meaning cannot be deduced from the individual words used. Expressions such as "to kick the bucket" and "doesn't have a leg to stand on" are idioms; you either know the meaning of the expression or you don't. You can't figure out an idiom's meaning from only a knowledge of the individual words.

The positive side of idioms is that they give your speech a casual and informal style; they make your speech sound like a speech and not like a written essay. The negative side of idioms is that they create problems for listeners who are not native speakers of your language. Many will simply not understand the meaning of your idioms. This problem is especially important because audiences are becoming increasingly intercultural and because the number of idioms we use is extremely high. If you're not convinced of this, read through any of the speeches in this text, especially in an intercultural group, and underline all idioms. You will no doubt have underlined a great deal more than most people would have suspected.

Vividness

Select words that make your ideas vivid and come alive in the minds of your listeners.

Use Active Verbs. Favor verbs that communicate activity rather than passivity. The verb "to be," in all its forms—is, are, was, were, will be—is relatively inactive. Try using verbs of action instead. Rather than saying "The teacher was in the middle of the crowd," say "The teacher stood in the middle of the crowd." Instead of saying "The report was on the President's desk for three days," try "The report rested (or slept) on the President's desk for three days." Instead of saying "Management will be here tomorrow," consider "Management will descend on us tomorrow" or "Management jets in tomorrow."

Use Strong Verbs. The verb is the strongest part of your sentence. Instead of saying "He walked through the forest," consider such terms as "wandered," "prowled," "rambled," or "roamed." Consider whether one of these might not better suit your intended meaning. Consult a thesaurus for any verb you suspect might be weak.

TIPS
from professional speakers

Of all the language problems in international communication, idiomatic usage ranks almost at the top of the list. *Idioms* are words and expressions peculiar to a language. They often have a meaning that differs from their logical or grammatical meaning and—here's the worse part—can't be translated literally into another language without confusing or losing the meaning. You know what that means, right? *Don't use idioms.*

Mary A. DeVries, expert on international communications, *Internationally Yours: Writing and Communicating Successfully in Today's Global Marketplace.* (Boston: Houghton Mifflin, 1994): 83.

A good guide to identifying weak verbs is to look at your use of adverbs. If you use lots of adverbs, you may be using them to strengthen weak verbs. Consider cutting out the adverbs and substituting stronger verbs.

Use Figures of Speech. Figures of speech help achieve vividness. Figures of speech are stylistic devices that have been a part of rhetoric since ancient times. Table 16.1 contains 10 figures you might use in your speech, along with definitions and examples.

Use Imagery. Appeal to the senses, especially our visual, auditory, and tactile senses. Make us see, hear, and feel what you're talking about.

Visual Imagery. In describing people or objects, create images your listeners can see. When appropriate, describe such visual qualities as height, weight, color, size, shape, length, and contour. Let your audience see the

Never use a metaphor, simile, or other figure of speech which you're used to seeing in print. Never use a long word when a short one will do. If it is possible to cut a word out, always cut it out. Never use the passive when you can use the active. Never use a foreign phrase, a scientific word, or a jargon word if you can think of an everyday English equivalent. Break any of these rules sooner than say anything outright barbarous.
—George Orwell

TABLE 16.1 Figures of Speech

Can you create an original expression using each of these 10 figures?

Type	Definition	Example
Alliteration	Repetition of the same initial sound in two or more words.	fifty famous flavors; the cool calculating leader
Antithesis	Presentation of contrary ideas in parallel form	my loves are many; my enemies are few; "It was the best of times, it was the worst of times." (Dickens)
Climax	The arrangement of individual phrases or sentences in ascending order of forcefulness.	as a child he lied, as a youth he stole, as a man he killed
Hyperbole	The use of extreme exaggeration.	he cried like a faucet; your obedient and humble servant; I'm so hungry I could eat a whale
Irony	The use of a word or sentence whose literal meaning is the opposite of that which is intended.	a teacher handing back failing examinations might say, "So pleased to see how many of you studied so hard."
Metaphor	The comparison of two unlike things.	she's a lion when she wakes up; all nature is science; he's a real bulldozer
Metonymy	The substitution of a name for a title with which it's closely associated.	"City Hall issued the following news release" where "City Hall" is used instead of "the mayor" or the "city council"
Personification	The attribution of human characteristics to inanimate objects.	This room cries for activity. My car is thirsty and wants a drink.
Rhetorical question	the use of a question to make a statement or to produce a desired effect rather than secure an answer.	Do you want to be popular? Do you want to get well?
Simile	The comparison of two unlike objects by using "like" or "as"	he charges in like a bull; the manager is as gentle as a lamb

sweat pouring down the faces of the coal miners; let them see the short, overweight executive in a pin-striped suit smoking a cigar.

Here Stephanie Kaplan (Reynolds and Schnoor, 1991), a student from the University of Wisconsin, uses visual imagery to describe the AIDS Quilt:

> *The Names Project is quite simply a quilt: Larger than 10 football fields, and composed of over 9,000 unique 3-feet by 6-feet panels each bearing a name of an individual who has died of AIDS. The panels have been made in homes across the country by the friends, lovers, and families of AIDS victims.*

Auditory Imagery. Appeal to our sense of hearing by using terms that describe sounds. Let your listeners hear the car screeching, the wind whistling, the bells chiming, the angry professor roaring.

Tactile Imagery. Use terms referring to temperature, texture, and touch to create tactile imagery. Let your listeners feel the cool water running over their bodies and the punch of the fighter; let them feel the smooth skin of the newborn baby.

These suggestions for using imagery were offered as aids to making your speech more vivid than it would normally be in, say, conversation. However, there's some evidence to show that too many vivid images may actually make your speech less memorable and less persuasive than it would be without them (Frey and Eagly, 1993). When images are too vivid, they divert the brain from following a logically presented series of thoughts or arguments. The brain focuses on these extremely vivid images and loses the speaker's train of thought. The advice, therefore, is to use vividness when it adds clarity to your ideas. When there's the suspicion that your listeners may concentrate on the imagery rather than the idea, drop the imagery.

Appropriateness

Use language that is appropriate to you as the speaker. Also, use language that is appropriate to your audience, the occasion, and the speech topic. Here are some general guidelines to help you achieve this quality.

Speak on the Appropriate Level of Formality. The most effective public speaking style is less formal than the written essay but more formal than conversation. One way to achieve an informal style is to use contractions. Say "don't" instead of "do not," "I'll" instead of "I shall," and "wouldn't" instead of "would not." Contractions give a public speech the sound and rhythm of conversation, a quality that most listeners react to favorably.

Use personal pronouns rather than impersonal expressions. Say "I found" instead of "it has been found," or "I will present three arguments" instead of "three arguments will be presented."

Do remember, as noted in the previous unit, that the expected and desirable level of formality will vary greatly from one culture to another.

Avoid Unfamiliar Terms. Avoid using terms the audience doesn't know. Avoid foreign and technical terms unless you're certain the audience is familiar with them. Similarly, avoid jargon (the technical vocabulary of a specialized field) unless you're sure the meanings are clear to your listeners. Some acronyms (NATO, UN, NOW, and CORE) are probably familiar to most audiences; most, however, are not. When you wish to use any of these types of expressions, explain fully their meaning to the audience.

Avoid Slang. Avoid offending your audience with language that embarrasses them or makes them think you have little respect for them. Although your listeners may themselves use such expressions, they often resent their use by public speakers.

Avoid Racist, Sexist, and Heterosexist Terms. According to Andrea Rich (1974), "any language that, through a conscious or unconscious attempt by the user, places a particular racial or ethnic group in an inferior position is racist." Racist language expresses racist attitudes. Racist language emphasizes differences rather than similarities and separates rather than unites members of different cultures.

Avoid referring to culturally different groups with terms that carry negative connotations or picturing them in stereotypical and negative ways. At the same time, avoid slighting members who may represent only a minority of your audience. Include references in fairness to all groups in your examples and illustrations.

Use nonsexist language. Use "human" instead of "man" to include both sexes; use "she and he" instead of "he"; use "police officer" instead of "policeman" and "firefighter" instead of "fireman."

Avoid gender role stereotyping. Avoid, for example, making the hypothetical elementary school teacher female and the college professor male. Avoid referring to doctors as male and nurses as female. Avoid noting the gender of a professional with terms such as "female doctor" or "male nurse." When you're referring to a specific doctor or nurse, the person's gender will become clear when you use the appropriate pronoun.

Avoid heterosexist language, language that disparages gay men and lesbians. As with racist language, we see heterosexism in the derogatory terms used for lesbians and gay men as well as in more subtle forms of language usage. For example, when you qualify a profession—as in "gay athlete" or "lesbian doctor"—you're in effect stating that athletes and doctors are not normally gay or lesbian.

Still another instance of heterosexism is the presumption of heterosexuality. Usually, people assume the person they are talking to or about is heterosexual. Usually, they are correct since the majority of the population is heterosexual. At the same time, however, note that it denies the lesbian and gay identity an appropriate legitimacy. The practice is similar to the presumption of whiteness and maleness that we have made significant inroads in eliminating.

Once brought to awareness, most people recognize the moral legitimacy of using language that is inclusive, language that is nonracist, sexist, or heterosexist. There are also rhetorical reasons for avoiding such language:

- It's likely to offend a significant part of your audience.
- It's likely to draw attention to itself and away from what you're saying.
- It's likely to reflect negatively on your credibility.

Avoid Ethnic Expressions (Generally). Ethnic expressions are words and phrases that are peculiar to a particular ethnic group. At times these expres-

Why are such expressions as "female physician" or "gay doctor" offensive? What do such expressions imply? What impression do you get of a speaker who uses such expressions?

sions are known only by members of the ethnic group, and at other times they are known more widely but still recognized as ethnic expressions.

In speaking to a multicultural audience it's generally best to avoid ethnic expressions unless they're integral to your speech and you explain them. Such expressions are often interpreted as exclusionist; they highlight the connection between the speaker and the members of that particular ethnic group and the lack of connection between the speaker and all others who are not members of that ethnic group. And, of course, ethnic expressions should never be used if you're not a member of the ethnic group.

If, on the other hand, you're speaking to an audience from one ethnic group and if you're also a member, then such expressions are fine. Politicians who run in districts in which they and the voters are of the

LISTEN TO THIS How to Listen without Racist, Sexist, or Heterosexist Attitudes

Just as racist, sexist, and heterosexist attitudes will influence your language, they also influence your listening. In this type of listening you hear what the speaker is saying filtered through your stereotypes of sex, race, or affectional orientation.

When you dismiss a valid argument or attribute validity to an invalid argument, when you refuse to give someone a fair hearing, or when you give less credibility (or more credibility) to a speaker because the speaker is of a particular sex, race, or affectional orientation, you're practicing sexist, racist, or heterosexist listening. Put differently, sexist, racist, or heterosexist listening occurs when you listen differently to a person because

of his or her sex, race, or affectional orientation when these characteristics are irrelevant to the communication. It's sexist listening to assume that only one sex has anything to say that's worth hearing or that what one sex says can be discounted without a fair hearing. The same is true when listening through a person's race or affectional orientation.

Can you identify instances where you have engaged in sexist, racist, or heterosexist listening? Have others ever listened to you unfairly because of your sex, race, or affectional orientation?

(The next Listen to This box appears on page 341.)

same national origin or language community will frequently use ethnic terms or even phrases in the native language of the audience. In these cases, ethnic expressions may well prove effective since they are part of the common language of speaker and audience and will help to stress your own similarities with the audience.

Use Preferred Cultural Identifiers. Perhaps the best way to avoid sexism, heterosexism, and racism is to learn the cultural identifiers to use (and not to use) in talking about members of different cultures. As always, when in doubt, find out. The preferences and many of the specific examples identified here are drawn largely from the findings of the Task Force on Bias-Free Language of the Association of American University Presses (Schwartz 1995). Do realize that not everyone would agree with these recommendations; they're presented here—in the words of the Task Force—"to encourage sensitivity to usages that may be imprecise, misleading, and needlessly offensive" (Schwartz 1995, p. ix). They're not presented so that you can "catch" someone being "politically incorrect" or label someone "culturally insensitive."

Generally: the term "girl" should only be used to refer to very young females and is equivalent to "boy." Neither term should be used for people older than, say, 13 or 14. "Girl" is never used to refer to a grown woman, nor is "boy" used to refer to persons in blue collar positions, as it once was. "Lady" is negatively evaluated by many because it connotes the stereotype of the prim and proper woman. "Woman" or "young woman" is preferred. "Older person" is preferred to "elder," "elderly," "senior," or "senior citizen" (which technically refers to someone older than 65).

Generally: "Gay" is the preferred term to refer to a man who has an affectional orientation for another man and "lesbian" is the preferred term for a woman who has an affectional orientation for other women. [*Lesbian* means "homosexual woman" so the phrase *lesbian woman* is redundant.] This preference for the term *lesbian* is not universal among homosexual women; in one survey, for example, 58 percent preferred "lesbian" and 34 percent preferred "gay" (Lever 1995). "Homosexual" refers to both gay men and lesbians but more often to a sexual orientation to members of one's own sex. "Gay" and "lesbian" refer to a life style and not just to sexual orientation. "Gay" as a noun, although widely used, may prove offensive in some contexts, for example, "We have two gays on the team." Although used within the gay community in an effort to remove the negative stigma through frequent usage, the term *queer*—as in "queer power"— is often resented when used by outsiders. Because most scientific thinking holds that one's sexuality is genetically determined rather than being a matter of choice, the term "sexual orientation" rather than "sexual preference" or "sexual status" (which is also vague) is preferred.

Generally: Most African Americans prefer "African American" to "black" (Hecht, Ribeau, and Collier 1993) though *black* is often used with *white*. *Black* is also used in a variety of other contexts (for example, Department of Black and Puerto Rican Studies, the *Journal of Black History*, and Black History Month). The American Psychological Association recommends that both terms be capitalized, but the *Chicago Manual of Style* (the manual used by most newspapers and publishing houses) recommends using lower case letters. The terms "negro" and "colored," although used in the names of some organizations (for example, the United Negro College Fund and the National Association for the Advancement of Colored People) are not used outside of these contexts.

"White" is generally used to refer to those whose roots are in European cultures and who are not Hispanics. On the analogy of *African American* comes the phrase "European American." Few European Americans, however, would want to be called that; most would prefer their national origins emphasized, for example, *German American* or *Greek American.* This preference may well change as Europe moves into a more cohesive and united entity. "People of color"—a more literary sounding term appropriate perhaps to public speaking but sounding awkward in most conversations—is preferred to "nonwhite" which implies that whiteness is the norm and nonwhiteness is a deviation from that norm. The same is true of the term "non-Christian."

Generally: "Hispanic" is used to refer to anyone who identifies himself or herself as belonging to a Spanish-speaking culture. "Latina" (female) and "Latino" (male) refer to those whose roots are in one of the Latin American countries, for example, the Dominican Republic, Nicaragua, or Guatemala. "Hispanic American" refers to those U.S. residents whose ancestry is a Spanish culture and includes Mexican, Caribbean, and Central and South Americans. In emphasizing a Spanish heritage the term is really inadequate in referring to those large numbers in the Caribbean and in South America whose origins are French or Portuguese. "Chicana" (female) and "Chicano" (male) refer to those with roots in Mexico, though it often connotes a nationalist attitude (Jandt 1999) and is considered offensive by many Mexican Americans. "Mexican American" is preferred.

"Inuk" (pl. "Inuit") was officially adopted at the Inuit Circumpolar Conference to refer to the group of indigenous people of Alaska, Northern Canada, Greenland, and Eastern Siberia. This term is preferred to "Eskimo" (a term the United States Census Bureau uses), which was applied to the indigenous peoples of Alaska by Europeans and derives from a term that means "raw meat eaters" (Maggio 1997).

"Indian" refers only to someone from India and is incorrectly used when applied to members of other Asian countries or to the indigenous peoples of North America. "American Indian" or "Native American" are preferred, even though many Native Americans refer to themselves as *Indians* and *Indian people.* The term "native American" (with a lower case *n*) is most often used to refer to persons born in the United States. Although the term technically could refer to anyone born in North or South America, people outside the United States generally prefer more specific designations such as *Argentinean, Cuban,* or *Canadian.* The term "native" means an indigenous inhabitant; it's not used to mean "someone having a less developed culture."

"Muslim" is the preferred form (rather than the older "Moslem") to refer to a person who adheres to the religious teachings of Islam. "Quran" (rather than "Koran") is the preferred term for the scriptures of Islam. The terms "Mohammedan" or "Mohammedanism" are not considered appropriate since they imply worship of Muhammad, the prophet, "considered by Muslims to be a blasphemy against the absolute oneness of God" (Maggio 1997, p. 277).

Although there's no universal agreement, generally "Jewish people" is preferred to "Jews"; and "Jewess" (a Jewish female) is considered derogatory. "Jew" should only be used as a noun and is never correctly used as a verb or an adjective (Maggio 1997).

When history was being written with a European perspective, it was taken as the focal point and the rest of the world was defined in terms of its location from Europe. Thus, Asia became the east or the orient and Asians became "Orientals"—a term that is today considered inappropriate or "Eurocentric." Thus, people from Asia are *Asians* just as people from Africa are *Africans* and people from Europe are *Europeans*.

Personal Style

Audiences favor speakers who speak in a personal rather than an impersonal style, who speak *with* them rather than *at* them.

Use Personal Pronouns. Say *I* and *me* and *he* and *she* and *you*. Avoid such impersonal expressions as *one* (as in "One is lead to believe . . .) or "this speaker," or "you, the listeners." These expressions distance the audience and create barriers rather than bridges.

Use Questions. Ask the audience questions to involve them. In a small audience, you might even briefly entertain responses. In larger audiences, you might ask the question, pause to allow the audience time to consider their responses, and then move on. When you direct questions to your listeners, they feel a part of the public speaking transaction.

Create Immediacy. Immediacy is a connectedness, a relatedness with one's listeners. Immediacy is the opposite of disconnected and separated. Here are some suggestions for creating immediacy through language:

- Use personal examples.
- Use terms that include both you and the audience, for example, *we* and *our*.
- Address the audience directly, say *you* rather than *students;* say "you'll enjoy reading . . . " instead of "everyone will enjoy reading." Say "I want you to see" instead of "I want people to see."
- Use specific names of audience members when appropriate.
- Express concern for the audience members.
- Reinforce or compliment the audience.
- Refer directly to commonalities between you and the audience; for example, "We are all children of immigrants" or "We all want to see our team in the playoffs."
- Refer to shared experiences and goals; for example, "We all want, we all need, a more responsive PTA."
- Recognize audience feedback and refer to it in your speech. Say, for example, "I can see from your expressions that we're all anxious to get to our immediate problem."

Forcefulness/Power

Forceful or powerful language will help you achieve your purpose, whether it be informative or persuasive. Forceful language enables you to direct the audience's attention, thoughts, and feelings. To achieve more forceful language, eliminate weakeners, vary intensity as appropriate, and avoid bromides and clichés.

Eliminate Weakeners. Delete phrases that weaken your sentences. Among the major weakeners are uncertainty expressions and weak modifiers. Phrases that express uncertainty such as *I'm not sure of this but, perhaps it might,* or *maybe it works this way* communicate a lack of commitment and conviction and will make your audience wonder if you're worth listening to. Weak modifiers such as "It works *pretty* well," "It's *kind of like* . . . ", or "It *may be* the one we want" make you seem unsure and indefinite about what you're saying.

Cut out any unnecessary phrases that reduce the impact of your meaning. Instead of saying "There are lots of things we can do to help," say "We can do lots of things to help." Instead of saying "I'm sorry to be so graphic, but Senator Bingsley's proposal . . . " say "We need to be graphic. Senator Bingsley's proposal . . . ." Instead of saying "It should be observed in this connection that, all things considered, money is not productive of happiness," say "Money does not bring happiness." Consider the suggestions in Table 16.2 for achieving more powerful language. These suggestions are not limited in application to public speaking; they relate as well to interpersonal and small group communication.

Vary Intensity as Appropriate. Much as you can vary your voice in intensity, you can also phrase your ideas with different degrees of stylistic intensity. You can, for example, refer to an action as "failing to support our

TABLE 16.2 Suggestions for More Powerful Speech

What other suggestions can you offer for making speech more powerful?

Suggestions	Examples	Comments
Avoid hesitations	I-er want to say that -ah this one is -er the best, you know . . .	Hesitations make you sound unprepared and uncertain.
Avoid too many intensifiers	Really, this was the greatest; it was truly phenomenal.	Too many intensifiers make your speeches all sound the same, and don't allow for intensifying what should be emphasized.
Avoid tag questions	I'll review the report now, okay? That's a great proposal, don't you think?	Tag questions ask for another's agreement and therefore signal your need for approval and your own uncertainty or lack of conviction.
Avoid self-critical statements	I'm not very good at this. This is my first speech.	Self-critical statements signal a lack of confidence and make public your inadequacies.
Avoid slang vulgar expressions	"!!#//***," No problem.	Slang and vulgarity signal a low social class and hence little power; it may also communicate a lack of respect for your audience.

position" or as "stabbing us in the back"; you can say that a new proposal will "endanger our goals" or "destroy us completely"; you can refer to a child's behavior as "playful," "creative," or "destructive." Vary your language to express different degrees of intensity—from mild through neutral to extremely intense.

Avoid Bromides and Clichés. Bromides are sentences that are worn out because of constant usage. Here are some examples.

- She's as pretty as a picture.
- Honesty is the best policy.
- If I can't do it well, I won't do it at all.
- I don't understand modern art, but I know what I like.

When you hear them, you recognize them as unoriginal and uninspired.

Clichés are phrases that have lost their novelty and part of their meaning through overuse. Clichés call attention to themselves because of their overuse. Some clichés to avoid are identified in Practically Speaking 16.2 on page 335.

PHRASING SENTENCES

Give the same careful consideration that you give to words to your sentences as well. Some guidelines follow.

Use Short Sentences. Short sentences are more forceful and economical. They are easier to comprehend, and they are easier to remember. Listeners don't have the time or the inclination to unravel long and complex sentences. Help them listen more efficiently. Use short rather than long sentences.

Use Direct Sentences. Direct sentences are easier to understand. They are also more forceful. Instead of saying, "I want to tell you of the three main reasons why we should not adopt Program A," say "We should not adopt Program A. There are three main reasons."

Use Active Sentences. Active sentences are easier to understand. They also make your speech seem livelier and more vivid. Instead of saying "The lower court's decision was reversed by the Supreme Court," say "The Supreme Court reversed the lower court's decision." Instead of saying "The proposal was favored by management," say "Management favored the proposal."

Use Positive Sentences. Positive sentences are easier to comprehend and remember. Notice how sentences (a) and (c) are easier to understand than sentences (b) and (d).

a. The committee rejected the proposal.
b. The committee did not accept the proposal.
c. This committee works outside the normal company hierarchy.
d. This committee does not work within the normal company hierarchy.

Vary the Types of Sentences. The advice to use short, direct, active, and positive sentences is valid most of the time. Yet too many sentences of the

TIPS from professional speakers

You don't need to be a speech writer or have a graduate degree in literature to brighten up your vocabulary. Just read and listen more attentively. Make an appeal to the ear. Instead of "The office is full of activity," say "The office is humming, buzzing, pulsating, exploding with activity." (Choose just one, of course).

Elizabeth Urech, international communication specialist and founder of "Speak for Yourself," *Speaking Globally: Effective Presentations Across International and Cultural Boundaries.* (Dover, NH: Kogan Page, 1998): 39.

Hush little bright line
Don't you cry . . .
You'll be a cliché
Bye and bye.
—Fred Allen

same type or length will make your speech sound boring. Use variety while following (generally) the preceding advice.

Here are a few special types of sentences that should prove useful, especially for adding variety, vividness, and forcefulness to your speech.

Parallel Sentences. Phrase your ideas in parallel (similar, matching) style for ease of comprehension and memory. Note the parallelism in (a) and (c) and its absence in (b) and (d).

a. The professor prepared the lecture, graded the examination, and read the notices.
b. The professor prepared the lecture, the examination was graded, and she read the notices.
c. Love needs two people to flourish. Jealousy needs but one.
d. Love needs two people. Just one can create jealousy.

Antithetical Sentences. Antithetical sentences juxtapose contrasting ideas in parallel fashion. John Kennedy used antithetical sentences when he said:

If a free society cannot help the many who are poor, it cannot save the few who are rich.

In his inaugural speech, President Kennedy phrased one of his most often quoted lines in antithetical structure.

Ask not what your country can do for you; ask what you can do for your country.

Periodic Sentences. In periodic sentences, you reserve the key word until the end of the sentence. In fact, the sentence is not grammatically complete until you say this last word. For example, in "Looking longingly into his eyes, the old woman fainted," the sentence doesn't make sense until the last word is spoken.

MAKING YOUR SPEECH EASY TO REMEMBER

If your aim is to communicate information and argument to a listener, then surely part of your job is to ensure that your listeners remember what you say. Here are a few techniques you might use in helping your audience remember your speech.

Stress Interest and Relevance

We learn more easily and remember better that which is interesting and relevant to our own lives because we give it greater attention. Almost automatically we relate this new information to our own lives and to what we already know. This association of the new with the old helps us remember the information.

Listeners will also think more about material they find interesting and relevant. This "active rehearsal" significantly aids all kinds of memorization. You would probably have little trouble remembering the address for a job interview that promises $1,500 per week to start, nor are you likely to

You never know when you're making a memory.
—Rickie Lee Jones

forget the amount of money being offered. You might, however, have difficulty learning a complex set of numbers if they bore no relevance to your immediate life.

Create Connections

In trying to get someone to remember anything, associate it with what is already known. If a new theory resembles a theory the audience is familiar with, mention this and then point out its differences. If, for example, feedback in communication works like feedback in a thermostat (with which the audience is already familiar), mention that.

Pattern Your Messages

Things are more easily remembered if they are presented in an organized pattern. Consider this experiment. College students tried to memorize a list of words shown to them one at a time. Without any pattern, they had great difficulty. One group, however, was told that they should organize the words alphabetically. Each word began with a different letter. In recalling the list, the experimenters advised, they should go through the alphabet, recalling first the A word, then the B word, and so on. Not surprisingly, the group working with a pattern, in this case the alphabet, did significantly better. The pattern or organizational scheme helped the students structure the information and thus increased their ability to remember the words. Use this insight and likewise assist the listeners to remember what you say in the speech.

The organizational patterns considered in the discussion of organization and outlining (Units 12, 13, and 14) help you present the listeners with patterns to aid their memory. Time sequences and spatial sequences, for example, are obvious examples of using known organizational patterns to assist memory. A useful aid to help remember is the mnemonic device.

Mnemonic Devices. A widely used memory system is the mnemonic device. (The word *mnemonic* comes from the Greek goddess of memory, Mnemosyne.) For example, if I were to ask how many days there are in November, you might go through the mnemonic rhyme, "Thirty days have September, April, June, and November."

A useful mnemonic device is the mediated associate. I remember the spelling distinction between *angle* and *angel* by recalling that the sequence *el* goes up physically, as do angels. I remember the 12 cranial nerves from college physiology because of the sentence "On old Olympus towering top a fine and gentle vision stands high." The initial letters in this sentence remind me of the first letter of each of the cranial nerves. Similarly, I remember the order of the colors of the spectrum (red, orange, yellow, green, blue, indigo, and violet) by the name "Roy G. Biv."

You might consider coining a mnemonic to help your audience remember the points of your speech. But, as you can see, this technique can get very corny if carried too far. Use such devices sparingly and with originality.

Focus Audience Attention

The best way to focus the listeners' attention is to tell them to focus their attention. Simply say, "I want you to focus on three points that I will make in this speech. First, . . . " Then repeat at least once again (but preferably two or three times) these very same points. With experience in public speaking, you will be able to do this with just the right combination of subtlety and directness.

UNIT IN BRIEF

Choose Your Words to Achieve an Effective Public Speaking Style	**Clarity**: be economical; be specific; use guide phrases; use short, familiar terms; use repetition and restatement; avoid misusing commonly confused words. **Vividness**: use active verbs; use strong verbs; use figures of speech; use imagery. **Appropriateness**: speak on the appropriate level of formality; avoid unfamiliar terms; avoid slang and vulgar terms; avoid racist, sexist, and heterosexist expressions, avoid ethnic expressions (generally), use the preferred cultural identifiers. **Personal terms**: use personal pronouns; ask questions; create immediacy. **Forcefulness**: eliminate weakeners; vary intensity as appropriate; avoid bromides and clichés.
Construct Sentences to Achieve Clarity and Forcefulness	Use short rather than long sentences. Use direct rather than indirect sentences. Use active rather than passive sentences. Use positive rather than negative sentences. Vary the types and lengths of sentences, making use of parallel, antithetical, and periodic sentences.
Make Your Speech Easy to Remember	Make your material interesting and relevant to your audience. Connect what the audience knows with what you're talking about. Give your listeners an organization or pattern to follow. Focus your listeners' attention on the main points of your speech.

THINKING CRITICALLY ABOUT EFFECTIVE PUBLIC SPEAKING STYL

REVIEWING KEY TERMS AND CONCEPTS IN PUBLIC SPEAKING STYLE

1. Review and define the key terms used in this unit:

□ periodic sentences (p. 332) □ mnemonic device (p. 333)

2. Review and explain the key concepts discussed in this unit:

- What are the characteristics of style that should influence word choice?
- How might sentences be structured for greatest effect?
- How might you help your listeners remember your speech?

DEVELOPING STRATEGIES IN PUBLIC SPEAKING STYLE

1. Shandra is being interviewed for a managerial position at Cybox Corporation. As part of the second interview, Shandra is asked to give a speech to a group of analysts she'll supervise (as well as to the management that will make the hiring decision). Shandra knows very little about the corporate culture; people working there describe it as "conservative," "professional but friendly," and "hard-working." What advice would you give Shandra concerning her speaking style? For example, should she strive for a personal style or an impersonal one? A powerful style? Should she strive for immediacy or should she signal distance? Would your advice differ if Shandra were significantly older than the group she would be supervising? Would your advice differ if Shandra were significantly younger than the group?

2. Francisco is scheduled to give two speeches, one to a predominantly female audience of nurses and one to a predominantly male audience of store owners. His topic for both groups is the same: neighborhood violence. What stylistic advice—if any—would you give Francisco for tailoring his speech to the two different audiences? If you would not offer advice, why not?

EVALUATING STYLE IN PUBLIC SPEECHES

1. Review any one of the speeches contained in this text for each of the characteristics of language discussed in this unit: clarity, vividness, appropriateness, personal style, and forcefulness. Can you find specific examples of each?

2. Review any one of the speeches contained in this text for examples of effective sentences. Do you find direct and indirect sentences? Active and passive sentences? Positive and negative sentences? Which types of sentences seem to work best?

3. Review any one of the speeches contained in this text. Can you find examples of parallel sentences, antithetical sentences, and periodic sentences?

USING TECHNOLOGY IN PUBLIC SPEAKING STYLE

1. If you're having trouble with grammar or just want to polish your speaking style, visit http://www.cc.columbia.edu/acis/bartley/strunk for a wealth of suggestions.

2. Continue your study of language by examining what's available at http://www.blackwellpublishers.co.uk/linguist/lingres.htm#overview. There's something here for everyone.

PRACTICALLY SPEAKING

16.1 Short Speech Technique

Prepare and deliver a two-minute speech in which you:

a. analyze an advertisement in terms of clarity, vividness, appropriateness, personal style or forcefulness (choose one or two).

b. describe the language of a person you consider forceful or weak.

c. describe an object in the room using visual, auditory, and tactile imagery.

d. explain the meaning of some popular idioms.

16.2 Rephrasing Clichés

Clichés are expressions whose meaning has become worn out from excessive usage. Many clichés are also idioms, expressions whose meanings are not easily deduced from the individual words but which must be understood as a single linguistic unit, much like a single word. Thus, in using clichés you betray a lack of originality. When they are idioms, clichés can easily create special problems for non-native speakers of the language. The clichés and idioms listed here will provide a useful opportunity to practice your abilities to use language effectively. Rephrase each of these clichés/idioms, so that they are—following the guidelines for language given in this unit—clear, vivid, appropriate, personal, and forceful.

- Heads will roll.
- It's a blessing in disguise.
- You have to take the bitter with the sweet.
- Her problem was that she burned the candle at both ends.
- What can I add? That's the way the cookie crumbles.
- He meant well but he drove everyone up the wall.
- So, I told her: either fish or cut bait.
- He just has to get his act together.
- She has a heart of gold.
- I talked and talked but it was in one ear and out the other.
- Lighten up; keep your shirt on.
- He let it slip through his fingers.
- That Stephen King movie will make your hair stand on end.
- Well, it's easy being a Monday-morning quarterback.

- Don't put all your eggs in one basket.
- It's just water over the dam.
- He ran out with his tail between his legs.
- They gave the detective a real snow job.
- It was fun but it wasn't what it was cracked up to be.
- I was so excited I had my heart in my mouth.
- Wow, you're touchy. You get up on the wrong side of the bed?

16.3 Talking about Cultural Identities

Anonymously on an index card write one of your cultural identities (race, religion, nationality) and three strengths that you feel a significant number of members of this cultural group possess. The cards should be collected, randomized, and read aloud. This brief experience—along with any discussion it generates—should make the following clear:

1. People have diverse cultural identities; each person has several.

2. Each identity has its own perceived strengths. Even the "strengths" themselves may not be recognized as "strengths" by members of other cultures.

3. The most effective individual is likely to be the one who recognizes and welcomes the strengths of different cultures.

Characteristics
of Delivery

If you're like my own students, delivery creates more anxiety for you than any other aspect of public speaking. Few speakers worry about organization or audience analysis or style. Many worry about delivery, so you have lots of company. This unit examines the general methods and principles for effectiveness in presentation. You can then adapt them to your own personality. In the next unit, specific suggestions for effectively presenting your speech are offered.

METHODS OF DELIVERY

Speakers vary widely in their methods of delivery: some speak "off-the-cuff," with no apparent preparation; others read their speeches from manuscript; some memorize their speeches word for word; others construct a detailed outline and actualize the speech itself at the moment of delivery. Speakers use all four of these general methods of delivery: impromptu, manuscript, memorized, and extemporaneous. Each has advantages and disadvantages.

Speaking Impromptu

When you speak impromptu you speak without any specific preparation. You and the topic meet for the first time and immediately the speech begins.

On some occasions you will not be able to avoid speaking impromptu. In a classroom, after someone has spoken, you might comment on the speaker and the speech you just heard—this requires a brief impromptu speech of evaluation. In asking or answering questions in an interview situation you're giving impromptu speeches, albeit extremely short ones. At meetings, you may find yourself explaining a proposal or defending a plan of action. These, too, are impromptu speeches. The ability to speak impromptu effectively depends on your general public speaking ability. The more proficient a speaker you are, the better you'll be able to function impromptu. Suggestions unique for speaking impromptu are offered by Wanda Vassallo in the accompanying TIP and in Practically Speaking 17.2.

The impromptu experience provides excellent training in the different aspects of public speaking, for example, maintaining eye contact, responding to audience feedback, or gesturing. The impromptu speech experi-

It usually takes me more than three weeks to prepare a good impromptu speech.
—Mark Twain

ence can also provide practice in basic organization and in development of examples, arguments, and appeals.

The major disadvantage is that impromptu speaking focuses on appearances. The aim is often to *appear* to give an effective and well-thought-out speech. Another disadvantage is that it does not permit attention to the details of public speaking such as audience adaptation, research, and style. Because of this inadequacy, the audience is likely to get bored. This in turn may make the speaker feel uncomfortable.

Speaking from Manuscript

In the manuscript method, you read the entire speech. The speech is constructed in the same way you would construct any speech. After you construct the detailed preparation outline, you write out the entire speech, exactly as you want it to be heard by your audience. You then read this speech to the audience.

The major advantage of a manuscript speech is that you can control the timing precisely. This is particularly important when delivering a recorded speech (on television, for example). You don't want your conclusion cut off so the fifty-ninth rerun of "Roseanne" can go on as scheduled. Also, there's no danger of forgetting, no danger of being unable to find the right word. Everything is there for you on paper, so, you probably will be less anxious.

Still another advantage is that it allows for you to use the exact wording you (or a team of speech writers) want. In the political arena this is often crucial; an ambiguous phrase that might prove insulting or belligerent could cause serious problems. The manuscript speech also has the advantage that it's already written out so you can distribute copies and are, therefore, less likely to be misquoted.

The most obvious disadvantage is that it's difficult to read a speech and sound natural and nonmechanical. Reading material from the printed page (or even from a teleprompter) with liveliness and naturalness is itself a skill that is difficult to achieve without considerable practice. Audiences don't like speakers to read their speeches. They prefer speakers who speak with them.

Reading a manuscript makes it difficult (even impossible) to respond to feedback from your listeners. With a manuscript you're committed to the speech word for word and cannot make adjustments on the basis of audience feedback.

When the manuscript is on a stationary lectern, as it most often is, it's impossible for you to move around. You have to stay in one place. The speech controls your movement or, rather, your lack of movement.

Still another disadvantage is that it takes lots of time to write out a speech word for word, time that is much better spent working on the substance of your speech.

Speaking from Memory

The memorized method involves writing out the speech word for word (as does the manuscript speech), but instead of reading it, you commit it to memory and recite it or "act it out."

TIPS from professional speakers

Don't panic. There is a way out without falling flat on your face, and short of dropping dead on the spot.

First of all, don't apologize. Don't say that you had no idea you were going to be called on to say something. Act poised—even if you don't feel poised. Who knows? You might even fool yourself.

Realize that the audience doesn't expect a magnificent speech on the spur of the moment.

Wanda Vassallo, professional speaker and author, *Speaking with Confidence: A Guide for Public Speakers* (Crozet, VA: Betterway Publications, 1990): 117.

Spontaneous speeches are seldom worth the paper they are written on.
—Leslie Henson

The memorized method allows you to devote careful attention to style. As in the manuscript speech, you can carefully review the exact word, phrase, or sentence and eliminate any potential problems in advance. In politically sensitive cases or in cases where media impose restrictions, the memorized method may prove useful.

One of the reasons the memorized delivery is popular is that it has all the advantages of the manuscript method; at the same time, however, it allows you freedom to move about and otherwise concentrate on delivery.

The major disadvantage, of course, is that you might forget your speech. In a memorized speech each sentence cues the recall of the following sentence. Thus, if you forget one sentence, you may forget the rest of the speech. This danger, along with the natural nervousness that speakers feel, makes this method a poor choice in most situations.

Another disadvantage is that the memorized method is even more time-consuming than the manuscript method since it involves additional time for memorization. When you recognize that you may easily forget the speech, even after spending hours memorizing it, it hardly seems worth the effort.

Still another disadvantage is that the memorized method does not allow for ease in adjusting to feedback. In fact, there's less opportunity to adjust to listener feedback than even in the manuscript method. And if you're not going to adjust to feedback, you lose the main advantage of face-to-face contact.

Speaking Extemporaneously

Extemporaneous delivery involves thorough preparation and a commitment to memory of the main ideas and their order. It may also involve a commitment to memory of the first and last few sentences of the speech. There is, however, no commitment to exact wording for the remaining parts of the speech.

Advantages. The extemporaneous method is useful in most speaking situations. Good college lecturers use the extemporaneous method. They prepare thoroughly and know what they want to say and in what order they want to say it, but they have given no commitment to exact wording.

This method allows you to respond easily to feedback. Should a point need clarification, you can elaborate on it when it will be most effective. This method makes it easy to be natural because you're being yourself. It's the method that comes closest to conversation or, as some theorists have put it, enlarged conversation. With the extemporaneous method, you can move about and interact with the audience.

Disadvantages. The major disadvantage to extemporaneous speaking is that you may stumble and grope for words. If you've rehearsed the speech a number of times, however, this is not likely to happen. Another disadvantage is that you cannot give the speech the attention to style that you can with other methods. You can get around this disadvantage too by memorizing those phrases you want to say exactly. There's nothing in the extemporaneous method that prevents your committing to memory selected phrases, sentences, or quotations.

I am the most spontaneous speaker in the world because every word, every gesture, and every retort has been carefully rehearsed.
—George Bernard Shaw

What are your personal reactions to someone who gives an impromptu speech? From manuscript? From memory? Extemporaneously?

Guidelines for Speaking Extemporaneously. Having stated a clear preference for the extemporaneous method, I do suggest that you memorize three parts of such a speech. Memorize your opening lines (perhaps the first few sentences), your closing lines (perhaps the last few sentences), and your major propositions and the order in which you'll present them.

Memorizing the opening and closing lines will help you focus your complete attention on the audience and will also put you more at ease. Once you know exactly what you'll say in opening and closing the speech, you'll feel more in control. Memorizing the main ideas will free you from relying on your notes and will make you feel more in control of the speech and the speech-making situation.

LISTEN TO THIS   How to Listen without Being Difficult

The poet Walt Whitman once said, "To have great poets, there must be great audiences too." The same is true of communication; to have great communication, there must be great listeners as well as great speakers. Here are some general types of listeners that make public speaking difficult. As you read this list, ask yourself what you can do as a speaker to help your listeners become less difficult. And, as a listener, what can you do to prevent yourself from becoming one of these difficult listeners?

- The **static listener** gives no feedback, remains relatively motionless and expressionless, and you wonder: "Why isn't she reacting? Can't she hear me?"
- The **monotonous feedback giver** seems responsive but the responses never vary; regardless of what you say, the response is the same: "Am I making sense? Why is he still smiling? I'm being dead serious."
- The **overly expressive listener** reacts to just about everything with extreme responses: "Why is she so expressive? I didn't say anything that provocative. She'll have a heart attack when I get to the punchline."
- The **reader/writer** reads or writes, while "listening" and only occasionally glances up, and you start to think: "Am I that boring? Is last weeks' newspaper more interesting than what I'm saying?"
- The **eye avoider** looks all around the room and at others but never at you: "Why isn't he looking at me? Do I have spinach on my teeth?"
- The **preoccupied listener** listens to other things at the same time, often with headphones: "When is she going to shut that music off and really listen? Does my speech need background music?"
- The **waiting listener** listens for a cue to interrupt, and you wonder: "Is he listening to me or rehearsing his next interruption?"

[The next Listen to This box appears on page 358.]

CHARACTERISTICS OF EFFECTIVE DELIVERY

Strive for a delivery that is natural, reinforces the message, is appropriate, is varied, and is conversational.

Effective Delivery Is Natural

Listeners will enjoy and believe you more if you speak naturally, as if you were conversing with a small group of people. Don't allow your delivery to call attention to itself. Your ultimate aim should be to deliver the speech so naturally that the audience won't even notice your delivery. This will take some practice, but you can do it. When voice or bodily action are so prominent that they're distracting, the audience concentrates on the delivery and fails to attend to your speech.

Effective Delivery Reinforces the Message

Effective delivery should aid instant intelligibility. Your main objective is to make your ideas understandable to an audience. A voice that listeners have to strain to hear, a decrease in volume at the ends of sentences, and slurred diction obviously hinder comprehension.

When you give a public speech, everything about you communicates. You cannot prevent yourself from sending messages to others. The way in which you dress is no exception. In fact, your attire will figure significantly in the way your audience assesses your credibility and even the extent to which they'll give you attention. In short, it will influence your effectiveness in all forms of persuasive and informative speaking. Unfortunately, there are no rules that will apply to all situations for all speakers. Thus, only general guidelines are offered here. Modify and tailor these for yourself and for each unique situation.

- Avoid extremes: don't allow your clothes to detract attention from what you're saying.
- Dress comfortably: be both physically and psychologically comfortable with your appearance so that you can concentrate your energies on what you're saying.
- Dress appropriately: your appearance should be consistent with the specific public speaking occasion.

Effective Delivery Is Varied

Listening to a speech is hard work. Flexible and varied delivery relieves this difficulty. Be especially careful to avoid monotonous and predictable patterns.

Speakers who are monotonous keep their voices at the same pitch, volume, and rate throughout the speech. The monotonous speaker maintains one level from the introduction to the conclusion. Like the drone of a motor, it easily puts the audience to sleep. Vary your pitch levels, your volume, and your rate of speaking. In a similar way, avoid monotony in bodily action. Avoid standing in exactly the same position throughout the speech. Use your body to express your ideas, to communicate to the audience what is going on in your head.

TIPS

from professional speakers

For the person who feels uncomfortable using hand gestures, I suggest this: Force yourself to try some. One simple type is to hold up fingers when enumerating key points. ("My third suggestion is . . .") Continue to experiment with gestures, and make them bigger—more expansive. Your listeners will not sense this exaggeration but will get the impact of your gesture.

Paul R. Timm, author and communication trainer and popular speaker, *How to Make Winning Presentations* (Franklin Lakes, NJ: Career Press, 1997): 72.

A predictable vocal pattern is one in which, for example, the volume levels vary but always in the same pattern. Through repetition, the pattern soon becomes predictable. For example, each sentence may begin at a loud volume and then decline to a barely audible volume at the sentence end. In bodily action, the predictable speaker repeatedly uses the same movements or gestures. For example, a speaker may scan the audience from left to right to left to right throughout the entire speech. If the audience can predict the pattern of your voice or your bodily action, it will almost surely be ineffective. It will draw their attention away from what you're saying and toward this patterned and predictable delivery.

Effective Delivery Is Conversational

Although more formal than conversation, delivery in public speaking should have some of the most important features of conversation. These qualities are immediacy, eye contact, expressiveness, and responsiveness to feedback.

Immediacy. Just as you can create a sense of immediacy through language, you can also create it with delivery. Make your listeners feel that you're talking directly and individually to each of them. You can communicate immediacy through delivery in a number of ways:

- Maintain appropriate eye contact with the audience members.
- Maintain a physical closeness that reinforces a psychological closeness; don't stand behind the desk or lectern.
- Smile.
- Move around a bit; avoid the appearance of being too scared to move.
- Stand with a direct and open body posture.
- Talk directly to your audience and not to your notes or to your visual aid.

Eye Contact. When you maintain eye contact (in addition to communicating immediacy), you make the public speaking interaction more conversational. Look directly into your listeners' eyes. Make a special effort to make eye contact. Lock eyes with different audience members for short periods.

Expressiveness. When you're expressive, you communicate genuine involvement in the public speaking situation. You can communicate this quality of expressiveness, of involvement, in several ways:

- Express responsibility for your own thoughts and feelings.
- Vary your vocal rate, pitch, volume, and rhythm to communicate involvement and interest in the audience and in the topic.
- Allow your facial muscles and your entire body to reflect and echo this inner involvement.
- Use gestures to communicate involvement—too few gestures may signal disinterest, too many may communicate uneasiness, awkwardness, or anxiety.

Start being expressive when you get up from your seat and walk to your speaking position. Certainly, avoid expressing signs of discomfort or displeasure. Your listeners will respond more favorably if they feel you're enjoying the experience and you're in control of the situation.

My basic rule is to speak slowly and simply so that my audience has an opportunity to follow and think about what I am saying.
—Margaret Chase Smith

TIPS
from professional speakers

Engage your audience by reaching out to them. As you speak, think that all who sit in front of you are your friends, with whom you will share something useful, valuable, or at least sufficiently attractive to absorb their attention for a few moments. If you are successful, you will have imparted a message that will be understood, retained, and even acted on.

Jack Valenti, president of the Motion Picture Association of America and former speech writer to President Lyndon Johnson. *Speak Up with Confidence: How to Prepare, Learn, and Deliver Effective Speech* (New York: William Morrow, 1982): 75–76.

Continue to be expressive even after you've spoken your last lines. Maintain eye contact with the audience for a second or two and then walk (do not run) to your seat. Once you sit down, avoid expressing signs of relief; don't sigh or in any way indicate that you're relieved or pleased that the experience is over.

Responsiveness to Feedback. Read carefully the feedback signals sent by your audience. Then respond to these signals with verbal, vocal, and bodily adjustments. For example, respond to audience feedback signals communicating lack of comprehension or inability to hear with added explanation or increased volume.

USING NOTES

For many speeches it may be helpful to use notes. A few simple guidelines may help you avoid some of the common errors made in using notes.

Keep Notes to a Minimum

The fewer notes you take with you, the better off you'll be. The reason so many speakers bring notes with them is that they want to avoid the face-to-face interaction required. With experience, however, you should find this face-to-face interaction the best part of the public speaking experience.

Resist the normal temptation to bring with you the entire speech outline. You may rely on it too heavily and lose the direct contact with the audience. Instead, compose a delivery outline (see pp. 298–299), using only key words. Bring this to the lectern with you—one side of an index card or at most an 8 1/2-by-11 inch page should be sufficient. This will relieve anxiety over the possibility of your forgetting your speech, but it will not be extensive enough to interfere with direct contact with your audience.

Use Notes with "Open Subtlety"

Don't make your notes more obvious than necessary. At the same time, though, don't try to hide them. Don't gesture with your notes and thus

Can you identify public speaking situations in which notes would be considered inappropriate?

make them more obvious than they need be. At the same time, don't turn away from the audience to steal a glance at them either. Use them openly and honestly but gracefully, with "open subtlety." To do this effectively, you'll have to know your notes intimately. Rehearse at least twice with the same notes that you'll take with you to the speaker's stand.

Don't Allow Your Notes to Prevent Directness

When referring to your notes, pause to examine them. Then regain eye contact with the audience and continue your speech. Don't read from your notes, just take cues from them. The one exception to this is an extensive quotation or complex set of statistics that you have to read; then, almost immediately, resume direct eye contact with the audience.

UNIT IN BRIEF

Methods for Delivering Public Speeches	**Impromptu**: speaking without preparation; useful in training certain aspects of public speaking. **Manuscript**: reading from a written text; useful when exact timing and wording are essential. **Memorized**: acting out a memorized text; useful when exact timing and wording are required. **Extemporaneous**: speaking after thorough preparation and memorization of the main ideas; useful in most public speaking situations.
Characteristics of Effective Delivery	**Natural**: appears genuine, does not call attention to itself. **Reinforces the message**: aids audience comprehension. **Varied**: monotony and predictable patterns of voice and bodily action are avoided. **Conversational**: possesses some of the essential qualities of effective conversation such as immediacy, eye contact, expressiveness, and responsiveness to feedback.
Guidelines for Using Notes	Use few notes—the fewer the better. Use notes with "open subtlety," neither obviously nor secretly; be so familiar with your notes that you'll be able to concentrate on your audience. Don't allow your notes to interfere with maintaining direct contact with your audience.

THINKING CRITICALLY ABOUT DELIVERY

REVIEWING KEY TERMS AND CONCEPTS IN PUBLIC SPEAKING DELIVERY

1. Review and define the key terms used in this unit:

- ❑ impromptu speaking (p. 338)
- ❑ manuscript speaking (p. 339)
- ❑ memorized delivery (p. 339)
- ❑ extemporaneous speaking (p. 340)
- ❑ monotonous patterns (p. 342)
- ❑ predictable patterns (p. 343)
- ❑ immediacy (p. 343)
- ❑ expressiveness (p. 343)

2. Review and explain the key concepts discussed in this unit:
   - What are the four main methods of delivery, their advantages, and their disadvantages?
   - What are the characteristics of effective delivery?
   - What guidelines can you suggest for using notes?

DEVELOPING DELIVERY STRATEGIES

1. Michael has a very formal personality; he's very restrained in everything he does. But he wants to try to project a different image—a much more personable, friendly, informal type of guy—in his speeches. What advice would you give Michael?

2. Pat, a new teacher at the elementary school, is to address a group of parents at a PTA meeting. (Let's assume that these parents are like the parents of the students in this public speaking class.) Pat is to be one of four speakers and is wondering what would be appropriate dress? What advice would you give if Pat were a man? If Pat were a woman?

EVALUATING SPEECHES

1. How would you describe the delivery method of any lecturer at your college? What general method is used? Is it used effectively?

2. Watch one of the monologues of a standup comedian—Jay Leno, David Letterman, Ellen DeGeneres, Jerry Seinfeld, Kathy Griffin, Chris Rock, Paula Poundstone, Margaret Cho, for example—and analyze his or her delivery in terms of the characteristics of effective delivery noted here.

USING TECHNOLOGY IN PUBLIC SPEAKING DELIVERY

1. Review a video of a speaker on the Web. Which delivery mannerisms work for the speaker? Which work against the speaker?

2. Access Psychlit through a CD ROM database or Internet site your college library subscribes to and look for studies on memory. Can you find any advice for the public speaker wanting to make her or his speech easier for the audience to remember?

PRACTICALLY SPEAKING

17.1 Short Speech Technique

Prepare and deliver a two-minute speech in which you:

a. describe the delivery of some noted personality (real or fictional).
b. compare the delivery styles of any two television personalities.
c. describe the delivery styles of men and women.
d. introduce an excerpt from literature and read the excerpt as you might a manuscript speech.

17.2 Developing the Impromptu Speech

The following experience may prove useful as an exercise in delivery. Students should be given three index cards each. Each student should write an impromptu speech topic on each of the cards. The topics to be used for impromptu speaking should be familiar but not clichés. They should be worthwhile and substantive, not trivial. They should be neither too simplistic nor too complex. The cards should be collected and placed face down on a table. A speaker is chosen through some random process and selects two cards, reads the topics,

selects one of them, and takes approximately one or two minutes to prepare a two-to-three minute impromptu speech. A few guidelines may prove helpful.

1. Don't apologize. Everyone will have difficulty with this assignment, so there's no need to emphasize any problems you may have.

2. Don't express verbally or nonverbally any displeasure or any negative responses to the experience, the topic, the audience, or even to yourself. Approach the entire task with a positive attitude and a positive appearance. It will help make the experience more enjoyable for both you and your audience.

3. When you select the topic, jot down two or three subtopics that you'll cover and perhaps two or three bits of supporting material that you'll use in amplifying these two or three subtopics.

4. Develop your conclusion. It will probably be best to use a simple summary conclusion in which you restate your main topic and the subordinate topics that you discussed.

5. Develop an introduction. Here it will probably be best simply to identify your topic and orient the audience by telling them the two or three subtopics that you'll cover.

Effective Speech Delivery

UNIT CONTENTS	UNIT OBJECTIVES
	After completing this unit, you should be able to:
Voice	Explain how to maximize your use of vocal volume, rate, and pitch.
Articulation and Pronunciation	Explain the nature of and problems associated with articulation and pronunciation.
Pauses	Explain the function of pauses in public speaking and how you might use them more effectively.
Bodily Action	Explain how you might effectively deal with each of the major aspects of bodily action: eye contact, facial expression, posture, gestures, movement, and proxemics.
Rehearsal: Practicing and Improving Delivery	Explain the suggested rehearsal procedures.

What specifically can you do to improve your presentation skills—your voice and your bodily action? This unit answers that important question and also offers some suggestions for rehearsing your speech and for undertaking a long-term improvement program.

VOICE

Three dimensions of voice are significant to the public speaker: volume, rate, and pitch. Your manipulation of these elements will enable you to control your voice to maximum advantage.

Volume

Volume refers to the relative intensity of the voice. Loudness, on the other hand, refers to the perception of that relative intensity. In an adequately controlled voice, volume will vary according to a number of factors. For example, the distance between speaker and listener, the competing noise, and the emphasis the speaker wishes to give an idea will all influence volume.

The problems with volume are easy to identify in others, though difficult to recognize in ourselves. One obvious problem is a voice that is too soft. When speech is so soft that listeners have to strain to hear, they'll soon tire of expending so much energy. On the other hand, a voice that is too loud will prove disturbing because it intrudes on our psychological space. However, it's interesting to note that a voice louder than normal communicates assertiveness (Page and Balloun, 1978) and will lead people to pay greater attention to you (Robinson and McArthur, 1982). On the other hand, it can also communicate aggressiveness and give others the impression that you may be difficult to get along with.

The most common problem is too little volume variation. A related problem is a volume pattern that, although varied, varies in an easily predictable pattern. If the audience can predict the pattern of volume changes, they'll focus on it and not on what you may saying.

Fading away at the end of sentences is particularly disturbing. Here the speaker uses an appropriate volume but ends sentences speaking the last few words at an extremely low volume. Be particularly careful when finishing sentences; make sure the audience is able to hear these at an appropriate volume.

If you're using a microphone, test it first. Whether its a microphone that clips around your neck, one you hold in your hand, or one that is stationed to the podium, try it out first. Some speakers—talk show host Montel Williams is a good example—use the hand microphone as a prop and flip it in the air or from hand to hand as they emphasize a particular point. For your beginning speeches, it's probably best to avoid such techniques and to use the microphone as unobtrusively as you can.

Rate

Rate refers to the speed at which you speak. About 150 words per minute seems average for speaking as well as for reading aloud. The problems of rate are speaking too fast or too slowly, or with too little variation or too predictable a pattern. If you talk too fast you deprive your listeners of time they need to understand and digest what you're saying. If the rate is extreme, the listeners will simply not spend the time and energy needed to understand your speech.

If your rate is too slow, it will encourage your listeners' minds to wander to matters unrelated to your speech. Be careful, therefore, not to bore the audience by presenting information at too slow a rate; yet don't give them information at a pace that is too rapid to absorb. Strike a happy medium. Speak at a pace that engages the listeners and allows them time for reflection without boring them.

Like volume, rate variations may be under used or totally absent. If you speak at the same rate throughout the entire speech, you're not making use of this important speech asset. Use variations in rate to call attention to certain points and to add variety. If you speak of, for example, the dull routine of an assembly line worker in a rapid and varied pace, or of the wonder of a circus in a pace with absolutely no variation, you're surely misusing this important vocal dimension. Again, if you're interested in and conscious of what you're saying, your rate variations should flow naturally and effectively. Too predictable a rate pattern is sometimes as bad as no variation at all. If the audience can predict—consciously or unconsciously—your rate pattern, you're in a vocal rut. You're not communicating ideas but words you've memorized.

Pitch

Pitch refers to the relative highness or lowness of your voice as perceived by your listener. More technically, pitch results from the rate which your

TIPS
from professional speakers

Speaking a little faster than usual certainly beats talking too slow. Fast-paced talking requires keener listening and will make the audience pay more attention. It also gives them the subliminal message that this speech is not going to go on all day and all night. You don't want to sound like an auctioneer, but pick up the pace a little more than your regular conversational speech. . . . .

Another benefit of a fast-paced dialogue is that when you do slow down, or stop dead, the audience is alerted to the fact that "this must be important." It's a great way to emphasize.

Don Aslett, writer and professional speaker, *Is There a Speech Inside You?* (Cincinnati, Ohio: Writer's Digest Books, 1989): 70.

TIPS
from professional speakers

In every sentence, one word or phrase is more important than the rest. Read this sentence out loud: "The company was forced to ask him for his resignation." If you were a company spokesperson, you might consider "forced" to be the most important word. If you were a colleague of the person told to resign, you might consider "resignation" to be the key word.

Whatever your choice, you want to emphasize that word or phrase to make your point to your audience. This technique is called "punching" it. Speech writers underline the words they want the speaker to hit. You can do the same on your outline.

Marjorie Brody and **Shawn Kent**, both communication consultants and trainers, *Power Presentations: How to Connect with Your Audience and Sell Your Ideas* (New York: Wiley, 1993): 31.

vocal folds vibrate. If they vibrate rapidly, listeners will perceive your voice as having a high pitch. If they vibrate slowly, they'll perceive it as having a low pitch.

Pitch changes often signal changes in the meanings of many sentences. The most obvious is the difference between a statement and a question. Thus, the difference between the declarative sentence, "So this is the proposal you want me to support" and the question "So this is the proposal you want me to support?" is inflection or pitch. This, of course, is obvious. But note that, depending on where the inflectional change is placed, the meaning of the sentence changes drastically. Note also that all of the following questions contain exactly the same words, but they each ask a different question when you emphasize different words:

- Is **this** the proposal you want me to support?
- Is this the **proposal** you want me to support?
- Is this the proposal you want **me** to support?
- Is this the proposal you want me to **support**?

The obvious problems of pitch are levels that are too high, too low, and too patterned. Neither of the first two problems is common in speakers with otherwise normal voices, and you can correct a pitch pattern that is too predictable or monotonous with practice. With increased speaking experience, pitch changes will come naturally from the sense of what you're saying. Because each sentence is somewhat different from every other sentence, there should be a normal variation—a variation that results not from some predetermined pattern but rather from the meanings you wish to convey to the audience.

ARTICULATION AND PRONUNCIATION

Articulation and pronunciation are similar in that they both refer to enunciation, the way in which you produce sounds and words. They differ, however, in a technical sense. Articulation refers to the movements the speech organs make as they modify and interrupt the air stream you send from the lungs. Different movements of these speech organs (for example, the tongue, lips, teeth, palate, and vocal cords) produce different sounds. Pronunciation refers to the production of syllables or words according to some accepted standard, identified in any good dictionary. Our concern here is with identifying and correcting some of the most common problems associated with faulty articulation or pronunciation.

What do you feel are the most common problems of voice among public speakers? What one suggestion would you offer speakers to improve their vocal delivery?

Errors of Omission

Omitting sounds or even syllables is a major articulation problem, but it is one we can easily overcome with concentration and practice. Here are some examples:

Not This	This
gov-a-ment	gov-ern-ment
hi-stry	hi-story
wanna	want to
fishin'	fishing
studyin'	studying
a-lum-num	a-lum-i-num
hon-orble	hon-or-able
comp-ny	comp-a-ny
vul-ner-bil-ity	vul-ner-a-bil-ity

Errors of Substitution

Substituting an incorrect sound for the correct one is another easily corrected articulation problem. Among the most popular are substituting "d" for "t" and "d" for "th," illustrated by the first three examples.

Not This	This
wader	waiter
dese	these
beder	better
ax	ask
undoubtebly	undoubtedly
ekcetera	etcetera
ramark	remark
lenth	length
dormatory	dormitory

Errors of Addition

When we make errors of addition, we add sounds where they don't belong. Some examples include:

Not This	This
acrost	across
airaplane	airplane
athalete	athlete
Americer	America

Sir, you have tasted two whole worms; you have hissed all my mystery lectures and have been caught fighting a liar in the quad; you will leave by the next town drain.
—attributed to Reverend W. A. Spooner (from whose name we get the word *spoonerism:* the interchanging of initial sounds with sounds in other words)

TIPS
from professional speakers

Violin virtuoso Isaac Stern was once asked how it was that all professional musicians could play the right notes in the right order, but some made beautiful music while others did not. He replied, "The important thing is not the notes. It's the intervals between the notes." Just as the best musicians add an extra shade of meaning—the difference between good music and great music—by spacing their notes, the best speakers know the value of pausing for effect.

Sandy Linver, a communication consultant and President, Speakeasy, Inc., *Speaking and Get Results: The Complete Guide to Speeches and Presentations that Work in Any Business Situation*, revised and updated. (New York: Simon & Schuster [Fireside], 1994): 139.

idear	idea
filim	film
lore	law

If you make any of these errors, you can easily correct them by following these steps:

- come conscious of your own articulation patterns (and the specific errors you might be making)
- listen carefully to the articulation of prominent speakers (for example, broadcasters)
- practice the correct patterns until they become part of your normal speech behavior

Errors of Pronouncing Silent Sounds

For some words, the acceptable pronunciation is to not pronounce certain sounds, as in the following examples:

Not This	This
often	offen
homage	omage
Illinois	Illinoi
evening	evning
burgalar	burglar

The best way to deal with pronunciation problems is to look up in a good dictionary any words whose pronunciation you're not sure of. Learn to read the pronunciation key in your dictionary, and make it a practice to look up words you hear others use that seem to be pronounced incorrectly or that you wish to use yourself but are not sure how to pronounce.

PAUSES

Pauses come in two basic types: filled and unfilled. Filled pauses are pauses in the stream of speech that we fill with vocalizations such as "-er," "-um," "-ah," and the like. Even expressions such as "well" and "you know," when used just to fill up silence, are called **filled pauses**. These pauses are ineffective and weaken the strength of your message. They'll make you appear hesitant, unprepared, and unsure of yourself.

Unfilled pauses are silences interjected into the normally fluent stream of speech. Unfilled pauses can be especially effective if used correctly. Here are just a few examples of places where unfilled pauses—silences of a few seconds—should prove effective.

1. Pause before beginning your speech. Instead of starting your speech as soon as you get to the front of the room, pause and survey your audience; engage their attention. Then begin your speech.
2. Pause at transitional points. This will signal that you're moving from one part of the speech to another or from one idea to another. It will help the listeners separate the main issues you're discussing.

The right word may be effective but no word was ever as effective as mighty timed pause.
—Mark Twain

3. Pause at the end of an important assertion. This will allow the audience time to think about the significance of what you're saying.

4. Pause after asking a rhetorical question. This will provide the necessary time so the audience can think of how they would answer the question.

5. Pause before an important idea. This will help signal that what comes next is especially significant.

6. If there's a question period following your speech and you're in charge of it, pause after you've completed your conclusion and ask the audience if they have any questions. If there's a chairperson who will recognize audience members, pause after your conclusion, and then nonverbally indicate to the chairperson that you're ready to entertain questions. If there's no question period, pause after the last statement of your conclusion, before leaving the front of the room.

Like most good things, pauses can be overdone. Used in moderation, however, they can be powerful aids to comprehension and persuasion.

BODILY ACTION

Your body is a powerful instrument in your speech. You speak with your body as well as with your mouth. The total effect of the speech depends not only on what you say but also on the way you present it. It depends on your movements, gestures, and facial expressions as well as your words.

Six aspects of bodily action are especially important in public speaking: eye contact, facial expression, posture, gestures, movement, and proxemics.

Eye Contact

The most important single aspect of bodily communication is eye contact. The two major problems with eye contact are not enough eye contact and eye contact that does not cover the audience fairly. Speakers who don't maintain enough eye contact appear distant, unconcerned, and less trustworthy than speakers who look directly at their audience. And, of course, without eye contact, you'll not be able to secure that all-important audience feedback.

Maintain eye contact with the entire audience. Involve all listeners in the public speaking transaction. Communicate equally with the members on the left and on the right, in both the back and the front.

Use eye contact to secure audience feedback. Are they interested? Bored? Puzzled? In agreement? In disagreement? Use your eyes to communicate your commitment to and interest in what you're saying. Communicate your confidence and commitment by making direct eye contact; avoid staring blankly through your audience or glancing over their heads, at the floor, or out the window.

Facial Expression

Facial expressions are especially important in communicating emotions—your anger and fear, boredom and excitement, doubt and surprise. If you feel committed to and believe in your thesis, you'll probably display your meanings appropriately and effectively.

I'm going to milk those greedy pauses till they're udderless.
—Richard Burton

TIPS
from professional speakers

Within many cultures around the world, it is believed that the eyes are the windows to the soul. In public speaking, since we usually want to arouse both spirit and soul, the eyes become the most important physical equipment of all.

Start by thinking about one-on-one conversations. Have you ever conversed with someone who kept looking away constantly, avoiding eye contact? This behavior often illustrates discomfort or dishonesty. Conversely, the person who maintains good eye contact is displaying sincerity, attention, and respect.

Roger E. Axtell, *Do's and Taboos of Public Speaking: How to Get Those Butterflies Flying in Formation* (New York: Wiley, 1992): 67.

Nervousness and anxiety, however, may at times prevent you from relaxing enough so that your emotions come through. Fortunately, time and practice will allow you to relax, and the emotions you feel will reveal themselves appropriately and automatically.

Generally, members of one culture will be able to recognize the emotion displayed facially by members of other cultures. There are differences, however, in what each culture considers appropriate to display. Each culture has its own "display rules" (Ekman and Friesen 1972). For example, Japanese Americans watching stress inducing film, spontaneously displayed the same facial emotions as did other Americans when they thought they were unobserved. But, when an observer was present, the Japanese masked (tried to hide) their emotional expressions more than did the Americans (Gudykunst and Kim 1992a).

Posture

When delivering your speech, stand straight but not stiff. Try to communicate a command of the situation without communicating the discomfort that is actually quite common for beginning speakers.

Try to avoid the common mistakes of posture such as putting your hands in your pockets or leaning on the desk, the podium, or the chalkboard. With practice you'll come to feel more at ease and will communicate this by the way you stand before the audience.

Gestures

Gestures in public speaking help illustrate your verbal messages. We do this regularly in conversation. For example, when saying "Come here," you probably move your head, hands, arms, and perhaps your entire body to motion the listener in your direction. Your body as well as your verbal message say "Come here."

Avoid using your hands to preen, for example, fixing your hair or adjusting your clothing. Avoid fidgeting with your watch, ring, or jewelry. Avoid keeping your hands in your pockets or clasped in front or behind your back.

Effective bodily action is spontaneous and natural to you as the speaker, to your audience, and to your speech. If they seem planned or rehearsed, they'll appear phony and insincere. As a general rule, don't do anything with your hands that doesn't feel right for you; the audience will recognize it as unnatural. If you feel relaxed and comfortable with yourself and your audience, you'll generate natural bodily action without conscious and studied attention.

Movement

Movement refers here to your large bodily movements. Move around a bit as you speak; it keeps both you and the audience more alert. Even when speaking behind a lectern, you can give the illusion of movement. You can step back or forward or flex your upper body so it appears that you're moving more than you are.

Avoid these three problems of movement: too little, too much, and too patterned. Speakers who move too little often appear strapped to the podium, afraid of the audience, or too disinterested to involve themselves fully. With too much movement, the audience begins to concentrate on the movement itself, wondering where the speaker will wind up next. With too patterned a movement, the audience may become bored—too steady and predictable a rhythm quickly becomes tiring. The audience will often view the speaker as nonspontaneous and uninvolved.

Use gross movements to emphasize transitions and to emphasize the introduction of a new and important assertion. Thus, when making a transition, you might take a step forward to signal that something new is coming. Similarly, this type of movement may signal the introduction of an important assumption, bit of evidence, or closely reasoned argument.

Proxemics

Proxemics refers to the way you use space in communication. In public speaking, the space between you and your listeners and among the listeners themselves is often a crucial factor. If you stand too close to the audience, they might feel uncomfortable, as if their personal space is being violated. If you stand too far away from your audience, you might be perceived as uninvolved, uninterested, and uncomfortable. Watch where your instructor and other speakers stand and adjust your own position accordingly.

If you're using a lectern, you may wish to signal transitions by stepping to the side or in front of it and then behind it again as you move from one point to another. Generally, it's best to avoid the extremes; both too much movement around the lectern and no movement are to be avoided. You may wish to lean over it when, say, posing a question to your listeners or when advancing a particularly important argument. But, never lean on the lectern; never use it as support.

REHEARSAL: PRACTICING AND IMPROVING DELIVERY

Use your rehearsal time effectively and efficiently to achieve the following goals:

- to develop a delivery that will help you achieve the purposes of your speech.
- to time your speech; if you time your rehearsals, you'll be able to see if you can add material or if you have to delete something.
- to see how the speech will flow as a whole and to make any changes and improvements you think necessary.
- to test out the presentation aids, to detect any technological problems, and to resolve them.
- to help you learn the speech effectively.
- to reduce apprehension and give you confidence.

The following procedures should assist you in achieving these goals.

Rehearse the Speech as a Whole

You should rehearse your speech from beginning to end. Do not rehearse in parts. Rehearse it from getting out of your seat, through the introduction, body, and conclusion, to returning to your seat. Be sure to rehearse

I like people who refuse to speak until they are ready to speak.
—Lillian Hellman

the speech with all the examples and illustrations (and audiovisual aids, if any) included. This will enable you to connect the parts of the speech and to see how they interact with each other.

Time the Speech

Time your speech during each rehearsal. Make the necessary adjustments on the basis of this timing. If you're using computer presentation software, you'll be able to time your speech very precisely. It will also enable you to time the individual parts of your speech so you can achieve the balance you want—for example, you might want to spend twice as much time on the solutions than on the problems, or you might want to balance the introduction and conclusion so that they each constitute about 10 percent of your speech.

Approximate the Actual Speech Situation

Rehearse the speech under conditions as close as possible to those under which you'll deliver it. If possible, rehearse the speech in the same room in which you'll present it. If this is impossible, try to simulate the actual conditions as close as you can—in your livingroom or even bathroom. If possible, rehearse the speech in front of a few supportive listeners. It's always helpful (especially for your beginning speeches) that your listeners be supportive rather than too critical. Merely having listeners present during your rehearsal will further simulate the conditions under which you'll eventually speak. Get together with two or three other students in an empty classroom where you can each serve as speaker and listener.

THE ETHICS OF Questions and Answers

The speaker's ethical obligations don't stop with the speech. Rather, ethical issues have to be considered during the question and answer period as well. Consider the following situations that might arise in a public speaking situation. How would you respond?

1. You've just given a speech to a high school class on why they should consider attending your college. One audience member asks if you're allowed to keep animals in the dorm. You simply don't know the answer. What do you say?

2. You've just given a speech advocating banning alcohol on campus and in the speech you claimed that over 70 percent of the students favor banning alcohol. At the end of the speech, you realize that you made a mistake and that only 30 percent favor banning alcohol. Because you were nervous, you mixed up the figures. There's a question and answer period

but no one asks about the figures. What do you say?

3. Representing the college newspaper, you ask the Student Government to increase funding. The Student Government objects to allocating extra money because the paper has favored many causes that are unpopular with most students. You feel that it's essential for the paper to represent the disenfranchised and fully expect to continue to do just exactly as you have in the past. But, if you say you'll give primary coverage to majority positions, you'll get the extra funding that the paper needs to survive. What do you say?

What ethical standards did you use in answering these questions? How might you phrase these standards as a code of ethics for answering questions?

[The next Ethics in Public Speaking box appears on page 392.]

See Yourself as a Speaker

Rehearse the speech in front of a full-length mirror. This will enable you to see yourself and to see how you'll appear to the audience. This may be extremely difficult at first, and you may have to force yourself to watch. After a few attempts, however, you'll begin to see the value of this experience. Practice your eye contact, your movements, and your gestures in front of the mirror. Consider too the value of incorporating the insights from cognitive restructuring and performance visualization into your rehearsal (see Unit 3).

Incorporate Changes and Make Delivery Notes

Make any changes in the speech that seem appropriate between rehearsals. Don't interrupt your rehearsal to make notes or changes. If you do, you may never experience the entire speech from beginning to end. While making these changes, note too any words whose pronunciation or articulation you wish to check. Also, insert pause notations ("slow down" warnings and other delivery suggestions) into your outline.

If possible, record your speech (ideally, on videotape) so you can hear exactly what your listeners will hear: your volume, rate, pitch, articulation and pronunciation, and pauses. You'll thus be in a better position to improve these qualities.

Rehearse Often

Rehearse the speech as often as seems necessary. Two useful guides are: (1) rehearse the speech at least three or four times, less than this is sure to be too little; (2) rehearse the speech as long as your rehearsals result in improvements in the speech or in your delivery.

Undertake a Long-Term Delivery Improvement Program

Consider the value of undertaking a long-term delivery program to help you continue to perfect your public speaking skills. Here are a few suggestions.

1. Approach this task with positive thinking. This will help a great deal in setting up an attitude that will help you become a truly effective public speaker. Tell yourself that you can do it and that you will do it.

2. Seek feedback from someone whose opinion and insight you respect. Your public speaking instructor may be a logical choice, but someone majoring in communication or working in a communication field might also be appropriate. Get an honest and thorough appraisal of both your voice and your bodily action.

3. Learn to hear, see, and feel the differences between effective and ineffective patterns. Learn to hear, for example, the patterned nature of your pitch or your too-loud volume. A tape recorder will be very helpful. Learn to feel your rigid posture or your lack of arm and hand gestures. Once you've perceived these differences, concentrate on learning more effective patterns. Practice a few minutes each day. Avoid becoming too conscious

from professional speakers

Practice was particularly important for me because I began my speaking career before I had achieved fluency in the English language. As an undergraduate student at Mount Olive College in North Carolina, I began speaking to people about my native country, and someone would pass the hat.

People in small churches were willing to accept a young foreign student's imperfect English. But my career aims were higher than that. I wanted to communicate my way to success, and that meant learning to use the English language fluently and skillfully. This called for practice. If English is your native tongue, you have a head start on me. But you still need practice to achieve true greatness as a communicator.

Nido R. Qubein, chair of an international consulting firm and popular public speaker and author, *How to be a Great Communicator: In Person, on Paper, and on the Podium* (New York: Wiley, 1997): 16.

How to Listen to Question Type

In addition to listening to the question content, listen also to the type of question. **Open questions** give you considerable freedom in your response ("Could you explain your position on abortion?"). **Closed questions**, on the other hand, restrict your response sometimes to a "yes" or "no" answer ("Is Netscape better than Internet Explorer?"). Realize, however, that even if you're asked a yes/no question, there's no reason why you have to respond with only "yes" or "no"; as the speaker you have the right to elaborate as you wish. If you were on the witness stand at a trial, your options would not be so broad.

Primary questions introduce a topic and **follow-up questions** ask for elaboration on what was just said. Generally, audience members should be allowed at least one follow-up question. So, don't move too quickly to the next questioner; the last one may have a follow-up question.

Direct questions ask for a very specific response; **indirect questions** allow greater freedom in how you answer and may even allow you the option of avoiding an answer. This aspect of questions will vary greatly from one culture to another. In the United States, be prepared for rather direct questions. In many Asian cultures, listeners very rarely ask questions, and if they do the questions are usually indirect.

Neutral questions don't specify any answer as more appropriate than any other, for example, "What do you think of MMX technology?" **Biased or loaded questions** specify the answer the listener expects or wants, for example, "Don't you think nuclear energy creates more problems than it solves?" If you don't want to be pushed into the expected answer, consider rephrasing the question, saying something like "I think nuclear energy can create problems, but it doesn't have to if proper planning is taken. And that's what I'm talking about—proper planning." Or, you might consider pointing out the bias, saying something like, "Well, I guess I don't agree with that position. My feeling is. . . . "

(The next Listen to This box appears on page 364.)

of any source of ineffectiveness. Just try to increase your awareness and work on one problem at a time. Don't try to change all your patterns at once.

4. Seek additional feedback on the changes. Make certain that listeners agree that the new patterns you're practicing are really more effective. Remember that you hear yourself through air transmission as well as through bone conduction. Others hear you only through air transmission, so, what you hear and what others hear will be different.

5. For voice improvement, consult a book on voice and diction for practice exercises and for additional information on the nature of volume, rate, pitch, and quality.

6. If any of these difficulties persist, see a professional. For voice problems, see a speech clinician. Most campuses have a speech clinic. You can easily avail yourself of their services. For bodily action difficulties, talk with your public speaking instructor.

7. Seek professional help if you're psychologically uncomfortable with any aspect of your voice or your bodily action. It may be that all you have to do is to hear yourself or see yourself on a videotape—as others see and hear you—to convince yourself that you sound and look just fine. Regardless of what is causing this discomfort, however, if you're uncomfortable, do something about it. In a college community there's more assistance available to you at no cost than you'll ever experience again. Make use of it.

UNIT IN BRIEF

Voice Problems	**Volume**: overly soft, loud, or unvaried, and fading away at ends of sentences. **Rate**: too rapid, too slow, too little variation, and too predictable a pattern. **Pitch**: overly high, low, monotonous, or too predictable a pattern.
Problems in Articulation and Pronunciation	Errors of omission. Errors of substitution. Errors of pronouncing silent sounds.
The Functions of Pauses	Signal transitions between parts of the speech. Give the audience time to think. Allow listeners to ponder rhetorical questions. Signal approach of important ideas.
Effective Bodily Action	Maintain eye contact. Allow facial expressions to convey thoughts and feelings. Use posture to communicate command of the speech experience. Gesture naturally. Move around a bit Position yourself neither too close nor too far from the audience.
Rehearsal Procedures	Rehearse the speech as a whole. Time the speech. Approximate the actual speech situation. See yourself as a speaker. Incorporate changes and delivery notes. Rehearse often. Undertake a long-term delivery improvement program.

THINKING CRITICALLY ABOUT EFFECTIVE SPEECH DELIVERY

REVIEWING KEY TERMS AND CONCEPTS IN EFFECTIVE SPEECH DELIVERY

1. Review and define the key terms used in this unit:

   - ❏ vocal volume (p. 348)
   - ❏ vocal rate (p. 349)
   - ❏ vocal pitch (p. 349)
   - ❏ articulation (p. 350)
   - ❏ pronunciation (p. 350)
   - ❏ pause (p. 352)
   - ❏ proxemics (p. 355)

2. Review and explain the key concepts discussed in this unit:

   - What are the dimensions of voice and the major problems associated with each?
   - What are articulation and pronunciation and the major problems associated with each?
   - What are the types of pauses and how might they be used effectively in delivering a speech?
   - What are the dimensions of bodily action and how might these be used most effectively?
   - What are the major rehearsal suggestions?

DEVELOPING EFFECTIVE SPEECH DELIVERY STRATEGIES

1. After sitting through two rounds of speeches, Tom wonders if the class wouldn't be ready for a speech spoken at noticeably higher volume than normal—rather like advertisements on television are played at a greater volume than the regular broadcast. What would you advise Tom to do?

2. Rosa has been invited to speak to the fitness club members on stretching exercises. Rosa has a Spanish accent and wonders if she should say anything about this to the members during her introduction. What would you advise Rosa to do?

EVALUATING PUBLIC SPEECHES

1. Watch a speaker deliver a speech and describe his or her delivery style in terms of voice, articulation and pronunciation, pausing, and bodily action. What did the speaker do particularly well? What could have been improved?

2. Compare your own delivery style with a public performer or speaker you admire. Focusing on this one person, try to identify characteristics of this person's delivery style that you could perhaps emulate.

USING TECHNOLOGY IN PUBLIC SPEAKING

1. Visit an interesting Web site for public speakers at http://speeches.com/index.shtml. It contains a variety of speeches and speaker resources. What advice on delivery can you find at this Web site?

2. Access ERIC, Psychlit, or Sociofile and look for research on one of the topics of delivery that interested you, perhaps, eye contact, facial expression, or posture. What can you learn from these studies that might help you improve your own public speaking delivery?

PRACTICALLY SPEAKING

18.1 Short Speech Technique

Prepare and deliver a two-minute speech in which you:

a. describe your growth as a public speaker over the last several months.

b. describe the delivery of a speaker you consider effective or ineffective.

c. outline the steps you intend to take to continue your learning of communication skills.

d. compare the delivery styles of any two prominent people from the arts or politics.

e. describe the delivery style of a prominent comedian or compare the delivery styles of any two comedians.

18.2 Communicating Vocally but Nonverbally

This exercise is designed to give you practice in communicating effectively with your voice and body. In this exercise a person recites the alphabet attempting to communicate each of the following emotions: anger, nervousness, fear, pride, happiness, sadness, jealousy, satisfaction, love, and sympathy.

The person may begin the alphabet at any point and may omit and repeat sounds, but may use only the names of the letters of the alphabet to communicate these feelings.

The speaker should first number the emotions in random order so that he or she will have a set order to follow that is not known to the audience, whose task it will be to guess the emotions expressed.

As a variation, have the speaker go through the entire list of emotions twice: once facing the audience and employing any nonverbal signals desired, and once with his or her back to the audience without employing any additional signals. Are there differences in the number of correct guesses depending on which method is used? Why?

After the exercise is completed, consider some or all of the following questions:

1. What vocal cues are used to communicate the various emotions?

2. Are some cues useful for communicating some emotions and not useful (or even detrimental) for communicating others? Explain.

3. What bodily cues are useful in communicating these various emotions?

4. Are some bodily cues useful for communicating some emotions and not useful for others? Explain.

5. Are there significant gender differences for effectively communicating these emotions? That is, should men and women use different cues in communicating these emotions?

The Informative Speech

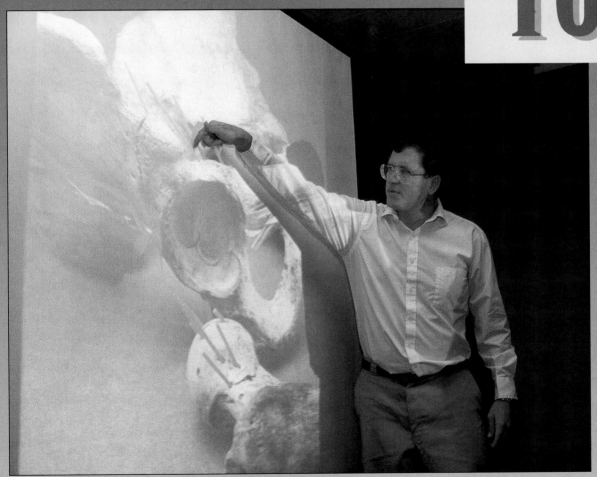

In this unit we look at the informative speech. First, a series of general principles useful for all informative speaking are presented and second, the three types of informative speeches are explained.

PRINCIPLES OF INFORMATIVE SPEAKING

When you communicate "information" you tell your listeners something they don't know, something new. You may tell them of a new way of looking at old things or an old way of looking at new things. You may discuss a theory not previously heard of or a familiar one not fully understood. You may talk about events that the audience may be unaware of or may have misconceptions about. Regardless of what type of informative speech you intend to give, the following principles should help.

Limit the Amount of Information

There's a limit to the amount of information that a listener can take in at one time. Resist the temptation to overload your listeners with information. Limit the breadth of information you communicate and, instead, expand its depth. It's better to present two new items of information and explain these with examples, illustrations, and descriptions than to present five items without this needed amplification.

Here, for example, is the type of thing you should avoid:

In this speech I want to discuss the differences between women and men. I'm going to focus on the physiological, psychological, social, and linguistic differences.

Clearly the speaker is trying to cover too much. The speaker is going to be forced to cover these four areas only superficially with the result that little new information will be communicated. Instead, select one area and develop it in depth:

In this speech I want to discuss some of the linguistic differences between women and men. I'm going to focus on two linguistic differences: differences in language development and differences in language problems. Let's look first at the way in which girls and boys develop language.

In this speech, the speaker now has the opportunity to cover an area in depth. As a result the listeners are more likely to learn something that they didn't know.

Adjust the Level of Complexity

As you know from attending college classes, information can be presented in very simple or very complex form. The level of complexity that you communicate your information on should depend on the wide variety of factors considered throughout this book: the level of knowledge your audience has, the time you have available, the purpose you hope to achieve, the topic on which you're speaking, and so on. If you simplify a topic too much, you risk boring or, even worse, insulting your audience. On the other hand, if your talk is too complex, you risk confusing your audience and failing to communicate your message.

Generally, however, beginning speakers err by being too complex and not realizing that a five or 10 minute speech isn't very long to make an audience understand sophisticated concepts or complicated processes. At least in your beginning speeches, try to keep it simple rather than complex. Make sure the words you use are familiar to your audience or, if not, explain and define them as you use them. Remember too that jargon and technical vocabulary familiar to the computer hacker may not be familiar to the person who still uses a typewriter. Always see your topic from the point of view of the audience; ask yourself how much they know about your topic and its unique language.

Stress Relevance and Usefulness

Listeners remember information best when they see it as relevant and useful to their own needs or goals. Notice that as a listener you regularly follow this principle. For example, in class you might attend to and remember the stages in the development of language in children simply because you'll be tested on the information and you want to earn a high grade. Or you might remember information because it will help you make a better impression in your job interview or make you a better parent or enable you to deal with relationship problems. Like you, listeners attend to information that will prove useful to them.

If you want the audience to listen to your speech, relate your information to their needs, wants, or goals. Throughout your speech, but especially in the beginning, make sure your audience knows that the information you're presenting is relevant and useful to them now or in the immediate future. For example, you might say something like:

We all want financial security. We all want to be able to buy those luxuries we read so much about in magazines and see every evening on television. Wouldn't it be nice to be able to buy a car without

TIPS
from professional speakers

Many years ago, a mentor gave me this bit of homespun advice about life: "Buy low, sell high . . . and never walk behind a manure spreader."

The corollary is "Learn the value of good timing. And, then, don't ever do anything stupid!"

Applying this advice to public speaking means: Know *when* to speak but also *when not* to speak. Speak *only* when you know the subject. *Decline* to speak if you are unsure about or unprepared for the topic. Otherwise, you may do something stupid . . . and end up walking behind that manure spreader.

Roger E. Axtell, *Do's and Taboos of Public Speaking: How to Get Those Butterflies Flying in Formation* (New York: Wiley, 1992): 67.

worrying about where you're going to get the down payment or how you'll be able to make the monthly payments? Actually, that is not an unrealistic goal as I'll demonstrate in this speech. In fact, I'll show you several methods for investing your money that will enable you to increase your income by at least 20 percent.

In recent research on relevance, communication researchers investigated what students felt made their college lectures relevant to their personal and professionals goals (Frymier and Shulman 1995). They found that the greater the relevance of the lecture, the more the students were motivated to study. It seems reasonable to extend these findings and argue that the more relevant a speech, the more an audience will be motivated to listen and even to further pursue this new interest. Here are a few of the most frequently noted ways for stressing relevance the researchers found, stated in the form of suggestions for informative speaking:

- Use examples that make content relevant.
- Use exercises or explanations to show the content's importance to your listeners.
- Explain how the content is related to career goals of your listeners.
- Stimulate your listener's thinking about how the content applies to their goals.
- Use your own or your listeners' own experiences to stress the importance of the content of your talk.
- Relate current events to the content of your talk.

Relate New Information to Old

Listeners will learn information more easily and retain it longer when you relate it to what they already know. So, relate the new to the old, the

---

How to Listen to New Ideas

Ideally, informative speeches will communicate information that is new and potentially useful to you as a listener. A useful technique in listening to new ideas is PIP'N, a technique that derives from the insights of Carl Rogers (1970) on paraphrase as a means for ensuring understanding and of Edward deBono's (1976) PMI (plus, minus, interesting) technique. PIP'N involves four steps:

P = ***Paraphrase.*** *State in your own words what you think the other person is saying. Your paraphrase will help you understand and remember the idea.*

I = ***Interesting.*** *Consider why the idea is interesting.*

P = ***Positive.*** *Think about what's good about the idea. Might it solve a problem or improve a situation?*

N = ***Negative.*** *Think about any negatives that the idea might entail. Might it be expensive? Difficult to implement? Is it directed at insignificant issues?*

Try using PIP'N the next time you hear a new idea. For practice, you may want to try PIP'N on the PIP'N technique itself.

(The next Listen to This box appears on page 433.)

Can you identify any additional principles that might be useful in informing an audience?

unfamiliar to the familiar, the unseen to the seen, the untasted to the tasted. Here, for example, Betsy Heffernan, a student from the University of Wisconsin (Reynolds and Schnoor 1991), relates the problem of sewage to a familiar historical event:

> *During our nation's struggle for independence, the citizens of Boston were hailed as heroes for dumping tea into Boston Harbor. But not to be outdone, many modern day Bostonians are also dumping things into the harbor. Five-thousand gallons of human waste every second. The New England Aquarium of Boston states that since 1900, Bostonians have dumped enough human sewage into the harbor to cover the entire state of Massachusetts chest deep in sludge. Unfortunately, Boston isn't alone. All over the country, bays, rivers and lakes are literally becoming cesspools.*

In this next example, Teresa Jascob, a student from Ohio State University (Schnoor, 1997, p. 97) relates the problems of drug interactions (the new) to mixing chemicals in the school lab (the old or familiar):

> *During our high school years, most of us learned in a chemistry class the danger of mixing harmless chemicals in lab. Add one drop of the wrong compound and suddenly you've created a stink bomb, or worse, an explosion. Millions of Americans run the same risk inside their bodies each day by combining drugs that are supposed to help restore or maintain good health.*

Vary the Levels of Abstraction

You can talk about freedom of the press in the abstract by talking about the importance of getting information to the public, by referring to the Bill of Rights, and by relating a free press to the preservation of democracy. That is, you can talk about the topic on a relatively high level of abstraction. But, you can also talk about freedom of the press by citing specific examples: how a local newspaper was prevented from running a story critical of the town council or about how Lucy Rinaldo was fired from the Accord Sentinel after she wrote a story critical of the mayor. You can talk about the topic on a relatively low level of abstraction, a level that is specific and concrete.

Combining the high abstraction and the specific seems to work best. Too many high abstractions without the specifics or too many specifics without the high abstractions will generally prove less effective than the combination of abstract and specific.

Here, for example, is an excerpt from a speech on the homeless. Note that in the first paragraph we have a relatively abstract description of homelessness. In the second paragraph, we get into specifics. In the last paragraph, the abstract and the concrete are connected.

> *Homelessness is a serious problem for all metropolitan areas throughout the country. It's currently estimated that there are now over 200,000 homeless in New York City alone. But, what is this really about? Let me tell you what it's about.*

> *It's about a young man. He must be about 25 or 30, although he looks a lot older. He lives in a cardboard box on the side of my apartment house. We call him Tom, although we really don't know his name. All his possessions are stored in this huge box. I think it was a box from a refrigerator. Actually, he doesn't have very much and what he has easily fits in this box. There's a blanket my neighbor threw out, some plastic bottles he puts water in, and some styrofoam containers he picked up from the garbage from Burger King He uses these to store whatever food he finds.*

> *What is homelessness about? It's about Tom and 200,000 other "Tom's" in New York and thousands of others throughout the rest of the country. And not all of them even have boxes to live in.*

THE SPEECH OF DESCRIPTION

When you describe, you're concerned with explaining an object, person, event, or process. Here are a few examples:

Describing an Object or Person

- the structure of the brain
- the contributions of Thomas Edison
- the parts of a telephone
- the layout of Philadelphia
- the hierarchy of a corporation
- the human body
- the components of a computer system

Describing an Event or Process

- the bombing in Oklahoma City
- the events leading to World War II
- organizing a body building contest

- the breakdown of Russian communism
- how a newspaper is printed
- the process of buying a house
- purchasing stock
- how a child acquires language
- how to read a textbook

Strategies for Describing

Here are some suggestions for describing objects and people, events and processes.

Select an Appropriate Organizational Pattern. Consider using a spatial or a topical organization when describing objects and people. Consider using a temporal pattern when describing events and processes. For example, if you were to describe the layout of Philadelphia, you might start from the north and work down to the south (using a spatial pattern). If you were to describe the contributions of Thomas Edison, you might select the three or four major contributions and discuss each of these equally (using a topical pattern).

If you were describing the events leading up to World War II, you might use a temporal pattern and start with the earliest and work up to the latest. A temporal pattern would also be appropriate for describing how a hurricane develops or how a parade is put together.

Use a Variety of Descriptive Categories. Describe the object or event with lots of descriptive categories. Use physical categories and ask yourself questions such as these:

- What color is it?
- How big is it?
- What is it shaped like?
- How high is it?
- How much does it weigh?
- How long or short is it?
- What is its volume?
- How attractive/unattractive is it?

Also, consider the social, psychological, and economic categories. In describing a person, for example, consider such categories as friendly/unfriendly, warm/cold, rich/poor, aggressive/meek, and pleasant/unpleasant.

Consider Using Presentation Aids. Presentation aids such as those described in Unit 9 will help you describe almost anything. Use them if you possibly can. In describing an object or person, show your listeners a picture; show them pictures of the brain, the inside of a telephone, the skeleton of the body. In describing an event or process, show them a diagram or flowchart to illustrate the stages or steps; show them a flowchart representing the stages in buying stock, in publishing a newspaper, in putting a parade together.

Consider Who? What? Where? When? and Why? These categories are especially useful when you want to describe an event or process. For example, if you're going to describe how to purchase a house, you might want to consider the people involved (who?), the steps you have to go through (what?), the places you'll have to go (where?), the time or sequence in which each of the steps have to take place (when?), and the advantages and disadvantages of buying the house (why?).

Developing the Speech of Description

Here are two examples of how you might go about constructing a speech of description. In this first example, the speaker describes four suggestions for increasing assertiveness (following a temporal sequence). Notice that the steps follow the order one would follow in becoming more assertive.

GENERAL PURPOSE: to inform

SPECIFIC PURPOSE: to describe how we can become more assertive

THESIS: assertiveness can be increased (How can assertiveness be increased?)

   I. Analyze assertive behaviors.
  II. Record your own assertive behaviors.
 III. Rehearse assertive behaviors.
 IV. Act assertively.

In this second example, the speaker describes the way in which fear works in intercultural communication.

GENERAL PURPOSE: to inform

SPECIFIC PURPOSE: to describe the way fear works in intercultural communication

THESIS: fear influences intercultural communication (How does fear influence intercultural communication?)

   I. We fear disapproval.
  II. We fear embarrassing ourselves.
 III. We fear being harmed.

In delivering such a speech, a speaker might begin by saying:

There are three major fears that interfere with intercultural communication. First, there's the fear of disapproval—from members of our own group as well as from members of the other person's group. Second, we fear embarrassing ourselves, even making fools of ourselves, by saying the wrong thing or appearing insensitive. And third, we may fear being harmed—our stereotypes of the other group may lead us to see their members as dangerous or potentially harmful to us.

Let's look at each of these fears in more detail and we'll be able to see how they influence our own intercultural communication behavior.

Consider first the fear of disapproval.

THE SPEECH OF DEFINITION

What is leadership? What is a born-again Christian? What is the difference between sociology and psychology? What is a cultural anthropologist? What is safe sex? These are all topics for informative speeches of definition.

A definition is a statement of the meaning or significance of a concept or term. Use definitions when you wish to explain difficult or unfamiliar concepts or when you wish to make a concept more vivid or forceful.

In defining a term or in giving an entire speech of definition, you may focus on defining a term, a system or theory, or the similarities and/or differences among terms or systems. It may be a subject new to the audience or one familiar to them but presented in a new and different way. Here are some examples:

Defining a Term
- What is multiculturalism?
- What is drug addiction?
- What is machismo?
- What is creativity?
- What is affirmative action?
- What is classism?
- What is political correctness?
- What is inflation?

Defining a System or Theory
- What is the classical theory of public speaking?
- What are the parts of a generative grammar?
- Confucianism: its major beliefs
- What is expressionism?
- What is futurism?
- The "play theory" of mass communication

Defining Similar and Dissimilar Terms or Systems
- Football and soccer: What is the difference?
- Communism and socialism: some similarities and differences
- What do Christians and Muslims have in common?
- Oedipus and Electra: How do they differ?
- Genetics and heredity
- Ballet and square dancing
- Differences between critical and creative thinking
- Animal and human rights
- Key word and directory searches
- Freshwater and saltwater fishing

Strategies for Defining

There are several approaches to defining your topic. Here are some suggestions.

Use a Variety of Definitions. When explaining a concept, it's helpful to define it in a number of different ways. Here are some of the most important ways to define a term.

The beginning of wisdom is the definition of terms.
—Socrates

Define by Etymology. One way to define a term is to trace its historical or linguistic development. In defining the word "communication," for example, you might note that it comes from the Latin *communis,* meaning "common"; in "communicating" you seek to establish a commonness, a sameness, a similarity with another individual.

And "woman" comes from the Anglo-Saxon *wifman,* which meant literally a "wife man," where the word man was applied to both sexes. Through phonetic change *wifman* became *woman.* Most larger dictionaries and, of course, etymological dictionaries will help you find useful etymological definitions.

Or, you might define a term by noting, not its linguistic etymology, but how it came to mean what it now means. For example, you might note that "spam" on the Net comes from a Monty Python television skit in which every item on the menu contained the product Spam. And much as the diner was forced to get Spam, so the Net surfer gets spam—even when he or she wants something else.

Define by Authority. A term can often be clarified by explaining how a particular authority views it. You might, for example, define "lateral thinking" by authority and say that Edward deBono, who developed lateral thinking in 1966, has noted that "lateral thinking involves moving sideways to look at things in a different way. Instead of fixing on one particular approach and then working forward from that, the lateral thinker tries to find other approaches."

Or you might use the authority of cynic and satirist Ambrose Bierce and define love as nothing but "a temporary insanity curable by marriage," and friendship as "a ship big enough to carry two in fair weather, but only one in foul."

Define by Negation. You might also define a term by noting what the term is not, that is, defining by negation. "A wife," you might say, "isn't a cook, a cleaning person, a babysitter, a seamstress, a sex partner. A wife is . . . " or "A teacher isn't someone who tells you what you should know but rather one who . . . ." Here Michael Marien (1992) defines futurists first negatively and then positively:

> *Futurists do not use crystal balls. Indeed, they're generally loathe to make firm predictions of what will happen. Rather, they make forecasts of what is probable, sketch scenarios of what is possible, and/or point to desirable futures—what is preferable and what strategies we should pursue to get there.*

Define by Direct Symbolization. You might also define a term by direct symbolization, by showing the actual thing or a picture or model of it. For example, a sales representative explaining a new computer keyboard would obviously use an actual keyboard in the speech. Similarly, a speech on magazine layout or types of fabrics would include actual layout pages and fabric samples.

Use Definitions to Add Clarity. If the purpose of the definition is to clarify, then it must do just that. This would be too obvious to mention except for the fact that so many speakers, perhaps for want of something to say, define terms that don't need extended definitions. Some speakers use def-

To define is to exclude and negate.
—Jose Ortega Y Gasset

initions that don't clarify, and that, in fact, complicate an already complex concept. Make sure your definitions define only what needs defining.

Use Credible Sources. When you use an authority to define a term, make sure the person is in fact an authority. Tell the audience who the authority is and the basis for the individual's expertise. In the following excerpt, note how Russell Peterson (1985) uses the expertise of Robert McNamara in his definition:

> When Robert McNamara was president of the World Bank, he coined the term "absolute poverty" to characterize a condition of life so degraded by malnutrition, illiteracy, violence, disease and squalor, to be beneath any reasonable definition of human decency. In 1980, the World Bank estimated that 780 million persons in the developing countries lived in absolute poverty. That's about three times as many people as live in the entire United States.

Proceed from the Known to the Unknown. Start with what your audience knows and work up to what is new or unfamiliar. Let's say you want to explain the concept of phonemics (with which your audience is totally unfamiliar). The specific idea you wish to get across is that each phoneme stands for a unique sound. You might proceed from the known to the unknown and begin your definition with something like this:

> We all know that in the written language each letter of the alphabet stands for a unit of the written language. Each letter is different from every other letter. A "t" is different from a "g" and a "g" is different from a "b" and so on. Each letter is called a "grapheme." In English we know we have 26 such letters.

> We can look at the spoken language in much the same way. Each sound is different from every other sound. A "t" sound is different from a "d" and a "d" is different from a "k" and so on. Each individual sound is called a "phoneme."

> Now, let me explain in a little more detail what I mean by a "phoneme."

Developing the Speech of Definition

Here are two examples of how you might go about constructing a speech of definition. In this first example, the speaker explains the parts of a resume and follows a spatial order, going from the top to the bottom of the page.

GENERAL PURPOSE: to inform

SPECIFIC PURPOSE: to define the essential parts of a resume

THESIS: there are four major parts to a resume (What are the four major parts of a resume?)

   I. Identify your career goals.
   II. Identify your educational background.

TIPS from professional speakers

To introduce new material to an audience, you must allow their brains to hook into old, well-known, comfortable information-processing systems. To absorb new material or make sense of any material, your audience needs for you to follow a logical progression. In real life "A" does truly come before "B" and "C." So it must in your presentation. Start at the beginning.

Sonya Hamlin, communication consultant, *How to Talk So People Listen: The Real Key to Job Success* (New York: Harper & Row, 1988): 99.

    III. Identify your work experience.
    IV. Identify your special competencies.

In this second example, the speaker selects three major types of lying for discussion and arranges these in a topical pattern.

GENERAL PURPOSE: to inform

SPECIFIC PURPOSE: to define lying by explaining the major types of lying misdirection

THESIS: there are three major kinds of lying (What are the three major kinds of lying?)

    I. Concealment is the process of hiding the truth.
    II. Falsification is the process of presenting false information as if it were true.
    III. Misdirection is the process of acknowledging a feeling but misidentifying its cause.

In delivering such a speech, a speaker might begin the speech by saying:

A lie is a lie is a lie. True? Well, not exactly. Actually, there are a number of different ways we can lie. We can lie by concealing the truth. We can lie by falsification, by presenting false information as if it were true. And, we can lie by misdirection, by acknowledging a feeling but misidentifying its cause. Let's look at the first type of lie— the lie of concealment.

Most lies are lies of concealment. Most of the time when we lie we simply conceal the truth. We don't actually make any false statements. Rather we simply don't reveal the truth. Let me give you some examples I overheard recently.

THE SPEECH OF DEMONSTRATION

In using demonstration (or in a speech devoted entirely to demonstration), you explain how to do something or how something operates. Here are some examples:

Demonstrating How to Do Something

    ■ how to give mouth-to-mouth resuscitation

What types of definitions might you use in an informative speech on "technological advances in communication?"

- how to balance a checkbook
- how to pilot a plane
- how to drive defensively
- how to set up a Web site
- how to say "no"
- how to prevent burnout
- how to ask for a raise
- how to burglar-proof your house
- how to develop your body
- how to use PowerPoint

Demonstrating How Something Operates

- how the body maintains homeostasis
- how a thermostat operates
- how perception works
- how the Internet works
- how divorce laws work
- how e-mail works
- how probate works
- how a hurricane develops
- how a heart bypass operation is performed

Strategies for Demonstrating

In demonstrating how to do something or how something operates, consider the following guidelines.

Use Temporal Organization. In most cases, a temporal pattern will work best in speeches of demonstration. Demonstrate each step in the sequence in which it's to be performed. In this way, you'll avoid one of the major difficulties in demonstrating a process, backtracking. Don't skip steps even if you think they're familiar to the audience. They may not be. Connect each step to the other with appropriate transitions. For example, in explaining the Heimlich maneuver you might say:

> Now that you have your arms around the choking victim's chest, your next step is to. . . ."

Assist your listeners by labeling the steps clearly, for example, "the first step," "the second step," and so on.

Begin with an Overview. It's often helpful when demonstrating to give a broad general picture and then present each step in turn. For example, let's say you were talking about how to prepare a wall for painting. You might begin with a general overview and say this:

> In preparing the wall for painting, you want to make sure that the wall is smoothly sanded, free of dust, and dry. Sanding a wall isn't like sanding a block of wood. So, let's look at the proper way to sand a wall.

In this way, your listeners will have a general idea of how you'll go about demonstrating the process.

Consider the Value of Presentation Aids. Presentation aids are especially helpful in showing the steps of a process in sequence. A good example of this is the signs in all restaurants demonstrating the Heimlich maneuver. These signs demonstrate each of the steps with pictures as well as words. The combination of verbal and graphic information makes it easy to understand this important process. In a speech on this topic, however, the best aid would be just the pictures so that the written words will not distract your audience from your oral explanation.

Developing the Speech of Demonstration

Here are two examples of the speech of demonstration. In this first example, the speaker explains the proper way to argue by identifying the ways we should not argue. As you can see, these unproductive fight strategies are all about equal in value and are arranged in a topical order.

GENERAL PURPOSE: to inform

SPECIFIC PURPOSE: to demonstrate how to fight fairly by identifying and demonstrating four unfair conflict strategies.

THESIS: conflict can be made more productive (How can conflict be made more productive?)

   I. Blame the other person.
  II. Unload all your previous grievances.
 III. Make light of the other person's displeasure.
 IV. Hit the other person with issues he or she can't handle effectively.

In the next example, the speaker identifies and demonstrates how to listen actively.

GENERAL PURPOSE: to inform

SPECIFIC PURPOSE: to demonstrate three techniques of active listening

THESIS: we can learn active listening (How can we learn active listening?)

   I. Paraphrase the speaker's meaning.
  II. Express understanding of the speaker's feelings.
 III. Ask questions.

In delivering the speech, the speaker might begin by saying:

Active listening is a special kind of listening. It's listening with total involvement, with a concern for the speaker. It's probably the most important type of listening you can engage in. Active listening consists of three steps: paraphrasing the speaker's meaning, expressing understanding of the speaker's feelings, and asking questions.

Your first step in active listening is to paraphrase the speaker's meaning. What is a paraphrase? A paraphrase is a restatement in your own words of the speaker's meaning. That is, you express in your own words what you think the speaker meant. For example, let's say that the speaker said. . . .

The three types of informative speeches identified here—description, demonstration, and definition—are just one way of looking at informative speaking. Here are some classifications of information speeches offered by other writers in public speaking. These will give you additional ideas for informative speeches.

Isa Engleberg (1994) classifies informative speeches into three groups:

- New information, for example, telling someone how to do something
- Enhance information, for example, detailing the recent research in AIDS
- Clarify information, for example, safe ways to lose weight

Stephen Lucas (1998) uses a four-part classification:

- Speeches about objects, persons, places, or things, for example, the contributions of a noted scientist or philosopher
- Speeches about processes or a series of actions, for example, explaining how to do something
- Speeches about events or happenings, for example, your first date
- Speeches about concepts, beliefs, or ideas, for example, theories of economics

George Rodman and Ron Adler (1997) offer a four-part classification for classroom speeches:

- Introductions of yourself as well as of objects, events, and concepts
- Instructions to do something, for example, how to use a scanner
- Demonstrations to show how something works, for example, how CPR works
- Explanations to explain why something works, for example, why cocaine has the effects it does

Joe Ayres and Janice Miller (1994) identify five types of informative speeches:

- Description, "to give a vivid, accurate picture of a person, place, event, or object"
- Lecture, for example, the classroom lecture
- Report, for example, the classroom oral report
- Instructions, explanations of how to do something
- Demonstration of a process, explaining how something works

UNIT IN BRIEF

Principles of Informative Speaking	Limit the amount of information you communicate.
	Adjust the level of complexity.
	Stress the relevance and the usefulness of the information to your audience.
	Relate new information to old.
	Vary the levels of abstraction.

Three Major Types of Informative Speeches	**Description**: describing a process or procedure, an event, an object, or a person.
	Definition: defining a term, system, or theory, or similarities and/or differences among terms.
	Demonstration: demonstrating how to do something or how something operates.

THINKING CRITICALLY ABOUT INFORMATIVE SPEAKING

REVIEWING KEY TERMS AND CONCEPTS IN INFORMATIVE SPEAKING

1. Review and define the key terms used in this unit:

- ❏ informative speaking (p. 362)
- ❏ limiting the amount of information (p. 362)
- ❏ adjusting the level of complexity (p. 363)
- ❏ stressing relevance and usefulness (p. 364)
- ❏ relating new information to old (p. 364)
- ❏ vary the levels of abstraction (p. 365)
- ❏ speeches of description (p. 366)
- ❏ speeches of definition (p. 369)
- ❏ speeches of demonstration (p. 372)

2. Review and explain the key concepts covered in this unit:

- ▪ What are the principles of informative speaking?
- ▪ What is the speech of description? What are the suggested strategies for developing the speech of description?
- ▪ What is the speech of definition? What are the suggested strategies for developing the speech of definition?
- ▪ What is the speech of demonstration? What are the suggested strategies for developing the speech of demonstration?

DEVELOPING INFORMATIVE SPEAKING STRATEGIES

1. You want to give an informative speech on virtual reality simulation but most of your audience members have never experienced it. How would you communicate this concept and this experience to your audience?

2. You're planning to give an informative speech on defensive driving and are considering the strategies that you might use. What organizational pattern would be appropriate? What types of presentation aids might you use? How will you define "defensive driving"? How will you introduce your speech?

3. You're scheduled to be the third speaker in a series of six presentations today. Unfortunately, the first speaker presented a really excellent speech on the same topic you're speaking on—how the Internet works. What should you do?

EVALUATING PUBLIC SPEECHES

1. Select an advertisement (television or print) and examine how closely it follows the principles of informative speaking identified here. In what ways does an advertisement differ from a speech?

2. Look over your first speech for the principles of information speaking. How closely did you follow the principles? What would you do now that you didn't think of at the time you prepared that speech?

USING TECHNOLOGY IN PUBLIC SPEAKING

1. Visit the Web site of the Society for Technical Communication at http://www.stc-va.org/ for guides for writing and speaking on technical matters.

2. Visit the Hypertext Webster Interface at http://c.gp.cs.cmu.edu:5103/prog/webster/ for an unusual dictionary that provides hypertext definitions so that you can get definitions of the words in the definition itself.

3. Visit the eclectic writer Web site at http://www.eclectics.com/writing/writing.html. What information on this Web site might prove useful to the public speaker?

PRACTICALLY SPEAKING

19.1 Short Speech Technique

Prepare and deliver a two-minute speech in which you:

a. describe some common object in the classroom.

b. define one of the following terms: love, friendship, power, pride, jealousy, truth, freedom, honesty, or faithfulness (use at least two different types of definitions).

c. demonstrate—without the aid of the object—how to tie a shoelace, use a blender, make a phone call, sew on a button, open a door with a credit card, move a bloc of text on a computer, print out a computer file, or use a template.

d. explain one of the principles of informative speaking using a variety of examples.

e. explain how one or more of the principles of informative speaking are used or violated in one of your textbooks.

19.2 Analyzing an Informative Speech

This exercise is designed to help you identify the major parts of an informative speech and the way they fit together. First, carefully read the speech by Cindy Weisenbeck, "False Memory Syndrome" presented here. For your first reading, ignore the critical thinking questions on the right. After you've read the entire speech, then reread it, this time reading and responding to the critical thinking questions. These questions should help you analyze the speech and help you see the principles of public speaking in clear application.

FALSE MEMORY SYNDROME

Connie Chung on the CBS evening news of August 25, 1993, stated, "(But) memories are far from perfect; there are some things that happen that we can't remember, then there are things we remember that never happened." Stephen Cook might finally agree. After his suit accusing Cardinal Bernardin of childhood sexual abuse was highly publicized, the Boston Globe of March 1, 1994, reported that he has since dropped all charges realizing his memories of abuse were purely fictitious. Stephen Cook's story embodies what the psychological community terms False Memory Syndrome. *Time* of November 29, 1993, describes False Memory Syndrome as "a troubling psychological phenomenon that is harming patients, devastating families, influencing legislation, taking up courtroom time and stirring fierce controversy." The magnitude of this problem is highlighted by the fact that both *Time* and *U.S. News & World Report* featured False Memory Syndrome as their cover stories during the week of November 29, 1993. Considering the sheer number of Americans in counseling or therapy today, the reality is that anyone of us could either be manipulated into developing our own false memories or be accused of abuse or other crimes based on someone else's false memories. In order to realize how we can protect ourselves from this phenomenon, we first need to investigate how False Memory Syndrome is destroying the lives of both the accused as well as the accuser. Then, we'll come to see how the psychological and legal communities are perpetuating this syndrome. And finally, we'll pursue solutions to ensure that none of us are

What functions does this introduction serve? What specifically gains your attention?

What connects the speaker, audience, and topic?

How does the speaker orient the audience?

Does the speaker draw you into the topic and make it interesting to you? How?

wrongly accused of childhood sexual abuse based solely on someone's false memories.

There is little question, given the number of cases throughout the country, that False Memory Syndrome both exists and is devastating individuals. The Gannett News Service on March 16, 1994, reported that the False Memory Syndrome Foundation, headquartered in Philadelphia, fielded calls from over 11,000 individuals who were either therapy patients persuaded to believe they were victims of sexual abuse or by individuals accused of abusing someone in the past. Through therapy, memories of abuse are "discovered," and given current legal trends, are then used to potentially convict the accused. States the *Skeptical Inquirer* of Summer 1993, juries today are finding patients guilty with no evidence except therapist-induced memories.

The result, as described by Dr. Richard Ofshe in *Society* of March/April 1993, is that "because the memories implicate family and community members of horrible crimes, the trauma of this therapy radiates outward to involve often dozens of innocent people. . . . Thousands of families have already been shattered. The possibilities for fracturing family groups are all being realized: the accused spouse is divorced; siblings are forced to choose sides; grandparents are denied access to their grandchildren; grandchildren lose contact with their grandparents, and so on."

Unfortunately, False Memory Syndrome does not only harm the accused, for the therapy patients themselves are also victimized. The November 29, 1993, issue of *Time* magazine relates the story of 39-year-old Melody Gavigan. She had checked herself into a local psychiatric hospital for depression. There, her counselor suggested incest. Through a therapist, she recovered extensive memories of molestation from ages one through five. She became so convinced of the memories that she confronted her father, severed all ties with him and formed an incest survivors group. Once away from therapy, Melody realized that her memories were simply not true. She is currently seeking to repair her familial relationships and is suing the hospital for malpractice. The devastation for Ms. Gavigan, as well as all victims of False Memory Syndrome, was expressed by Psychiatrist John J. Cannell in the *Missoulian* of February 21, 1993. "[But] there is no healing if someone relies on something that is false to explain their problems. The pain is still there. People won't get well unless you search for the real causes of their pain." Clearly, our society's attempts to aid the true victims of childhood sexual abuse have left us with extensive and destructive problems.

With this devastation in mind, let's try to understand how and why false memories are created. Three critical underlying factors are responsible, for false memories are created through hypnosis

What organizational structure is signaled by this orientation? How else might this have been presented?

Are you convinced that the accusation of Stephen Cook against Cardinal Bernardin was a case of false memory syndrome? If not, what evidence would you want?

What level of credibility do you ascribe to the skeptical inquirer? How might the speaker have insured that you would have a high level of credibility for these publications?

How effective was the story of Melody Gavigan?

How effective is this transition?

and sustained because of a profit motive and current laws.

In examining how false memories are created, it is important to keep in mind that repressed memories themselves are not the problem, but rather how those memories are uncovered. The *U.S. News & World Report* of November 29, 1993, reports that the American Medical Association has repeatedly cited hypnosis as the critical underlying factor in current cases of False Memory Syndrome. Though hypnosis can be effective for a variety of needs, memory recall is not one of them. Dr. George Ganway explains in the May 17, 1993, *New Yorker* that memories recovered in hypnosis are more likely to contain a mixture of fact and fantasy.

By convincing patients that they were abused and should prosecute, the therapist is creating a source of income for years to come. *Newsweek* of December 13, 1993, reported that therapists justify legal action as a legitimate way to pay for the cost of therapy. Dr. Michael Yapko, a Psychologist and Expert of suggestive therapies, claims, "in essence, therapists create the problem they have to treat."

Finally, the third institution that fuels the production of false memories is our current legal system. Two recent legal trends in the United States are responsible for false memories entering the courtroom. First, according to *Society* of March/April, 1993, within the last two years, 15 states have decided to allow therapy-induced memories to serve as actual evidence in childhood sexual abuse cases. What we must understand is that under current law, once we are accused, we have virtually no way of defending ourselves against the testimony of the alleged victim and their therapist. The memories, whether real or false, can serve as grounds to convict us. Additionally, states the *Minneapolis Star and Tribune* of October 10, 1993, 23 states have enacted laws extending the statute of limitations for sexual abuse cases from three to nine years after the memory is recalled. This opens the door for more therapy patients to act on the suggestions of their therapists, filling our courtrooms with cases that consist of no more than fabricated evidence.

With the precedent toward hypnosis, combined with a legal system that drives therapists' profits, the stage is set for intense victimization of families. In order to end the needless destruction of American families, three steps need to be taken.

Eleanor Goldstein in her 1992 book, *Confabulations,* argues that the first step to ending the injustice is through legislation. *The New York Times* of March 27, 1994, reported that Illinois has recently introduced a bill "to protect people from lawsuits based on psychological quackery." This bill will reduce the statute of limitations for sexual abuse cases based on therapy-induced memories. Furthermore, the 15 states that currently allow therapy-induced memories to serve as evidence need to rescind

How effectively are the three underlying factors stated? How might they have been stated differently?

How effectively does the speaker establish the profit motive as one of the factors underlying false memory syndrome? What else might the speaker have said?

How effectively does the speaker establish that the current laws are a factor in false memory syndrome?

What additional information would you have liked to have included in the speech?

How effective is this internal summary and transition? Would you have preferred to have a brief preview of the three steps? Would this have helped you follow the remainder of the speech?

their laws. The remaining states that have no legislation dealing with these issues need to pass laws that do not allow therapy-induced memories into the courtroom. Therefore, the only way we can protect ourselves from being wrongly accused or even imprisoned is by insisting that these laws are changed in each of our own states.

Second, the psychiatric community needs regulations regarding the use of hypnosis as a treatment for sexual abuse. As a model for our own personal advocacy, we can turn to the state of Ohio. According to the June 20, 1993, issue of the Athens, Ohio "Messenger," a citizen group asked the State Board of Psychology to establish guidelines pertaining to therapy for patients who may have been abused or molested. We must confront our own State Boards of Psychology and demand that rigorous regulations be placed on counselors and therapists, declaring hypnosis and memory-induced therapies unethical.

Third, and most importantly, we must be willing to take the time to protect ourselves. Before seeing a therapist of any kind for any reason, there are two things you need to ask your potential therapist: first, ask what percentage of the therapist's patients have been diagnosed as victims of childhood sexual abuse. If the number is unusually high and makes you uncomfortable, ask a second question. Find out what types of therapy the therapist tends to rely on. If the answer is hypnosis or suggestive therapy, seek out another therapist. Only by questioning our potential therapists can we ensure that our problems are accurately and fairly diagnosed.

By better understanding the problems created by False Memory Syndrome, how and why false memories are created and how we can protect ourselves, it is clear that reliance on memory is far from foolproof. As more of us turn to the aid of therapy to understand our problems, it is essential that the advice we receive is accurate and, ultimately, healing. By allowing false memories to be created, we undermine the very point of mental health. Our alarm must produce change. Change that will protect not only the legitimate victims of abuse, but more importantly, the truly innocent.

SOURCE: This speech was given by Cindy Weisenbeck, a student at the University of Wisconsin—Eau Claire, Wisconsin. She was coached by Tom Glauner. The speech is reprinted from *Winning Orations of the Interstate Oratorical Association*, Larry G. Schnoor, ed. (1994), with permission of the Interstate Oratorical Association.

Did the speaker effectively make the case for "ending the injustice through legislation"? What else might have been included?

Are you convinced that the psychiatric community needs to be regulated in its use of hypnosis in treating sexual abuse cases?

What do you think of the speaker's recommendations for taking charge of our own lives when, for example, seeking a therapist?

What percentage of patients diagnosed as victims of childhood sexual abuse would you consider high? 10%, 25%, 40%, 55%, 70%, 85% How would you have handled this if you were the speaker?

Are you ready to rule out hypnosis as a viable therapeutic procedure for childhood sexual abuse?

Was the type of evidence appropriate to the speech and topic? How effectively did the speaker integrate the research?

Assuming your class as your audience, how would you have titled the speech?

What effect did the speech have on you? Did it inform? Did it strengthen or change your attitudes and beliefs about false memory syndrome? Will it move you to any specific action (perhaps at a later date)?

The Persuasive Speech

UNIT CONTENTS	UNIT OBJECTIVES
	After completing this unit, you should be able to:
Attitudes, Beliefs, Values, and Behaviors	Define *attitude, belief, value,* and *behavior* as used in persuasion.
Facts, Values, and Policies	Define and distinguish among questions of fact, value, and policy.
Principles of Persuasion	Explain the principles of persuasion: selective exposure, cultural difference, audience participation, inoculation, magnitude of change, identification, consistency, logos, pathos, and ethos.
The Speech to Strengthen or Change Attitudes or Beliefs	Define and explain the strategies for developing the speech to strengthen or change attitudes or beliefs.
The Speech to Stimulate Action	Define and explain the strategies for developing the speech to stimulate action.

Most of the speeches you hear are persuasive. The speeches of politicians, advertisers, and religious leaders are clear examples. In most of your own speeches, you too will aim at persuasion. You'll try to change your listeners' attitudes and beliefs or perhaps get them to do something. In school you might try to persuade others to (or not to) expand the core curriculum, use a plus-minus or a pass-fail grading system, disband the basketball team, allocate increased student funds for the school newspaper, establish competitive majors, or eliminate fraternity initiation rituals. On your job you may be called upon to speak in favor of (or against) having a union, a wage increase proposal, a health benefit package, or the election of a new shop steward.

In this unit we focus on the nature of attitudes, beliefs, values, and behaviors; the principles for making your persuasive speeches more effective; and the ways to prepare the two major types of persuasive speeches.

ATTITUDES, BELIEFS, VALUES, AND BEHAVIORS

In your persuasive speeches you might want to strengthen or change the attitudes, beliefs, or values of your listeners. Or, you might want to get them to do something; that is, you might want to influence their behaviors. Let's define more specifically what is meant by attitudes, beliefs, values, and behaviors. You may wish to review Unit 10, "The Audience: Sociological Analysis and Adaptation," where these terms were discussed in the context of audience analysis.

An **attitude** is a tendency to behave in a certain way. If, for example, you have a favorable attitude toward chemistry, you would be more apt to select chemistry courses, to read about chemistry, to talk about chemistry, and to conduct chemistry experiments. If you have an unfavorable attitude toward chemistry, you would avoid chemistry courses, not read about chemistry, and so on. If you have a negative attitude toward horror films, you would resist going to see them and might try to discourage your friends or family from seeing them as well.

A **belief** is a conviction in the existence or reality of something or in the truth of some assertion. You may believe that there's justice in the world or that there's life after death. You may believe that democracy (or socialism or communism) is the preferred system of government or that children should be seen and not heard. You may believe that power corrupts, that soft drugs lead to hard drugs, or that television contributes to teenage violence.

A **value** is a indicator of what you feel is good or bad, ethical or unethical, just or unjust. Generally, values are heavily influenced by the culture in which you were raised. For example, you probably feel that caring for the poor and the sick is good, but that killing and stealing is bad. You positively value caring for the poor and negatively value the killing and stealing. Similarly, you probably place a positive value on love and honesty and a negative value on hate and dishonesty.

Behavior in persuasion refers to overt, observable actions: voting for Tania for class president, buying a Ford, reading to a sightless student, studying for an economics final, and saying "Yes, I will marry you" are all examples of behaviors. They're all actions that you can observe. Beliefs, attitudes, and values, on the other hand, are not directly observable. Rather, you have to infer they exist from a person's behavior. So, for example, you might observe a person giving money to a particular charity and on that basis you might infer that this person has a favorable attitude toward this particular charity, that he or she believes that the charity does good work, and that he or she positively values helping others.

Now, the reason why beliefs, attitudes, and values are so important in persuasion is simply that people's behavior—which is what you ultimately want to influence—depends on their attitudes, beliefs, and values. So, if you can change their beliefs, say, about abortion, you might get them to vote one way or another or you might get them to contribute to a particular abortion position. If you can change the values that people have toward animals and toward animal experimentation, you might get them to boycott cosmetics that use animals in their testing.

Further, the audience's beliefs, attitudes, and values will influence how they respond to your thesis, your propositions, your arguments, your evidence, and just about everything else you do in your speech. For example, if you were going to give a speech defending physician-assisted suicide, it would be crucial for you to know the beliefs, attitudes, and values that your audience has before you can frame and support your propositions. You have to prepare very different speeches for an audience that believes that suicide of any kind is morally wrong and an audience whose concern centers on how physician-assisted suicides can be monitored to prevent violating the patients' wishes. So, in constructing your persuasive speeches and in using the 10 principles of persuasion discussed later in this unit, be sure to take into consideration the beliefs, attitudes, and values of the audience as these relate to *anything* you'll say in your speech—but particularly to your thesis, main propositions, and main supports.

There is nothing in the world like a persuasive speech to fuddle the mental apparatus and upset the convictions and debauch the emotions of an audience not practiced in the tricks and illusions of oratory.
—Mark Twain

FACTS, VALUES, AND POLICIES

A useful way to look at the issues you'll be dealing with in your persuasive speeches (whether as your thesis or a particular proposition) is to view them as questions of facts, values, or policies.

Questions of Fact

Questions of fact concern what is or is not true, what does or does not exist, what did or did not happen. Recently, the media of the entire country was focused on what did or did not take place between the president and a White House intern and whether or not what was said constitutes perjury—questions of fact. Sometimes a speaker will formulate a thesis around a question of fact in such speeches as:

- Iraq is hiding (not hiding) chemical weapons.
- This company has (doesn't have) a glass ceiling for women.
- Wellington was (wasn't) slandered (or libeled or defamed).
- Ali's death was (wasn't) a case of physician-assisted suicide.
- Marijuana does (not) lead to hard drugs.
- Gay men and lesbians make (don't make) competent military personnel.
- Television violence leads (doesn't lead) to violent behavior in viewers.

At other times, you may want to establish a question of fact as one of your major propositions. So, for example, let's say you're giving a speech advocating that the military give gay men and lesbians full equality. In this case, one of your propositions might focus on a question of fact, and here you might seek to establish that gay men and lesbians make competent military personnel. Once that is established, you might then be in a better position to argue for equality in military policy.

Questions of Value

A question of value concerns what you consider good or bad, moral or immoral, just or unjust. Theses devoted to questions of value might look something like this:

- IQ tests are biased.
- Bullfighting is inhumane.
- The death penalty is morally unjustifiable.

And, in the same way as with questions of fact, you might have a speech in which one of your propositions is a question of value. For example, you might want to establish that IQ tests are biased as one of your propositions, with your thesis being that IQ tests should be discontinued at your school. Or you might want to show that bullfighting is inhumane in a speech with the thesis that bullfighting should be declared illegal throughout the world.

Questions of Policy

Questions of policy concern what should be done, what procedures should be adopted, what law should be changed, in short, what policy

Using the classification of fact, value, and policy, how would you classify the majority of speeches given at ceremonial functions such as that pictured here? Speeches given by politicians to potential voters? Speeches given by religious leaders to their followers? Speeches within a business organization?

should be followed. Frequently persuasive speeches revolve around questions of policy, for example:

- What should the college's sexual harassment policy be?
- What should our drug policy be?
- What immigration policy should we adopt?
- What alcohol level should be used to establish "drunk driving"?
- What should our position be on affirmative action?

Generally, questions of policy are used as theses more often than as major propositions. Still, in some instances, you might phrase a major proposition around a policy issue. For example, a lawyer might want to argue that the alcohol level that should be used to establish "drunk driving" should be much higher than it currently is in a speech designed to get her or his client off a driving-while-intoxicated charge.

As noted here, any of these questions can be used to help you conceptualize a thesis statement or to frame a major proposition. A single speech, of course, may involve questions of fact, value, and policy. For example, you might argue, first, that the number of homeless people is growing (question of fact) and, second, that everyone is responsible for the less fortunate (question of value), and then conclude with your thesis that legislation must be enacted to reduce homelessness (question of policy).

PRINCIPLES OF PERSUASION

Your success in strengthening or changing attitudes or beliefs and in moving your listeners to action will depend on your use of the principles of persuasion. These principles will be useful to you in all your attempts at persuasion; they're summarized in Table 20.1.

Selective Exposure

Your listeners (in fact, all audiences) follow the "law of selective exposure." It has at least two parts:

TABLE 20.1 Ten Principles of Persuasion

The first seven of these principles are discussed in detail in this unit. The last three—logos, pathos, and ethos—are the most important. They are identified here to position them as principles of persuasion and are then discussed in detail, each in a separate unit: Unit 21 discusses logic and reasoning, Unit 22 considers emotional appeals, and Unit 23 focuses on making yourself credible.

Principle	Advice
Selective Exposure	Anticipate selective exposure when you challenge existing attitudes, beliefs, and values.
Cultural Differences	Take into consideration cultural differences placed on persuasive appeals and patterns.
Audience Participation	Actively involve the audience; make them a part of the process.
Inoculation	Strive for small gains with an inoculated audience; proceed inductively when attacking inoculated beliefs; refute counter arguments when strengthening an audience's beliefs.
Magnitude of Change	Strive for small gains; get your "foot in the door" by beginning with a very small request and leading up to your real request; get the "door in your face" by beginning with a request larger than you really want and following it with a smaller request.
Identification	Establish common ground with the audience; emphasize similarities and points of agreement.
Consistency	Show the audience how their beliefs and values are consistent with what you're urging them to believe or do.
Logos, logical appeals	Use reliable and valid evidence and sound argument to prove your case.
Pathos, motivational appeals	Arouse the emotions of the audience, appeal to the motives that influence their behavior.
Ethos, credibility appeals	Establish your own believability by stressing your competence, character, and charisma.

1. Listeners actively seek out information that supports their opinions, beliefs, values, decisions, and behaviors.
2. Listeners actively avoid information that contradicts their existing opinions, beliefs, attitudes, values, and behaviors.

Of course, if you're very sure that your opinions and attitudes are logical and valid, then you might not bother to seek out supporting information. In fact, you may not actively avoid contradictory messages. You exercise selective exposure most often when your confidence in your opinions and beliefs is weak.

So, if you want to persuade an audience that holds attitudes different from your own, anticipate selective exposure operating and proceed inductively; that is, hold back on your thesis until you've given them your evidence and argument. Only then relate this evidence and argument to your thesis.

If you were to present them with your thesis first, they might tune you out without giving your position a fair hearing. So, become thoroughly familiar with the attitudes of your audience if you want to succeed in making these necessary adjustments and adaptations.

Let's say you're giving a speech on the need to reduce spending on college athletic programs. If your audience was composed of listeners who agreed with you and wanted to cut athletic spending, you might lead with your thesis. Your introduction might go something like this:

> *Our college athletic program is absorbing money that we can more profitably use for the library, science labs, and language labs. Let me explain how the money now going to unnecessary athletic programs could be better spent in these other areas.*

On the other hand, let's say that you were addressing alumni who strongly favored the existing level of spending on athletic programs. In this case, you might want to lead with your evidence and hold off stating your thesis until the end of your speech.

Cultural Differences

Members of different cultures respond very differently to persuasive attempts (Lustig and Koester 1999; Dodd 1995). In some cultures, for example, credibility is extremely influential in persuasion. If the religious leader says something, it's taken as true and therefore believed. In other cultures, the religious leader's credibility would be assessed individually—not all religious leaders are equally believable. In still other cultures, the religious leader's credibility would be assessed negatively.

The schools in the United States teach students to demand logical and reliable evidence before believing something. The critical thinking emphasis throughout contemporary education and in this text are good examples of this concern with logic, argument, and evidence. Other cultures give much less importance to these forms persuasion.

Some audiences favor a deductive pattern of reasoning. They expect to hear the general principle first and the evidence, examples, and argument second. Other audiences favor a more inductive pattern (Asian audiences are often cited as examples) where the examples and illustrations are given first and the general principle or conclusion is given second.

Still other cultures expect a very clear statement of the speaker's conclusion. Low-context cultures (the United States, Germany, and Sweden, for example) generally expect an explicit statement of the speaker's position and an explicit statement of what he or she wants the audience to do. Low-context cultures prefer to leave as little unspoken as possible. High-context cultures (Japanese, Chinese, and Arabic, for example) prefer a less explicit statement and prefer to be lead indirectly to the speaker's conclusion. An explicit statement ("Vote for Smith" or "Buy Viterall") may be interpreted as too direct and even insulting.

Audience Participation

Persuasion is greatest when the audience participates actively in your presentation. In experimental tests the same speech is delivered to different audiences. The attitudes of each audience are measured before and after

To please people is the greatest step toward persuading them.
—Lord Chesterfield

the speech. The difference between their attitudes before and after the speech is taken as a measure of the speech's effectiveness. For one audience the sequence consists of (1) pretest of attitudes, (2) presentation of the persuasive speech, and (3) post-test of attitudes. For another audience the sequence consists of (1) pretest of attitudes, (2) presentation of the persuasive speech, (3) audience paraphrases or summarizes the speech, and (4) post-test of attitudes. Researchers consistently find that those listeners who participated actively (as in paraphrasing or summarizing) are more persuaded than those who received the message passively. Demagogues and propagandists who succeed in arousing huge crowds often have the crowds chant slogans, repeat catch phrases, and otherwise participate actively in the persuasive experience.

The implication here is simple: persuasion is a transactional process. It involves both speaker and listeners. You'll be more effective if you can get the audience to participate actively in the process.

Here's a good example involving a simple show of hands, given by Ernest W. Deavenport (1998), Chair and CEO of Eastman Chemical Company in a speech to the Chief Executive Club of Boston:

If given a choice, what do you think employees would prefer, several weeks of training or a $1,000 bonus? Let me see a show of hands of how many of you think the average employee would go for the training?

As a matter of fact, almost all of the employees in a recent N-A-M focus group said they would take several weeks of training over the $1,000 bonus.

Inoculation

Suppose that you lived in a germ-free environment. Upon leaving this germ-free environment and upon exposure to germs, you would be particularly susceptible to infection because your body has not built up an immunity—it has no resistance. Resistance, the ability to fight off germs, might be achieved by the body, if not naturally, through some form of inoculation. You could, for example, be injected with a weakened dose of the germ so that your body fights off the germ by building up antibodies that create an "immunity" to this type of infection. Your body, because of the antibodies it produced, is able to fight off even powerful doses of this germ.

The principle of inoculation in persuasion works similarly. Some of your attitudes and beliefs have existed in a "germ-free" environment; they have never been attacked or challenged. For example, many of us have lived in environments in which the values of a democratic form of government, the importance of education, and the virtues of capitalism have not been challenged. Consequently, we have not been "immunized" against attacks on these values and beliefs. We have no counterarguments (antibodies) prepared to fight off these attacks on our beliefs, so if someone were to come along with strong arguments against these beliefs, we might be easily persuaded.

Contrast these "germ-free" beliefs with issues that have been attacked and for which we have a ready arsenal of counterarguments. Our attitudes on the draft, nuclear weapons, war, government corruption, athletics, and

Beware of people carrying ideas. Beware of ideas carrying people.
—Barbara Grizzuti Harrison

thousands of other issues have been challenged in the press, on television, and in our interpersonal interactions. As a result of this exposure, we have counterarguments ready for any attacks on our beliefs concerning these issues. We have been inoculated and immunized against attacks should someone attempt to change our attitudes or beliefs.

If you're addressing an inoculated audience, take into consideration the fact that they have a ready arsenal of counterarguments to fight off your persuasive assault. For example, if you're addressing heavy smokers on the need to stop smoking or alcoholics on the need to stop drinking, you should assume that these people have already heard your arguments and that they have already inoculated themselves against them. In such situations, be prepared, therefore, to achieve only small gains. Don't try to totally reverse the beliefs of a well-inoculated audience. For example, it would be asking too much to get the smokers or the alcoholics to quit their present behaviors as a result of one speech. But, it might not be too much to ask to get them—at least some of them—to attend a meeting of a smoking clinic or Alcoholics Anonymous.

If you're trying to persuade an uninoculated audience, your task is often much simpler since you don't have to penetrate a fully developed immunization shield. For example, it might be relatively easy to persuade a group of high school seniors about the values of a college core curriculum since they probably have not thought much about the issue and probably don't have arguments against the core curriculum at their ready disposal.

Do recognize, however, that even when an audience has not immunized itself, they often take certain beliefs to be self-evident. As a result they may well tune out any attacks on such cherished beliefs or values. This might be the case, for example, if you try to persuade an audience of socialists to support capitalist policies. Although they may not have counterarguments ready, they may accept their communal welfare beliefs as so fundamental that they simply will not listen to attacks on such beliefs. Again, proceed slowly and be content with small gains. Further, an inductive approach would suit your purposes better here. Attacking cherished beliefs directly creates impenetrable resistance. Instead, build your case by first presenting your arguments and evidence and gradually work up to your conclusion.

Magnitude of Change

The greater and more important the change you want to produce in your audience, the more difficult your task will be. The reason is simple: we normally demand a greater number of reasons and lots more evidence before we make important decisions—career changes, moving our families to another state, or investing our life savings in certain stocks.

On the other hand, we may be more easily persuaded (and demand less evidence) on relatively minor issues—whether to take a course in "Small Group Communication" rather than "Persuasion," or to give to the United Heart Fund instead of the American Heart Fund.

People change gradually, in small degrees, over a long period of time. And although there are cases of sudden conversions, this general principle holds true more often than not. Persuasion, therefore, is most effective when it strives for small changes and works over a considerable period of time. For example, a persuasive speech stands a better chance when it tries to get the alcoholic to attend just one AA meeting rather than to give up alcohol for life. If you try to convince your audience to change their attitudes radically or to engage in behaviors to which they're initially opposed, your attempts will probably backfire. In this type of situation, the audience may tune you out, closing its ears to even the best and most logical arguments.

When you have the opportunity to try to persuade your audience on several occasions (rather than simply delivering one speech), two strategies will prove relevant: the foot-in-the-door and the door-in-the-face techniques.

Foot-in-the-Door Technique. As its name implies, this technique involves getting your foot in the door first. That is, you first request something small, something that your audience will easily comply with. Once this compliance has been achieved, you then make your real request (Freedman and Fraser, 1966; Dejong, 1979; Cialdini, 1984; Pratkanis and Aronson, 1991). Research shows that people are more apt to comply with a large request after they have complied with a similar but much smaller request. For example, in one study the objective was to get people to put a "Drive Carefully" sign on their lawn (a large request). When this (large) request was made first, only about 17 percent of the people were willing to comply. However, when this request was preceded by a much smaller request (to sign a petition), between 50 and 76 percent granted permission to install the sign. The smaller request and its compliance paved the way for the larger request and put the audience into an agreement mode.

In using this strategy, be sure that your first request is small enough to gain compliance. If it isn't, then you miss the chance ever to gain compliance with your desired larger request.

Door-in-the-Face Technique. This technique is the opposite of foot-in-the-door (Cialdini and Ascani, 1976; Cialdini, 1984). In this strategy you first make a large request that you know will be refused (for example, "We're asking most people to donate $100 for new school computers). Later, you make a more moderate request, the one you really want your listeners to comply with (for example, "Might you be willing to contribute $10?"). In changing from the large to the more moderate request, you demonstrate your willingness to compromise and your sensitivity to your listeners. The general idea here is that your listeners will feel that since you've made concessions, they will also make concessions and at least contribute something. Listeners will probably also feel that $10 is actually quite little, considering the initial request. Research shows, people are more likely to comply and will donate the $10.

In using this technique, be sure that your first request is significantly larger than your desired request but not so large as to seem absurd and be rejected out of hand.

Identification

If you can show your audience that you and they share important attitudes, beliefs, and values, you'll clearly advance your persuasive goal. Other similarities are also important. For example, in some cases similarity of cultural, educational, or social background may help you identify yourself with your audience. Do beware, however, that insincere or dishonest identification is likely to backfire and create problems for the speaker. So, avoid even implying similarities between yourself and your audience that don't exist.

Consistency

People strive for consistency among their attitudes, beliefs, values, and behaviors. We expect there to be logical relationships among them, and when that relationship exists we feel comfortable. When they contradict each other, we feel uncomfortable and we seek change—usually just enough to restore balance and comfort.

Consistency is the more common case, and you can probably see lots of examples in your own thoughts and behaviors. For example, if you have positive attitudes toward, say, animal rights, then you probably believe that animals do in fact have rights that have to be recognized and that, were you in a position to do something for animal rights, you would do it.

Inconsistency or dissonance occurs when, say, attitudes contradict behavior. For example, if you have positive attitudes toward helping the homeless but don't actually do anything about it, you're probably in a state of dissonance or discomfort—not always, but just when you think about the homeless and particularly when you bring to consciousness this discrepancy between attitude and behavior. And, when dissonance occurs, you'll try to do something to reduce it. For example, if your dissonance becomes too uncomfortable, you might decide to give money to the homeless shelter or to buy coffee for the homeless man who sits by your apartment building.

Generally, direct your propositions at increasing the audience's sense of consistency. Show them that, by accepting your thesis, their attitudes and behaviors will be consistent and in harmony. You might remind your audience of their positive attitudes to helping those less fortunate and then show them that by doing as you advise that their behavior will be consistent with their attitudes. The salesperson uses this technique regularly: "You want status, you want performance, you want luxury; a BMW, it's your only choice." In this case, buying the BMW brings your behavior into consistency with your attitudes and values.

If the audience is experiencing dissonance, try to connect your thesis or your propositions to its reduction. For example, let's say you're giving a speech to persuade the neighborhood merchants to recycle more carefully. Although they believe in recycling, they aren't following the rules because, they say, it takes too much time. Here is a situation in which the audience is experiencing dissonance—their belief in the value of recycling is contradicted by their nonrecycling behavior. As a speaker, your task would be to show the audience how they can reduce dissonance by, for example, following a few simple rules or by using color-coded trash cans. If you can show them how they can easily change their behavior to be consistent with their attitudes, you'll have a favorably disposed audience.

Logos

Generally, persuasion is best achieved when logical reasons are given, when you can provide listeners with solid evidence and sound argument to prove your case. This principle is probably more true with educated audiences than with uneducated audiences, but it's a useful generalization for all audiences. Because of the importance of sound evidence and argument, this particular principle of persuasion is discussed at length in Unit 21, "Developing Arguments."

Pathos

Although people are logical, they're also emotional and as such are greatly influenced by appeals to their emotions. If you can arouse an audience's emotions, you're in a much better position to persuade them. This topic is discussed at length in Unit 22, "Motivating Behavior."

Ethos

You'll be more persuasive if your listeners see you as credible. If your listeners see you as competent, knowledgeable, of good character, and charismatic or dynamic, they will think you credible. As a result you'll be more effective in changing their attitudes or in moving them to do something. Unit 23, "Speaker Credibility," considers this principle at length and offers a variety of specific suggestions on how you can enhance your own credibility.

THE ETHICS OF Propaganda Techniques

Here are four propaganda techniques that are generally considered unethical but are in wide use in public speeches and in the appeals of advertisers (Lee and Lee 1972, 1995).

Name-Calling. Here the speaker gives an idea, a group of people, or a political philosophy a bad name ("atheist," "Neo-Nazi") to try to get you to condemn the idea without analyzing the argument and evidence. The opposite of name-calling is "glittering generality" in which the speaker tries to make you accept some idea by associating it with things you value highly ("democracy," "free speech," "academic freedom"). By using "virtue words," the speaker tries to get you to ignore the evidence and simply approve of the idea.

Transfer. Here the speaker associates her or his idea with something you respect (to gain your approval) or with something you detest (to gain your rejection). For example, a proposal for condom distribution in schools may be characterized as a means for "saving our children from AIDS" (to encourage acceptance) or as a means for "promoting sexual promiscuity" (to encourage disapproval). Sports car manufacturers try to get you

to buy their cars by associating them with high status and sexual appeal, and exercise clubs and diet plans by associating them with health, self-confidence, and interpersonal appeal.

Testimonial. This device involves using the image associated with some person to gain your approval (if you respect the person) or your rejection (if you don't respect the person). This is the technique of advertisers who use people dressed up to look like doctors or plumbers or chefs to sell their products. Sometimes this technique takes the form of using only vague and general "authorities," for example, "experts agree," "scientists say," "good cooks know," or "dentists advise."

Plain Folks. Using this device, the speaker identifies himself or herself with the audience. The speaker is good-the "reasoning" goes-because he or she is one of the people, just "plain folks" like everyone else.

Can you identify specific print advertisements that make use of one or more of these propaganda techniques?

[The next Ethics in Public Speaking box appears on page 413.]

THE SPEECH TO STRENGTHEN OR CHANGE ATTITUDES, BELIEFS, OR VALUES

Many speeches seek to strengthen existing attitudes, beliefs, or values. Much religious and political speaking, for example, tries to strengthen beliefs and values. People who listen to religious speeches usually are already believers, so these speeches strive to strengthen the beliefs and values the people already hold. Here the audience is already favorable to the speaker's purpose and is willing to listen. Speeches designed to change attitudes or beliefs are more difficult to construct. Most people resist change. When you try to get people to change their beliefs or attitudes, you're fighting an uphill (but not impossible) battle.

Speeches designed to strengthen or change attitudes or beliefs come in many forms. Depending on the initial position of the audience, you can view the following examples as topics for speeches to strengthen or change attitudes, or beliefs.

- Marijuana should be legalized.
- General education requirements should be abolished.
- Expand college athletic programs.
- History is a useless study.
- Television shows are mindless.
- CDs and tapes should be rated for excessive sex and violence.
- Puerto Rico should become the fifty-first state.

Strategies for Strengthening or Changing Attitudes, Beliefs, and Values

When you attempt to strengthen or change your listeners' attitudes, beliefs, and values, consider the following principles.

Estimate Listeners' Attitudes, Beliefs, and Values. Carefully estimate—as best you can—the current state of your listeners' attitudes, beliefs, and values. If your goal is to strengthen these, then you can state your thesis and your objectives as early in your speech as you wish. Since your listeners are in basic agreement with you, your statement of your thesis will enable you to create a bond of agreement between you. You might say, for example:

> Like you, I am deeply committed to the fight against abortion. Tonight, I'd like to explain some new evidence that has recently come to light that we must know if we are to be effective in our fight against legalized abortion.

If, however, you're in basic disagreement and you wish to change their attitudes, then reserve your statement of your thesis until you've provided them with your evidence and argument. Get listeners on your side first by stressing as many similarities between you and your audience members as you can. Only after this should you try to change their attitudes and

TIPS
from professional speakers

Know exactly what response you hope to evoke. This should be thought through and determined in advance. Are you in the spotlight to motivate your audience, to rouse them, to produce or sell more, to educate, share information, raise their morale, or challenge them? You should know specifically what you want to accomplish and organize your thoughts, material, and delivery to that end.

Buck Rogers, former vice president of marketing at IBM and, according to *USA Today*, one of the most requested speakers in America, *Getting the Best Out of Yourself and Others* (New York: HarperCollins, 1987): 203–04.

Habits can't be thrown out the upstairs window. They have to be coaxed down the stairs one step at a time.
—Mark Twain

beliefs. Continuing with the abortion example (but this time with an audience that is opposed to your antiabortion stance), you might say:

We're all concerned with protecting the rights of the individual. No one wants to infringe on the rights of anyone. And it is from this point of view—from the point of view of the inalienable rights of the individual—that I want to examine the abortion issue.

In this way, you stress your similarity with the audience before you state your antiabortion position to this pro-abortion audience.

Seek Small Changes. When addressing an audience that is opposed to your position and your goal is to change their attitudes and beliefs, seek change in small increments. Let's say, for example, that your ultimate goal is to get an antiabortion group to favor abortion on demand. Obviously, this goal is too great to achieve in one speech. Therefore, strive for small changes. Here, for example, is an excerpt in which the speaker attempts to get an antiabortion audience to agree that some abortions should be legalized. The speaker begins as follows:

One of the great lessons I learned in college was that most extreme positions are wrong. Most of the important truths lie somewhere between the extreme opposites. And today I want to talk with you about one of these truths. I want to talk with you about rape and the problems faced by the mother carrying a child conceived in this most violent of all the violent crimes we can imagine.

Notice that the speaker does not state a totally pro-abortion position but instead focuses on one area of abortion and attempts to get the audience to agree that in some cases abortion should be legalized.

Demonstrate Your Credibility. Show the audience that you're knowledgeable about the topic (demonstrating your competence), have their own best interests at heart (demonstrating your good character), and that you're willing and ready to speak out in favor of these important concerns (demonstrating your dynamism and charisma). More specific ways of demonstrating credibility are covered in Unit 23.

Give Listeners Good Reasons. Give your audience good reasons for believing what you want them to believe. Give them hard evidence and arguments. Show them how such attitudes and beliefs relate directly to their goals, their motives. (Evidence and argument are covered in Unit 21 and motivational appeals in Unit 22.)

Developing the Speech to Strengthen or Change Attitudes, Beliefs, and Values

Here are some examples to clarify the nature of this type of persuasive speech. These examples present the specific purpose, the thesis, and the question asked of the thesis to help identify the major propositions of the speech.

This first example deals with birth control and uses a topical organizational pattern.

GENERAL PURPOSE: to persuade [to strengthen or change attitudes, beliefs, and values]

SPECIFIC PURPOSE: to persuade my audience that advertisements for birth control devices should be allowed in all media

THESIS: media advertising of birth control devices is desirable (Why is media advertising desirable?)

I. Birth control information is needed.
   A. Birth control information is needed to prevent disease.
   B. Birth control information is needed to prevent unwanted pregnancies.

II. Birth control information is not available to the very people who need it most.

III. Birth control information can best be disseminated through the media.

In this second example, the speaker uses a problem-solution organizational pattern, first presenting the problems created by cigarette smoking and then the solution.

GENERAL PURPOSE: to persuade [to strengthen or change attitudes, beliefs, and values]

SPECIFIC PURPOSE: to persuade my audience that cigarette advertising should be banned from all media

THESIS: cigarette advertising should be abolished (Why should it be abolished?)

I. Cigarette smoking is a national problem.
   A. Cigarette smoking causes lung cancer.
   B. Cigarette smoking pollutes the air.
   C. Cigarette smoking raises the cost of health care.

II. Cigarette smoking will be lessened if advertisements are prohibited.

III. Fewer people would start to smoke.

IV. Smokers would smoke less.

In delivering such a speech, a speaker might begin like this:

I think we all realize that cigarette smoking is a national problem that affects each and every one of us. No one escapes the problems caused by cigarette smoking—not the smoker and not the nonsmoker. Cigarette smoking causes lung cancer. Cigarette smoking pollutes the air. And cigarette smoking raises the cost of healthcare for everyone.

Let's look first at the most publicized of all smoking problems: lung cancer. There can be no doubt—the scientific evidence is overwhelming—that cigarette smoking is a direct cause of lung cancer. Research conducted by the American Cancer Institute and by research institutes throughout the world all come to the same conclusion: cigarette smoking causes lung cancer. Consider some of the specific evidence. A recent study—-reported in the June 1999 issue of the . . . .

THE SPEECH TO STIMULATE ACTION

Speeches designed to stimulate the audience to action or to engage in some specific behavior are referred to as **speeches to actuate**. The persuasive speech addressed to motivating a specific behavior may focus on just about any behavior imaginable. Here are some possible topics:

- Vote in the next election.
- Vote for Smith.
- Don't vote for Smith.
- Give money to the American Cancer Society.
- Buy a ticket to the football game.
- Watch "20/20."
- Major in economics.
- Take a course in computer science.
- Buy a Pontiac.

Strategies for Stimulating Listeners to Action

When designing a speech to get listeners to do something, keep the following principles in mind.

Be Realistic. Set reasonable goals for what you want the audience to do. Remember you have only 10 or 15 minutes and in that time you cannot move the proverbial mountain. So, ask for small, easily performed behaviors—to sign a petition, to vote in the next election, to donate a small amount of money.

Demonstrate Your Own Compliance. As a general rule, never ask the audience to do what you have not done yourself. So, demonstrate your own willingness to do what you want the audience to do. If you don't, the audience will rightfully ask, "Why haven't you done it?" In addition to your having done what you want them to do, show them that you're pleased to have done so. Tell them of the satisfaction you derived from donating blood or from reading to blind students.

Stress Specific Advantages. Stress the specific advantages of these behaviors to your specific audience. Don't ask your audience to engage in behaviors solely for abstract reasons. Give them concrete, specific reasons why they will benefit from the actions you want them to engage in. Instead of telling your listeners that they should devote time to reading to blind stu-

TIPS
from professional speakers

In preparing your speech, isolate the most important points and make sure you present them in the most dynamic and positive way possible. Don't bury them among a hodge-podge of thought or sandwich them between your laughs. Give them the kind of attention you'd expect from an advertising agency—that is, make sure that the most important points are distinguishable and as memorable as possible.

Buck Rogers, former vice president of marketing at IBM and, according to *USA Today,* one of the most requested speakers in America, *Getting the Best Out of Yourself and Others* (New York: HarperCollins, 1987): 204.

dents because it's the right thing to do, show them how much they will enjoy the experience and how much they will personally benefit from it.

Developing the Speech to Stimulate Action

Here are a few examples of the speech to actuate. The first outline is from a speech on devoting time to helping people with disabilities. The speaker asks for a change in the way most people spend their leisure time. It uses a topical organizational pattern; each of the subtopics is treated about equally.

GENERAL PURPOSE: to persuade [to stimulate action]

SPECIFIC PURPOSE: to persuade my audience to devote some of their leisure time to helping people with disabilities.

THESIS: leisure time can be well used in helping people with disabilities (How can leisure time be spent helping people with disabilities? or What can we do to help people with disabilities?)

  I. Read for the blind.
    A. Read to a blind student.
    B. Make a recording of a textbook for blind students.

  II. Run errands for students confined to wheelchairs.

  III. Type for students who can't use their hands.

In this second example the speaker tries to persuade the audience of parents and teachers to see the advantages of the new multicultural curriculum at the town's high school and stresses two major issues.

GENERAL PURPOSE: to persuade [to strengthen and change attitudes]

SPECIFIC PURPOSE: to persuade my audience to believe that the multicultural curriculum should be adopted

THESIS: the multicultural curriculum is beneficial [Why is the multicultural curriculum beneficial?]

  I. The multicultural curriculum will teach tolerance.

  II. The multicultural curriculum will raise all students' self-esteem.

In delivering the speech, the speaker might say:

We've all heard about the new multicultural curriculum proposed for the high schools in our county. After years of research I can tell you what we know about the effects of multicultural education on students. And what we know is that multicultural education—such as that presented in the curriculum before you—teaches tolerance for all people and all groups and, equally important, raises the self-esteem of all our sons and daughters. Let me explain how this curriculum teaches tolerance.

TIPS
from professional speakers

Every good salesperson knows that you don't mention price too early. That's a surefire way to lose a sale. Why? You haven't built value. People will find the money if they believe you have something they need. But if you start with the price, people won't be motivated to listen—in fact, they'll screen you out. So state listeners' needs, offer your ideas, and build your case.

Diane DiResta, international communications coach and speaker, *Knockout Presentations: How to Deliver your Messages with Power, Punch, and Pizzazz* (Chander House Press: Worcester, MA, 1998): 170.

UNIT IN BRIEF

Attitudes, Beliefs, Values, and Behaviors	**Attitudes**: tendency to behave. **Beliefs**: conviction in existence. **Values**: measure of goodness. **Behaviors**: observable actions.
Facts, Values, and Policies	Questions of fact focus on what is or is not. Questions of value focus on what is good or bad. Questions of policy focus on what the policy should be.
Principles of Persuasion	Selective exposure. Cultural difference. Audience participation. Inoculation. Magnitude of change. Identification. Consistency. Logos. Pathos. Ethos
The Speech to Strengthen or Change Attitudes, Beliefs, or Values	Estimate the current status of your listeners' attitudes, beliefs, and values. Seek change in small increments. Demonstrate your credibility. Give your listeners logical and motivational reasons.
The Speech to Stimulate Action	Be realistic in what you ask listeners to do. Ask for small, easily performed behaviors. Demonstrate your own willingness to do what you're asking your listeners to do. Stress the specific (rather than the general).

THINKING CRITICALLY ABOUT PERSUASIVE SPEAKING

REVIEWING KEY TERMS AND CONCEPTS IN PERSUASIVE SPEAKING

1. Review and define the key terms used in this unit:

- ❑ attitudes (p. 382)
- ❑ beliefs (p. 383)
- ❑ behaviors (p. 383)
- ❑ selective exposure principle (p. 385)
- ❑ cultural differences principle (p. 387)
- ❑ audience participation principle (p. 387)
- ❑ inoculation principle (p. 388)
- ❑ magnitude of change principle (p. 389)
- ❑ foot-in-the-door technique (p. 390)
- ❑ door-in-the-face technique (p. 390)
- ❑ identification (p. 390)
- ❑ consistency and dissonance (p. 391)
- ❑ logos (p. 391)
- ❑ pathos (p. 392)
- ❑ ethos (p. 392)
- ❑ speeches to strengthen or change attitudes or beliefs (p. 393)
- ❑ speeches to stimulate action (p. 396)

2. Review and explain the key concepts discussed in this unit:

- ■ How would you explain attitude, belief, value, and behavior and their relationship to each other?
- ■ How would you define and distinguish among questions of fact, value, and policy?
- ■ What are the major principles of persuasion?
- ■ How would you describe the speech to strengthen or change attitudes and beliefs? What strategies might you use in developing the speech to strengthen or change attitudes and beliefs?
- ■ How would you describe the speech to stimulate action? What strategies might you use in developing the speech to stimulate action?

DEVELOPING PERSUASIVE SPEAKING STRATEGIES

1. Pat is planning to give a persuasive speech advocating more conscientiousness in recycling to two very dif-

ferent audiences. One audience is composed solely of women and the other audience solely of men. Otherwise the audience members are similar: around 30 years old, college-educated, and professional. In what ways would the two speeches differ? What general principles or assumptions about gender would Pat be justified in making an attempt to adapt these two speeches to these different audiences?

2. You want to get your listeners to contribute one-hour a week to the college's program of helping high school students prepare for college. You're considering using the foot-in-the-door or the door-in-the-face technique. How would you develop each of these strategies? Which would you eventually use?

EVALUATING PERSUASIVE SPEECHES

1. Read a persuasive speech, focusing on the principles of persuasion noted in this unit. Does the speaker make use of any of these principles? What persuasive principles can you identify from reading this speech?

2. Examine a speech for questions of fact, value, and policy. How are these issues used in the speech?

USING TECHNOLOGY IN PERSUASIVE SPEECHES

1. Visit the National Press Club Web site for complete texts of the speeches from the National Press Club's luncheons at http://npc.press.org/. Read one of the speeches and evaluate it in terms of the principles of persuasion discussed in this unit. This is also an excellent research Web site; the guides will prove useful for just about any topic.

2. Visit "The Speaker's Companion" Web site at http://www.lm.com/~chipp/spkrhome.htm. How would you compare the principles discussed in this unit with the principles used in this program?

PRACTICALLY SPEAKING

20.1 Short Speech Technique

Prepare and deliver a two-minute speech in which you:

a. explain an interesting attitude, belief, or value that you've come across.

b. explain how a speech strengthened or changed one of your attitudes or beliefs.

c. explain an advertisement in terms of the principles of persuasion.

d. explain cultural differences in popularly held beliefs regarding such concepts as God, life, death, family, happiness, education, law, or men and women.

20.2 Developing Persuasive Strategies

The objective of this exercise is to stimulate the discussion of persuasive strategies on a variety of contemporary cultural situations. It may be completed individually, in small groups, or with the entire class.

What persuasive strategies would you use to convince your class of the validity of either side in any of these points of view? For example, what persuasive strategies would you use to persuade your class members that interracial adoption should be encouraged or discouraged? Do realize that these points of view are simplified for purposes of this exercise and shouldn't be taken to suggest that the viewpoints given here are complete descriptions of these complex issues.

Point of View: Interracial Adoption. Those in favor of interracial adoption argue that the welfare of the child—who might not get adopted at all if not by someone of another race—must be considered first. Adoption (regardless of race) is good for the child and therefore is a positive social process. Those opposed to interracial adoption argue that children need to be raised by those of the same race if the child is to develop self-esteem and become a functioning member of his or her own race. Interracial adoption is therefore a negative social process.

Point of View: Women and the Church. Many women (and men)—both Catholic and non-Catholic—believe that women should be allowed to become priests and advance in the hierarchy of the Catholic church just as a man can. The sexes are equal and therefore should have equal opportunities, and that includes in the church. The Catholic Church rejects this idea and refuses to ordain women as priests; their argument is basically that Jesus (to whom the Catholic church traces itself back to) established a church with only men as its priests and that's the way it must remain.

Point of View: Gays and Lesbians and the Military. Regardless of the status of the current law, a large group within the United States military are opposed to gay men and lesbians in the military. The gay and lesbian communities argue that gay men and lesbians should be accorded exactly the same rights and privileges as heterosexuals—no more, no less. Those opposed argue that gay men and lesbians will undermine the image of the military and will make heterosexuals uncomfortable, leading to a lack of trust within military units.

Point of View: Interracial Marriage. Those in favor of interracial marriage argue that everyone has the right to make his or her own decision and if you fall in love with someone of a different race, the decision is a personal one, not a social one. Those opposed to interracial marriage argue that it dilutes the purity of the races (with the minority races suffering the most) and even threatens the continuance of the race. Given our current society, it also makes life difficult for the children.

Point of View: Affirmative Action. Those in favor of affirmative action argue that because of the injus-

tices in the way certain groups (racial, national, gender) were treated, they should now be given preferential treatment to correct the imbalance caused by the social injustices. Those opposed to affirmative action argue that merit must be the sole criterion for promotion, jobs, entrance to graduate schools, etc. and that affirmative action is just reverse racism; one form of injustice cannot correct another form of injustice.

20.3 Analyzing a Persuasive Speech

This exercise is designed to help you further understand the principles of public speaking in general and of persuasive speaking in particular and to see how they are used in an actual speech. Read the speech without looking at the critical thinking questions. Then reread the speech, this time responding to the questions. This speech was given by William E. Franklin, President of Franklin International, LTD to the Graduate School of Business of Columbia University at the Japan Business Association & International Business Society, New York City, April 8, 1998.

FROM: *Vital Speeches of the Day* 64 (September 15, 1998), pp. 719–721.

CAREERS IN INTERNATIONAL BUSINESS FIVE IDEAS OR PRINCIPLES
*Address by William E. Franklin, President, Franklin International, LTD
Graduate School of Business, Japan Business Association &
International Business Society, New York, New York, April 8, 1998*

I have been asked to lead a discussion today about careers in international business. I am honored and pleased to do so. Thank you for coming. There is a Japanese proverb that says "Rongo yomi no rongo shirazu" . . . just because you read Confucius does not necessarily ;mean you understand what he says. Just because I have worked and studied in Asia the past 25 years does not mean I understand everything about Asia. In fact, I spend more time studying about Asia today than when I first moved to Tokyo in 1973. So I would like to have this be a dialogue, more than a lecture a sharing of experiences and ideas.

After I accepted your invitation I read the report on rankings of business schools and learned Columbia was awarded an overall ranking of 99%. And also, not unimportant, you rank number one in placement success with a median starting salary of $88,000 . . . a higher starting salary than graduates of any other business school in the world. With that kind of success perhaps you should be leading

Notice the mixture of expertise (he has worked and studied in Asia for 25 years) and modesty (he doesn't understand everything about Asia and wants to dialogue rather than lecture) in this first paragraph. How appropriate and effective do you think this introduction was?

the discussion, with me in the audience. I really do want to hear your ideas, your questions . . . your comments, business questions, personal questions . . . anything that is on your mind.

I recently saw some demographic information which may help to bring perspective on your opportunities and responsibilities, some perspective on your place or role in the world.

If we shrink the world's 5.7 billion population to a village of 100 people . . . with all existing human ratios remaining the same, here is the resulting profile.

Of these 100 people 57 are Asian, 21 European, 14 from North and South America and eight from Africa.

51 female, 49 male

80 live in sub-standard housing

70 cannot read

Half suffer from malnutrition

75 have never made a phone call

Less than one is on the Internet

Half the entire village's wealth would be in the hands of 6 people.

Only one of the hundred have a college education.

You are in a very elite group of only 1% who have a college education. But you are even more elite and distinctive because you will soon graduate from what many consider to be the number one Graduate School of Business. The dictionary definition of elite is "the choice part" . . . "a powerful minority group." Whether you realize it or not the fact is that you are the choice part . . . and you have the power of education and knowledge.

Of course that does not guarantee you a good life . . . having that degree does not guarantee you anything. Your graduation will merely be the beginning of a new phase of learning in your life. I personally think the most valuable thing you can learn in any university is to develop your own personal method of learning so you can be a good student the rest of your life.

But being part of this very elite group does give you the potential for power and wealth . . . probably much more than you now realize. Many of you will be important global business leaders . . . some of you will be important government leaders. You will have far more power then you now realize . . . power to enhance the quality of your personal life . . . power to help others in the world who are less fortunate than yourself. It's not too early to begin thinking seriously about your personal values . . . and how you will use your power.

Now why do I talk about all that? Well, you don't have very much uncertainty about finding a job and I would imagine most of you have given a lot of thought to selecting a challenging career.

Your larger question will be "how will you create a rich and rewarding and balanced life?" There are two things to aim for in life. One, to get what you want in life and two, to enjoy it. Only the wisest of women and men achieve the second.

I will share with you 5 ideas or principles about careers, and about life because it is difficult to have a full discussion about your

What function does this paragraph serve? If you were in the audience, would this make you receptive to the speech?

Here's an excellent example of statistics that are made meaningful to an audience that will hear the figures just once. Do these figures gain and maintain your attention? Do they effectively support the speaker's point?

How does the speaker achieve a speaker-audience-topic relationship?

In what ways does the speaker orient the audience?

lifetime career without talking about your total life.

FIRST IDEA . . . Learn from other cultures. Let me read a quote from a speech by an American . . . see if you can guess who said this, "we have a favorable balance of trade. But if you think you can maintain that balance just by sending salesmen to Japan and China as you would to Montana or Chicago, you are mistaken. You must send people to live there to learn the culture, to learn the language, to learn the way of doing business there." John Wheeler said that in his inaugural speech as the first President of the United States Chamber of Commerce in 1912.

Sometimes we are very diligent in learning about other cultures . . . but to be good leaders we want to learn from other cultures. The other day I was looking at some speeches I made 8 or 9 years ago . . . attempting to persuade skeptical American audiences that American business and American ideas were not finished . . . and that Asia was not going to take over the world. You may remember how pessimistic everyone was about America then.

Now in 1998, with America's current up cycle and Asia's economic problems, there is a temptation of totally flip-flop and say, only the American way is the right way . . . and reject all Asian values.

As future global leaders, I ask you to think about the possibility that a more rewarding approach is to learn from each other . . . and try to adopt and adapt the best from each culture.

Isis Berlin said "the great human delusion is monism . . . the proposition that there is a single, final solution . . . the ultimate overarching truth." Sometimes Americans are so passionate about our ideals that we want the whole world to accept our ideals . . . and we feel some obligation to have all countries adopt our form of democracy . . . now. To accept our concept of human rights . . . now. to accept our rule of law . . . now. I think most Americans do this out of a sense of good purpose . . . but when we think that our ideals and institutions are the one best way for all cultures we automatically forgo the possibility of learning that other social and economic systems may have equal validity.

On my first trip to China almost 20 years ago, as part of a government delegation, I had the opportunity to meet Mr. Deng Xiao Peng. After the official government discussions he turned to me and said "I understand your company has expertise in tree growing and in utilization of the forest resource. Our country needs to improve both . . . Will you help us?" We then met with Minister of Forestry and that led to us becoming the principal forestry advisor to the PRC during the early 1980s. Mr. Deng said "it does not matter whether the cat is black or white as long as it helps to improve our country" . . . he was open to ideas from other cultures.

One time my friend, Mogi-san, was attempting to explain Japanese business philosophy to us. He said "you Americans always talk about fairness, arms length business transactions, objectivity, no favor to friends . . . very detailed contracts" all words that are pleasing to the ears of most American business women and men. He went on to say,

Notice how the speaker uses the audience participation principle. Where else in this speech might the speaker encourage audience participation?

What image do you get of the speaker as you read these experiences?

"if we think that is a very cold way to do business we wouldn't want to do business the way. We want to do business with friends."

And later many American companies learned that in order to have a total quality system we needed to adopt some Japanese ideas with respect to customer and supplier relationships. Which, by the way, many Japanese tell me they learned a lot about from Dr. Frederic Demming. We learned from each other.

There is a Zen saying . . . "in a beginners mind there are many possibilities, in the experts mind, there are none." I have observed in myself that I am a much better leader when I think of myself as a student of Asia than when I think of myself as an expert on Asia.

To be a good international leader it is not enough just to study other cultures. We need to learn from other cultures.

SECOND POINT. And closely related to the first point. This may sound contradictory to the first point, but it is not. We need to be very conscious of our personal values . . . personal values as defined by our behavior . . . not just what we say . . . but how we spend our time each day. Write them down so you can look at them . . . and update as you get new insights. Be aware you are forming habits today, good habits today, good habits and bad habits, that you may have the rest of your life.

When you are selecting a company to join, do some research to see if the companies values are consistent with your personal values. This is important. You will not do your best work with an organization and people whose values are incompatible with your values.

When I was at another university recently a student asked me "what's the biggest mistake you ever made?" My first response was that I had made so many it would be difficult to say which is the biggest. But later, after I had an opportunity to reflect, I said to this student "the biggest mistake I ever made was the time I compromised my personal values."

And it usually does not happen in big ways with big issues . . . my values get compromised in small ways for small gains or no gains. One time I was offered a bribe of $1,000,000 on a project in southeast Asia. That was a no brainer, it is easy for anyone to decide what to do in a circumstance that is that black and white. But on a daily basis the choices are always in the gray areas where it is not so clear and the decision may seem so unimportant. But the cost for small compromises in your values is cumulative . . . and it can be a big cost to your effectiveness as a leader . . . a big cost to your total being. One needs to be vigilant every moment to see that doesn't happen.

I heard John Wayne say once ". . . perversion and corruption masquerade as ambiguity. I don't like ambiguity. I don't trust ambiguity." I don't like ambiguity either, but ambiguity is part of reality for an international leader. Your day to day life will not be so black and white as we like to see in John Wayne's movies. Always seek clarity, but learn to live with complexity and ambiguity.

And it is my observation that individuals who have strong personal values have the most freedom and ability and perspective to learn

The speaker uses a wide variety of personal examples throughout the speech. What do you think of the personal examples used in the discussion of this first idea, that we need to learn from (not just about) other cultures? Did the speaker convince you of the importance of this first idea?

Would an example of choices "in the gray areas" have helped you appreciate this idea?

from other cultures. This is even more important in Asia. There is a generalization that Japanese business leaders are selected based on their character, American business leaders selected for their competence. I believe that is changing; the integrity and character of an American business leader is more important than it may have been at one time . . . and Japanese are giving more weight to competence.

When I moved back to my home country last year I saw a survey that says a majority of Americans think a businessman will do anything for money. A politician will do anything for a vote. A journalist will do anything for a story. That simply is not true.

Be true to your personal values. That will be your greatest strength.

THIRD POINT. Leadership. Take any opportunity to experience leadership. It is helpful to study leadership, and study other great leaders. But you only learn leadership by experiencing leadership. You only learn leadership by being a leader. You learn leadership by leading a study project, by being secretary of the camera club, by having a part time job by introducing a speaker.

The call to uphold our personal values in our actions is a relatively abstract principle that is often difficult to make clear to an audience. How effectively does the speaker handle this?

There will always be temporary shortages of certain technical skills but the law of supply and demand will correct the imbalance. But I have never been in any organization that has enough proven leadership.

Some say leaders are made. Some say leaders are born. It is really not too important whether leaders are made or born . . . because all of us have leadership potential that is never discovered . . . or discovered late in life. I'm talking about leaders who bring about win-win solutions. It's been my experience whether it be trade negotiations or internal corporate competition, only win-win solutions last.

The opening of the Japan building products market is an example of a win-win outcome. I will relate it to you briefly because it has some applicability to trade negotiations in general.

The principle that leadership can only be learned by actually leading is a good one. What types of supporting materials does the speaker use in explaining this principle?

Twenty years ago Japan's residential building codes included many restrictive materials based specifications. Wood was excluded from many uses. Working cooperatively, the North American and Japanese industry and government groups asked the Japanese regulatory agencies to consider using scientific tests to move from materials-based specifications to performance-based specifications. Wood would be required to pass the same fire and earthquake tests as steel, concrete or any other building material . . . but not be prohibited just because it is wood.

After a very long process the regulations were modified to be more performance base. Because leaders in Japan and North America took a win-win approach there is a true win-win outcome. Japanese producers have more business. Foreign suppliers have more business. Wood housing boomed in Japan.

And, most important, the Japanese people are the big winners with high quality, lower cost, safe wood homes. During the Kobe earthquake, 2x4 wood frame homes proved to be the safest of all. In the 21st century effective leaders will be win-win leaders.

When you have different job opportunities ask yourself which job will give me the best opportunity to experience leadership. When you are starting out with your career many times the worst place to work is the corporate headquarters . . . because a young person has so little opportunity to experience leadership. You are usually better off to take any job in the field where you have measurable account-ability for the results of an operation, no matter how small.

Don't confuse being close to leaders at the corporate headquarters with leading. Don't confuse having proximity to power with actually having power. Experience leaderships.

FOURTH POINT. Persevere. Johann Goethe, the German philoso-pher said "in the realm of ideas everything depends on enthusiasm . . . in the real world all rests on perseverance." I heard Paul Newman being interviewed recently. He was asked what makes the difference . . . "why do some actors become very successful and some do not . . . is it luck, it timing, is it connections . . . or, in the end, doesn't talent rule out?" His response "no . . . the most important element for an ac-tor to succeed is tenacity.

Nothing will be more important to your getting what you want than perseverance . . . many times making that one final effort when you feel mentally and physically exhausted will be just enough to put you across the finish line.

When you join your new organization you will see many things that need to be changed. I don't know about universities but in corpo-rations you are going to find many people are opposed to change, they will persuasively deny it's necessary. There's a line in a Grateful Dead song, "Denial ain't just a river in Egypt."

Many years ago I heard Jack Welsh being quizzed about how he was bringing about change at GE. He said "change has no constituen-cy." Don't confuse what I said about win-win solutions with waiting until you get consensus before implementing needed changes . . . it will be a long wait. Don't expect applause for making change at least not while you are doing it. Expect failure, rejection and humiliation sometimes.

I keep something on my desk that says "growth involves confusion and pain, moving from the comfortable known to the uncomfortable unknown." Most of us do not welcome confusion and pain . . . even when it is necessary and beneficial for us. You will need persever-ance to bring about change.

There is a Zen saying "before enlightenment chop wood, carry wa-ter . . . after enlightenment . . . chop wood, carry water.' An effective international leader does a lot of chopping wood and carrying water. Perseverance.

And finally. Network. Network. Network. If the U.S. is character-ized as a market economy then Japan might be called a network sys-tem. And that is true to some degree in many Asian countries. In any culture that is influenced more by rule of man rather than rule of law, networking is not an optional part of doing business . . . it's a require-ment for successful business. In many Asian countries it is more cus-tomary to do business with friends. And traditional Chinese take it even one step further . . . the business is most often a family business.

Many of us talk about when China adopts the rule of law . . . as if

Do you find the juxtaposition of the great philosopher Goethe, the highly successful actor and entrepreneur Newman, and the lyrics from the Grateful Dead an effective persua-sive device?

The speaker draws on an amazingly wide range of materials. In what ways does this help establish the speaker's credibility?

Did the speaker succeed in convinc-ing you of the importance of net-working to your own professional success?

that is inevitable and imminent. Many Chinese do not feel the rule of law is a necessary aspect of the human condition. Confucius said laws are too inflexible to handle all the diversity of human experiences. Chinese say they prefer to trust people, not laws.

Akio Morita, the co-founder of Sony, a fine man and a global thinker long before most of us . . . was being questioned at a dinner one day about the closed Japan market. Finally Morita-san said "well, technically the Japan market is open, it's just that sometimes the door is so small that it's hard for you big going to get in." His good humor got him off the hook that day but there was as much truth as humor in what he said. The system is designed to do business the Japanese way. Networking is not something you do in your spare time, it's an essential part of business.

To summarize

FIRST IDEA. Learn from other cultures.

SECOND. Be true to your personal values. You will learn that success, on the whole, success depends more on character than either intellect or luck.

THIRD IDEA. Take any opportunity to experience leadership. Leadership must be experienced to be learned.

AND FINALLY. Network. Network. Network.

Baron Charles Montesquie said a couple hundred years ago, "Commerce is the best cure for prejudice, peace is the natural effect of trade." If that was true in the 18th century it will be even more true in the 21st century. Trade and investment bring more than just money and goods, they bring ideas. As 21st century leaders you have great opportunity to help us all to overcome prejudice and bring about understanding and peace for all people. I have great confidence that is what you will do.

What type of organizational pattern did the speaker use? Was this an effective pattern? What other patterns might have also worked with this topic?

What functions does the speaker's conclusion serve? Can you identify a summary, a motivation, and a closing statement?

Developing Arguments

UNIT CONTENTS	UNIT OBJECTIVES
	After completing this unit, you should be able to: Define *argument* and *evidence*.
Argument and Evidence	
Reasoning from Specific Instances and Generalizations	Explain the nature of reasoning from specific instances and generalizations, the major tests, and the guidelines to follow in using this form of reasoning.
Reasoning from Analogy	Explain the nature of reasoning by analogy, the major tests, and the guidelines to follow in using reasoning from analogy.
Reasoning from Causes and Effects	Explain the nature of cause-effect reasoning, the major tests, and the guidelines to follow in using cause-effect reasoning.
Reasoning from Sign	Explain the nature of reasoning by sign, the major tests, and the guidelines to follow in using reasoning by sign.

This unit introduces a three-sequence section dealing with proof, the means you use to persuade an audience to think or do as you wish. This three part division, developed in the classical rhetorics of ancient Greece and Rome, consists of (1) logical argument and evidence, (2) appeals to the audience's emotions, and (3) appeals based on the credibility of the speaker. In this unit we begin with the logical part and consider how to develop and evaluate arguments. Units 22 and 23 focus on emotional appeals and speaker credibility.

ARGUMENT AND EVIDENCE

An argument consists of evidence (for example, facts) and a conclusion. Evidence plus the conclusion that the evidence supports equal an argument. Reasoning is the process you go through in forming conclusions on the basis of evidence. For example, you might reason that since college graduates earn more money than nongraduates (evidence), Jack and Jill should go to college if they wish to earn more money (conclusion).

When you present an argument in a public speech, you attempt to prove something to your listeners. You want to prove that what you say is true or practical or worth pursuing. In the vast majority of cases, you cannot prove in any objective sense that marijuana should or should not be legalized or that the death penalty would benefit or harm society. Rather, you seek, as a speaker, to establish the probability of your conclusions in the minds of the listeners. Thus, the process is in part a logical one of demonstrating that what you say is probably true. The process is, however, also a psychological one of persuading your listeners to accept the conclusions as you have drawn them.

The information presented here applies to the speaker in constructing the speech, to the listener in receiving and responding to the speech, and to the speech critic or analyst in analyzing and evaluating the speech. A poorly reasoned argument, inadequate evidence, and stereotypical thinking, for example, need to be avoided by the speaker, recognized and responded to by the listener, and negatively evaluated by the critic.

Argument and Evidence in Cultural Perspective

Before getting to the specific forms of argument, recall the general tests of support applicable to all forms of argument that we introduced in Unit 7 as tests of research. Recall these specifically from a multicultural perspective.

Is the Support Recent? Recency is especially important in technologically advanced societies because technology and all its influences change so rapidly. In some agrarian cultures, recency is much less important. In matters of soil cultivation, for example, the recency of a technique may make people suspicious.

Is There Corroborative Support? In collectivist cultures members are expected to share responsibility and blame and to protect other members. They're expected to provide corroboration for the ideas and behaviors of colleagues or friends. In such situations, for example, when colleagues publicly agree with an individual, it offers no evidence. Instead, it offers respect and shows that members are being polite and are following the rules of etiquette. This is much less true in individualist cultures where competition is emphasized and where a colleague's support is not written into the rules of etiquette.

Are the Sources Unbiased? In American courts of law, for example, eyewitness testimony from an unbiased source is extremely powerful evidence and will count heavily in the minds of both judge and jury. In certain African cultures, however, an eyewitness's testimony would not count as evidence because the people believe if you speak up, you obviously have something to gain (Lustig and Koester 1999).

In evaluating the evidence of others as listeners and critics and in using these forms of reasoning, remember that different people see things differently—even in matters of logic, argument, and evidence.

> *When a subject is highly controversial, one cannot hope to tell the truth. One can only show how one came to hold whatever opinion one does hold. One can only give one's audience the chance of drawing their own conclusions as they observe the limitations, the prejudices, the idiosyncrasies of the speaker.*
> —Virginia Woolf

Here political activist and filmmaker Oliver Stone delivers a speech. Can you identify a few ways in which films are similar to persuasive speeches? How are they different?

REASONING FROM SPECIFIC INSTANCES AND GENERALIZATIONS

In reasoning from specific instances (or examples), you examine several specific instances and then conclude something about the whole. This form of reasoning, known as induction, is useful when you want to develop a general principle or conclusion but cannot examine the whole. For example, you sample a few communication courses and conclude something about communication courses in general; you visit several Scandinavian cities and conclude something about the whole of Scandinavia.

You probably follow this same general process in dealing with another person. For example, you see Samantha in several situations and conclude something about Samantha's behavior in general; you date Pat a few times, or maybe even for a period of several months, and on that basis draw a general conclusion about Pat's suitability as a life partner.

Here Karen Bowers, a student from Bradley University (Schnoor 1994, p. 61) uses specific instances to support the generalization that the work environment can be a dangerous one:

> "141 Men and Girls Die in Triangle Shirtwaist Factory Fire; Street Strewn With Bodies; Piles of Dead Inside," reported the headline of The New York Times on March 26, 1911. Today, we generally view this "ancient history" as a tragedy of the industrial era. Is it? 25 employees die in Hamlet, North Carolina, Imperial Food Product Plant Fire, reported Time magazine on September 16, 1991. There was little chance for escape because most emergency exits had been locked. The 11-year-old plant had never been inspected. Unfortunately, this is not unusual. The January 28, 1991, edition of The Nation notes, "Work kills more people than die from drugs, AIDS, or car accidents."

Technically, you may also argue in the other direction—namely, from a general principle to some specific instance. That is, you begin with some general statement or axiom that is accepted as true by the audience and argue that since something is true of the entire class, it must also be true of the specific instance, which is a member of that class.

Reasoning from general principles—actually, more a way of presenting your argument than a type of reasoning—is useful when you wish to argue that some unexamined instance has certain characteristics. You would, for example, note the general principle and show that an unexamined item is a member of that general principle. You would then draw the conclusion that, therefore, the item also possesses the qualities possessed by the whole (or covered by the general principle).

Note in this excerpt from Ken Lonnquist's speech, "Ghosts," how he argues against abortion from the general principle that one does not have control over the body of another.

> We say that it is our right to control our bodies, and this is true. But there is a distinction that needs to be made, and that distinction is this: Preventing a pregnancy is controlling a body—controlling your body. But preventing the continuance of a human life that is not your own is

murder. If you attempt to control the body of another in that fashion, you become as a slave master was—controlling the lives and the bodies of his slaves—chopping off their feet when they ran away, or murdering them if it pleased him. This was not his right; it is not our right.

Critically Evaluating Reasoning from Specific Instances to a Generalization

Apply these tests in reasoning from specific instances.

Were enough specific instances examined? Obviously there will be a limit to the number of specific instances you can examine. After all, your time, energy, and resources are limited. Yet it's important that you examine enough instances to justify your conclusion. Exactly how much is enough will vary from one situation to another. You cannot spend three days in a foreign country and conclude something about the entire country. You cannot interact with three Australians and conclude something about all Australians.

Two general guidelines might prove helpful in determining how much is enough. First, the larger the group you wish covered by your conclusion, the greater the number of specific instances you should examine. If you wish to draw conclusions about a class of 75 million Martians, you'd have to examine a considerable number of Martians before drawing any valid conclusions. On the other hand, if you're attempting to draw a conclusion about a bushel of 100 apples, sampling a few is probably sufficient.

Second, the greater the diversity of items in the class, the more specific instances you will have to examine. Some classes or groups of items are relatively homogeneous, whereas others are more heterogeneous; this will influence how many specific instances constitute a sufficient number. Spaghetti in boiling water are all about the same; thus, sampling one usually tells you something about all the others. On the other hand, communication courses are probably very different from each other, so valid conclusions about the entire group of communication courses will require a much larger sample.

Were the specific instances representative? Specific instances must be representative. If you wish to draw conclusions about the entire class, examine specific instances coming from all areas or subclasses within the major class. If you wanted to draw conclusions about the student body of your school, you could not simply examine communication majors or physics majors or art majors. Rather, you'd have to examine a representative sample. Similarly, you could not survey only members of one culture and conclude something about members of other cultures. If you wish to draw conclusions about the whole, be sure you examine all significant parts of that whole.

Are there significant exceptions? When you examine specific instances and attempt to draw a conclusion about the whole, take into consideration the exceptions. Thus, if you examine the GPA of Astrology majors and discover that 70 percent have GPAs above 3.5, you might be tempted to draw the conclusion that Astrology majors are especially bright. But what about the 30 percent who have lower GPAs? How much lower are these scores?

This may be a significant exception that must be taken into account when drawing your conclusion and would necessitate qualifying your conclusion in significant ways. Exactly how many exceptions constitute "significant exceptions" depends on the unique situation.

As a speaker, you should disclose significant exceptions to your listeners. To hide these would be dishonest and also usually ineffective from a persuasive point of view because, more often than not, the audience either has heard or will hear of these exceptions. If you haven't mentioned them, they'll become suspicious of your overall honesty and your credibility will quickly decline.

Critically Evaluating Reasoning from a Generalization to Specific Instances

In testing reasoning from general principles to specific instances, apply these two tests.

Is the general principle true or at least probably true? Obviously, if the general principle is not true, it would be useless to apply it to any specific instance. In most instances you cannot know if a general principle is true simply because you cannot examine all instances of the class. If you did examine all instances of the class, there would be no reason to use this form of reasoning since you would have already examined the instance to which you wish to apply the general principle. For example, if you examine all the apples in the bushel, there's no reason to formulate the general conclusion that all the apples are rotten and to say that, therefore, one particular apple is rotten. In examining all the apples you will have examined that specific apple. Consequently, what we are really dealing with is a general principle that seems to be "usually" and "probably" true. Thus, our conclusions about any specific instance will also only be "usually" or "probably" true.

Is the unknown or unexamined item clearly a specific member of the class? If you want to draw a conclusion about a particular Atlantan and want to reason that this person is assertive because all Atlantans are assertive, you have to be certain that this person is in fact a member of the class of Atlantans.

Using Specific Instances and Generalizations

In reasoning from specific instances to general principles, stress that your specific instances are sufficient in number to warrant the conclusion you're drawing. Demonstrate that the specific instances are in fact representative of the whole. Show that there are no significant exceptions.

In using reasoning from general principles to specific instances, make certain that the audience accepts your general principle. This is especially important when your audience consists of members from different cultures. Depending on the cultures represented, you might not be able to assume that all members accept the idea that democracy is the best form of government, that capitalism is good, that state and church should be kept separate, or that men and women are equal. If the basic principle is not accepted by your audience, any attempt to use it as evidence concerning a specific instance will be doomed to failure. Conduct a thorough audience analysis before using this type of argument. The general principle must be

The best argument is that which seems merely an explanation.
—Dale Carnegie

THE ETHICS OF [More] Propaganda Techniques

Here are four more propaganda techniques. The first two come from the work of Lee and Lee (1972, 1995); the last two come from Pratkanis and Aronson 1991).

Card-Stacking. The speaker here selects only the evidence and arguments that support the case and might even falsify evidence and distort the facts to better fit the case. Despite these misrepresentations, the speaker presents the supporting materials as "fair" and "impartial."

Bandwagon. Using this method, the speaker persuades the audience to accept or reject an idea or proposal because "everybody's doing it" or because the "right" people are doing it. The speaker persuades you to jump on this large and popular bandwagon. This is a popular technique in political elections where results of polls are used to get undecided voters to jump on the bandwagon with the candidate leading in the polls. After all, you don't want to vote for a loser.

Agenda-Setting. In agenda-setting a speaker might argue that XYZ is the issue and that all others are unimportant and insignificant. This appeal is heard frequently: Balancing the budget is the key to the city's survival. There's only one issue confronting elementary education in our largest cities and that is violence. In almost all situations, however, there are many issues and many sides to each issue. Often the person proclaiming X is the issue really means "I'll be able to persuade you if you focus solely on X and ignore the other issues."

Attack. Attack involves accusing another person (usually an opponent) of some serious wrongdoing so that the issue under discussion never gets examined. Arguments such as "How can we support a candidate who has been unfaithful (smoked pot, avoided the military)?" are often heard in political discussions. When personal attack is used to draw attention away from other issues, it becomes unethical.

Can you identify a television or Internet advertisement that makes use of one or more of these techniques?

(The next Ethics in Public Speaking box appears on page 427.)

---

accepted before you use it as a basis for a conclusion about an unexamined specific instance.

REASONING FROM ANALOGY

In reasoning from analogy, you compare like things and conclude that, since they're alike in so many respects, they're also alike in some as-yet unknown or unexamined respect. For example, you reason that since the meat at Grand Union is fresh, the fish will be also. In this simple bit of reasoning, you compared two like things (the two foods, meat and fish) and concluded that what was known to be true about one item (that the meat was fresh) would also be true of the unknown item (the fish).

Analogies may be literal or figurative. In a literal analogy the items being compared are from the same class—foods, cars, people, countries, cities, or whatever. For example, in a literal analogy one might argue that (1) word processing, database, and desktop publishing software are all similar to tax preparation software—they're all popular, have been around for about the same number of years, and have been revised repeatedly; (2) these software packages have all been easy to learn and use; (3) therefore, tax preparation software will be easy to learn and use. Here, then, we've taken a number of similar items (types of computer software), and then reasoned that the similarity would also apply to the unexamined item (tax preparation software). In a figurative analogy, the items compared are from different classes. For example, you might draw an analogy between children and birds: as birds are free to roam all over the world, children need to be free to roam all over their new and unexplored universe. These analogies are useful for amplification but do not constitute logical proof.

Here, for example, Leanne Bennett (Schnoor, 1996, p. 53), a student from William Carey College, uses an analogy to introduce the topic of insurance discrimination. The analogy doesn't prove that insurance discrimination exists but it makes the audience feel what such discrimination might feel like:

> *Consider this scenario: A young boy walks into the room. One look around tells him he is different. The teacher tells him to go sit in the back of the room, not because those are the only seats left, but because that's where his kind belong. Throughout the day he tries to understand but his uplifted hand is ignored by a teacher who is blind to his type. He goes home discouraged, disheartened, and dejected. Will he try again tomorrow? Only tomorrow knows.*

Critically Evaluating Reasoning from Analogy

In testing the adequacy of a literal analogy, ask two questions:

Are the two cases being compared alike in essential respects? In the example of the tax preparation software, one significant difference was not noted: to use that software effectively, you really have to know the rules and regulations governing taxes. You can learn to use word-processing software without going beyond the information contained in the manual; but to learn to use tax-preparation software you have to know what is in the manual as well as the tax code.

Do the differences make a difference? In any analogy, regardless of how literal it is, the items being compared will be different: no two things are exactly the same. But in reasoning with analogies, ask yourself if the differences make a difference. Obviously, not all differences make a fundamental difference. The difference in the knowledge you need for the various software programs, however, is a substantial difference that needs to be considered.

Using Reasoning from Analogy

Stress the numerous and significant similarities between the items being compared and minimize the difference between them. Mention differences that do exist and that the audience will think of, but show that these do not destroy the validity of your argument. If the audience knows that there are differences, but you don't confront these differences squarely, your argument is going to prove ineffective. The listeners will be wondering, "But what about the difference in . . . ?"

For example, let's say you're giving a speech in favor of instituting the honor system at your college. You might argue from the analogy of West Point and say something like:

> *The honor system has worked at other colleges. West Point is perhaps the most famous example. At West Point students take their examinations without any proctors. They're totally on their own honor.*

But, your audience may well reject this analogy and say to themselves (and perhaps in the question period) that West Point is a very different type of college. Therefore, you need to confront the difference between West Point and your school. You might begin by saying:

I know that many of you are thinking that West Point is a very different type of school from ours. But, in matters that relate to the honor system, it's not different. Let me show why these two colleges are actually alike in all essential respects. First, both our schools enroll students of approximately the same academic abilities. SAT scores, for example, are almost identical, as are high school grades. Second, both schools . . . .

REASONING FROM CAUSES AND EFFECTS

In reasoning from causes and effects, you may go in either of two directions. You may reason from cause to effect (from observed cause to unobserved effect) or from effect to cause (from observed effect to unobserved cause).

Here, for example, a speaker (Ling 1993, p. 100) reasons from known causes (one of which is the growth of the aged population in Japan) to effects (health care problems for global corporations, the topic of the entire speech):

A second, related dynamic is a dramatic acceleration in the silvering of Japan.

Over 30 percent of the health insurance costs in this country are for people over 70 years old.

By the year 2000, 25 percent of the population will be over 65. Just for comparison, the aging of the Japanese population is advancing five times faster than France, and almost twice that of Germany and the U.K.

In this excerpt Amanda Hickman (Schnoor 1997, p. 102), a student from Miami University, reasons from effect (infectious disease crisis) to possible cause (exposure of bacteria to antibiotics):

Our infectious disease crisis can also in large part be blamed on the way we have treated them in the past. Bacteria are able to mutate when they are continually exposed to an antibiotic, rendering the antibiotic virtually useless against it. And the frequency in which antibiotics are prescribed today makes our pharmacies virtual classrooms for infections.

Critically Evaluating Reasoning from Causes and Effects

In testing reasoning from cause to effect or from effect to cause, ask yourself the following questions.

Might other causes be producing the observed effect? If you observe a particular effect (say, high crime or student apathy), you need to ask if

causes other than the one you're postulating might be producing these effects. Thus, you might postulate that poverty leads to high crime, but there might be other factors actually causing the high crime rate. Or poverty might be one cause, but it might not be the most important cause. Therefore, explore the possibility of other causes producing the observed effects.

Is the causation in the direction postulated? If two things occur together, it's often difficult to determine which is the cause and which is the effect. For example, a lack of interpersonal intimacy and a lack of self-confidence are often seen in the same person. The person who lacks self-confidence seldom has intimate relationships with others. But which is the cause and which is the effect? It might be that the lack of intimacy "causes" low self-confidence; it might also be, however, that low self-confidence "causes" a lack of intimacy. Of course, it might also be that some other previously unexamined cause (a history of negative criticism, for example) might be producing both the lack of intimacy and the low self-confidence.

Is there evidence for a causal rather than merely a time-sequence relation-ship? Two things might vary together, but they may not be related in a cause-effect relationship. Divorce frequently results after repeated instances of infidelity, but infidelity itself may not be the cause of the divorce rate. Rather, some other factor may be leading to both infidelity and divorce. Thus, even though infidelity may precede divorce, it may not be the cause of it. When you assume that a temporal relationship implies a causal relationship, you're committing a fallacy of reasoning called *post hoc ergo propter hoc* ("after this, because of this").

Using Cause-Effect Reasoning

Stress the causal connection by pointing out that:

1. other causes are not significant and may for all practical purposes be ruled out,
2. the causal connection is in the direction postulated, that is, that the cause is indeed the cause and the effect is the effect, and
3. the evidence points to a causal connection—that the relationship is not merely related in time.

Furthermore, depending on the specific purpose of your speech, make the audience realize that this causal connection can be altered to their advantage. Tell them that the effect may be strengthened (if the effect is desirable) or broken (if the effect is undesirable).

REASONING FROM SIGN

Some years ago I went to my doctor because of a minor skin irritation. Instead of looking at my skin, the doctor focused on my throat, noticed that it was enlarged, felt around a bit, and began asking me a number of questions. Did I tire easily? Yes. Did I drink lots of liquid? Yes. Did I

Student government debates, such as the one in which this speaker is engaged, rely heavily on logical arguments. What types of logical arguments would prove most effective in convincing an audience of your peers that (1) condoms should be distributed in high schools, (2) tuition must be raised, and (3) dress codes should be instituted at this school?

always feel thirsty? Yes. Did I eat a great deal without gaining any weight? Yes. She then had me stretch out my hand and try to hold it steady. I couldn't do it. These indicators were signs of a particular illness. Based on these signs, she made the preliminary diagnosis that I had a hyperthyroid condition. The results of blood and other tests confirmed the preliminary diagnosis. I was promptly treated, and the thyroid condition was corrected.

Medical diagnosis is a good example of reasoning by sign. The general procedure is simple. If a sign and an object, event, or condition are frequently paired, the presence of the sign is taken as proof of the presence of the object, event, or condition. Thus, the tiredness, extreme thirst, and overeating were taken as signs of hyperthyroidism since they frequently accompany the condition. When these signs (or symptoms) disappeared after treatment, it was taken as a sign that the thyroid disease had been arrested. Further tests confirmed this as well.

Here, for example, a speaker (Rolland 1993, p. 524) reasons from a number of signs to the conclusion that Americans are willing to sacrifice to achieve health care reform:

For example, a nationwide Wall Street Journal/*NBC poll in March found:*
—66 percent willing to pay higher taxes so everyone can get health insurance;
—52 percent willing to accept limit on the right to choose their own doctor; and
—46 percent even willing to accept higher insurance deductibles and copayments.

Critically Evaluating Reasoning from Sign

In reasoning from sign, ask yourself these questions.

Do the signs necessitate the conclusion drawn? Given the extreme thirst, overeating, and the like, how certain may I be of the "hyperthyroid" conclusion? With most medical and legal matters we can never be absolutely certain, but we can be certain beyond a reasonable doubt.

Are there other signs that point to the same conclusion? In the thyroid example, the extreme thirst could have been brought on by any number of factors. Similarly, the swollen throat and the overeating could have been attributed to other causes. Yet, taken together they seemed to point to only one reasonable diagnosis. This was later confirmed with additional and more sophisticated signs in the form of blood tests and thyroid scans. Generally, the more signs that point toward the conclusion, the more confidence we can have that it's valid.

Are there contradictory signs? Are there signs pointing toward contradictory conclusions? If, for example, "Higgins" had a motive and a history of violence (signs supporting the conclusion that Higgins was the murderer), but also had an alibi for the time of the murder (a sign pointing to the conclusion of innocence), the conclusion of guilt would have to be reconsidered or discarded. So, if you train yourself to look for signs pointing in different directions, you'll be less likely to miss contradictory signs.

Using Reasoning from Sign. Stress the certainty of the connection between the sign and the conclusion. Make the audience see that because these signs are present, no other conclusion is likely. Let them see that for all practical purposes, all other conclusions are ruled out.

This is the procedure followed in law. The guilt of an individual must be established not conclusively but beyond all reasonable doubt. The audience should be made to see that your conclusion drawn from sign is the best—the most reasonable—conclusion possible.

Make the connection between the signs and the conclusions clear to the audience. If you, as a speaker, know of the connection between, say, enlarged eyes and hyperthyroidism, this does not mean that the audience knows it. State explicitly that enlarged eyes can only be produced by hyperthyroidism and that, therefore, the sign (enlarged eyes) can lead to only one reasonable conclusion (hyperthyroidism).

UNIT IN BRIEF

Reasoning from Specific Instances and Generalizations	From specific instances to generalization: 1. Examine a valid number of specific instances. 2. Examine specific instances that are representative. 3. Account for the significant exceptions. This is most effective when you: 1. Stress the sufficiency and representativeness of the sample. 2. Account for exceptions. From a generalization to a specific instance: 1. The principle should be generally true. 2. The unexamined instance should be covered by the generalization. This is most effective when the principle is accepted by the audience.

Reasoning from Analogies	1. Use cases that are alike in essential respects. 2. Use cases in which the differences don't make a significant difference. This is most effective when: 1. Similarities are stressed. 2. The importance of differences is minimized. 3. Differences are confronted squarely.
Reasoning from Causes and Effects	1. Be sure that other causes are not producing the observed effect. 2. Be sure the causation is in the direction postulated. 3. Be sure there's evidence for a causal rather than simply a temporal relationship. This is most effective when: 1. Other possible causes are ruled out. 2. The causation is in the postulated direction. 3. The relationship is causal.
Reasoning from Sign	1. Use signs that clearly support the conclusion. 2. Identify other signs that point in the same direction. 3. Account for contradictory signs. This is most effective when: 1. The certainty of the connection between sign and conclusion is stressed. 2. The major counter-arguments are answered.

THINKING CRITICALLY ABOUT ARGUMENTS

REVIEWING KEY TERMS AND CONCEPTS IN DEVELOPING ARGUMENTS IN PUBLIC SPEAKING

1. Review and define the key terms used in this unit:

- ❏ argument (p. 408)
- ❏ evidence (p. 408)
- ❏ reasoning from specific instances and generalizations (p. 410)
- ❏ reasoning from analogy (p. 413)
- ❏ literal analogy (p. 413)
- ❏ figurative analogy (p. 413)
- ❏ reasoning from causes and effects (p. 415)
- ❏ reasoning from sign (p. 416)

2. Review and explain the key concepts discussed in this unit:

- ■ What is argument and evidence? In what ways does culture influence the appropriateness of argument and evidence?
- ■ How would you describe reasoning from specific instances to a generalization or from a generalization to a specific instance? How would you critically evaluate such reasoning?
- ■ How would you describe reasoning by analogy? How would you critically evaluate such reasoning?
- ■ How would you describe reasoning from causes and effects? How would you critically evaluate such reasoning?
- ■ How would you describe reasoning from sign? How would you critically evaluate such reasoning?

DEVELOPING STRATEGIES FOR ARGUMENTS IN PUBLIC SPEECHES

1. Devon is planning to give a speech in favor of the college restricting access to certain lifestyle Web sites. Devon knows that his audience is very likely to be opposed to his position and so he wonders what types of arguments will work best. What advice would you give Devon?
2. Ticha is preparing a speech arguing that psychic phone lines should not be allowed to advertise on television. What types of arguments would Ticha need if she were presenting this speech to your class? If she were presenting this speech to the typical audience of the Jerry Springer show?

EVALUATING EVIDENCE AND ARGUMENTS IN PUBLIC SPEECHES

1. Review the persuasive speech, "XXX Has Got to Go," in Unit 5. What evidence and arguments can you identify? How would you evaluate this evidence and argument?

2. Select two or three advertisements from a newspaper or magazine. What is their main argument? What form of reasoning did the advertiser use to support the argument?

USING TECHNOLOGY IN PUBLIC SPEECHES

1. Using the search engines and directories in Table 7.1, search for newsgroups or listservs that deal with a topic that interests you. Lurk for a while, reading as many of the posts as you can. Can you identify examples of the types of arguments discussed in this unit: specific instance and generalization, analogy, cause and effect, and sign? Can you find examples of both well-reasoned and faulty reasoned arguments?
2. Visit http://www.bris.ac.uk/Depts/Philosophy/VL and search for links related to logic, reasoning, and argument. In what ways might this material supplement what is presented in this unit?

PRACTICALLY SPEAKING

21.1 Short Speech Technique

Prepare and deliver a two-minute speech in which you:

a. develop an argument for or against the legalization of steroids.
b. develop an argument from specific instances to support one of these generalizations: (1) hard work leads to rewards, (2) people who agree with others become leaders, or (3) inflation will increase.
c. develop an analogy to help explain one of the following concepts: teaching, research, parenting, happiness, philosophizing, therapy.
d. develop a cause-effect or effect-cause argument for any of the following propositions: (1) cigarette advertising should be prohibited, (2) divorces should be easier to obtain, or (3) open a retirement account now.
e. develop an argument from sign to support any of the following conclusions: (1) the economic value of a college education has lessened over the last few decades, (2) exercise regularly, or (3) immigration policies need to be revised.
f. select one newspaper feature (advice to the lovelorn, astrology, medical advice column, celebrity news,

editorial, or letters to the editor, for example) and describe the types of evidence used

21.2 Evaluating the Adequacy of Reasoning

Here are, in brief, a few arguments. Read each of them carefully and (1) identify the type of reasoning used, (2) apply the tests of adequacy discussed in this unit, and (3) indicate what could be done to make the reasoning more logical and more persuasive.

1. Dr. Manchester should be denied tenure for being an ineffective teacher. Two of my friends are in Manchester's statistics course and they hate it; they haven't learned a thing. Manchester's student evaluation ratings are way below the department and college average, and the readings Manchester assigns are dull, difficult, and of little relevance to students.
2. The lack of success among the Martians who have settled on Earth is not difficult to explain. They simply have no ambition, no drive, no desire to excel. They're content to live on welfare, drink cheap wine, and smoke as much grass as they can get their hands on.

3. I went out with three people I met at clubs—they were all duds. In the club they were fine but once we got outside I couldn't even talk with them. All they knew how to do was wear freaky clothes and dance. So when Pat asked me out I said, "No." I decided it would be a waste of time.

4. One recent sociological report indicates some interesting facts about Theta Three. In Theta Three there are, as most of us know, few restrictions on premarital sexual relations. Unlike in our country, the permissive person is not looked down on. Social taboos in regard to sex are few. Theta Three also has the highest suicide rate in the galaxy. Suicide is not infrequent among teenagers and young adults. This condition must be changed. But, before it's changed, life must be accorded greater meaning and significance. Social, and perhaps legal, restrictions on premarital sexual relations must be instituted.

5. Pat and Chris are unhappy and should probably separate. The last time I visited, Pat told me that they just had a big fight and mentioned that they now fight regularly. Chris spends more time with the kids than with Pat and frequently goes out after work with people from the office. Often, Chris has told me, they sit for hours without saying a word to each other.

21.3 Analyzing Arguments with the Toulmin Model

An excellent way to analyze arguments is with the model developed by Stephen Toulmin, a British philosopher and logician. In Toulmin's model there are three essential parts and an additional three parts that may be used depending on the argument and the audience. The three essential parts include claim, data, and warrant.

The **claim** is the conclusion you wish the audience to accept; it's the proposition you want the audience to believe is true or justified or right. For example: Tuition must be increased.

The **data** are the facts and opinions—the evidence—used to support your claim. For example: The college has recently incurred vast additional expenses.

The **warrant** is the connection leading from the data to the claim. The warrant is the principle or the reason why the data justify (or warrant) the claim. For example: *Tuition has been in the past and is likely to continue to be the principal means by which the college pays its expenses.*

In addition to these three elements (which are essential to all arguments), there are three other optional elements that may or may not be present depending on the

type of argument advanced and the nature of the audience to be persuaded.

The **backing** is the support for the warrant—the supporting material that backs up the principle or reason expressed in the warrant. Backing is especially important if the warrant is not accepted or believed by the audience. For example: Over the last 40 years, each time the college incurred large expenses, it raised tuition.

The **qualifier** is the degree to which the claim is asserted; it's an attempt to modify the strength or certainty of the claim. The qualifier is used only when the claim is presented with less than total certainty. Examples of qualifiers include "probably," and "most likely."

The **reservation** (or rebuttal) specifies those situations under which the claim might not be true. For example: . . . unless the college manages to secure private donations from friends and alumni.

Usually these six parts of an argument are laid out in diagrammatic form to further illustrate the important relationships. See Figure 21.1.

The main value of Toulmin's system is that it provides an excellent method for analyzing arguments, which is especially appropriate to the public speaking situation. The following questions may also help you to analyze the validity and possible effectiveness of your arguments:

1. Are the data sufficient to justify the claim? What additional data are needed?

2. Is the claim properly (logically) qualified? Is the claim presented with too much certainty?

3. Is the warrant adequate to justify the claim on the basis of the data? Does the audience accept the warrant or will it need backing? What other warrants might be utilized?

4. Is the backing sufficient for accepting the warrant? Will the audience accept the backing? What further support for the warrant might be used?

5. Are the essential reservations stated? What other reservations might the audience think of that should be included here?

Test your understanding of these six elements of the Toulmin model by identifying which element each of the following statements represents. They're presented here in random order.

_____1. Cicero College must adopt a policy of training all its students in computer literacy.

_____2. Employers are demanding computer literacy for all positions.

_____3. This new emphasis must take place as soon as possible.

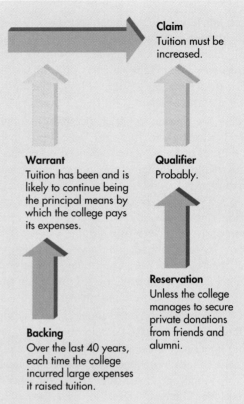

FIGURE 21.1

A diagram of the parts of an argument in a Toulmin analysis.

Data
The college has recently incurred vast additional expenses.

Claim
Tuition must be increased.

Warrant
Tuition has been and is likely to continue being the principal means by which the college pays its expenses.

Qualifier
Probably.

Reservation
Unless the college manages to secure private donations from friends and alumni.

Backing
Over the last 40 years, each time the college incurred large expenses it raised tuition.

_____4. Colleges are obligated to prepare students for the job market.

_____5. Colleges that have failed to prepare students for the job market have found themselves without students.

_____6. Unless the job market changes drastically

_____7. Unless Cicero becomes a college devoted solely to the fine arts

_____8. Tawny Bay, Middlecenter, and Mt. Hill Colleges all neglected computer literacy and have declined 30% in enrollment.

_____9. All students should be trained in computer science with the possible exception of those in the fine arts.

Answers: 1 = claim; 2 = data; 3 = qualifier; 4 = warrant; 5 = backing; 6 = reservation; 7 = reservation; 8 = backing; 9 = qualifier.

Now that the mechanics of this model are clear, select one of the "claims" that follow and construct and diagram an argument using Toulmin's system. Include all six parts of the argument: claim, data, warrant, backing, qualifier, and reservation. After each person has constructed and diagrammed one argument, the papers should be collected, randomized, and redistributed so that each student has a diagrammed argument developed by someone else. In groups of five or six (or with the class as a whole), each student should analyze the argument, evaluating its validity and its potential rhetorical effectiveness for an audience composed of students from your class. The five questions presented previously might provide a useful starting place.

Claims

1. Senator Smiley should be reelected.

2. College football should be abolished,

3. Everyone has ESP.

4. Take a course in critical thinking.

5. Exercise daily.

6. Support the college athletic fund.

7. Keep a daily journal.

8. Express your opinions to your local representative.

9. Trace your family origins.

10. Visit India.

Motivating Behavior

	UNIT OBJECTIVES
	After completing this unit, you should be able to:
	Explain the role of motivational appeals in persuasion and the principles governing motivation.
	Explain the variety of motivation appeals and how they may work in public speaking.
	Explain the suggested guidelines for evaluating motivational appeals.

Motivational appeals—appeals to needs, desires, and wants—are the most powerful means of persuasion you possess. Because of their importance, this entire unit is devoted to explaining what motivational appeals are and how you can use them effectively.

When you use motivational appeals you appeal to your listeners' needs and desires. You appeal to those forces that energize or move or motivate a person to develop, change, or strengthen particular attitudes or ways of behaving. For example, one motive might be the desire for status. This motive might lead you to develop certain attitudes about what occupation to enter, the importance of saving and investing money, and so on.

One of the most useful analyses of motives is Abraham Maslow's fivefold classification, reproduced in Figure 22.1. One of the assumptions contained in it is that you seek to fulfill the need at the lowest level first. Only when those needs are satisfied do the needs at the next level begin to exert influence on your behavior. Thus, for example, you would not concern yourself with the need for security or freedom from fear if you were starving (if your need for food has not been fulfilled). Similarly, you would not be concerned with friendship if your need for protection and security has not been fulfilled. The implication for the speaker is clear: you need to know what needs of your audience are unsatisfied. These are the needs you can appeal to in motivating them.

PRINCIPLES OF MOTIVATION

Let's first consider some principles of motivation so that you'll be able to use motivational appeals discussed in the next section more effectively in your own speeches.

Motives Differ

We should often be ashamed of our finest actions if the world understood our motives.
—Francois, Duc de La Rochefoucauld

Motives are not static, nor do they operate in the same way with different people. Motives differ from one time to another and from one person to another. Think of the motives that are crucial to you at this time in your life and that motivate your current thinking and behavior. These motives, however, may not be significant in 10 or even two years. They may fade

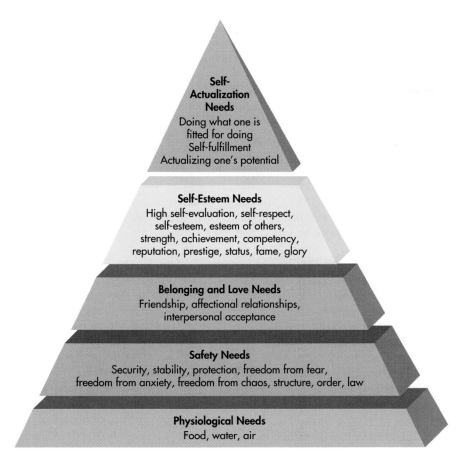

FIGURE 22.1

Maslow's "Hierarchy of needs."
SOURCE: Based on Abraham Maslow, *Motivation and Personality.* New York: HarperCollins, 1970.

and others may take their place. Now, for example, attractiveness may be one of the more dominant motives in your life. You have a strong need to be thought attractive by your peers. Later in life this motive may be replaced by, for example, the desire for security, for financial independence, or for power.

Motives also function differently with different people. This is simply a specific application of the general principle: people are different. Consequently, different people will respond differently to the very same motive.

Motives Are Ordered

Not all motives are equal in intensity. Some are powerful and exert a strong influence on behavior; others are less powerful and may influence behavior only slightly. Motives exist in varying degrees of intensity. Some motives are strong, some are weak, and the vast majority are somewhere in between. Since motives vary in intensity and strength, they vary in the influence they have on the individual. Determining which motives your audience holds strongly and which weakly may be one of your most difficult tasks. But, if you can identify those motives that will strongly influence the audience, you won't need to waste time on motives that are ineffective in influencing behavior.

He who gives food to the people will win.
—Lech Walesa

Further, motives may be ordered in terms of their degree of generality or specificity. Motives are general classes of needs and desires. The status motive may include a host of specifics that, taken together, make up and define status for a specific person. But, as you know, people are not motivated by appeals to abstract and general motives but rather to specific aspects of these motives. Thus, to appeal to status you would need to appeal to, for example, the desire to be recognized by others on the street, having a job that is respected by family and friends, or having a home in an exclusive part of town.

The more specific your appeal, the more effective your appeal will be in persuading your audience. Consider, for example, the difference between the teacher's appeal to read this book because it will help make you an educated person versus the appeal to read this book because it will help you pass this course or the next test.

Motives Interact

Motives rarely operate in isolation; a collection of motives usually operates together. Sometimes these motives operate in the same direction, all influencing behavior in the same way. At other times, motives conflict with one another, each stimulating behavior in somewhat different directions.

In cases where a number of motives influence behavior in the same direction, your appeal should be directed to a number of motives rather than limited to just one. For example, if you want an audience to contribute money to AIDS research, appeal to a variety of influential motives—safety for oneself and one's family and friends, altruism, control over the environment, and so on.

In cases where motives conflict with one another, your task is more difficult. Let's say, for example, that humanitarian motives would lead your audience to give money to AIDS research, but their desire to use their money for personal luxuries would lead them not to donate funds. In this case you might propose that the humanitarian motives are more noble or perhaps that the amount of money involved is not so great that they would impoverish themselves.

Motives Are Culturally Influenced

Throughout this discussion, keep in mind that the listener's culture will greatly influence the motives he or she will be responsive to. Members of highly individualistic cultures—the United States, Sweden, Germany, Norway, for example—are likely to be moved by appeals to status (which itself is an individualistic motive) and perhaps not moved as much by the desire to conform. Members of highly collective cultures—such as Arabic, Japanese, Latin American, and Chinese cultures—are more likely to be moved by appeals to conformity but not as much to status. To complicate matters even more, members of collective cultures may think it inappropriate for a speaker to appeal to motives of status and self-reward.

The motives discussed here are those that are judged potent in much of the United States. Researchers in communication and psychology, for example, find these motives operating in a variety of situations and, of course, advertisers and the media appeal to these motives in designing

TIPS

from professional speakers

Making the listener want to hear you is primary.

Right. But now that you think about it, why would someone else spontaneously get interested in your vested stuff? You'd need a propellant—something that could make a difference, something that could actively turn your audience to your pursuit and away from theirs. What? When what you have to say clearly intersects with what the other person wants or needs or cares about.

Sonya Hamlin, president, Sonya Hamlin Communications, a communications consulting firm, *How to Talk So People Listen: The Real Key to Job Success* (New York: HarperCollins, 1988): 22-23. Reprinted by permission.

Emotional appeals are all around. Persons who want to censor the Internet might appeal to the audience's fear of their children accessing pornographic materials; those who want to restrict the media's portrayal of violence may appeal to the audience's fear of increased violence in their community. Similarly, the real estate broker appealing to your desire for status, the friend who wants a favor appealing to your desire for social approval, and the salesperson appealing to your desire for sexual rewards are familiar examples. The question, of course, is, are these emotional appeals ethical? Here are a few questions to get you thinking about the ethical issues in the use of emotional appeals:

- Is it ethical for parents to use fear appeals to dissuade their teenage children from engaging in sexual

relationships? From interacting with teens of other races? Are the parents' motives relevant in deciding whether such appeals are ethical or unethical?

- Is it ethical to use fear appeals in public speeches or in advertisements to prevent sexually transmitted diseases? Is it ethical to use the same appeals if the motive is to sell condoms?
- Is it ethical for religious organizations to use fear appeals to get people to live their lives as the religion holds?

What ethical guidelines would you propose for the use of fear and emotional appeals in persuasion?

(The next Ethics in Public Speaking box appears on page 442.)

their ads, their magazines, and their sitcoms. As you read these discussions, consider how these needs might work in other cultural situations.

MOTIVATIONAL APPEALS

In reviewing these motivational appeals, try to visualize how you would use each one in your next speech. If that's too easy, try visualizing how you would use these motives on widely different audiences, for example, a group of college professors, members of the American Medical Association, the local PTA, or members of your class. Try also to apply these motives in speeches addressed to audiences composed of members from cultures differing widely from your own.

Altruism

Altruism, some argue, does not exist. It's often said that all motives are selfish, and perhaps this is right. Any action, any belief, any attitude can usually be traced to a motive that might be regarded as selfish—to greed, to sensory pleasure, to personal power. But it's equally true that most of us want to believe that our motives are altruistic, at least sometimes. We want to do what we consider the right thing; we want to help others; we want to contribute to worthy causes. We want to help the weak, feed the hungry, cure the sick. The fact that we derive some kind of selfish pleasure from these actions does not militate against our viewing them as being motivated by altruism. From a recent poll of 1,000 *Newsweek* readers (*Newsweek,* July 20, 1998) the researchers conclude: "The 'get ahead at any expense' attitude of the 1980s has fallen to the wayside in American culture. Instead, in the 1990s, *people want to help others,* spend time with their families and live how they see fit."

Appeals to altruism are most effective when done with moderation. If they're not moderate, they'll seem unrealistic and out of touch with the way real people think in a world that is practical and difficult to survive in.

Here's an especially good example of an appeal to altruism from a speech advocating that we become actively involved in the fight against AIDS by a student from Louisiana State University, Jimmy Rubio (Schnoor 1995, p. 43):

> *So, finally, the decision comes to you. The realistic choice requires only two steps: education, learning about AIDS, and action, simply remembering universal values. . . . [W]e all have a part of ourselves— be it our careers, our hobbies, or even our dreams—that can benefit someone who needs and appreciates us. It doesn't matter whether we are talking about specific love or general decency, we all have the impulse to care.*

Fear and Safety

We are motivated in great part by a desire to avoid fear. We fear the loss of those things we desire. We fear the loss of money, family, friends, love, attractiveness, health, job, and just about everything we now have and value. We also fear punishment, rejection, and failure. We fear the unknown, the uncertain, the unpredictable.

The use of fear in persuasion has been studied extensively, and the results show that strong amounts of fear work best (Boster and Mongeau, 1984; Allen and Preiss, 1990). With low or even moderate levels of fear, the audience is not motivated sufficiently to act; with high levels of fear, they perk up and begin to listen.

The other side of fear is safety. We all have a need for safety. Maslow put safety at the second level, just above the satisfaction of the physiological need for food and drink. We want to feel protected, to be free of fear. Sometimes the safety motive is seen in the individual's desire for order, structure, and organization. We fear what is unknown, and order and structure make things predictable and, hence, safe.

In this excerpt, Edwin J. Feulner Jr. (1995, p. 411) appeals to the desire for safety:

> *It is a false economy to withdraw any more of our 100,000 troops from Europe because Russia is not an immediate danger. To those who say, "Well, we'll just come back when Russia is a threat again." I say, "You mean like we did in 1944 on the beaches of Normandy?" And to those who ask "Why should America pay anything to defend Europe or East Asia?" I say, "We're not paying for Europe's defense or Japan's defense. We're paying for our defense."*

Individuality and Conformity

These two conflicting motives are discussed together because they're opposite sides of the same coin. Each pulls us in a different direction, and each lessens the effects of the other. Many people have a desire to be individuals yet also one of the crowd. In individualistic cultures, the desire to stand out, to be one-of-a-kind is the stronger motive in most situations. In collectivist cultures, the desire to be one of a group, to conform to the group standards and rules, is the stronger motive in most situations.

Power, Control, and Influence

We want power, control, and influence. First, we want power over ourselves—we want to be in control of our own destinies, we want to be responsible for our own successes. As Emerson put it, "Can anything be so elegant as to have few wants, and to serve them one's self?"

We also want control over other persons. We want to be influential. We want to be opinion leaders. We want others to come to us for advice, for guidance, for instruction. Similarly, we want control over events and things in the world. We want to control our environment. You'll motivate your listeners when you enable them to believe that they can increase their power, control, and influence as a result of their learning what you have to say or doing as you suggest.

Self-Esteem and Approval

"In his private heart," wrote Mark Twain, "no man much respects himself." And perhaps because of this, we have a need for a positive self-image, to see ourselves in the best possible light. We want to see ourselves as self-confident, as worthy and contributing human beings. Inspirational speeches, speeches of the "you're the greatest" type, never seem to lack receptive and suggestive audiences.

Self-esteem is, at least in part, attained by gaining the approval of others (something that is more important in collectivist cultures than it is in individualistic cultures). Most people are concerned with peer approval but also want approval from family, teachers, elders, and children. Somehow the approval of others makes us feel positive about ourselves. Approval from others also ensures the attainment of related goals. For example, if you have peer approval, you probably also have influence. If you have approval, you're likely to have status. In relating your propositions to your audience's desire for approval, avoid being too obvious. Few people want to be told that they need or desire approval.

Love and Affiliation

We are motivated to love and be loved. For most persons, love and its pursuit occupy a considerable amount of time and energy. If you can teach your audience how to be loved and how to love, you'll have not only an attentive but also a grateful audience.

We also want affiliation—friendship and companionship. We desire to be a part of a group despite our equally potent desire for independence and individuality. Notice how advertisements for discos, singles bars, and dating services emphasize this need for affiliation. On this basis alone they successfully gain the attention, interest, and participation of thousands. Again, such affiliation seems to assure us that we are, in fact, worthy creatures. If we have friends and companions, surely we are people of some merit.

Power only means the ability to have control over your life. Power implies choice.
—Nikki Giovanni

Love is much nicer to be in than an automobile accident, a tight girdle, a higher tax bracket or a holding pattern over Philadelphia.
—Judith Viorst

In this excerpt, Leo Buscaglia (1988), noted author and lecturer, appeals to our desire for love and affiliation:

Relationships that are based on little more than a steamy attraction more often than not end by leaving us bewildered, wondering what went wrong when we find that we are no longer "happily-ever-aftering." We usually discover that it was the small conflicts, the petty peeves, the infantile rigidity and stubbornness, the disillusionment and the refusal to forgive.

There is no simple formula for making us better lovers. At best we can base our love on certain tried-and-true rules that can make a positive beginning.

Achievement

We want to achieve in whatever we do. As students you want to be successful students. We want to achieve as friends, as parents, as lovers. This is why we read books and listen to speeches that purport to tell us how to be better achievers. We also want others to recognize our achievements as real and valuable. "Being successful in my work" is extremely important to most college students.

In using the achievement motive, be explicit in stating how your speech, ideas, and recommendations will contribute to the listeners' achievements. At the same time, recognize that different cultures will view achievement very differently. To some achievement may be financial, to others it may be group popularity, to still others it may mean security. In the survey referred to earlier, 1,000 *Newsweek* readers (*Newsweek,* July 20, 1998) ranked the following as "very important" and may be taken as one indication of how this group defined "achievement" (the percentage in parentheses indicates the percentage of people who ranked this item as "very important"):

- Freedom of choice in how to live my life (94%)
- To be able to have a good family life (89%)
- To own a home (70%)
- To be able to have a rewarding career (70%)
- To be able to afford to do the things you want to do (66%)
- To help others (57%)
- To be active in your community (34%)
- To be able to start a business of my own (33%)
- The ability to become wealthy (29%)

Show your audience how what you have to say will help them achieve these goals and you'll likely have an active and receptive audience. In this speech, for example, Raymond W. Smith (1995, p. 360), CEO of Bell Atlantic, used the achievement motive in persuading his audience (Advertising Women of New York) of the importance of interactive advertising:

Barry Diller bought QVC at the very same time that Sears closed its franchise catalog business. Diller saw the future; Sears could only mourn the past.

Which of you will be the pioneers of the new interactive medium? You'd better decide quick, because it won't be "new" very long. The leaders will establish themselves very fast. The rest will have trouble ever catching up.

Yogi Berra once said, "When you come to a crossroads—take it!" I couldn't have said it better myself.

The great rule is not to talk about money with people who have much more or much less than you.
—Katharine Whitehorn

Financial Gain

Most people are motivated to some extent by the desire for financial gain—for what it can buy, for what it can do. We may be concerned with buying necessities, luxuries, or even time. Concerns for lower taxes, for higher salaries, or for fringe benefits are all related to the money motive. Show the audience that what you're saying or advocating will make them money and they'll listen with considerable interest, much as they read the current get-rich-quick books that flood the bookstores.

In a speech showing the problems of the rising number of lawsuits from prison inmates, Adam Childers (Schnoor 1997, p. 78), a student from the University of Oklahoma, focuses on the financial problems this increase is causing:

This trend [toward the increase in the number of lawsuits] should alarm all of us, for two reasons. First, millions of dollars of our tax money are being spent needlessly on these lawsuits every year. But, even more importantly, these lawsuits are putting a financial strain on an already overburdened penal system—helping to create a situation in which our prisoners are being released early.

Status

One motive that accounts for a great deal of our behavior is our desire for status. In our society our status is measured by our occupation and wealth; often job and money are positively related.

But there are other kinds of status: the status that comes from competence on the athletic field, from excelling in the classroom, or from superiority on the dance floor. To be most effective, link your propositions with your specific audience's desire for status.

In this excerpt Kelly Zmak (Boaz and Brey, 1987), a student from San Jose State University, appeals to the audiences' desire for status and success:

You know, as college people we all have something in common. We want to be successful. The levels of our success vary, but to be successful is something that we all strive for. Having an advantage in today's world is something none of us would mind. But having a disadvantage is something that none of us can afford. I would say that there are many of you here today that are not capitalizing on your potential, because you don't own a personal computer. And for those of you who do, listen up. Your computer may not have the power, the capabilities, and the features needed to give the home user, the student, and the businessperson an advantage in today's world.

Self-Actualization

The self-actualization motive, according to Maslow (1970), only influences attitudes and behaviors after all other needs are satisfied. And since these other needs are very rarely all satisfied, the time spent appealing to self-actualization might better be spent on other motives. And yet, it seems that regardless of how satisfied or unsatisfied your other desires are, you have a desire to self-actualize, to become what you feel you're fit for. If you see yourself as a poet, you must write poetry. If you see yourself as a teacher, you must teach. Even if you don't pursue these as occupations, you nevertheless have a desire to write poetry or to teach. Appeals to self-actualization encourage listeners to strive for their highest ideals and are often welcomed. Here, for example, Julia Hughes Jones (1998, pp. 279–280) appeals to an audience of the Junior League of Jacksonville, Florida, and their desire for self-actualization.

> *Each of us is capable of becoming an effective leader by recognizing that leadership is not only responsibility, but character. Character has to do with who we are as human beings, and it has to do with the forces that have shaped us into who we are. Character continually evolves as we grow and develop through self-knowledge as well as continual self-assessment. People win and lose based not only on their knowledge of conditions but also on their knowledge of themselves.*

A somewhat different perspective is provided by research on compliance-gaining strategies. This research focuses on persuasion in an interpersonal relationship, but, as you can see from Table 22.1 detailing six strategies, it can easily prove useful to the public speaker trying to persuade an audience.

CRITICALLY EVALUATING MOTIVATIONAL APPEALS

As shown, motivational appeals are all around us. People use them on us and we use them on others. In dealing with motivational appeals, whether as speaker or listener, ask yourself these questions:

Of all the motives discussed here, which two do you think will prove most effective with members of your class?

TABLE 22.1 Compliance-Gaining Strategies

These six strategies are from the research of Marwell and Schmitt (1967) and Miller and Parks (1982). What other compliance-gaining strategies can you think of?

Compliance Gaining Strategy	Definition	Example
Promise	Promise the audience that they'll receive some kind of reward if they do as you request.	The time you spend organizing your finances will be cut in half with this new computer program.
Threat	Threaten the audience with some form of punishment if they don't do as you suggest.	If we don't elect Senator Underdog, you can kiss Social Security goodbye.
Self-feelings	Make the audience see that they'll feel better about themselves if they do as you suggest (or worse about themselves if they don't do as you suggest).	Charity doesn't only help those who need it, it helps those who give.
Altercasting	Cast your listeners in the role of the "good" person (or "bad" person) and argue that they should comply with your suggestion because a person with "good" qualities would comply (while a person with "bad" qualities would not).	Let's side with those who are trying to do something to help the homeless and not with the landlords and insurance companies who want the homeless to have no rights.
Debt	Make the audience realize that they have a debt, an obligation, to do as you suggest.	Look at everything the school has done for us; it's time we did something for the school.
Moral appeals	Make the audience see that what you're advocating is moral and right and that their moral responsibility is to do as you suggest (as it would be immoral to not do what you suggest).	It would be totally immoral to do nothing, to allow the homeless to be without shelter any longer. Building these shelters is the only moral alternative.

LISTEN TO THIS   How to Listen to Emotional Appeals

Part of the art of public speaking is to use emotional appeals appropriately; the other part is to listen to them appropriately. Here are three suggestions for listening to emotional appeals.

- Realize that emotional appeal does not constitute proof. No matter how passionate the speaker is, it does not prove the case.
- Realize that as a listener you really can't tell with certainty what the speaker is actually feeling. The speaker may, in fact, be using a wide variety of facial management techniques that help to communicate emotions without actually feeling them.
- Realize that some speakers may use emotional appeals instead of evidence and logical arguments. Some, in fact, may try to divert attention away from the lack of evidence with emotional appeals.

(The next Listen to This box appears on page 447.)

Are the motivational appeals being used instead of argument and evidence? Especially ask yourself, are they being used to the exclusion of argument and evidence? Does the speaker (or the advertisement) seek to arouse our emotions so we forget the fact that there's no evidence to support his or her position? If so, then we need to ask why.

Some ethicists claim that motivational appeals that "short circuit" the reasoning process are unethical (Haiman 1958, Johannesen, 1996). These are appeals that seek to get you to believe or do something purely on the basis of your emotional response and in fact discourage logical analysis and evaluation.

Are the appeals to high or low motives? It's often relevant to ask if the motives being appealed to are basically high or low. For example, in asking for a charitable donation, an organization may appeal to such high or positive motives as your altruism or your desire to help those less fortunate than you. Or it can play on your lower or more base motives such as guilt and, to some extent, pity. It can present images of children playing and learning as a result of your contributions or it can present images of children eating garbage and dying of starvation with the clear message that your lack of contributions is causing this situation to continue.

A speaker can seek to arouse feelings of love and peace but also feelings of hatred and war. Speeches at rallies often run the gamut from emphasizing the positive emotions of companionship, faith, and love to the negative emotions of prejudice, hatred, and divisiveness.

UNIT IN BRIEF

Principles of Motivation	Motives differ from one person to another. Motives are ordered, varying in intensity and generality. Motives interact, sometimes in concert and sometimes in conflict. Motives are culturally influenced.
Popular Motivational Appeals	Altruism Fear Individuality and conformity Power, control, and influence Self-esteem and approval Love and affiliation Achievement Financial gain Status Self-actualization
Thinking Critically about Motivational Appeals	1. Are they used instead of or to divert attention from the absence of logical appeals? 2. Are the appeals to our better selves?

THINKING CRITICALLY ABOUT MOTIVATION

REVIEWING KEY TERMS AND CONCEPTS IN MOTIVATING BEHAVIOR

1. Review and define the key terms used in this unit:

   - ❏ motive (p. 424)
   - ❏ hierarchy of needs (p. 425)
   - ❏ motivational appeals (p. 427)
   - ❏ altruism (p. 427)
   - ❏ self-actualization (p. 432)
   - ❏ compliance-gaining strategies (p. 433)

2. Review and explain the key concepts discussed in this unit:

   - What principles govern the way motives work?
   - What are some of the major motivational appeals useful to the public speaker?
   - What critical guidelines should you use in evaluating motivational appeals?

DEVELOPING STRATEGIES FOR MOTIVATIONAL APPEALS

1. Kelly is planning to give a speech to a group of junior high school students on why they need to stay away from drugs. It's estimated that 35 percent of the students in this school are casual to regular users of some form of drug. Most of the students are middle class; their parents are largely professionals. What motives would you advise Kelly to concentrate on?

2. What motives would you appeal to in persuading your class to:

   - vote for (against) affirmative action proposals?
   - support (don't support) a multiculturalism requirement?
   - support (don't support) the building of a homeless shelter in their neighborhood?

3. How would you use any one of the compliance-gaining strategies to persuade others and accomplish each of the following goals:

   - to persuade a friend to cut class and go to the movies.
   - to persuade a group to vote in favor of building a senior citizen center.
   - to persuade an audience to reaffirm their faith in the government.
   - to persuade an audience to manage their time more efficiently.
   - to persuade an audience to change their telephone company to Expand-a-Phone.

EVALUATING MOTIVATIONAL APPEALS IN PUBLIC SPEECHES

1. Read a speech and analyze it for motivational appeals. To what specific motives did the speaker appeal? Were they effectively presented?

2. Watch television advertisements that are addressed to an adult and then some addressed to a child. What motives are used to appeal to the adult? To the child?

USING TECHNOLOGY IN MOTIVATING APPEALS

1. Visit http://www.webcom.com/~lewrose/home/html, a Web site devoted to advertising law. In what ways do the laws and standards deal with the motivational appeals used in advertising?

2. How would you compare the motivational appeals used by advertisers on the Web with television advertisers? In answering this question try to draw on specific examples where the same product is advertised in both media.

PRACTICALLY SPEAKING

22.1 Short Speech Technique

Prepare and deliver a two-minute speech in which you:

a. analyze a current print or television advertisement for its motivational appeal.

b. explain how fear is used in education.

c. analyze the appeals used on a typical cover of an issue of the *National Enquirer,* the *Star,* or the *Globe.*

d. use at least three motivational appeals to support any of the following propositions: (1) buy this used car, (2) give to AIDS research, (3) make meditation a part of your day, (4) buy generic, or (5) join a gym.

22.2 Constructing Motivational Appeals

Select any combination of specific "Purposes" and "Audiences" that follow and develop a motivational appeal based on one or more of the motivational appeals discussed in this unit. After constructing these appeals, share the results of your labors with others, either in small groups or in the class as a whole. In your discussion you may wish to consider some or all of the following questions.

1. Why did you assume that this (these) appeal(s) would prove effective with the topic and the audience selected?

2. Might some of the appeals backfire and stimulate resentment in the audience? What precautions might be taken by the speaker to prevent such resentment from developing?

3. What are the ethical implications of using these motivational appeals?

Purposes

1. Marijuana should (not) be made legal for all those over 18 years of age.

2. Cigarette smoking should (not) be banned in all public places.

3. Capital punishment should (not) be law in all states.

4. Social Security benefits should be increased (decreased) by at least one-third.

5. Retirement should (not) be mandatory at age 65 for all government employees.

6. Police personnel should (not) be permitted to strike.

7. National health insurance should (not) be instituted.

8. Domestic partnerships should (not) be accorded the same rights and privileges as marriages

9. Teachers should (not) be paid according to performance rather than (but according to) seniority, degrees earned, or publications.

10. Divorce should (not) be granted immediately when the parties request it.

Audiences

1. Senior citizens of Metropolis

2. Small Business Operators Club of Accord

3. American Society of Young Dentists

4. Vietnam Veterans

5. Los Angeles Society of Interior Designers

6. Society for the Rehabilitation of Ex-Offenders

7. Catholic Women's Council

8. National Council of African American Artists

9. Parent-Teacher Association of New Orleans Elementary Schools

10. Midwestern Council of Physical Education Instructors

Speaker Credibility

If you were giving a speech on, say, the need for recycling, how believable would you be to other members of your class? How believable would you be apart from any evidence or argument you might advance? What is there about you as a person that makes people believe or not believe you? These are questions of credibility, the focus of this unit.

WHAT IS CREDIBILITY?

You've probably made judgments about speakers apart from any arguments, evidence, or motivational appeals they offered. Often you believe or disbelieve a speaker because of who the speaker is, not because of anything the speaker said. You may, for example, believe certain information or take certain action solely by virtue of Oprah Winfrey's or Rosie O'Donnell's reputation, personality, or character.

This quality of believability is called speaker credibility. Credibility is not something the speaker has or doesn't have in any objective sense; rather, it's what the audience thinks of him or her. In reality the speaker may be a stupid, immoral person, but, if the audience perceives him or her as intelligent and moral, then that speaker has high credibility. Further, research tells us, the audience will believe this speaker. Figure 23.1 explains how you form credibility impressions.

Much contemporary research focuses on what makes a person believable. Advertisers are interested because it relates directly to the effectiveness or ineffectiveness of their ad campaigns. Is Jerry Seinfeld an effective

*Some judge of authors names, not works, and then
Nor praise nor blame the writings, but the men*
—Alexander Pope

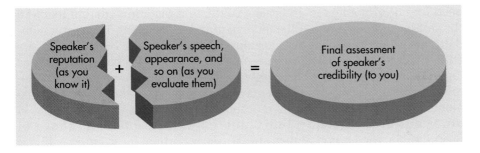

FIGURE 23.1

How You Form Credibility Impressions.

You form a credibility impression of a speaker on the basis of two sources of information: (1) the reputation of the speaker as we know it; this is *initial* or what theorists call *extrinsic* credibility and (2) the confirmation or disconfirmation of that reputation by what the speaker says and does during the speech; this is *derived* or *intrinsic* credibility. In other words, you combine what you know about the speaker's reputation with the more immediate information you get from present interactions and form a collective final assessment of credibility.

spokesperson for American Express? Is Michael Jordan an effective spokesperson for Nike? Is Susan Lucci an effective spokesperson for Ford? Would Madonna be a good spokesperson for Sara Lee? For K-Mart clothing? For Lean Cuisine?

Credibility is important to the politician because it determines in great part how people vote. It influences education—the students' perception of teacher credibility will determine the degree of influence the teacher has on a class. There seems no communication situation that credibility does not influence. We can identify three major qualities of credibility:

- **Competence:** the knowledge and expertise the audience thinks the speaker possesses
- **Character:** the intentions and concern of the speaker for the audience
- **Charisma:** the personality and dynamism of the speaker

Credibility and Culture

What makes a speaker credible will vary from one culture to another. In some cultures, people would claim that competence is the most important factor in, say, choosing a teacher for their preschool children. In other cultures the most important factor might be the goodness or morality of the teacher or perhaps the reputation of the teacher's family.

At the same time, each culture may define each of the characteristics of credibility differently. For example, "character" may mean following the rules of a specific religion to some and following one's individual conscience to others. The Quran, the Torah, and the New Testament, for example, will all have very different levels of credibility ascribed to them depending on the religious beliefs of the audience. This will be true even when all three religious books say essentially the same thing.

Similarly, members of different cultures may perceive the credibility of the various media very differently. For example, members of a repressive society in which the government controls television news may come to attribute little credibility to such broadcasts. After all, this person might reason, television news is simply what the government wants you to know. This may be hard to understand or even recognize by someone raised in the United States, for example, where the media are free of such political control.

The recommendations that follow are based largely on persuasion research conducted in the United States. When dealing with multicultural audiences, adjust your appeals accordingly. A good example of this

TIPS
from professional speakers

A businessperson in New York said that two of his contacts in Southeast Asia dropped him and his company before negotiations were barely warm. To this day, he's not completely sure why, but he now suspects that when he tried to convey his credentials and the qualifications of his company to supply the foreign firm with tools, his message came across as "Our companies are better than your companies." The wrong slant or one sentence too many can turn an honest attempt to convey information into unintentionally obnoxious boasting.

Mary A. DeVries, international communication expert, *Internationally Yours: Writing and Communicating Successfully in Today's Global Marketplace* (Boston: Houghton Mifflin, 1994): 193.

There is one principal 'credibility blunder' in most interracial situations: the how-do-you-feel or what-do-you-think syndrome. . . . The 'credibility blunder' assumes that the other communicator is omniscient on matters relating to his own ethnic group. This means, in the mind of the communicator initiator, that there should be nothing the ethnic person should not know about any other person from that ethnic group.
—Molefi Asanti

need for cultural adjustment is seen in the first recommendation made in the self-test, namely, to tell listeners of your competence. The recommendation is a generally good one for most audiences you'll encounter in the United States. In some cultures—notably collectivist cultures such as Japanese, Chinese, and Korean, for example—to stress your own competence or that of your corporation may be taken to mean that your audience members are inferior or that their corporations are not as good as yours. In other cultures—notably individualist cultures such as those of Scandinavia, the United States, and Western Europe, for example—if you don't stress your competence, your listeners may assume it's because you don't have any.

Before reading any further about credibility, you may wish to take the self-test, "How Credible Are You?"

TEST YOURSELF
How Credible Are You?

Respond to each of the following phrases as you think members of this class (your audience) see you when you deliver a public speech. Use the following scale:

5=Definitely true
4=Probably true
3=Neither true nor untrue
2=Probably untrue
1=Definitely untrue

_____ 1. Knowledgeable about the subject matter
_____ 2. Experienced
_____ 3. Confident
_____ 4. Informed about the subject matter
_____ 5. Fair in the presentation of material(evidence and argument)
_____ 6. Concerned with the audiences' needs
_____ 7. Consistent over time on the issues addressed in the speech
_____ 8. Similar to the audience in attitudes and values
_____ 9. Positive rather than negative
_____10. Assertive in personal style
_____11. Enthusiastic about the topic and in general
_____12. Active rather than passive

This test is designed to stimulate you to focus on yourself as a credible spokesperson. The test focuses on the three qualities of credibility: competence, character, and charisma and is based on a large body of research (for example, McCroskey 1997, Riggio 1987). Items 1 through 4 refer to your perceived competence: How competent or capable does the audience see you when you give a public speech? Items 5 through 8 refer to your perceived character: Does the audience see you as a person of good and moral character? Items 9 through 12 refer to your perceived charisma: Does the audience see you as dynamic and active rather than as static and passive? What specific steps can you take to change any audience perception with which you may be unhappy?

What three people do you ascribe high credibility to in matters of education? Politics? Morality? How do these three groups of people differ from each other?

COMPETENCE

Competence refers to the knowledge and expertise an audience thinks you have. The more knowledge and expertise the audience sees you as having, the more likely the audience will believe you. Similarly, you're likely to believe a teacher or doctor if you think he or she is knowledgeable on the subject.

Competence is logically subject-specific. Usually, competence is limited to one specific field. A person may be competent in one subject and totally incompetent in another. Often, however, you don't make the distinction between areas of competence and incompetence; thus, you may perceive a person you think is competent in politics as competent in general and in many fields. This is the halo effect—when listeners generalize their perception of competence to all areas. Listeners see the speaker's competence as a general trait.

This halo effect also has a counterpart—the reverse halo. Here the person, seen as incompetent in, say, mathematics, is perceived to be similarly incompetent in most other areas as well. As a critic of public speaking, be particularly sensitive to competence being subject-specific and to both the halo and reverse halo effects.

You can demonstrate your competence to your audience in a variety of ways.

Tell Listeners of Your Competence

Let the audience know the special experience or training that qualifies you to speak on this specific topic. If you're speaking on communal living and you've lived on a commune yourself, then say so in your speech. Tell the audience of your unique and personal experiences when these contribute to your credibility. Here, for example, comedian Bob Newhart

Everything nourishes what is strong already.
—Jane Austen

(1997), in a commencement address to students of Catholic University of America, establishes his competence by demonstrating his range of knowledge and depth of reading.

A recurrent theme running throughout commencement addresses is that what the speaker does for a living is worthwhile. So I will now attempt to justify what I do for a living. I was amazed when I re-read some of the books I had previously read on humor and laughter by the breadth of people who have written on the subject, starting with Aristotle, Plato, Hobbes, Freud (who devoted an entire treatise on it), Kant, Schopenhauer, Spenser, and Arthur Koestler, who devoted the first 90 pages of his book The Act of Creation *to humor and its place in the creative process.*

Cite a Variety of Research Sources

Make it clear to your audience that you've thoroughly researched your topic. Do this by mentioning some of the books you've read, the persons you've interviewed, the articles you've consulted. Weave these throughout your speech. Don't bunch them together at one time.

Look at any of the student speeches included throughout this book or in the appendix. Note that the speakers cite a wide variety of research sources—books, articles, interviews. Because of these citations—neatly woven into the speech—we get the impression that the speaker is knowledgeable about the topic and has thoroughly researched it.

Stress the Competencies of Your Sources

If your audience isn't aware of them, then emphasize the particular competencies of your sources. In this way it becomes clear to the audience that you've chosen your sources carefully and with a view toward providing the most authoritative sources possible. For example, saying simply,

---

THE ETHICS OF Credibility

Triple Academy Award winner Ingrid Bergman once said, "It's not whether you really cry. It's whether the audience thinks you are crying." Now, you'd probably agree that there's nothing unethical about actors fooling you by faking their emotions or presenting themselves to be people they aren't. As an audience member you go to the movies prepared and expecting to be fooled. But what about public speaking? Communication theorists tell us that, like acting, what makes for effective persuasion is not whether you really are competent or moral but whether the audience thinks you are. Unlike the movies, however, public speaking audiences don't ex-

pect to be fooled; they expect speakers to present themselves honestly.

At what point does following the principles for increasing credibility, such as those covered in this unit, raise ethical issues? For example, is it unethical for speakers to make the audience see them as more competent than they really are? Is it ethical for a lawyer to make himself or herself appear competent (though really not competent) to effectively represent a client? Is it ethical for the lawyer to do otherwise?

(The next Ethics in Public Speaking box appears on page 471.)

"Senator Cardova thinks . . ." does nothing to establish the senator's credibility. Instead, consider saying something like "Senator Cardova, who
headed the finance committee for three years and was formerly Professor
of Economics at MIT, thinks . . . ."

Avoid Apologizing

Don't needlessly call attention to your inadequacies as a spokesperson or
to any gaps in your knowledge. No one can know everything. Your audience doesn't expect you to be the exception. Stress your competencies, not
your inadequacies. Avoid such statements as "I know I'm no expert in
toxic waste but . . . . ," "I really should have looked into this more carefully but time was short. But, I did read . . . . ," or "I didn't read the opposing arguments because I don't believe they can possibly be right."

CHARACTER

You perceive a speaker as credible if you perceive that speaker as having
high moral character. Here your concern is with the individual's honesty
and basic nature—you want to know if you can trust that person. You
believe a speaker you can trust.

An individual's motives or intentions are particularly important in judging character. When an audience perceives the speaker's intentions as
good for them (rather than for his or her personal gain), they'll think the
speaker credible and they'll believe.

You can establish your high moral character in a number of ways.

Stress Similarities

Emphasize the ways in which you're similar to your audience, particularly in beliefs, attitudes, values, and goals. We perceive as believable people
who are like ourselves, especially in basic values. The more similar people
are to our own attitudes, beliefs, and goals, the more likely we will perceive them as credible. Consider this excerpt from President Bush's (1988)
acceptance speech. Note how he attempts to achieve similarity with his
widely diverse audience:

> But that's not what community means, not to me. For we are a nation
> of communities, of thousands and tens of thousands of ethnic, reli-
> gious, social, business, labor union, neighborhood, regional and
> other organizations, all of them varied, voluntary and unique.

> This is America: the Knights of Columbus, the Grange, Hadassah, the
> Disabled American Veterans, the Order of Ahepa, the Business and
> Professional Women of America, the union hall, the Bible study
> group, LULAC, Holy Name—a brilliant diversity spread like stars,
> like a thousand points of light in a broad and peaceful sky.

A more recent example comes from Madeleine K. Albright (1998, p.
518) who stresses the similarities between the United States and the NATO
countries:

*Character isn't inherited. One
builds it daily by the way one
thinks and acts, thought by
thought, action by action.*
—Helen Gahagan Douglas

The history of the 20th century has taught us that we need a partnership in which you can count on us and we can count on you. Our goals are enduring—providing security, ensuring prosperity and defending democracy. The institutions that unite us in pursuit of these goals are well-established. They include not only NATO but the OSCE and the relationship between the United States and the European Union.

The immediate challenges we face together are ambitious. They include completing the integration of Europe, including Russia and Ukraine; deepening the ties between the U.S. and Europe; and establishing more effective mechanisms for America and Europe to pursue common interests in Europe and beyond.

Stress Fairness

If delivering a persuasive speech, stress that you've examined both sides of the issue (if, indeed, you have). If you're presenting both sides, then make it clear that your presentation is an accurate and fair one. Be particularly careful not to omit any argument the audience may already have thought of—this is a sure sign that your presentation isn't a fair and balanced one. Tell the audience that you would not advocate a position if you did not base it on a fair evaluation of the issues.

Demonstrate Long-Term Consistency

We feel more comfortable putting our trust in someone who has been consistent over time. We become leery of persons who flit from one issue to another or from one team to another. If you've been supporting the Drug Hotline for the last few years, then tell the audience. For example:

I began working as a volunteer for the Drug Hotline when I first entered college, four years ago. Now that I'm ready to graduate I want to tell you about the work the Hotline is doing and why you should get involved in one of the most important projects I've ever worked on.

Stress Concern for Audience

Make it clear to the audience that you're interested in their welfare rather than seeking self-gain. If the audience feels that you're "out for yourself," they'll justifiably downgrade your credibility. Make it clear that the audience's interests are foremost in your mind. Tell your audience how the new legislation will reduce *their* taxes, how recycling will improve *their* community, how a knowledge of sexual harassment will make *their* workplace more comfortable and stress-free.

Stress Concern for Enduring Values

We view speakers who are concerned with small and insignificant issues as less credible than speakers who demonstrate a concern for lasting truths and general principles. Thus, make it clear to the audience that your position—your thesis—is related to higher-order values; show them exactly how this is true.

Notice how former President George Bush (1988) stresses his concern for such enduring values as family, religion, tradition, and individual power in his speech accepting the Republican nomination:

At the bright center is the individual. And radiating out from him or her is the family, the essential unit of closeness and of love. For it is the family that communicates to our children—to the 21st century—our culture, our religious faith, our traditions and history.

From the individual to the family to the community, and so out to the town, to the church and school and, still echoing out, to the country, the state, the nation—each doing only what it does well, and no more. And I believe that power must always be kept close to the individual, close to the hands that raise the family and run the home.

CHARISMA

Charisma is a combination of the speaker's personality and dynamism as seen by the audience. You perceive as credible (and believable) speakers you like rather than speakers you don't like. You perceive as credible speakers who are friendly and pleasant rather than aloof and reserved.

Similarly, you favor the dynamic over the hesitant, nonassertive speaker. You perceive as less credible the shy, introverted, soft-spoken individual than the extroverted and forceful individual. Perhaps you feel that the dynamic speaker is open and honest in presenting herself or himself whereas the shy, introverted individual may be hiding something. As a speaker there's much that you can do to increase your charisma and hence your perceived credibility.

Demonstrate a Positive Outlook

Show the audience that you have a positive orientation to the public speaking situation and to the entire speaker-audience encounter. We see positive and forward-looking people as more credible than negative and backward-looking people. Stress your pleasure at addressing the audience. Stress hope rather than despair; stress happiness rather than sadness. Note how Dennis W. Archer (1998, p. 340), the Mayor of Detroit, projects positiveness about his invitation to speak and about the city of Detroit:

Thank you very much. It is a pleasure and a privilege to join each of you here today. I certainly appreciate the presence of the elected officials who are with us, as well as some of our nation's principal leaders of business, education, government and law.

I am honored by the invitation to speak to the Winter Luncheon Meeting of the Economic Club of Washington.

Perhaps no other podium provides a speaker with such a well-informed, well-connected—and, indeed, high-powered audience.

I appreciate the opportunity to share the progress that the City of Detroit is making. Step by step—day by day, we are taking on challenges that affect all American cites in one way or another.

TIPS
from professional speakers

Sometimes . . . you have to work at uncovering why the material is important to you. Here are two helpful rules:

1. Learn everything you can about your subject. The more you know about it, the more excited and passionate you'll become.

2. As you learn, ask yourself. "How does this relate to me?" "Do I care?" "What does this mean to me?" For example: "The disease of muscular dystrophy, which I am discussing with this group, could it strike my little girl?" Or, "The beautiful car I am presenting to this customer, would it make my own family happy?"

Lilyan Wilder, communication consultant and coach, *Talk Your Way to Success* (New York: Simon & Schuster [Fireside Book], 1986).

Act Assertively and Confidently

Show the audience that you're a person who will stand up for your rights. Show them that you'll not back off simply because the odds may be against you or because you're outnumbered.

If you followed the 10 steps for preparing a public speech, you probably have considerable confidence in your speech. Communicate that confidence to the audience. Let them know that you're comfortable and at ease in speaking with them. If, for example, you're using presentation aids, become so familiar with them that you know exactly what order they're in and exactly at what point you'll use each.

Demonstrate Enthusiasm

The lethargic speaker, the speaker who somehow plods through the speech, is the very opposite of the charismatic speaker. Try viewing a film of Martin Luther King Jr. or Billy Graham speaking—they're totally absorbed with the speech and with the audience. They're excellent examples of the enthusiasm that makes speakers charismatic. Lilyan Wilder, in the accompanying "TIP," provides some useful suggestions for developing this needed enthusiasm.

Be Emphatic

Use language that is emphatic rather than colorless and indecisive. Use gestures that are clear and decisive rather than random and hesitant. Demonstrate a firm commitment to the position you're advocating; the audience will be much more likely to agree with a speaker who believes firmly in the thesis of the speech.

Here's an excerpt from one of the most famous of all speeches designed to establish credibility, Richard Nixon's "Checkers Speech." Nixon's credibility was severely shaken by allegations of misappropriation of campaign funds in the Senate campaign of 1950. In this speech he defended himself from these allegations and as a suitable vice-presidential candidate to run with Dwight D. Eisenhower. This speech is referred to as the "Checkers Speech" because of Nixon's reference to the family dog, Checkers. How effectively does Nixon establish his credibility?

> Then, in 1942, I went into the service. Let me say that my service record was not a particularly unusual one. I went to the South Pacific. I guess I'm entitled to a couple of battle stars. I got a couple of letters of commendation.
>
> But I was just there when the bombs were falling. And then I returned to the United States, and in 1946 I ran for Congress.
>
> When we came out of the war, Pat and I—Pat during the war had worked as a stenographer, and in a bank, and as an economist for a government agency, and when we came out, the total of our savings, from both my law practice, her teaching, and all the time I was in the war, the total for that entire period was just a little less than $10,000—every cent of that, incidentally, was in government bonds—well, that's where we start, when I got into politics.

How to Listen to Empower

Much as you can empower others by complimenting or constructively criticizing or in the way you ask questions, you can also empower others through your style of listening. When you wish to empower through listening, consider these suggestions:

1. Act like you're listening willingly and eagerly. This makes the speaker feel that what he or she is saying is valuable and important. Focus on the speaker as exclusively as possible and try to block out your focus on anything else. Nothing is worse than speaking to an audience that seems focused on what time it is or what others in the room are doing.

2. Listen supportively. Let the speaker see that you're responding favorably to him or her. An occasional smile or a special look of interest will go a long way to helping the speaker feel confident and empowered.

3. If there's a question session, ask a question. Your question will show that you did in fact listen carefully and also provide the speaker with added insight.

4. If appropriate and if true, let the speaker know privately that you enjoyed the presentation.

(The next Listen to This box appears on page 486.)

GENERAL GUIDELINES

In addition to these specific suggestions for projecting competence, character, and charisma, here are four general guidelines for becoming a more credible speaker.

Develop Credibility Characteristics

Develop or strengthen these characteristics of competence, character, and charisma as a person as well as a speaker. This is easy to say but may be extremely difficult to put into practice; nevertheless, it's important to have these goals. The actual development of these qualities is the best insurance to make you credible in public speaking situations.

Establish Your Credibility Directly

Whether you introduce yourself or whether someone else does it, it's helpful to legitimize yourself to the audience, especially in the introduction. If you have a broad knowledge of the topic or firsthand experience, tell the audience as early as possible. For example, a speaker might say something like this:

I've just returned to the states after spending two years in the Peace Corps. I worked in Guatemala for 10 months and in Chile for 14 months. I taught the people about farming, irrigation, and crop rotation. In just the short time that I was in these places, we managed to increase the vegetable crops by over 300 percent. I want to apply some of that same information we used in Guatemala and Chile to the problems you're now facing on your own farms.

If there's a formal introduction to your speech, you may have references integrated into this introduction to help establish your credibility.

Don't compromise yourself. You are all you've got.
—Janis Joplin

When teachers introduce themselves to their classes, they often establish their credibility. They might, for example, refer to their degrees, where they studied, or some research project on which they're working. At first glance this may seem immodest, but as long as the references are true, such credibility-establishing references allow the audience to better appreciate the information the teacher will communicate.

Use Varied Methods to Establish Credibility

Don't rely on the same few methods to build your credibility. Use a number of different methods and be sure to consider all three components of credibility: competence, character, and charisma.

An excerpt from U.S. Senator Edward Kennedy's "Chappaquiddick" speech follows. In 1969, Senator Edward Kennedy drove off a bridge in Chappaquiddick, killing his secretary, Mary Jo Kopechne. Because of the mysterious nature of this incident and because Kennedy had pleaded guilty to leaving the scene of the accident, it was necessary to defend himself if he was going to run again as Senator from Massachusetts. How effectively does Kennedy establish his general credibility?

> *The people of this state, the state which sent John Quincy Adams and Daniel Webster and Charles Sumner and Henry Cabot Lodge and John Kennedy to the United States Senate, are entitled to representation in that body by men who inspire their utmost confidence. For this reason, I would understand full well why some might think it right for me to resign. For me this will be a difficult decision to make.*

> *It has been seven years since my first election to the Senate. You and I share many memories—some of them have been glorious, some have been very sad. The opportunity to work with you and serve Massachusetts has made my life worthwhile.*

> *And so I ask you tonight, People of Massachusetts, to think this through with me. In facing this decision, I seek your advice and opinion. In making it, I seek your prayers. For this is a decision that I will have finally to make on my own.*

CRITICALLY EVALUATING CREDIBILITY APPEALS

In using and in listening to credibility appeals, critically evaluate them. Here are three questions that will be helpful to ask:

Is the dimension of credibility used relevant to the issue at hand? For example, is the politician's family (nice as they may be) relevant to his or her position on gun control or social security or immigration? Is the person's former military service or the lack of it relevant to the issue being discussed?

Are credibility appeals being used instead of argument and evidence? Just as motivational appeals can be used instead of or to divert attention from logical reasons and evidence, so too can credibility appeals. You see this regularly in the political debates and accusations and defenses that appear in the news. Too often, the argument revolves around issues of credibility that often—though not always—are irrelevant to the issues.

Are the credibility appeals true? For example, should the actor who advertises toothpaste dressed as a dentist in a dentist's office environment be accorded credibility? Do you unconsciously associate credibility because of the uniform? Is the advertiser ethical in conveying this misleading image of the actor—despite the frequent disclaimer at the bottom of the screen, "This is a dramatization"?

I resent the idea that people would blame the messenger for the message, rather than looking at the content of the message itself.
—Anita Hill

UNIT IN BRIEF

Definitions of Credibility	Credibility: the audience's perception of the speaker's believability.
	Initial or extrinsic credibility: the reputation of the speaker.
	Derived or intrinsic credibility: the impression derived from the speaker's speech.
Components of Credibility	Competence: the knowledge and expertise the speaker is thought to possess.
	Character: the honesty and integrity the speaker is perceived to possess.
	Charisma: the speaker's personality and dynamism as perceived by the audience.
Critically Evaluating Credibility Appeals	1. Is the appeal relevant?
	2. Are credibility appeals used to divert attention from the argument and evidence?
	3. Are the credibility appeals true?

THINKING CRITICALLY ABOUT SPEAKER CREDIBILITY

REVIEWING KEY TERMS AND CONCEPTS IN SPEAKER CREDIBILITY

1. Review and define the key terms used in this unit:

   - ❏ speaker credibility (p. 438)
   - ❏ initial or extrinsic credibility (p. 439)
   - ❏ derived or intrinsic credibility (p. 439)
   - ❏ halo effect (p. 441)
   - ❏ competence (p. 441)
   - ❏ character (p. 443)
   - ❏ charisma (p. 445)

2. Review and explain the key concepts discussed in this unit:

   - What is speaker credibility and how are impressions formed?
   - What is competence and how might a speaker establish his or her competence?
   - What is character and how might a speaker establish his or her character?
   - What is charisma and how might a speaker establish his or her charisma?

- What general guidelines might a speaker use in establishing credibility?
- What critical guidelines should be used in evaluating credibility appeals?

DEVELOPING STRATEGIES FOR SPEAKER CREDIBILITY

1. Karen is giving a speech on the failure of the juvenile prison system in your state. Much of what Karen knows comes first hand, from serving 1½ years at a juvenile detention center. Karen wonders if mentioning this would increase or lessen her credibility. What would you advise Karen to do? If you would suggest that Karen reveal this information, when and how would you suggest she do this?

2. Thom is giving a speech on the gay and lesbian civil rights movement and wonders if revealing to the audience that he's gay would help or hinder his credibility. Consider your public speaking class as the target audience. If you would suggest that Thom reveal this, when and how would you suggest he do this?

EVALUATING CREDIBILITY APPEALS IN PUBLIC SPEECHES

1. Read a speech in this text or in some other source and identify the ways in which the speaker established her

or his credibility. Try to identify instances of competence, character, and charisma.

2. Review your last speech with special reference to credibility. How might you have more effectively established your own competence, character, and charisma?

USING TECHNOLOGY IN SPEAKER CREDIBILITY

1. Visit one of the Web sites devoted to a specific personality, for example, a movie star, musician, politician, sports figure, or film director and examine it for references to credibility. Use one of the search engines listed in Table 7.1, page 134, to help you locate the Web site for someone you're interested in and would like to know more about. Can you find instances where the competence, character, and charisma of the individual are discussed?

2. Visit a few college and university Web sites. Use one of the search engines identified in Table 7.1, page 134, or go to http://www.globalcomputing.com/universy.html for links to the Web sites of over 500 colleges and universities. What contributes to your impression of the credibility of the college?

PRACTICALLY SPEAKING

23.1 Short Speech Technique

Prepare and deliver a two-minute speech in which you:
a. explain why you think a particular person is credible or not credible.
b. explain the credibility of a television personality such as Oprah Winfrey, Geraldo Rivera, Montel Williams, Sally Jesse Raphael, Jerry Springer, Ricki Lake, Regis Philbin, Cathy Lee Gifford.
c. explain why you think a particular person would be a great spokesperson for a particular product—consider playing the role of the advertising executive trying to convince your client to hire your choice for product spokesperson.
d. explain how credibility operates in (1) dating and meeting your partner's family, (2) teaching, (3) inter-

viewing for a job, or (4) sales.
e. introduce yourself to your audience; tell them about yourself and especially about your credibility—develop this speech so that it would be appropriate for someone else to give in introducing you.

23.2 Comparing Credibility

Credibility judgments are made both absolutely and comparatively. Thus, for example, you may judge the credibility of a witness at a trial or a newspaper reviewer or a local religious leader on the basis of some absolute standards you may have. Even in making this absolute judgment, though, you're probably also comparing this person with others who are similar and are probably positioning this person somewhere on a scale along with these others. Similarly, you may make a comparison credibility judgment of the three candidates running for Mayor and vote for the one to whom you attribute the highest credibility. So, your judgment for Senator Smith is made not just absolutely but also in comparison with the others in the race.

This exercise emphasizes this concept of comparative credibility judgments and asks you to rank order the following people, roles, and institutions: Use 3 for the highest credibility and 1 for the lowest.

1. Talk show host on cultural differences.
_____ Oprah Winfrey
_____ Jerry Springer
_____ Sally Jesse Raphael

2. Talk show hosts on the male reluctance to express himself.
_____ Montel Williams
_____ Cathy Lee Gifford
_____ Geraldo Rivera

3. Financial news periodicals.
_____ *Money* magazine
_____ *The Wall Street Journal*
_____ *Barron's*

4. Newscasters.
_____ San Donaldson
_____ Dan Rather
_____ Connie Chung

5. U.S. politicians on the role of the politician in today's world.
_____ Bill Clinton
_____ Newt Gingrich
_____ Jesse Jackson

6. Speaker on leading a happy life.
_____ professor
_____ physician
_____ lawyer

7. Institutions on community service.
_____ bank
_____ insurance company
_____ hospital corporation

8. Authors of exercise books on the proper way to exercise.
_____ Richard Simmons
_____ Jane Fonda
_____ Arnold Schwarzenegger

9. Sources of accurate and up-to-date information on film and television.
_____ "Entertainment Tonight"
_____ *The National Enquirer*
_____ *People* Magazine

10. Scholar on the meaning of life.
_____ philosopher
_____ minister/priest/rabbi
_____ scientist

After completing these ratings, consider, for example: (1) What reasons did you use in constructing your rankings? What qualities of credibility did you consider in your ranking? (2) Do any of your rankings illustrate the notion that credibility depends on the subject matter? (3) Are there certain qualities that make you believe someone regardless of the subject matter? (4) Which of the three major characteristics of credibility (competence, character, charisma) would you consider the most and the least important for: (a) a family physician, (b) a college professor, (c) a divorce lawyer, (d) a romantic-life partner, (e) a best friend? (5) Are any of your credibility judgments gender-related? That is, do you attribute higher credibility to women on some issues and to men on others? (6) Are any of your credibility judgments culture-related? That is, might you attribute high or low credibility ratings to people or products or institutions because of their culture?

23.3 Analyzing Gender Credibility

Following is a chart for recording the topics of public speaking for which you think an audience would perceive men and women to have different degrees of credibility and also for recording those topics for which gender wouldn't influence perceived credibility. Fill in each space. After you've completed the chart, compare your responses with those of others in a small group or with the entire class. One interesting way to do this is for one person to read out a topic (without revealing where he or she put it) and see if others can identify the "appropriate" place. This experience will give you a general idea of how widely held are beliefs about the credibility that men and women are seen to possess.

	Men	Women
Extremely high credibility; gender is highly relevant.	1. _____	1. _____
	_____	_____
	2. _____	2. _____
	_____	_____
	3. _____	3. _____
	_____	_____

	Men	Women
Gender doesn't contribute to credibility.	1. _____ _____	1. _____ _____
	2. _____ _____	2. _____ _____
	3. _____ _____	3. _____ _____
Extremely low credibility; gender is highly relevant	1. _____ _____	1. _____ _____
	2. _____ _____	2. _____ _____
	3. _____ _____	3. _____ _____

Why did certain topics seem more appropriately positioned in one place rather than another? What evidence did you use for classifying some topics as giving men greater credibility and others as giving women greater credibility? What specific advice would you give a speaker who is talking on a topic for which the audience is likely to see members of his or her gender as having little credibility?

The Special Occasion Speech

When you give a "special occasion" or "ceremonial" speech, you're giving a speech that is part information and part persuasion. These special occasion speeches are reviewed separately because their purposes are a bit more limited in scope. We discuss four special occasion speeches: (1) the speech of introduction, (2) the speech of presentation or acceptance, (3) the speech designed to create goodwill, and (4) the speech of tribute. These four speeches are certainly not the only special occasion speeches; rather, they're presented here because they're among the most popular and because they can easily be adapted to serve other purposes. Table 24.1 provides examples of a few additional types of special occasion speeches.

TABLE 24.1 Some Additional Special Occasion Speeches

Special Occasion Speech	Purposes
Speeches of Dedication	To give some special meaning to, say, a new research lab, a store opening, or the start of the building of a bridge.
Commencement Speeches	To congratulate and inspire the recent graduates, often intended as a kind of transition from school to the next stage in life.
Eulogies	A type of speech of tribute seeking to praise someone who died, to set their life and contributions in perspective and in a positive light.
Farewell Speeches	To say goodbye to a position or to colleagues; to signal that you're moving on and you want to express your feelings to those you're leaving.
Toasts	To say hello or good luck in a relatively formal sense; speeches at weddings, conferences, and banquets often include toasting the honorees.

THE SPEECH OF INTRODUCTION

The speech of introduction is usually designed to introduce another speaker or to introduce a general topic area and a series of speakers. Often, for example, before a speaker addresses an audience, another speaker sets the stage by introducing both the speaker and the topic. At conventions, where a series of speakers address an audience, a speech of introduction might introduce the general topic on which the speakers will focus and perhaps provide connecting links among the several presentations.

In giving a speech of introduction your main purpose is to gain the attention and arouse the interest of the audience. Your speech should pave the way for favorable and attentive listening. It should seek to create an atmosphere conducive to achieving the particular speech purpose. The speech of introduction is basically informative and follows the general patterns already laid down for the informative speech. The main difference is that instead of discussing a topic's issues, you would discuss who the speaker is and what the speaker will talk about. In your speeches of introduction, follow these general principles.

Establish the Significance of the Speech

Your major concern in introducing another speaker is to establish the importance of the speech for this specific audience. In this way you focus the audience's attention and interest on the main speaker.

Establish Relevant Connections

Establish a connection or relationship among the essential elements in the public speaking act. At a minimum, draw connections among the speaker, the topic, and the audience. Answer the implicit questions of the audience: Why should we listen to this speaker on this topic? Why is this speaker appropriate to speak on this topic? What do we (the audience) have to do with this speaker and this speech topic?

If you can answer such questions satisfactorily, you'll have done your job of establishing a ready and receptive audience for the speaker.

Stress the Speaker's Credibility

Establish the speaker's credibility. The speech of introduction is the ideal opportunity to present those accomplishments of the speaker that the speaker could not mention with modesty. Review the ways of establishing credibility (Unit 23) for some useful suggestions. The most general guideline is to try to answer the audience's question: What is there about this speaker that has earned her or him the right to speak on this topic, to this audience? In answering this question, you'll inevitably establish the speaker's credibility.

Be Consistent with the Main Speech

Make your speech of introduction consistent in style and manner with the major speech. To introduce a speaker on terminal diseases in a humorous and flippant style would clearly be inappropriate. Conversely, to introduce a humorist in a somber and formal style would be equally inappropriate.

TIPS
from professional speakers

How to Give a Winning Introduction

W: Explain *why* this particular speaker is addressing this audience today.

I: *Intrigue* the audience with a specific fact or question to get them sitting on the edges of their seats, curious and attentive.

N: Announce the speaker's *name* at the end of your introduction. Only now should the focus switch from you to the speaker.

Elizabeth Urech, international communication specialist and founder of "Speak for Yourself," *Speaking Globally: Effective Presentations Across International and Cultural Boundaries* (Dover, NH: Kogan Page, 1998): 130.

To make a speech immortal you don't have to make it everlasting.
—Leslie Hore-Belisha

In judging style and manner, predict the tone that the main speech will take. As you answer an invitation with the same degree of formality with which it is extended, you would introduce a speaker with the same degree of formality that will prevail during the actual speech. Otherwise, the speaker will have to counteract an inappropriate atmosphere created by the speech of introduction.

Be Brief

Remember that the audience has come to hear the main speaker, so be brief. In actual practice, speeches of introduction vary considerably in length—from "Ladies and Gentlemen, the President" to pages and pages. You'll have to judge how long is long enough. If the main speech is to be brief—say, 10 or 20 minutes—your speech of introduction should be no longer than 1 or 2 minutes. If, on the other hand, the main speech is to be an hour long, then your introduction might last 5 or 10 minutes or even longer. In estimating length, visualize yourself as a member of the audience listening to your own speech of introduction. How much would you want to hear?

Don't Cover the Speaker's Topic

Don't cover the substance of the topic or what the speaker will discuss. Clever stories, jokes, startling statistics, or historical analogies, which are often effective in speeches of introduction, will prove a liability if the guest speaker intended to use this same material. It's not uncommon to find a speaker without an introduction or a conclusion because the material was used in the speech of introduction. If you've any doubts, check with the speaker well in advance of the actual speech. In this way you'll avoid duplication and embarrassing the speaker and yourself.

Don't Oversell the Speaker

Speakers giving introductions have a tendency to oversell the guest speaker, the topic, or both. The speech of introduction should be complimentary but should not create an image impossible to live up to. To say, for example, that "Morso Osrom is not only the world's greatest living expert on baldness but a most fascinating, interesting, and humorous speaker as well" only adds difficulties to the speaker's task. It would be better to let the speaker demonstrate his or her own communicative abilities.

The same is true for the topic. To say that "this is the most important topic today" or "without the information given here we are sure to die paupers" will only encumber the speaker by setting unrealistic expectations for the audience.

Sample Speeches of Introduction

Here, for example, is a speech, given by Jack Shea, introducing the 1998 John Huston Awards.

Good evening, and welcome to the fifth annual John Huston Award Dinner, tonight honoring Tom Cruise. At past events, we've honored such staunch advocates of artists rights as Fred Zinnemann, Steven Spielberg, Martin Scorsese and Miloš Forman. Each evening has turned out to be celebratory, informative and entertaining—as well as inspiring—and tonight will be no exception. Now, helping to make this evening possible are our very generous sponsors: Sprint, Tiffen Manufacturing, DTS, and the Bandai Foundation. We also want to acknowledge United Airlines and Ray Ban Sunglasses for their support and contribution tonight. And, finally, we thank the Huston family and Robert Graham who has designed and created the John Huston Award.

"In keeping with the spirit of the event, we've taken into consideration that one of the basic rights of the artist is to not have to work on an empty stomach. So, we've opted to serve the dinner before the testimonials. While you're digesting, we've prepared a short film about who we are, why we are, and what we are, and where we would be probably if we weren't who, why, and what we are. Enjoy the film, enjoy the evening, and thank you all for coming.

Most of the introductory speeches will be similar to those given here and will generally follow the rules already noted. Next, however, is an introductory speech of a very different type. In this speech, Michael Greene, the president of the National Academy of Recording Arts & Sciences, seeks not to introduce another speaker but rather to set the activities within a context. He seeks to put the proceedings—in this case the Grammy Awards—into a social perspective. The speech is one of "introduction" because it introduces a theme or point of view that is to pervade the entire award presentation. At the same time, the speech puts the National Academy of Recording Arts & Sciences' position on funding for the arts on record and gives this position extremely wide circulation. The speech is, however, primarily one of persuasion and seeks to strengthen the attitudes and beliefs of the immediate audience and to move the more remote audience (the viewers) to action.

Good evening. I'm pleased to welcome all of you, more than a billion viewers in 167 countries, to the 37th Annual Grammy Awards. The extraordinary artists and recordings we pay tribute to here tonight remind us of music's powerful influence in our lives. Music and the arts are a healing, therapeutic force that lifts our spirits and unites us as a culture.

But the fact is, our culture is at serious risk. Viewers around the world may not be aware that the funding necessary to ensure the survival of our proud legacy of jazz, blues, and virtually all other forms of indigenous American music is being threatened. Our National Endowment for the Arts could have its budget slashed by forty percent next year, another forty percent the year after, finally "zeroed out" the year after that. And folks, National Public Radio and PBS will surely be next. We are here tonight on the brink of becoming the only industrialized nation in the world with no federal support for the arts.

THEY SAY IT'S A MATTER OF MONEY. Yet it costs taxpayers about a dollar a year to keep jazz, blues, folk, and classical music on the public radio airwaves, and for the Arts Endowment to bring theater, dance, and music to communities across America. Is it really about money? You know, if the Pentagon tried to operate on the Arts Endowment's annual budget, they'd have to shut down in just five hours.

The arts are an economic plus—second only to aerospace as our most lucrative national export. Despite all this, our Speaker of the House has yet to agree to meet with the chairman of the Arts Endowment. It's hard to imagine either the Secretary of Commerce or Defense being treated with such total disregard.

Since the Arts and Humanities Endowments were founded with bi-partisan support thirty years ago, they have enjoyed the support of every president, Republican or Democrat. Our leaders knew that politicizing America's arts agenda would cripple the accomplishments that make America a leading culture force.

We MUST NOT allow the arts to be politicized, privatized, commercialized, sanitized, neutralized, or "zeroed out."

Artists by their very nature stretch the limits. Controversy is both part of the price and the VALUE of artistic freedom. Lest we forget, one of the Endowment's most controversial grants was the funding of the Vietnam Veterans Memorial in Washington, D.C. Today it is the most heralded and visited tourist attraction in our nation's capital. To see to it that the arts retain their proper place within our society, grab a pencil and I'll tell you what you can do.

On Tuesday, March 14, a campaign of unprecedented scope will be waged; it's called the National Call in Day for Arts and Culture. This campaign begins tonight by your calling 1-800-225-2007 for options that will see to it that your congressional representatives know that you support the continued funding for these vital programs. When Winston Churchill was asked during World War II to cut the British Arts Council Budget, he didn't waste words. "Hell no," said Churchill, "what have we been fighting for?"

Folks, without arts education and the Arts Endowment, music and the love of it will no longer be a cultural treasure, but more a privilege tied to personal, family, and class economics.

Let's join together tonight in a triumphant effort to keep the arts alive. Our very culture depends on it. Thank you.

THE SPEECH OF PRESENTATION OR ACCEPTANCE

We consider speeches of presentation and speeches of acceptance together because they frequently occur together and because the same general principles govern both types of speeches.

In a speech of presentation you seek to (1) place the award or honor in some kind of context, and (2) give the award an extra air of dignity or status. A speech of presentation may focus on rewarding a colleague for an important accomplishment (Teacher of the Year) or recognizing a particularly impressive performance (Academy Award winner). It may honor an employee's service to a company or a student's outstanding grades or athletic abilities.

The speech of acceptance is the counterpart to this honoring ceremony. Here the recipient accepts the award and also attempts to place the award in some kind of context. At times the presentation and the acceptance speeches are rather informal and amount to a simple "You really deserve this" and an equally simple and direct "Thank you." At other times, as, for example, in the presentation and acceptance of a Nobel Prize, the speeches are formal and are prepared in great detail and with great care. Such speeches are frequently reprinted in newspapers throughout the world. Somewhere between these two extremes lies the average speech of presentation and acceptance. In your speeches of presentation, follow these two principles.

State the Reason for the Presentation

As the presenter, make clear why this particular award is being given to this particular person. If a scholarship is being awarded for the best athlete of the year, then say so. If a gold watch is being awarded for 30 years of faithful service, say this.

State the Importance of the Award

The audience (as well as the group authorizing or sponsoring the award) will no doubt want to hear something of the importance of the award. You can state this in a number of different ways. For example, you might refer to the previous recipients (assuming they're well known to the audience), the status of the award (assuming that it's a prestigious award), or its influence on previous recipients.

A Sample Speech of Presentation

This speech was given by Michael Greene, immediately after he gave the introductory speech reprinted earlier. Here Greene presents five Life Achievement awards, and, in a relatively short speech, succeeds in highlighting the careers and contributions of five outstanding recording artists.[1]

> Just as the Grammy Awards represent the best in today's music, our Life Achievement and Trustees Awards recognize individuals whose careers and cumulative contributions have had a profound effect on our culture. This year's five recipients, through their artistry and vision, have both enriched and advanced the recording medium.
>
> Our first recipient is Barbra Streisand. She recorded her first album in 1962 and since then 50 albums have borne her artistic stamp, earning her eight

[1] This speech, delivered March 1, 1995, was transcribed from the televised presentation.

Grammy Awards and a worldwide audience. A singer at heart, she's achieved unprecedented success as an actress, director, and producer as well. She is also a spokesperson for many humanitarian causes.

Henry Mancini. A twenty time Grammy winner, redefined the art of composing for film while carving out an equally enviable career as a conductor, instrumentalist, songwriter, and arranger. A tireless supporter of arts education, the recording industry and the academy are deeply in the debt of this extraordinary gentleman.

Patsy Cline. The female country star who crossed over to pop and to timeless ballads. We lost Patsy far too soon, but her music continues to exert a powerful influence on several generations of country and pop artists.

Curtis Mayfield. Singer, songwriter, producer, guitarist, and record executive. The Chicago-born pioneer of the soul era influenced attitudes and opinions around the world with his socially relevant songs. A Grammy legend, award winner last year, his energy and creativity continue to inspire us all.

And Miss Peggy Lee. "Why Don't You Do Right" was the title of her first hit with Benny Goodman and she's been doing right ever since—as a jazz and pop vocalist and song writer. Forever identified with such classics as "Manana," "Fever," and "Is That All There Is?" Peggy is the embodiment of coolness, hipness, and sophistication.

With us in the house this evening are two of our Life Achievement honorees. Please help me acknowledge Curtis Mayfield and Peggy Lee.

In preparing and presenting your speech of acceptance, follow these three principles.

Express Thanks

Thank the people responsible for sponsoring and awarding you the award—the academy members, the board of directors, the student body, your fellow teammates.

Acknowledge Others Who Helped

Much as an author will thank those persons who helped her or him in the writing of a particular book (see, for example, the acknowledgments in the preface of this book), the award recipient should thank those instrumental in achieving the award. In thanking such people, be specific without boring the audience. It's not necessary to detail exactly what each person contributed, but it's interesting to the audience to learn, for example, that Pat Tarrington gave you your first role in a soap opera or that Chris Willis convinced you to play the role in the film that led to your first Academy Award.

Convey Your Feelings

Put the award into personal perspective. Tell the audience what the award means to you right now and perhaps what it will mean to you in the future. Allow the audience a personal closeness to you that they might not experience otherwise.

What would you say in a speech of acceptance if you received the award for outstanding student of the year?

Sample Speeches of Acceptance

Here is an exceptionally moving and provocative acceptance speech that clearly illustrates how closely tied together are the speaker, audience, and occasion. The speech was given by Elizabeth Taylor in acceptance of the Jean Hersholt Humanitarian Award, given for her great humanitarian work on behalf of people with AIDS. It was presented by Angela Lansbury for the Academy of Motion Picture Arts and Sciences on March 29, 1993. The speech was transcribed from television.

I have been on this stage many times as a presenter. I have sat in the audience as a loser. And I've had the thrill and the honor of standing here as a winner. But, I never, ever thought I would come out here to receive this award.

It is the highest possible accolade I could receive from my peers. And for doing something I just have to do, that my passion must do.

I am filled with pride and humility. I accept this award in honor of all the men, women, and children with AIDS who are waging incredibly valiant battles for their lives—those to whom I have given my commitment, the real heroes of the pandemic of AIDS.

I am so proud of the work that people in Hollywood have done to help so many others, like dearest, gentle Audrey. And while she is, I know, in heaven, forever guarding her beloved children, I will remain here as rowdy an activist as I have to be and, God willing, for as long as I have to be. [Applause]

Tonight I am asking for your help. I call upon you to draw from the depths of your being, to prove that we are a human race, to prove that our love outweighs our need to hate, that our compassion is more compelling than our need to blame, that our sensitivity to those in need is stronger than our greed, that our ability to reason overcomes our fear, and that at the end of each of our lives we can look back and be proud that we have treated others with the kindness, dignity, and respect that every human being deserves.

Thank you and God bless.

Here's a brief speech of acceptance, given by a college professor upon receiving honorary membership in the Golden Key Honor Society for excellence in teaching:

I must confess that I was not aware that there was an organization—an honor society—so dedicated to excellence. And the more I thought about it the more important I realized it was. And I thought it especially appropriate—though perhaps a bit embarrassing—that it was founded by students.

The great thing about Golden Key and about this award is that you help make excellence respectable, worthy of having as a goal, as a way of learning and a way of life—and a little bit less scary. You seek out excellence, reward it, and thereby provide useful models.

I hope that we will also—students and teachers—seek out and speak out when excellence does not prevail where it should prevail. The need for this is now, when our educational system (especially in places like New York City) seems to be growing more concerned with the numbers of students being graduated from high schools and colleges rather than with the quality of their education and where the curriculum we may or may not teach in elementary school is being dictated by ignorance and prejudice, instead of knowledge, fairness and justice.

I thank the Golden Key for giving excellence such a prominent voice and I thank you for asking for excellence from me and for telling me that I'm on the right track. I'm honored, I'm flattered. I thank you.

Here is Tom Cruise's speech of acceptance of the John Huston Award.

Well this is a pretty overwhelming evening for me. Thank you, Steven, and everyone who came here tonight. My friends, people who've inspired me, who've been so generous to me, and for all of the kind words; this is a night that I will certainly remember forever.

In receiving this award, it seems to me that it involves more than accepting an honor. It's a responsibility, It's a responsibility to protect our movies from unwanted and unwarranted change. And I'm very, very honored to receive this, and somewhat troubled by your expression of confidence. Troubled because I can think of few things more critical to the preservation of film than explaining it to others. An I can think of even fewer things more difficult than trying to explain the importance without sounding either self-serving, or, I guess, pretentious. And yet I believe the preservation of our work involves more than artist's rights—not to have our work altered, defaced or mutilated. It involves more than the consequent damage to the reputations, as artists. But finally, it involves the rights of the audience—past, present, and future. Popular movies can and have passed into the culture and language. "Casablanca," "Maltese Falcon," "Sands of Iwo Jima," "Yankee Doodle Dandy" are an integral part of our collective experience and our common memory.

Movies both document and create our history. To change them is to change history, alter memory, and tear at the fabric of our shared experiences. To change them is to injure the ability of one generation to understand and appreciate another. And these are, I think, very, very serious injuries. And while history alone may decide which movies, in the fullness of time, are worthy of being considered fine art, if nothing else, they do need to be preserved—as they were made—in order for history to make that judgment. And whether they're art or entertainment, they do need and deserve to be protected. So men from time out of mind have understood the need to protect those things that tell them who they are, where they have been, and where they might be going.

And I accept this award, and I accept it very, very gratefully and gladly, and I assure you that I will do everything that I can to preserve our work. So thank you very much for this evening, and it's an evening that I certainly will never, ever forget.

This next example is quite different. This speech by William Faulkner, one of the leading American writers of the twentieth century, was given in acceptance of the Nobel Prize for Literature. Faulkner delivered the speech on December 10, 1950, in Stockholm, Sweden, reportedly in his first dress suit and before television cameras for the first time. The speech is one of the best acceptance speeches ever recorded and is especially noteworthy for its clarity of style and purpose and for its universal theme.

I feel that this award was not made to me as a man, but to my work—a life's work in the agony and sweat of the human spirit, not for glory and least of all for profit, but to create out of the materials of the human spirit something which did not exist before. So this award is only mine in trust. It will not be difficult to find a dedication for the money part of it commensurate with the purpose and significance of its origin. But I would like to do the same with the acclaim too, by using this moment as a pinnacle from which I might be listened to by the young men and women already dedicated to the same anguish and travail, among whom is already that one who will someday stand here where I am standing.

Our tragedy today is a general and universal physical fear so long sustained by now that we can even bear it. There are no longer problems of the spirit. There is only the question: when will I be blown up? Because of this, the young man or woman writing today has forgotten the problems of the human heart in conflict with itself which alone can make good writing because only that is worth writing about, worth the agony and the sweat.

He must learn them again. He must teach himself that the basest of all things is to be afraid; and, teaching himself that, forget it forever, leaving no room in his workshop for anything but the old verities and truth of the heart, the old universal truths lacking which any story is ephemeral and doomed—love and honor and pity and pride and compassion and sacrifice. Until he does so, he labors under a curse. He writes not of love but of lust, of defeats in which nobody loses anything of value, of victories without hope, and, worst of all, without pity or compassion. His griefs grieve on no universal bones, leaving no scars. He writes not of the heart but of the glands.

Until he relearns these things, he will write as though he stood among and watched the end of man. I decline to accept the end of man. It is easy enough to say that man is immortal simply because he will endure; that when the last dingdong of doom has clanged and fades from the last worthless rock hanging tideless in the last red and dying evening, that even then there will still be one more sound. That of his puny inexhaustible voice, still talking. I refuse to accept this. I believe that man will not merely endure: he will prevail. He is immortal, not because he alone among creatures has an inexhaustible voice, but because he has a soul, a spirit capable of compassion and sacrifice and endurance. The poet's, the writer's, duty is to write about these things. It is his privilege to help man endure by lifting his heart, by reminding him of the courage and honor and hope and pride and compassion and pity and sacrifice which have been the glory of his past. The poet's voice need not merely be the record of man; it can be one of the props, the pillars, to help him endure and prevail.

Don't Misjudge the Importance of the Award

Neither underestimate nor overestimate the importance or significance of an award. Most speakers err in the direction of exaggeration. When this is done the presenter, the recipient, and the entire situation can appear ludicrous. Be realistic. A good guideline to follow is to ask yourself what this award will mean next year or five years from now to these very same people. Will they remember it? Will it have exerted a significant influence on their lives? Will the local or national newspapers report it? Is it a likely item for a television spot? Obviously, the more questions you answer "yes," the less likelihood of your exaggerating. The more "no" answers, the more reserved you need to be.

Don't Be Long-Winded

Few people want to hear long speeches of presentation or acceptance. Normally, these awards are given at dinners or at some other festive function, and people are generally anxious to get on with other activities. If there are many awards to be given on this same occasion, then you've added reason to be especially brief. We see this very commonsense principle violated yearly on the Academy Awards show. The story told by news correspondent Charles Osgood in the accompanying "TIP" may be taken as a reminder (rather than as specific advice) against delivering too long of a speech of acceptance.

Generally, the length of the speech should be proportional to the importance of the award. Awards of lesser importance should be presented and accepted with short speeches. Awards of greater significance may be presented and accepted with longer speeches. When acknowledging those who helped you, be selective. Don't include everyone you've ever known; select the most significant few and identify these. Everyone knows that there were others who influenced you, so it's unnecessary to state the obvious: "And there are many others too numerous to mention who helped me achieve this wonderful award."

Don't Talk in Platitudes and Clichés

Platitudes and clichés abound in speeches of presentation and acceptance. Be especially careful not to include expressions that will lead your audience to think that this is a canned presentation and that the entire ceremony is perfunctory. Obvious examples to avoid are these:

This award-winner is so well known that no introduction is necessary.

I really don't deserve this award.

There's no one more deserving of this award than this year's recipient.

THE SPEECH TO SECURE GOODWILL

The speech to secure goodwill is a peculiar hybrid. It's part information and part persuasion, and it's difficult to determine where one ends and the other begins. In fact, the strength of the goodwill speech often depends on the extent to which the information and the persuasion are blurred in the minds of the audience.

On the surface, the speech to secure goodwill informs the audience about a product, company, profession, institution, way of life, or person. (When this "person" is the speaker, we often refer to this as a speech of **self-justification**.) Beneath this surface, however, lies a more persuasive purpose: to heighten the image of a person, product, or company—to create a more positive attitude toward this person or thing.

Many speeches of goodwill have a still further persuasive purpose: to get the audience to ultimately change their behavior toward the person, product, or company. Such a speech functions to create goodwill but invariably also functions to alter behavior. The securing of goodwill and the changing of behavior are not, in reality, separable.

A special type of goodwill speech is the speech of self-justification, where the speaker seeks to justify his or her actions to the audience. Political figures do this frequently. Richard Nixon's "Checkers Speech," his Cambodia-bombing speeches, and, of course, his Watergate speeches, are clear examples of self-justification. Edward Kennedy's Chapaquiddick speech, in which he attempted to justify what happened when Mary Jo Kopechne drowned, is another example. (Excerpts from these speeches are provided in Unit 23.) The most famous contemporary example is, of course, President Clinton's speech to the nation on the Monica Lewinsky affair. This entire speech is reprinted later in this unit.

Whenever there's a significant loss of credibility, the speaker will be called upon to offer a speech of self-justification. As any political leader's image goes down, the frequency of the self-justifying speeches goes up.

In securing goodwill, whether for another person or for yourself, the following principles should prove helpful.

TIPS from professional speakers

When Marlene Dietrich sent Mikhail Baryshnikov to pick up her award from the Council of Fashion Designers in New York, the great dancer asked her what she wanted him to say. She said, "Take the thing, look at it, thank them, and go." Mikhail said, "That's it?" and she said, "That's it! They don't have time to listen anyway."

Charles Osgood, CBS news correspondent and anchor of the "CBS Sunday Night News." *Osgood on Speaking: How to Think on Your Feet Without Falling on Your Face* (New York: Morrow, 1988): 39.

When you sit back after a good dinner and listen to others speak, you tend to make very simple judgments of their performance:

Do you like them?

Can you hear them?

Have they interested or amused you?

Was it well presented?

Were they relevant?

Were they succinct?

When you prepare a speech, if you try and see yourself as your audience will see you, then hopefully you can please them.

Martin Nicholls, *After Dinner Speeches* (London, Ward Lock Limited, 1989): 11.

Demonstrate the Contributions that Deserve Goodwill

Demonstrate how the audience may benefit from this company, product, or person. Or at least (in the speech of self-justification), show how the audience has not been hurt or not been hurt willfully. Often this is accomplished obliquely. When IBM demonstrates that they have accomplished a great deal through research, they also stress implicitly and sometimes more directly that these developments make it easier to function in business or in the home. General Electric's "We bring good things to life," Radio Shack's "You've got questions. We've got answers," and Microsoft's "Where do you want to go today?" are designed to secure goodwill and to demonstrate that the company benefits the audience—with more free time, less hard labor, and more accessible and inexpensive entertainment.

Stress Uniqueness

In a world dominated by competition, the speech to secure goodwill must stress the uniqueness of the specific company, person, profession, and so on. Distinguish it clearly from all others, otherwise any goodwill you secure will be spread over the entire field.

Establish Credibility

Speeches to secure goodwill must also establish credibility, thereby securing goodwill for the individual or commodity. To do so, concentrate on those dimensions of credibility discussed earlier (see Unit 19). Demonstrate that the subject is competent, of good intention, and of high moral character. Examine how Lee Iacocca does this in his speech on the odometer on page 467. Who could not have goodwill toward such an individual, product, or business?

Don't Be Obvious

An ineffective goodwill speech is an obvious advertisement; an effective one is not. The effective goodwill speech looks, on the surface, very much like an objective informative speech. It will not appear to ask for goodwill, except upon close analysis.

Don't Plead for Goodwill

This admonition is especially appropriate in the speech of self-justification. Criers may achieve some goals, but in the long run they seem to lose out. Few people want to go along with someone who appears weak. If you attempt to justify some action, justify it with logic and reason. Don't beg for goodwill—demonstrate that it's due you. Most audiences are composed of reasonable people who prefer to act out of logic, who recognize that not everyone is perfect, and who are ready to establish or reestablish goodwill toward an individual.

Don't Overdo It

Overkill is ineffective. You'll turn off your audience rather than secure their goodwill. Remember: your perspective and the perspective of your audience are very different. Your acquaintance with the product may fully convince you of its greatness, but your audience does not have that acquaintance. Consequently, they will not appreciate too many superlatives.

Sample Speeches to Secure Goodwill

A particularly effective example of the speech to secure goodwill is the following speech by Lee Iacocca, former CEO of Chrysler Corporation. Here Iacocca was presented with a particularly difficult problem. Chrysler was accused of disconnecting its odometers so that the cars would appear to be new, despite the 40 miles of road test. This was not a particularly horrible offense since most car buyers know that their cars are put through various tests, yet it presented Iacocca with a credibility problem. He met this head on with a series of print and television advertisements in which he admitted the error and spelled out what he would do to correct this error of judgment.

> Testing cars is a good idea. Disconnecting odometers is a lousy idea. That's a mistake we won't make again at Chrysler. Period.
> —Lee Iacocca

Let me set the record straight.

1. For years, spot checking and road testing new cars and trucks that come off the assembly line with the odometers disengaged was standard industry practice. In our case, the average test mileage was 40 miles.
2. Even though the practice wasn't illegal, some companies began connecting their odometers. We didn't. In retrospect, that was dumb. Since October 1986, however, the odometer of every car and truck we've built has been connected, including those in the test program.
3. A few cars—and I mean a few—were damaged in testing badly enough that they should not have been fixed and sold as new. That was a mistake in an otherwise valid quality assurance program. And now we have to make it right.

What we're doing to make things right.

1. In all instances where our records show a vehicle was damaged in the test program and repaired and sold, we will offer to replace that vehicle with a brand new 1987 Chrysler Corporation model of comparable value. No ifs, ands, or buts.
2. We are sending letters to everyone our records show bought a vehicle that was in the test program and offering a free inspection. If anything is wrong because of a product deficiency, we will make it right.
3. Along with free inspection, we are extending their present 5 year or 50,000 mile protection plan on engine and powertrain to 7 years or 70,000 miles.

4. And to put their minds completely at ease, we are extending the 7 year or 70,000 mile protection to all major systems: brakes, suspension, air conditioning, electrical, and steering.

The quality testing program is a good program. But there were mistakes and we were too slow in stopping them. Now they're stopped. Done. Finished. Over.

Personally, I'm proud of our products. Proud of the quality improvements we've made. So we're going to keep right on testing. Because without it we couldn't have given America 5 year 50,000 mile protection five years ahead of everyone else. Or maintained our warranty leadership with 7 years 70,000 mile protection. I'm proud, too, of our leadership in safety-related recalls.

But I'm not proud of this episode. Not at all.

As Harry Truman once said, "The buck stops here." It just stopped. Period.

Another type of goodwill speech is the speech of apology, a speech in which the speaker apologizes for some transgression and tries to restore his or her credibility. Three particularly dramatic examples of this type of speech, given by President William Jefferson Clinton, are presented below. As you read these speeches try visualizing yourself as Clinton's head speech writer and consider—using the benefit of hindsight—what you would change if these speeches were submitted to you as drafts to be edited and approved.

The first speech was given to the nation on August 17, 1998 after Clinton testified to a grand jury about a variety of issues. The issue that the nation and the media focused on, however, was his affair with Monica Lewinsky and the extent to which he misled the country and whether he obstructed justice. This speech was almost universally criticized for not expressing enough of an apology, for not asking the people to forgive him, and for attacking the opposition rather than taking responsibility himself.

Good evening. This afternoon in this room, from this chair, I testified before the Office of Independent Counsel and a grand jury. I answered their questions truthfully, including questions about my private life, questions no American citizen would ever want to answer.

Still I must take complete responsibility for all my actions, both public and private. And that is why I am speaking to you tonight.

As you know, in a deposition in January, I was asked questions about my relationship with Monica Lewinsky. While my answers were legally accurate, I did not volunteer information. Indeed I did have a relationship with Miss Lewinsky that was not appropriate. In fact it was wrong.

It constituted a critical lapse in judgment and a personal failure on my part for which I am solely and completely responsible.

But I told the grand jury today, and I say to you now, that at no time did I ask anyone to lie, to hide or destroy evidence, or to take any other unlawful action.

I know that my public comments and my silence about this matter gave a false impression. I misled people. Including even my wife. I deeply regret that.

I can only tell you I was motivated by many factors. First, by a desire to protect myself from the embarrassment of my own conduct. I was also very concerned about protecting my family. The fact that these questions were being asked in a politically inspired lawsuit which has since been dismissed was a consideration too.

In addition, I had real and serious concerns about an independent counsel investigation that began with private business dealings 20 years ago—dealings, I might add, about which an independent Federal agency found no evidence of any wrongdoing by me or my wife over two years ago.

The independent counsel investigation moved on to my staff and friends. Then into my private life. And now the investigation itself is under investigation. This has gone on too long, cost too much, and hurt too many innocent people.

Now this matter is between me, the two people I love most, my wife and our daughter, and our God. I must put it right. And I am prepared to do whatever it takes to do so.

Nothing is more important to me personally, but it is private. And I intend to reclaim my family life for my family. It's nobody's business but ours. even Presidents have private lives. It is time to stop the pursuit of personal destruction and the prying into private lives and get on with our national life.

Our country has been distracted by this matter for too long, and I take my responsibility for my part in all of this. That is all I can do. Now it is time, in fact it is past time, to move on. We have important work to do, real opportunities to seize, real problems to solve, real security matters to face.

And so tonight I ask you to turn away from the spectacle of the past seven months, to repair the fabric of our national discourse and to return our attention to all the challenges and all the promise of the next American century.

Thank you for watching and good night.

The next two speeches were delivered on February 12, 1999 after the Senate acquitted President Clinton in the impeachment trial. The first was read to the nation and the second was sent as an e-mail to the White House staff. These last two speeches were received much more favorably than the first one by both the people and the media.

[Speech to the Nation]

Now that the Senate has fulfilled its constitutional responsibility, bringing this process to a conclusion, I want to say again to the American people how profoundly sorry I am for what I said and did to trigger these events and the great burden they have imposed on the Congress and on the American people.

I also am humbled and very grateful for the support and the prayers I have received from millions of Americans over this past year.

Now I ask all Americans, and I hope all Americans here in Washington and throughout our land, will rededicate ourselves to the work of serving our nation and building our future together. This can be and this must be a time of reconciliation and renewal for America.

Thank you very much.

[E-mail to White House Staff]

I want to thank you personally for all you are doing for this Administration and our nation. Working at the White House is a great privilege, but I know it is also often a burden on you, and on the family and friends to whom you turn for support. That has meant long days, late nights, and many weekends here—and I want you to know how grateful I am.

The past year has been especially difficult for you. I know that my actions and the events they triggered have made your work even harder. For that, I am profoundly sorry. In all this, under the most extraordinary of circumstances, you never lost sight of your first obligation—to serve the people of our nation. For that, I am profoundly grateful.

The remaining years of this Administration can and must be a time of great achievement for our nation. I know you share my pride in what we have accomplished already to strengthen America at home and abroad, including over the past year, when we created the first surplus in three decades and continued dramatic advances in education and other vital areas.

Now, together we have much more to do to meet our obligations to future generations. We have set out our goals before the American people—from saving Social Security and Medicare, to strengthening education and health care, to advancing peace and security around the world—and I know you share my determination to act on those priorities. Today, the nation we love is strong and confident. In the months to come, we can move beyond the divisions of the past year to build a nation that is stronger and more united as it enters the 21st century.

Your dedication and loyalty have meant more to me than you can ever know. The best way I can repay you is to redouble my own efforts on behalf of the ideals we share, and to make the most of every day we are here, I thank you again for everything you are doing—and I ask you to keep working hard in the months ahead. Together, we can achieve great things for the American people.

THE SPEECH OF TRIBUTE

The speech of tribute encompasses a wide variety of speeches. All, however, are designed to pay some kind of tribute to a person or event. They include the eulogy, designed to praise the dead; the farewell; the dedication; the commendation, praising some living person; and the commemoration of some particular event or happening. The general purpose of the speech of tribute is to inform the audience of some accomplishment or of the importance of some event. It should also heighten the audience's awareness of the occasion, accomplishment, or person; strengthen or

THE ETHICS OF Electronic Communication

Credo for Free and Responsible Use of Electronic Communication Networks

The principles of free and responsible communication have long been a hallmark of communication study. Since 1963, the National Communication Association has included among its core documents a Credo for Free and Responsible Communication in a Democratic Society. Recognizing the advent of electronic means of global communication that are accessible to the general public, we members of the National Communication Association endorse the following statement of principles relating to electronic communication:

We take the concept of "free speech" literally: there is limited freedom of expression if access to the means of expression is limited by financial ability. We, therefore, urge the development of free and low-cost means of accessing the means for processing and distributing information in electronic forms.

We realize that access is limited if specialized expertise is required to take advantage of the necessary technology. We, therefore, urge the development of hardware and software that requires minimal training but that still allows wide use of worldwide electronic resources.

We support freedom of expression and condemn attempts to constrain information processing or electronic communication, especially expressions that are offensive to some or even most of the populace. Likewise, we support a right to privacy, both in the ability to maintain the integrity of individual message exchanges and in the ability to shield oneself from unwanted messages.

While supporting free expression, we nevertheless consider the maintenance of intellectual property rights to be crucial to the encouragement of creativity and originality. We, therefore, urge the designers and regulators of electronic forms of communication to use special vigilance to insure that the works of individuals or groups are protected from unfair use by others.

We encourage communication researchers to produce findings that will guide policy decisions concerning the social impact of electronic communication and to make those findings available widely. Likewise, we encourage the designers and regulators of electronic forms of communication to take credible findings about the social impact of their work into account as they implement new products and services.

We accept the need to teach students not only how to use electronic forms of communication but how to use them both wisely and well.

Finally, we call upon users of information processing and distribution networks to do so responsibly, with respect for language, culture, gender, sexuality, ethnicity, and generational and economic differences they may encounter in others.

Adopted 1994

How would you apply these guidelines to: (1) a Web site devoted to advancing the principles of the Ku Klux Klan? (2) a newsgroup devoted to pornography? (3) a listserv focusing on ways to cheat on your income tax?

create positive attitudes; and make the audience more appreciative. On the surface, then, the purpose is informative; below the surface, it's persuasive. In the speech of tribute, these principles should prove effective.

Involve the Audience

Involve the audience in some way. This is not always easy. Some tributes seem only to involve the individual being praised and some abstraction such as history, posterity, or culture. Make any history, posterity, or culture relevant to this specific audience. For example, if you were giving a eulogy, you would relate the meaning and accomplishments of the individual being eulogized to the specific audience. You would, in other words, answer the listeners' question, "What did this person's life mean to me?"

State the Reason for the Tribute

It's frequently helpful to give the audience some idea of why you're making this tribute. Often it's obvious: the teacher praises the student; the president congratulates the employee; the student eulogizes the teacher, and so on. The connections in these cases are obvious, and when they are, don't belabor them. But when they aren't obvious to the audience, tell the audience why you're the person giving this tribute.

Be Consistent with the Occasion

Construct and present a speech that is consistent with the specific occasion. This does not mean that all eulogies must be somber or that all sports award presentations must be frivolous. It is to say only that the speech should not contradict the basic mood of the occasion.

Don't Go Overboard

The speech of tribute records the positive, and the speech should be positive. But don't go overboard and overplay the specific accomplishments of an individual. This is dishonest and usually ineffective. State the person's accomplishments realistically. With some eulogies it's difficult to recognize the real person for all of the unrealistic and undeserved (and dishonest) praise.

A Sample Speech of Tribute

In the following speech former President Ronald Reagan pays tribute to the astronauts who died in the space shuttle Challenger explosion in 1986. The occasion was an extremely sad one. Most of the nation watched the tragedy on television just hours before. The speech reflects this sadness and mourning and will surely become a classic of the genre.

> Ladies and gentlemen, I planned to speak to you tonight to report on the State of the Union, but the events of earlier today have led me to change those plans.

Today is a day for mourning and remembering. Nancy and I are pained to the core by the tragedy of the shuttle Challenger. We know we share this pain with all of the people of our country. This is truly a national loss.

Nineteen years ago, almost to the day, we lost three astronauts in a terrible accident on the ground, but we've never lost an astronaut in flight; we've never had a tragedy like this. And perhaps we've forgotten the courage it took for the crew of the shuttle but they, the Challenger seven, were aware of the dangers and overcame them and did their jobs brilliantly.

We mourn seven heroes: Michael Smith, Dick Scobee, Judith Resnik, Ronald McNair, Ellison Onizuka, Gregory Jarvis and Christa McAuliffe. We mourn their loss as a nation, together.

The families of the seven—we cannot bear, as you do, the full impact of this tragedy but we feel the loss and we're thinking about you so very much. Your loved ones were daring and brave and they had that special grace, that special spirit that says, "Give me a challenge and I'll meet it with joy." They had a hunger to explore the universe and discover its truths. They wished to serve and they did—they served all of us.

We've grown used to wonders in this century; it's hard to dazzle us. For 25 years the United States space program has been doing just that. We've grown used to the idea of space, and perhaps we forget that we've only just begun. We're still pioneers. They, the members of the Challenger crew, were pioneers.

And I want to say something to the schoolchildren of America who were watching the live coverage of the shuttle's takeoff. I know it's hard to understand that sometimes painful things like this happen. It's all part of the process of exploration and discovery; it's all part of taking a chance and expanding man's horizons. The future doesn't belong to the fainthearted. It belongs to the brave. The Challenger crew was pulling us into the future, and we'll continue to follow them.

I've always had great faith in and respect for our space program, and what happened today does nothing to diminish it. We don't hide our space program, we don't keep secrets and cover things up. We do it all up front and in public. That's the way freedom is and we wouldn't change it for a minute. We'll continue our quest in space. There will be more shuttle flights and more shuttle crews and, yes, more volunteers, more civilians, more teachers in space. Nothing ends here. Our hopes and our journeys continue.

I want to add that I wish I could talk to every man and woman who works for NASA, or who worked on this mission, and tell them: "Your dedication and professionalism have moved and impressed us for decades, and we know of your anguish. We share it."

There's a coincidence today. On this day 390 years ago, the great explorer Sir Francis Drake died aboard ship off the coast of Panama. In his lifetime the great frontiers were the oceans, and a historian later said. "He lived by the sea, died on it, and was buried in it." Well, today we can say of the Challenger crew, their dedication was, like Drake's, complete. The crew of the space shuttle Challenger honored us by the manner in which they lived their lives. We will never forget them nor the last time we saw them this morning as they prepared for their journey and waved goodbye and "slipped the surly bonds of earth to touch the face of God."

Thank you.

THE SPECIAL OCCASION SPEECH IN CULTURAL PERSPECTIVE

Like all forms of communication, the special occasion speech must be developed with a clear understanding of the influence of culture. In the discussion of the speech of introduction, for example, the suggestion was made not to oversell the speaker and in the discussion of the speech of tribute the suggestion was made not to go overboard in praising the person. Excess exaggeration is generally evaluated negatively in much of the United States. On the other hand, it's often expected in, for example, some Latin cultures.

Culture will also influence the way in which an acceptance should be framed. Not surprisingly, collectivist cultures would suggest that you give lots of credit to the group whereas individualist cultures would suggest that taking self-credit (when it's due) is appropriate. Thus, if you were accepting an award for a performance in a movie, an extreme collectivist orientation would lead you to give great praise to others and to claim that without others you never could have accomplished what you did. An extreme individualist orientation would lead you to accept the award and the praise for yourself; after all, you did it! In the media business, as you see from the numerous televised award shows, everyone give thanks to almost everyone connected with the project. That's the custom; the collectivist form of expression has become the norm at least in the show business context.

Speeches at college graduation, as you'll discover, are often of the "inspirational" type. What principles would you suggest the inspirational speaker follow? What pitfalls would you suggest this speaker avoid?

In the discussion of the speech of goodwill, the suggestion was offered to present yourself as being worthy of the goodwill rather than as a supplicant begging for it. In some cultures, however, this attitude might be seen as arrogant and disrespectful to the audience. Pleading for goodwill in, for example, some Asian cultures would be seen as suitably modest and respectful of the audience.

In introducing or in paying tribute to someone, consider the extent to which you wish to focus on the person's contribution to the group or to individual achievement. An audience with a predominantly collectivist orientation will expect to hear group-centered achievements whereas an audience of predominantly individualist orientation will expect to hear more individually focused achievements.

All this is not to say that you should simply give the audience what it wants or expects but rather than these expectations need to be considered as you develop your speech.

Never rise to speak unless you have something to say; and when you have said it, cease.
—John Witherspoon

UNIT IN BRIEF

Speech of Introduction	Establishes a connection among speaker, topic, and audience. Establishes the speaker's credibility. Is consistent in style and manner with the major speech. Is brief. Avoids covering what the speaker intends to discuss. Avoids overselling the speaker.
Speeches of Presentation and Acceptance	[Speech of presentation] States the reason for the presentation. States the importance of the award. [Speech of acceptance] Thanks those who gave the award. Thanks those who helped. States the meaning of the award to you. [Both speeches] Avoid misjudging the importance of the award. Avoid giving too long a speech. Avoid talking in platitudes and clichés.
The Speech to Secure Goodwill	Stresses the benefits the audience may derive. Stresses uniqueness. Establishes your credibility and the credibility of the subject. Avoids being obvious in securing goodwill. Avoids pleading for goodwill. Avoids overdoing the superlatives.
The Speech of Tribute	Involves the audience. States the reason for the tribute. Is consistent with the occasion. Avoids disproportionate praise.

The Special Occasion Speech in Cultural Perspective	Develop the special occasion speech with an understanding of the influence of culture, considering, for example, how the audience's culture looks upon:
	Praise for an individual as in a speech of introduction
	Credit for achievement
	Seeking goodwill
	Individual versus group achievement

THINKING CRITICALLY ABOUT SPECIAL OCCASION SPEAKING

REVIEWING KEY TERMS AND CONCEPTS IN SPECIAL OCCASION SPEECHES

1. Review and define the key terms used in this unit:

- ❏ speech of introduction (p. 455)
- ❏ speech of presentation (p. 459)
- ❏ speech of acceptance (p. 459)
- ❏ speech to secure goodwill (p. 465)
- ❏ speech of tribute (p. 470)

2. Review and explain the key concepts discussed in this unit:

- ▪ What are the characteristics of an effective speech of introduction?
- ▪ What are the characteristics of an effective speech of presentation? Of acceptance?
- ▪ What are the characteristics of an effective speech to secure goodwill?
- ▪ What are the characteristics of an effective speech of tribute?
- ▪ What cultural considerations should be kept in mind in developing and presenting the special occasion speech?

DEVELOPING STRATEGIES FOR THE SPECIAL OCCASION SPEECH

1. Jay is scheduled to give a wedding toast at his best friends' wedding. He was told that it should be about two minutes long. What advice would you give Jay if his friends were 18 years old? If they were in their 50s?

2. Mollie has been asked by her catering firm—which was recently cited by the Board of Health for a variety of unsafe practices and was shut down for six months—to present their case for the catering contract to approximately 20 members of the Board of Education. These members all know the history of the catering company and why it was shut down; they've agreed to hear Mollie but are generally reluctant to hire this firm again. After all, they figure, if it happened once, it will happen again. What advice would you give Mollie for this speech to secure goodwill (and another chance).

EVALUATING SPECIAL OCCASION SPEECHES

1. Compare and contrast the two speeches designed to secure goodwill—the speech of Lee Iocacca and the speech of President Clinton (pp. 468–469). What are the major differences you find in these speeches? If you were hearing the speeches when they were originally delivered, which you would consider the more effective? Which would have the greater persuasive impact on you?

2. Read the five speeches of acceptance—those by Elizabeth Taylor, Tom Cruise, and William Faulkner (in this unit) and those by Martin Scorsese and Nelson Mandela (in the Appendix). What unifying theme appears throughout these speeches? Which of these would you consider the most effective speech? Why?

USING TECHNOLOGY IN SPECIAL OCCASION SPEAKING

1. Using one of the search engines (see Table 7.1 for examples) look for one of the types of special occasion speeches discussed here. Are you surprised at how many of these speeches are on the Web? Of what value is it to have these speeches on the Web?

2. Visit the Obituary Daily Times at http://www.best.com/~shuntsbe/obituary/ to help you locate information about someone you admire. Write a brief two-minute eulogy for this person.

PRACTICALLY SPEAKING

24.1 Short Speech Technique

Prepare and deliver a two-minute speech in which you:

a. introduce any speaker you wish, speaking to any audience you wish, on any subject you wish.

b. present an award for the best speaker of the year, the best quarterback, the best actor, the best firefighter, the best police officer, or the best teacher.

c. explain how an advertisement is like a speech to secure goodwill.

d. toast your friend's new relationship commitment.

e. say thanks for a group of your friends who just surprised you with a birthday party; they're all clapping and yelling "speech, speech."

f. eulogize a person.

24.2 Developing the Speech of Introduction

Prepare a speech of introduction approximately two minutes long. For this experience you may assume that the speaker you introduce will speak on any topic you wish. Do, however, assume a topic appropriate to the speaker and to your audience—your class. You may wish to select your introduction from one of the following suggestions.

1. Introduce a historical figure to the class.

2. Introduce a contemporary religious, political, or social leader.

3. Prepare a speech of introduction that someone might give to introduce you to your class.

4. Introduce a famous media (film, television, radio, recording, writing) personality—alive or dead.

5. Introduce a series of speeches debating the pros and cons of multicultural education

24.3 Developing the Speech of Presentation/Acceptance

Form pairs. One person should serve as the presenter and one as the recipient of a particular award or honor. The two people can select a situation from the following list or make one up themselves. The presenter should prepare and present a two-minute speech in which she or he presents one of the awards to the other person. The recipient should prepare and present a two-minute speech of acceptance.

1. Academy Award for best performance

2. Gold watch for service to the company

3. Ms. or Mr. America

4. Five million dollars for the college library

5. Award for contributions to intercultural understanding

6. Book of the year award

7. Mother (Father) of the Year award

8. Honorary Ph.D. in communication for outstanding contributions to the art

9. Award for outstanding achievement in architecture

10. Award for raising a prize hog

24.4 Developing the Speech to Secure Goodwill

Prepare a speech approximately three to five minutes long in which you attempt to secure the goodwill of your audience toward one of the following:

1. your college (visualize your audience as high school seniors).
2. a particular profession or way of life (teaching, religious life, nursing, law, medicine, bricklaying, truck driving, etc.).
3. this course (visualize your audience as college students who have not yet taken this course).

4. the policies of a particular foreign country now in the news.
5. a specific multinational corporation.

24.5 Developing the Speech of Tribute

Prepare a speech approximately three to five minutes long in which you pay tribute to one of the following persons:

a. a politician for supporting AIDS research.
b. a scientist for advances in cancer research.
c. a visitor from another planet.
d. a famous athlete for building a children's hospital.
e. a consumer advocate for exposing fraud in advertising.

Speaking in Small Groups

UNIT OBJECTIVES

After completing this unit, you should be able to:
Define the small group and explain the group as a culture.

Describe problem solving, idea generation, and information sharing groups.

Explain small group tasks of both members and leaders.

Explain the panel, symposium and team presentations, symposium forum, and oral and written reports as ways of presenting a group's thinking.

There is somebody wiser than any of us, and that is everybody.
—Napoleon Bonaparte

Very likely you're a member of several small groups. The family is the most obvious example, but you're also a part of a team, a class, a collection of friends, and so on. Some of your most important and most personally satisfying communications take place within small groups. This unit focuses on speaking in small groups, offering a kind of bridge connecting public speaking to small group communication, and it covers the nature of the small group, how to communicate effectively in small groups, and guidelines for presenting a group's findings, conclusions, or recommendations.

THE SMALL GROUP

A small group is a relatively small collection of individuals (usually around five to 12) who are related to each other by some common purpose and have some degree of organization among them. People on a bus would not constitute a group, since they're not working at some common purpose. Should the bus get stuck in a ditch, however, the riders may quickly become a group and work together to get the bus back on the road.

Before beginning your study of small group communication, examine how apprehensive you are in group discussions and in meetings by taking the following self-test.

TEST YOURSELF
How Apprehensive Are You in Group Discussions and Meetings?

Just as you have apprehension in public speaking and conversations (Unit 3), you probably also experience apprehension in group discussions and in meetings. This brief test is designed to measure your apprehension in these small group situations.

This questionnaire consists of 12 statements concerning your feelings about communication in group discussions and meetings. Please indicate in the space provided the degree to which each statement applies to you. There are no right or wrong answers. Some of the statements are similar to other statements. Don't be concerned about this. Work quickly; just record your first impression.

1 = Strongly Agree
2 = Agree
3 = Are Undecided
4 = Disagree
5 = Strongly Disagree

_____ 1. I dislike participating in group discussions.
_____ 2. Generally, I am comfortable while participating in group discussions.
_____ 3. I am tense and nervous while participating in group discussions.
_____ 4. I like to get involved in group discussions.
_____ 5. Engaging in a group discussion with new people makes me tense and nervous.
_____ 6. I am calm and relaxed while participating in group discussions.
_____ 7. Generally, I am nervous when I have to participate in a meeting.
_____ 8. Usually, I am calm and relaxed while participating in meetings.
_____ 9. I am very calm and relaxed when I am called upon to express an opinion at a meeting.
_____ 10. I am afraid to express myself at meetings.
_____ 11. Communicating at meetings usually makes me uncomfortable.
_____ 12. I am very relaxed when answering questions at a meeting.

This test will enable you to obtain two subscores, one for group discussions and one for meetings. To obtain your scores use the following formulas:

For group discussions compute your score as follows:
1. Begin with the number 18; this is just used as a base so that you won't wind up with negative numbers.
2. To 18, add your scores for items 2, 4, and 6.
3. Subtract your scores for items 1, 3, and 5 from your Step 2 total.

For meetings compute your score as follows:
1. Begin with the number 18; this is just used as a base so that you won't wind up with negative numbers.
2. To 18, add your scores for items 8, 9, and 12.
3. Subtract your scores for items 7, 10, and 11 from your Step 2 total.

Scores above 18 show some degree of apprehension. How do these scores compare with your scores from the public speaking and conversation apprehension tests presented in Unit 3? What factors contribute to your apprehension in small discussion groups and meetings? Might the suggestions offered in Unit 3 for managing apprehension also prove useful here?

The Small Group as a Culture

Many groups—especially long-standing work groups—develop into small cultures with their own norms. These norms are the rules or standards of behavior, the rules that say which behaviors are appropriate (for example, willingness to take on added tasks or directing conflict toward issues rather than toward people) and which are inappropriate (for example, coming late or not contributing actively). Sometimes these rules for appropriate behavior are explicitly stated in a company contract or policy: all members must attend department meetings. Sometimes rules are implicit: members should be well-groomed. Regardless of whether norms are spelled out or not, they're powerful regulators of members' behaviors.

Norms may apply to individual members as well as to the group as a whole and, of course, will differ from one group to another (Axtell, 1990a, b 1993). For example, in Japan and in many Arab countries it's customary to begin meetings with what many Americans would think is unnecessary socializing. While many Americans prefer to get right down to business, the Japanese, for example, prefer rather elaborate socializing before getting to the business at hand. They want to first experience confidence and trust (DeVries 1994).

In the United States men and women in business are expected to interact when making business decisions as well as when socializing. In Muslim and Buddhist societies, however, there are religious restrictions that prevent mixing the sexes. In the United States, Bangladesh, Australia, Germany, Finland, and Hong Kong, for example, punctuality for business meetings is very important. But in countries such as Morocco, Italy, Brazil, Zambia, Ireland, and Panama, for instance, time is less highly regarded and being late is no great insult and is even expected. In the United States, and in much of Asia and Europe, meetings are held between two groups. In many Persian Gulf nations, however, the business executive is likely to conduct meetings with several different people—sometimes dealing with totally different issues—at the same time. In this situation, you have to expect to share what in the United States would be "your time" with these other parties. In the United States very little interpersonal touching goes on during business meetings; in Arab countries, however, touching (for example, hand holding) is common and is a gesture of friendship.

Norms that regulate a particular member's behavior, called role expectations, identify what each person in an organization is expected to do; for example, Pat has a great computer setup and so should play the role of secretary.

You're more likely to accept the norms of your group when you:

- want to continue your membership in the group;
- feel your group membership is important;
- are in a group that is cohesive, when you and the other members are closely connected;
- are attracted to each other and depend on each other to meet your needs;
- would be punished by negative reactions or exclusion from the group for violating the group norms (Napier and Gershenfeld 1989).

Cross cultural studies show that members of different cultures have different tendencies to conform to group norms—even when these conflict with their own perceptions. For example, in a classic study, a subject is seated with confederates of the experimenter who misjudge the length of a line shown on a screen (Asch 1946). Does the subject report what he or she

Society in its full sense . . . is never an entity separable from the individuals who compose it.
—Ruth Benedict

really sees or go along with the majority? The answer is that many people do contradict their own perceptions to go along with the group, but it varies with the culture. For example (and contrary to popular stereotypes), German and Japanese respondents are less conformist than North Americans or Chinese (Moghaddam, Taylor, and Wright 1993). It's also interesting to note that people are showing less conformity to group norms today than they did when the original studies were conducted in the 1950s (Moghaddam, Taylor, Wright 1993).

TYPES OF SMALL GROUPS

Several group situations call for the skills of public speaking. Here three such groups are considered: the problem-solving group, the idea-generation group, and the information-sharing group.

Problem-Solving Groups

A problem-solving group is a collection of individuals who meet to solve a problem or to reach a decision. In one sense this is the most exacting kind of group. It requires not only a knowledge of small group communication techniques, but also a thorough knowledge of the particular problem. We look at this group first in terms of the classic and still popular problem-solving approach, identifying the steps you'd go through in solving a problem. These steps are, in one sense, the group's agenda; they're the main activities of the group.

Most groups have an agenda. An agenda is simply a list of the group's tasks. It's an itemized listing of what the group hopes to consider. At times, the agenda is prepared by the supervisor or consultant or CEO and is simply presented to the group. The group is then expected to follow the agenda item by item. At other times, the group will develop its own agenda, usually as its first or second order of business.

Generally, the more formal the group, the more important this agenda becomes. In informal groups, the agenda may simply be general ideas in the minds of the members (for example, we'll review the class assignment and then make plans for the weekend). In formal business groups the agenda will be much more detailed and explicit. Some agendas specify not only the items that must be covered, but also the order in which they should be covered, and even the amount of time that should be devoted to each item.

The agenda must be agreed upon by the group members. If it's imposed by the CEO, for example, then there's little doubt that the group members will accept it and follow it. If it's one that the group itself develops, then both leader and members must make sure that members agree to follow it. At times, it might be helpful to have a brief discussion of the agenda and a commitment from all members to follow it.

The Problem-Solving Sequence. The problem-solving approach, which owes its formulation to the philosopher John Dewey's steps in reflective thinking, identifies six steps (see Figure 25.1). These steps are designed to make problem solving more efficient and effective.

Steps in problem-solving discussion.

While most small group theorists would advise you to follow the problem-solving pattern as presented here, others would alter it somewhat. For example, some would advise you to reverse Steps 2 and 3, to identify possible solutions first and then consider the criteria for evaluating them (Brilhart and Galanes 1992). The advantage of this approach is that you're likely to generate more creative solutions since you will not be restricted by standards of evaluation. The disadvantage is that you might spend a great deal of time generating solutions that would never meet the standards you'll eventually propose.

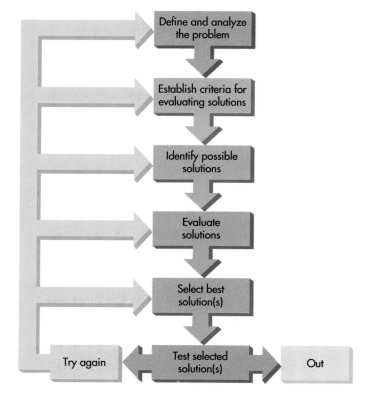

Step 1. Define and Analyze the Problem. Generally, it's best to define the problem as an open-ended question ("How can we improve the student newspaper?") rather than as a statement ("The student newspaper needs to be improved") or a yes/no question ("Does the student newspaper need improvement?"). The open-ended question allows for greater freedom of exploration.

Limit the problem so that it identifies a manageable area for discussion. A question such as, "How can we improve the university?" is too broad and general. Rather, it would be more effective to limit the problem and to identify one subdivision of the university on which the group might focus: the student newspaper, student-faculty relationships, registration, examination scheduling, or student advisory services, for example.

Step 2. Establish Criteria for Evaluating Solutions. Before any solutions are proposed, decide how to evaluate the solutions. Identify the standards or criteria that you'll use in evaluating the solutions or in selecting one solution over another.

Consider both practical and value criteria. Focusing on the practical, you might decide that the solutions must not increase the budget, must lead to a higher number of advertisers, must increase the readership by at least 10 percent, and so on. In focusing on the value criteria, you might consider that the newspaper must be a learning experience for all those who work on it or that it must reflect attitudes consistent with the university's mission statement.

Step 3. Identify Possible Solutions. Identify as many solutions as possible. Focus on quantity rather than quality. Brainstorming may be particularly

A problem well stated is a problem half solved.
—Charles F. Kettering

useful at this point (see discussion of idea-generation groups on page 488). Solutions to the student newspaper problem might include incorporating reviews of faculty publications; student evaluations of specific courses; reviews of restaurants in the campus area; outlines for new courses; and employment information.

Step 4. Evaluate Solutions. After all the solutions have been proposed, go back and evaluate each according to the practical and value criteria already established. For example, to what extent does incorporating reviews of area restaurants meet the criteria for evaluating solutions? Would it increase the budget? Would it lead to an increase in advertising revenue? Match each potential solution against the criteria. A useful procedure in analyzing any kinds of issues is provided by critical thinking pioneer Edward deBono. The technique is explained in Table 25.1.

Step 5. Select the Best Solution(s). Select the best solution or solutions. For example, if "reviews of faculty publications" and "outlines for new courses" best meet the criteria for evaluating solutions, the group might then decide that these are its solutions.

Some problems are so complex that you have to be highly intelligent and well informed just to be undecided about them.
—Laurence J. Peter

TABLE 25.1 The Six Critical Thinking Hats Technique

Critical thinking pioneer Edward deBono (1987) suggests that in defining and analyzing problems, you use six thinking hats. With each hat you look at the problem from a different perspective. The technique provides a convenient and interesting way to further explore a problem from a variety of different angles.

Hat	Focuses on	Questions to Ask
The fact hat	The data, the facts and figures that bear on the problem.	What are the relevant data on the newspaper? How can you get more information on the paper's history? How much does it cost to print? How much advertising revenue can you get?
The feeling hat	Our feelings, emotions, and intuitions concerning the problem.	How do you feel about the newspaper and about making major changes?
The negative argument hat	The negative possibilities or downside that might result if the idea or solution is accepted.	Why might this proposal fail? What are the problems with publishing reviews of courses? What is the worst-case scenario?
The positive benefits hat	The positive benefits or upside that might result if the idea or solution is accepted.	What are the opportunities that this new format will open up? What benefits will reviewing courses provide for the students? What would be the best thing that could happen?
The creative new idea hat	New ways of looking at the problem and can be easily combined with the techniques of brainstorming discussed later in this chapter.	What other ways can you use to look at this problem? What other functions can a student newspaper serve that have not been thought of? Can the student paper provide a service to the nonacademic community as well?
The control of thinking hat	What you have done and are doing and asks that you reflect on your own thinking processes and synthesize the results of your thinking.	Have you adequately defined the problem? Are you focusing too much on insignificant issues? Have you given enough attention to the possible negative effects?

It's interesting to note the differences between groups in the United States and in Japan. In the United States groups are supposed to reach decisions relatively quickly; speed is always important. In Japan groups are expected to be more deliberate and to make decisions after greater reflection. From even this seemingly simple difference, it's easy to see how members from the United States might view Japanese groups as indecisive and unwilling to commit to a decision. Equally, it's easy to see how members from Japan might view groups from the United States as impulsive, thoughtless, and more interested in getting the job done than in thinking about it carefully and fully (Lustig and Koester 1999, Samovar and Porter, 1995).

Step 6. Test Selected Solution(s). After the solution(s) are selected, the group might decide to put them into operation to test their effectiveness. For example, the group might decide to run the two new features in the next several months' issues. Then, the group might poll students about the new newspaper or examine the number of copies purchased. Or it might analyze the advertising revenue or see if readership did increase 10 percent. If the feedback is positive, the group might then recommend these solutions as permanent changes.

If these solutions prove ineffective, the group would go back to one of the previous stages and repeat part of the process. Often this takes the form of selecting other solutions to test. It may also involve going further back to, for example, a re-analysis of the problem, an identification of other solutions, or a restatement of criteria.

Problem-Solving in Business. The problem-solving sequence discussed here is used widely in business in a variety of different types of groups. Here

---

LISTEN TO THIS   How to Listen for Groupthink

Listen carefully for groupthink, a group attitude that develops when members are more concerned with agreeing with each other than with careful analysis of a problem (Janis, 1983). Groupthink is likely to occur when group members limit discussion to only a few alternative solutions or when it doesn't reexamine its decisions despite indications of possible dangers. In groupthink, members are extremely selective in the information they consider seriously. While facts and opinions contrary to the group's position are generally ignored, those that support the group's position are readily and uncritically accepted. The following symptoms should help you listen more critically and recognize groupthink in the groups you observe or participate in:

- Group members think the group and its members are invulnerable.
- Members create rationalizations to avoid dealing with warnings or threats.
- Members believe their group is moral.
- Those opposed to the group are perceived in simplistic, stereotyped ways.
- Group pressure is applied to any member who expresses doubts or questions the group's arguments or proposals.
- Members censor their own doubts.
- Group members believe all are in unanimous agreement, whether this is stated or not.
- Group members emerge whose function it is to guard the information that gets to other members, especially when it may create diversity of opinion.

are three groups popular in business that rely largely on problem solving: the nominal group technique, the Delphi technique, and quality circles.

The Nominal Group Technique. The nominal group is a method of problem solving that uses limited discussion and confidential voting to obtain a group decision. It's especially helpful when some members may be reluctant to voice their opinions in a regular problem-solving group or when the issue is controversial or sensitive. With this technique, each member contributes equally and each contribution is treated equally. Another advantage of this technique is that it can be accomplished in a relatively short period of time. The nominal group technique can be divided into seven steps (Kelly 1994):

1. The problem is defined and clarified for all members.
2. Each member writes down (without discussion or consultation with others) his or her ideas on or possible solutions to the problem.
3. Each member—in sequence—states one idea from his or her list which is recorded on a board or flip chart so everyone can see it. This process is repeated until all suggestions are stated and recorded. Duplicates are then eliminated. Group agreement is secured before ideas are combined.
4. Each suggestion is clarified (without debate). Ideally, each suggestion should be given equal time.
5. Each member rank orders the suggestions.
6. The rankings of the members are combined to get a group ranking which is then written on the board.
7. Clarification, discussion, and possible reordering may follow.

The highest ranking solution might then be selected to be tested, or perhaps several high-ranking solutions may be put into operation.

The Delphi Method. In the Delphi method, a group of experts is established, but there's no interaction among them; instead they communicate by repeatedly responding to questionnaires (Tersine and Riggs 1980, Kelly 1994). The method is especially useful when you want to involve people who are geographically distant from each other as, for example, if your sales staff is distributed throughout the United States and Asia while management is in San Francisco. The Delphi method is also useful when you want all members to act as part of the solution and to uphold it, and when you want to minimize the effects of dominant members or even of peer pressure. The method is best explained as a series of steps (Kelly 1994).

1. The problem is defined (We need to improve intradepartmental communication). What each member is expected to do is specified (Each member should contribute five ideas on this specific question).
2. Each member then contributes anonymously five ideas in writing. This stage used to be completed through questionnaires sent through traditional mail but is now more frequently done through e-mail. This greatly increases the speed with which the entire process can be accomplished.
3. The ideas of all members are combined, written up, and distributed to all members who may be asked to, say, select the three or four best ideas from this composite list.

4. Members then select the three or four best ideas and submit these.
5. From these responses another list is produced and distributed to all members who may be asked to select the one or two best ideas.
6. Members then select the one or two best ideas and submit these.
7. From these responses another list is produced and distributed to all members. The process may be repeated any number of times, but usually three rounds are sufficient for achieving a fair degree of agreement.
8. The "final" solutions are identified and are communicated to all members.

Quality Circles. In quality circles, groups of workers (usually from about six to 12) investigate and make recommendations for improving the quality of some organizational function. The members are drawn from the workers whose area is being studied. Thus, if the problem is to improve advertising on the Internet, then the quality circle membership would be drawn from the advertising and computer departments. Generally, the motivation for establishing quality circles is economic; the company's aim is to improve quality and profitability. Another related goal is to improve worker morale; because quality circles involve workers in decision making, workers may feel empowered and more essential to the organization (Gorden and Nevins 1993).

The basic idea is that people who work on similar tasks will be better able to improve their departments or jobs by pooling their insights and working through problems they share. The quality circle style of problem solving is often considered one of the major reasons for the success of Japanese businesses where it's widely used. In the United States, hundreds of organizations use quality circles but generally with less success than those in Japan (Gorden and Nevins 1993).

Quality circle members investigate problems using any method they feel might be helpful, for example, face-to-face problem-solving groups, nominal groups, or delphi methods. The group then reports its findings and its suggestions to those who can do something about it. In some cases the quality circle members may implement their solutions without approval from upper management levels.

The Idea-Generation Group

Many small groups exist solely to generate ideas and often follow a formula called brainstorming, a technique for bombarding a problem and generating as many ideas as possible (Osborn, 1957). Advertisers developing an advertising campaign or creating a slogan, Jay Leno's writing team, teachers trying to develop a new curriculum, and an electronics' firm trying to find ways to cut costs would all make use of some form of brainstorming.

Brainstorming occurs in two phases. The first is the brainstorming period proper; the second is the evaluation period. In the brainstorming period, a problem is selected that is amenable to many possible solutions or ideas. Group members are informed of the problem to be brainstormed before the actual session so they can think about it. When the group meets, each person contributes as many ideas as possible. All ideas are recorded either in writing or on tape. During this idea-generating session, four general rules are followed.

TIPS
from professional speakers

Establish a method for recording the session. A tape recorder works well. A blackboard or flip chart may slow the flow of ideas, but has the advantage of keeping ideas where people can see them and build on them. If you record the session on a blackboard or flip chart, rotate note takers.

Sam Deep, organizational consultant and trainer, and Lyle Sussman, professor, *Smart Moves* (Reading, MA: Addison-Wesley, 1990): 203.

Don't Criticize. No criticism is allowed. All ideas are recorded. They're not evaluated nor even discussed. Any negative criticism—whether verbal or nonverbal—is itself criticized by the leader or the members.

Work for Quantity. The more ideas the better. Somewhere in a large pile of ideas will be one or two good ones. The more ideas generated, the more effective the brainstorming session.

Combine and Extend Ideas. While you may not criticize a particular idea, you may extend it or combine it in some way. The value of a particular idea may well be in the way it stimulates someone to combine or extend it.

Think Wild. The wilder the idea, the better. It's easier to tone an idea down than to spice it up. A wild idea can easily be tempered, but it's not so easy to elaborate on a simple or conservative idea.

After all the ideas are generated—a period lasting no longer than 15 or 20 minutes—the entire list of ideas is evaluated. The ones that are unworkable are thrown out; the ones that show promise are retained and evaluated. During this phase negative criticism is allowed.

Communicating New Ideas. If a group develops an idea, it will generally seek in some way to put this idea into operation. Often it's necessary to convince others that the idea is workable and cost effective. Here are a few suggestions for communicating new ideas more effectively:

- Attach the new idea to an old one, if possible. People are more apt to understand and accept new ideas when they somehow resemble old and more comfortable ones. If it's a new rule, show how it's related to the old rule.
- Present the idea in a nonthreatening manner. New ideas often frighten people. If your ideas might lead people to feel insecure about their jobs, then alleviate these worries before you try to explain the idea in any detail. And, generally, it's best to proceed slowly.
- Present new ideas tentatively. You may be taken with the flash of inspiration and not have reasoned out the practical implications of the idea. So, if you present your ideas tentatively and they're shown to be impractical or unworkable, you will be less hurt psychologically and—most important—will be more willing to try presenting new ideas again.
- In many instances, it will prove helpful to link changes and new ideas to perceived problems in the organization or relationship. If you're going to ask employees to complete extensive surveys, then show them how this extra work will correct a problem and benefit them and the organization.
- Say why you think the idea would work. Give the advantages of your plan over the existing situation and explain why you think this idea should be implemented. The patterns for organizing a public speech will prove helpful in accomplishing this.
- State the negatives (there usually are some with most ideas) as you understand them and, of course, why you think the positives outweigh them.
- Relate the new ideas to the needs and interests of those on whom the innovation will impact.
- Persuasion research suggests that you proceed inductively when you anticipate objections. When presenting ideas to a hostile or potentially hostile audience, give the benefits before introducing the new idea. Ideally, move your audience into wanting the benefits and values of the new idea before they ever hear of the idea itself.

The best way to have a good idea is to have a lot of ideas.
—Linus Pauling

TIPS from professional speakers

In a perfect world, perfectly good ideas would be implemented. You have to understand political realities of the workplace—pressures from colleagues, customers, and co-workers that may force others to veto your idea and plans. Find ways to help people handle those realities rather than expect them to become martyrs for your sake.

Dianna Booher, business communication consultant and president of Booher Consultants, *Communicate with Confidence!* (New York: McGraw-Hill, 1994): 100.

The wisest mind has
something yet to learn.
—George Santayana

Information-Sharing Groups

The purpose of information-sharing groups is to acquire new information or skills through shared knowledge. In most information-sharing groups, all members have something to teach and something to learn, for example, a group of students sharing information to prepare for an examination. In others, the interaction takes place because some have information and some don't, for example, a discussion between patients and health care professionals.

Educational or Learning Groups. Members may follow a variety of discussion patterns. For example, a historical topic (for example, the development of free speech or equal rights) might be developed chronologically, with the discussion progressing from the past into the present and perhaps predicting the future. Issues in developmental psychology, such as a child's language development or physical maturity, might also be discussed chronologically. Other topics lend themselves to spatial development. For example, the development of the United States might take a spatial pattern—from east to west—or a chronological pattern—from 1776 to the present. Other suitable patterns, depending on the topic and the group's needs, might be causes and effects, problems and solutions, or structures and functions.

Perhaps the most popular is the topical pattern. A group might discuss the legal profession by itemizing and discussing each of its major functions. A corporation's structure might also be considered in terms of its major divisions. As can be appreciated, each of these topics may be further systematized by, say, listing the legal profession's functions in terms of importance or complexity and ordering the corporation's major structures in terms of decision-making power.

Focus Groups. A different type of learning group is the focus group, a kind of depth interview of a small group. The aim here is to discover what people think about an issue or product. What do men between 18 and 25 think of the new aftershave lotion and its packaging? What do young executives earning over $100,000 think of buying a foreign luxury car?

In the focus group the leader tries to discover the beliefs, attitudes, thoughts, and feelings that participants have so as to better guide decisions on, for example, changing the scent or redesigning the packaging or constructing advertisements for luxury cars. It's the leader's task to prod members to analyze their thoughts and feelings on a deeper level and to react to or elaborate on the thoughts and feelings of others in the group.

For example, in one study the researcher tried "to collect supplementary data on the perceptions graduates have of the Department of Communication at ABC University" (Lederman 1990). Two major research questions, taken directly from Lederman's study, motivated this focus group:

- What do graduates of the program perceive the educational effectiveness of their major at ABC?
- What would they want implemented in the program as it exists today?

Group participants then discussed their perceptions that were organized around the following questions (Lederman 1990):

- The first issue to discuss is what the program was like when you were a major in the department. Let's begin by going around the table and making introductions. Will you tell me your name, when you graduated from ABC, what you're doing now, and what the program was like when you were here, as you remember it?
- Based on what you remember of the program and what you have used from your major since graduating, what kinds of changes, if any, would you suggest?

MEMBERS AND LEADERS IN SMALL GROUPS

In this section we consider the roles or functions of small group members and leaders. By gaining insight into the roles of both members and leaders, you'll be in a better position to analyze your own small group behavior and to modify it as you wish.

Members in Small Groups

What are the major roles that members serve in small group communication? How can you become more effective participants in small groups?

Member Roles. Member roles can be divided into three general classes (Benne and Sheats 1948). These roles are, of course, frequently served by leaders as well. **Group task roles** are those that help the group focus more specifically on achieving its goals. For example, one person may almost always seek the opinions of others, another may concentrate on elaborating details, another on evaluating suggestions, and still another on stimulating the group to greater activity. Usually it's better for the roles to be spread about evenly among the members so that each may serve many group task roles.

Group building and maintenance roles focus not only on the task to be performed but on interpersonal relationships among members. Members might positively reinforce others, try to resolve conflict, keep the channels of communication open, or mediate the differences between group members.

Individual roles are counterproductive. They hinder the group's achieving its goal and are individual rather than group-oriented. Such roles, often termed dysfunctional, hinder the group's productivity and member satisfaction. Examples of individual roles include expressing negative evaluation, trying to focus attention on oneself, trying to dominate the group, or pleading the case of some special group.

Member Participation. Another perspective on group membership may be gained from looking at the recommendations for effective participation in small group communication.

- Be Group-Oriented. In the small group you're a member of a team, a larger whole. Your participation is of value to the extent that it advances the goals of the group and promotes member satisfaction. Your task is to pool your talents, knowledge, and insight so that the group may arrive at a better solution than any one person could have developed.
- Center Conflict on Issues. Conflict is a natural part of the small group process. It's particularly important in the small group to center conflict on issues rather than on personalities. When you disagree, make it clear

Do not wait for leaders, do it alone, person to person.
—Mother Teresa

that your disagreement is with the solution suggested or the ideas expressed, and not with the person who expressed them.

■ Be Critically Open-Minded. Come to the group with a mind open to alternatives. Don't come with your mind already made up. When this happens, the small group process degenerates into a series of individual debates in which each person argues for his or her own position.

■ Ensure Understanding. Make sure that your ideas are understood by all participants. If something is worth saying, it's worth saying it clearly. Don't hesitate to ask if something you said was clear.

Leaders in Small Groups

In many small groups, one person serves as leader. In others, leadership may be shared by several persons. In some groups, a person may be appointed the leader or may serve as leader because of her or his position within the company or hierarchy. In other groups, the leader may emerge as the group proceeds in fulfilling its functions or may be voted as leader by the group members. In any case the role of the leader or leaders is vital to the well-being and effectiveness of the group. (Even in leaderless groups, where all members are equal, leadership functions must still be served.)

Before examining leadership any further, you should find it interesting to analyze your own views on and style of leadership by taking the accompanying self-test: What Kind of Leader Are You?

TEST YOURSELF
What Kind of Leader Are You?*

Respond to each of the following statements by indicating YES if the statement is a generally accurate description of your leadership style and NO if it's not.

_____ 1. I would speak as a representative of the group.
_____ 2. I would settle conflicts when they occur in the group.
_____ 3. I would be reluctant to allow the others freedom of action.
_____ 4. I would decide what should be done and how it should be done.
_____ 5. I would refuse to explain my actions when questioned.
_____ 6. I would allow members complete freedom in their work.
_____ 7. I would permit the others to use their own judgment in solving problems.
_____ 8. I would let the others do their work as they think best.
_____ 9. I would allow the others a high degree of initiative.
_____ 10. I would permit the group to set its own pace.

These questions come from an extensive leadership test and should help you focus on some ways a leader can accomplish a task and ensure member satisfaction. Questions 1-5 are phrased so a leader concerned with completing the group's task would answer YES. Questions 6-10 are phrased so a leader concerned with ensuring that the group members are satisfied would answer YES. Think about your own style of leadership. Are you generally more concerned with task or people? Do you adjust your style on the basis of the specific group or do you have one style that you use in all situations?

SOURCE: "T-P Leadership Questionnaire: An Assessment of Style" from J. W. Pfeiffer and J. E. Jones, *Structured Experiences for Human Relations Training*. Copyright by the American Educational Research Association. Reprinted by permission of the publisher.

Three types of leadership styles are often distinguished: laissez-faire (the leader lets the group members do as they wish and only offers information when asked); democratic (the leader provides direction but allows the group to make its own decisions and progress the way its members wish); and authoritarian (the leader dominates the group and makes the decisions regardless of what the group members may want). Which type of leader would you find most difficult to work under in, say, a work team? Which style are you most likely to adopt with, say, subordinates at work?

Leaders need to be concerned with task and people, though each situation will call for a somewhat different combination of task and people concerns (Hersey and Blanchard 1988). For example, a group of scientists working on AIDS research would probably need a leader who provides them with the needed information to accomplish their task. They would be self-motivating and would probably need little in the way of social and emotional encouragement. On the other hand, a group of recovering alcoholics might require leadership that stresses the social and emotional needs of the members.

Leadership effectiveness depends on combining the concerns for task and people according to the specifics of the situation.

Leader's Functions: Task and People. With this situational view of leadership we can look at some of the major functions leaders serve. In relatively formal small group situations, as when politicians plan a strategy, advertisers discuss a campaign, or teachers consider educational methods, the leader has several specific functions.

The following functions are not the exclusive property of the leader. Nevertheless, when there's a specific leader, he or she is expected to perform those functions. Leadership functions are best when performed unobtrusively—in a natural manner.

■ Activate Group Interaction. Perhaps the group is newly formed and the members feel a bit uneasy with one another. Don't expect diverse members to sit down and discuss a problem without becoming familiar with each other. As the group leader you would stimulate the members to interact. You would also serve this function when members act as individuals rather than as a group.

■ Maintain Effective Interaction. Even after the group is stimulated to group interaction, see that members maintain effective interaction and that all members have an opportunity to express themselves. When the discussion begins to drag, prod the group to effective interaction: "Do we have any additional comments on the proposal?" "Would anyone like to add anything?"

Leadership is action, not position
—Donald H. McGannon

Do you think you'd have greater power in a group if you emphasized your ability to do a task (for example, you maintained eye contact, sat at the head of the table, used a relatively rapid speech rate, spoke fluently, and gestured appropriately) or if you tried to dominate or threaten members (for example, spoke in a loud and angry voice, pointed fingers, maintained rigid posture, used forceful gestures, and lowered your eyebrows)? Most people, research finds, would follow the leader who used task cues (Driskell, Olmstead, and Salas 1993). Group members will also see such people as more competent and more likable. People using dominance cues, on the other hand, are seen as less competent, less influential, less likable, and more self-oriented. So, if you wish to gain influence in a group (and be liked), use task cues and avoid dominance cues. Can you see this difference operating in your work environment? Among your friends?

- Keep Members on the Track. As the leader, keep all members reasonably on track by asking questions, interjecting internal summaries as the group goes along, or providing transitions so that the relationship of an issue just discussed to one about to be considered is clear.
- Ensure Member Satisfaction. If a group is to be effective, it must meet not only the surface purposes of the group, but also the underlying or interpersonal purposes that motivated many of the members to come together in the first place.
- Encourage Ongoing Evaluation and Improvement. Most groups encounter obstacles as they try to solve a problem, reach a decision, or generate ideas. Most groups could use some improvement. If the group is to improve, it must focus on itself. Along with trying to solve some external problem, it must try to solve its own internal problems as well, for example, personal conflicts, failure of members to meet on time, or members who come unprepared. As the leader you would try to identify any such difficulties and encourage and help the group resolve them.
- Prepare Members for the Discussion. This may involve preparing the members for the small group interaction as well as for the discussion of a specific issue or problem. If members are to discuss a specific problem, it may be necessary to brief them. Or, perhaps you would need to distribute certain materials before the actual discussion or tell members to read certain materials or view a particular film or television show. Whatever the preparations, the leader would organize and coordinate them.

PRESENTING THE GROUP'S THINKING

The purpose of small group interaction isn't completed when the group has reached its decision. Rather, these decisions (findings, conclusions, recommendations) need to be presented to some larger group—the entire union membership, your class as a whole, the board of directors. There are lots of ways in which these decisions may be presented. Here's just a sampling.

The Panel

In the panel, the group members are cast in the role of "experts" and participate informally and without any set pattern of who speaks when. The procedure is similar to that of the regular small group interaction, except that the group is really discussing the issue to inform an audience who is present but which does not participate in the actual discussion.

A variation is the two-panel format, with an expert panel and a lay panel. The expert panel includes the members who participated in the group and who ideally have information that the lay panel members do not. The information is shared by the interaction between the lay and the expert panel.

Notice that this is the format followed by many talk shows, such as Oprah Winfrey. In these cases, the moderator is the host (Winfrey). The "expert panel" is the group of guests (the dysfunctional family, the gossip columnists, the political activists). And the lay panel are the members of the studio audience who ask questions or offer comments. Another lay panel consists of the at-home audience who can often call in or who probably talk to others in the home or on the phone about the discussion.

Here are a few suggestions for making these presentations more effective:

- Always treat the questions and the questioners with respect. You'll notice this on the popular talk shows. No matter how stupid the question is, the moderator treats it as serious, though often restructuring it just a bit so that it makes more sense. Treat the questions objectively; don't try to bias the question or the answer through your verbal or nonverbal responses.
- Speak in short turns. The group's interaction should resemble a conversation, rather than individual public speeches. Resist the temptation to tell long stories or go into too much detail.
- Try to spread the conversation around the group. Generally, try to give each member the opportunity to speak about equally.

The Symposium and Team Presentation

In the symposium, each member delivers a prepared presentation, a public speech. All speeches are addressed to different aspects of a single topic. In the symposium, the leader introduces the speakers, provides transitions from one speaker to another, and may provide periodic summaries.

The team presentation is popular in business settings where two or three members of the group will report the group's findings to a larger group. In some situations, the team presentations may amount to "positive papers," in which the report of the majority and the minority are presented, as does the Supreme Court. Or if, say, the group is considering new scheduling systems, members of a team might each present one of the proposed systems.

Here are a few suggestions for making these presentations more effective.

- Coordinate your presentations very carefully. Team presentations and symposia are extremely difficult to synchronize. Make sure that everyone knows exactly what he or she is responsible for. Make sure there's no (or very little) overlap among the presentations.
- Much as you would rehearse a public speech, try to rehearse these presentations and their coordination. This is rarely possible to do in actual practice, but it's still a useful ideal.
- Select a strong leader to introduce the presentations and to manage audience questions.
- Keep last-minute changes to a minimum. When they're unavoidable, make sure that all members know about the changes.

TIPS
from professional speakers

As the conference moderator, you need to provide a running commentary which links one speaker to the other and gives the audience a thoughtful framework. At the end of the conference, a final summary is in order. Ideally you will energetically sum up each speaker's contribution and add a final dynamic, just like the ending of an individual speech. And you want to end on time while the delegates are still sitting in the audience and not on their way to the airport.

Elizabeth Urech, international communication specialist and founder of "Speak for Yourself," *Speaking Globally: Effective Presentations Across International and Cultural Boundaries* (Dover, NH: Kogan Page, 1998): 129.

- Adhere carefully to time limits. If you speak for more time than allotted, that time is deducted from that of a later speaker. As you can appreciate, violating time limits will severely damage the entire group's presentation.
- Provide clear transitions between the presentations. Internal summaries work especially well as connectives between one speech and the next: "Now that Judy has explained the general proposal, Peter and Margaretta will explain some of the advantages and disadvantages of the proposal. First, we'll hear from Peter with the advantages and then from Margaretta with the disadvantages."

The Symposium-Forum

The symposium-forum consists of two parts: a symposium, with prepared speeches (as just explained), and a forum, with questions from the audience and responses by the speakers. The leader introduces the speakers and moderates the question-and-answer session.

The suggestions for making these presentations more effective are essentially the same as for the panel and the symposium.

Oral and Written Reports

In many cases, the group leader will make a presentation of the group's findings, recommendations, or decisions to some other group—the class as a whole, the entire student body, the board of directors, the union membership, or the heads of departments.

Depending upon the specific situation, these reports may be similar to speeches of information or speeches of persuasion. For example, your task might be to simply inform the other group of the recommendations of your committee, for example, the ways to increase morale, the new pension proposals, or new developments in competing organizations. In other cases, your report will be largely persuasive, for example, to convince the larger group to give you increased funding so that your group's decisions can be implemented.

In some situations, a brief oral report and a more extensive written report are required. A good example of this is the press conference. In this situation, your oral report would be delivered to members of the press who would also receive a written report. The press would then question you after your report for further details. Here are a few suggestions for more effective oral and written reports.

- Write the written report as you would a term paper and from that develop a summary of the report in the form of a public speech, following the 10 steps explained throughout this text.
- Don't read the written report. Even though the oral and the written report may cover essentially the same content, they're totally different in development and presentation. The written report is meant to be read, the oral report is meant to be listened to.
- In some instances it's helpful to distribute the written report and use your oral report to highlight the most essential aspects of the report. Members may then refer to the report as you speak—a situation not recommended for most public speeches.

- In very rare instances, you may choose to distribute the written report only after you have completed your oral report. Generally, people don't like this procedure; they prefer the option of thumbing through the report as they listen or reserving reading until they've heard the oral report.

UNIT IN BRIEF

The Small Group	A small group is a collection of individuals that is small enough for all members to communicate with relative ease as both senders and receivers. The members are related to each other by some common purpose. Most small groups develop norms identifying what is considered appropriate.
Types of Groups	The problem-solving group attempts to solve a particular problem or at least to reach a decision. The idea-generation group tries to generate as many ideas as possible. The information sharing group attempts to acquire new information through sharing of knowledge or insight.
Members and Leaders in Groups	Members should be group-oriented, center conflict on issues, be critically open-minded, and ensure understanding. Leaders should seek to address the task and the interpersonal needs of members, and should activate the group interaction, maintain effective interaction, keep members on the track, ensure member satisfaction, encourage ongoing evaluation, and prepare members for discussion.
Presenting the Group's Thinking	Small groups make use of four major formats: the panel, the symposium and team presentations, the symposium forum, and oral and written reports.

THINKING CRITICALLY ABOUT SMALL GROUP COMMUNICATION

REVIEWING KEY TERMS AND CONCEPTS IN SPEAKING IN SMALL GROUPS

1. Review and define the key terms used in this unit:

- □ small group (p. 480)
- □ small group norms (p. 481)
- □ problem-solving group (p. 483)
- □ groupthink (p. 486)
- □ idea generation group (p. 488)
- □ information-sharing group (p. 490)
- □ small group role (p. 491)
- □ small group leadership (p. 492)
- □ panel (p. 494)
- □ symposium (p. 495)
- □ team presentation (p. 495)
- □ forum (p. 496)
- □ oral report (p. 496)

2. Review and explain the key concepts covered in this unit:

- What is the nature of the small group?
- What are the major types of small groups and how are they each conducted?
- What roles do group members and leaders serve?
- In what ways might the group's thinking be presented? What guidelines can you offer for making these presentations most effective?

DEVELOPING STRATEGIES FOR SPEAKING IN SMALL GROUPS

1. Kim is scheduled to lead a group of financial analysts in a brainstorming session designed to discover ways of

getting new clients. None of the analysts really want to participate in this; since they're not paid commission, they really don't care if they get new clients or not. Given this situation, what kind of introduction would you suggest Kim give the group? Would your advice be different if the analysts were earning commissions?

2. At *Ditto Magazine* six teams of 10 to 12 people each have been created to consider ways to increase readership. The plan is to have a representative from each team report to the entire staff the deliberations and recommendations of his or her team. Jesse is scheduled to give his team's report next week and wants to present his report as a slide show (as discussed in Unit 9). What advice would you give Jesse on handouts? What types should he use (if any) and how should he distribute and use them?

EVALUATING SPEAKING IN SMALL GROUPS

1. Watch a sitcom in which there are frequent group conversations—"Newsradio," "Friends," or "Frasier" or reruns of "Seinfeld," "MASH," or "Murphy Brown" are good examples. What principles of group communication can you see in these interactions?

2. Recall a recent small group experience you had at school or work. What did you do to contribute to the group's progress? Did you do anything that hindered its progress? What might you have done to have been a more effective member?

USING TECHNOLOGY IN SPEAKING IN SMALL GROUPS

1. Visit an Internet chat room and lurk for a time before writing anything yourself. What principles of group communication can you detect in this group? Is there an obvious leader? Do certain members play certain roles—roles similar to those discussed here? A good starting place is http://www.abeamoflight.com/hot/chat-a-htm which will provide you with links to just about any kind of chat room you might want.

2. Visit http://unix1.sncc.lsu.edu/internet/usenet/usenet-etiquette.html which provides information on how to politely post a message to a newsgroup. What small group communication norms can you detect from these suggestions? After you read this, visit one or a few newsgroups. Can you see these norms manifested in the way in which the messages are posted?

PRACTICALLY SPEAKING

25.1 Short Speech Technique

Prepare a two-minute speech in which you:

a. explain the functions of a group to which you belong.

b. explain the leadership qualities of a person you know or have read about.

c. explain your own leadership traits and abilities.

d. illustrate how a problem might be solved by tracing the six stages in the problem-solving process.

e. explain how you see decisions made by authority, majority rule, and consensus in the groups with which you're familiar.

f. explain how a problem could be analyzed with the six thinking hats technique.

25.2 Solving Problems in Groups

Together with four, five, or six others, form a problem-solving group and discuss one of the following questions:

- What should we do about the homeless?
- What should we do to improve student morale?
- What should we do to better prepare ourselves for the job market?
- What should we do to improve student-faculty communication?
- What should be the college's responsibility concerning AIDS?

Before beginning the discussion, each member should prepare a discussion outline, answering the following questions:

- What is the problem? How long has it existed? What caused it? What are the effects of the problem?
- What criteria should be used to evaluate possible solutions?
- What are some possible solutions?
- What are the advantages and disadvantages of each of these possible solutions?

- What solution seems best (in light of the advantages and disadvantages)?
- How might we put this solution to a test?

After the group discussion, the findings of each group should be presented using one of the following methods or some combination of them:

a. a panel discussion
b. a symposium
c. a two- or three-person team presentation
d. a symposium forum
e. a simulated press conference
f. an oral report

APPENDIX

Thinking Critically About Speeches

Student Speeches for General Analysis

1. Matthew Sanchez, Diplomatic Immunity Unjustified
2. Jocelyn So, Crash of the Internet
3. Maria Lucia R. Anton, Sexual Assault Policy a Must
4. Sara Mitchell, Homosexuals and the Military

Student Speeches for Focused Analysis

1. Meleena Erikson, See Jane, See Jane's Dilemma [Analysis focus: **Audience Analysis and Adaptation**]
2. Amy Celeste Forman, What Exactly Are We Working For? [Analysis focus: **Research and Supporting Materials**]
3. Adam Childers, The Cost of Justice [Analysis focus: **Organization**]
4. Steven N. Blivess, Medical Miscommunication: Improving the Doctor-Patient Interaction [Analysis focus: **Style and Language**]

Professional Speeches for General Analysis

1. Judith Humphrey, Executive Eloquence
2. Nelson Mandela, Nobel Prize Acceptance Speech
3. Nancy W. Dickey, A Window of Opportunity: Meeting the Challenges of Medicine's Agenda
4. Carolyn Woo, Living Up to Your Fullest Potential
5. Martin Scorsese, Acceptance Speech for the John Huston Award for Artists Rights
6. James C. McCroskey, Why We Communicate the Ways We Do: A Communibiological Perspective

The speeches in this appendix are included here as models of the effective application of the principles of public speaking to a wide variety of topics intended for a wide variety of listeners. The speeches are grouped into three categories.

Student speeches for general analysis contains four speeches given by college students. Each of these speeches is annotated with questions to guide your analysis of the speech. These annotations and questions cover the entire public speaking process.

Student speeches for focused analysis also contains four speeches by college students. These annotations, however, focus on specific concepts in public speaking: audience analysis and adaptation, research and supporting materials, organization, and style and language. Analyzing these speeches will help you focus on specific aspects of public speaking and the way in which they are treated in excellent speeches.

Professional speeches for general analysis contains six speeches given by people used to public speaking. A general guide for analyzing these speeches is presented as a preface to them and follows the principles of public speaking identified in Unit 2.

Use any and all of these speeches as learning tools, as models. Ask yourself what you can learn from the speeches that will help you perfect your own public speaking skills.

Student Speeches for General Analysis

1. Matthew Sanchez, Diplomatic Immunity Unjustified
2. Jocelyn So, Crash of the Internet
3. Maria Lucia R. Anton, Sexual Assault Policy a Must
4. Sara Mitchell, Homosexuals and the Military

Diplomatic Immunity Unjustified

Matthew Sanchez

Imagine an evening outing: you and your two children decide to have a fun night out. You look up to your rearview mirror to see a car slam into the back of you car—WHAM—killing your children. You survive the crash and so does the individual who rear-ended you. You are told by the police that the driver was drunk the night of the accident, but that no crimes applied to him. Murder, vehicular homicide, and driving under the influence of alcohol are just meaningless statements to this person.

According to the *USA Today* of June 4, 1996, "There are more than 18,000 of these individuals, not including their family members, who are immune to all law in the U.S." And the one thing that they have in common is that they are foreign diplomats.

What was once thought to be a great international resolution is quickly becoming a great international dilemma. Despite repeated derogatory reports about diplomatic immunity, UN policy officials fail to reform diplomatic international law.

Today, I would like to speak to all of you about why diplomatic immunity's current application is not justified.

First, we will examine the purpose of diplomatic immunity. Second, I will explain the problem that diplomatic immunity has created. And third, I will offer an amendment to diplomatic immunity.

First, we will examine the purpose of diplomatic immunity. According to the *U.S. Department of State Dispatch* on June 28, 1996, "Diplomatic immunity is defined as a principle of international foreign law in which certain foreign government officials are not subject to local courts and/or

Did the title grab your attention? Do you think it was effective for the speaker to reveal his purpose and thesis in the title?

Did the speaker establish the relevance of the topic? If you were in the audience, would you be concerned about this topic?

How effective was the speaker's orientation?

Did the speaker establish an S-A-T connection? How would you have done it?

other authorities." Simply put, you do not have to obey the law if you are a foreign diplomat. This concept is derived from the premise that upon entering into another country, you may be unaware of their laws and societal norms. But the question arises, is it possible to be a foreign diplomat and at the same time be unaware of laws in other nations?

The Economist of October 13, 1996, gives us the answer to this question: "In 1961 the Vienna Convention of Consular Practices established most modern diplomatic relations, including the concept of diplomatic immunity. Today there are more than 160 nations including the U.S. who are members of these treaties. These treaties grant foreign diplomats and their families complete immunity to all aspects of Foreign Law in hopes of protecting them from unfair prosecution at the hands of a foreign court."

Notice the transition from the first point (the purpose of diplomatic immunity) to the second point (the problems of diplomatic immunity). In what other ways might you have phrased this transition?

Now that we have examined the purpose of diplomatic immunity, let us look at the problems that diplomatic immunity has created. *Time* magazine of November 2, 1996, states that foreign diplomats living in New York City often refuse to pay their debts. This leaves little recourse for U.S. creditors since it is impossible to sue a foreign mission. *New York Magazine* of the same month goes on to say that "Total estimated foreign diplomatic debt is between 5.3 and 7 million dollars." Take a moment, please, and imagine the adverse ramifications that a deficit of 7 million dollars would have on your city's budget. Where in the world is your city going to get that kind of money? Unfortunately the first place that local government goes to for money is our taxpayer dollars. Instead of building better parks, schools, and highways, our taxes will be spent on foreign diplomat debt. On January 17, 1997, ABC interviewed New York Mayor Rudolph Guiliani as to what he thought about diplomatic immunity and he had quite a bit to say. He poured out that the Russian Federation alone owes over 15,000 unpaid traffic violations to the city of New York. Furthermore, when one of his officers accosted a man about parking in front of a fire hydrant, the man responded by punching out the officer. After subduing the culprit and taking him to jail the police found out three things about him. First, that he was drunk, second that he was a diplomat, and third that because of diplomatic immunity nothing could be done to this criminal and he had to be released back out onto the streets of New York. In a current dispute, Friday April 18, 1997, carloads of diplomats from the Russian Embassy blocked in a moving van on a public street in Washington, DC, that was transporting Russian Artifacts from one museum to another. The diplomats parked one car in front of the van and one car in back of the van and did not move for days.

Specific examples are essential to a speech topic like this. How would you have handled the examples? Would you have used fewer examples but developed them in more detail? Or, would you have used more examples but developed them in less detail?

These are reasons enough that diplomatic immunity must be amended. But they are nothing compared to what CBS News states on January 17, 1997. In 1981 a British police woman was out patrolling her nightly route, when she was shot in the head by a Libyan sniper. This assassin also happened to be a member of the Libyan Embassy and was therefore immune to prosecution. Furthermore, Jud Aspen in the book *Diplomatic Crime* writes after getting into an argument with a bartender, a Brazilian official then decided to leave, only to come back with a 45 caliber handgun and kill the bartender. He then fled the U.S. and because of diplomatic immunity's sanctions, nothing could be done to this cold-blooded murderer.

In yet another example, the son of the attaché from Ghana came to the U.S. in 1986 and raped his first victim. Since then he has caught onto his freedom from law in other nations and has raped over 16 other women in the New York area alone. New York Detective Pat Christenson said that after he released the handcuffs, the diplomat laughed in his face, laughed in the rape victim's face and then left the office. The victim asked the detective why her rapist was let go and he responded, "Ma'am, I am sorry; there is nothing I can do. He is the son of a diplomat."

On January 15, 1997, UPI stated "Second ranked Georgian Diplomat Gregory Makardze was allegedly under the influence of alcohol and when driving in a downtown Washington area, his car collided with a set of parked cars, killing 16-year-old Jovianna Waltrick." Joseph A. Thomasino, student of International Law at Johns Hopkins University, told me that unless Georgian President Eduard Shevardnadze decides to waive diplomatic immunity, we cannot sue this diplomat. Fortunately, Shevardnadze did waive diplomatic immunity in this case. However, Washington, DC, *News Online* updated April 15, 1997 stated that Makardze pleaded not guilty. But realize relying on another country's goodwill to waive diplomatic immunity is not the solution, because the problem of diplomatic immunity still exists.

Notice how you pay especially close attention to the anecdotes. And notice too how much easier they are to follow than other parts of the speech. For example, you could probably repeat the anecdote about the moving van or about the rapist without any difficulty. But, you'd probably have a hard time repeating the first major proposition of the speech. Which of these examples was the most compelling? Why?

As citizens of the USA we should be appalled that a person foreign to our country can walk into our own backyard and get away with murder. But, we should also be embarrassed that on January 4, 1997, CNN stated that one of our own diplomats was in Russia in 1986 and while driving under the influence of alcohol killed a woman and her three children while they were peacefully walking alongside of the road.

As Julius Caesar once wrote, "The inviolability of diplomats is acknowledged by most civilized people, but there must be a limit. How do you protect, for example, people guilty of cold-blooded murder?"

I have defined the problems resulting from diplomatic immunity; now let us look at the solution. Moderate Exemption Directive Reform is the solution to diplomatic immunity, wherein foreign diplomats and their families remain immune to all aspects of foreign law, except for two: theft and the violation of safety of others. These two concepts are universal in nature. That means all 160 nations in the UN label them as crimes. So there is no confusion on the part of the diplomat for not knowing any better since his own country prosecutes these crimes. Mortimer J. Adler in the book *Six Great Ideas* states, "Justice is fairness; it is giving to each what he is due."

How effective is this transition? Would it have been more effective to summarize both major propositions and then introduce the solution? In what other ways might you have phrased this transition?

How effective were the several quotations the speaker used? How did they contribute to the overall effectiveness of the speech?

Diplomatic immunity is not just; it is not fair because it does not punish criminals. Moderate Exemption Directive Reform is just because it does punish criminals. It gives them what they are due. Therefore, your tax dollars are safe, because people not paying what they owe is a form of theft. And rapists like the son of the attaché from Ghana shall be put behind bars because when they violate the safety of another human being it is considered a crime.

Does the speaker succeed in convincing you that Moderate Exemption Directive Reform is an effective solution?

So, let us recap. The original intent of diplomatic immunity was to protect diplomats from unfair prosecution in a foreign court. We have discovered that diplomatic immunity has long since gone out of control and that something must be done. The solution is to have moderate exemption amend the way that diplomatic immunity is currently administered.

How effective is the speaker in summarizing the major points of the speech?

How would you evaluate the speaker's use of research materials? How effectively did the speaker integrate the materials into the oral presentation?

How effective is the speaker's closing? How would you have closed the speech?

In closing, diplomatic immunity has proven itself to be retrogressive to a foreign diplomat's mission and abusive to a hosting country and its citizens. Nolan Kirkpatrick in the book *Living Issues in Ethics* states "Moral choices reside upon an understanding of Justice." Making diplomats accountable for their actions will, in turn, enable them to become better decision makers. But for now, your brother's murder, your close friend's sexual assault, and worst of all, those children whom you love so much that lost their lives to a drunk driver one night, could all end up victims to the international criminal otherwise known as the foreign diplomat.

SOURCE: Matthew Sanchez (1997). "Diplomatic Immunity Unjustified," *Winning Orations of the Interstate Oratorical Association*, pp. 19–21, ed. Larry Schnoor. Mankato, MN: Interstate Oratorical Association. Matthew Sanchez, a student at Florida Community College, was coached by Carol Grimes.

Crash of the Internet

Jocelyn So

What do you think of the speech title? After you complete the speech, return to the title and try to create alternative titles.

How effectively does the description of a cartoon introduce the topic? Did it gain your attention? Did it focus your attention on the topic to be discussed?

In the cartoon strip *Over the Hedge,* Verne the turtle feels compelled to cross-post his spam and potato chip recipe to every newsgroup in existence. So, he sends 6,897,435,987 messages across the Internet. After a traditional Ka-boom cloud appears over his computer, the strip ends with Verne saying in dazed disbelief, "I broke the Internet."

Now, while a rather caffeinated computer programmer may be the only one who thinks this strip is funny, cartoonist Fry Lewis isn't too far off the mark. Every day, people communicate with one another via electronic mail, students and professionals access Internet databases for research, and companies use World Wide Web sites to advertise and keep in touch with their customers. Unfortunately, the more the Internet is used, the slower it becomes. In the words of Mike Roberts, vice president of the Internet standards firm Educom, as stated in the October 1996 edition of *PC World,* "At a minimum, we're in for a lot of bad hair days on the Internet."

The fact is, the Internet you log onto every day to get the latest sports scores is the same one your bank uses to transfer funds around the world. And just because you may not have a modem doesn't mean that your doctor or your employer doesn't. Whether you're an active Internet user, or just an impartial observer, if the Internet crashes, we're all going down with it. For, the Internet is already being strained past its breaking point, and while we can't save it ourselves, at least we can get it back on track.

Notice that the speaker makes an attempt to include those who use the Internet as well as those whose data are stored electronically and accessed through the Internet. How effective is the speaker in accomplishing this goal? Do you feel included? Why?

How effectively does the speaker explain what she'll cover in the speech?

In order to ensure that our next trip down the information super highway doesn't end in a million car pile up, we'll first find out how bad the Internet's bugs really are. Then, we'll browse through the causes of the problems, so that finally we can download some simple steps that you can take to save the Internet.

From college students, to the Olympics, to every commercial and sitcom on television, it seems that everyone is on the Net. And that's the problem. According to the *Christian Science Monitor* of September 13, 1996, as more and more people log onto the Net, the slower and less efficient the process becomes, defeating the whole point of working on-line in the first place. The resulting frustration coincides with two major problems: information and productivity loss.

Because the Internet was designed from the start to transfer information, when the system breaks down, the flow of information does as well. The previously cited *Christian Science Monitor* explains that phone company MCI's network alone carries enough Internet data each month to fill nine million sets of encyclopedias. And while losing volume M of the Encyclopedia Britannica may not be the end of the world, according to a *Gartner Group* research article published September 23, 1996, every second, more than 4,000 stock market transactions are sent worldwide over the Net, and each transaction lost represents millions of dollars disappearing into thin air. The problem hinges on the fact that while network technology has grown steadily over the years, the ability of companies to implement the technology hasn't—leaving the Internet users of the nineties stuck in the technology of the seventies. Unfortunately, *Newsweek* of September 16, 1996, reports that "Everyone complains of brown-outs everyday, and it's going to get a lot worse."

But the brown-out has already begun, and our productivity is going with it. On August 7, 1996, America Online, the world's largest on-line company, and its 6 million customers went off-line for 19 hours due to Internet failures. The loss of a day meant the loss of billions of dollars to the thousands of U.S. companies that rely on AOL to provide much needed electronic mail and World Wide Web services. According to *Business Week* of August 26, 1996, AOL Chairman Stephen Case wrote in an apology letter to subscribers, "I wish I could tell you this will never happen again, but frankly I can't make that commitment." Case didn't know how right he was. America Online went off-line again on January 23, 1997, and once more on February 5, according to the February 6, 1997, edition of the *Washington Post*. And even without these large-scale failures, productivity is lost every day by people who must spend working hours just trying to access the already overburdened Internet. According to the January 26, 1997, edition of the *San Francisco Examiner*, "Attempting to log on is like trying to solve the *New York Times* crossword puzzle. You know you'll never make it, but you try anyway."

Did the speaker strengthen or change your belief that the Internet is overloaded?

Even with the thousands of failures the Internet experiences every day, few individuals have done anything to fix its problems. To do so, we must focus on the internal structure of the Internet, the Internet service providers, and our own unmoderated use.

When users access the Internet they're really making a connection from their computer to many other computers. To understand how it works, think back to when you were a kid and played the game telephone. Someone would come up with a message, tell the next person in line, and so on until the message, at this point completely distorted, reaches the last person. The Internet works the same way, hopefully without the distorted message. According to the previously cited edition of *PC World*, the typical Internet connection involves more than 2 dozen computers, each passing on a message that needs to be sent. In the center of the Internet are hubs, multimillion dollar computer facilities that direct most of the Internet's traffic. Unfortunately, when a hub goes down, it forces all the other computers to pick up the load, making them work even harder. Imagine a game of telephone in which a kid in the middle of the line goes home for dinner—makes it much more difficult to get even a distorted message through. But the consequences of a botched game of telephone pale in comparison to the warning stated in the previously cit-

What opinion are you forming of the speaker's credibility? What specific things contribute to your credibility impression?

ed *Gartner Group* article: it would only take the failure of two major hubs to bring half the worldwide Internet to a standstill.

The second problem is the Internet service providers, or ISPs, themselves. These companies purchase phone lines and computer connections from the major phone companies and then sell access to you and me. According to the February 2, 1997, edition of the *St. Louis Dispatch,* ISPs are offering low flat rates for unlimited Internet access, usually about $20 a month. These aggressive marketing tactics have induced many people to sign up, but the ISP's have made a big mistake—they've sold more people access than can possibly use the system and when that happens, the system slows down and can crash.

And we're partially to blame. We've become people who want information now, not later. *The New York Times* of July 21, 1996, explains that within 24 hours of putting up a dedication page to the friends of families of TWA Flight 800, Montoursville, Pennsylvania, resident Scott Frye counted nearly 100,000 hits, or computer visits, to the Web site and over 500 pieces of e-mail. The response was so overwhelming that it actually overloaded the server in his area, causing several Pennsylvania towns to lose access to the Internet completely. And while losing access to the Net may not seem like a big deal, to those whose livelihood depends on the Internet, that's simply not the case. Conon Cocallas told the previously cited *San Francisco Examiner,* "I run a small business and I rely on e-mail from clients for orders. When I can't log on, I am shut down."

Think about the last time you logged onto the Net. You probably checked your e-mail, sent a few messages and then started browsing the Web. Did you stop to think about the thousands of computers you were affecting just so you could download yesterday's Dilbert cartoon? We wouldn't let a child play with something they could break, so why do we all do it thousands of times a day? Let's face it, the Internet's grown up; it's time we did as well.

The key to saving the Internet is responsibility. Fortunately, it's not too late to take a few simple steps that may help prevent traffic jams on our information super highway.

First, shop carefully for an Internet Service Provider. Before signing up, ask the ISP representative for a map that pinpoints their network's proximity to the major hubs. The more direct the connection, the less likely that you will experience service slow downs or brown-outs.

Second, the May 23, 1996, *Chicago Sun Times* recommends scheduling your access times to avoid peak periods, after the prime-time crowd has gone to bed. Early morning or late evening works best. Besides, trying to access the Internet in the middle of the day will normally take you three times as long.

Finally, beyond solutions for the individual user, companies are developing technologies that may help alleviate Net congestion. According to the July 18, 1996, edition of *Top View,* several vendors are gearing up to produce high speed cable modems, which make use of the cable connections that already exist in a majority of homes in the United States. Unfortunately, cable companies have been reluctant to invest in these new technologies, fearing a lack of demand. So, provide some incentive. Contact your cable company and let them know that you support the development of a cable network. If enough of their subscribers express interest, cable companies

What do you think of newspapers as research sources? Which newspapers would have the most credibility for your public speaking class?

Did the speaker offer useful suggestions for helping to relieve traffic jams? Will you follow them?

How would you evaluate the source material used in this speech? How effectively did the speaker integrate the research and references into the oral speech?

What might the speaker have said if she wanted to include a final motivational appeal? Do you think that would have been effective?

will be far more inclined to get this technology out onto the market.

By giving us the ability to contact people all over the world and access information from a wide array of sources, the Internet really is becoming a way of life. But unless we start taking responsibility for our actions, we're all going to have little Ka-boom clouds appearing over our computers. And unlike the cartoon, it won't be nearly as funny when it happens to us.

SOURCE: Jocelyn So (1997). "Crash of the Internet." *Winning Orations of the Interstate Oratorical Association*, pp. 115-118, ed. Larry Schnoor. Mankato, MN: Interstate Oratorical Association. Jocelyn So, a student from the University of Pennsylvania, was coached by Todd Anten and Paul Higday.

Notice how effectively the speaker summarizes her two major points in this final paragraph. In what other ways might you have summarized this speech?

Do you think the closing sentence relating back to the opening reference to the cartoon was effective?

Sexual Assault Policy a Must
Maria Lucia R. Anton

"If you want to take her blouse off, you have to ask. If you want to touch her breast, you have to ask. If you want to move your hand down to her genitals, you have to ask. If you want to put your finger inside her, you have to ask."

What effect do the opening lines of the speech have on you? Do they gain your attention?

What I've just quoted is part of the freshman orientation at Antioch College in Ohio. In the sexual offense policy of this college, emphasis is given to three major points: (1) If you have a sexually transmitted disease, you must disclose it to a potential partner; (2) To knowingly take advantage of someone who is under the influence of alcohol, drugs and/or prescribed medication is not acceptable behavior in the Antioch community; (3) Obtaining consent is an on-going process in any sexual interaction. The request for consent must be specific to each act.

The policy is designed to create a "safe" campus environment according to Antioch President Alan Guskin. For those who engage in sex, the goal is 100 percent consensual sex. It isn't enough to ask someone if they would like to have sex, you have to get verbal consent every step of the way.

This policy has been highly publicized and you may have heard it before. The policy addresses sexual offenses such as rape, which involves penetration, and sexual assault, which does not. In both instances, the respondent coerced or forced the primary witness to engage in nonconsensual sexual conduct with the respondent or another.

Sexual assault has become a major problem on U.S. campuses today. However, in spite of increased sexual assaults on campuses, many still go without a policy to protect their students. The University of Guam, where I am a senior, is one example.

Sexual assault has become a reality on many campuses across the nation. Carleton College in Northfield, Minnesota, was sued for $800,000 in damages by four university women. The women charged that Carleton was negligent in protecting them against a known rapist. From the June 3, 1991, issue of *Time* magazine:

Amy had been on campus for just five weeks when she joined some friends to watch a video in the room of a senior. One by one the other students went away, leaving her alone with a student whose name she didn't even know. "It ended up with his hands around my

What effect does this extended quotation have? Might it have been more effective were the story told in the speaker's own words?

throat," she recalls. In a lawsuit she has filed against the college, she charges that he locked the door and raped her again and again for the next four hours. "I didn't want him to kill me, I just kept trying not to cry." Only afterwards did he tell her, almost defiantly, his name. It was on top of the "castration list" posted on women's bathroom walls around campus to warn other students about college rapists. Amy's attacker was found guilty of sexual assault but was only suspended.

Julie started dating a fellow cast member in a Carleton play. They had never slept together, she charges in a civil suit, until he came to her dorm room one night, uninvited, and raped her. She struggled to hold her life and education together, but finally could manage no longer and left school. Only later did Julie learn that her assailant was the same man who had attacked Amy.

What are the purpose and thesis of the speech? Note that these are not stated explicitly until later in the speech. Should they have been stated earlier?

Ladies and gentlemen, the court held that the college knew this man was a rapist. The administration may have been able to prevent this from happening if they had expelled the attacker, but they didn't. My campus has no reports of sexual assault; is administration waiting for someone to be assaulted before they formulate a sexual assault policy? This mistake has been made elsewhere. We don't have to prove it again.

Perhaps some statistics will help you understand the magnitude of the problem. According to *New Statesman & Society*, June 21, 1991, issue:

- A 1985 survey of sampled campuses by *Ms.* magazine and the National Institute of Mental Health found that 1 in every 4 college women were victims of sexual assault. Seventy-four percent knew their attackers. Even worse, between 30 to 40 percent of male students indicated that they might force a woman to have sex if they knew they would escape punishment.

How effectively does the speaker make the case that sexual assault on college campuses is a real problem? Assume the audience did not believe this was a real problem—would the speaker have convinced them?

- In just one year, from 1988 to 1989, reports of student rape at the University of California increased from 2 to 80.

These numbers are indeed disturbing. But more disturbing are the effects of sexual assault. A victim feeling the shock of why something this terrible was allowed to happen. Having intense fears that behind every dark corner could be an attacker ready to grab her, push her to the ground and sexually assault her. Many waking moments of anxiety and impaired concentration as she remembers the attack. Countless nights of reliving the traumatic incident in her sleep. Mood swings and depression as she tries to deal internally with the physical hurt and the emotional turmoil that this attack has caused.

Does the speaker make the effects of sexual assault real to the audience? Would both men and women understand the speaker equally? How would you have made this point to members of your class?

Many campuses are open invitations for sexual assault. The absence of a policy is a grand invitation. I have never been sexually assaulted so why do I care so much about a policy? You know why, because I could be assaulted. I won't sit and wait to be among 1 out of every 4 women on my campus to be assaulted. The first step to keep myself out of the statistics is to push for a sexual assault policy on my campus. One way to do this is through a petition to the university.

In what way does the speaker establish her credibility here?

Although the Antioch policy sounds a little far-fetched and has been the target of criticism in comedy routines such as those on "Saturday Night Live," although students feel this is unnatural, many campuses are taking heed and revising their own policies. Campuses like mine don't have a sexual policy to revisit. Does yours?

By far the most controversial policy today is that of Antioch. I'm not saying that we need one as specific as theirs, but every university has a responsibility to provide a safe environment for its students. Universities have an obligation to provide a sexual assault policy to protect their students.

The following points are fundamental to the safety of the students and need to be addressed by universities:

1. Every campus should have a sexual assault policy that is developed with input from the students, faculty, staff, and administration. The policy then needs to be publicized in the student handbook. The school newspaper should print and campus radio broadcast the policy periodically to heighten awareness.
2. Campuses must institute programs to educate students and other campus personnel. Examples of these include discussing the sexual assault policy during mandatory student orientation and conducting special workshops for faculty and other staff.
3. Outline a step-by-step written procedure to guarantee that sexual assault victims are assisted by the university. It is pertinent that they are not without support at this very critical time.

How reasonable do you find the speaker's proposals?

My vision is a campus where there is no place for any sexual assault. I want to leave my classroom at night knowing that my trip from the building to the car will not be one of fear for my personal safety.

Does the speaker effectively answer the question of the audience member who says to himself or herself, "Why can't the police handle these cases?" Is this issue relevant to the speaker's specific purpose?

You may be saying to yourself that there are laws to handle crimes like these. From *The Chronicle of Higher Education*, May 15, 1991, Jane McDonnell, a senior lecturer in women's studies at Carleton, says colleges cannot turn their backs on women. "We'd be abandoning victims if we merely sent them to the police," she says. "The wheels of justice tend to grind slowly and rape has one of the lowest conviction rates of any crime."

How would you evaluate the adequacy of research for the speech? How would you evaluate its integration into the speech?

Without a policy, most institutions lack specific penalties for sexual assault and choose to prosecute offenders under the general student-conduct code. In cases such as Carleton College, Amy's attacker was allowed back on campus after his suspension and consequently he raped again.

Although the policy may not stop the actual assault, would-be offenders would think twice before committing sexual assault if they knew they would be punished. In addition, it guarantees justice for victims of sexual assault. We need to make it loud and clear that sexual assault will not be tolerated.

Yes, universities have a big task in the struggle to prevent sexual assault.

You and I can actively assist in this task and can make a giant contribution to move it forward. On my campus students have not only voiced their concerns but we have also started a petition demanding that the university formulate a sexual assault policy.

The bottom line is, we need to prevent sexual assault on campus. The key to prevention is a sexual assault policy. If you don't have a policy, then you need to petition your administration to have one. I know I won't stop my advocacy until I see a policy on my campus.

What functions does the speaker's conclusion serve?

What would you have titled this speech if you were delivering it to your class?

SOURCE: Maria Lucia R. Anton, University of Guam (1994). She was coached by Don R. Swanson. Reprinted with permission of the Interstate Oratorical Association, *Winning Orations*, Larry G. Schnoor, editor.

Homosexuals and the Military

Sara Mitchell

Does the opening story gain your attention? Why or why not?

When I went home for the holidays last December, my cousin, Ellen, announced that she's in love and this time she thinks it's forever. Her lover's name is Linda. Twelve years after acknowledging to herself that she is a lesbian, Ellen decided to come out. She was tired of lying about who she is.

Does the speaker make the topic relevant to the audience? What do you think of as the speaker stresses the topic's relevance?

Gays and lesbians are our cousins, our brothers and sisters, sons and daughters, even mothers and fathers. A recent article in *Science* magazine estimates the homosexual population at between 4 percent and 10 percent. Odds are all of us have known numerous homosexuals, with or without being aware of it.

As you read the next few paragraphs, consider how the speaker seems to have estimated her audience's initial attitudes toward homosexuals in the military. What adaptations do you feel she may have made?

What is homosexuality? Until recently, most people believed it was a disease which could be cured or that it was willful immoral conduct. However, more and more recent studies suggest what most gays have long felt. Sexual orientation is not a choice. It is biologically determined and trying to change it would be like trying to change the color of your eyes.

This changing definition of homosexuality has resulted in a lot of controversy and has complicated the issue of whether homosexuals should be allowed to serve in the United States armed forces. This is the topic of my speech today: Homosexuals and the Military.

Is the orientation sufficiently clear?

First, I would like to examine the current policy on gays in the military. Second, I will explore the rationale (or irrationality) behind it.

The current policy is the result of a compromise between the Clinton administration, Congress and the military leadership. It attempts to distinguish homosexuality from homosexual behavior. The policy states, "Homosexual orientation is not a bar to service . . . unless manifested by homosexual conduct."

Is the distinction between homosexuality and homosexual behavior sufficiently clear?

What constitutes homosexual conduct? Sex with someone of the same gender, of course. But holding hands and same-sex dancing are also grounds for discharge. And statements interpreted by anyone as indicating homosexuality could launch an investigation. Anthony Rotundo states in a March, 1993, issue of *The Chronicle of Higher Education* that many famous 19th century men such as Abraham Lincoln and Daniel Webster had romantic friendships with other men. Alexander Hamilton, while serving under George Washington, wrote to another man:

> I wish [to] convince you that I love you. I shall only tell you that 'til you bade us adieu. I hardly knew the value you had taught my heart to set upon you.

What effect does the example of Alexander Hamilton have on you? What do the letter and the investigation it would have caused have on your thinking about homosexuals and the military?

Today, this letter, which is preserved in Hamilton's papers, would certainly cause an investigation and that investigation would probably end with Hamilton's discharge.

At what point did this speech become persuasive? What is the earliest reference that this was a persuasive rather than an informative speech?

What about same-sex dancing? Does that mean all kinds of dancing? Is that slam-dancing or just slow-dancing? My sister and I went out not too long ago, and our dates didn't feel like dancing so we danced together. I guess that was an incestuous as well as a homosexual act.

John Money, professor emeritus of medical psychology at Johns

Hopkins University, points out that during the Vietnam War draftees claimed homosexuality to avoid service. Suppose we became involved in another unpopular war? Simply holding hands with someone of the same gender could make anyone ineligible for service.

The wording of the policy is ridiculous at best and at worst could pose serious problems for the military.

Now I will discuss the rationale behind the policy on gays in the armed forces. As I said, it is the result of a compromise. Its stated intent is to allow homosexuals to serve their country—as long as they deny their homosexuality, that is. Actually, its aim is to keep gays out of the military.

In what other ways might the speaker have phrased her transition?

Those who vehemently insist that homosexuals should not be allowed to serve in the military have a multitude of reasons. For many it is a moral issue. Others fear the spread of AIDS or cite problems due to lack of privacy. Perhaps the strongest argument against allowing gays and lesbians to serve is that it will hurt morale and unit cohesion. These are all valid concerns and I will address each one separately.

Does the speaker select the most important issues for discussion?

Morality. We should respect and accommodate each other's moral beliefs as much as possible, but we should also respect each other's rights and personal freedom. Many people feel that extramarital sex of any kind is immoral, but no one is asking single heterosexual men and women to take vows of celibacy to serve their country. Behavior that does not cause harm to others should be at least tolerated if not condoned.

How effective is the argument used in this section on morality? What else might the speaker have said?

AIDS. Most people seem to be unaware of the military's AIDS testing program. Every single recruit is tested and rejected if the results are positive. Once in the military, mandatory testing continues on a regular basis. The armed forces probably have a lower AIDS rate than any other segment of the population.

Lack of Privacy. Before I address this concern, I'd like to say that I am a veteran. I served four years in the Army and three in the Army Reserves, including seven months of active duty during the Gulf War. And, by the way, I'm straight. During my four years in the regular Army, I went to the field countless times and often lived in tents with the men in my platoon. During Desert Storm, I went to the Gulf with a combat engineering company of about 150 men and three women. We lived in the desert for six months. At one point, my whole battalion, 700 men and 30 women, lived together under one roof in a warehouse. We managed to live peacefully together and, with a little consideration, give each other necessary privacy. The few problems we did have were the result of attitudes not circumstances.

What effect does this discussion have on your perception of the speaker as a credible spokesperson on this topic? Would it have been more effective if the speaker discussed this earlier in the speech?

It could be argued that this is not the same as gays and straights living together. Heterosexual men seem particularly concerned about being the object of unwanted lust and sexual advances. Forgive me for enjoying that they are frightened of being in the same position women have always been in. The simple solution is absolute zero tolerance of sexual harassment of any kind.

What effect did the discussion of the heterosexual male have on your perception of the speaker?

And finally, morale. The current Department of Defense directive states that: "The presence of [homosexuals] adversely affects the ability of military services to maintain discipline, good order and morale; to foster mutual trust and confidence among service-members." General

How effectively does the speaker argue for the proposition that homophobic attitudes, not homosexuality, are the cause of the difficulties with homosexuals in the military?

What functions did the conclusion serve? Were these functions served effectively?

Was the evidence sufficient? Were the sources cited appropriate to the topic? What other evidence would you have used?

What organizational changes would you have made in this speech?

What other titles might have been appropriate? How would you title this speech for an audience that favors including homosexuals in the military? For an audience opposed to including homosexuals in the military?

Schwarzkopf, testifying before the Senate Armed Forces Committee, said that introducing homosexuality into any military organization would destroy "the very bonding that is so important for the unit's survival in war." This stance ignores what James Burk, associate professor of sociology at Texas A&M University, points out is an "undisputed" fact. "Homosexuals have always served in the military (often with exemplary records) and will continue to do so." Homosexuality is not the problem. Homophobic attitudes are, and attitudes, unlike sexual orientation, can be changed.

I have discussed the ban on gays in the military and the reasons behind it. I have attempted to show why the ban is unacceptable and that the reasons for the ban are invalid. In conclusion, I'd like to say that all Americans who are willing to serve their country should be given that opportunity without having to deny their very nature. Let us respect each other's rights and let us respect each other.

SOURCE: This speech was given by Sara Mitchell, Tennessee Technological University. She was coached by Graham Kash. Reprinted with permission of the Interstate Oratorical Association, *Winning Orations*, 1994, Larry G. Schnoor, editor.

Student Speeches for Focused Analysis

1. Meleena Erikson, See Jane, See Jane's Dilemma [Analysis focus: **Audience Analysis and Adaptation**]
2. Amy Celeste Forman, What Exactly Are We Working For? [Analysis focus: **Research and Supporting Materials**]
3. Adam Childers, The Cost of Justice [Analysis focus: **Organization**]
4. Steven N. Blivess, Medical Miscommunication: Improving the Doctor-Patient Interaction [Analysis focus: **Style and Language**]

Analysis Focus: **Audience Analysis and Adaptation**

See Jane, See Jane's Dilemma
Meleena Erikson

Would the title grab the attention of your public speaking class members?

Would the opening paragraph secure the attention of members of your class? With what types of audiences might this introductory section not work?

Is this a common topic around your dinner table? How would the speaker's statement that this is a common table topic have different effects depending on whether or not this really is a common topic?

Jane is a seventh grader and one day during lunch she finally approached a teacher to let her know that Joey, a fellow seventh grader, was spreading rumors that Jane had to go to the hospital to get a hot dog removed from her vagina. We must question why this behavior occurs so young. We must question why according to the American Association of University Women 85 percent of girls and 76 percent of boys feel that they have been sexually harassed.

Ever since the Anita Hill, Clarence Thomas case broke into the media in the early 1990s, sexual harassment has become a common topic around dinner tables across America. The media has had a field day, laws have been made and court dates have been set. However, through all the discussion, and all the changes, one group of people have gone unnoticed. Teenagers.

In order to find a solution to the chaos surrounding this issue we must first examine why it is a problem, how did it reach this level without being stopped. Second we will look at the causes of sexual harassment in high schools, and then how to stop this atrocious crime.

Sexual harassment has grown in schools, and is plaguing America's youth. In the Eve Bruneau case in October of 1996, she was rewarded with a settlement after being called a "dog-faced bitch" and a "prostitute." *The New York Times* article October 21, 1996, called it: "One of the most disturbing and destructive cases of teenage sexual harassment." Eve had not been alone in her predicament. The same boys that called her names had also grabbed other girls' breasts and cut their hair. This behavior is unacceptable, and is running rampant through our schools. The *Times Education* October 8, 1993, brought us the results of two more studies that indicated four out of five students felt as though they had received some form of unwanted sexual attention during their education.

Now that we have seen how this problem manifests itself in our schools, and now that we have seen that sexual harassment in schools is truly no laughing matter, we can examine some of the main causes of sexual harassment in schools. The first cause that we will look at today is that of ignorance. A lot of students in grades 6–12 are unclear of what sexual harassment is exactly. There is a thin line between teasing and bullying, between flirting and sexual harassment. According to the November 1994 *Educational Leadership* an incident at a midwestern high school led several boys and girls to call another girl a whore, slut and bitch. They then spread a rumor that she had AIDS. The teacher on duty dismissed the behavior as ignorance on the subject matter and did not consider it to be sexual harassment. But as attorney Verna Williams, who is with the National Woman's Law Center put it: "Sometimes it's not just a kiss on the cheek. Sometimes it's very, very serious, and very, very damaging."

Now that we have seen how ignorance affects teenage sexual harassment we will look into the second cause which is that of teenage cruelty. Being a teenager is never an easy thing. The emotional and physical changes that come with puberty often add to the stress of pre-teens and teenagers causing them to tease one another. Each of us have experienced a time when we have either picked on or been picked on. But where does that thin line get drawn? Eve Bruneau's attorney Books Burdette, said of her case: "There's a difference between flirting and hurting. What happened in our case was systematic. It was a lot more than childhood horseplay." Eve Bruneau's case is a classic one. Was the verbal harassment that she dealt with day in and day out just simply kids being cruel? Were the boys rubbing their hands up and down her back simple flirting? Title IX of the education Amendments of 1972 says it is sexual harassment. The amendment states: "Requiring that schools take adequate steps to stop unwelcome verbal or physical conduct of a sexual nature, when it becomes severe, persistent or pervasive." In Eve's case, it was all these. The final cause that we will look at today is that of letting this crime go. From 1991–93, Jessica and Jacquelyn Fowler were groped and harassed by obscene taunts and gestures by their fellow high school students on their 45 minute bus ride to school. Although the girls did tell their parents, and their parents called the school, nothing was done. The school dismissed the problem. When taken to court, 245 instances in which this harassment took place were discovered. This is why we cannot, as students, parents and teachers, let this crime go. Katherine Nurdock, the attorney of the Oregon Department of

Is your class concerned with sexual harassment directed at teenagers? If not, what might the speaker have done to make them concerned?

Is this a topic that different cultures would view differently and have different attitudes about?

Do you think that gay men and lesbians, on the one hand, and heterosexual men and women, on the other, would respond differently to this speech? How would you have adapted the speech if it were to be delivered to an all gay and lesbian audience? To an all heterosexual audience?

How do you think teenagers would respond to this speech? People in their 30's and 40's? People in their 70's and 80's?

Does the speaker relate this topic to both men and women? Does the title? Do the examples? How might you change this speech if it were to be delivered to an all-male audience? An all-female audience?

Would blue-collar and white-collar listeners respond to this speech differently? How would you adapt the speech to relate it more closely to the interests and needs of blue-collar listeners? To white-collar listeners?

Would the language used in the speech be appropriate to an audience of your public speaking class? Can you identify language choices you would have made differently?

If this speech was to be twice as long as it is now and was to be delivered to a cross section of students from your college, which sections would you suggest the speaker elaborate upon? Can you offer specific adaptation suggestions?

Visualizing your public speaking class as the audience:

- *How willing would they be to listen to this speech and to openly think about the speaker's thesis?*
- *How favorable would they be to the speaker's thesis?*
- *How actively involved would the audience be?*
- *How knowledgeable would the audience be?*

Education said: "Educators need to make schools a place where respectful behavior among students is an expected norm." Another example of a case that went unnoticed because a student kept quiet was the case of young Jane of whom I spoke of earlier. It took her several weeks to tell a teacher, and during this time the harassment continued. By ignoring the hurtful comments Jane simply allowed herself to be victimized over and over again.

Now that we have seen some of the major causes of sexual harassment we can look at some things that we can all do, as parents, teachers and students, to stop sexual harassment in our schools. There are two ways to prevent these causes from reoccurring. The first is education and the second is immediate action.

To solve the problem of ignorance among students and faculty, we must educate them about what sexual harassment is and how harmful it can be. Since many students in grades 6–12 don't know what sexual harassment is, we should tell them. When the concept of sexual harassment came up in one eighth grade classroom, the teacher Nan Higginson took matters into her own hands. With the help of the school social worker and psychologist, they put together a statement defining sexual harassment. Their definition is as follows: "Sexual harassment is not an issue of sex, but of power. Sexual harassment is coerced, unethical and unwanted intimacy. The Supreme Court ruled that remarks, gestures and even graffiti can be considered forms of sexual harassment." Mrs. Higginson and her crew cleared up misconceptions, did role playing and finally asked the students to design a policy for the school. The class eventually decided that education could prevent most problems. I will say again, education is the key way to solve most problems. It is time that more teachers take action as Mrs. Higginson did. It is time we follow in the steps of Nan Higginson. By developing school policies on sexual harassment not only are you making it known that it is a crime, but you are also defining it for teachers and students as well as making it clear that it will not be tolerated.

The second solution that we need to look at is that of immediate action. As educators, teachers must encourage students to bring sexual harassment complaints when they begin. This way, sexual harassment would be nipped in the bud. Teachers and guidance counselors need to be prepared to take sexual harassment complaints seriously and take action against the perpetrator. The victims need to tell the perpetrator to stop immediately and let them know that they are not going to take that kind of abuse. It is vital to set limits. People also need to report sexual harassment if they see it happening. By not saying anything, the spectator is just as guilty as the perpetrator. Merrick Rossein, a University of New York Law professor, said in relation to the Eve Bruneau case: "The fact that it hurt the girls a lot and silenced them and prevented them from participating in academic programs wasn't recognized by the school." If immediate action is taken then the fear of sexual harassment will diminish.

So today, we have looked at why sexual harassment has become such a large problem in our schools, the causes of this problem and some ways it can be solved.

In the case of Jane and Joey, it seemed that Joey had not been alone in harassing Jane. The parents of the boys were notified and a letter of apology was sent to Jane. In return, Jane told them how upset she was to have those things said about her. Although it helped to talk about it, there are scars that will take much longer to heal.

SOURCE: Meleena Erikson (1997). "See Jane, See Jane's Dilemma," *Winning Orations of the Interstate Oratorical Association*, pp. 61-64, ed. Larry Schnoor. Mankato, MN: Interstate Oratorical Association. Meleena Erikson , a student from Emerson College, was coached by Matthew Sobnosky.

Analysis focus: **Research and Supporting Materials**

What Exactly Are We Working For?

Amy Celeste Forman

One morning in the fall of 1994, Harvard president Neil Rudenstine over-slept. While we're all prone to occasionally hitting the snooze too many times, for Rudenstine, who was in the middle of planning a $1 million a day fund-raising campaign, this was a cause for alarm. He had a habit of making notes late into the night, to the football coach, to *Harvard Crimson* editors, to residence hall staff. His sleep habits were scrambled, his daily life was plagued with unfinished tasks. In short, Neil Rudenstine was suffering from the same problem most Americans are, but fail to recognize. He was facing the problem of working too hard, and taking too little time for himself. *The Annals of Internal Medicine* reports that 24 percent of people surveyed complained of fatigue that lasts longer than two weeks. As a society, we're all feeling the effects of the Information Age, where we're bombarded by work to be done, information to digest, and the fear of falling behind. As a nation, we are exhausted to the breaking point.

How would you describe the opening example? Did it get you involved in the topic and in the thesis of the speech?

Because of the nature of this problem, it is one that is seldom ad-dressed. People who put in 60 or 70 hours a week at their jobs are looked at as a real asset. Students who study constantly are viewed as models. It's only when we consider the results that this "all work and no play" attitude have on us emotionally, physically, and in our relationships with friends and family that the problem emerges. Today, we will exam-ine exactly what the problem is, the effects it has on us, and how we can bring balance and control back into our lives.

Before I even began writing this speech, I described the topic to my friends. In doing so, each one of them made remarks such as "Sounds like the story of my life" or "I can sure relate to that." According to *Newsweek*, March 6, 1995, fatigue is now among the top five reasons people call their doctor. As a nation of achievers—baby boomers still trying to get ahead and college students fighting to not live up to the Generation X slack-er stereotype—we are in a constant juggling act, where our juggling pins are things as precious as our families, friends, jobs, education, and activi-ties. The essence of the problem is that somehow we have received the message that we should be able to take on more and more and do it per-fectly. The simple fact is that we cannot without heavy cost to ourselves.

How would you describe the types of sources the speaker uses? Are these appropriate given her topic and, let's assume, your public speaking class as the audience?

The problem of exhaustion is not a new one, in fact it is as old as sleep. George Washington used to disappear for months because of nerves. But in the past several years, it has been brought into the lime-light. According to *Sports Illustrated*, January 30, 1995, sports figures

Does the speaker effectively establish the credibility of the sources used?

Did the speaker effectively integrate the source material into the text of the speech?

Can you identify examples of narration?

Can you identify with the type of person the speaker is talking about? What did the speaker say that enables you to feel that this applies to you?

such as Don Nelson, former coach of the Golden State Warriors, are prime examples of dedication gone too far, to the point of exhaustion. During the O.J. trial, attorneys William Hodgman and F. Lee Bailey were hospitalized because of fatigue and stress. Due to these famous cases, the problem has received new attention. But mental and physical exhaustion continue to plague everyday people in everyday jobs. Dr. Rupert C. Burtan, a specialist in occupational medicine, says, "Many workers have too much dumped on their desks and not enough time in which to get it all done." This very thing makes secretaries' jobs tough, as well as teachers or journalists. But many experts say the hardest job of all is that of the working mom. *Parents Magazine,* July 1996 gives an example of Barbara, who spent the first seven months of her daughter's life in a fog. Her daughter, Shelby had jaundice and would sleep for only two hours at a time. One afternoon, when Shelby was seven months old, Barbara was gripped by chest pains and her husband rushed her to the ER. The doctors couldn't find anything wrong, and kept Barbara overnight to await tests in the morning. That night Barbara got over eight hours of sleep and woke feeling normal for the first time in months. The doctor's diagnosis was complete physical exhaustion.

Overextending ourselves affects us in more ways besides leaving us physically exhausted. The mental exhaustion or numbness that we also face has a wide range of negative effects on us. In her book, *Working Ourselves to Death,* Diane Fassel describes Elizabeth, a woman whose busy schedule and obsession with order has made her a chronic list maker. If something does not appear on this list, it will not get done, no matter how important it is. And if something trivial is on the list, Elizabeth will do it, no matter how much time she wastes. She won't even spend time with her children unless she writes "2 PM to 4 PM—spend time with the kids" on the list. This behavior is characteristic of burnout. According to the *Journal of Applied Psychology,* April 1996, burnout consists of three dimensions: emotional exhaustion, depersonalization, and diminished personal accomplishment. We start out by working ourselves into a state of emotional exhaustion, then this causes us to distance ourselves from loved ones, until finally we are accomplishing less than we were to begin with. Diane Fassel constructed a scale for measuring work addiction, which she described as a disease. The early stage consists of difficulty sleeping, periods of comatose staring into space, and blackouts at work or on the road. The late stage can bring a stroke or serious illness, emotional deadness, and moral and spiritual bankruptcy. The third stage can end in death.

Even if we are well aware that we are on the road to complete mental exhaustion and know how it will affect us, what can we do? Few of us can just quit a job and we hate to give up our commitments. As Dr. Dean Ornish of the Preventative Medicine Research Institute of California has written, "We can't always change other people. We can't always change jobs or families. But we can change our perceptions." We have to learn to view down time as important as work time. We feel so tied to work today because technology keeps us literally in constant connection with work. *Newsweek,* March 6, 1995, says that five million cell phones were sold last year and that almost 25 million beepers are in use; more than 50 percent of users are between 18 and 29 years old. While abstinence from working is rarely an option, we can change the job or job field we are currently in. And we can limit the intrusions work makes in our lives by limiting the work we do. Turning off the beeper or fax machine when we sit down to dinner gives us some peaceful, reflective time away from work. We can discuss with our bosses ways to change our job duties so that we have better job performance. Many employers now offer a mental health day, which is similar to a sick day in that you have a certain number of days you can take off when you're feeling over-stressed and need to take some time off yourself.

Did the speaker effectively establish the authority of the people she quoted? Were you as a reader willing to accept their authority on the basis of what the speaker said?

As students and competitors in forensics, we must also find a solution to the exhaustion and stress that come from working to be our best. We have to realize that it's the quality that matters, not the quantity. So what if you're taking seven events to a tournament next weekend? If you've been losing sleep just to throw together a paper you barely understand or a speech you don't care about, what have you accomplished? The exhaustion is not worth it if we have seven events we can't be proud of.

And instead of working ourselves to death in our private lives, we can enlist help there, too. If we have children we should realize that we can't do it all ourselves and taking time off is just as important as the time spent with them.

Would you have included more statistics here and perhaps throughout the speech? If so, what purpose would you want the statistics to serve?

But most importantly, we have to know ourselves, know what we're capable of. For some, chairing two committees is no problem, for others even being involved in one is difficult enough. We need to learn our limits and work within them. And we must appreciate the importance of keeping ourselves healthy. Researchers led by University of Michigan sociologist James House concluded that overworking and isolating ourselves is statistically just as dangerous as smoking, high blood pressure, or lack of exercise.

What types of presentation aids might have been of value in this speech? What would you include in a word chart designed to summarize the major parts of the speech?

Today, we have examined the problem of all work and no play. We have seen the effects, physically and mentally, that it can produce. And most importantly, we have examined some solutions to the problem. It is important for our physical and mental health that we each take stock of the effects work is having on us and obtain a balance between work and play. After all, what are we working for if we're too busy or exhausted to enjoy the results?

SOURCE: Amy Celeste Forman (1997), a student from Morehead State University, "What Exactly Are We Working For?" *Winning Orations of the Interstate Oratorical Association,* pp. 50-52, ed. Larry Schnoor. Mankato, MN: Interstate Oratorical Association. Amy Celeste Forman was coached by Tony Glover and Lisa Shemwell.

Analysis focus: **Organization**

The Cost of Justice

Adam Childers

You know, there are just some things in life that you have to fight for—like your right to crunchy style peanut butter. And that is why, when inmate Kenneth Parker, of Nevada State Prison, was given creamy instead of crunchy peanut butter by his prison canteen two years ago, he filed a civil rights lawsuit. In this lawsuit, he demanded $5,500 dollars for the mental

Does the speaker effectively capture your attention early in the introduction? How does he do this?

Does the speaker establish a speaker-audience-topic connection? Does the speaker effectively explain his interest and concern for this topic and how it is related to the audience?

Does the speaker effectively orient the audience? Do you have a very clear idea of how the speech will be developed? What are the speaker's three major propositions? How might these be stated in a preparation outline?

Did the speaker commit any of the faults common in introductions, for example, apologizing or relying on gimmicks?

Do you agree with the speaker's decision to state his thesis early in the speech? With what type of audience do you think it might have been wiser to delay the statement of the thesis until the evidence and argument had been presented?

How does the speaker make the transition to the first major proposition?

and emotional pain that he suffered, without the PB of his choice. Two years later, after countless hours spent by the Attorney General's office, and over $10,000 spent in taxpayer's money, this case was dismissed. As nutty as this story may sound, sadly, it is fast becoming the norm. That is because according to *Trial* magazine of May 1995, the number of inmate civil lawsuits nationwide, has risen to 35,000 per year—which is roughly thirty percent of all civil lawsuits filed in the United States annually. This trend should alarm all of us, for two reasons. First, millions of dollars of our tax money are being spent needlessly on these lawsuits every year. But, even more importantly, these lawsuits are putting a financial strain on an already overburdened penal system—helping to create a situation in which our prisoners are being released early.

Today we will examine this growing problem of frivolous inmate civil lawsuits. By first, uncovering their origins; secondly, understanding the problems associated with them; we will, finally, discover a few viable solutions to this current crisis.

Initially, we must understand where these lawsuits are coming from. To do so, we must take a look at Section 1983, Title 42, of the United States Code. The March 1995 edition of *Federal Probation,* reports that this statute was established shortly after the Civil War, and it grants the right to citizens to sue local and state government officials when policies and practices fall below Constitutional standards. During the 1960s, the Supreme Court extended the power of this act, to give the right to prisoners to challenge their confinement—on the grounds that it violated their Constitutional rights. Over the years, these cases have proven to be instrumental in forcing improvement in prison medical care, legal access, and inmate treatment. The problem though, as the March 21, 1995, *New York Times* can attest, is that along with these landmark cases have come a bounty of frivolous and costly complaints. New York State Attorney General Oliver Koppel, stated in a January 1996 press release, that these cases consume over twenty percent of his department's resources—and he concluded by saying, "there has to be a way for prisoners to complain, but this it not it." In Mr. Koppel's home state of New York, there are 28,000 inmate lawsuits backlogged, waiting to be heard. As astounding as their figure is, it is eclipsed by the states of California, Texas, Missouri, and Florida. We can only expect these numbers to rise as these lawsuits are so easy to file. Most prisoners can cite poverty and avoid the $120 dollar filing fee. In addition, prisons are required to provide inmates with legal access and even postage to mail off their complaints. And this does not even take into account what the August 7, 1995, *National Law Journal* calls "loneliness lawsuits." This is the trend of prisoners who have nothing else better to do, filing lawsuits—to while away their time. Case in point, inmate Jerry Young of Connecticut who has congested our federal court system with a record 98 civil lawsuits in the past twelve years alone.

With an understanding of the origins, and the severity of inmate civil litigation in hand, we can now turn, and understand how these lawsuits are adversely affecting our prison population and society at large.

Time magazine, of February 7, 1995, points out that our prison population has doubled in recent decades—reaching 925,000 prisoners in 1995. These prisoners do not come cheaply either. The October 17, 1995, edition of *Fortune* notes that each and every one of these prison-

ers costs an estimated $36,500 to house per year. With conditions such
as these, obviously every dime counts. Which makes it even more unfor-
tunate, that as this same article pointed out, last year alone over
$181,000,000 was spent on inmate civil lawsuits.

But, even more worrisome than this, is the detrimental effects that these
lawsuits are having on the societal level. The January 1995 *ABA Journal*
points out that the average American prisoner spends only forty-one percent of his appointed time in jail, and that since 1991, 43,000 convicts
have been rearrested after an early release that was due to financial troubles. Financial troubles, that according to the August 30, 1995,
Washington Post, are due in large part to these frivolous inmate lawsuits.
Money wasted on these suits cannot solve our prison's problems outright,
but they can help shore up a penal system that has run amok. Whether it
be money spent on: Roy Clenidnen's one million dollar suit for the right to
ice cream in his New York prison, or Reginald Troy's battle for veal and
oysters in his Texas prison, or even Keith Polloidian's pending suit in the
state of Florida, over the razor wire that encircles his prison—which he
insists could severely lacerate him—if he chose to escape. All of this money is sorely needed to ensure that our prisoners are rehabilitated, and
that law-abiding citizens are kept safe.

The problems associated with inmate civil lawsuits are quite evident, but,
fortunately, so too are the solutions. There are steps that we may take to alleviate this problem on a state, federal, and finally, an individual level.

First, state prisons deal with the bulk of inmate lawsuits (97% to be
precise). The May 2, 1995, *Fortune* notes that the best step for these institutions is to require a one to five dollar filing fee of the prisoner's
wages. The Federal District of New York recently began this practice,
and has enjoyed a thirty-five percent decrease in cases filed.

The federal government can help lend a hand as well, with the Civil
Rights of Institutionalized Persons Act, also known as CRIPA. CRIPA enables
the United States Attorney General and the federal courts to certify state administrative grievance mechanisms—such as a screening process that
would hear all cases, checking them for validity before they advance to the
trial stage. CRIPA authorizes state and federal courts to mandate the exhaustion of these sort of grievance mechanisms before inmate cases reach
the court docket. In a January 1995 United States Department of Justice report entitled, "Challenging the Conditions of our Prisons and Jails," researchers concluded that the leadership of the Districts of the United States
Courts of Appeals must encourage state correctional agencies to submit
new grievance mechanisms to help ensure that CRIPA is implemented.

That means that the only question left now is, What can we do to help?
And, the answer is—get involved. In a telephone interview, conducted on
January 23, 1996, Assistant Attorney General of Florida, Joe Bizarro, explained to me that it is only with the efforts of citizens' group s that are dedicated to tort reform that we can expect any sort of significant change.
Such a group is CALA—Citizens Against Lawsuit Abuse. Based out of
Houston, Texas, this is a nationwide grass-roots organization that is resolved to fight for legal reform. One of their major goals is curbing frivolous
inmate lawsuits. The means that they use to achieve this end, sometimes,
can be as simple as a bumper sticker sent out to all those who contact their
organization. But, they can also be as complex as the many lobby groups

What organizational pattern is the speaker following? Might other organizational patterns work as well?

What additional transitions can you locate in this speech? Are they effective?

Does the speaker use any internal summaries?

How effectively does the speaker summarize his major points?

Does the speaker motivate his audience to do something about the problem?

they have formed around the nation, that are currently urging both state legislatures as well as the federal government, to change existing laws that allow these frivolous inmate lawsuits to occur. In order that you may be able to contact this organization, at the conclusion of this speech, I will distribute a card with the address and phone number of CALA—which will enable all of you to make a choice, a choice to get involved.

How does the speaker close the speech? Is this effective?

Today, we have examined the growing problem of frivolous inmate civil lawsuits by examining their origins and implications, and by, finally, highlighting some concrete solutions to their existence.

Does the speaker commit any of the faults common to the conclusion, for example, introducing new material or diluting the position taken in the speech?

The story of Kenneth Parker, and his fetish for crunchy style peanut butter is a funny one. But, for every story like his, there is another like the one documented in the February 17, 1995, *New York Times*. This story tells of a fifteen-year-old Ohio girl who was caught running away from home, and sent to jail for the night. There, she was raped by a prison guard. She subsequently filed a civil rights lawsuit against the prison, but, her case was backlogged by numerous, frivolous inmate lawsuits. By the time that her case was heard—over one year later—over one hundred more children had spent time in that same jail cell. It lies in our hands to ensure that travesties of justice like this one do not take place in the future. Not only for the safety of our prisoners, but, for our own as well.

Can you create a brief key word delivery outline for this speech?

SOURCE: Adam Childers (1996). "The Cost of Justice," *Winning Orations of the Interstate Oratorical Association*, pp. 78–80, ed. Larry Schnoor. Mankato, MN: Interstate Oratorical Association. Adam Childers, a student from the University of Oklahoma, was coached by Jerry Miller.

Analysis focus: **Style and Language**

Medical Miscommunication: Improving the Doctor-Patient Interaction

Steven N. Blivess

How direct do you find the speaker's introduction? Can you identify specific examples of direct and indirect language?

A week after graduation, Harvard medical school student Jody Heymann woke up in a hospital emergency room. The doctors working on her didn't tell her where she was, how she'd gotten there, or what was wrong with her. Further, throughout her 18-month stay, no one explained to her why a 90-minute operation lasted 10 hours. And still later, because of her medication, she began vomiting a brilliant green fluid, the resident refused her request to change her medication. This lack of communication between Heymann and her physicians is a problem that continually plagues today's medical industry. And while communication may be at the heart of the practice of medicine, according to the May 1, 1995, *Hartford Courant*, miscommunication can cause a psychological barrier that will prevent people from getting the medical care they need. For us to see how both doctors and patients are responsible for miscommunications, we will first examine common communication problems that afflict physicians. Next, we will look at how the patients' ineffective communication skills contribute to the problem. And finally, we will uncover solutions to help ourselves become better and more effective participants in our medical treatment.

Our first step towards rebuilding the bridge of doctor-patient communication begins with the physician. While doctors face a myriad of communication problems, we will focus on three of the more pressing issues: the power relationship, the doctor's rhetorical insensitivity, and communicating across a gender gap. The first major problem the doctor faces arises from their view of the so-called "power relationship." Because many doctors continue to harbor the archaic belief that the patient is subservient to them, according to the 1995 edition of the *Journal of Social Science & Medicine*, the questions that they ask, "are mostly closed-ended: a yes or no answer is all that is expected." The effect of this often condescending attitude is that vital information can be lost. Take the case of Michael James, as chronicled in the February 26, 1995, *Pittsburgh Post Gazette.* Having entered the hospital with complaints of a debilitating headache, we must wonder why the doctors on duty never asked about the head injury he had suffered during a mugging the previous year. Perhaps a simple inquiry into his background could have prevented a barrage of tests he would later receive.

The second major problem facing today's medical practitioner, according to Dr. Gary Kreps, the foremost expert on health communication, lies in their rhetorical insensitivity. In a telephone interview on March 13, 1996, Dr. Kreps stated that doctors often offer explanations that are saturated with technical jargon that create a language barrier. Further, Dr. Dewitt Baldwin of the American Medial Association explained in a telephone interview that also took place on March 13, 1996, that by comparing patient satisfaction to the occurrence of malpractice cases he discovered that physicians who spend little time explaining technical language to their patients see an increased instance of dissatisfaction and malpractice suits. The March 1, 1995, *Journal of the American Medical Association* collaborates with this assessment when it reports that "the result of language barriers is often poor compliance, inappropriate follow-up, and patient dissatisfaction."

A final problem facing physicians is related to gender differences. According to the 1995 edition of the *Journal of Woman and Health,* "medical discourse tends to marginalize" the information brought by women to the physicians, labeling it as trivial, troublesome, and irrelevant to diagnosis. This blatant disregard for what women are saying eliminates the opportunity for women to get comprehensive examinations or effective treatments. The April 11, 1995, *New York Times* reports that District Attorney Michael McCann has considered filing charges against a New York doctor for misdiagnosing cervical cancer. Because the doctor failed to take the complaints of his patient seriously, her pap smear was misdiagnosed and the patient, ultimately, died.

While doctors may take the majority of the blame for miscommunication, we as patients are also at fault for the widening communication gap between ourselves and our doctors. The first problem we face as patients is that we acquiesce as passive consumers. We consciously don't take an active role as a participant in the medical give and take process. One factor, according to the April 14, 1995, *St. Louis Post-Dispatch*, is the stress of the situation. The anxiety of being confronted with an unfamiliar illness leads to details being lost. For an example, let's look, once again, at the Michael James case. Earlier, we bashed the doctors for not asking about his previous medical history. However, we must also note that James

How would you describe the language in terms of abstraction? Can you identify an example from the first paragraph of a high and a low level abstraction? Does this help gain and focus your attention on the topic?

Do you get the feeling that both you and the speaker share similar connotative meanings for such terms of power relationship, rhetorical insensitivity, and gender gap?

Can you identify any instances of polarization, fact-inference confusion, allness, static evaluation, or indiscrimination?

How would you describe the speaker's style? Is it basically an oral style? Does it contain elements of written style?

Do you find the language clear? For example, is the language economical? Are specific rather than general terms used? Are guide phrases provided?

failed to volunteer his history to help doctors diagnose his symptoms.

The second problem facing patients is that we haven't adequately prepared ourselves for the doctor-patient interaction. In many cases, we simply don't know the correct medical terminology. Take as a metaphor the auto repair industry. We have all at some point said that our car is making a pinging noise, yet we are unable to articulate further as to the specifics of the problem. The same holds true in the medical repair industry. We tell doctors our stomach is making gurgling sounds without clarity and expect instant diagnosis. Unfortunately, doctors can't check under the hood, or put us up on the rack. Both our passive nature and inadequate preparation can force doctors to make assumptions that lead down the wrong diagnostic path, or force the doctor to assume an over-authoritative role which just perpetuates the problematic cycle.

How vivid do you find the language? Are the verbs active and strong? Does the speaker use figures of speech and imagery? Is this level of vividness appropriate to the topic and the audience?

Having diagnosed the problems, it's time to prescribe some solutions for more effective doctor-patient communication. There are several steps we as patients can take. First, collaborate in the search for information. According to the 1995 article *Patients as Partners* by Carnegie Mellon University researcher Amanda Young, collaboration offers an additional strategy for care giving. By structuring the dialogue between the patient and the doctor towards working together, a partnership is formed in interpreting symptoms, recognizing their effects and planning an effective treatment plan. In addition, a collaborative effort includes being willing to ask for written material to accompany oral instruction. According to a personal correspondence with Lorraine Jackson, a professor at the California Polytechnical Institute, that took place on March 11, 1996, written material can be kept, reread and referred to thus increasing the probability that information will be followed and treatment will be completed.

Does the speaker speak on the appropriate level of formality given the topic and, let's assume, your public speaking class as the audience?

Second, select a doctor with whom you are comfortable. Although in the age of HMOs it may be hard—shop around. In his book *Communicating With Your Doctor*, Dr. Gary Kreps, the previously mentioned health communication expert, says that finding a doctor that suits your personality goes a long way towards good communication. One characteristic Dr. Kreps advises us to look for is what kind of approach does the doctor take towards medicine. Dr. Dewitt Baldwin also stated in the previously mentioned interview that a humanistic approach to medicine provides for increased interaction between the patient and the doctor. A humanistic approach means that the physician uses eye contact to establish trust, listens without interrupting to avoid prejudging, and encourages the patient to open up. By looking for doctors who employ these few simple techniques, we vastly improve our ability to communicate with our physicians.

Do you find the language appropriately personal?

Do you find the language appropriately forceful and powerful? Do you think a more forceful style would have been more effective? Might a less forceful style have been more effective?

Finally, we need to be able to relate our symptoms, which means knowing the correct medical terminology. To this end the March 1995 *American Health* reports that there are medical books that have been designed with the lay person in mind. One example would be the American Medical Association's *Home Medical Encyclopedia*. While purchasing one of these books is recommended, it should never be used to replace a visit to our doctor, but instead be used as a tool to supplement the visit. Ultimately, what each of these solutions boils down to is effective communication only becomes possible when both the doctor and the patient, can and do, work together to find a cure for the patient's ailment.

How would you describe the sentence structure used in the speech?

Medical care isn't just a matter of diagnosis and prescription; it's also a matter of social relations finely adjusted by language. Without the ability to communicate, we as social animals would find ourselves lost in the barren wasteland that is silence. Yet, we, as patients, continue to hinder our ability to communicate with our doctors, and vice versa. Having looked at the problems from both perspectives, we have determined that miscommunications between doctors and patients, is, in fact, a significant problem in today's society. Fortunately, we have also learned some steps we can take as medical consumers to begin to re-establish the lines of communication between ourselves and our physicians. So as we move into the future secure in our ability to communicate, we can be sure that if we wake to find ourselves in the emergency room someday, we will be able to find out where we are, how we got there, and what was wrong with us.

Will you remember this speech? Will you remember the speaker's major propositions? What did the speaker do to make his speech easy to remember?

SOURCE: Steven N. Blivess (1996), "Medical Miscommunication: Improving the Doctor-Patient Interaction," *Winning Orations of the Interstate Oratorical Association*, pp. 87–89, ed. Larry Schnoor. Mankato, MN: Interstate Oratorical Association. Steven N. Blivess, a student from Pennsylvania State University, was coached by Enrico Pucci.

Professional Speeches for General Analysis

1. Judith Humphrey, Executive Eloquence
2. Nelson Mandela, Nobel Prize Acceptance Speech
3. Nancy W. Dickey, A Window of Opportunity: Meeting the Challenges of Medicine's Agenda
4. Carolyn Woo, Living Up to Your Fullest Potential
5. Martin Scorsese, Acceptance Speech for the John Huston Award for Artists Rights
6. James C. McCroskey, Why We Communicate the Ways We Do: A Communibiological Perspective

Here is a collection of six contemporary speeches given by people who are superior public speakers. The speeches represent a variety of types and styles. They also deal with widely different topics. Each of these topics, however, should prove of considerable interest to you, and you're likely to learn a great deal from the content of each speech.

Our primary concern here, however, is to learn the principles of public speaking through the use of models such as these. So, after you read a speech, reflect on its attention to the principles of public speaking that were introduced in Unit 2 and followed throughout the text (omitting rehearsal and delivery since these can't really be discussed from reading the written text):

1. Was the topic an appropriate one given the speaker and the audience to be addressed? Was it sufficiently limited in focus?
2. Did the speaker adapt the speech to his or her specific audience? Can you identify parts of the speech that address the immediate audience specifically?
3. Did you feel the topic and the speech generally were well researched? Did you feel that the speaker had a good command of the topic? On what basis did you get this impression?

4. What was the thesis of the speech? What were the speech's major propositions? Did each of the propositions support the thesis?
5. Did the speaker effectively support each of the major propositions?
6. Were the speech materials effectively organized? Was the pattern of organization apparent to you as you read the speech?
7. Was effective style and language used throughout the speech? Was the style clear, vivid, appropriate, personal, and forceful?
8. Did the introduction serve to gain attention, establish a connection among the speaker, audience, and topic, and orient the audience as to what was to follow? Did the conclusion summarize, motivate, and close the speech?

Executive Eloquence

Judith Humphrey

Every day in corporate board rooms this scene is repeated over and over again. An executive walks to the front of the room, turns on the overhead projector, and begins a narration that bores both speaker and audience.

The same scene is repeated in external conferences, although perhaps with more panache. Speakers with impressive titles walk to the podium on a much larger stage, the lights flash, visuals come to life on the big screen, and the speaker begins a narration that bores both speaker and audience.

As the head of a firm that provides speech coaching to executives, I have worked with hundreds of business leaders who know that something is not right with this scene. In a situation that should be one of their best leadership opportunities, they feel uneasy and frustrated by their lack of impact.

Take the situation I observed, when asked to observe a CEO at the podium. It was felt I could help this newly-appointed Chief Executive Officer become a stronger leader. It seemed like an excellent opportunity to assess the new leader's strengths, and possibly work with him.

The CEO droned on for almost an hour. Although he was known as a bright individual, he came across as dull and without clarity of thought. In a dutiful fashion, he worked his way through mounds of material. No aspect of his company's technology offering was left untouched. No corporate stone was left unturned. No visual left out. The audience was restless and unmistakably disappointed. Eventually people began to leave, even while the executive was still talking.

Sadly, this new CEO had missed out on a wonderful leadership opportunity. He lost out on a chance to inspire his audience—including many potential customers—with management's vision of where his company was going.

What goes wrong? Why do executives often speak too long, say too little, and lose their audience? I've found that it's not lack of motivation. Nor is it lack of ability. The truth is that great speaking is an art that must be developed throughout learning and practice.

Indeed, today executives need to be more inspirational than ever. They must deliver ideas and beliefs that excite the minds and hearts of their audiences. Leadership is not conferred by title. It is achieved every time an executive moves an audience. In today's competitive world, customers, employees, management, boards and shareholders must be turned into believers.

Today I'd like to discuss the art of eloquence. I'll draw upon observations of public speakers and the knowledge that we in The Humphrey Group have gained from working with many leaders over the past decade.

My message is this: executives who want to motivate audiences can do so by following seven steps.

Step 1: Begin with commitment.

A speech must begin with a serious commitment on the part of the executive. No speech or presentation will be successful unless the speaker has a deep desire to reach a particular audience. This deep involvement should be demonstrated in several ways.

Accept speaking engagements only when you think you can make a difference. You have to feel a sense of purpose, of urgency, a sense of your own leadership. What's your motive?

If possible, write the speech or presentation yourself. Many great speakers—Abraham Lincoln, Winston Churchill, and Martin Luther King, Jr., for example—wrote their own speeches.

Or work closely with a speechwriter. John F. Kennedy worked very closely with Theodore Sorensen, his speechwriter, and they were a creative, forceful team. In guiding your speechwriter, make sure the speech captures your thinking. After all, you're going to have to bring it to life at the podium.

I'm impressed by the willingness of many top executives to prepare their own remarks. And I'm equally impressed by the results. Many of the CEOs and senior executives we coach spend valuable hours writing their own speeches. When I set up The Humphrey Group, one senior banking executive asked if we'd design a speech writing course for him. That way he'd be able to prepare his own remarks or guide a speechwriter. This course has become a mainstay in our executive program.

In fact, a CEO told me that he could not in good conscience pay one cent to have his annual meeting speech written for him. He preferred to invest in our Executive Speechwriting Program which would show him how to write that year's talk, as well as the ones that would follow. The result was a great, deeply felt speech.

Step 2: Know your audience.

The second step in developing an inspirational leadership style is having a strong sense of your audience.

The best speakers tailor their remarks for the individuals they will address. They mentally switch places with their listeners, and ask themselves, "What do I want to hear from this speaker?"

Good speakers find out as much as they can about their audience. If you are delivering an internal speech, conduct interviews to test your ideas. Those exchanges might uncover objections to your ideas. You'll also be alerted to questions that many of your listeners might have.

An appreciation of the outlook of the audience should lead you to adopt the right one. Don't preach to or bully your listeners. Rather your talk should inspire and motivate them. But it should do so because it respects the feelings, experiences, and intellect of the audience. An executive who says: "I give orders . . . other listen and do what I say," will not find many receptive ears in the audience.

I'm amazed at how often speakers concentrate so fully on their own "agenda" that they forget the audience's perspective. A company that has been going through rough times, for example, needs a positive approach from their leader. Her sense of urgency should be translated into a positive, motivational message, not a critical one that could demoralize the troops.

Step 3: Develop a clear message.

The third step in becoming an inspirational leader is developing a strong, clearly-defined message. Corporate executives are asked to speak because of their vision. Knowing their subject is not enough. They must have something clear and convincing to say about it. When Lou Gerstner joined IBM he developed a forceful vision: IBM must lead big companies into the brave new networked world. This message has been articulated by management at all levels, and it has given IBM its direction.

Too many corporate speakers ramble on, lacking coherence or direction because their address is without a central argument. As a result, they come across as having nothing—or, paradoxically, too many things—to say. Such speeches are literally pointless, as is the act of listening to them.

Canadians look to Prime Minister Jean Chrétien for a coherent message about Canada's future. Few find it. This lack of a vision was particularly disturbing during the key months leading up to the 1995 Quebec referendum. Political leaders must help people understand and believe in their nation's future.

President Clinton began office with a weak message. "We must reinvent America" was the anaemic theme of his first inaugural speech. Hence many feel that he has lacked leadership, and his accomplishments fail to reflect a coherent vision.

How do you develop a message? Begin by realizing that you must focus. Churchill said, "A speech is like a spotlight: the more focused it is, the more intense the light with a smaller area covered." A message that's too general will sound superficial. "We had a great year" is not a message to inspire the troops. But John F. Kennedy's message in his first inaugural speech was clear and forceful: "Let every nation know, whether it wishes us well or ill, that we shall pay any price, bear any burden, meet any hardship, support any friend, oppose any foe, to assure the survival and the success of liberty."

Corporate messages come in many forms. One CIO we worked with had a terse but powerful message to his troops: "We're at war." Whatever your main idea, state it boldly in your introduction. For example, the speaker might say: "If there's one message I'd like to leave with you today, it's that." That single argument should shape the entire speech. And it should be restated in the conclusion.

Once you grasp the importance of a clear message, its power quickly becomes apparent. A Hewlett-Packard executive told me that the concept of message is enabling him to achieve much greater leadership at staff meetings.

He used to open quarterly sales meetings by asking each regional sales executive to provide an "update." Now he asks them to summarize their results in a sentence and then elaborate. And he closed each meeting with a summary of these results—and a statement of his vision.

Finally, remember that a message is important even in the most informal talks. Even if you are speaking for four minutes, addressing an informal luncheon, or handling questions and answers, you should set forth your main idea. Otherwise your remarks will be a jumble.

The very last words of your speech should be a Call to Action in which you urge your audience to act upon your message.

Step 4: Build a persuasive structure.

The fourth step toward inspirational leadership is developing a persuasive structure.

To begin with, the structure must support the message. Too many executive presentations or speeches simply ramble on, from topic to topic. When a structure elaborates an idea, it takes on an excitement, and energy. It has a pulse to it.

Take the speech given some time ago by the CEO of TRW to investment analysts. His message implied a strong, powerful structure: "There's just one message I have for you today. It's that there are nine excellent reasons for recommending our stock." The structure would then consist of nine points or "reasons" why the stock should be seen as a "buy."

Most speeches can be structured by one of five common patterns.

First is the one we call the "Four Reasons" speech—although it might be the three reasons or nine reasons speech. It's a clear, powerful format.

Second is the "Ways" speech, which demonstrates the ways or areas in which the main idea can be shown to be true.

Next is "Problem and Solution." It's a good way of first addressing a problem and then showing how you'll solve it. It's great for customer presentations.

There's also the "Process" or "Chronological" model. You discuss a sequence of steps. This talk with its seven-fold path to eloquence follows that model.

Last is the "Present Situation/Future Outlook" talk. Annual meeting speeches often take this approach. You tell your audience that while this year's results were good, we will restructure to make the future still brighter for the company.

Step 5: Use language of leadership.

The fifth step in becoming an inspirational speaker is choosing words and expressions that underscore your leadership. Several imperatives accompany this one.

Be genuine. So many speakers fail to inspire their audiences because they speak an artificial language. Even when putting forth his best programs, Brian Mulroney's language betrayed him. His sentences were too long, his words too abstract. Audiences have trouble believing a speaker who uses such prose.

Be clear. Avoid the jargon that's all too common in presentations. If language is a reflection of the speaker's mind, then what can we deduce about the minds that produce the following: "I can approach others to leverage our capabilities and maximize yields on our investments." Or, "We are an industry of provisionaries of networks . . ." Or, "We must place the funnel as equal to, or even more important than, account-based cleanups."

Eliminate clutter. Too many speakers fill their talks with unnecessary clutter—often to buy time while they're thinking. Expressions such as "to be honest," "I have to admit that," "you know," or "um," are verbal junk.

Eliminate this verbiage, and you'll sound more polished and clear-minded.

Be confident. Your language should exude confidence. Be very sparing in your use of qualifiers such as "I think," "I guess," or "hopefully." If you have to guess or you're just hoping for a certain outcome, rethink your approach.

Too many executives—especially female executives—use language that undercuts their message. Be careful not to tell your audience: "I just have two items to discuss, or "It's only my view, but . . ." As well, emotional language conveys weakness and undercuts leadership. Be very sparing in the use of expressions such as, "I'm unhappy about the way things are proceeding," "It would be greatly appreciated if you could . . ." or "I want to thank you with all my heart." Such language works better in the home than in the office.

The words executives use should reflect their leadership. Language should be genuine, clear, free of clutter, and confident.

Step 6: Make yourself the visual.

Visual aids are the bane of corporate presentations. They're uninspiring, and too often dull, cluttered and difficult to decipher. More significantly, they upstage the speaker and make that individual appear to be less of a leader. My advice? Use visuals only when they are absolutely necessary.

Think of yourself as the best visual. Have your audience focus on you—your energy, your conviction, your inspirational qualities. Don't confine yourself to the sidelines. Be the focus of the audience's attention.

I once heard about a presenter who wanted to impress his audience with the best, most colorful state-of-the-art, glitzy visuals. At the end of the talk, a number of people came up to ask for a business card—not his, but the individual who had created the graphics!

I've worked with enough executives to know that some corporate cultures insist on visuals—at least in presentations. If you must use them, avoid word slides. You want your audience listening to you, not reading while you're talking. Project a simple corporate logo if you need an image. Some material—an organizational chart, a network diagram—can be presented visually. But if you do, keep your visual simple. No one should have to study or decipher an image to determine what you're showing.

Step 7: Let your delivery style show your leadership.

Seventh, and finally, your delivery style should affirm your leadership, not undercut it. A compelling style combined with a good text will allow you to achieve your goal: inspiring and motivating your audience.

Here are some guidelines for developing a leadership presence when you speak.

Use gestures sparingly. Most executives think they're more inspirational if they move a lot. But keep the words of Peter Ustinov in mind: "The secret of acting is to reduce everything to absolute stillness. If you are absolutely still, when you move it registers; if you move the whole time, nothing registers."

Stand tall. Leadership is best expressed by a tall, aligned body, with feet squarely planted on the floor. Whatever your height or sex, imagine yourself on a string (hung from a ceiling), and lift your body accordingly. It's amazing what this will do for you. Why don't speakers naturally do this?

Some executives think they're too tall, so they slouch. Others show their discomfort with speaking by making themselves smaller. They hunch over. Resist the temptation to make yourself small or cozy. Your audience will not be inspired.

Look at people. It's amazing how rarely executive speakers look at their audiences. Many look above the heads of the audience, others graze the room with their eyes, and still others bury their eyes in their speech or visual aids. Remember, people listen with their eyes. They may hear the words with their ears, but they think about what you're saying when your eyes are locked with theirs. So look at the audience when you are about to say something, and when you complete your thought.

And really look at people, one at a time. Remember, there are two kinds of animals: predators and prey. Predators have their eyes in front of their head, prey have them on the side of their head. So, use your eyes to take control of the room. Jen Monty, the president of BCE Inc., has incredible eye contact. Even when he steps out of an elevator, he takes control with his eyes. He owns the space, and people feel that he does.

Pace yourself. Speak with lots of pauses. Too many people rush. But consider this: when does the audience think? Not while you're speaking, because they can't think about an idea until it's delivered. They think during the pauses. But if there are no pauses, they won't think. They won't be moved. They won't act upon what you say. The degree to which you want to involve the audience is reflected in the length of your pauses. Use a tone that inspires. Find a tone that's close to your best conversational voice, and make sure it's full of leadership.

The single most common tonal problem we come across in coaching executives is the artificial tone of someone whose voice says, "I am giving a speech." In other words, they're more conscious of themselves than they are of their message. That's deadly, for if you are not involved in your message, how can the audience be? Listen to yourself on audio tape or video. See how you react to your own voice. Do you sound real?

Avoid a tone that's too loud, too brash, too bland, too sweet or too didactic. So many executives are still unconsciously caught up in "male" or "female" stereotypes that undercut leadership. The voices of men can be too strident and arrogant, or dull and controlled. The voices of female executives are frequently too soft, nice, or pretty. Executives need a tone that has both power and warmth. Carol Stephenson, president and CEO of Stentor Resources Centre Inc., is a good example of such vocal strength.

Your voice should also reflect the material you're delivering. Convey the excitement and conviction that's in your text. Present your bold structural statements with more emphasis than your supporting statements.

These are the seven steps to inspirational speaking. In numerology, seven is the number closely associated with inspiration. Certainly there is no greater goal for a leader than to inspire an audience—whether that audience is a CEO, a room of shareholders, a group of customers, or employees.

The question is, can everybody be inspiring? The answer: if they believe they can, and work at it, they can. Consider the great speakers of history. They applied themselves to crafting their remarks. Winston Churchill fainted out of fear at one of his first public speeches. But he got better. In fact he became one of the world's greatest statesmen, because he had a mission. And executives have a similar mission in their companies.

John Caldwell, President and CEO of CAE Inc., once told me: "The reality is, you've got to set a direction for your company, and then you've got to help people get on that bandwagon."

This ability to move the hearts and minds of employees, customers, and other stakeholders is the primary role of senior executives. To achieve this goal takes concentration, desire, and hard work. But when you achieve this leadership, it's worth it.

"Where there is no vision, the people perish," we read in Proverbs 29:18. But where there is vision, people flourish. That is the work of the inspirational leader.

SOURCE: This speech was given by Judith Humphrey, president of The Humphrey Group, to The Board of Trade, Metropolitan Toronto, Toronto, Canada, November 25, 1997. The text is reprinted from *Vital Speeches of the Day* 64 (May 15, 1998):468–71.

Nobel Prize Acceptance Speech
Nelson Mandela

Your Majesty the King,
Your Royal Highness,
Honourable Prime Minister,
Madame Gro Brundtland,
Ministers,
Members of Parliament and Ambassadors,
Esteemed Members of the Norwegian Nobel Committee,
Fellow Laureate, Mr. F. W. de Klerk,
Distinguished guests,
Friends, ladies and gentlemen:

I am indeed truly humbled to be standing here today to receive this year's Nobel Peace Prize.

I extend my heartfelt thanks to the Norwegian Nobel Committee for elevating us to the status of a Nobel Peace Prize winner.

I would also like to take this opportunity to congratulate my compatriot and fellow laureate, State President F. W. de Klerk, on his receipt of this high honour.

Together, we join two distinguished South Africans, the late Chief Albert Luthuli and His Grace Archbishop Desmond Tutu, to whose seminal contributions to the peaceful struggle against the evil system of apartheid you paid well-deserved tribute by awarding them the Nobel Peace Prize.

It will not be presumptuous of us if we also add, among our predecessors, the name of another outstanding Nobel Peace Prize winner, the late African American statesman and internationalist, the Rev. Martin Luther King Jr.

He, too, grappled with and died in the effort to make a contribution to the just solution of the same great issues of the day which we have had to face as South Africans.

We speak here of the challenge of the dichotomies of war and peace, violence and non-violence, racism and human dignity, oppression and repression and liberty and human rights, poverty and freedom from want.

We stand here today as nothing more than a representative of the millions of our people who dared to rise up against a social system whose very essence is war, violence, racism, oppression, repression, and the impoverishment of an entire people.

I am also here today as a representative of the millions of people across the globe, the anti-apartheid movement, the governments and organisations that joined with us, not to fight against South Africa as a country or any of its peoples, but to oppose an inhuman system and sue for a speedy end to the apartheid crime against humanity.

These countless human beings, both inside and outside our country, had the nobility of spirit to stand in the path of tyranny and injustice, without seeking selfish gain. They recognized that an injury to one is an injury to all and therefore acted together in defense of justice and a common human decency.

Because of their courage and persistence for many years, we can, today, even set the dates when all humanity will join together to celebrate one of the outstanding human victories of our century.

When that moment comes, we shall, together, rejoice in a common victory over racism, apartheid, and white minority rule.

That triumph will finally bring to a close a history of five hundred years of African colonization that began with the establishment of the Portuguese empire.

Thus, it will mark a great step forward in history and also serve as a common pledge of the peoples of the world to fight racism wherever it occurs and whatever guise it assumes.

At the southern tip of the continent of Africa, a rich reward is in the making, an invaluable gift is in the preparation, for those who suffered in the name of all humanity when they sacrificed everything—for liberty, peace, human dignity and human fulfillment.

This reward will not be measured in money. Nor can it be reckoned in the collective price of the rare metals and precious stones that rest in the bowels of the African soil we tread in the footsteps of our ancestors. It will and must be measured by the happiness and welfare of the children, at once the most vulnerable citizens in any society and the greatest of our treasures.

The children must, at last, play in the open field, no longer tortured by the pangs of hunger or ravaged by disease or threatened with the scourge of ignorance, molestation, and abuse, and no longer required to engage in deeds whose gravity exceeds the demands of their tender years.

In front of this distinguished audience, we commit the new South Africa to the relentless pursuit of the purposes defined in the World Declaration on the Survival, Protection and Development of Children.

The reward of which we have spoken will and must also be measured by the happiness and welfare of the mothers and fathers of these children, who must walk the earth without fear of being robbed, killed for political or material profit, or spat upon because they are beggars.

They too must be relieved of the heavy burden of despair which they carry in their hearts, born of hunger, homelessness, and unemployment.

The value of that gift to all who have suffered will and must be measured by the happiness and welfare of all the people of our country, who will have torn down the inhuman walls that divide them.

These great masses will have turned their backs on the grave insult to human dignity which described some as masters and others as servants, and transformed each into a predator whose survival depended on the destruction of the other.

The value of our shared reward will and must be measured by the joyful peace which will triumph, because the common humanity that bonds both black and white into one human race, will have said to each one of us that we shall all live like the children of paradise.

Thus shall we live, because we will have created a society which recognises that all people are born equal, with each entitled in equal measure to life, liberty, prosperity, human rights, and good governance.

Such a society should never allow again that there should be prisoners of conscience nor that any person's human rights should be violated.

Neither should it ever happen that once more the avenues to peaceful change are blocked by usurpers who seek to take power away from the people, in pursuit of their own, ignoble purposes.

In relation to these matters, we appeal to those who govern Burma that they release our fellow Nobel Peace Prize laureate, Aung San Suu Kyi, and engage her and those she represents in serious dialogue, for the benefit of all the people of Burma.

We pray that those who have the power to do so will, without further delay, permit that she uses her talents and energies for the greater good of the people of her country and humanity as a whole.

Far from the rough and tumble of the politics of our own country, I would like to take this opportunity to join the Norwegian Nobel Committee and pay tribute to my joint laureate, Mr. F. W. de Klerk.

He had the courage to admit that a terrible wrong had been done to our country and people through the imposition of the system of apartheid.

He had the foresight to understand and accept that all the people of South Africa must, through negotiations and as equal participants in the process, together determine what they want to make of their future.

But there are still some within our country who wrongly believe they can make a contribution to the cause of justice and peace by clinging to the shibboleths that have been proved to spell nothing but disaster.

It remains our hope that these, too, will be blessed with sufficient reason to realise that history will not be denied and that the new society cannot be created by reproducing the repugnant past, however refined or enticingly repackaged.

We live with the hope that as she battles to remake herself, South Africa will be like a microcosm of the new world that is striving to be born.

This must be a world of democracy and respect for human rights, a world freed from the horrors of poverty, hunger, deprivation, and ignorance, relieved of the threat and the scourge of civil wars and external aggression and unburdened of the great tragedy of millions forced to become refugees.

The processes in which South Africa and Southern Africa as a whole are engaged, beckon and urge us all that we take this tide at the flood and make of this region a living example of what all people of conscience would like the world to be.

We do not believe that this Nobel Peace Prize is intended as a commendation for matters that have happened and passed.

We hear the voices which say that it is an appeal from all those, throughout the universe, who sought an end to the system of apartheid.

We understand their call, that we devote what remains of our lives to the use of our country's unique and painful experience to demonstrate, in practice, that the normal condition for human existence is democracy, justice, peace, non-racism, non-sexism, prosperity for everybody, a healthy environment, and equality and solidarity among the peoples.

Moved by that appeal and inspired by the eminence you have thrust upon us, we undertake that we too will do what we can to contribute to the renewal of our world so that none should, in future, be described as the wretched of the earth.

Let it never be said by future generations that indifference, cynicism, or selfishness made us fail to live up to the ideals of humanism which the Nobel Peace Prize encapsulates.

Let the strivings of us all, prove Martin Luther King Jr. to have been correct, when he said that humanity can no longer be tragically bound to the starless midnight of racism and war.

Let the efforts of us all, prove that he was not a mere dreamer when he spoke of the beauty of genuine brotherhood and peace being more precious than diamonds or silver or gold.

Let a new age dawn!

Thank you.

SOURCE: This speech was given by Nelson Mandela, president of the African National Congress, in his acceptance of the Nobel Peace Prize in 1993. The text is taken from the Internet Web site at http://www.anc.org.za/ancdocs/speeches/nobelnrm.http.

A Window of Opportunity: Meeting the Challenges of Medicine's Agenda

Nancy W. Dickey

Good morning. When they told me I would be giving the challenge address for this conference, I knew I had my work cut out for me. Because as physicians, the last thing we need right now is another challenge. We're challenged every day as it is.

Hassles from government, onerous regulations from insurers, and an array of outside forces telling us how to run our practices and care for our patients are making an already challenging profession even more difficult.

Not to mention all the complex issues on our plates right now: patient protection legislation, E & M guidelines, Medicare, medical liability, troubling public health issues like tobacco, accusations of fraud and abuse and the criminalization of medicine, and wide-ranging ethical dilemmas.

And that's just some of what faces us before we put on our white coats in the morning and see our first patient.

And once we do, there are the many clinical challenges awaiting us. The technological and scientific advances our profession is making are occurring so fast; it can be difficult to keep up sometimes. I would venture to say that 80 percent of the prescriptions I write today were not even around when I graduated from medical school 22 years ago.

Likewise, we use cutting-edge procedures in medicine today that we couldn't even have imagined even just a decade ago.

Yes, being a physician these days is already extraordinarily challenging. Yet, we've come to this conference because we're willing to do more. Because we know we have to do more. I guess no one said being a leader was easy.

Up until now, we've spent this conference discussing some of the important issues facing medicine and we've shared with you some strategies for addressing them.

Now, as we enter the homestretch, it's time to set our sights higher and challenge ourselves to do something positive and productive with the information and strategies we've been given.

Over the past three days we've heard from some of America's most prominent voices.

General Colin Powell who talked about the importance of reaching out to our young people and making a commitment in America's future.

And from Supreme Court Justice Scalia who talked about law and the Constitution—and how medicine's issues fit into both.

We've heard from President Clinton and Speaker of the House Gingrich—and other top political leaders on both sides of the aisle—tell us how extremely important our voice is in shaping health care change.

These influential leaders came here to speak with us because our voice and actions as physicians do matter—and because we can make a meaningful difference for all of America's patients. Today, let me add to those challenges and tell you why your leadership is so critical these days.

If nothing else, we hope this conference has afforded you a brief respite from all that you're doing back home and given you a chance to focus on health care's big picture.

And as you have, I hope you have seen what I have, that a growing dissatisfaction with the current health care system on many fronts, has given us a real window of opportunity right now to fix some things.

Specifically, a window of opportunity to take back control of our medical profession, ensuring that physicians, not others, are making the medical decisions. And that patients, not profits or politics, are the top priority.

As you know, physicians have been unhappy with the current system for quite some time. For the past decade, the so-called "cost-control decade," we have seen our relationships with patients threatened.

During the same time, we have seen our autonomy slide, our paperwork mount and our frustrations escalate as various forces have conspired, it seems, to make our jobs more difficult, if not impossible.

But to tell you the truth, no one seemed to care too much if physicians were unhappy. Many said we were more interested in our paychecks than our patients and they would run the health care system as they saw fit.

Well, they ran it all right—right into crisis.

Because lately, we find we're not the only ones who are unhappy. Increasingly, patients are voicing their dissatisfaction as well. Too many of them feel they have to jump through hoops just to see their doctor or get the care they need. And even when they do get to see us, they are not sure who or what is driving the medical decision-making affecting their care these days.

Some are concerned—and rightfully so—that health plans, not physicians, are calling the shots. Others fear that health plan bonus incentives—not their individual well-being—may be determining their health care options.

And they express other concerns as well, ones that have become all too familiar to us:

"I never see the same doctor twice . . .," they say.

Or "By the time my records get to a plan, my employer changes plans and I have to find another doctor . . ."

And "How can I ever have trust? I never get a chance to learn my new doctor's name before I move on to someplace else."

But even unhappy patients and physicians have not provided the leverage needed to create this current window of opportunity.

No, the real reason it exists is this: CEOs are starting to join physicians and patients in the ranks of the dissatisfied. And no wonder. Current grumblings within the health care marketplace suggest that health care costs are about to rise again. A sign, perhaps, that a decade of cost-cutting measures has finally "maxed out," and that new answers really are needed.

Organized medicine can and should—in fact, it must—provide those answers. But how well we do it will depend largely on the leadership right here in this room. That is why I am bringing this challenge to your attention today.

Because you are the heart and soul of organized medicine—not to mention the brains and the brawn—and without your active participation, the plans and strategies put forth during this conference will die right at that door.

None of us can afford to let that happen. So with that in mind, let me target three areas where your leadership is desperately needed in the days and months ahead.

First and foremost, we need your leadership in recommitting medicine to the core values of ethics and professionalism. That means remembering the core principles on which medicine was founded, honoring those principles, and encouraging—even demanding—that our colleagues do the same.

In this current "outcomes-based" generation, it's not enough to just say that we are committed to ethics and professionalism. We have to demonstrate it in measurable, visible, ways. To put it another way: If we can't document it—we're probably not doing it. And if our patients can't see it, it really doesn't matter anyway.

Now, a big part of our recommitment is recognizing the damage that's been done to our relationships with patients—both individually and collectively. And then, doing all we can to fix it, because medicine's credibility absolutely depends upon it.

True, part of our credibility is based on scientific knowledge and our ability to diagnose and treat disease. But an equal part is based on the commitment we show to our patients.

Because, clinical expertise aside, patients need to know that when we enter the exam room or the surgical suite or the emergency department, we are there to do what's best for them. Not what's best for the accountants, the plan or the insurance industry as a whole, or even what's best for the new relationships we may be developing with networks, hospitals, or other associations.

It must be clear to everyone, that we're there to do what's best and right for our patient. And if we do not strengthen our credibility and repair the damage that has been caused in our essential patient relationships then much of what we talk about here is moot. It will never be accomplished.

So, first, a recommitment to ethics and professionalism.

Second, we also need your leadership in the health care marketplace. Using our collective voice and political clout to shape a better health care delivery system for patients and physicians alike.

Not only to speak out and to eliminate current problems, like onerous government regulations or dangerous managed care policies; but also to outline and advocate for principles and provisions that can actually improve the current system.

Principles like choice. Because let's face it, America is not a "one-size-fits-all" country. Just look around this room or outside this hotel and see all the choices that are available to us.

From the clothes we wear—to the cars we drive. From our choice of medical specialty—to the hours that we work. Americans value freedom of choice, and we want that freedom in most areas of our life—and health care is no exception.

A second concept we need to push in the marketplace is individual ownership of our health plans.

Today, and ever since the 1930s, this country has favored employer-purchased health plans. But as long as the employer chooses, health care plans don't really belong to our patients. And many of them will continue to feel alienated and detached from the benefits their plans do, or do not, provide.

Allowing patients to own and choose their own health care plans will go a long way toward making patients feel in control and toward taking responsibility for their health care—something desperately missing in today's environment.

Now don't get me wrong, I'm not suggesting that employers have no responsibility in this new and improved delivery system. Because historically, and at least for the time being, most health care will continue to be employer-funded.

Not so that patients and physicians can have their cake and eat it too, but because it's the financially responsible thing to do.

Keep in mind that ever since employers first offered health insurance to their employees, they have used it as a factor in determining wage increases. Workers have accepted smaller wage increases over that time because of trade-offs for benefits.

Now, to tell employers that they no longer have to pay for health insurance, without providing an equivalent wage increase, is robbing American workers of 40 or 50 years of compensation. And that is intolerable and simply not an option.

So, at least for a significant transition period, employer funding will and should remain an important component of health care delivery.

Having said that, I am not insensitive to the concerns of employers, who must deal with unpredictable and rising insurance premiums. As director of a residency training program, I share those concerns. I have to budget insurance expenses for 16 residents and a half-dozen faculty members, and fluctuating charges, specifically those higher than anticipated, wreak havoc with my budget. So, one final concept we need to introduce to the marketplace is budget predictability.

But how do we get the predictability?

One possible solution is defined contributions. A situation in which an employer might say to an employee—

"I'll give you $3,000 dollars and you can purchase any plan you want. You can add your own money to purchase a more expensive plan—or you can pick one that is completely covered by the company's contribution."

"It's completely up to you."

And that should be our goal, and the marketplace we strive for. One in which the selection and ownership of health care plans is completely up to our patients—but one that gives employers budget predictability and maintains a basic benefit that workers have helped finance for the past 50 years.

To accomplish all this, however, there will have to be regulatory and legislative changes—not just rhetoric. And that means we need to raise our voices, both as community members and as professionals, and begin to initiate these changes.

Helping our legislators understand why choice and individual owner-ship are good in the long run. But also showing them that we understand the concerns of employers and that we are willing to develop a solution that works for all.

So, we need your leadership to recommit to ethics and professionalism and to speak out for health system reform and find ways to make it work.

Third and finally, we need your leadership in the advocacy arena.

We've touched upon so many areas during this conference where your advocacy and leadership are absolutely essential. Here in Washington, back home in your statehouses, within the House of Medicine itself. Each of these areas needs your voice and your actions.

But think more broadly, as well. Because advocacy is about so much more than just placing a call to your congressional representative when you get a blast fax from the AMA.

It's keeping in contact with your representative and senators through-out the year, letting them know our primary concern is our patients, not our paychecks.

Call them even when a vote is not coming up. Now, he or she might wonder what you're up to the first few times, especially when you're not asking them to vote on something; but after a while, they will learn your name and may even learn to value your opinion that much more when their vote really is needed.

Advocacy is also making sure that your colleagues and your patients know what's at stake.

You know, there are 1,000 physicians attending this conference, but there are tens of thousands more, who have no idea about how—or what goes into—tackling the problems we are addressing at this conference.

Our patients know even less.

Go home and tell them what needs to be done, why it needs to be done and how to go about it. Make them advocates, too.

Speak up at your county, state and specialty society meetings, or your local Kiwanis and Rotary meetings. Anyplace you can think of—right down to your patient reception areas, to educate those around you about the im-portant issues facing health and health care because they do affect us all.

And by doing so, you will make medicine's voice bigger, and stronger and more effective.

Finally, one more specific issue that needs your advocacy.

It's one that doesn't get much of our attention, though it has been firm-ly supported by AMA policy for more than a decade.

And I call your attention to it not only because it presents the ultimate challenge in our recommitment to medical ethics and professionalism, but also because I know of no other group that can put forth more powerful or compelling support on its behalf than the one assembled right here.

I'm talking about universal access to care for all patients in this country. And as physician leaders, I'm asking you to speak up strongly and bravely on behalf of this issue.

Because while we can say that the uninsured ultimately do get care, one way or another, let's not pretend, not even for a minute, that we provide this care in an effective or efficient manner.

Too many patients come to us late in their disease. They're sicker than they should be and suffer more than they should have to. And many—too many, are treated in piecemeal fashion—never getting the referrals they really need to treat a chronic condition.

Today, there are more than 40 million uninsured Americans living in this country. And by the end of the century, that number is expected to rise another two to three million. That's 15 percent of the American population. And if we do not speak up for these individuals now, their numbers will only continue to grow.

For too long now, we've either ignored the issue or have been unfocused in our response to it. That must change now and that change must begin with us.

As physicians, we know the importance of every American having access to basic, high-quality, health care. And as leaders, we must fight to see that America's patients get it, each and every one of them.

Not only because it's the right thing to do, but because it's part of our professional and ethical obligation to the American public. And because if we don't make universal access a priority, no one else will.

But to achieve that access, we have to do it through the marketplace, with a government single-payor solution. What I'm talking about is developing a mosaic of solutions for getting these patients care.

It's back to that idea of choice. It's choosing different approaches in developing different solutions for different patients.

Answers built on personal responsibility where possible. On professional generosity where necessary. For example, sliding scale "buy-ins" where appropriate. And partnering with medical education where available. An American solution for our public and our patients.

In closing, just let me say it again; organized medicine needs your leadership. This country needs your leadership.

We need it to help us recommit to the ethics and professionalism that have so long served as the hallmark of American medicine. The very reason that Nathan Davis and his colleagues founded the AMA 150 years ago.

We need your leadership in the marketplace, giving patients choice and ownership of their health plans. Giving employers budget predictability, even while we look for alternate ways to fund the system.

Finally, we need your leadership in all our advocacy efforts—to speak up for those with no voice of their own. And most of all, to make universal access a reality for all Americans.

Now, that's a lot to accomplish. But it pales in comparison to some of the accomplishments physicians work toward each and every day.

Think about it: our physician intellect and commitment have allowed us to diagnose, and cure, cancers.

To move HIV from a sure death sentence toward a chronic disease—and hopefully, in our lifetime, toward a disease that we can cure.

And to be able to identify human genes and then use that knowledge to prevent disease and chronic conditions from ever occurring in the first place.

That intellect and commitment that shows what physicians can accomplish when we focus our efforts and our energies and then dedicate ourselves fully to reaching our goal.

Let's show the same focus and dedication in addressing these current challenges. Because there is a window of opportunity in front of us—but we need your leadership and your commitment—to widen that window for patients, physicians and for our profession. Let's begin today—and let's do it together.

SOURCE: This speech was given by Nancy W. Dickey, M.D., President-Elect of the American Medical Association at the 1998 AMA National Leadership Conference in Washington, D.C., March 10, 1998. The text is reprinted from *Vital Speeches of the Day* 64 (May 15, 1998):456–59.

Living Up to Your Fullest Potential

Carolyn Woo

Thank you very much for inviting me to share this special day with you. I would like to congratulate all the degree candidates as well as the parents, spouses, siblings, relatives, friends, and faculty who have been with you on this journey. A day like this celebrates not only the achievements of the candidates, but also the people who have loved and affirmed you, and whose dreams and aspirations are intertwined with yours. Congratulations to all.

While today celebrates the end of one phase, it also marks the beginning of the many experiences you will choose to undertake. While the word "retirement" seems increasingly limited, the term "commencement" has become even more appropriate as we move into what is now known as the "Knowledge Economy." "Commencement" indicates to us that all the years of study are about preparation so that we may "begin," "launch," "initiate," "originate," or "bring forth,"—all synonyms of the verb "to commence."

I am excited for you because you are entering a world that holds tremendous opportunities. Despite concerns we may have, I think we can all agree that the technologies for a better life and the politics for a better world are emerging everyday. A forecast from Batelle, a leading "think tank," offers a list of innovations which will be very much a part of our lives in the next five to fifteen years. These include:

1. Pharmaceutical products that will treat many diseases, including cancer, multiple sclerosis, osteoporosis, Lou Gehrig's disease, Alzheimer's and AIDS.
2. Home health monitors that are simple to use, inexpensive, and non-invasive. These will allow us to check on liver, kidney, cholesterol level, triglycerides,

sugar, hormones, water, salt, potassium. Monitoring our health will be as simple as weighing ourselves everyday.

3. Anti-aging and weight control products, a cure for baldness. While we will still age, it may lessen the physical trauma and enhance our well-being.

4. "Smart" materials that will give off a warning when they are under excessive stress. Sensors will be built in so that we can detect deterioration in car or aircraft components, bridges, or pipelines.

5. Advancing from the personal computer, we will have personalized computers that will be adapted to follow our voices, to record our preferences and interests, and to do searches (for shopping bargains, holiday bookings, news updates) tailored to our own preferences.

These are exciting because they can better our lives and more importantly, create many career opportunities for you. You will be working on products, performing functions and creating solutions that are new to your parents and your instructors. These are your frontiers and over the past years, you have already added to your tool kit for this journey.

I remember being in your shoes and wondering: this is all very exciting, but will I succeed? What will I need to do? Is there anything I can be sure of? I believe there are two things you must do, and if you give your heart to these, you will succeed. The most important two things are: living up to your fullest potential, and developing the potential of your team or community.

LIVE UP TO YOUR FULLEST POTENTIAL

I am reminded of a story of a man walking around in a circus. He saw the troupe of elephants; each was tied to a stake in the ground. He asked the elephant keeper: how long must this stake be to hold the elephant to this spot? The elephant keeper pulled it out and it was only a normal stake you would use for any tent: no more than about 15 inches.

It was the idea of the stake, the picture of the stake that sometimes holds us back. I am sure each of us has our stake and we imagine it deeper in the ground than what it really is.

I also recall the story of one of my students. She had a major mishap that caused her to lose the whole grade on a project in one course. When she came to see me, she was devastated: convinced that her career was over before it started. I logically did the calculation and showed her that this mishap carried the weight of less than one percent in her total GPA. This did not console her. She extended this to probable failure in getting an internship and, of course, probable failure in everything afterwards. After half an hour when my efforts went nowhere, I finally said, you are indeed right—you will probably encounter total failure. For the scariest thing about life is that it is a self-fulfilling prophecy. You will go exactly as high or as low as you think you will go. She was stunned by my comments, picked herself up and went on to a very successful internship.

Living up to our fullest potential requires at least four things:

A. In the "Knowledge Economy," the most important source of competitive advantage for the company and source of power for the individual is knowledge. Based on a report by the National Alliance of Business, a high school graduate earns 53% more than one who does not complete high school. A person with a two-year degree earns 37% above a high school graduate—an additional two years of college will bring a similar increase. This gap nearly doubled in the last 15 years.

Correspondingly, companies also benefit significantly from education. A study at the University of Pennsylvania shows that a 10% increase in the education level of a company's workforce (approximately one year of education) increases productivity by 8.5% in manufacturing businesses and 13 percent in the non-manufacturing sector. As you all know, learning has become much more accessible through a variety of media such as CD ROM, the Internet and teleconferencing. Many companies now support or require continuing education for all levels of employees. The barriers to learning are disappearing quickly. But one thing remains the same—the onus for learning is still on the individual learner. It is completely up to each one of you to cultivate his or her own curiosity for new knowledge and to have the discipline to engage in these programs.

B. In addition to learning, we must also be willing to take risks. We know the future holds many uncertainties and that we must be adaptable, versatile and flexible. As companies move into new arenas and re-design processes and structure, we find ourselves in new territories: creating, experimenting, improvising, modifying and changing. All these require us to take risks, and not be afraid of what we don't know, what we have not done, and what we cannot predict. A recent card I got said: Get out on a limb: that's where the fruit is.

C. Taking risks means facing the possibility of something that is not working out—that means setbacks and flops. If we reach beyond the comfortable, these are definite possibilities. The ability to take risks rests on our ability to rebound, regroup, re-energize after a tough spell. Mary Pickford once said: "You may have a fresh start any moment you choose, for this thing that we call 'failure' is not falling down, but the staying down."

I have found that of my own setbacks, I am less forgiving of myself than others are. Issues of image and ego often drive my feelings of embarrassment. I have actually found a greater dose of support and graciousness on the part of good friends and supportive supervisors who base their assessment on efforts and intent, and less so on the need for perfection or flawless appearance.

As a result, I have learned that if I put aside the questions "what do people think?" or "do I look foolish?" I recover more quickly and become bolder. I find that taking risk requires something as deep as inner strength and as pragmatic as a "nest egg," or the "rainy day fund." I have learned that equally important, I must be humble enough to ask for the support of good friends and supportive colleagues. In the end, a strong dose of self-confidence and humor will go a long way. I am reminded of what Linda Ellerbee once said, "Laughter in the face of reality is probably the finest sound there is. In fact, a good time to laugh is any time you can."

D. Finally, living up to our potential requires a tremendous amount of energy, discipline, and sacrifice. It is hard to give at that level unless you are driven by a sense of passion for causes and work you feel deeply about. But don't sit on the fence answering this question. Go out and take action. Explore—give different options a chance, develop interests, and most importantly, cultivate the capacity to care. Some of you are already there; for some it will take time. Listen to your heart for your aspirations and your ideals. They are the fuel that will keep you going the extra mile. As Cardinal Mercier once said, "We must not only give what we have, we must also give what we are." In response, we must know who we are, what we stand for and what we care about. When we honor these, we are more likely to reach our fullest potential.

I want to move from the notion of "Building You" to "Building Us."

The notion of "Building Us" is as simple and as humbling as what is noted in this Irish proverb, "It is in the shelter of each other that the people live." All of us would agree that little is done except in collaboration with each other. Teamwork, work groups, collaboration, alliances, partnerships, networks, consortia: these are key words in the lexicon which describes how business has been and will be done. Harold Leavitt, a senior management scholar at Stanford, wrote: "To get the world's work done, people have to get along with one another, and getting along requires empathy, sensitivity, and feelings of boundedness and membership."

"Building us" or building community is about creating a sense of the common good and fostering ownership by all members for the success of the group. It requires a commitment to "win-win" solutions and decision making, which does not create persistent winners and losers. Community is based on inclusiveness and respect; it welcomes differences while seeking common ground. Community in the workplace uses hierarchy and structure for coordinating work, not for designating who is more or less important. Community building takes place everywhere in our lives: within families, work groups, church groups, and in our neighborhoods. It is the glue that gives us the whole, and a whole that is bigger than all its parts.

Most of us are familiar with Adam Smith's notion of the "Invisible Hand": i.e., allowing the market to sort out the strong from the weak, the winners from the losers. Adam Smith also wrote another book, *Theory of Moral Sentiments*, in which he identified "sympathy" or the proper regard for others as the basis of a civilized society. It is indeed the joint workings of the "Invisible Hand" and the "Invisible Handshake" that allows all of us to prosper.

Building community is based on the recognition of our interdependence and a deep respect for each other. I recall from my own commencement speaker a definition of charisma: "To take people as we find them, to like them for what they are and not to despise them for what they are not." To me, leadership is the ability to bring out the best in people, to unite and build trust, and to forge collaboration among people for meaningful and significant endeavors.

In conclusion, I am excited about the possibilities you face. Your analyses, efforts, and decisions will collectively shape our tomorrow. Education has always held a special place for me, and increasingly so as I grow older. I am reminded of the capital campaign tag line at Purdue University: Touching Tomorrow Today. It is a well-known sentiment that our students are the messages and the messengers we send to a time we won't see. Each generation passes the baton, a continuous process punctuated with specific events like the one we are celebrating today.

And on this journey forward, there will be many satisfying and glorious moments; there will be ones that bring disappointment and hopefully re-assessment and renewal.

But always remember that we are never alone on our journey, but in the presence of God as His children. I would like to end with a quote from Mother Theresa, "I know God will not give me anything I can't handle. I just wish He didn't trust me so much."

God bless you and make joy a part of each day.

SOURCE: This speech was given by Carolyn Woo, Dean of the University of Notre Dame's College of Business Administration, at the commencement at Holy Cross College, South Bend, Indiana, May 9, 1998. The text is reprinted from *Vital Speeches of the Day* 64 (August 15, 1998):670–72.

Acceptance Speech for the John Huston Award for Artists Rights

Martin Scorsese

Thank you. I'm very honored to receive this award.

You've just heard me talk at length, maybe too much at length, about the way I feel on these issues.

The end of the '80s saw a new awareness about reassessing the conditions of our film heritage. What was particularly new was that people in the creative community were beginning to get involved. In fact, within a few months from each other, in a spontaneous, independent way, two organizations were set up by filmmakers: the Artists Rights Foundation, set up to fight for the integrity of our work, and The Film Foundation, set up to take action with the studios to preserve the films in their vaults.

In the spring of 1990, I was in Milan working on a documentary, when I received a letter from Elliot Silverstein expressing concern about the two organizations overlapping. On my return, Elliot and I met at Wally and Joseph's restaurant, on 49th Street, by the Brill Building (I was editing "Cape Fear" at the time), to discuss this. Over dinner we came to realize that, without planning it, we had been dealing all along with two sides of the same issue:

1. The actual preservation of film.
2. The recognition of moral rights of filmmakers.

As I've said repeatedly, you can't have one without the other. Lots of films are already gone, many recent films are in need of restoration. My own film, "Taxi Driver," made in 1976, was just restored, and the "Star Wars" trilogy is now in the process of being restored.

This is why we're here tonight. It's great to get awards but we're not here only to congratulate each other. Rather, what this event does is to focus once more on what we're concerned about. It's another great opportunity to keep on spreading the message.

And I always look at these events with the hope of some forward motion, of seeing some real progress. And there is some progress tonight. The fact that I'm being presented this award by Jack Valenti, who is the spokesman for the MPAA, shows this. Since I first met Jack, in 1970 at the Sorrento Film Festival, he has always been a supporter of my artists' rights. As we found out through the work of The Film Foundation on film preservation, the studios and the archives are coming together. And if tonight is any indication, the same can happen with artists' rights. At least we're talking.

Look let's face it, the cinema—the classical cinema—is gone. It's over. The cinema as we know it up to now, is disappearing. It doesn't mean that cinema is dead. Rather, it's evolving. It's new, totally new. So new, that some of us may not even be aware of what changes will occur in the next decade.

We're witnessing a new cinema being born and that's exciting. However, whatever cinema evolves into, you still need an author.

Cinema is not just technology. It's not impersonal. The "author" is not an abstract corporation. It didn't just drop from the sky. It isn't off an assembly line, like you make a car. Film is not factory made, it's a human creation. And so what we're saying is, let's keep the "human" in the creative process.

Look, the reality is that cinema is an art. It may not all be great art. Like all art, you have good, bad, mediocre, indifferent art. But when it comes to film, lots of people feel you can do whatever you want with it—cut it, manipulate it any way you want. But you have to be very careful about deciding what is art and what isn't. There are dangers in making hasty judgments about which filmmakers are more important. Take for instance Alfred Hitchcock. Young people today who study his work may find it hard to believe that, in his time, despite his work being enjoyed and being commercially successful, it was not taken seriously. Some felt his films were just "thrillers," or clever story-telling.

Or for instance, "film noir." Those post-war low-budget, gritty black and white films of the '40s and '50s. Films of urban violence and paranoia that may not have been viewed as the highest form of cinema at the time, but films that in the 1960s were rediscovered by critics and audiences and viewed as a major proof of film as an artistic medium. Thank God all of these films were not tossed out at the time, like many of the silent films were, which were considered too insignificant to be passed on to future generations. You see, in those days it was more important to save the silver in the film stock than film itself. Today "film noir" has generated new genres, evolved into big movies—blockbusters in fact, which are the heart of the industry—the summer movies.

So, what are we really talking about when we say artists' rights? Studios, corporations own movies. Because they own it, it doesn't mean they should update them, revise them, distort them, or let them rot in their vaults. In fact, in light of the new technologies and possible future uses, you never know when you'll have to go back to the original negatives.

And what does this say about the owners of the work? It says really that they are custodians. They may own it, but they have a responsibility. The work belongs to the world. They are custodians.

As far as the American tradition goes, there is nothing new about this responsibility. Years ago, wealthy families—Carnegie, Rockefeller—who helped build American industry, shared the notion that if you had great wealth you held it as a kind of custodian on behalf of society and you had a responsibility to use that wealth for that society's benefit. It used to be called stewardship. In the film industry, we're asking studios to show that stewardship by preserving their films and by respecting its integrity.

But I go further. Major corporations own some studios today and they have received so much from film, they should give something back and render a great service to the nation. They should preserve not only their own libraries but help in the preservation of orphan films: documentaries, independent films, and most of all, newsreels—which are historical documents. There are a hundred million feet of nitrate film, at a cost of $2.00 per foot. It's $200 million that needs to be transferred to safety. By losing them, we lose an important part of our history, our culture.

I'll come to ask your help on this. I promise.

What concerns me is that our attitude towards art and culture reflects how our own society sees itself—what it thinks of itself.

And we will be judged in the future, among other things, by the way we treat our art and our culture. In fact, we're being judged in our own time. Like jazz, we must remember that cinema is the great indigenous American art form, and all we're saying is that we want it to be preserved and we want it to be shown, now and in the future, the way it was meant to be, by those who originally created it.

Thank you.

SOURCE: This speech was given by film director Martin Scorsese in his acceptance of the John Huston Award for Artists Rights, February 16, 1996. The text of the speech is taken from ["mail to:webmaster@godamongdirectors.com">E-mail The Webmaster]

Why We Communicate the Ways We Do: A Communibiological Perspective

James C. McCroskey

I wish to begin by expressing my appreciation to the selection committee for choosing me to present this lecture. I am deeply honored. As the first non-dean chosen to deliver the Arnold lecture, I find it a difficult challenge to follow the superb lectures which many of you heard presented by Dean Wartella and Dean Zarefsky at our last two conventions. However, as the first, but certainly not the last, former student of Professor Arnold to present this lecture in his honor, I will do my best to reflect positively on his memory. Since Carroll was always open to new ways of looking at our field, and willing to give new approaches a fair hearing, I believe he would have appreciated the comments I will be making.

I wish to share my thoughts with you concerning a new perspective on communication research, and ultimately a new way of thinking about and understanding how human communication behaviors are formed, repeated, and changed. It is what my colleague, Professor Michael Beatty, and I have chosen to call the "communibiological perspective." While we refer to this as a "new perspective," some who have read our unpublished work suggest it actually is a call for adoption of a "new research paradigm." I will let you decide. Before I directly consider this "new" approach, it is important that we understand how we arrived where we are and the nature of the status quo perspective which I will argue should be changed.

The Traditional Rhetorical Perspective

The rich rhetorical perspective which we inherited from the ancients was the dominant orientation of most people in this field through the first half of the 20th century, and continues to be a focal point of study and teaching in the field today. This perspective centers on communication within a one-to-many context where sources and audiences are clearly distinguishable and play very different roles. The classical rhetorical view, which I was privileged to study with Professor Arnold, focused much attention on audience analysis and adaptation. Aristotle, for example, emphasized this and spent a considerable portion of *The Rhetoric* explaining why people behave as they do. It was felt that to be an effective persuader, one needed to understand the people to be persuaded and adapt one's message to them. This view remains at the core of persuasion theory today.

By the mid-1960s a different perspective was striving for our attention, and beginning to receive it. This was a time of massive change in our society, and even more dramatic change within the academy. Many of us who lived through the sixties did not fully understand at the time the profound changes in our field which were occurring. Women, minorities, and white males of the middle and lower classes flowed into high schools and colleges in enormous numbers. The interests of these individuals were not fully consistent with those of the former occupants of higher education—those representing the economic and cultural elite. Many of these "new students" did not envision themselves as future public speakers. Instead, they saw their communication future to be involved primarily in dyadic and/or group contexts, and their goals to be both cooperative and persuasive. This gave birth to what we now recognize as the "interpersonal perspective," an orientation which is very influential in many of our institutions today.

With the advent of the interpersonal perspective the concepts of "sources" and "receivers" began to blur. Scholars began to recognize that these distinctions were much less useful in interpersonal communication than in one-to-many communication. Everyone in a small group or dyadic encounter is both a source and a receiver. Viewing communication primarily as an interpersonal encounter caused us to see old concepts in new ways. When we took a traditional rhetorical perspective, we learned that "stage fright" was a severe problem for some people. When we adopted an interpersonal perspective we learned that about one person in five had similar problems in virtually all communication contexts—and we came to study communication apprehension, shyness, and reticence. While we had looked at trait personality variables as matters sources needed to understand in order to persuade audiences, with our interpersonal perspective we came to recognize these same traits (and subsequently many others) had direct impact on both source and receiver behaviors in interpersonal contexts—in social, organizational, educational, and service encounters. We looked to our colleagues in personality psychology for help. We learned about extraversion, dogmatism, Machiavellianism, and other personality traits.

At this point some people in our field began to develop programs of research investigating the impact of traits on communication behaviors or communication outcomes. Others were distracted for a while by concerns about whether human communication behavior is a function of the context within which the communication takes place or the traits of the individuals communicating. Once we recognized that the impact of any context was mediated by how people perceived that context, and that such perceptions are also trait-based, we began to comprehend the overpowering potential of traits. People have trait responses to contexts. Highly apprehensive people might perceive the context of giving a two-minute speech in a classroom as being more threatening than a less apprehensive person in our field would see giving a lecture such as this! Simply put, in terms of impact on communication behavior the context does not exist separate from the trait-based perceptions of the people within that context.

Clearly people vary greatly in their trait communication behavior patterns. And this is true in all cultures. In addition, an individual's trait communication behavior pattern usually is quite consistent across contexts. However, I do not argue that people are perfectly consistent in their behavior across communication contexts. Certainly our behavior can vary from one context to another. In fact many believe, myself included, that such versatility is highly indicative of our level of communication competence. Nevertheless, most of us communicate the ways we do, most of the time, with minimal variation produced by the context of the behavior. Our communication behaviors are mostly trait-driven. It is no longer a question as to whether individuals' traits impact their communication behavior; the questions are: 1) Which traits are most important? and 2) How do those traits come to exist?

We will leave the first of these questions for another time. Tonight, I will focus on the second. How do communication traits come to exist? Two views have existed throughout time. The dominant view for the past thirty-plus years has been that communication traits are primarily learned by exposure to one's environment—culture, parents, schools, peers, siblings, etc. The other view is that traits are primarily inborn, the product of the biological reproduction process of genetic replication. We will consider the learning explanation first.

The Social Learning Model

The fields of educational and social psychology have directed a great deal of attention throughout much of this century to determining how people learn. Conditioning, reinforcement, and modeling approaches were among the many explanations which were advanced, and enormous amounts of research were devoted to each. Each had its devotees in psychology, and subsequently in communication. The work of Bandura and his social learning/modeling theory captured much of the attention in this field. His theory, and the fascinating research associated with it, was as intuitively compelling as it was ultimately unpredictive. However, the learning approaches fit well within the religious and political views of the time. The field's commitment to the idea of "free will" and the rejection of inborn differences reflected the dominant protestant religious views of most of the leadership in the speech field and the political unacceptability in the United States of anything that reminded people of the Nazi genetic research prior to and during World War II. To put it in the modern context, the social learning approach was "politically correct" for its time.

When we began applying learning theories (Educational Psychology was my doctoral minor) to interpersonally based constructs such as communication apprehension and verbal aggressiveness, we found them to predict very little variance in human behavior. Similarly, while social learning theory seemed to explain why people in different cultures communicate in somewhat different ways, it simply could not account for why there was so much more variance in communication behavior within any given culture than there was between any two cultures—when all the people in a given culture were exposed to repeated doses of the same or highly similar models. Also, as observers of mass communication, we were initially convinced that children (and some adults) learned all kinds of anti-social behavior from watching television (as we had been told about comic books a generation earlier). But we became disillusioned with the theory when we realized it could not explain why only a minority of viewers usually seemed to be affected. We were forced to recognize that individual differences in viewers were probably more important than what actually appeared on the screen (or in the comic book).

But, do not mistake my point here. People *do* learn by imitating others around them and by imitating what they see on TV (and in movies, and in comic books, etc.) Indeed, this is how the culture maintains and changes itself. But this does not explain why people differ so dramatically from one another even though they have essentially the same models in their environment. Research based on this theory rarely accounts for more than 5 to 10 percent in the variance in communication behavior—and often far less than that.

Let's give social learning more credit than it has earned and double the amount of variance it predicts—make it 10 to 20 percent predictable. When multiple applications of a theory leave 80 to 90 percent of the variance unexplained, it is not a strong theory. It probably should be discarded, or at least relegated to the classification of "minor theory." It is not so much "wrong" as that it has been demonstrated to be of limited value. As one of my hard-science colleagues once commented to me, "We would never have gone to the moon if we could have explained only ten percent of how to get there!" We have been following the siren's song. This theory and research paradigm normally explains a trivial amount of variability in human communication behavior, so little that many authors wishing to avoid public embarrassment do not even report the effect sizes they obtain in their studies. We are not approaching our research and theory goals of explaining human communication behavior. As every serious theorist is well aware, the predictive power of a theory is the most important criterion for determining its value. Without predictive power, a theory's elegance, parsimony, and intuitive appeal are nothing more than window dressing.

We must move on. If traits are produced either by learning or by biology (or a combination), and learning leaves at least 80 percent of the variance unexplained, it may be that if we turn to the biology of communication traits we will be better able to make more progress toward our goals. Scientists in other fields have already made this move.

Contemporary Science in Other Fields

In recent years psychobiologists have been working mostly under the rubric of *temperament*, which is seen as individual, biologically based differences in behavioral tendencies across various kinds of situations and times. They have made impressive advances in the understanding of human behavior, especially in social contexts. In addition to providing extremely strong evidence for the biological bases of traits, much of the foundation of this evidence comes from behaviors which are easily recognizable as what scholars in our field consider to be interpersonal communication behaviors. Shyness, extraversion, communicator style, aggressiveness, assertiveness, and empathy, all have been strongly linked to inherited neurobiological processes. And these are just a few examples, ones which are very obviously communication-centered. Consequently, no theory of human interaction can be taken seriously unless it is informed by this massive body of research literature that has already established strong effects for inborn, individual differences in neurobiological processes that underlie major dimensions of social behavior.

It should be noted, that no reference to any work in our field is present in this literature, nor is this work generally acknowledged in our field. While Joe Cappella, as well as Mark Knapp and his colleagues, has at least written articles suggesting we should pay attention to some of this work, the only study in this area conducted by a person in our field was one reported by Cary Horvath in *Communication Quarterly* in 1995. Incredibly, this research was done for her M.A. thesis! The psychobiological work is extremely significant scientific research on interpersonal communication, and it is not informed by work in our field.

The work conducted by the psychobiologists and neurobiologists is part of a ground-swell of scholarship investigating genetic differences in humans. The Human Genome project may well be the most important scientific project ever undertaken. Its ultimate purpose is to map every human gene. Already this work has enabled development of prenatal genetic tests for 450 genetically based diseases. Genetic bases of anxiety also have been identified, which certainly have implications for those of us concerned with communication apprehension.

Much of the most revealing research has involved comparative studies of identical versus non-identical twins. This is because identical twins share the same set of genes whereas non-identical twins are no more genetically alike than other siblings. The degree to which the correlation of traits between identical twins is larger than that for non-identical twins provides a conservative estimate of the variability which cannot be attributed to sharing a common environment (learning), and thus what can be attributed to the twins' shared genetics. A couple of examples can illustrate this approach. The results of one study indicated that if one twin has agoraphobia, it is five times more likely that her/his twin will have that phobia also if they are identical twins than if they are non-identical twins. In another study seventy percent of obesity was found to be predictable in identical twins, whereas only 40 percent was predictable in non-identical twins. Interestingly, particularly for those who wish to cling to the learning theory of traits, research comparing adult identical twins with non-identical as well as identical twins who had lived their lives near each other, found that identical twins, whether they were separated at birth or lived their whole lives near one another, became more alike as they got older, whereas the non-identical twins did not.

It is clear that science is producing one breakthrough after another which indicates the powerful impact of genetics of human traits. Many of these traits are the foundation of human interaction. We cannot continue to ignore what is going on around us. Conducting our learning experiments and writing our insightful ethnographies will not make us relevant in a future we can now see—a society that understands and adapts to the fact that much of human communication behavior is genetically influenced and difficult to control or change. Certainly some communication behavior is learned—otherwise we would all speak the same language with the same accent and people in all cultures would engage in highly similar nonverbal communication behaviors. Hence, some work with the learning model will certainly continue. However, if the failure to learn certain communication skills is not the cause of a problem, our normal skills-training course is not likely to be the solution. We cannot be part of the solution if we do not understand the problem. That is why I call for a shift of emphasis to the communibiological perspective in both our scholarship and our teaching.

The Communibiological Perspective

I do not have time this evening to outline fully the communibiological perspective which Professor Beatty and I are advancing, much less to provide the detailed support for each of the five central propositions of this approach. Fortunately, a pre-publication copy of our book which includes chapters related to this work is available at the Hampton Press display area at this conference, and two articles have been accepted for publication (by *Communication Monographs* and *Communication Quarterly*) and will be available shortly for those of you who wish to probe this area more deeply. I will, however, try to provide an overview of this approach which may help you decide if you want to consider it for your use.

Although the five propositions I will delineate shortly represent a radical departure from current thinking about human communication on the part of serious communication scholars, these propositions are widely accepted among psychobiologists. These propositions are parallel to those which form the underpinnings of psychobiology.

> *Proposition 1: All psychological process—including cognitive, affective, and motor—involved in social interaction depend on brain activity, making necessary a neurobiology of communication.*

Simply stated, theoretical speculation about thinking, feeling, and behaving during human interaction must be consistent with available knowledge regarding brain and brain-related functioning. Although the communication literature is replete with constructs positing processes that hint at neurobiological activity of some sort (e.g., assembling, differentiating, selecting), communication scholars have not yet specified the neurological activity expected to underlie the supposed processes, nor have they validated the constructs against appropriate neurological criteria. We do not know whether cognitive or affective processes inferred by scholars from the behavior of communicators exist within neurobiological reality. In our field conceptual labels, whether referring to processes or traits, are merely metaphoric surrogates for complex neurobiological systems. As such, most of the constructs in our field represent starting points, requiring further elaboration which consists of linking proposed constructs to specific neurobiological operations. In the absence of these linkages, such so-called theories are no more than word games—they provide no method of scientific verification or disproof.

While our scholars have been prolific in generating speculations about what goes on in people's heads (often based on ex post facto self-reports), psychobiologists have been making considerable headway mapping the neurobiological circuitry associated with psychological processes. Although the neurobiological functions are not yet totally understood, much is now known about extroverted social behavior, shyness, hostility and aggression, self-imposed constraint in social situations, impulsivity, approach and avoidance behavior, selective attention, focus, and memory. The importance of this work to the study of communication was made explicit by one temperament researcher when he stated "there is general agreement that temperament is manifest largely in the context of social interaction."

Proposition 2: Brain activity precedes psychological experience.

Scholars addressing issues regarding the nature of the relationship between brain activity and subjective experience (often referred to as the "mind-brain" problem) have taken one of three stances: 1) *Physical reductionism* holds that all psychological experience is a product of brain functioning: 2) *Mentalism* posits the existence of a non-biological form of consciousness that directs brain activity and efforts to carry out its will; 3) *Interactionism*, assumes that both reductionists and mentalists are partly correct. The communibiological perspective is decidedly reductionistic. We see no scientific grounds to be otherwise.

If scholars insist the psychological processes underlying communicative behavior are subject to autonomous control, they must describe the mechanisms making such processes possible. Certainly, scholars taking a mentalist or interactionist position on the mind-brain problem take on the obligation to describe the circuitry that allows an extra-physical mind to orchestrate changes in the physical brain. It is noteworthy that mentalist and interactionist philosophies emerged at a time and in a culture in which church and state were not separate and such positions were often required to make room for religious convictions in the concepts of "spirit" and "free will." These are the same forces which led to our listening to the siren's song of social learning—and much earlier holding fast to the theory that the Earth was flat and the sun, moon, and stars revolved around it. This time, we choose not to listen.

Proposition 3. The neurobiological structures underlying temperament traits and individual differences are mostly inherited.

As I mentioned before, traits are labels used by theorists to describe collective samples of cognition, affect, or behavior. As such, traits are not inherited, but the neurobiological structures are mostly due to heredity. Recent studies of identical twins have produced strong evidence for this position regarding a wide-range of socially significant results. On a wider variety of variables there has been little difference observed between the correlations for identical twins who were raised apart and those who were raised together. This indicates that shared environment is of little importance for these traits. Some of these variables include altruism, empathy, nurturance, aggressiveness, assertiveness, constraint, and (most importantly) general happiness. In the latter case, many studies have indicated that at least 50 percent of general happiness is genetically based. However, the most recent study indicated that approximately 80 percent was genetic.

Some may question, if our proposition is true, why we don't anticipate genetics predicting 100 percent of the variance in communication behavior. First, as with all social science research, a variety of methodological imperfections attenuates the observed effects. If better measures of the traits were developed, more predictable variance should be expected—but probably never 100 percent, for we are unlikely ever to have perfect measures. Second, there are other (unmeasured) biological influences which can have an impact on neurobiological influences (nutrition, prenatal drug or alcohol use, etc.) beside heredity. And, of course, we do not rule out the existence of learning effects. This proposition says "mostly inherited," not "entirely inherited." Given our generous estimate of 20 percent learning effect to 80 percent error, the genetic explanation certainly promises to be at least as parsimonious as the learning perspective, and probably more so. In addition, it is highly likely that genetics and learning interact with each other to influence communication behavior.

Proposition 4: Environment or "situation" has only a negligible effect on interpersonal behavior.

The research on "happiness" or "well-being" helps to illustrate this proposition. While the research clearly indicates that these feelings are genetically based traits, that does not mean that we don't feel good when we get a raise or have a personal success, nor that we don't feel bad if we fail a test or lose our job. However, as intense as these feelings are at a given time, they are merely fluctuations about a stable temperamental set point (another term for trait) that is characteristic of us.

The principle that boundaries of individual reactions to environmental stimuli are defined by individual temperament is embedded in the concept of *temperamental set points.* In the case of communication apprehension, for example, a person's specific response to a given demand for social interaction is difficult to predict, for there are other traits which will normally also be in operation as well as the communication apprehension trait. However, the class of responses to communication apprehension can be predicted with considerable accuracy when several members of the class are observed. So called "situational" effects are most likely the impact of genetically based differences in temperamental set points.

Proposition 5: Differences in interpersonal behavior are principally due to individual differences in neurobiological functioning.

Traits are based on neurobiological structures. Various neurobiological structures underlie clusters of various social behaviors. Since different individuals will differ in their neurobiological structures, they will engage in different interpersonal behaviors. No one knows precisely how many distinguishable and relevant traits there are at this point. But we do know that sometimes an individual may have traits that conflict. In these cases it is difficult to predict one's behavior, because he or she is a unique neurological being. These conflicting orientations can be referred to as "competing traits" and it is believed that these are most likely to arise from different neurological systems.

To understand the importance of competing traits, consider a young man with extremely high stage fright. Presume also, that he does not need to take a public speaking class to graduate. His behavior is highly predictable—odds are very good he won't take the class. However, presume he must pass a public speaking course with a "B" to graduate. He is now motivated by the desire to graduate and inhibited by his fear of public speaking. He may give up on graduating (and experience sanctions for the behavior) or try to give the speech (and experience extreme stress). He may lose either way, for his stress may make it impossible to give the quality of speech necessary. However, predicting which option will be chosen will be difficult even if we know both (or all) of the traits involved, and probably impossible if we do not. What is much more likely is that this young man will spot this potential conflict in advance and behave in such a way as to prevent the conflict from coming to fruition. He may transfer to a new major where public speaking is not required, or to a different college or university where the requirement is not present. He will try to make his world fit him if he perceives his traits do not fit his world.

Each of us recognizes these kinds of conflicts in our own lives—and we behave as much as possible so that we don't get forced into those choices. That is, we try to place ourselves in situations where our traits do not come into conflict. Simply put, we impact our situations rather than letting our situations impact us. We behave in ways consistent with all of our traits rather than having to choose just one.

These are the propositions underlying the communibiological perspective—or paradigm if you prefer. If you are, like me, one who bought into the social learning model over the years, it may be difficult to swallow all of this in one bite. I encourage you to read more widely in this area. While I have emphasized in my remarks problems with some of the science in our field, the implications of these remarks may be even more crucial for qualitative scholars and teachers. Research in this area suggests that our traits drive our qualitative scholarship, just as they drive our other communication behavior. Qualitative researchers are no less susceptible to social learning's call than quantitative researchers. It is our vision of the nature of human communication and its precursors which needs to be re-examined, not just the approach by which we choose to study it.

I was honored by your attendance and I appreciate your attention.

Notes

My co-authors and I have addressed the importance of traits in considerable detail elsewhere:

Beatty, M. J., & McCroskey, J. C. (1998). Interpersonal communication as temperamental expression: A communibiological paradigm. In McCroskey, J. C., Daly, J. A., Martin, M. M., & Beatty, M. J., Eds. *Communication and Personality: Trait Perspectives*, Cresskill, NJ: Hampton Press.

Beatty, M. J., & McCroskey, J. C., (In Press). It's in our nature: Verbal ag-

gressiveness as temperamental expression, *Communication Quarterly*.
Beatty, M. J., McCroskey, J. C., & Heisel, A. D. (In Press).
Communication apprehension as temperamental expression: A communibiological paradigm, *Communication Monographs*.

SOURCE: This speech was given by communication professor James McCroskey at the Carroll C. Arnold Distinguished Lecture at the annual convention of the National Communication Association, Chicago, Illinois, November 20, 1997. The text of the speech is taken from the booklet James C. McCroskey, *Why We Communicate the Ways We Do: A Communibiological Perspective.* Boston, MA: Allyn & Bacon, 1998. It is reprinted by permission of James C. McCroskey.

BIBLIOGRAPHY

Adams, Dennis M., and Hamm, Mary E. (1990). *Cooperative Learning: Critical Thinking and Collaboration across the Curriculum.* Springfield, IL: Charles C. Thomas.

Adams, Linda, with Lenz, Elinor. (1989). *Be Your Best.* New York: Putnam.

Addeo, Edmond G., and Burger, Robert E. (1973). *Egospeak: Why No One Listens to You.* New York: Bantam.

Adler, Mortimer J. (1983). *How to Speak, How to Listen.* New York: Macmillan.

Adler, Ronald B. (1977). *Confidence in Communication: A Guide to Assertive and Social Skills.* New York: Holt, Rinehart and Winston.

Ailes, Roger (1988). *You Are the Message.* New York: Doubleday.

Akinnaso, F. Niyi (1982). On the Differences between Spoken and Written Language. *Language and Speech* 25, part 2, 97–125.

Albrecht, Karl (1980). *Brain Power . . . Learn to Improve Your Thinking Skills.* Englewood Cliffs, NJ: Prentice Hall [Spectrum].

Albright, Madeleine K. (1998). *Vital Speeches of the Day* 64 (June 15):518–520.

Alessandra, Tony (1986). How to Listen Effectively, *Speaking of Success* (Video Tape Series). San Diego, CA: Levitz Sommer Productions.

Alisky, Marvin (1985). *Vital Speeches of the Day* 51 (January 15).

Allen, Mike, and Preiss, Raymond W. (1990). Using Meta-Analysis to Evaluate Curriculum: An Examination of Selected College Textbooks. *Communication Education* (April):103–116.

Allen, Steve (1991). *Dumbth and 81 Ways to Make Americans Smarter.* Buffalo, NY: Prometheus Books.

American Psychiatric Association (1980). *Diagnostic and Statistical Manual,* 3rd ed. Washington, DC: American Psychiatric Association.

Anderson, Donna (1994). "Corporate Retiree Volunteerism," *Vital Speeches of the Day* 60 (December 15):138–40.

Archambault, David (1992). *Vital Speeches of the Day* (June 1):491–93.

Archer, Dennis W. (1998). *Vital Speeches of the Day* 64 (March 15):340–42.

Argyle, Michael (1988). *Bodily Communication,* 2nd ed. New York: Methuen.

Arliss, Laurie P. (1991). *Gender Communication.* Englewood Cliffs, N.J.: Prentice-Hall.

Arnold, Carroll C., and Bowers, John Waite, eds. (1984). *Handbook of Rhetorical and Communication Theory.*
Boston: Allyn & Bacon.

Aronson, Elliot (1980). *The Social Animal,* 3rd ed. San Francisco: Freeman.

Asch, Solomon (1946). Forming Impressions of Personality. *Journal of Abnormal and Social Psychology* 41: 258–90.

Authier, Jerry, and Gustafson, Kay (1982). Microtraining: Focusing on Specific Skills. In Marshall, Eldon K., Kurtz, P. David, and Associates. *Interpersonal Helping Skills: A Guide to Training Methods, Programs, and Resources.* San Francisco: Jossey-Bass, 93–130.

Axtell, Roger E. (1993). *Do's and Taboos Around the World,* 3rd ed. New York: Wiley.

Axtell, Roger E. (1990). *Do's and Taboos of Hosting International Visitors.* New York: Wiley.

Axtell, Roger E. (1999). *Do's and Taboos of Humor Around the World.* New York: Wiley.

Aylesworth, Thomas G., and Aylesworth, Virginia L. (1978). *If You Don't Invade My Intimate Zone or Clean Up My Water Hold, I'll Breathe in Your Face, Blow on Your Neck, and Be Late For Your Party.* New York: Condor.

Ayres, Joe (1986). Perceptions of Speaking Ability: An Explanation for Stage Fright. *Communication Education* 35:275–87.

Ayres, Joe, and Hopf, Tim S. (1992). Visualization: Reducing Speech Anxiety and Enhancing Performance. *Communication Reports* 5:1–10.

Ayres, Joe, and Hopf, Tim S. (1993). *Coping with Speech Anxiety.* Norwood, NJ: Ablex Publishing Corporation.

Aryes, Joe, and Hopf, Tim (1995). An Assessment of the Role of Communication Apprehension in Communicating with the Terminally Ill. *Communication Research Reports* 12 (Fall):227–34.

Ayres, Joe, and Miller, Janice (1994). *Effective Public Speaking,* 4th ed. Dubuque, IA: Brown & Benchmark.

Ayres, Joe, Hopf, Tim S. and Ayres, Debbie M. (1994). An Examination of Whether Imaging Ability Enhances the Effectiveness of an Intervention Designed to Reduce Speech Anxiety. *Communication Education* 43 (July):252–58.

Backrack, Henry M. (1976). Empathy. *Archives of General Psychiatry* 33:35–38.

Banach, William J. (1991). Are You Too Busy to Think? *Vital Speeches of the Day* 62 (March 15):351–52.

Barker, Larry and Gaut, Deborah (1996). *Communication,* 7th ed. Boston: Allyn & Bacon.

Barker, Larry, Edwards, R., Gaines, C., Gladney, K., and

Holley, F. (1980). An Investigation of Proportional Time Spent in Various Communication Activities by College Students. *Journal of Applied Communication Research* 8:101–09.

Barna, LaRay M. (1985). Stumbling Blocks in Intercultural Communication. In Samovar, Larry A., and Porter, Richard E., eds. *Intercultural Communication: A Reader,* 4th ed. Belmont, CA: Wadsworth, 330–38.

Barnlund, Dean C. (1970). A Transactional Model of Communication. In Akin, J., Goldberg, A., Myers, G., and Stewart, J., comps. *Language Behavior—A Book of Readings in Communication.* The Hague: Mouton.

Barnlund, Dean C. (1975). Communicative Styles in Two Cultures: Japan and the United States. In Kendon, A., Harris, R. M., and Key, M. R., eds. *Organization of Behavior in Face-to-Face Interaction.* The Hague: Mouton.

Baron, Robert A., and Byrne, Donn (1984). *Social Psychology: Understanding Human Interaction,* 4th ed. Boston: Allyn & Bacon.

Barrett, Karen (1982). Date Rape. *Ms.,* September: 48–51.

Beatty, Michael J. (1988). Situational and Predispositional Correlates of Public Speaking Anxiety. *Communication Education* 37:28–39.

Beck, Aaron (1988). *Love Is Never Enough.* New York: HarperCollins.

Beier, Ernst (1974). How We Send Emotional Messages. *Psychology Today* 8 (October): 53–56.

Benne, Kenneth D., and Sheats, Paul (1948). Functional Roles of Group Members. *Journal of Social Issues* 4:41–49.

Bennis, Warren, and Nanus, Burt (1985). *Leaders: The Strategies for Taking Charge.* New York: Harper & Row.

Berger, Charles R., and Chaffee, Steven H., eds. (1987). *Handbook of Communication Science.* Thousand Oaks, CA: Sage.

Bettinghaus, Erwin P., and Cody, Michael J. (1987). *Persuasive Communication,* 4th ed. New York: Holt, Rinehart & Winston.

Blankenship, Jane (1968). *A Sense of Style: An Introduction to Style for the Public Speaker.* Belmont, CA: Dickenson.

Blau, Shawn, and Ellis, Albert, eds. (1998). *The Albert Ellis Reader, Rational Emotive Behavior Therapy: A Guide to Well Being.* Secaucus, New Jersey: Citadel Press.

Blumstein, Philip, and Schwartz, Pepper (1983). *American Couples: Money, Work, Sex.* New York: Morrow.

Boaz, John K., and Brey, James R., eds. (1987). *1987 Championship Debates and Speeches.* Normal, IL: American Forensic Association.

Boaz, John K., and Brey, James R., eds. (1988). *1988 Championship Debates and Speeches.* Normal, IL: American Forensic Association.

Bochner, Arthur, and Kelly, Clifford (1974). Interpersonal Competence: Rationale, Philosophy, and Implementation of a Conceptual Framework. *Communication Education* 23:279–301.

Bok, Sissela (1978). *Lying: Moral Choice in Public and Private Life.* New York: Pantheon.

Bok, Sissela (1983). *Secrets.* New York: Vintage Books.

Borisoff, Deborah, and Merrill, Lisa (1985). *The Power to Communicate: Gender Differences as Barriers.* Prospect Heights, IL: Waveland Press.

Boster, Frank, and Mongeau, Peter (1984). Fear Arousing Persuasive Messages. In Bostrom, Robert, ed. *Communication Yearbook 8.* Thousand Oaks, CA: Sage, 330–77.

Boutras-Ghali, Boutros (1994). "Transnational Crime," *Vital Speeches of the Day* 60 (December 15):130–32.

Boyd, Stephen D., and Benz, Mary Ann (1985). *Organization and Outlining: A Workbook for Students in a Basic Speech Course.* New York: Macmillan.

Bradac, James J., Bowers, John Waite, and Courtright, John A. (1979). Three Language Variables in Communication Research: Intensity, Immediacy, and Diversity. *Human Communication Research* 5:256–69.

Bradley, Bert E. (1991). *Fundamentals of Speech Communication: The Credibility of Ideas,* 6th ed. Dubuque, IA: Brown.

Bransford, John D., Sherwood, Robert D., and Sturdevant, Tom (1987). Teaching Thinking and Problem Solving. In Joan Boykoff Baron and Robert J. Sternberg, eds., *Teaching Thinking Skills: Theory and Practice,* 162–81. New York: W. H. Freeman.

Brilhart, John, and Galanes, Gloria (1992). *Effective Group Discussion,* 7th ed. Dubuque, IA: Brown & Benchmark.

Brody, Jane F. (1991). How to Foster Self-Esteem. *New York Times Magazine.* (April 28):15.

Brougher, Toni (1982). *A Way With Words.* Chicago: Nelson-Hall.

Brown, Lee P. (1995). "International Drug Trafficking." *Vital Speeches of the Day* 61 (January 1):175–80.

Brownback, Sam, "Free Speech: Lyrics, Liberty and License," *Vital Speeches of the Day* 64 (May 15, 1998), 454–56.

Brownwell, Judi (1987). Listening: The Toughest Management Skill, *Cornell Hotel and Restaurant Administration Quarterly* 27:64–71.

Buchsbaum, S. J. (1991). *Vital Speeches of the Day* (December 15):150–55.

Buchstein, Frederick (1988). *Vital Speeches of the Day* (June 15):534–36.

Buckley, Reid (1988). *Speaking in Public.* New York: Harper & Row.

Buller, David B., LePoire, Aune, A. Beth, Kelly, and Eloy, Sylvie (1992). Social Perceptions as Mediators of the Effect of Speech Rate Similarity on Compliance. *Human Communication Research* 19 (December):286–311.

Burgoon, Judee K., Buller, David B., and Woodall, W. Gill (1995). *Nonverbal Communication: The Unspoken Dialogue,* 2nd ed. New York:McGraw-Hill.

Burke, Kenneth (1950). *A Rhetoric of Motives.* New York: Prentice-Hall.

Buscaglia, Leo (1988). Leo Buscaglia's Golden Rules of Love. *Woman's Day* (June 29).

Bush, George (1988). Acceptance Speech. *Vital Speeches of the Day* 55 (October 15).

Butcher, Willard C. (1987). *Vital Speeches of the Day* (September 1):680.

Carr, Harold (1987). *Vital Speeches of the Day* 53 (February 1).

Chang, Hui-Ching, and Holt, G. Richard (1996). The Changing Chinese Interpersonal World: Popular Themes in Interpersonal Communication Books in Modern Taiwan. *Communication Quarterly* 44 (Winter):85–106.

Cheek, Jonathan (1989). *Conquering Shyness: The Battle Anyone Can Win.* New York: Dell Trade.

Chisholm, Shirley (1978). *Vital Speeches of the Day* 44 (August 15).

Cialdini, Robert T. (1984). *Influence: How and Why People Agree to Things.* New York: Morrow.

Cialdini, Robert T., and Ascani, K. (1976). Test of a Concession Procedure for Inducing Verbal, Behavioral, and Further Compliance with a Request to Give Blood. *Journal of Applied Psychology* 61:295–300.

Clark, Herbert (1974). The Power of Positive Speaking. *Psychology Today* 8:102.

Clement, Donald A., and Frandsen, Kenneth D. (1976). On Conceptual and Empirical Treatments of Feedback in Human Communication. *Communication Monographs* 43:11–28.

Clinton, Bill (1994). "Invasion of Haiti Canceled," *Vital Speeches of the Day* 60 (October 1):740–41.

Coates, J., and Cameron, D. (1989). *Women, Men, and Language: Studies in Language and Linguistics.* London: Longman.

Collier, M. J., and Powell, R. (1990). Ethnicity, Instructional Communication and Classroom Systems. *Communication Quarterly* 38:334–49.

Condon, John C., and Yousef, Fathi (1975). *An Introduction to Intercultural Communication.* Indianapolis: Bobbs-Merrill.

Conrades, George (1998). *Vital Speeches of the Day* 64 (April 1):377–80.

Cooper, Kathleen B. (1994). "What Do I Recommend for Young Women?" *Vital Speeches of the Day* 61 (November 15):85–88.

Craig, Mary E., Kalichman, Seth C., and Follingstad, Diane R. (1989). Verbal Coercive Sexual Behavior Among College Students. *Archives of Sexual Behavior* 18 (October): 421–34.

Culick, S. (1962). *The East and West: A Study of Their Psychic and Cultural Characteristics.* Ruthland, UT: Charles Tuttle.

Dalton, John (1994). "The Character of Readiness," *Vital Speeches of the Day* 60 (March 1):296–99.

D'Angelo, Frank J. (1980). *Process and Thought in Composition,* 2nd ed. (1980). Cambridge, MA: Winthrop.

Deavenport, Earnest W. (1998). *Vital Speeches of the Day* 64 (June 1):501–03.

DeBono, Edward (1976). *Teaching Thinking.* New York: Penguin.

DeBono, Edward (1987). *The Six Thinking Hats.* New York: Penguin.

Dejong, W. (1979). An Examination of Self-Perception Mediation of the Foot-in-the-Door Effect. *Journal of Personality and Social Psychology* 37:2221–2239.

Delattre, Edwin (1988). *Vital Speeches of the Day* (May 15):467.

DeVito, Joseph A. (1965). Comprehension Factors in Oral and Written Discourse of Skilled Communicators. *Communication Monographs* 32 (1965):124–28.

DeVito, Joseph A. (1969). Some Psycholinguistic Aspects of Active and Passive Sentences. *Quarterly Journal of Speech* 55:401–406.

DeVito, Joseph A. (1970). *The Psychology of Speech and Language: An Introduction to Psycholinguistics.* New York: Random House.

DeVito, Joseph A. (1974). *General Semantics: Guide and Workbook,* Rev. ed. DeLand, Fla.: Everett/Edwards.

DeVito, Joseph A. (1976). Relative Ease in Comprehending Yes/No Questions. In Blankenship, Jane, and Stelzner, Herman G., eds., *Rhetoric and Communication.* Urbana, IL: University of Illinois Press, 143–54.

DeVito, Joseph A. (1986). *The Communication Handbook: A Dictionary.* New York: Harper & Row.

DeVito, Joseph A. (1989). *The Nonverbal Communication Workbook.* Prospect Heights, IL: Waveland Press.

DeVito, Joseph A. (1995). *The Interpersonal Communication Book,* 7th ed. New York: HarperCollins.

DeVito, Joseph A. (1996). *Messages: Building Interpersonal Communication Skills,* 3rd ed. New York: HarperCollins.

DeVito, Joseph A., and Hecht, Michael L., eds. (1990). *The Nonverbal Communication Reader.* Prospect Heights, IL: Waveland Press.

DeVito, Joseph A., Giattino, Jill, and Schon, T. D. (1975). *Articulation and Voice: Effective Communication.* Indianapolis: Bobbs-Merrill.

DeVries, Mary A. (1994). *Internationally Yours: Writing and Communicating Successfully in Today's Global Marketplace.* Boston: Houghton-Mifflin.

Dodd, Carley H. (1997). *Dynamics of Intercultural Communication,* 5th ed.Dubuque, IA: William C. Brown.

Dole, Bob (1995). *Vital Speeches of the Day* 61 (May 15):450–52.

Dresser, Norine (1996). *Multicultural Manners: New Rules of Etiquette for a Changing Society.* New York: Wiley.

Dreyfuss, Henry (1971). *Symbol Sourcebook.* New York: Mcgraw-Hill.

Driskell, James, Olmstead, Beckett, and Salas, Eduardo (1993). Task Cues, Dominance Cues, and Influence in Task Groups. *Journal of Applied Psychology* 78 (February):51–60.

Eakins, Barbara, and Eakins, R. Gene (1978). *Sex Differences in Communication.* Boston: Houghton-Mifflin.

Eisen, Jeffrey, with Farley, Pat (1984). *Power-Talk: How to Speak It, Think It, and Use It.* New York: Simon and Schuster.

Eisenberg, Nancy, and Strayer, Janet (1987). *Empathy and Its Development.* New York: Cambridge University Press.

Eitzen, D. Stanley (1998). *Vital Speeches of the Day* 64 (December 1): 122–26.

Ekman, Paul, and Friesen, W. V. (1971). Constants Across Cultures in the Face and Emotion. *Journal of Personality and Social Psychology* 17:124–29.

Ellis, Albert (1998). *How to Control Your Anxiety Before It Controls You.* New York: Birch Lane Press.

Ellis, Albert, and Harper, Robert A. (1975). *A New Guide to Rational Living.* Hollywood, CA: Wilshire Books.

Engleberg, Isa N. (1994). *The Principles of Public Presentation.* New York: HarperCollins.

Ennis, Robert H. (1987). A Taxonomy of Critical Thinking Dispositions and Abilities. In Baron, Joan Boykoff, and Sternberg, Robert J., eds., *Teaching Thinking Skills: Theory and Practice.* New York: Freeman: 9–26.

Faber, Adele, and Mazlisb, Elaine (1980). *How to Talk So Kids Will Listen and Listen So Kids Will Talk.* New York: Avon.

Ferguson, John F. (1995). *Vital Speeches of the Day* 61 (February 1):242–43.

Feulner, Edwin J., Jr. (1995). "A New Conservative Internationalist Foreign Policy," *Vital Speeches of the Day* 61 (April 15):406–10.

Filley, Alan C. (1975). *Interpersonal Conflict Resolution.* Glenview, IL: Scott, Foresman.

Floyd, James J. (1985). *Listening: A Practical Approach.* Glenview, IL: Scott, Foresman.

Folger, Joseph P., and Poole, Marshall Scott (1984). *Working Through Conflict: A Communication Perspective.* Glenview, IL: Scott, Foresman.

Fraser, Bruce (1990). Perspectives on Politeness. *Journal of Pragmatics* 14 (April):219–36.

Freedman, J., and Fraser, S. (1966). Compliance Without Pressure: The Foot-in-the-Door Technique. *Journal of Personality and Social Psychology* 4:195–202.

Frey, Kurt J. and Eagly, Alice H. (1993). Vividness Can

Undermine the Persuasiveness of Messages. *Journal of Personality and Social Psychology* 65 (July):32–44.

Frymier, Ann Bainbridge, and Shulman, Gary M. (1995). "What's In It For Me?": Increasing Content Relevance to Enhance Students' Motivation. *Communication Education* 44 (January):40–50.

Gabor, Don (1989). *How to Talk to the People You Love.* New York: Simon and Schuster.

Garner, Alan (1981). *Conversationally Speaking.* New York: McGraw-Hill.

Gephardt, Richard A. (1995). "The Democratic Challenge in the 104th Congress," *Vital Speeches of the Day* 61 (January 15):197–201.

Gibb, Jack (1961). Defensive Communication. *Journal of Communication* 11: 141–48.

Giles, Howard, Mulac, Anthony, Bradac, James J., and Johnson, Patricia (1987). Speech Accommodation Theory: The First Decade and Beyond, in Margaret L. McLaughlin, ed., *Communication Yearbook 10.* Thousand Oaks, CA: Sage, 13–48.

Glaser, Connie Brown, and Smalley, Barbara Steinberg (1992). *More Power to You! How Women Can Communicate Their Way to Success.* New York: Warner.

Glasser, William (1999). *Choice Therapy.* New York: HarperCollins.

Glucksberg, Sam, and Danks, Joseph H. (1975). *Experimental Psycholinguistics: An Introduction.* Hillsdale, NJ: Lawrence Erlbaum.

Gorden, William I., and Nevins, Randi J. (1993). *We Mean Business: Building Communication Competence in Business and Professions.* New York: Longman.

Gordon, Thomas (1975). *P.E.T.: Parent Effectiveness Training.* New York: New American Library.

Goss, Blaine (1989). *The Psychology of Communication.* Prospect Heights, IL: Waveland Press.

Goss, Blaine, Thompson, M., and Olds, S. (1978). Behavioral Support for Systematic Desensitization for Communication Apprehension. *Human Communication Research* 4:158–63.

Gronbeck, Bruce E., McKerrow, Raymie E., Ehninger, Douglas, and Monroe, Alan H. (1997). *Principles and Types of Speech Communication,* 13th ed. New York: HarperCollins.

Gross, Ronald (1991). *Peak Learning.* Los Angeles: Jeremy P. Tarcher.

Gudykunst, William B. (1991). *Bridging Differences: Effective Intergroup Communication.* Thousand Oaks, CA.: Sage.

Gudykunst, William B., and Nishida, T. (1984). Individual and Cultural Influences on Uncertainty Reduction. *Communication Monographs* 51:23–36.

Gudykunst, William B., and Kim, Young Yun (1992a). *Communicating with Strangers: An Approach to Intercultural Communication,* 2nd ed. New York: McGraw-Hill.

Gudykunst, William B. and Kim, Young Yun (1992b), eds. *Readings on Communication with Strangers: An Approach to Intercultural Communication.* New York: McGraw-Hill.

Gudykunst, William B., Yang, S. M., and Nishida, T. (1985). A Cross-Cultural Test of Uncertainty Reduction Theory: Comparisons of Acquaintance, Friend, and Dating Relationships in Japan, Korea, and the United States. *Human Communication Research* 11:407–55.

Guerra, Stella (1986). *Vital Speeches of the Day* (September 15):727.

Haiman, Franklyn S. (1958). Democratic Ethics and the Hidden Persuaders. *Quarterly Journal of Speech* 44 (December):385–92.

Hall, Edward T., and Hall, Mildred Reed (1987). *Hidden Differences: Doing Business with the Japanese.* New York: Doubleday, Anchor Books.

Hamlin, Sonya (1988). *How to Talk So People Listen.* New York: Harper & Row.

Haney, William (1973). *Communication and Organizational Behavior: Text and Cases,* 3rd ed. Homewood, IL: Irwin.

Hankin, Joseph N. (1997). *Vital Speeches of the Day* 64 (October 15):22–29.

Harnack, Andrew, and Kleppinger, Eugene (1997). *Online! The Internet Guide for Students and Writers.* New York: St. Martin's Griffin.

Hatfield, Elaine, and Rapson, Richard L. (1996). *Love and Sex: Cross Cultural Perspectives.* Boston: Allyn & Bacon.

Hayakawa, S. I., and Hayakawa, Alan R. (1990). *Language in Thought and Action,* 5th ed. New York: Harcourt Brace Jovanovich.

Hecht, Michael, and Ribeau, Sidney (1984). Ethnic Communication: A Comparative Analysis of Satisfying Communication. *International Journal of Intercultural Relations* 8:135–51.

Hecht, Michael L., Collier, Mary Jane, and Ribeau, Sidney (1993). *African American Communication: Ethnic Identity and Cultural Interpretation.* Thousand Oaks, CA: Sage.

Heinrich, Robert et al. (1983). *Instructional Media: The New Technologies of Instruction.* New York: Wiley.

Heldmann, Mary Lynne (1988). *When Words Hurt: How to Keep Criticism from Undermining Your Self-Esteem.* New York: Ballantine.

Henley, Nancy M. (1977). *Body Politics: Power, Sex, and Nonverbal Communication.* Englewood Cliffs, NJ: Prentice-Hall.

Hensley, Carl Wayne (1992). "What You Share Is What You Get: Tips for Effective Communication," *Vital Speeches of the Day* 59 (December 1):115–17.

Hensley, Carl Wayne (1994). "Divorce—the Sensible Approach," *Vital Speeches of the Day* 60 (March 1):317–19.

Hersey, Paul, and Blanchard, Ken (1988). *Management of Organizational Behavior: Utilizing Human Resources.* Englewood Cliffs, NJ: Prentice-Hall.

Hess, Ekhard H. (1975). *The Tell-Tale Eye.* New York: Van Nostrand Reinhold.

Hess, Jon A. (1993). Teaching Ethics in Introductory Public Speaking: Review and Proposal. In Lawrence W. Hugenberg, ed., *Basic Communication Course Annual* V Boston: American Press: (September), 101–126.

Hewitt, John, and Stokes, Randall (1975). Disclaimers. *American Sociological Review* 40:1–11.

Hickey, Neil (1989). Decade of Change, Decade of Choice. *TV Guide* 37 (December 9):29–34.

Hickson, Mark L., and Stacks, Don W. (1989). *NVC: Nonverbal Communication: Studies and Applications,* 2nd ed. Dubuque, IA: Brown.

Higgins, James M. (1994). *101 Creative Problem Solving Techniques.* New York: New Management Publishing Co.

Hocker, Joyce L., and Wilmot, William W. (1991). *Interpersonal Conflict,* 3rd ed. Dubuque, IA: Brown.

Hoft, Nancy L. (1995). *International Technical Communication: How to Export Information about High Technology.* New York: Wiley.

Hofstede, Geert (1980). *Culture's Consequences: International Differences in Work-Related Values.* Thousand Oaks, CA: Sage.

Hofstede, Geert (1997). *Cultures and Organizations: Software of the Mind.* New York: McGraw-Hill.

Infante, Dominic A. (1988). *Arguing Constructively.* Prospect Heights, IL: Waveland Press.

Infante, Dominic A., Rancer, Andrew S., and Womack, Deanna F. (1993). *Building Communication Theory,* 2nd ed. Prospect Heights, IL: Waveland Press.

Jackson, William (1985). *Vital Speeches of the Day* (September 15).

Jacob, John E. (1995). *Vital Speeches of the Day* 61 (July 1): 572–74.

Jacobs, Harvey (1985). *Vital Speeches of the Day* 51 (May 1).

Jacobs, John E. (1997). *Vital Speeches of the Day* 63 (May 15), 461–64.

Jaffe, Clella (1995). *Public Speaking: Concepts and Skills for a Diverse Society,* 2nd ed. Belmont, CA: Wadsworth.

Jaksa, James A., and Pritchard, Michael S. (1994). *Communication Ethics: Methods of Analysis,* 2nd ed. Belmont, CA: Wadsworth.

James, David L. (1995). *The Executive Guide to Asia-Pacific Communications.* New York: Kodansha International.

James-Catalano, Cynthia N. (1996). *Researching on the World Wide Web.* Rocklin, CA: Prima.

Jandt, Fred E. (1999). *Intercultural Communication: An Introduction,* 2nd ed. Thousand Oaks, CA: Sage.

Janis, Irving (1983). *Victims of Group Thinking: A Psychological Study of Foreign Policy Decisions and Fiascoes,* 2nd ed. Boston: Houghton-Mifflin.

Jensen, J. Vernon (1985a). Perspectives on Nonverbal Intercultural Communication. In Samovar, Larry, and Porter, Richard E., eds., *Intercultural Communication: A Reader,* 4th ed. Belmont, CA: Wadsworth, 256–72.

Jensen, J. Vernon (1985b). Teaching Ethics in Speech Communication, *Communication Education* 34:324–30.

Johannesen, Richard L. (1996). *Ethics in Human Communication,* 5th ed. Prospect Heights, IL: Waveland Press.

Johnson, Geneva B. (1991). *Vital Speeches of the Day* (April 15):393–98.

Johnson, Kenneth G., ed. (1991). *Thinking Creatically.* Concord, CA: International Society for General Semantics.

Jones, Julia Hughes (1998). "Tips for Effective Leadership." *Vital Speeches of the Day* 64 (February 15):278–81.

Kearns, David T. (1987). *Vital Speeches of the Day* 54 (December 15).

Kelly, P. Keith (1994). *Team Decision-Making Techniques.* Irvine, CA: Richard Chang Associates.

Kemp, Jerrold E., and Dayton, Deane K. (1985). *Planning and Producing Instructional Media,* 5th ed. New York: Harper & Row.

Keohane, Nannerl O. (1991). *Vital Speeches of the Day* (July 15):605–608.

Kersten, K., and Kersten, L. *Marriage and the Family: Studying Close Relationships.* New York: Harper & Row.

Kesselman-Turkel, Judi, and Peterson, Franklynn (1982). *Note-Taking Made Easy,* Chicago: Contemporary Books.

Kim, Hyun J. (1991). Influence of Language and Similarity on Initial Intercultural Attraction. In Ting-Toomey, Stella, and Korzenny, Felipe, eds., *Cross-Cultural Interpersonal Communication.* Thousand Oaks, CA: Sage, 213–29.

Kim, Young Yun, ed. (1986). *Interethnic Communication: Current Research.* Thousand Oaks, CA: Sage.

Kim, Young Yun (1991). Intercultural Communication Competence. In Ting-Toomey, Stella, and Korzenny, Felipe, eds., *Cross-Cultural Interpersonal Communication.* Thousand Oaks, CA: Sage, 259–75.

Kim, Young Yun, and Gudykunst, William B., eds. (1988). *Theories in Intercultural Communication.* Thousand Oaks, CA: Sage.

King, Robert, and DiMichael, Eleanor (1992). *Voice and Diction.* Prospect Heights, IL: Waveland Press.

Kinsley, Carol W. (1994), "What Is Community Service Learning?" *Vital Speeches of the Day* 61 (November 1):40–43.

Kleinke, Chris L. (1978). *Self-Perception: The Psychology of Personal Awareness.* San Francisco: Freeman.

Kleinke, Chris L. (1986). *Meeting and Understanding People.* New York: Freeman.

Kluge, Holger (1997). "Reflections on Diversity." *Vital Speeches of the Day* 63 (January 1): 171–75.

Knapp, Mark, and Hall, Judith (1992). *Nonverbal Behavior in Human Interaction,* 3rd ed. New York: Holt, Rinehart and Winston.

Kohn, Alfie (1989). Do Religious People Help More? Not So You'd Notice. *Psychology Today* (December):66–68.

Korzybski, Alfred (1933). *Science and Sanity: An Introduction to Non-Aristotelian Systems and General Semantics.* Concord, CA: International Society for General Semantics.

Kramarae, Cheris (1981). *Women and Men Speaking.* Rowley, MA: Newbury House.

Lambdin, William (1981). *Doublespeak Dictionary.* Los Angeles: Pinnacle Books.

Lamkin, Martha (1986). *Vital Speeches of the Day* (December 15):152.

Langer, Ellen J. (1978). Rethinking the Role of Thought in Social Interaction. In Harvey, J. H., Ickes, W. J., and Kidd, R. F., eds. *New Directions in Attribution Research,* vol. 2. Hillsdale, NJ: Erlbaum, 35–58.

Langer, Ellen J. (1989). *Mindfulness.* Reading, MA: Addison-Wesley.

Larson, Charles U. (1992). *Persuasion: Reception and Responsibility,* 6th ed. Belmont, CA: Wadsworth.

Leathers, Dale G. (1992). *Successful Nonverbal Communication: Principles and Applications,* 2nd ed. New York: Macmillan.

Lederman, Linda (1990). Assessing Educational Effectiveness: The Focus Group Interview as a Technique for Data Collection. *Communication Education* 39:117–27.

Lee, Alfred McClung, and Lee, Elizabeth Briant (1972). *The Fine Art of Propaganda.* San Francisco, CA: The International Society for General Semantics.

Lee, Alfred McClung, and Lee, Elizabeth Briant (1995). The Iconography of Propaganda Analysis, *ETC.: A Review of General Semantics* 52 (Spring):13–17.

Leeds, Dorothy (1988). *Powerspeak.* New York: Prentice-Hall.

Lever, Janet (1995). The 1995 Advocate Survey of Sexuality and Relationships: The Women, Lesbian Sex Survey. *The Advocate* 687/688 (August 22):22–30.

Levitt, Arthur (1995). "Consumer Protection." *Vital Speeches of the Day* 61 (January 15):194–97.

Lidstad, Richard (1995). *Vital Speeches of the Day* 61 (July 1): 559–61.

Lineberry, Robert L., Edwards, George C., and Wallenberg,

Martin P. (1994). *Government in America.* New York: Longman.

Ling, Joseph T. (1993). "Design for the Environment," *Vital Speeches of the Day* 59 (August 1):629–32.

Linkugel, Wil A., Allen, R. R., and Johannesen, Richard L., eds. (1978). *Contemporary American Speeches,* 4th ed. Dubuque, IA: Brown & Benchmark.

Littlejohn, Stephen W. (1992). *Theories of Human Communication,* 4th ed. Belmont, CA: Wadsworth.

Littlejohn, Stephen W., and Jabusch, David M. (1987). *Persuasive Transactions.* Glenview, IL: Scott Foresman.

Loden, Marilyn (1986). *Vital Speeches of the Day* (May 15):472–75.

Loftus, Elizabeth, and Palmer, J. C. (1974). Reconstruction of Automobile Destruction: An Example of the Interaction Between Language and Memory. *Journal of Verbal Learning and Verbal Behavior* 13:585–89.

Lucas, Stephen E. (1998). *The Art of Public Speaking,* 6th ed. New York: McGraw-Hill.

Lukens, J. (1978). Ethnocentric Speech. *Ethnic Groups* 2:35–53.

Lumsden, Gay, and Lumsden, Donald (1993). *Communicating in Groups and Teams.* Belmont, CA: Wadsworth.

Lunsford, Charlotte (1988). *Vital Speeches of the Day* (September 15):731.

Lurie, Alison (1983). *The Language of Clothes.* New York: Vintage.

Lustig, Myron W., and Koester, Jolene (1999). *Intercultural Competence: Interpersonal Communication Across Cultures,* 3rd ed. New York:Longman.

Mackay, Harvey B. (1991). *Vital Speeches of the Day* (August 15):656–59.

MacLachlan, John (1979). What People Really Think of Fast Talkers. *Psychology Today* 13 (November):113–17.

Maggio, Rosalie (1997). *Talking about People: A Guide to Fair and Accurate Language.* Phoenix, AZ: Oryx Press.

Malandro, Loretta A., Barker, Larry, and Barker, Deborah Ann (1989). *Nonverbal Communication,* 2nd ed. New York: Random House.

Marien, Michael (1992). *Vital Speeches of the Day* (March 15):340–44.

Markway, Barbara G., Carmin, Cheryl N., Pollard, C. Alex, and Flynn, Teresa. *Dying of Embarrassment: Help for Social Anxiety and Phobia.* Oakland, CA: New Harbinger Publications, 1992.

Marshall, Evan (1983). *Eye Language: Understanding the Eloquent Eye.* New York: New Trend.

Martel, Myles (1989). *The Persuasive Edge.* New York: Fawcett.

Martin, Matthew M., and Anderson, Carolyn M. (1995). Roommate Similarity: Are Roommates Who Are Similar in Their Communication Traits More Satisfied? *Communication Research Reports* 12 (Spring):46–52.

Marwell, G., and Schmitt, D. R. (1967). Dimensions of Compliance-Gaining Behavior: An Empirical Analysis. *Sociometry* 39:350–64.

Maslow, Abraham (1970). *Motivation and Personality.* New York: HarperCollins.

Matsumoto, David (1994). *People: Psychology from a Cultural Perspective.* Pacific Grove, CA: Brooks/Cole.

Matsuyama, Yukio (1992). *Vital Speeches of the Day* (May 15):461–66.

McCarthy, Michael J. (1991). *Mastering the Information Age.* Los Angeles: Jeremy P. Tarcher.

McCroskey, James C. (1997). *An Introduction to Rhetorical Communication,* 7th ed. Needham Hts., MA: Allyn & Bacon.

McCroskey, James C., and Wheeless, Lawrence (1976). *Introduction to Human Communication.* Boston: Allyn & Bacon.

McGill, Michael E. (1985). *The McGill Report on Male Intimacy.* New York: Harper & Row.

McLaughlin, Margaret L. (1984). *Conversation: How Talk Is Organized.* Thousand Oaks, CA: Sage.

McMahon, Ed (1986). *The Art of Public Speaking.* New York: Ballantine.

McNamara, Robert (1985). *Vital Speeches of the Day* (July 1):549.

Midooka, Kiyoshi (1990). Characteristics of Japanese Style Communication. *Media, Culture and Society* 12 (October):477–89.

Miller, Gerald, and Parks, Malcolm (1982). Communication in Dissolving Relationships. In Duck, Steve, ed., *Personal Relationships: 4. Dissolving Personal Relationships.* New York: Academic Press.

Miller, Sherod, Wackman, Daniel, Nunnally, Elam, and Saline, Carol (1982). *Straight Talk.* New York: New American Library.

Moghaddam, Fathali M., Taylor, Donald M., and Wright, Stephen C. (1993). *Social Psychology in Cross-Cultural Perspective.* New York: W. H. Freeman.

Morris, Desmond, Collett, Peter, Marsh, Peter, and O'Shaughnessy, Marie (1979). *Gestures: Their Origins and Distribution.* New York: Stein and Day.

Murphy, Lisa (1997). Efficacy of Reality Therapy in the Schools: A Review of the Research from 1980–1995. *Journal of Reality Therapy* 16 (Spring):12–20.

Murphy, Richard (1958). The Speech as Literary Genre. *Quarterly Journal of Speech* 44 (April): 117–27.

Naisbitt, John (1984). *Megatrends: Ten New Directions Transforming Our Lives.* New York: Warner.

Napier, Rodney W., and Gershenfeld, Matti K. (1989). *Groups: Theory and Experience,* 4th ed. Boston: Houghton-Mifflin.

Nelson, Alan (1986). *Vital Speeches of the Day* 52.

Newhart, Bob (1997). "Humor Makes Us Free." *Vital Speeches of the Day* (July 15):607–608.

Nichols, Michael P. (1995). *The Lost Art of Listening.* New York: Guilford Press.

Nichols, Ralph (1961). Do We Know How to Listen? Practical Helps in a Modern Age. *Communication Education* 10:118–24.

Nichols, Ralph, and Stevens, Leonard (1957). *Are You Listening?* New York: McGraw-Hill.

Nickerson, Raymond S. (1987). Why Teach Thinking? In Baron, Joan Boykoff, and Sternberg, Robert J., eds., *Teaching Thinking Skills: Theory and Practice.* New York: Freeman, 27–37.

Orr, James F., III (1993). "Learning to Learn." *Vital Speeches of the Day* 59 (September 15):725–28.

Orski, C. Kenneth (1986). *Vital Speeches of the Day* (February 1):274.

Osborn, Alex (1957). *Applied Imagination,* Rev. ed. New York: Scribners.

Page, Richard A., and Balloun, Joseph L. (1978). The Effect of Voice Volume on the Perception of Personality. *Journal of Social Psychology* 105:65–72.

Payan, Janice (1990). *Vital Speeches of the Day* (September 1):697–701.

Pearson, Judy C. (1985). *Gender and Communication.* Dubuque, IA: Brown.

Pearson, Judy C., West, Richard, and Turner, Lynn H. (1995). *Gender and Communication,* 3rd ed. Dubuque, IA: Brown.

Pease, Allen (1984). *Signals: How to Use Body Language for Power, Success and Love.* New York: Bantam.

Pei, Mario (1956). *Language for Everybody.* New York: Pocket Books.

Penfield, Joyce, ed. (1987). *Women and Language in Transition.* Albany: State University of New York Press.

Penn, C. Ray (1990). *Vital Speeches of the Day* (December 1): 116–17.

Peterson, Houston, ed. (1965). *A Treasury of the World's Great Speeches.* New York: Simon & Schuster.

Peterson, Russell W. (1985). *Vital Speeches of the Day* (July 1):549.

Peterson, Susan (1995). "Managing Your Communication," *Vital Speeches of the Day* 61 (January 1): 188–90.

Pratkanis, Anthony, and Aronson, Elliot (1991). *Age of Propaganda: The Everyday Use and Abuse of Persuasion.* New York: Freeman.

Price, Hugh B. (1995). "Public Discourse." *Vital Speeches of the Day* 61 (January 15):213–16.

Qubein, Nido R. (1986). *Get the Best from Yourself.* New York: Berkley.

Rankin, Paul (1929). Listening Ability. In *Proceedings of the Ohio State Educational Conference's Ninth Annual Session.*

Reed, Warren H. (1985). *Positive Listening: Learning to Hear What People Are Really Saying.* New York: Franklin Watts.

Reivitz, Linda (1985). *Vital Speeches of the Day* 52 (November 15):88–91.

Reynolds, Christina L., and Schnoor, Larry G., eds. (1991). *1989 Championship Debates and Speeches.* Normal, IL: American Forensic Association.

Rich, Andrea L. (1974). *Interracial Communication,* New York: Harper & Row.

Richardson, Margaret Milner (1995). "Taxation with Representation." *Vital Speeches of the Day* 61 (January 15): 201–203.

Richmond, Virginia P., and McCroskey, James C. (1997). *Communication: Apprehension, Avoidance, and Effectiveness,* 5th ed. Boston: Allyn & Bacon.

Richmond, Virginia, McCroskey, James, and Payne, Steven (1987). *Nonverbal Behavior in Interpersonal Relationships.* Englewood Cliffs, NJ: Prentice-Hall.

Riggio, Ronald E. (1987). *The Charisma Quotient.* New York: Dodd, Mead.

Roach, Carol A., and Wyatt, Nancy J. (1988). *Successful Listening.* New York: Harper & Row.

Robinson, Janet, and McArthur, Leslie Zebrowitz (1982). Impact of Salient Vocal Qualities on Causal Attribution for a Speaker's Behavior. *Journal of Personality and Social Psychology* 43:236–47.

Rockefeller, David (1985). *Vital Speeches of the Day* (March 15):328–31.

Rodman, George, and Adler, Ronald B. (1997). *The New Public Speaking.* Fort Worth, TX: Harcourt Brace.

Rogers, Carl (1970). *Carl Rogers on Encounter Groups.* New York: Harrow Books.

Rolland, Ian M. (1993). "Toward a *Working* Health Care System." *Vital Speeches of the Day* 59 (June 15):524–27.

Rosenthal, Peggy (1984). *Words and Values: Some Leading Words and Where They Lead Us.* New York: Oxford University Press.

Rosenthal, Robert, and Jacobson, L. (1968). *Pygmalion in the Classroom.* New York: Holt, Rinehart and Winston.

Rothwell, J. Dan (1982). *Telling It Like It Isn't: Language Misuse and Malpractice/What We Can Do About It.* Englewood Cliffs, NJ: Prentice-Hall.

Ruben, Brent D. (1985). Human Communication and Cross-Cultural Effectiveness. In Samovar, Larry A., and Porter, Richard E., eds. *Intercultural Communication: A Reader,* 4th ed. Belmont, CA: Wadsworth:338–46.

Rubenstein, Eric (1992). *Vital Speeches of the Day* (April 15):401–404.

Ruchlis, Hy (1990). *Clear Thinking: A Practical Introduction.* Buffalo, NY: Prometheus Books.

Ruggiero, Vincent Ryan (1987). *Vital Speeches of the Day* 53 (August 15).

Ruggiero, Vincent Ryan (1990). *The Art of Thinking: A Guide to Critical and Creative Thought,* 3rd ed. New York: HarperCollins.

Samovar, Larry A., and Porter, Richard E., eds. (1997). *Intercultural Communication: A Reader,* 8th ed. Belmont, CA: Wadsworth.

Samovar, Larry A., and Porter, Richard E. (1991). *Communication Between Cultures.* Belmont, CA: Wadsworth.

Samovar, Larry A., Porter, Richard E., and Jain, Nemi C. (1981). *Understanding Intercultural Communication.* Belmont, CA: Wadsworth.

Schaefer, Charles E. (1984). *How to Talk to Children About Really Important Things.* New York: Harper & Row.

Schmidley, Dianne, and Alvarado, Herman A. (1997). *The Foreign-Born Population in the United States: March 1997 (Update).* Washington, D.C., United States Bureau of the Census.

Schnoor, Larry G., ed. (1994). *1991 and 1992 Championship Debates and Speeches.* River Falls, WI: American Forensic Association.

Schnoor, Larry, ed. (1995). *Winning Orations of the Interstate Oratorical Association.* Mankato, MN. Interstate Oratorical Association.

Schnoor, Larry G., ed. (1996). *Winning Orations of the Interstate Oratorical Association.* Mankato, MN. Interstate Oratorical Association.

Schnoor, Larry G., ed. (1997). *Winning Orations of the Interstate Oratorical Association.* Mankato, MN. Interstate Oratorical Association.

Schwartz, Marilyn, and the Task Force on Bias-Free Language of the Association of American University Presses (1995) *Guidelines for Bias-Free Writing.* Bloomington: Indiana University Press.

Seidler, Ann, and Bianchi, Doris (1988). *Voice and Diction Fitness: A Comprehensive Approach.* New York: Harper & Row.

Silber, John R. (1985). *Vital Speeches of the Day* 51 (September 15).

Simonson, Brenda (1986). *Vital Speeches of the Day.* 52 (July 1).

Singer, Marshall R. (1987). *Intercultural Communication: A Perceptual Approach.* Englewood Cliffs, NJ: Prentice-Hall.

Smith, Raymond W. (1995). "Advertising and the Interactive Age." *Vital Speeches of the Day* 61 (April 1):358–61.

Snyder, Richard (1984). *Vital Speeches of the Day* 51 (January 1).

Spitzberg, Brian H., and Cupach, William R. (1984). *Interpersonal Communication Competence.* Thousand Oaks, CA: Sage.

Spitzberg, Brian H., and Cupach, William R. (1989). *Handbook of Interpersonal Competence Research*. New York: Springer-Verlag.

Spitzberg, Brian H., and Hecht, Michael L. (1984). A Component Model of Relational Competence. *Human Communication Research* 10:575–99.

Sprague, Jo, and Stuart, Douglas (1996). *The Speaker's Handbook*, 4th ed. San Diego: Harcourt Brace Jovanovich.

Sprague, Jo, and Stuart, Douglas (1988). *The Speaker's Handbook*, 2nd ed. San Diego: Harcourt Brace Jovanovich.

Stark, Peter B. (1985). *Vital Speeches of the Day* 51 (October 1).

Steil, Lyman K., Barker, Larry L., and Watson, Kittie W. (1983). *Effective Listening: Key to Your Success*. Reading, MA: Addison-Wesley.

Stephan, Walter G., and Stephan, Cookie White (1985). Intergroup Anxiety. *Journal of Social Issues* 41:157–75.

Stephan, Walter G., and Stephan, Cookie White (1996). *Intergroup Relations*. Dubuque, IA: Brown and Benchmark.

Sternberg, Robert J. (1987). Questions and Answers About the Nature and Teaching of Thinking Skills. In Baron, Joan Boykoff, and Sternberg, Robert J., eds., *Teaching Thinking Skills: Theory and Practice*. New York: Freeman: 251–59.

Swets, Paul W. (1983). *The Art of Talking so that People Will Listen*. Englewood Cliffs, NJ: Prentice-Hall [Spectrum].

Tannen, Deborah (1990). *You Just Don't Understand: Women and Men in Conversation*. New York: William Morrow and Co.

Teng-Hui, Lee (1995). *Vital Speeches of the Day* 61 (August 1): 611–13.

Tersine, Richard J., and Riggs, Walter E. (1980). The Delphi Technique: A Long-Range Planning Tool. In Ferguson, Stewart and Ferguson, Sherry Devereaux, eds., *Intercom: Readings in Organizational Communication*. Rochelle Park, N.J.: Hayden Book: 336–73.

Thorne, Barrie, Kramarae, Cheris, and Henley, Nancy, eds. (1983). *Language, Gender and Society*. Rowley, MA: Newbury House.

Toulmin, Stephen, Rieke, Richard, & Janik, Allen (1979). *An Introduction to Reasoning*. New York: Macmillan.

Trenholm, Sarah (1986). *Human Communication Theory*. Englewood Cliffs, NJ: Prentice-Hall.

Truax, C. (1961). A Scale for the Measurement of Accurate Empathy. *Wisconsin Psychiatric Institute Discussion Paper No. 20*. Madison, WI: Wisconsin Psychiatric Institute.

Valenti, Jack (1982). *Speaking Up with Confidence: How to Prepare, Learn, and Deliver Effective Speeches*. New York: Morrow.

Vasile, Albert J. and Mintz, Harold K. (1996). *Speaking with Confidence: A Practical Guide*. New York: HarperCollins.

Veit, Howard R., "Health Care Consumerism," *Vital Speeches of the Day 64* (July 1, 1998), 562–66.

Verderber, Rudolph F. (1991). *The Challenge of Effective Speaking*, 8th ed. Belmont, CA: Wadsworth.

Wade, Carole, and Tarvis, Carol (1990). *Learning to Think Critically: The Case of Close Relationships*. New York: HarperCollins.

Wallace, Karl (1955). An Ethical Basis of Communication. *Communication Education* 4 (January):1–9.

Warnick, Barbara, and Inch, Edward S. (1989). *Critical Thinking and Communication: The Use of Reason in Argument*. New York: Macmillan.

Watson, Arden K., and Dodd, Carley H. (1984). Alleviating Communication Apprehension through Rational Emotive Therapy: A Comparative Evaluation. *Communication Education* 33: 257–66.

Watzlawick, Paul (1978). *The Language of Change: Elements of Therapeutic Communication*. New York: Basic Books.

Watzlawick, Paul, Beavin, Janet Helmick, and Jackson, Don D. (1967). *Pragmatics of Human Communication: A Study of Interactional Patterns, Pathologies, and Paradoxes*. New York: Norton.

Weinstein, Fannie (1995). Professionally Speaking, *Profiles: The Magazine of Continental Airlines* 8 (April):50–55.

Weisinger, Hendrie (1990). *The Critical Edge: How to Criticize Up and Down Your Organization and Make It Pay Off*. New York: Harper & Row.

Wells, Theodora (1980). *Keeping Your Cool Under Fire: Communicating Non-Defensively*. New York: McGraw-Hill.

Wharton, Clifton R., Jr. (1995). "The Myth of Superpower." *Vital Speeches of the Day* 61 (January 15): 204–207.

Whitman, Richard F., and Timmis, John H. (1975). The Influence of Verbal Organizational Structure and Verbal Organizing Skills on Select Measures of Learning. *Human Communication Research* 1:293–301.

Williams, Andrea (1985). *Making Decisions*. New York: Zebra.

Wolf, Florence I., Marsnik, Nadine C., Tacey, William S., and Nichols, Ralph G. (1983). *Perceptive Listening*. New York: Holt, Rinehart and Winston.

Wolpe, Joseph. (1958). *Psychotherapy by Reciprocal Inhibition*. Stanford, CA: Stanford University Press.

Yoshida, Susumu (1995). *Vital Speeches of the Day* 61 (March 1):301–306.

CREDITS

Page 184: Figures 9.2a–d, graphs regarding "Cultural Diversity at Berkeley" data from *The New York Times,* June 4, 1995. Copyright © 1995 by The New York Times. Reprinted by permission.

Page 187: © Gazin/The Image Works

Page 188: Figure 9.4, "human ear" from *Psychology in Perspective,* 2/e by James Hasset. Copyright © James Hasset. Reprinted by permission of Addison Wesley Educational Publishers, Inc.

Page 203: © Mark Richards/Photo Edit

Page 208: © The Picture Cube

Page 210: © Frank Siteman/The Picture Cube

Page 216: Scott Foresman Photo

Page 229: © Bob Daemmrich/Stock Boston

Page 236: © Joel Gordon

Page 242: Scott Foresman Photo

Page 252: © Dick Blume/The Image Works

Page 261: © Bob Daemmrich/Stock Boston

Page 266: © Michelle Bridwell/Photo Edit

Page 275: © David Young-Wolff/Photo Edit

Page 280: © David Young-Wolff/Tony Stone Images

Page 286: © David Young-Wolff/Photo Edit

Page 292: © David Young-Wolff/Photo Edit

Page 300: © Photo Edit

Page 307: © Michael Newman/Photo Edit

Page 313: © Reuters/Gary Hershorn/Archive Photos

Page 318: © J. Sohm/The Image Works

Page 324: © Chronis Jons/Tony Stone Images

Page 337: © T. Russell/Sygma

Page 339: © J. Jacobson/The Image Works

Page 342: © Rashid/Monkmeyer

Page 347: © Stephen D. Cannerelli/The Image Works

Page 350: © Bob Daemrrich/Stock Boston

Page 361: © David J. Sams/Stock Boston

Page 365: © Consolidated/Archive Photos

Page 372: Scott Foresman Photo

Page 377: Weisenbech, Cindy "False Memory Syndrome." Reprinted with permission of the Interstate Oratorical Association, *Winning Orations,* 1994, Larry Schnoor, Editor.

Page 381: © Gary Conner/Photo Edit

Page 385: © John Coletti/Stock Boston

Page 400: Franklin, William, "Careers in International Business" from *Vital Speeches of the Day,* 9/15/98, pp. 719–721. Reprinted by permission of the author.

Page 407: © B. Daemmrich/Stock Boston

Page 409: © Halebran/Liaison International

Page 417: © Daemmrich/Stock Boston

Page 423: © Tom Sobolik/Black Star

Page 432: © Joel Gordon

Page 437: © Barry King/Gamma Liaison

Page 441: © Bob Daermmrich/Stock Boston

Page 453: © Frank Siteman/Stock Boston

Page 457: Jack Shea's introductory speech at the 1998 John Huston Award Dinner. Reprinted by permission of Jack Shea, President, Director's Guild of America and Chairman, Artists Rights Foundation.

Page 460: Speech given by Michael Greene during the 37th Annual Grammy Awards Telecast, March 1, 1995. Reprinted by permission of Michael Greene, President/CEO National Academy of Recording Arts and Sciences.

Page 461: © Los Angeles Daily News/Sygma

Page 462: Tom Cruise acceptance speech at the John Huston Award Dinner, 1998. Reprinted by permission of Creative Artists Agency and the speaker.

Page 467: Lee Iacocca speech "Testing Cars." Reprinted by permission of Daimler Chrysler Corporation.

Page 471: NCA creedo. Reprinted by permission of the National Communication Association.

Page 474: © Leslye Borden/Photo Edit

Page 479: © Paula Lerner/The Picture Cube

Page 480: "Self-Test: How Apprehensive Are You in Group Discussions and Meetings?" by James C. McCroskey from *An Introduction to Rhetorical Communication,* 7/e by James C. McCroskey. Reprinted by permission of James C. McCroskey.

Page 493: © Gary A. Conner/Photo Edit

Page 494: © Bonni Kamin/Photo Edit

Page 501: "Diplomatic Immunity Unjustified" by Matthew Sanchez, pp. 19–21. With permission "T-P Leadership Questionnaire: An Assessment of Style" from J.W. Pfeiffer and J.E. Jones, *Structured Experiences for Human Relations Training,* © 1969 American Educational Research Association.

Page 504: "Crash of the Internet" by Jocelyn So, p. 115. With permission from the Interstate Oratorical Association, Larry Schnoor, Executive Secretary, Mankato, MN, *Winning Orations,* 1997.

Page 507: "Sexual Assault Policy a Must" by Maria Lucia R. Anton. Reprinted with permission of the Interstate Oratorical Association from *Winning Orations,* 1994, Larry Schnoor, Editor.

Page 510: "Homosexuals and the Military" by Sara Mitchell. Reprinted with permission of the Interstate Oratorical Association from *Winning Orations,* 1994, Larry Schnoor, Editor.

Page 512: "See Jane, See Jane's Dilemma" by Meleena Erikson, pp. 61–64. With permission from the Interstate Oratorical Association, Larry Schnoor, Executive Secretary, Mankato, MN, *Winning Orations,* 1997.

Page 515: "What Exactly Are We Working For?" by Amy Celeste Forman, pp. 50–52. With permission from the Interstate Oratorical Association, Larry Schnoor, Executive Secretary, Mankato, MN, *Winning Orations,* 1997.

INDEX

Fear. *See also* Communication
apprehension
and confidence development,
51–52
of failure, 48
and intercultural situations, 47
as motivational appeal, 428
Feedback, 6
direct/indirect styles of, 65
speaker responsiveness to, 344
Feulner, Edwin J., Jr., 428
Figurative analogy, 413–414
Figures of speech, 323
Filled pauses, 352
Filtering out unpleasant messages,
as obstacle to listening,
69, 71
Financial gain, as motivational
appeal, 431
Fink, Ramona L., 38–41
First person narratives, 166
Fishbone diagram for limiting
speech topics, 112–113
5W organization, 257
Fletcher, Leon, 246
Flip charts, as presentation aid
media, 188–189
Floyd, James, 70
Focus, on audience, 237, 240
Focused analysis, speeches for,
501, 512–523
Focus groups, 490–491
Follow-up questions, 358
Foot-in-the-door technique in
persuasive speech, 390
Forceful language, 329–331
Forley, Maurice, 7
Formality
of language, 307–308
wording for appropriate level
of, 324
Forman, Amy Celeste, 500,
515–517
Franklin, William E., 400–406
Friend-or-foe factor, as obstacle to
listening, 68
Full outline, 201
Future, in conclusion of speech,
278–279

Gabor, Don, 267
"Galileo and the Ghosts"
technique, 117
Gelb, Michael J., 220
Gender. *See also* Sexist language
audience analysis and, 26–27,
217–220

as cultural variable, 14–15
listening and, 67–68, 304
nonverbal messages and, 218
preferred cultural identifiers
and, 327
Gender role stereotyping, avoiding,
325
General analysis speeches,
500–501, 501–512, 523–554
Generalizations
in audience analysis, 214
reasoning from, 409–413
General reference sources, 137–140
General research and opinion
posts, 144–145
"General Semantics," thinking
errors in, 308–310
Gephardt, Richard A., 165–166
Gestures, 354
"Ghosts" speech (Lonnquist),
excerpt, 410–411
Gibbon, Edward, 126
Gimmicks, avoiding, 275
Glaser, Connie Brown, 62, 315, 483
Glass, Lillian, 25
Glauner, Tom, 380
Glittering generality, 392
Goodwill speech, 465–470
characteristics of, 465, 467–468
principles of, 466–467
samples of, 467–470
Gopherspace, 128, 129
Government, U.S., research
sources from, 140
Graham, Billy, 446
Graphics, in computer assisted
presentations, 202
Graphs, 183–185
bar, 184
line, 184–185
pie chart, 183
Greene, Michael
introduction speech of, 457–458
presentation speech of, 459–460
Group building and maintenance
roles, 491
Group-orientation, 491
Groups, small. *See* Small groups
Group task roles, 491
Groupthink, listening for, 486
Guerra, Stella, 163–164
Guide phrases, 320

Halo effect, 441
Hamlin, Sonya, 371, 414, 426
Handouts, as presentation aid
media, 190

Hearing
honest, 67
vs. listening, 61
Heffernan, Betsy, 365
Hensley, Carl Wayne, 276–277
Heterogeneous audience, adapting
to, 237–238
Heterosexist language, 325, 326,
327
Hierarchy of needs (Maslow), 424,
425
High-context culture, 259
Historical justification standard of
criticism, 84–85
Hitler, Adolf, 85
Hoff, Ron, 88, 288
Hoft, Nancy L., 80, 193
Homogeneity of audience, 236–237
Homophobic language, 305
"Homosexuals and the Military"
(Mitchell), speech for general
analysis, 500, 510–512
Honest hearing, of listener, 67
Honest responding, of listener, 67
Humes, James C., 181
Humor, in introduction of speech,
269
Humorous style, 312–315
appropriateness in, 315
brevity in, 314
relevance in, 313–314
spontaneity in, 314–315
tastefulness in, 315
Humphrey, Judith, 500, 524–530
Hyperbole, 323

Iacocca, Lee, goodwill speech of,
467–468
Idea-generation group, 488–489
Idea generator, for speech topics,
103–109
Ideas, and symbols in outlines,
291–292
Identification principle of
persuasive speech, 390–391
Identification with audience, 233
Idiolect, 64
Idioms, 322
"I Have a Dream" speech (King),
84, 278
Illustrations, 161
in introduction of speech, 269
as presentation aids, 186–187
Imagery, 323–324
Immediacy
creating, 329
in speech delivery, 343